East European Integration
and East-West Trade

CONTRIBUTORS

Arpad Abonyi	Research Associate, Carleton University, Canada
Mark Allen	Economist, International Monetary Fund
Morris Bornstein	Professor of Economics, University of Michigan
Jozef M. van Brabant	Economist, United Nations, New York
Josef C. Brada	Associate Professor of Economics, Arizona State University
Lawrence J. Brainard	Vice President, Bankers Trust Co., New York
Robert W. Campbell	Professor and Chairman of Economics, Indiana University
James A. Caporaso	Andrew W. Mellon Professor of International Studies, University of Denver
Zdeněk Drábek	Lecturer and Deputy Chairman, Department of Economics, The University College at Buckingham, England
Zbigniew M. Fallenbuchl	Professor of Economics, University of Windsor, Canada
Gregory Grossman	Professor of Economics, University of California, Berkeley
Philip Hanson	Senior Lecturer in Economics, Center for Russian and East European Studies, University of Birmingham, England
Edward A. Hewett	Associate Professor of Economics, University of Texas at Austin
Franklyn D. Holzman	Professor of Economics, Tufts University and Fletcher School of Law and Diplomacy
Marvin Jackson	Professor of Economics, Arizona State University
Andrzej Korbonski	Professor of Political Science, University of California at Los Angeles
Carl H. McMillan	Associate Professor of Economics and Director, Institute of Soviet and East European Studies, Carleton University, Ottawa, Canada
Paul Marer	Associate Professor of International Business, School of Business, Indiana University
John Michael Montias	Professor of Economics, Yale University
Gur Ofer	Professor of Economics, Hebrew University, Jerusalem, Israel
Frederic L. Pryor	Professor of Economics, Swarthmore College
Theodore Shabad	Editor, *Soviet Geography*
Ivan J. Sylvain	Research Associate, Carleton University, Ottawa, Canada
Robert N. Taaffe	Professor and Chairman of Geography, Indiana University
Jan Vaňous	Assistant Professor of Economics, The University of British Columbia, Canada
Thomas A. Wolf	Associate Professor of Economics, Ohio State University
Adam Zwass	Senior Economist, The National Bank of Austria, Vienna

East European Integration
and East-West Trade

Edited by

PAUL MARER
Indiana University

JOHN MICHAEL MONTIAS
Yale University

INDIANA UNIVERSITY PRESS
BLOOMINGTON

Studies in East European and Soviet
Planning, Development, and Trade
International Development Institute
Indiana University, Bloomington, Indiana
Paul Marer, Editor
No. 28

Manufactured in the United States of America

Library of Congress Cataloging in Publication Data
Main entry under title:

East European integration and East-West trade.

81-1298

   (Studies in East European and Soviet planning, development, and trade; no. 28)
   Based on a conference held at Indiana University/Bloomington in Oct. 1976, which
was sponsored by the Joint Committee on Eastern Europe.
   1. Europe, Eastern—Economic integration—Congresses. 2. East-West trade
(1945-   )—Congresses. I. Marer, Paul. II. Montias, John Michael, 1928   III. Joint
Committee on Eastern Europe. IV. Series.
HC244.E22   337.47   79-3181
ISBN 0-253-16865-1   1 2 3 4 5 84 83 82 81 80

Contents

List of Tables

Acknowledgments

This book is based in part on some of the papers and formal discussions originally presented at the Conference on East European Integration and East-West Trade, held at Indiana University in Bloomington between October 28 and 31, 1976, and in part on additional studies commissioned after the conference. The Conference brought together specialists on central planning and on international trade and international relations. Among the one hundred participants were members of the academic community from various universities and colleges in the United States and abroad, as well as representatives of the business world, the banking community, and research, government, and international organizations. The Conference was commissioned and generously supported by a grant from the Joint Committee on Eastern Europe of the American Council of Learned Societies and the Social Science Research Council and funded in part by an additional grant from the U.S. Department of State. The Conference was organized under the sponsorship of the School of Business, the Russian and East European Institute, and the International Development Institute of Indiana University. Special thanks are due to John Ryan, the President of Indiana University; Howard C. Schaller, Executive Associate Dean of the School of Business; Alexander Rabinowitch, Director of the Russian and East European Institute; and William J. Siffin, Director of the International Development Institute, for their encouragement, advice, and participation in the Conference. Several universities and other institutions also made contributions by providing release time and covering travel expenses for their staff members. We express our appreciation to all these organizations.

The editors are deeply grateful to the formal participants in the Conference, especially the chairpersons, Professors Abram Bergson of Harvard University, Morris Bornstein of the University of Michigan, Gregory Grossman of the University of California, John Hardt of the Congressional Research Service and George Washington University, Marie Lavigne of the University of Paris, and Friedrich Levcik, Director of the Institute for International Comparison in

Vienna. They also helped us plan the conference and gave advice on the volume. Caroline Berg and other staff members of the International Development Institute, John Garland of the School of Business, and the Conference Bureau of Indiana University deserve special acknowledgment for helping with the paperwork and the logistics of organizing and running a large conference.

Many individuals contributed much time and effort to enable the editors to blend into a cohesive volume the revised versions of some of the Conference contributions and the additional papers and comments solicited subsequently. We wish, in particular, to thank our contributors who were gracious to put up with our numerous suggestions for revisions. We owe much to the careful editing and creative suggestions of Marianne Platt who also supervised the production of the volume, Barbara Dutton for the typesetting and the manuscript typing of Heather Taylor, sometimes delivered on very short notice. Janet Rabinowitch at the Indiana University Press was most helpful with her suggestions and for seeing the work through its various stages of publication.

The publication of this book was made possible by a Ford Foundation grant to Indiana University to support a problem-oriented interdisciplinary training and research program on Eastern Europe.

Paul Marer
J. Michael Montias

Paul Marer and John Michael Montias

Introduction

In October 1976, a Conference on East European Integration and East-West Trade was held at Indiana University/Bloomington, sponsored by the Joint Committee on Eastern Europe of the American Council of Learned Societies and the Social Science Research Council. The purpose was to commission and discuss studies that would

> constitute fundamental contributions to knowledge with a firm empirical base [intended] to establish a milestone in East European research and set new directions for the future.

This volume traces its origins to the Bloomington conference, but it is not a proceedings. It contains the revised versions of fewer than half of the papers presented and several subsequently commissioned contributions. The unifying theme is a focus on the role of foreign trade in the economies of the European members of the Council of Mutual Economic Assistance (CMEA), including the USSR. The unifying mode is an analytical approach to each topic.

Part I is an essay on CMEA integration written by the editors. It discusses Eastern and Western concepts and measures of economic integration, describes the impact of environmental, systemic, and policy variables on CMEA integration, outlines CMEA's institutional arrangements, and provides a topical guide to the remaining contributions.

Part II, "Theoretical Analysis," is comprised of three chapters. Hewett attempts to measure and explain differences between centrally planned and market economies in their foreign-trade behavior and outcomes, i.e., trade level, direction, and structure. Two short essays by political scientists follow. Abonyi and Sylvain critically examine the relevance of political science theories on international integration to the experience of CMEA. Caporaso contrasts the difference between the European Economic Community (EEC) and CMEA in terms of the historical, political, and socio-economic conditions present when the respective regions began their integration efforts and deduces conclusions regarding comparisons involving the EEC and CMEA. Wolf develops a framework for analyzing the short-run, macro-economic adjustments of both conventional centrally planned economies (CPEs) and "modified" CPEs, such as Hungary, to external economic disturbances, such as inflation or changes in terms of trade.

Part III, "Issues in CMEA Integration," contains essays on various aspects of the topic. Brainard's contribution focuses on the CMEA financial system. Fallenbuchl compares industrial policy in the CMEA and the EEC; that is, national and supranational efforts to promote industrial growth by encouraging structural changes in the branch or geographic composition of an industrial sector. His statistical comparison focuses on the steel industry. Vanous presents an econometric model of intra-CMEA foreign trade, a pioneering attempt to combine the rudiments of a theory of the key determinants of intrabloc trade with an empirical testing of the model.

Part IV, "Individual Country Perspectives," views integration and East-West trade issues from the perspective of several members of the CMEA. Shabad focuses on Soviet industrial location policy and poses the question: When Soviet planners decide on the location of new capacity, do they take into account total demand within CMEA as well as their trade with the West? Hanson contributes on a topic on which there is much controversy: How large are the gains to the USSR from its Western technology imports? His method is that of a detailed case study which focuses on the Soviet mineral fertilizer industry.

Three contributions present integration and East-West trade issues from the perspective of three East European countries: Bulgaria, Romania, and Poland. Ofer's contribution compares Bulgaria's growth and specialization strategies with those of the other East European nations and finds Bulgaria's strategy significantly different from those of the rest of the countries in the CMEA. Montias examines the role foreign trade has played in Romania's economic development, tests a hypothesis to explain the fluctuations in the share of the West in Romania's total machinery imports, and discusses some of the new trading problems Romania is likely to face during the 1980s. Korbonski examines the past, present, and prospective future relationship between Poland and the CMEA. His approach combines political, social, and economic considerations that influence Poland's attitude and policies toward that organization. Bornstein's brief essay calls attention to similarities and differences concerning the foreign trade of Romania and Poland.

All of the longer contributions are followed by one or more discussions that critique or elaborate on the essays; the shorter contributions stand without comment. While some of the comments made at the Conference were "taken over" by the authors, additional comments on some of the papers were invited by the editors for inclusion in the volume.

This volume is intended to establish a comprehensive and up-to-date Western perspective on where the field of foreign trade in CPEs stands today and to help set directions for future research. Since a similar goal was set, and successfully achieved, by another conference and another volume approximately a decade ago, let us compare and contrast the two endeavors.

In 1966, a Conference on International Trade and Central Planning was held at the University of Southern California in Los Angeles, sponsored by the Joint Committee on Slavic Studies of the American Council of Learned Societies and the Social Science Research Council. The purpose was to initiate a systematic study of centrally planned foreign trade, which had been a relatively neglected field. In 1968, a volume based on the conference, *International Trade and Central Planning* (edited by Alan A. Brown and Egon Neuberger) was published. In that volume, there was an emphasis on searching for what is different and unique about centrally planned foreign trade, as is appropriate for a new and emerging field of study. The contributions in the present volume take a more balanced approach, seeking to find both similarities and differences between CPEs and market-type economies, revealing that CPEs have important features that make it possible to compare them with nations outside of Eastern Europe. The contributions also recognize that the CPEs themselves should be increasingly differentiated—by size, level of development, historical and political tradition, and the extent of modifications in the traditional CPE system that nations may undertake in individual fashion.

A further distinction between the two works is that while most of the contributions in the Brown-Neuberger volume tended to be descriptive of CPE foreign-trade institutions and policies, necessary at an early stage of research, most of the contributions in this volume are analytical and theoretical, made possible by the fact that the authors could build on the earlier, and by and large still relevant, descriptive contributions. One aspect is the inclusion in this volume of several econometric studies, whereas there was neither a firm enough theoretical foundation nor adequate statistical information to attempt econometric work ten years ago. Thus, in this volume, relatively little attention is being paid to the institutional mechanisms of trading by a typical CPE because, fundamentally, not much has changed in these matters during the last decade, except in Hungary. (Regrettably, no contribution focuses specifically on the implications for foreign-trade institutions of Hungary's New Economic Mechanism, although some aspects of Hungary's trade policy are discussed in Wolf's contribution.)

With respect to the CMEA trading and coordinating mechanism, there has been, in our view, only one major new development during the last decade: the gradual emergence of a financial subsystem under which the settlement of a certain portion of intra-CMEA trade is made in convertible currencies. Brainard describes this new development and assesses its implication for CMEA integration. To be sure, there have been developments in the CMEA during the last decade that are of great importance for the member countries, such as changes in membership, adjustments in the foreign-trade pricing mechanism, the establishment of a regional investment bank, the setting up of some new CMEA planning and coordinating bodies and procedures, and the growing scale of so-called CMEA joint investment projects (see the contribution that follows this introduction). But these developments do not fundamentally alter the basic CMEA institutions and coordinating mechanisms, already in place during the 1960s.

Concerning future prospects, the only issue that received considerable attention in the Brown-Neuberger volume was the question of economic reforms, including reforms in the foreign-trade sector. It was recognized, especially by Grossman, that balance-of-payments problems would provide pressure for reforms in Eastern Europe— though not in the USSR—which would have as a main purpose to render these economies more effective as an earner of foreign exchange and as a gainer from the international division of labor. Yet it was felt, notably by Bergson, that CPEs would probably not move rapidly toward improved efficiency either in their domestic or in their foreign-trade sectors because serious obstacles remain against economic decentralization type reforms. These obstacles were identified by Neuberger as "legacies of a Soviet-type CPE": the absence of entrepreneurs interested and able to exploit profitable trading opportunities; investment by the state in "infants" that refuse to grow up; a high investment rate creating supply shortages which planners feel would get inflation out of control if they allowed enterprises too much room to maneuver; the difficulty of correcting a price system divorced from both domestic and foreign scarcity relations; and the absence, or relatively small number, of specialized and technologically advanced export sectors.

In retrospect, ten years later we find that this prediction was quite accurate, except in the case of Hungary which did overcome, against seemingly long odds, many of these obstacles and in 1968 introduced its New Economic Mechanism. (To what extent the Hungarian economy operates according to the "rules" of the New Economic Mechanism or on the basis of central direction and intervention is, to a Western observer, certainly not clear.)

It is interesting that no one even raised the possibility ten years ago that one policy option the CPEs might have is to borrow heavily from the West. The CMEA countries boosted sharply their imports from the industrial West during the 1970s to help modernize their economies with Western technology. They also required large increases of industrial materials purchased from the West to compensate for a slowdown in the growth of such imports from the USSR and from each other. Because the growth rate of exports was considerably slower than the tempo of imports, all these countries undertook heavy borrowing from the West, pushing the total net hard-currency debt of the CMEA countries from a few billion dollars ten years ago to well over $50 billion by the end of 1978.

Looking ahead, it is not difficult to predict that the large indebtedness, especially of the East European countries, will remain critically important in shaping not only East-West trade but also CMEA integration. But the fundamental question remains the evolution of the CPE system and the interaction between economic system and foreign trade. The evolution of the domestic economic mechanism in the East European countries is also linked closely to the question of progress in CMEA integration. Will progress be made toward integration during the 1980s, and, if yes, will it be by the imposition of supranational authority or by economic reforms in the planning and price mechanisms of the member countries, followed by the introduction of currency convertibility? It is not any easier to predict future prospects in these matters as we enter the 1980s than it was a decade ago.

There is one new issue that may have a significant impact on CMEA integration: the continuous enlargement of the CMEA by the incorporation of Mongolia and Cuba during the 1960s, Vietnam in 1978, and possibly the newly emerging communist countries in Asia (Laos, Afghanistan, and Cambodia?) and elsewhere during the 1980s. So far, the peripheral members have played only a marginal role in CMEA decisions. But membership by a growing number of less-developed countries enhances the possibility that subregional integration schemes may be promoted during the 1980s, among some of the more developed East European countries on the one hand and among the less-developed Asian or European countries on the other. We offer a few thoughts on this and other "future prospects" issues in "The Theory and Measurement of East European Integration," in this volume.

PART I
OVERVIEW

Paul Marer and John Michael Montias

Theory and Measurement of East European Integration

What Is Economic Integration and Can It Be Measured?

Economic integration has traditionally been equated with the division of labor in a geographical region, although it has not been made clear what minimum level of trade would justify speaking of integration. More recently, economic integration is said to consist not only of the internationalization of the markets for goods and services but also for those of capital and labor, technology and entrepreneurship, money and credit, as well as supporting economic institutions.

It is impossible to measure the institutional aspects of integration with statistical indicators, but their effects will presumably be reflected in the level and composition of trade and other kinds of measurable economic links among members of a regional group. In discussing integration in the Council for Mutual Economic Assistance (CMEA),[1] East European economists tend to focus on the CMEA institutions that foster or hinder integration; Western economists, by contrast, seek statistical measures of commercial ties among countries belonging to any regional group.

What are the key differences and similarities between capitalist and socialist economic integration? Can the Common Market and the CMEA be compared? To be sure, characterizing Common Market countries as "capitalist" and CMEA countries as "socialist" is an oversimplification. There is significant state ownership and control over the means of production in the Common Market as well as a degree of supranational planning. Conversely, market-type relations can be found both in the domestic economies of individual CMEA countries and in their relations with each other. Still, the basic features of the two integration groups justifies characterizing them as essentially capitalist or socialist.

The fundamental *difference* between capitalist- and socialist-type economic integration can be found in the institutions facilitating or hindering integration. In Western economies, in spite of the expansion of the public sector and other deviations from perfect competition, the bulk of international commerce is conducted by private enterprise, seeking profit opportunities wherever it can find them. Hence, a reduction in or elimination of barriers to the movement of goods, factors of production, and money across national boundaries goes a long way toward integration. By contrast, once the market is replaced by central planning, all movement of goods and factors within the region (as transactions with outsiders) requires an explicit action by the governments involved. The integration of centrally planned economies (CPEs) demands, therefore, more overt management and, thus, a more elaborate bureaucratic structure.

The fundamental *similarity* between capitalist- and socialist-type economic integration is that the purposes behind efforts to integrate tend to be similar: (1) better division of labor (i.e., improved specialization) desired as a source of economic growth; (2) economic discrimination in favor of members; and (3) enhanced political power for the integration group. The strongest country usually hopes that closer economic ties will lead to closer political ties and eventually to political unification, while weaker countries seek the benefits of being associated with a strong group but resist any significant loss of national independence and freedom of action in the international arena.

Focusing on market-type economies, Western economists and political scientists have developed sophisticated statistical indicators to measure aspects of integration from the point of view of a single member of a group of countries vis-à-vis other groups or the rest of the world. The indices that measure commercial ties can refer either to the *conditions* or to the *effects* of integration. Among the conditions are those that have the power to affect *mobility* (defined as elasticity in response to stimuli): One statistical approach is to quantify the obstacles to the free movement of goods or factors of production within a region. Among the *effects* are actual movements of goods and services, factors of production, technology, and money: One statistical approach is to measure changes in the level and composition of trade; another is to focus on changes in the relative prices of goods or factors of production within a region.

Statistical measures of integration, which will be discussed in greater detail in the next section, tend to give meaningful insights when applied to the same country or a group of countries over time. Less meaningful are attempts to compare integration among countries or groups of countries at any given moment. The reason is that it is so difficult to hold "all other things constant."

Among the important variables that will influence comparative outcomes are the economic size of the countries (regions) and the size disparities within the groups, level of development, resource endowment, distance from main suppliers and key markets, the economic policies pursued (such as import substitution vs. export expansion), the political objectives and relations of the countries within an integration group, and the group's economic and political relations with the rest of the world. It is not possible to isolate simultaneously the effects of these and other variables on integration outcomes because the statistical sample of integration groups is limited. No union of countries can, therefore, be compared meaningfully with the European Community (EC), which itself is changing as new members are added and political conditions in the member countries change.

In addition, attempted comparisons of the integration outcomes of market and planned economies, i.e., the EC vs. the CMEA, encounter special difficulties. One is the problem of calculating identical statistical measures for both groups. For example, if the CMEA is viewed as a Western-type custom union because its members discriminate against outsiders, this would be reflected in the CMEA countries' preference for higher priced or lower quality domestic or bloc suppliers. That is, the CMEA aggregates its preferential trading area by implicit quotas rather than by preferential tariffs or explicit quotas.[2] Moreover, even when it is possible to calculate nominally identical measures for the EC and the CMEA, institutional differences can undermine the validity of parallel statistical interpretation. Rather than indicating successful integration, a relatively large volume of intrabloc trade, like that which occurred during the 1950s, may only reflect underlying systemic or externally imposed commercial and financial barriers to extra-regional trade.[3]

To be sure, meaningful statistical comparisons of selected aspects of EC and CMEA integration can be made (see Fallenbuchl's contribution in this volume comparing the industrial policies of the two regions). But comprehensive statistical measures are not readily available to compare the degree of integration of the EC and the CMEA. Our efforts in the next section will, therefore, be limited to the conceptualization and measurement of economic integration in the CMEA.

Concepts and Measures of CMEA Integration

The economic integration of socialist countries may be seen from the vantage point of national authorities as they perceive the problem or as Western economists would envisage it, in theory or in practice. In this section, we present both points of view, along with some appropriate methods of measuring progress toward integration.

The way CMEA policymakers look at progress toward integration is undoubtedly more subtle and complex today than it was two or three decades ago. At that time, it was generally believed that any decision tending to increase trade among CMEA members at the expense of trade with nonmembers promoted bloc integration, which was deemed to be a good thing. A widely used indicator of such progress was the percentage of each member's total trade with other members of the bloc. Viewed thusly, the integration of the communist bloc reached its high point in the 1950s, when every member of the CMEA, including the Soviet Union, conducted a larger part of its trade with other members than it does today, even though the organization itself was dormant. Lack of opportunities to trade outside the bloc, largely due to the Western strategic embargo, contributed significantly to this apparent integration.

Today, CMEA policymakers concerned with the pace of integration place considerable weight on the "deepening" of the intra-CMEA division of labor, that is, on increased specialization within branches and on "vertical" specialization by two or more countries contributing inputs, components, or final assembling capacity to manufacture a product. "Deepening," of course, does not necessarily increase the share of intra-CMEA trade in the total trade of the bloc. Two CMEA members, each agreeing to specialize in a particular production line, may find that as their output and exports of products expand, their imports needed to sustain the increased output have to be stepped up *pari passu*. Gains in real income due to specialization may also lead to larger imports from nonmember countries.

A measure of integration commonly used by CMEA economists, as well as by the United Nations' Economic Commission for Europe, is the "delta coefficient," which is the ratio of a region's actual share of intrabloc trade to its hypothetical share. The ratio is calculated on the assumption that intrabloc trade is proportional to the region's share in total world exports and imports.[4] To illustrate, if the EC were to account for 35% of total world exports and 30% of total world imports, the hypothetical share of intra-EC trade would be 10.5% of world trade (35% × 30%). If the actual share were, say, 15.75%, the "delta coefficient" would be 1.5 (= .1575/.105).

According to a variant of this measure developed by an Austrian economist, where delta coefficients are scaled on the basis of their maximum attainable level (the maximum would be achieved if all the trade of a region were intrabloc), the highest degree of CMEA integration occurred in 1955 and again in 1962, and declined until 1975 (the last year included).[5] But, in our view, this and other related measures of integration are poor indicators of the extent to which a bloc of countries trading in a protected common market has achieved specialization according to its members' comparative advantage. One reason is that a bloc's share in world trade may be depressed by a policy of systematic "trade aversion" on the part of its member countries or by discrimination against the bloc by outsiders.[6] Yet, net "trade creation" in intrabloc exchanges may not be big enough to compensate for the drop in trade with the rest of the world. In such a case, the delta coefficient would rise without any increase in intrabloc specialization taking place. Stating the problem differently, if the EC's higher foreign-trade intensity, measured by trade/GNP ratios, is not properly considered, the delta coefficients will underestimate the trade integration of the EC and overstate that of the CMEA.[7]

There is a more fundamental problem, however, with any indicator that relies on changes in trade shares among members of a preferential group. A decrease in the share in the face of an increase in the absolute volume of intrabloc trade surely does not indicate a decline in regional integration, just as an increase in the share in the face of a stagnating or declining volume of intrabloc trade does not signal an increase in integration. Thus, the decline in the CMEA's delta coefficients between 1971 and 1976 was almost certainly due to increased Soviet and East European trade with the West rather than dis-integration of CMEA. Moreover, the requirement of bilateral balancing within the CMEA encourages tied trade and re-exports, so that even changes in the absolute volume of intrabloc trade may not necessarily indicate a corresponding change in the degree of integration.

A more promising approach consists in comparing actual trade within a bloc with potential trade, which is econometrically estimated on the basis of the distance between trading countries, their relative populations, and GNPs. Natural resource endowments and industrial structure also influence potential trade and should be included but are usually omitted from these "gravity models."[8] This is the route chosen by Hewett (in this volume), who analyzes differences in the foreign-trade outcomes between centrally planned and market economies. One difficulty these models face, as Hewett stresses, is how to allow for the impact on potential trade of policymakers' preferences for trading with partners in the bloc rather than with outsiders. Moreover, the potential is generally estimated from coefficients derived from the trading records of Western economies, which fail to exploit the full advantages of interindustry specialization.

The neo-classical approach to the definition and measurement of integration differs radically from those just examined. For example, consider a set of economies where all investment and output decisions are strictly consistent with the familiar requirements of "efficiency in production," yet trade among them is limited by artificial barriers (tariffs, quotas, exchange controls). Suppose that all impediments to trade among them—though not necessarily with the rest of the world—were removed. In the framework of the neo-classical paradigm, a necessary and sufficient condition for complete integration of this "bloc" would be that the relative prices of any pair of goods in every member country should be the same (adjusted for transportation costs). A *process of integration* would then consist in moving from an initial state, where relative prices differ significantly in each country, through a series of states, each marked by a convergence of relative prices compared to the last. Any temporary divergences in relative price trends due to exogenous events would eventually have to be reversed: that is, the trend toward equalization of relative prices in each country would have to be resumed as integration proceeded.

Among centrally planned economies (or, for that matter, among market economies where the state interferes with production or investment decisions), convergence toward equal price relatives is a necessary but not a sufficient condition for integration because government planners may order or induce levels of output or investment projects that are inconsistent with comparative advantage.

How can one tell whether a country is investing along the lines of comparative advantage?[9] Consider two countries, A and B, both producing some amounts of goods x and y in the presence of trade restrictions. Let coal-intensive good x be produced relatively cheaply in A and oil-intensive good y be produced relatively cheaply in B. When trade is facilitated by the removal of restrictions, A moves toward an output-mix richer in x and B toward a mix richer in y. The scarcities (or the shadow prices) of x and coal increase in A relative to the scarcities (or the shadow prices) of y and oil. The profitability (in terms of shadow prices) of producing x and coal increase in A, while that of producing y and oil increases in B. To be consistent with comparative advantage, investments and other resources must gravitate toward x and coal in A and toward y and oil in B. If, instead, prior to the removal of trade restrictions, large investments had flowed toward y and oil in A and toward x and coal in B, the same relative scarcities of these two pairs of goods might also have been attained in both countries, at which point no trade would take place even in the absence of restraints. If investment decisions are systematically made with an eye to equating relative scarcities within each country, then members of the bloc would cease engaging in any mutual trade, and perfect dis-integration would result.[10]

Let us now examine the problem of measuring progress toward integration along these lines. In light of our definition of an integration process, price and quantity indicators should be used to measure changes in the degree of integration. But in CPEs, prices and costs generally diverge from marginal rates of transformation in production (due, among other factors, to low capital charges and to large differences in the extent of indirect taxes and profits levied on various goods). Moreover, wholesale accounting and retail prices have not had much influence on the planners' choice of tradeable goods, nor have export and import prices been reflected systematically in wholesale and retail prices. In this situation, it would be difficult to use changes in the relative prices of goods to give even an impression of the extent to which relative scarcities within CMEA have tended to converge or to diverge over time.[11]

On the quantity side, the question is how to measure the convergence or divergence of relative outputs among countries over time. The method we suggest is analogous to the measurement of changes in the distribution of incomes or wealth using the Lorenz curve approach. Take as an example the production statistics of metal-cutting lathes, which we assume to be available for all CMEA countries in comparable measurement units. What is the percentage of the total CMEA output of these goods in a given year represented by the smallest producer (say, Bulgaria) or of the two smallest producers, and so forth, until the entire output is accounted for? The results may be plotted on a Lorenz curve, with the number of states shown on the abscissa and the cumulative shares of total output they represent on the ordinate. Of interest then would be the changes in the position of the curve observed through time. Clearly, progress toward integration will be marked by greater "inequality" or a larger coefficient of variation, that is, by each curve lying farther from the 45° line than the last.

To see what the results of a systematic study with this measure might yield, we selected a sample of 14 products from the CMEA statistical yearbooks. Data availability limited the samples to relatively highly aggregated products, such as lathes and tractors (see table 1). According to our definition, a movement toward specialization would show a more unequal distribution of production, i.e., the smallest three or four producers accounting for a declining share of total CMEA output over time. As could have been predicted, this indicator of integration during 1950-76 shows dis-integration among CMEA members for most products, largely because the countries that produced the smallest relative outputs during the 1950s (Bulgaria and Romania) have increased their shares of total bloc output over time. Table 1 reveals that during 1950-60, a trend toward specialization is

Table 1

Indicator of Product Specialization in CMEA:
Has the Distribution of Production Levels Among
CMEA Members Become More Unequal?

Product	1950-60	1960-70	1970-76
Investment goods			
Tractors	yes	no	no
Railway cars	no	yes	yes
Buses	no	no	yes
Lathes	n.a.	no	no
Intermediate goods			
Pig iron	no	no	no
Steel	no	no	no
Synthetic fertilizer	no	no	no
Consumer products			
Shoes	no	no	no
TV sets	no	yes	no
Radio sets	yes	yes	yes
Textile fabrics	no	no	no
Cigarettes	yes	yes	yes
Agricultural products			
Butter	no	no	yes
Meat	no	no	no

NOTE: The CMEA as here defined includes the USSR and the six East European countries of Bulgaria, Czechoslovakia, the GDR, Hungary, Poland, and Romania.

SOURCE: Based on production data in physical units reported in various CMEA statistical yearbooks. The method of calculation is described in the text.

found for only 3 out of 13, during 1960-70 for 4 out of 14, and during 1970-76 for 5 out of 14 products.

This particular application of the proposed measure is far from ideal, if only because we cannot rest a generalization about CMEA integration or dis-integration on 14 arbitrarily chosen and quite aggregated products. There is also a conceptual problem. One usually thinks of increased specialization as one country *expanding* output at the expense of other countries; but if one country *reduces* output to let several other countries expand production, might that not also be construed as a move toward increased specialization? This is, in fact, what we found in the case of tractors. During 1960-76, Hungary and the GDR were giving up the production of this item (their absolute production figures were declining); yet during the same period, the combined shares of the four smallest CMEA producers were rising. The statistical results, therefore, can give an ambiguous answer.

We computed the coefficient of variation of the percentages of output of the 14 commodities represented by the different members of CMEA. (The greater the coefficient, the greater in principle the degree of integration.) To refine this measure, which is strongly influenced by the USSR's large share (close to two-thirds) in the total CMEA output of most of these commodities and to detect whether subregional integration might be taking place among the six East European countries, the coefficient of variation is shown both including and excluding the Soviet Union.[12]

The results in table 2 do not contradict the conclusions noted above. First, in every instance, the coefficient of variation is significantly greater, as expected, among the CMEA seven than among the CMEA six (which excludes the USSR). Second, for the CMEA seven, between 1950 and 1960 the coefficient declines or remains essentially unchanged for 9 out of 14 commodities, between 1960 and 1970 again for 9 out of 14 commodities, and between 1970 and 1976 for 11 out of 14 products. The picture is somewhat different if we focus on the CMEA six. Between 1950 and 1960, the coefficient declined or remained essentially unchanged for 13 out of 14 commodities (the exception is tractors); between 1960 and 1970, it again declined or remained practically unchanged for 13 out of 14 commodities (except for cigarettes). But between 1970 and 1976, the coefficients increased for about half of the commodities, indicating that there may have been a movement toward specialization, although a significant increase is found only for TV and radio sets. Our tentative conclusion is that there appears to have been "dis-integration" in the CMEA between 1950 and 1970 as the less-developed countries began to produce many products that were previously the monopoly of the more industrialized members. But after 1970 this trend appears

TABLE 2

Indicator of Product Specialization in CMEA:
Coefficient of Variation of Percentages of
Output Levels for Selected Commodities, 1950-76

Product	CMEA Seven*				CMEA Six†			
	1950	1960	1970	1976	1950	1960	1970	1976
Investment goods								
Tractors	2.06	1.97	2.08	1.97	0.75	1.11	0.95	1.00
Railway cars	1.68	1.31	1.42	1.46	1.16	0.92	0.81	0.93
Buses	1.86	1.92	1.64	1.59	1.62	0.80	0.80	0.84
Lathes	1.42	1.41	1.45	1.54	1.04	0.83	0.42	0.35
Intermediate goods								
Pig iron	2.07	1.97	1.98	1.94	0.93	0.75	0.64	0.61
Steel	1.92	1.90	1.87	1.82	0.76	0.70	0.58	0.61
Synthetic fertilizer	1.49	1.37	1.56	1.64	1.98	1.51	0.87	0.78
Consumer products								
Shoes	1.63	1.59	1.53	1.43	0.74	0.54	0.51	0.48
TV sets	1.71	1.57	1.88	1.73	2.44	0.85	0.38	0.60
Radio sets	1.36	1.62	1.80	1.59	0.79	0.67	0.60	0.87
Textile fabrics	1.51	1.64	1.64	1.62	0.55	0.47	0.44	0.45
Cigarettes	1.46	1.58	1.45	1.42	0.45	0.47	0.57	0.64
Agricultural products								
Butter	1.73	1.64	1.64	1.60	0.98	0.90	0.86	0.90
Meat	1.24	1.41	1.42	1.26	0.89	0.62	0.55	0.53

SOURCE: See table 1.

*USSR and the six East European countries.

†Six East European countries only.

to have been halted and some specialization decisions implemented.

These statistical results illustrate the problem of quantifying the proposed measure of integration. One may argue, for example, that working with more disaggregated products, which would distinguish, say, lathes of various dimensions and degrees of automatic control, might show more positive results on specialization, since individual CMEA members are more willing to specialize in narrowly defined than in broadly defined product groups.[13] Fallenbuchl (in this volume) compares CMEA and EC integration in the steel sector. His measure analyzes the coefficient of variation of the narrowly defined physical outputs of steel products produced by the various members of a bloc.

A method of measuring progress toward integration in terms of prices and outputs may also be devised on the basis of index-number theory. First, calculate for certain benchmark years the aggregate output (GNP or industrial production, depending on whether only specialization in industrial goods is of concern) for any pair of countries A and B in CMEA using, alternatively, the prices of A and B to measure the aggregate. It is well known that the ratio of country A's output to B's will be larger when B's prices are used to weight the outputs of both A and B than when A's prices are used, if and only if the relative outputs of the two countries are inversely correlated with their prices. Otherwise, the result will be reversed.[14]

If the ratio in question, measured at two points in time with the same sets of prices drawn from A and from B, marks an increase, it will denote a trend toward greater integration. This is because the constancy in prices ensures that a rise in the ratio implies a greater divergence (variance) between the quantities produced in A and in B. To check whether prices have converged in a given period, a calculation can be made of the output ratio in the two countries at the beginning and at the end of the period, using beginning-of-the-period and end-of-the-period prices and keeping quantities constant. Needless to say, there is an underlying assumption that the quantities and prices entering the ratio in each period are representative of all the outputs and all the prices in each economy.

The neo-classical framework for analyzing specialization and integration has lately come under attack by Western economists. One of its chief drawbacks is that it has little to say about the extraordinarily rapid growth of intra-industry exchanges and about the related phenomenon of balanced trade within sectors and even within subsectors in trade among developed market economies.

The extraordinarily rapid growth of intra-industry specialization is obscured by the fact that for many developed countries the share of foreign trade in GNP has increased only moderately. But the intensity of trade *within* practically all *industrial* sectors has increased drastically, in some cases by some 50% to 100% during the last decade. The reason for this apparent paradox is that the composition of GNP of many industrial countries has shifted from high-trade to low-trade sectors, mainly from manufacturing to services, and public services in particular.[15]

What explains the success of increasing intra-industry and the failure to deepen inter-sectoral specialization after the elimination of tariffs? Balassa's explanation for the EC focuses on product differentiation and strong promises to protect existing industries. He found that "the increased exchange of consumer goods is compatible with unchanged production in the consumer goods industries of each of the participating countries while changes in product composition can be accomplished in the framework of existing machinery and intermediate products industries."[16]

Focusing on the effect of successive tariff reductions among GATT countries, Hufbauer and Chilas explained the failure to deepen intersectoral specialization in terms of the process of bargaining for the mutual concessions that paved the way for expanding trade among these developed nations. They argued that the negotiators, in the framework of GATT, swapped tariff concessions, which had to be more or less balanced to receive domestic support from the industries likely to be affected. Often the consent of a powerful firm could be obtained for an import that might threaten its sales only if a countervailing concession could be secured for one of its exports.[17]

With regard to the protection of domestic industries, the situation within CMEA seems to be analogous, particularly in the mutual trade of its East European members. CMEA negotiations on reciprocal deliveries take place within specialized commissions, one for each industrial sector, such as machine-building, chemicals, and textiles. In this framework, concessions are likely to be "balanced." There is little chance that one country would concede an export surplus to one or more other members in goods under the jurisdiction of one commission in exchange for the opportunity to run a surplus in goods subject to negotiation in another commission.

Trade in machinery within the CMEA illustrates the point. Table 3 shows the share of machinery in the total imports and exports of individual CMEA countries and of the bloc, with and without the USSR, for three five-year periods between 1960-64 and 1970-74. We find that trade in machinery has grown much faster than in other products, especially among the six East European countries, where in just ten years the share of machinery in their mutual trade increased from about 40% to 54%. The main reason for this is the rapid increase in the machinery exports of the less-developed countries, especially Bulgaria, Romania, and Poland, principally to the more developed

TABLE 3
Share of Machinery in Intra-CMEA Trade, 1960-74
(five-year arithmetic average percent)

Country	Imports			Exports		
	1960-64	*1965-69*	*1970-74*	*1960-64*	*1965-69*	*1970-74*
USSR	47.7	48.6	49.8	28.4	31.8	34.7
Eastern Europe						
Less developed						
Bulgaria	52.7	51.8	51.1	21.6	31.3	40.8
Romania	40.9	44.6	51.8	20.7	25.1	32.8
Medium developed						
Hungary	36.3	35.9	40.2	44.8	42.9	44.8
Poland	39.7	44.0	45.4	41.8	50.1	52.7
More developed						
GDR	21.2	31.3	40.4	55.3	58.3	59.9
Czechoslovakia	31.9	35.6	38.9	51.3	57.9	58.9
CMEA Seven	38.6	42.4	45.7	38.4	42.4	45.7
CMEA Six						
(excl. USSR)	41.2	48.9	54.3	40.3	48.9	54.2

SOURCE: Jan Vanous, computer printouts from *Project CMEA-FORTRAM Data Bank of Foreign Trade Flows and Balances of CMEA Countries, 1950-75* (Vancouver: Department of Economics, University of British Columbia).

markets of the GDR and Czechoslovakia. Thus, the large export and import surpluses of the 1950s and 1960s in intrabloc trade in machinery, and in the corresponding offset categories of raw materials and foodstuffs, have diminished over time as intra-industry reciprocal deliveries became the framework for trade within the CMEA.

Intra-industry trade among developed nations cannot be explained satisfactorily by specialized factor endowment or by any of the standard theories of the neo-classical paradigm. Neither can its advantages be measured in terms of the familiar gains-from-trade arguments. Theorists now think in terms of economies of scale and product differentiation in imperfectly competitive markets, while the advantages of trade without specialization may be attributed to the broadening of consumer choice, the limitation of the power of oligopolies, and the enlarged possibilities for the transmission of technology.[18] It can hardly be claimed that expansion of balanced intra-industry trade, so characteristic of exchanges among both Eastern and Western nations, promotes the type of integration that reduces or eliminates differences in relative scarcities among trading partners, at least to the same extent as intersectoral trade might be expected to. Despite the advantages that we have listed, its potential for facilitating growth or increasing consumers' welfare is definitely inferior to what we would associate with a freer type of trade.

Impact of the Economic System, Policy, and the Environment on CMEA Integration

Economic System and Integration

The foreign-trade activities of a traditional centrally planned economy (CPE) are determined or influenced by the following institutional arrangements:[19]

1. In each country, production and trade levels are set by highly placed officials in the party or in the government and carried out by the ministerial hierarchies concerned. Plans—sets of *ex ante* production and trade decisions slated to be carried out in a given period by producers and foreign-trade enterprises (FTEs)—are geared to a system of interlocking material balances. Decisions are implemented via orders that come down through hierarchic lines. Information about the environment of producers is transmitted chiefly from subordinates to superiors.

2. FTEs, subordinated to the Ministry of Foreign Trade, buy output from producers for export and sell imports to producers and wholesalers. On behalf of the FTEs, the monobank in each country pays producers for goods exported and charges consumers for goods imported in local currency. The producer of export and the user of import deals with the FTEs only: he is isolated from the foreign buyer or supplier. Managers of producing enterprises and FTEs are subject to material incentives for fulfilling physical output or foreign-trade plans, for cutting down on production costs, and for carrying out other assigned tasks.

3. Export and import transactions entered into by the FTEs with non-CMEA countries are valued according to current world market prices and settled in a convertible currency. With CMEA countries, transactions are valued according to an agreed upon set of past ("historical") world market prices (see the appendix) and settled in "transferable" rubles (TRs). The TR is an artificial accounting unit that takes a world market price expressed in a convertible currency and translates it into rubles at the prevailing official exchange rate.

4. The official exchange rates of the individual CMEA countries in terms of convertible currencies or vis-à-vis the TR are set arbitrarily and tend not to reflect or even approximate the equilibrium exchange rates based on the purchasing power of the currencies or some other equilibrium concept. FTEs, therefore, must keep two sets of books in domestic currency: one expressing the value of transactions with

foreign buyers and sellers translated into domestic currency via the official exchange rate, and the other expressing the value of transactions with domestic sellers of exports and users of import according to the domestic prices fixed (to some degree arbitrarily) by the domestic authorities in the country. The "gain" or "loss" on foreign transactions reflected by the difference in the two sets of books is settled automatically with the state budget, a procedure known as "automatic price equalization."

5. Within the CMEA, representatives of each country negotiate the pattern of production specialization with other CMEA members, bilaterally or multilaterally. The exchange of goods among countries is almost always agreed upon bilaterally. Prompted by the domestic planning system in the CMEA countries, which is based on "material balances," trade negotiations in the CMEA focus mainly on the type and quantity of goods each country wishes to import. Barter deals are then struck to keep bilateral accounts balanced. Any surplus demand beyond an exporter country's planned supply must be purchased outside the CMEA. For this reason, the value of a given surplus or deficit with one CMEA partner, expressed in TRs, is indeterminate and cannot be used automatically to offset deficits or surpluses with CMEA partners.[20] Lack of convertible currency sometimes leads to egregiously inefficient decisions. Hungary, for example, has a chemical complex whose operation requires a large quantity of salt. One of Europe's largest salt mines is across the border in Romania, about 35 miles from the complex. But Romania ships the salt to the US and other countries where it gets paid in convertible currency while Hungary imports salt from Algeria because there is no direct outlay of scarce hard currency required. Sometimes such problems are solved by agreeing to settle certain intra-CMEA trade transactions in convertible currency, a growing tendency that may favor bloc-wide integration insofar as it mitigates the integration-reducing effects of bilateral clearing accounts (see Brainard's contribution in this volume).

Since the early 1950s, when this "pure" foreign-trade system was in force throughout the bloc, partial reforms have been implemented by all CMEA countries, and in 1968 comprehensive reforms were introduced in Hungary.[21] Have economic reforms changed the basic mechanism of foreign trade within the CMEA?

There are three types of partial reform measures: in the planning mechanism, in the foreign trade monopoly, and in the domestic price and exchange rate systems.

The essence of planning reforms is a reduction in the number of quantitative plan targets set by the central planner, leaving some flexibility to the ministries and producing enterprises to determine the composition of output. Decisions to incorporate a line of production, an investment project, or an export or an import commitment into the plan may be based on, or justified by, calculations of costs and returns made with the aid of domestic or foreign-currency prices. Yet, the essential features of traditional material balancing and central supply allocation have remained unchanged in all countries except Hungary.

Reforms in the monopoly of foreign trade were prompted by a recognition that the functional separation of foreign trade from domestic production is inefficient. Various schemes have been introduced, therefore, to make FTEs and producing enterprises more equal partners, including the granting of foreign-trade rights to selected industrial firms. Still, the fundamental lack of interest of producing enterprises in earning more foreign exchange by improving the quality of products or by finding new export items has not changed.

Reforms in the domestic price system were undertaken so that prices would more accurately reflect production costs, including the cost of imports. But because there is no consensus in these countries on how to set prices to reflect both costs and relative scarcities or on how long prices should remain fixed, and because strong vested interests oppose any major price change, prices tend to be arbitrary and still play only a small allocative role. Various reforms were also undertaken to forge a more meaningful link between domestic and foreign prices. Exchange-rate-type coefficients are permitted to influence, to a greater or lesser degree, some export and import choices. But given the shortcomings of the domestic price systems and the mechanisms under which taxes and subsidies wipe out the greater part of enterprise profits and, eventually, all of its losses (bankruptcies are not permitted), these modifications in the price mechanism do not have a substantially different effect on enterprise decisions than the automatic price equalization did under the traditional system. The central features of Hungary's comprehensive economic reform in 1968 were abolishing detailed plan instructions to enterprises, basing prices on factor costs and allowing some prices to be flexible to reflect demand, and establishing more realistic exchange rates to link foreign and domestic markets operationally. But the influence of the market is still circumscribed by the monopoly power of many enterprises, which remain protected from foreign competition, and by using many direct and indirect instruments of state intervention.

We conclude that, notwithstanding the introduction of partial reforms in all CMEA countries since the late 1950s and the nurturing of the comprehensive reform in Hungary since 1968, the "traditional" foreign-trade mechanism is still essentially intact. But what forces are generated by the "system" for and against CMEA integration?

First, the system places on producers constraints that are not conducive to integration with foreign markets. Since producing for the
foreign market is more difficult as a rule than supplying the domestic
market, most firms are fundamentally disinterested in exports. The
enterprise is ordered to export to fulfill the plan rather than to make a
profit; the firm's existence in most cases is not threatened in any
fundamental way by its inability to export or to compete efficiently
with imports. Since most exporting firms also produce for the domestic market, even when managerial bonuses are tied to foreign exchange earnings, the maximum bonus can usually be achieved more
easily by skillful bargaining with the planning authorities or by
fulfilling the domestic plan than by gearing up for exports. Even when
nominal bonuses for exports expansion are substantial, the marginal
taxation rate of personal income is so high that the *de facto* export
incentive is insignificant. These generalizations seem to be valid even
for the majority of Hungarian industrial producers. There are exceptions, to be sure, in all CMEA countries: enterprises that have a long
tradition of producing for foreign markets (e.g., pharmaceuticals in
Hungary, optical equipment in the GDR, ships in Poland) or
enterprises whose top management is entrepreneurial and has strong
lobbying power to obtain the resources necessary to produce for
export. (This does not mean, of course, that these firms efficiently
deal with the cost of earning a unit of foreign exchange.)

The information system in CMEA countries is much too coarse to
enable the policymaking hierarchy to make fine-tuned specialization
and trade decisions based on small differences in relative scarcities
between their country and other CMEA members. In the late 1960s,
when Poland and Czechoslovakia agreed to produce tractor parts and
components for each other's markets, there was so much uncertainty
and debate about the worth of each part or component that they
finally entered into a barter agreement in which 10 kg. of exports was
exchanged for 10 kg. of "similar type" imports. The uncertainty
about whether this kind of specialization yielded gains or losses was a
factor in the decision to abandon the agreement.

Indeed, decisionmakers in the CMEA countries probably do not
perceive the necessity of balancing relative scarcities among countries. They are moved to action by perceived shortages and deficits in
the availability of goods or by calculations of costs and returns showing a conspicuous advantage in engaging in certain lines of exports or
in replacing expensive domestic production by imports. Neither the
material balances (which at least ensure a modicum of consistency
between input and output decisions) nor the calculations comparing
foreign exchange prices with domestic costs (based ultimately on

administered prices) can supply accurate guidelines for specialization and trade policies.[22] Consider a tentative plan for the year which differs from last year's actual plan only in that there is a gap between the expected supply and demand of good y. Imports of the gap-bridging quantity of y can be paid for by an increase in the export of good x. Assume that the import can be arranged with a CMEA member with a perceived surplus of y, and that this same country is willing to take the appropriate quantity of x in exchange.[23] The export and the import decisions in the two countries are now incorporated into the plan, and suitable modifications are made in a few of the material balances on which the plan is based to assign responsibility for the production of the additional inputs needed to produce the increment in the production of x for export.

In a market economy, changes would occur in relative costs and returns if additional quantities of x were exported and y were imported. This would stimulate investments in x (to eliminate the extra costs due to the declining productivity of variable inputs pressing on a given capacity in the x industry) and discourage investments in y. It is not clear through what information channel or as a result of what calculation either of these effects would be induced in a CPE.

The first effect—investment in the export industry—may occur, not as part of a cost-reducing operation but with the aim of expanding exports for balance-of-payments reasons or, in the case of the less-developed members of CMEA, because exports in certain "modern" branches of manufacturing are prestigious. There is no *a priori* reason to believe that the resulting investments would be efficient in volume or in composition. For example, about ten years ago Bulgaria decided to specialize in electronic pocket calculators. It started to export calculators to Hungary (and probably to other CMEA countries) for 100 TR each. Finding the price too high, Hungary attempted import substitution and started to produce calculators. But since it found that the value of the components it had to import from the West was $15 and that it could import the finished product for about the same price, Hungary stopped production and began to import calculators from Hong Kong.[24]

The second effect—curtailment of investments in the industry competing with the imported good—is also problematic. From the viewpoint of the employees of a project-making bureau attached to an industrial ministry, importing y may be a signal to step up rather than to choke off investments in production. For many decisionmakers in CPEs, every imported good is a "deficit item," and any branch of domestic production that can be expanded to replace it is a worthy candidate for investments. While there may be no policy of "import-substitution across the board" handed down from the highest levels of the government, such an attitude is fostered for balance-of-payments reasons, by a misperception of scarcity and by a fear that dependence on inputs imported from socialist partners may jeopardize fulfillment of the plans in case of supply breakdowns.[25] Diversification of production to hedge against the vicissitudes of supply may be just as rational a response to this source of uncertainty at the national level as it is at the enterprise level. This pattern of enterprise behavior in CPEs is conventional wisdom in the East European and Western literature on the topic. Unless the import supply of *y* can be nailed down through a CMEA-sponsored specialization agreement supplemented by an enforceable long-term contract with the exporting country, it is likely that the one-time "shortage" will sooner or later disappear as a result of a capacity-expanding investment in the importing country. But, paradoxically, attempted import substitution cannot reduce the imports of the relatively small countries of Eastern Europe; it only transforms their composition. If the country was previously importing commodities that have been replaced with new domestic capacity, then the import requirements will consist of goods made necessary by the process of import substitution itself.[26]

This discussion of systemic considerations leads us to conclude that decisions by branch ministries, industrial associations, or enterprises are unlikely to move the system in the direction of intrabloc comparative advantage and may well move it in the opposite direction. An active integration policy must be conducted at the top to combat tendencies toward isolationism in the lower levels.

Economic Policy and Integration

Given the economic system in the CMEA countries and the system-determined mechanism of foreign trade in the bloc, what *integration policies* are pursued by CMEA members? First we will discuss the evolution of key policy recommendations for integration, especially those by the Soviet Union, and the concrete measures taken up to now to implement them. Next we will call attention to certain *domestic policies* of the CMEA countries, which affect regional integration outcomes directly or indirectly.

INTEGRATION POLICIES IN THE CMEA

The economic system described above perpetuates the producers' fundamental lack of interest in becoming integrated with customers and suppliers in other countries. For this reason, the integration policies of member countries must focus on the mechanism of state-to-state relations rather than on domestic economic policies that would make CMEA integration more attractive to producers and consumers. That is, integration must be planned by the state at the highest level and imposed on the ministries, trusts, and enterprises.

Tracing the efforts during the three decades of CMEA existence to find policies acceptable to all members reveals how difficult it is first to reach agreement about specialization, then to find a workable CMEA mechanism, and finally to implement policies effectively in each country. Linked closely with alternative policies on specialization, suggestions for reforming the CMEA mechanism have ranged from proposals for a supranational authority, which would create the traditional institutions of central planning at the regional level, to those favoring greater reliance on market mechanisms.

The best known proposed integration policy was that advocated by the Soviet Union during 1962-64 for CMEA to become a supranational organ. The Soviets proposed that CMEA make decisions and allocate resources *ex ante* rather than try to coordinate *ex post* the decisions made by the national planning authorities. This proposal brought to the surface the fear of the comparatively small East European countries that bloc integration under a supranational authority would mean more and more Soviet domination. Romania took the most uncompromising stand against this type of integration. Its ruling party issued a famous 1964 statement, bringing the conflict to world attention:

> . . . forms and measures have been proposed such as a joint plan and a single planning body for all member countries. . . . The idea of a single planning body for all CMEA countries has the most serious economic and political implications. The planned management of the national economy is one of the fundamental, essential, and inalienable attributes of sovereignty of the socialist state . . . transmitting such levers to the competence of superstate or extrastate bodies would turn sovereignty into a meaningless notion.[27]

In the face of Romania's firm stand—and perhaps remembering that intensified pressure on Albania a few years earlier had led to that country's defection from the bloc—the USSR decided not to press its proposals.

The 1964-70 period was one of much discussion, debate, and experimentation in each CMEA country about needed reforms in the traditional CPE system. In addition, the proposals usually contained suggestions to reform the CMEA mechanism. One such proposal, most clearly articulated by Hungarian economists, favored a greater reliance on market mechanisms for socialist integration. The advocates of this approach predicted better prospects for realizing gains from regional specialization and for maintaining greater national autonomy. Other proposals, including those made by Soviet economists, favored planned integration relying on the traditional concepts and institutions of central planning.[28]

After the Czechoslovak events of 1967-68, it became more urgent for the Soviet Union to promote the cohesiveness of the CMEA network, through which it could maintain its dominion without using coercion.[29] The Soviet Union probably also wanted a system of regional integration that would place external limits on the economic reforms undertaken by any East European country. At the same time, this system would better compensate the Soviets as an increasingly large net supplier of energy and raw materials to Eastern Europe than the then current CMEA price and trading system. Accordingly, Soviet economists began to float new proposals in the late 1960s. Realizing that supranational planning was not politically feasible, they thought that it could be approximated, nevertheless, through joint planning of the regional economy's key sectors.[30]

The outcome of this debate was the 1971 *Comprehensive Program* for socialist integration. Although the document appears to be a compromise between those advocating market mechanisms and those favoring a joint planning approach, the emphasis has been clearly on joint planning and the initiation of joint investment projects in priority sectors. The aspects of the Comprehensive Program that stress the market approach to socialist integration, such as its timetable to introduce a degree of convertibility into CMEA currency relations, appear to have been mere lip service, or perhaps a recognition of need rather than a statement of resolution.[31] However, to reduce the fears of the East European countries about compulsory supranationalism, one important compromise was made and appears to have become a permanent feature of the CMEA: the "interested party principle," which permits member countries to participate only in those CMEA projects or programs in which they have a material "interest."

Three types of activities contained in the Comprehensive Program have been stressed: improved plan coordination, joint CMEA investment projects, and cooperation in long-term "target" programs. It is difficult to learn from the CMEA literature how much has been agreed upon in principle only, whether comprehensive and detailed blueprints for implementation have yet been accepted, or the extent to which implementation of these programs is underway. Our understanding of the status of these activities at the end of 1978 is as follows:

Improved plan coordination is to proceed on the basis of a 1973 agreement specifying that each country must include a special section in its national plan document for 1976-80 elaborating the specific economic details of its integration measures. The special sections consist of two parts:

1. A listing of resources allocated for the construction of CMEA joint projects and of the reciprocal commodity deliveries resulting from the projects.

2. A listing of resources devoted to the construction and operation of domestic industries that have bilateral or multilateral specialization agreements with other CMEA countries and the reciprocal commodity deliveries resulting from these agreements.

Plan coordination thus appears to involve a standardization of economic information concerning projects that involve a long-term linking of two or more CMEA economies. This should facilitate a better assessment of what is happening in the CMEA and checking the bilateral and multilateral consistency of national plans, but it does not, of course, affect the substance of CMEA integration.

Joint CMEA investment projects represent the major new form of CMEA activity. About a dozen such projects are being implemented during the current five-year plan (1976-80), most of them located in the USSR. The biggest by far is the Orenburg gas pipeline; others include asbestos mining facilities at Kiembayev, a cellulose plant at Ust Ilim, and an electric power transmission line between the USSR and Hungary. The planned value of joint CMEA projects in 1976-80 was 9 billion TR (approximately $14.5 billion), about half financed by the USSR the other half by the East European countries.[32] Since the Comprehensive Plan was accepted, the Soviet Union has been pressing the other countries to participate in such projects, pointing out that its territory has the natural resources which most of these joint projects are designed to exploit or transport, and that these investments represent partial compensation for supplying its CMEA partners with energy and raw materials—hard goods that the Soviets can readily sell to Western countries for convertible currency.

The East European countries argue, on the other hand, that investing in the so-called CMEA joint projects—which take the form of the delivery of labor, capital and consumer goods, and the provision of technical know-how for projects located on Soviet soil—are not necessarily economically beneficial from their point of view. They cite the high manpower and hard-currency costs of these projects, the low interest rates received, and the disadvantageous terms of repayment, made in kind, yet valued in continually depreciating TRs as intra-CMEA prices follow the rise of prices on the world market. The East European countries recognize, however, that these liabilities must be juxtaposed with assurance that the promised supplies will be available in the future.

Strong disagreements among the CMEA countries regarding the economic viability of the joint projects have apparently triggered a 1979 decision by the USSR not to press the East European countries to participate in new joint projects during the first half of the 1980s. Instead, the Soviet Union is reportedly pressing for greater cooperation in other integration programs.

Cooperation in long-term target programs calls for most CMEA countries to agree voluntarily on meaningful, CMEA-wide plan coordination and on joint planning for selected sectors and key projects. The blueprint for this type of cooperation reportedly consists of:[33]

1. Joint forecasting for 15 to 20 years of production, consumption, and trade trends to identify prospective shortages and surpluses.

2. Coordination of medium- and long-term plans for the sector's main branches of production and key commodities.

3. Joint planning of the production of selected key commodities and joint research and development programs.

4. Continuous exchange of information of planning experiences. It has been agreed that cooperation in long-term target programs should encompass five sectors: fuels, energy, and raw materials; machine building; industrial consumer goods; agriculture, especially foodstuffs; and transportation. Joint planning of production has been agreed on in principle for selected commodities.

Implementing these programs would appear to involve substantial investments. At the 32nd CMEA session in Bucharest in mid-1978, the Soviet Union was still urging the rapid formulation of concrete plans in the first three of these sectors, so that implementation could begin with the next five-year plan (starting in 1981). Thus, it appears that cooperation in long-term target programs has not yet advanced beyond a general statement of goals and intent.

DOMESTIC POLICIES AFFECTING INTEGRATION

While the system determines or narrowly confines the channels through which policies can be implemented and the environment imposes restrictions on each country's actions, policymakers are still able to impose their preferences on matters of integration. First, the preferences of the highest authorities in the CMEA countries and the policies that they inform differ a good deal with respect to the nature and the extent of specialization they are willing to accept. Bulgaria, as Gur Ofer and Mark Allen point out in this volume, has specialized in exports of agricultural products, both raw and processed, as far as was compatible with her goal of rapid industrialization. In contrast, Romania, as Montias and the discussants to his paper indicate, until recently neglected her agriculture to press all available resources into industrial expansion. Within the industrial sector, Romania and Bulgaria also differed in that the former insisted on "balanced, complex, multisided development," meaning that no branch of industry was to be sacrificed for the sake of reaping the advantages of specialization, whereas the latter was distinctly more willing to go along with CMEA-wide specialization.[34]

Not all members of CMEA have the same preference, relative to the other goals they may pursue, for promoting the economic interests of CMEA as a whole. In more recent years, the Soviet Union at times appears to have forsaken its short-term economic advantage by its willingness, for example, to become an increasingly large net supplier to Eastern Europe of oil and other "hard goods" at a time when those commodities could have been sold more advantageously on the world market.[35] This policy no doubt involves a trade-off between its economic and political aims. Furthermore, it is our impression that the leaders of tbe GDR and perhaps Bulgaria have at times been more willing to accommodate the larger interest of the bloc, especially that of the USSR, than the other members.[36] To establish this point firmly, however, would require more systematic study. An interesting approach in the case of Poland is taken by Korbonski who, in his contribution to this volume, examines the forces generated by the process of integration that influence political decisionmakers to move toward closer or looser integration within the CMEA.

The attitude of individual CMEA members toward trade and industrial cooperation with Western countries and their reliance on Western credits differ considerably. The Western share in the total trade of the European CMEA countries ranges from about 20% for Bulgaria to almost 50% for Romania and Poland. Only Romania and Hungary permit equity joint ventures with Western corporations (Poland also permits small-scale joint ventures in certain sectors). The acceptance of Western credits, or the active search for them since the early 1970s, ranges from extremely eager in the case of Poland and Bulgaria to zealous in the case of Hungary and Romania to cautious in the case of Czechoslovakia.[37] Western credits facilitate the expansion of trade with the West, both through an immediate rise in imports by the credited nation and an eventual rise in exports to repay the loans.

In spite of these differences within the CMEA, there was a substantial expansion of all CMEA countries' trade with the West during the 1970s. Increasing reliance on Western imports—whether energy, raw materials, semi-manufactures, grain, technology, or consumer products—reflects the growing unavailability (in adequate quantities or quality) of products most in demand from CMEA suppliers (which may be a consequence of the economic system), the easy availability of Western credits, and new policies by the CMEA countries.

The relationship between East-West trade and CMEA integration can be both complementary and competitive.[38] Complementarity obtains insofar as the inflow of Western goods, technology, and managerial know-how may give an impetus to product specialization in the CMEA. Some Western imports and a few industrial cooperation agreements with Western firms are motivated in part by the desire of the smaller East European countries to be designated the sole (or at least the principal) supplier of machinery or other products under CMEA specialization agreements. For Western corporations, the possibility of penetrating CMEA and especially the Soviet market through industrial cooperation with an East European partner can be an important commercial motive.[39]

These kinds of complementarities are illustrated by the 1972 agreement between the US firm International Harvester and the Polish firm BUMAR to jointly manufacture crawler tractors in Poland.[40] One of BUMAR's motives in entering into industrial cooperation with a Western firm was to gain a competitive edge within the CMEA, especially on the Soviet market, by obtaining specialization rights for certain types of construction machinery. In 1974, under a CMEA agreement, Poland (i.e., mainly BUMAR) was granted specialization rights in the CMEA for dozens of different types of construction machinery and equipment. "We could develop exports to the socialist countries even more," stated an executive of BUMAR, "if we offered a greater number of machines built in cooperation with American partners." One of International Harvester's motives in entering into industrial cooperation with a Polish firm was to gain entry into those CMEA markets where its market penetration was limited. International Harvester benefits from Poland's CMEA arrangements directly through royalties and the export of components essential to the production of these machines and indirectly because it can help promote sales in other CMEA countries. For example, even before its initial agreement with BUMAR was signed, we understand that the Soviet Union switched some of its purchases of crawler tractors to the American firm because it assumed that the Polish firm would be able to provide spare parts and service.

This example of complementarity between East-West commerce and CMEA integration does not suggest that the two are typically complementary and mutually reinforcing. Many examples can illustrate the opposite. The CMEA countries have no common agreed-upon strategy regarding the purchase of Western technology or industrial cooperation with Western firms.[41] This causes unnecessary duplication of effort among them. For example, during the first half of the 1970s, every European CMEA country bought similar PVC technology from the West and planned to export a large part of the output to pay for the import. Lack of coordination in the CMEA, inadequate CMEA-wide planning for domestic utilization of the output, and long delays in putting the plants on stream (during which worldwide over-production had cut the world price of PVC by nearly half) have resulted in excess production capacity and cutthroat competition to sell PVC for convertible currency.

East-West trade and CMEA integration can also be competitive in other respects. The substantial expansion of the CMEA countries' trade with the West during the 1970s has created economic links that cannot easily be severed. The large indebtedness of the CMEA countries to the West mortgages a significant share of East Europe's future exports to the West, with self-evident consequences for CMEA integration.

Environmental Variables and Integration

REGIONAL FACTORS

The most remarkable aspect of the CMEA environment in contrast to the EC's is the disparity in size, resource endowment, and political power among its members. The Soviet Union accounts for roughly two-thirds of the population and aggregate GNP of the bloc; and it is endowed with over nine-tenths of its crude oil, gas, and iron ore resources.

As well endowed as the Soviet Union is, there is a deficit supply in the communist bloc in natural resources, minerals, foodstuffs, and other primary commodities. This is in part a consequence of forced industrialization, which required a growing quantity of these resources for domestic industries and for exports and the wasteful use of materials in production. The deficit is also caused because primary commodities can be traded more easily outside the bloc for convertible currencies and because in the CMEA they are underpriced relative to manufactured products (as compared to world market prices). This relative underpricing—much less pronounced since 1975—is the outcome of the bargains struck by individual CMEA members in bilateral and multilateral negotiations and, hence, of the policies underlying the negotiating stance of each member.[42] But once prices have been decided on, the relative scarcity of "hard goods" and the abundance of "soft goods" become exogenous (i.e., part of the environment) for each CMEA member.

Countries relatively well supplied with natural resources, or which are net exporters, are pressed by those that cannot provide these scarce "hard goods." The former, chiefly the Soviet Union but also Poland and Romania, hold the trump cards. They exert bargaining power by tying their deliveries of primary products to sales of soft goods, chiefly manufactured commodities that the purchasers would not otherwise have wished to buy. Jan Vanous' contribution in this volume builds an econometric model of intra-CMEA foreign trade that explicitly recognizes the tying of hard and soft goods in bilateral trade among CMEA countries.

The disparities in industrial development levels of CMEA members inhibits integration. One might expect that the faster growth of the least advanced members (Bulgaria and Romania) and the gradual evening out of development levels in the bloc would tend in the long run to reduce the importance of this impediment to integration.[43] This, however, is by no means certain, in view of the "brute-force" nature of the development of the latecomers to industrialization. As long as the technological gap between the more and the less advanced members of the bloc persists, the former will not, in general, abandon lines of production to the latter and become dependent on suppliers that may not be capable of meeting their requirements.[44] The technological gap is not likely to narrow as rapidly as disparities in GNP per capita.

The enlargement of the CMEA by the incorporation of Mongolia in the early 1960s, Cuba in the early 1970s, and Vietnam in 1978 (Laos, Afghanistan, and Cambodia during the 1980s?) makes integration more difficult for political and institutional reasons, even if these countries play only a marginal role in CMEA specialization agreements. Given their locations, their membership would appear to serve principally Soviet foreign policy interests, according to which the East European countries are called upon to subsidize these less-developed allies of the USSR.

A critical environmental factor for CMEA is the extremely low mobility of factors of production between the socialist countries, especially within Eastern Europe proper. The failure to open Eastern Europe to the free movement of labor and capital may stem originally from Soviet policies imposed on East European clients in the early postwar period. This actively discouraged forming deep commercial ties among East European countries.[45] But these policies eventually became a part of the CMEA economic environment. For example, with few exceptions there have been no significant transfers of labor within the bloc.[46] In addition, these economies do not take advantage of low-cost foreign labor from countries outside the bloc, such as the EC imports from Portugal, Spain, Greece, Turkey, and Yugoslavia.

Capital exports from one CMEA nation to another have also been small and are often determined *ex post*, when credits are granted to finance an unplanned imbalance (visible and invisible) in trade flows or because of political considerations. An example of the latter is the flow of Soviet credits granted to several East European countries to finance their deteriorating terms of trade with the USSR after 1975 when energy prices were raised. Such Soviet credits often cannot be fully utilized by the East European countries because the goods they need the most (energy and raw materials) are not available and what is readily available (e.g., standard machinery, watches, cameras) is not wanted. Credits are also involved in the so-called joint CMEA investment projects discussed earlier.

According to the neo-classical theory of international trade, given differences in factor endowment in a group of countries, low factor mobility should be conducive to even greater intensity of trade than if factors were free to move.[47] But under conditions where intra-industry trade, which is not particularly related to specific factor endowments, predominates, lack of mobility is likely to impede trade rather than promote it. CMEA integration, no matter how defined, would move to higher levels if energetic measures were taken to transfer labor and capital across those frontiers where they might be expected to be most productive on the margin. But such transfers are impeded by the inability to reliably calculate the benefits and costs of such integration measures.

INTERNATIONAL FACTORS

The rapid growth of trade with the West during the 1970s has made the East European countries, and to a lesser extent the Soviet Union, increasingly sensitive to international economic disturbances, such as the OPEC-triggered energy crisis, rapid world inflation, and Western recession. OPEC's action in 1973-74 increased the opportunity cost to the Soviet Union of supplying energy and raw materials to Eastern Europe, thus intensifying pressure for the USSR to reorient its export supplies to the West. Although the actual reorientation was modest because of political considerations, it has forced the East European countries to rely more on alternative sources for energy and raw materials. This is clearly dis-integrative. However, to the extent that the world market price explosion increased the cost of Soviet energy and raw materials to Eastern Europe (although with some time lag), the East European countries have had to export more to the USSR to finance their deteriorating terms of trade. They also had to become more willing to invest in the large energy and raw material projects located in the USSR. Both of these outcomes are integrative, even though the cost-benefit calculations on the joint projects are unclear and the terms of investment participation are in dispute.

Perhaps the most important effect of world events since 1973 on CMEA integration was the impact of developments on the international financial markets. Large OPEC surplus funds had to be recycled just when the deep Western recession reduced corporate demand for loanable funds, creating large excess liquidity on the world financial markets. The recession also induced Western governments to subsidize the financing of their country's exports. These developments, combined with the new political environment created by détente, caused the West to offer exceedingly large private and official credits to the CMEA countries. At the end of 1978, the indebtedness of the six East European countries and the USSR to the West exceeded $50 billion.[48] Because of the availability of these credits, the extraordinarily rapid expansion of imports from the West was not, in our view, at the expense of CMEA integration (induced as the expansion was in part by the shortcomings of CMEA). Intra-bloc trade continued to expand during this same period, although at a slowed rate.

The impact of CMEA's large indebtedness on the future of CMEA integration is exceedingly difficult to assess. Much will depend on the productivity of the borrowed resources in terms of generating hard-currency exports. Although the debt may continue to rise—some experts foresee the possibility that it may double during the 1980s—the need to service the debt mortgages resources. As the ability of the CMEA countries to import from the West is impaired by the requirements of debt service, this may promote an improved intrabloc division of labor.

There is another environmental consideration: Successive international crises and the growing difficulties that CMEA countries are encountering on Western markets due to protectionism are supporting those in Eastern Europe who argue that the CMEA, and especially the Soviet Union, offers a more stable and more easily accessible market and source of supply than does the West.

No simple generalizations can be made about the impact of the external economic environment on CMEA integration. The expansion of East-West commerce has set in motion both centrifugal and centripetal forces in the CMEA; their strength and impact differ from time to time and from country to country.[50]

Conclusions

Where does the CMEA stand today, as it begins the fourth decade of its existence, and what are its prospects for the 1980s?

It is our impression that, once again, the CMEA has reached an impasse. No significant initiatives appear to have been taken in recent years to more efficiently conduct intra-CMEA economic relations. Coordination of national plans and joint planning focus on the last stage of production for key commodities, without much attention given to the interconnectedness of production with the other branches. While there are a number of highly visible CMEA mining and transport projects, these undertakings can be justified for the most part by natural resource endowment or engineering considerations. Even on these projects, there is much dispute between the host and the investing countries about who is contributing how much and how equitable the repayment arrangements are. For this reason, CMEA joint projects apparently will be relied on much less extensively during the 1980s. Joint projects in manufacturing, which must be based on commercial considerations and supported by cost calculations and financial arrangements acceptable to all parties, have not yet materialized on any significant scale. Successful CMEA integration, i.e., increased specialization in manufactures, requires uniform valuation criteria among the countries. This in turn becomes possible if, in every CMEA country, domestic price relatives of tradeables approximate prices on the world market and national currencies become convertible. As a minimum, the prices and exchange rates used to make decisions on CMEA specialization must simulate world market prices and equilibrium exchange rates.[51]

There are two key determinants of the future of CMEA integration: First, the course of domestic economic reforms in individual CMEA countries is important because the fundamental systemic constraints to CMEA integration are rooted in the domestic institutions of CPEs, whether traditional or partially reformed. Second, the attitudes of the USSR are important because the policies of the East European members of the CMEA are to some extent constrained by the policies adopted by the organization's most powerful member. East European countries are fundamentally much less conservative about comprehensive economic reforms than the USSR, not only for political reasons but also because the role of foreign trade is relatively small in the Soviet economy. Soviet leaders are less willing to tamper with the country's domestic economic mechanisms or move toward currency convertibility, which would necessitate changing domestic prices. For East European countries, on the other hand, improved efficiency of foreign trade, including a more effective CMEA integration, is very important, although the constellation of economic and political forces supporting and opposing comprehensive reform differs from country to country. Paradoxically, one of the reasons the issue of improved regional integration is pressing on all members is the rising cost of energy and their large indebtedness to the industrial West. This makes it imperative for all countries to use their resources and to trade more efficiently.

Given all the obstacles that must be overcome to achieve integration in today's environment and in the framework of a central planning system that is not conducive to this end, in the long run there appear to be only two ways to cut the Gordian knot. One option is to impose supranational authority over the members, resulting in policies working for integration being ordered by the "center." Although Moscow probably prefers this solution, Kremlin leaders know that the Soviet Union incurs significant political costs when it uses overt force to gain its ends. This gives the East European states some room for maneuver. The second option is to develop comprehensive economic reforms, which must encompass economic (as opposed to administrative) decentralization, a reform in the price mechanism, and the introduction of currency convertibility. At the very least, the evaluation of proposed CMEA projects and specialization agreements must be based on generally accepted cost-benefit calculations, even if the CMEA trade and financial mechanism remains unchanged for the time being. A further intermediate solution might lie in a smaller group of East European countries undertaking comprehensive domestic economic reforms and simultaneously moving toward sub-regional integration. In any event, the key to the choice lies in the politico-economic preferences of the Soviet leaders. They will choose among these options to achieve more rapid and far-reaching integration if and only if the gains they expect from this "common good" outweigh the expected political losses they are likely to suffer under any alternative course.

Appendix
Institutional Arrangements in the CMEA
(as of 1978)

Membership and Affiliation

There are four types of affiliation with the CMEA: full membership, associate membership, non-socialist "cooperant" status, and "observer country" status. In addition, several countries have been identified as "interested" in some form of affiliation.

Ten countries had *full membership* at the end of 1978. The six nations that formed the CMEA in January 1949: the USSR, Bulgaria, Czechoslovakia, Hungary, Poland, and Romania (Albania joined about a month later but has taken no part in CMEA's activities since 1961); the GDR (1950), Mongolia (1962), Cuba (1972), and Vietnam (1978). Members can decide whether or not to participate in CMEA programs according to the "interested party" provision of the charter.

Associate membership status governs the affiliation of Yugoslavia since 1964, participating in 21 of 32 key CMEA institutions as if it were a full member.

Non-socialist cooperant status has been granted to three countries: Finland in 1973 and Iraq and Mexico in 1976. Since these countries have no foreign-trade plans and their governments cannot conclude agreements on behalf of firms, they do not participate in the work of CMEA organizations. Each country has mixed commissions, com-

CHART 1
CMEA Organization Chart

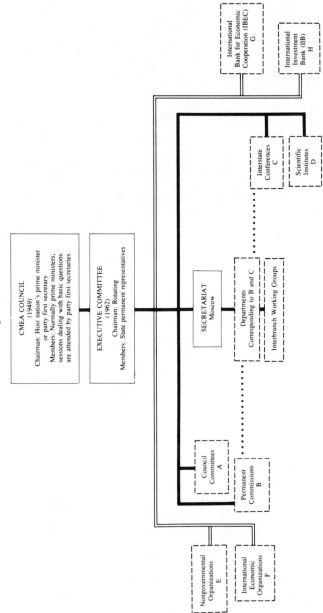

CMEA COUNCIL
(1949)
Chairman: Host nation's prime minister or party first secretary
Members: Normally prime ministers; sessions dealing with basic questions are attended by party first secretaries

EXECUTIVE COMMITTEE
(1962)
Chairman: Rotating
Members: State permanent representatives

SECRETARIAT
Moscow

Departments Corresponding to B and C

Interbranch Working Groups

Council Committees A

Permanent Commissions B

Interstate Conferences C

Scientific Institutes D

International Bank for Economic Cooperation (IBEC) G

International Investment Bank (IIB) H

Nongovernmental Organizations E

International Economic Organizations F

Legend:

Relations of superiority and subordination

Advisory relationship

Functional relationship

SOURCE: Harry Trend, "Economic Integration and Plan Coordination Under COMECON," in James F. Brown, ed., *Eastern Europe's Uncertain Future* (New York, Praeger, 1978).

posed of government and business representatives, which sign various kinds of "framework" agreements with CMEA's Joint Commission on Cooperation, especially established for this purpose. The agreements are subsequently "accepted" by the relevant permanent commission of the CMEA, but the implementation is up to the interested CMEA country(ies) and cooperant country firms.

Observer status appears to be a designation applied to a mixed group of communist or communist-leaning governments. The group's composition changes from time to time, depending mainly on political developments. At one time, for example, the People's Republic of China and North Korea were "observers." At the end of 1978, Afghanistan, Angola, Cambodia, Ethiopia, Mozambique, and South Yemen had negotiations underway with the CMEA to explore the possibility of a Yugoslav-type associate membership. Occasionally, some countries in this group are invited to attend CMEA Council sessions as observers.

Interested country appears to be a designation for a group of less-developed countries whose composition has also changed over time. For example, Egypt, Chile under Allende, and Bangladesh were at one time interested countries. At the end of 1978, seven less-developed countries reportedly had an interest in the possibility of a Finland-type cooperant status: Guyana and Jamaica, with which official talks were said to have been underway, and Angola, Colombia, Costa Rica, India, and Venezuela, which were said to have been considering the matter.

Organizations

CMEA's main policy and administrative organizations and the linkages are shown in chart 1.[52]

The CMEA Council is the organization's supreme policymaking body; each full member has one vote. The Council is convened about once a year; sessions deciding important matters are usually attended by the party first secretaries. The Council's recommendations must be approved by each country, after which bilateral or multilateral agreements or treaties must be signed as a basis for implementation.

The Executive Committee is the executive body of the Council. It proposes statements and recommendations for consideration by the Council, supervises the work of all other CMEA bodies, and monitors the implementation of CMEA agreements and treaties. It meets at least once every two months.

The Secretariat, located in Moscow, carries out the day-to-day operations of the CMEA. It has a large, multinational staff headed by a Soviet citizen. Many of its departments correspond in name and function to those of the various special-purpose Council committees and permanent commissions (see below); other departments are responsible for interbranch coordination, arranging interstate conferences and other functions.

The key line functions of the CMEA are performed by three *Council* committees, set up in 1971, and a large number of *permanent commissions,* most of them established during the 1950s and 1960s. The *Committee on Cooperation in Planning,* comprised of the chairmen of the central planning bodies of the member countries, comes close to being a supranational planning agency for dealing with specific economic problems. This committee is the main CMEA body responsible for the coordination of the five-year and long-term plans of the member countries. It has a special permanent working group on energy. The other two *Council* committees are the *Committee on Scientific Technological Cooperation* and the *Committee on Cooperation in Material and Technical Supply,* each dealing with problems suggested by its name.

The *permanent commissions* are generally organized along branch lines, but some are responsible for functional areas, such as health, statistics, currency, and standardization.

In addition, the CMEA also has two regional banks (see below), a large number of scientific institutes, interstate conferences on *ad hoc* problems, intergovernmental commissions dealing with specific issues, and many conferences of non-governmental organizations that maintain loose ties to CMEA organs. It has been estimated that more than 100,000 persons are involved directly in carrying out various CMEA functions and sponsored activities.[53]

Of special interest in connection with CMEA integration is a new type of organization created in the early 1970s, the International Economic Organization (IEO). Its purpose is "the *concrete* coordination . . . of joint economic activities in the fields of research and development, production, services, and foreign trade."[54] IEOs can be established either by international law or by a civil law contract between the founding members, which are never the countries themselves but their industrial associations, enterprises, or FTEs. The IEOs are legal entities of the country in which their headquarters is located. They are thus not organs of the CMEA, although they do have a close working relationship with CMEA bodies, especially the permanent commissions.

The significance of the IEO concept lies in the possibility that IEOs may provide the legal and experimental basis for creating socialist multinational corporations, which potentially could play an important role in CMEA integration. To be sure, the consensus of Western opinion is that the difficulties of accurately determining costs, prices, and meaningful exchange rates, as well as other problems, have greatly limited the scope and operation of the IEOs, which *cannot* be considered socialist multinational enterprises.[55]

In 1977, Machowski published the most comprehensive Western study on IEOs.[56] He identified eleven IEOs and classified them into two types: international economic associations (IEAs) and joint enterprises (JEs).

International economic associations have mainly a coordinating function so that they do not directly carry out productive activities. Machowski identified seven IEAs whose founding members and purposes (with year of founding and the headquarters shown in parentheses) are:

1. *Interatominstrument* (1972; Warsaw) by the six European members of CMEA except Romania: cooperation in research, production and sales of nuclear-technical equipment, with authorization to trade with third countries.

2. *Interatomenergo* (1973; Moscow) by the seven European members plus Yugoslavia: cooperation in research, planning, construction and supply of nuclear power plants.

3. *Assofoto* (1973; Moscow) between the USSR and the GDR: joint planning in the photo-chemical industry.

4. *Intertextilmash* (1973; Moscow) by the seven European members plus Yugoslavia: cooperation in research, production, and sales of textile machinery, with trade with third countries to be authorized "in the future."

5. *Mongolsovtsvemet* (1973; Ulan Bator) between the USSR and Mongolia: coordination of prospecting, mining, and processing of nonferrous metal ores.

6. *Interkhimvolokno* (1974; Bucharest) by the seven European members plus Yugoslavia: cooperation in research, production, and sales of chemical fibers.

7. *Domokhim* (1974; Moscow) between the USSR and the GDR: joint planning in domestic (household?) chemical products, with company sales outlets in the founding countries.

Joint enterprises are authorized to perform production operations. Machowski identified four:

1. *Haldex* (1959; Katowice, Poland) between Hungary and Poland: extraction and processing of coal waste products.

2. *Druzhba* (1972; Zawiercie, Poland) between the GDR and Poland: production of cotton yarns.

3. *Erdenet* (1973; Erdenet, Mongolia) between the USSR and Mongolia: mining and processing of copper and molybdenum ores.

4. *Service* (1976; Zielona Gora, Poland), a subsidiary of *Interatominstrument* (see above): maintenance of nuclear-technical equipment imported by Poland.

While not part of the formal CMEA structure, the two regional banks must be discussed along with other CMEA institutions.

The *International Bank for Economic Cooperation* (IBEC) was established in 1964 by the full members of the CMEA to perform bookkeeping operations arising from commercial transactions among the members, to issue trade credits and thereby promote multilateralism within the region, and to carry out financial operations with banking institutions outside the region. IBEC's statutory capital was set at 300 million transferable rubles (TR)—an artificial unit of account described in the following section. Each country's quota was determined in proportion to its share in intra-CMEA trade. But since loanable TRs can be "created" only through an export surplus in intra-CMEA trade and since all members cannot be net exporters simultaneously, it is not clear how, or whether, the paid-up capital in TRs has actually been transferred to the Bank, as prescribed, by all members.

IBEC does perform its intra-CMEA bookkeeping function and has been expanding considerably the volume of transactions with Western banks in convertible currencies, but it has not promoted multilateralism in any significant way.[58]

The *International Investment Bank* (IIB) was established in 1971 by the full members of the CMEA to help finance investments in member countries, including the joint CMEA projects. Statutory capital was set at 1 billion TR, 30% payable in convertible currency, the rest in TR. Each country's quota is proportional to its share in intra-CMEA trade. As with IBEC, how the IIB "creates" loanable TR funds is not clear. The fundamental issue is that when the Bank issues paper credits in TRs, what freedom does the recipient country have in choosing the investment goods it needs from the other CMEA countries to build a project? This point has not been clarified in the CMEA literature. One possibility is that a member's TR quota subscription takes the form of a hypothetical (or tentative) list of pledged investment goods. Another possibility is that a granting of IIB credits must be preceded by successfully concluded negotiations between the prospective debtor and creditor countries, specifying the investment and repayment commodities that will be shipped, including all terms and conditions. In either case, the mobilization of TR credits must be exceedingly difficult.

In recent years, the IBEC and the IIB have both borrowed substantial convertible currency sums from Western financial institutions. Brainard's contribution shows how the convertible currency operations of these banks have promoted regional integration, while their intended purpose, promoting CMEA integration through the introduction and increased use of the TR, has not been achieved.

PART II
THEORETICAL ANALYSIS

Edward A. Hewett

Foreign Trade Outcomes in Eastern and Western Economies

The majority view among Western scholars is that central planning in the Soviet Union and Eastern Europe has had substantial impact on all aspects of those countries' foreign-trade outcomes: the level of trade, its commodity composition, and its geographic distribution. The *level* of eastern trade[1] has received the most attention. Numerous Western studies have concluded that because of central planning, Eastern trade/GNP ratios are lower than those typical of Western developed countries. Many scholars see the effects of central planning in the *commodity composition* of Eastern trade, particularly in the relatively low share of machinery, equipment, and consumer goods in exports to the West, and the low share of consumer goods in total imports. Finally, it is a common supposition that central planning and Soviet-East European political relations explain the relatively high share of intra-CMEA trade in Eastern countries' total trade; thus, central planning also affects the *geographical distribution* of trade.

Western hypotheses on Eastern foreign trade fall into two groups: (1) other things equal, Eastern foreign-trade outcomes diverge from those typical of Western economies; and (2) central planning provides the primary explanation for that divergence. Testing hypotheses from the first group requires estimating a model that predicts Western foreign-trade outcomes, then comparing predictions of Eastern outcomes (based on that model) with actual Eastern foreign-trade outcomes. Empirical studies of this form, which are discussed in the next section, weakly corroborate some hypotheses in this first set and refute none.

Therefore, additional variables must be introduced to explain the variance in Western and Eastern foreign-trade outcomes, hence to derive estimates of typical foreign-trade outcomes taking into account the special characteristics of all countries in the sample. This is the spirit behind the second set of hypotheses which see the missing variables in central planning. But none of these hypotheses has been tested, nor are they even formulated in testable form. To date, the reasoning has gone something like this: Eastern countries have unusual foreign-trade outcomes, and they use central planning, which includes within it well-known biases against foreign trade; therefore, central planning must explain the unusual foreign-trade behavior. However, there may be other variables important in explaining the East-West differences, and which are uncorrelated with central planning or the policies associated with it. For example, differences in levels of development may serve to explain part of the East-West differences in foreign-trade outcomes.

The variable "central planning" must also be very carefully defined. One must separate the consequences of central planning *as a system* from the consequences of using central planning *as a tool* to implement policies adopted in particular Eastern countries. If, for example, the high investment/GNP ratio in Eastern countries affects foreign-trade outcomes, it would be an error to attribute that to central planning. A high investment/GNP ratio is not an indisputable part of central planning as a system; rather, central planning provides an efficient vehicle for enforcing high investment ratios.

This paper builds on previous work on differences in Eastern and Western foreign-trade outcomes and recent work in economic systems theory—particularly the work of Montias and Koopmans—to develop a theoretical model useful in explaining the variance in foreign-trade outcomes between systems. It is basically a theoretical paper which identifies the major variables that must be accounted for in "other things equal" before one can begin to sort out the effects of system and policy on foreign-trade outcomes.

Summary and Critique of Previous Research on Eastern Foreign-Trade Outcomes

The traditional approach to foreign-trade planning in the Eastern countries, predating economic reforms of the mid-1960s in Eastern Europe (but still intact in the USSR), is composed of several elements:

1. A state monopoly controls all important foreign transactions and all movements of capital.

2. Control over all export and import activities is focused in the state planning committee, the ministry of foreign trade, and the other ministries. The determination of exports and imports occurs as part of the annual planning process. Enterprises have no formal authority to make export or import decisions on their own.

3. Domestic and foreign prices are separated from each other by an elaborate system of taxes and subsidies. Domestic wholesale prices are set for a long time period on the basis of average costs of production by industry, and enterprises buy (sell) imports (exports) from (to) foreign-trade organizations (FTO's) at domestic wholesale prices. Consequently, domestic enterprises face export and import prices that provide no information on relative world market prices for traded goods. FTO's may buy and sell at prices different from domestic prices times the exchange rate, and state subsidies and taxes make up the difference.

4. Plans are formulated through an administrative process supervised by the state planning committee in the course of which this committee and the ministries use material balances for key commodities in an effort to construct a consistent plan.

In some of the Eastern countries, the reforms of the 1960s had a substantial impact on the system as it relates to foreign trade. In other countries, there was practically no effect. In the USSR, for example, the system as outlined above remains intact. At the other end of the spectrum as part of the New Economic Mechanism in Hungary, direct planning of foreign trade and detailed material balance planning were abandoned, subsidies and taxes separating domestic and foreign prices are being phased out, and consequently domestic prices (especially wholesale prices) are beginning to align with foreign prices. While FTO's still exist and handle many foreign transactions, a number of individual enterprises in Hungary now have rights to independent export and import, decisions that are controlled principally through a licensing system.

Reforms in the other Eastern countries have had effects on foreign trade, although not such radical effects as in the Hungarian case. Their common characteristic would seem to be a retention of substantial central control, particularly over imports, but simultaneously some attempt to allow world market prices to exert an influence on domestic wholesale prices. Consumer prices are still to a great extent protected from world market price changes for political reasons.[2]

A Review of the Literature

Several scholars have written on the determinants of differences in Eastern and Western foreign-trade outcomes. The major studies are considered here under the level of trade, its commodity composition, and its geographic distribution.

THE LEVEL OF TRADE

Hypotheses: Conceptual work on Eastern foreign-trade outcomes has focused primarily on the effects of central planning and the policies typically associated with it on the level of foreign trade. Brown, Holzman, van Brabant, and Wiles[3] provide a representative sample of the approaches to this problem. They share the conclusion that central planning drives the level of foreign trade away from optimal or efficient levels; and they share the supposition that divergence also means that Eastern foreign-trade levels diverge from actual levels of Western foreign trade. They differ, however, on whether factors other than central planning are important, and on whether the level of Eastern trade may be higher or lower than efficiency, optimality, and Western typical trade would suggest.

Holzman contends that planners, in their strong desire for self-sufficiency (which he defines as autarky), set policies to minimize the level of foreign trade. Likewise, the system itself contains several biases against foreign trade, the most important of which are the foreign-trade monopoly and the separation of domestic and foreign-trade prices.

Van Brabant agrees that Eastern countries show a downward bias in their foreign trade, and that at least part of the explanation lies in the central planning system and in the preferences of central planners.[4] Traditional material balance techniques are unable to deal with the broadened options presented by foreign trade; therefore, planners avoid choosing among the options by insulating the domestic economy from foreign trade.[5] Central planners also have an unusually strong preference for stability, even at a substantial cost in efficiency; and *the monopoly* for foreign trade provides such stability.

In addition to central planning, van Brabant sees broader historical forces at work in the anti-foreign-trade bias. For example, Eastern Europe's interwar experience with foreign trade highlighted the foreign sector's potential for transmitting devastating cycles into the domestic economy, a lesson that East European planners are not likely to forget.[6]

Wiles defines autarky two ways: as an unwillingness to enter into foreign commerce, and as the gap between actual trade, and trade which would obtain, *ceteris paribus*, under conditions of perfect competition.[7] He contends that although Eastern trade levels have been autarkic under both definitions, there is now an opposite danger of over-trading, which he calls *hyperpoly*, with two potential sources. First, the tendency in many Eastern countries to underprice imports encourages "hyperpolistic" imports that must be financed with abnormally high levels of exports. Secondly, Eastern attempts in the 1950s to develop the capacity to produce a broad range of commodities, regardless of comparative advantage considerations, have possibly driven imports above what they would otherwise have been as the requisite raw materials and semifabricates could not be produced domestically and had to be imported.[8]

Alan Brown agrees that Eastern planners show strong autarkic *as-pirations*, but he sees strong forces pushing for higher levels of trade, primarily planners' use of foreign trade in implementing a rapid growth strategy and the constant use of foreign trade to break bottlenecks. Brown concludes that, although planners may aspire to depress the level of trade, in fact their policies and reactions to those policies within the system may push actual foreign-trade outcomes toward hyperpoly.[9]

Empirical tests: Table 1 summarizes results of the major empirical tests for differences in the level of Eastern and Western foreign trade spanning the 1955-70 period. All the studies share the use of mul-tivariate techniques to estimate hypothetical trade flows. Typically, trade is treated as a non-linear function of GNP and population. In most cases, the equations are estimated using data for developed Western countries. Thus, the coefficients are an estimate of the in-fluence of GNP and population on Western trade. Then Eastern GNPs and populations are substituted into the equations to estimate Eastern trade if it were related to GNP and population, as is typical among Western countries. For example, in van Brabant's 1960 sample (Row 5), Bulgaria's actual imports in 1960 are 83% of what his regression for that year predicted they would be on the basis of Bulgarian GNP and population and the experience of 11 West European countries.

These data *seem* to provide strong confirmation of the autarky hypothesis, particularly for the 1950s. Yet such strong conclusions are inappropriate in light of uncertainties concerning the reliability of the estimates of hypothetical trade and of problems in the data.

It is important to be clear about the econometric problems involved in interpreting these results. The denominators in table 1 are answers to questions of the form, ". . . if there were a Western country with GNP and population identical to that of Eastern country Z, then what would that hypothetical country's trade be?" This is the equivalent of *forecasting* in a time-series problem, and there are standard econometric techniques for making forecasts and for indicating their reliability. The appropriate econometric answer to the question is not a single number, but "there is a 95% probability that trade for a hypothetical country with population and GNP equal to that of East-ern country Z will be $2 billion plus or minus $200 million," where $2 billion represents predicted trade. If the actual trade for Eastern coun-try Z were $1.8 billion, then the entry in table 1 for that country would be .82-1.00 (1.8/2.2 – 1.8/1.8) with a probability of .95 that the true ratio lay somewhere in the interval.

Consequently, in place of each ratio in table 1, there should be an interval, a "confidence band." For countries where the bands do not

TABLE 1
Actual/Predicted Trade for Eastern Countries, 1955-70

Author and sample year	Row	Actual trade divided by predicted trade for:							Geometric Avg.*	
		Bulgaria	Czechoslovakia	GDR	Hungary	Poland	Romania	USSR	incl. USSR	excl. USSR
Pryor, 1955A	(1)	.35	.45	.46	.50	.36	.31	.28	.38	.40
Pryor, 1955B	(2)	.22	.29	.29	.33	.28	.21	—	—	.27
van Brabant, 1955	(3)	.58	.78	.90	.78	.76	.50	.63	.69	.70
UNECE, 1953-1957 avg.	(4)	.85	.64	.81	.81	.91	1.40	—	—	.88
van Brabant, 1960	(5)	.83	.90	.95	.92	.76	.56	.62	.78	.81
Broner, 1960	(6)	1.27	.82	.75	.97	.75	.98	.75	.88	.91
UNECE, 1958-1962 avg.	(7)	1.03	.59	.72	.80	.90	1.20	—	—	.85
van Brabant, 1965	(8)	.97	.95	.82	.95	.74	.55	.54	.77	.81
UNECE, 1963-1967 avg.	(9)	1.13	.61	.65	.80	.81	1.02	—	—	.82
Broner, 1970	(10)	2.04	.84	.78	1.34	.83	1.06	.49	1.08	.96

SOURCES: Available from author.

*These numbers are in many cases transformed from results presented in a different form.

TABLE 2

95 Percent Confidence Bands for Actual/Predicted Trade Ratios
(selected countries and years)

Study	Bulgaria	Czechoslovakia	GDR	Hungary	Poland	Romania	USSR	Geometric Averages inc. USSR	exc. USSR
Pryor 1955A	.20-.49	.26-.63	.27-.65	.29-.70	.21-.51	.18-.44	.16-.39	.22-.53	.23-.53
van Brabant									
1955	.39-.71	.52-.95	.60-1.09	.52-.95	.51-.92	.33-.61	.42-.77	.46-.84	.47-.85
1965	.60-1.61	.59-1.58	.51-1.36	.59-1.58	.46-1.23	.34-.91	.34-.90	.48-1.28	.40-1.84
Broner 1970	.22-14.10	.10-5.80	.09-5.40	.15-9.28	.10-5.75	.11-7.34	.05-3.39	.10-7.48	.09-6.65

SOURCE: These are the numbers in table 1 multiplied by .9 to adjust for differences between intra-CMEA and world market prices, then divided in each case, respectively, by the upper bound and lower bound ratios discussed in the Appendix.

include unity (bands such as .4 − .8), we could know with a given probability that that country's trade was less than predicted for a similar, but hypothetical Western country.

There are also data problems associated with these numbers. First and most obvious is that none of the studies has adjusted Eastern trade data for inflated intra-CMEA trade prices. For the period of this sample, intra-CMEA trade was conducted at prices which, at official exchange rates, were approximately 20-25% above world market prices.[10] Therefore, total Eastern trade is overstated by different amounts for different Eastern countries (since shares of intra-CMEA trade differ and bilateral price levels differ somewhat from the average). On average, the overstatement is at least 10%.[11]

The price problem and the need for confidence bands are the two most obvious impediments to properly interpreting the results. It is possible to approximate on the basis of data reported for the regressions in Pryor's, Broner's, and van Brabant's studies what the confidence bands would be at their narrowest points, close to the mean of the independent variables (see table 2 and the Appendix for details). Also, the numbers have been adjusted downward 10% as a conservative correction for over-valuation in total trade steming from intra-CMEA prices.

These are not the true confidence bands; there was not sufficient information to compute those. Instead, these are probably narrower than the true intervals. For countries whose populations and GNPs are atypical of the sample used to estimate the regression (Western Europe for van Brabant and Pryor, developed and underdeveloped countries for Broner), the actual bands are much wider than those shown, a particularly important point for the USSR ratios for all the studies and (in the van Brabant and Pryor samples) for Bulgaria and Romania.

Even these crude and very conservative adjustments provide a somewhat firmer foundation for interpreting the results of the studies reported in table 1. Both Pryor's and van Brabant's results support the hypothesis that in 1955 Eastern trade was below trade typical of similar Western countries. Van Brabant finds higher ratios, and the GDR ratio could be unity; in addition, the USSR band is most likely much wider than the one indicated here. Van Brabant's 1965 results are far less conclusive, partly because he found higher ratios and partly because the confidence bands are wider. Broner's results are obviously useless. Even the narrowest confidence band is so wide that nothing interesting can be concluded about the trade ratios.

In sum, it is simply not clear from table 2 whether actual-predicted trade ratios for Eastern countries are different from unity. With these specifications, more precise answers could be obtained by estimating regressions and computing the actual confidence bands. However, there are also major improvements needed in specifications and sample choices before a more satisfactory answer can be obtained to the question of whether Eastern trade levels systematically diverge from those of Western countries.

THE COMMODITY COMPOSITION OF TRADE

Hypotheses: Most analyses of Eastern foreign trade devote little attention to the commodity structure of trade, the one exception being van Brabant who discusses throughout his *Bilateralism and Structural Bilateralism* various hypotheses concerning the determinants of all foreign-trade outcomes. He hypothesizes that Eastern industrialization policies substantially affected the product composition of imports. At first, massive investment programs meant a rapid increase in machinery and equipment imports. Later, because many industries were created without adequate regard for input supplies, unusually high levels of intermediate commodity imports resulted from increased production in the new industries.[12] He also notes that, in general, Eastern planners show strong interest in the structure of trade, particularly in intra-CMEA trade, where countries frequently try to balance their trade bilaterally in large product groups (what van Brabant called "structural bilateralism," and what is frequently referred to as the "one-to-one rule").[13]

Another proposition is that Eastern countries export an abnormally low amount of sophisticated manufacturers to the West, while intra-CMEA trade contains an abnormally high proportion of the same commodities. Central planning is the major explanation on the Western export side: the way the system is structured, Eastern producers have neither the information nor the incentive to try to compete in the highly demanding Western markets.[14] The high level of intra-CMEA trade in these products is presumably a manifestation of structural bilateralism.

Empirical test: Van Brabant estimates potential imports for 1955, 1960, and 1965 for the four commodity groups typically used by the CMEA countries to report their trade data: machinery and equipment, primary and semi-finished products, foodstuffs, and manufactured consumer goods.[15] The models are similar to those used to estimate total trade flows, with the addition of several variables to capture factors particular to various sectors. He concludes that Eastern countries import more machinery and equipment than is typical for Western European countries, and that they import far fewer consumer goods. For machinery and equipment in 1965, the ratios of actual to predicted trade range from .72 for East Germany to 3.1 for the USSR, their geometric average being .62. The differences between actual and predicted trade are small for the other two product groups.

As in the regressions for total trade, these results should have confidence bands around them. Also, intra-CMEA prices distort the results, even more than for total trade, since machinery and equipment and manufactured consumer goods are the two commodity groups in which CMEA foreign-trade price/world market price ratios are relatively high.[16] In the mid-1960s, machinery and equipment prices were probably about 25% above those on the world market and manufactured consumer goods prices about 40% above.[17] Since only a portion of imports in these two groups originated in CMEA, it is assumed here that the total flow is inflated in value by about half of the CMEA flow, that is, by about 15% and 20%.[18]

Table 3 presents van Brabant's results for these two product groups, corrected for price distortions and with confidence bands estimated at their narrowest point according to the methodology discussed in the Appendix. For the other two commodity groups, the bands obviously include unity and are not reported here. For manufactured consumer goods, the confidence bands exclude unity for both averages and all the individual countries with the exception of the USSR, where the actual confidence band is surely much wider. Obviously, Eastern countries have imported far fewer consumer

TABLE 3

95% Confidence Bands for
Actual/Predicted Trade Ratios, 1965
(selected commodity groups)

	Machinery and Equipment	Manufactured Consumer Goods
Bulgaria	.94-1.35	.27-.51
Czechoslovakia	.81-1.15	.26-.47
East Germany	.53-.75	.21-.38
Hungary	.67-.95	.31-.56
Poland	1.08-1.53	.43-.79
Romania	1.02-1.45	.40-.73
USSR	2.27-3.21	1.49-2.73
Geometric Average:		
including USSR	.95-1.35	.38-.70
excluding USSR	.82-1.16	.31-.56

SOURCE: Original data are from Jozef M. P. van Brabant, *Bilateralism and Structural Bilateralism in Intra-CMEA Trade* (Rotterdam: Rotterdam University Press, 1973), pp. 197, 244. The machinery and equipment ratios were multiplied by .87 and the manufactured consumer goods ratios by .83 to adjust for relatively high prices on the CMEA portion of those imports. The method of computation for the confidence bands is discussed in the appendix.

goods than hypothetical developed Western countries with identical GNP's and populations.

The results for machinery and equipment are ambiguous. The 95% confidence bands around the averages both include unity, as do the confidence bands for five of the seven countries. Therefore, contrary to van Brabant's clear conclusion, it cannot be said with any certainty that Eastern countries imported an unusually large amount of machinery and equipment, at least not in 1965.[19]

Van Brabant made pioneering efforts concerning the commodity composition of Eastern trade, but much remains to be done. Because Eastern countries may trade less than Western countries overall, an attempt to compute actual/predicted ratios of the *level* of imports by commodity group will guarantee that trade by commodity group for some or all commodity groups will fall below predicted levels. Therefore, the hypotheses should be tested for proportions of trade allocated to certain commodity groups to remove the total trade bias.

THE GEOGRAPHIC DIRECTION OF TRADE

Hypotheses: This has probably received the least attention of the three foreign-trade outcomes in terms of quantitative research. Again, van Brabant has examined this problem. He articulates the generally accepted view that intra-CMEA trade is abnormally high compared to total trade for two reasons: (1) a preference among policymakers "for clearing trade needs with ideological partners"; and (2) Eastern countries using material balances for planning need commitments on trade, which foreign trade agreements with other Eastern countries provide.[20]

While intra-Eastern trade is a relatively high share of total Eastern trade, it is not clear that there is an unusual bias towards trading with each other. CMEA is an economic union and as such can be expected to have a protective effect on mutual trade. The question is whether intra-Eastern trade is a higher proportion of their trade than is typical of similar Western countries in their intra-union trade. I have attempted to answer that question by estimating a trade gravity model for 1970 trade between the members of CMEA, EFTA, and the EEC.[21] Dummy variables for each economic union were introduced to capture their effect on trade and dummy variables were introduced for each Eastern country to capture the effect of central planning on their overall trade. The results suggested that the EEC and EFTA almost doubled trade among their members, while CMEA increased trade by almost 16 times what typical trade would have been between a CMEA member and nonmember country.

Implications for Further Research

While there are many valuable insights and results in the literature discussed here, a great deal remains to be done and, in some cases, re-done. Previous work is plagued by different combinations of data problems, weaknesses in econometric techniques, poor specifications, and unduly restrictive samples.

Data problems are the constant companion of the empirical researcher. Prices make Eastern trade and GNP data treacherous. Many times adjustments of the data are not possible; all that may be known is that there are errors, with no information about their direction. In these cases, sensitivity tests on the results for various possible values of the variables might be fruitful.

Econometric techniques are only beginning to make their way seriously into the study of Eastern economies, and it is quite natural for early efforts to rely heavily on models in other fields. Hopefully, in the future we shall see more experimentation with models that conform more closely to the special characteristics and data availabilities associated with Eastern countries.

With the exception of van Brabant's study and the Chenery study that Pryor used, the samples used in estimating equations to test for East-West differences have been taken from Western Europe. This sample choice has serious drawbacks since few of the Eastern countries approach EEC development levels. In terms of per capita GNP, they lie in the thinly populated space of countries that are certainly not underdeveloped, but are also not wealthy. They share with developed countries per capita incomes above the world average, yet they share with many underdeveloped countries the problems of nations seeking to industrialize. Their intermediate position in the world economy suggests that models used to estimate their potential foreign-trade outcomes should be estimated with data from both developed and underdeveloped countries. Only then can Eastern countries' outcomes be judged in terms of both where they have been and where they seem to be going.

MODEL SPECIFICATION

Model specification has been a major weakness in previous research. The goal of much of the literature to date is to show that, *ceteris paribus,* central planning has an impact on foreign-trade outcomes. Yet to adequately test that hypothesis, the researcher must build a complete model that identifies all variables that influence foreign-trade outcomes, including economic systems. One could go about this in one of two ways. One approach would be to quantify all of the variables that influence foreign-trade outcomes, including the system. This involves quantifying the system as a variable, conceptually and empirically a difficult task.[22] A second and possibly more promising approach is to treat the effects of the system much like those of technology, as an inexplicable residual after all other major variables are accounted for. This may be empirically more tractable, although one can never be sure whether random disturbances and the system are all that are left.

In either case, it is necessary to build a model. None of the studies reviewed above has explicitly attacked this task in its full complexity. Many implicitly assume that the differences in foreign-trade outcomes between Eastern and Western countries can only be attributed to those of central planning in the East and its absence in the West—not a very convincing "model." Others, van Brabant, for example, have introduced a much broader range of considerations into the determinants of foreign-trade outcomes. But these considerations never find their way into the empirical specifications.

Whichever modeling approach one chooses, certain basic requirements must be satisfied:

1. Before the influence of systems on foreign-trade outcomes can be ascertained, the first step is to account for the determinants of foreign-trade outcomes other than systems.

2. To isolate the impact of "system" on foreign-trade outcomes, policies must be separated from the system.

The next two sections are devoted to discussing an analytical framework which seeks to meet these two requirements and which should prove useful in structuring future empirical research in this area.

A Model of the Determination of Foreign-Trade Outcomes

This section introduces a framework suitable for analyzing the major determinants of all outcomes, with special attention to foreign-trade outcomes. The next section discusses its specific application to the problem of East-West differences. The framework is not specific to Eastern systems; rather, systems are treated as variables which influence and are influenced by outcomes.

The approach is similar to that used in specifying any econometric model. The problem is to specify *a priori* the important variables that influence foreign-trade outcomes and to specify how they are related to the dependent variables and to each other. Determinants of all outcomes in all systems, including foreign-trade outcomes, are divided into three classes: (1) the environment within which that system operates; (2) the character of the system itself, and (3) the policies that governments seek to realize through the system. The variation in those variables serve to explain variation in foreign-trade outcomes among countries. A simplified view of these variables' interrelationship is presented in figure 1.

Definitions and Concepts

The major definitions are taken from the work of Koopmans and Montias, although I have considerably modified parts of their framework to highlight foreign-trade outcomes and some special features of systems to which they gave relatively little attention.[23] The four basic definitions are:

1. An *economic system* is some subset of a total system where the latter "includes all political, social, and economic institutions, organizational structures, laws and rules (and the extent of their enforcement and voluntary observance), and all traditions, religious and secular beliefs, attitudes, values, taboos, and the resulting systematic or stochastic behavior patterns."[24]

2. *Policies* are "classes of decisions adopted in order to economize on decision time and effort and, in many cases, made known in order to create stable expectations about future decisions."[25]

3. *Outcomes* "are all aspects or consequences of the system, and of the policies, decisions, or actions of all participants"[26] (e.g., firm, individual) at a specific time. Decisions are commitments to several related actions.

4. The *environment* of the economic system includes resources, human and physical capital, technology, external factors, the impact of random events on these, initial preferences, and "incomplete interactions," simple examples of which would be unfulfilled economic commitments.

It is useful for present purposes to expand considerably on the notions of "outcome" and "policy" and to introduce the new concept of "norms."

OUTCOMES

I distinguish here between foreign-trade outcomes and other outcomes, the important foreign-trade outcomes being the level, commodity composition, and geographic distribution of trade. I shall ignore other variables that could be included in this category, such as the terms of trade and international factor flows. They are relegated to the "other" outcome category.

POLICY

Governments set policies that affect foreign-trade outcomes, but so do other organizations involved in economic activity. The large corporation that has rules of thumb or "policies" for buying and selling

FIGURE 1
The Determinants of Foreign Trade Outcomes

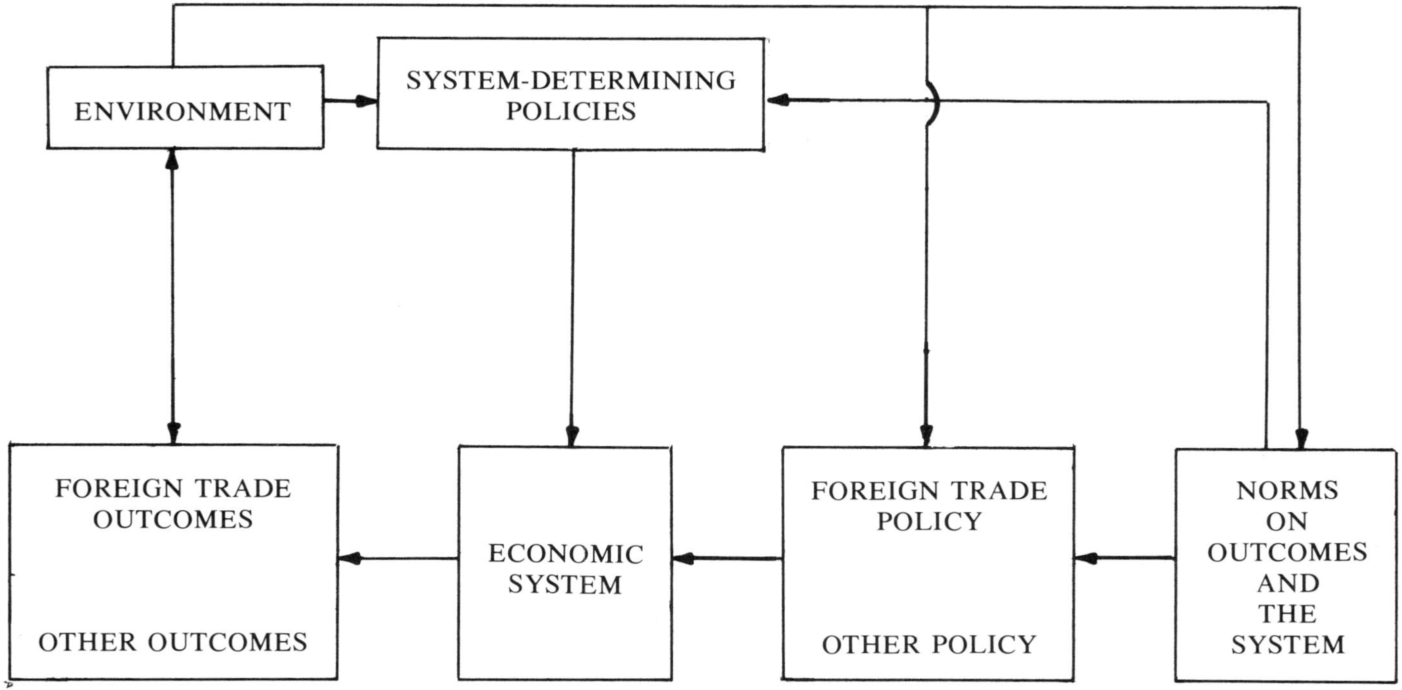

currencies or commodities affects through its policies foreign-trade outcomes in the system of which it is a part. In this model, explicit consideration is given only to government policies; the policies of nongovernmental organizations are treated as part of the system. Nevertheless, the policies of nongovernmental organizations are a crucial part of the story, for they influence the success of governmental policies. If, for example, an Eastern government institutes a policy stating that its enterprises can only export commodities that exhibit domestic currency/hard currency price ratios below a fixed cut-off point, enterprises will probably respond with their own policies concerning the determination of accounting costs of the portion marketed abroad.[27]

For brevity, the term "policies" will refer only to governmental policies. I shall distinguish here between *system-determining policies* and *policies within the system*. Both types of policies are divided into those directly relating to foreign trade ("foreign trade policies") and "other" policies.

System-determining policies refer to governmental decisions about how other decisions in the system will be made; that is, they relate to the very essence of the economic system. These could include a policy in an Eastern country about the incentive system used in stimulating technical change, or in a Western country about the structure of an industry (both in the "other" category). In both systems, the government is exercising its power to determine part of the character of the system. The government is only one force influencing the character of any system. In addition, beliefs, attitudes, values, and the enforcement of laws are all part of the system over which governments exert varying degrees of imperfect influence.

Policies *within* the system are those governmental policies that seek to change outcomes without changing the system. For example, in making decisions on import quotas in an Eastern country or setting tariffs in a Western country, the government can vary the policy and seek to affect outcomes by *using* the system rather than changing it. Governments set policicies within the system to which nongovernmental organizations react. Therefore, there is no direct causality from policy to outcomes: policy triggers responses from other organizations which, when combined with policy, determine outcomes.

NORMS AND PREFERENCES

A complete model of outcomes requires a theory of policy-formation. Without such a theory, policy remains an exogenous variable, seemingly unrelated to other parts of the system. But policy is influenced by the system, the environment, and outcomes, just as it influences those variables. I assume that policymakers monitor outcomes of interest to them and change policies when outcomes deviate from either explicit or implicit norms.[28] Policymakers in Western economies may have a norm that the rate of unemployment shall not rise above 5%, nor the rate of inflation above 6%. When outcomes exceed those levels, policies begin to change. Eastern economies also have norms concerning the rates of inflation and unemployment, but with much lower values. Norms are "rules of thumb," representing the outcome of a constrained choice problem policymakers face when they balance their *preferences* over all outcomes with the constraints they face.

In fact, policymakers have preferences over many outcomes and face many constraints both from the environment (e.g., production possibilities, outcomes in other systems, past norms, and political stability of the government) and also from the system itself (e.g., the lowest possible unemployment rate, given the system for allocating labor resources). And norms can change in one system (or vary among systems) either because preferences change (preferences are different) or constraints change (constraints are different), or some combination. As will be discussed in the next section, this is important for understanding the source of differences in Eastern and Western norms concerning the share of manufacturing in GNP.

The Model

Figure 1 depicts interrelationships among aspects that could be identified in any economic system. It is a picture of what could be written as a set of simultaneous equations if all the functional relationships were known and quantifiable. Norms formed in the environment are constantly compared to outcomes, and, as a consequence, decisions are made on policies. Presumably, there is a convention, or what one might call an "inertia function," that specifies which policies are changed with most frequency and which are changed with less frequency and more reluctance. As a rule, policies within the system will be changed with less reluctance than system-determining policies or norms themselves. It is easier to manage and the effects are more easily focused.

Policy changes (about and within the system) interact with the system to produce changes in outcomes (foreign trade and other). These in turn feedback as performance indicators to be compared with norms, and so on. Outcomes become part of the environment for future periods in the form of new capital stock, stocks of other goods, readings on production possibilities that may generate a change in norms, or possibly effects on other countries, which in turn affect the environment of the country in question.

The model is fully simultaneous. Were one able to specify all the equations implied here with the appropriate lags, then the model would be closed, dynamic, and sufficient to explain the evolution not only of outcomes, but also changes in policies and the system itself. Our present knowledge is inadequate, however, to quantify this model.[29]

In this framework, one cannot simply say that "norms drive the system" or that "preferences determine policies." There is very little one-way causality, but rather mutual interaction. One-way causality comes through the environment. For example, should the terms of trade move against an Eastern economy (those being an exogenous part of the environment for most Eastern economies), then the balance-of-payments falls below the norm, triggering policy changes, changes in outcomes, and possibly a further change in norms or more policy changes. In this sense, a shock from outside the system "drives" the system.

This framework can be used either to describe the evolution of foreign-trade outcomes in one system over time or to describe variance in the foreign-trade outcomes among systems at a point in time. The latter is the subject of this paper, and the next section discusses how variations in policies, systems, and environments among countries at a point in time can influence their foreign-trade outcomes.

Differences in Foreign-Trade Outcomes Among Systems

The framework of the previous section is useful for restating the issues surrounding variations in the three major foreign trade outcomes: the level of trade, its direction, and commodity composition. Two countries could show differences in foreign-trade outcomes from combinations of variations in three basic determinants: the environment, system-determining policy, and policy within the system.

Variations in the Environment

The environment includes all that is not part of policy or system. The effects of the environment on foreign-trade outcomes must be neutralized in order to earn the right to certify that other things are indeed "equal." The four classes of variables with the greatest potential importance for foreign-trade outcomes are: traditional economic factors, preferences, actions of other countries, and political-economic factors.

TRADITIONAL ECONOMIC FACTORS
These include human and physical capital, technical know-how,

organizational know-how, and natural resource endowments. World market prices give economic meaning to all these variables. Organizational skills (including planning skills) are part of human capital.

These factors share certain characteristics: they are the determinants of relative costs of production, comparative advantage, and the potential gains from trade. All except world market prices are stocks that change gradually. Outside of natural resource endowments, the stocks are records of past outcomes in the system, a physical record of the country's economic history. They are an appropriate index for the level of economic development. Physical capital stock reflects past investment decisions, the quality of output of domestic machine-building industry, and past import policies. Human capital reflects previous educational policies and the initial literacy of the population.

In analyzing variations in foreign-trade outcomes, some decision must first be made on how these variables will be handled. If the issue is the effects of policy and system in a particular year, then two countries will have to be found or simulated with approximately the same economic history. Only in two countries with the same production possibilities frontier can one explore the effects of policy and system on foreign-trade outcomes.

PREFERENCES

Preferences are part of the environment; they influence norms, policies, the system, and outcomes without, in turn, being influenced by those variables. For simplicity, most trade models for Western countries assume the similarity of preferences across countries; but when one is studying East-West differences, this assumption is *too* simple. Planners in Eastern countries are able to enforce their preferences with considerable (though not total) disregard for the preferences of the populace. Therefore, even if all other parts of the environment can be brought into equality between an Eastern and Western country, differences in preferences may in turn influence norms, policy, and the system, and consequently create differences in outcomes. One can argue that in some sense these are really system differences affecting outcomes. It is the system that minimizes popular influence on central decisions concerning resource allocation. Whether or not one subscribes to that interpretation, it is important to separate out this influence on outcomes, from influences coming, for example, from unintended or unwanted consequences flowing directly from the resource allocation mechanism being used. If Eastern trade is indeed lower than that typical in Western countries, and if it is that way because policymakers prefer it and not because the system they have chosen has such an effect as an externality, then those who condemn low imports are condemning planners' preferences, not the system.

ACTIONS OF OTHER COUNTRIES

Actions of other countries are a potentially important part of the environment which may influence trade. Trade embargos are an obvious consideration, as are loan conditions. The latter can work both ways. For example, many Western countries have recently offered particularly generous state-supported loans to subsidize exports to Eastern countries. These loans permit levels of imports that, *ceteris paribus,* would have been otherwise unattainable through import substitution. This affects the domestic output mix and the level and composition of potential exports, and, therefore, future foreign-trade outcomes.

POLITICAL-ECONOMIC FACTORS

Decisions on norms and policies in all systems occur in a political-economic environment that can impose constraints, with potentially important consequences for foreign-trade outcomes. The political-economic constraints may preclude the choice of certain policies and, therefore, are important in explaining decisions on policies. Two examples are the traditions of protectionism in Eastern Europe and the political legitimacy of current regimes.

Eastern Europe has a long tradition of state protection of industry.[30] During the Great Depression, East European countries engaged in bitter trade wars that resulted in a virtual collapse of trade. Protectionism in the post-war period took the form of policies that aimed at the development in each Eastern country of its own machine-building production and exports.[31]

Problems with political legitimacy in Eastern Europe can circumscribe planners' ability to impose their preferences in selected areas. The present ruling elite came into power with the help of outside forces and retains power through a combination of economic benefits to the populace and Soviet support. They must, so to speak, live off "current income" for their continued existence. If, for example, planners are "buying" their legitimacy with full employment and price stability, then whatever their preferences, they take care to set policies that protect these economic indicators. The significance of this for foreign trade is that to gradually open the economy to competition from abroad seems a potentially unpopular measure because it creates uncertainty for workers. Therefore, problems with legitimacy may enhance protectionist sentiments on the part of Eastern planners so that, other things equal, an Eastern country would protect trade more than a Western country. Only politically secure regimes can manage to decrease trade barriers, given the strong and well-organized interests (producers, workers) hurt by such moves and the diffuse interests (consumers) that benefit from such policies.

Variations in System-Determining Policy

A fundamental difference between Eastern and Western economies lies in their policies toward the system itself. Eastern governments take a much more active role in seeking to shape the character of the system by forbidding or discouraging certain organizational forms and ways of motivating people and encouraging others. One way in fact to distinguish between Eastern and Western economies is that in Western economies the government makes policies about far fewer aspects of the system than is typical in Eastern economies. In Western countries, systems evolve according to their own dynamics. If governments have system-determining policies, they are intended primarily to influence system change rather than to dictate it. Eastern governments, on the other hand, seek to initiate and control system change.

The range of system characteristics on which governments set policy varies between Eastern and Western governments; this in itself is a potentially important determinant of variation in foreign-trade outcomes. These differences have potential effects on all functions of the system: production, distribution, and foreign trade. Foreign-trade outcomes can be influenced by system-determining policies directly related to foreign trade and other system-determining policies.

POLICIES DIRECTLY RELATED TO FOREIGN TRADE

The monopoly of foreign trade typical of Eastern countries separates producers from the foreign sector, interposing the state as the final arbiter of what should be exported and imported. The price system and the exchange rates support this organizational separation; consequently, producers have neither sufficient incentive nor sufficient information to export goods Eastern countries produce relatively inexpensively. Planners may have the incentive, but they have difficulty gathering sufficient data to maximize their economy's gains from trade.[32] This almost certainly means that the actual gains from trade will fall far below their potential. But whether this will be the result and if there will be too much or too little trade cannot be predicted based on system characteristics alone. One needs a theory of how planners deal with uncertainty concerning the gains from trade.

OTHER SYSTEM-DETERMINING POLICIES

System characteristics not directly related to foreign trade may still influence foreign-trade outcomes. Of particular importance is the strong Eastern preference for organizational forms and incentives toward technical change.

The interest of Eastern governments in systems touches not only major aspects of the system, such as ministry-enterprises relations and foreign trade, but also specific details, including the organization of the enterprise itself. In Eastern countries, nearly all enterprises are state property, and the state exercises its authority by specifying the organization of the firm. In effect, the state imposes its organizational preferences on the production and distribution processes. There is considerably more freedom of choice concerning the organization of production and distribution in Western countries.

In Western countries, competing firms tend toward organizational forms best suited to the tasks they perform, and these apparently differ among industries.[33] In Eastern countries, central authorities exhibit a strong preference for uniform multi-level hierarchies across industry. The enforcement of uniformity around this particular form will have an effect on relative costs of production, increasing them the most, *ceteris paribus*, compared to Western countries, in those products least amenable to production organized through multi-level hierarchies (e.g., requiring close coordination between research, production, and marketing organizations in the system).

If comparative costs were known and part of the planners' calculus, then Eastern economies would move toward specializing in products that are amenable to production organized the way planners prefer. Indeed, some such specialization occurs now in East-West commerce, where Eastern countries specialize in assembly line production, which is most amenable to multi-level hierarchical control, and Western countries specialize in marketing and research and development, activities much better handled by less formal organizational forms. But since comparative costs are only imperfectly known, planners may attempt to export products which, given their organizational preferences, should really be imported (e.g., advanced manufactured products where technology is changing rapidly). Again, this will decrease the gains from trade, but its effects on the commodity structure of trade are not clear. Eastern planners could heavily subsidize exports of high-cost manufactured goods and come close to, say, the typical proportion for Western countries of manufactures in total exports, but at a substantial cost in the gains from trade.

The relatively strong bias against technical change in most Eastern economies is related to the organizational preference problem but it deserves special attention. There are apparently both systemic and policy causes for the bias against technical change. Among the systemic characteristics important in varying degrees in all Eastern countries are the separation of the R&D functions from production activities, high concentration ratios, and protection of domestic industry. The policies most biased against technical change are the importance given to gross output growth, the lack of strong incentives to encourage technological change, and the pricing systems.[34]

As a consequence of this bias, Eastern countries are considerably hampered in their attempts to export to international markets, where competition for sales of many products is precisely in terms of their technological characteristics. This will tend to lower the level of Eastern exports of machinery, equipment, and other manufactured goods, and may increase the level of imports of similar goods.

Other systemic characteristics important to foreign-trade outcomes must at least be mentioned. Holzman lists the use of material balances planning, quantity targeting, and taut planning as three system characteristics with important implications for foreign-trade outcomes. Brown stresses the detrimental effects on foreign trade of the highly irregular time path of production resulting directly from the incentives in the system.[35] Neither author explores the full implications of these characteristics for foreign trade, although Brown does base much of his case for hyperpoly on tautness, which leaves the system with chronic low reserves; hence, there is a constant need to resort to imports to relieve bottlenecks.

Variations in Policies Within the System

Policies within the system seek to work within the current resource allocation mechanism to change outcomes. In a Western economy, a change in tariffs is a change in non-system policy; it seeks to change the domestic/foreign consumption mix while maintaining (and in fact using) markets as the fundamental resource allocation mechanism. I shall distinguish between policies directed specifically at foreign trade and those not immediately related to foreign trade, but which nevertheless have an important impact on foreign-trade outcomes.

FOREIGN TRADE POLICY WITHIN THE SYSTEM

Eastern and Western governments share a desire to protect domestic manufacturers from foreign competition. The difference is that Western governments must consciously act to block imports that otherwise will occur, while Eastern governments consciously choose their imports that otherwise are automatically blocked.

In both systems, a myriad of small decisions on what to trade, and with whom, combine into aggregate indicators of foreign-trade outcomes. Policies are designed to directly affect the individual decisions. In Western countries, the government must primarily rely on fully visible public means to influence private decisions. It must either influence the variables that influence private decisionmakers, such as prices and credits or it must prevent some transactions as a matter of public policy.

In Eastern countries, the governments' communications on foreign-trade policy are intra-bureaucratic rather than public. Consequently, it is exceedingly difficult to find out just what Eastern foreign-trade policy really is. In many cases, government policy and foreign-trade decisions merge, such as when a foreign-trade organization receives an order to import x Hungarian buses as part of a USSR-Hungarian foreign-trade agreement. Policy and foreign-trade decisions are more separated in areas where organizations operate according to rules, such as "do not import a product into the USSR if it is produced in the USSR." In the first case, the policy is not even visible. In the second case, it is visible (if it is a published law and not an unpublished instruction or informal command), but the problem is still whether the law, so stated, is being enforced.

It is difficult, then, to generalize about differences between Eastern and Western governments' policies relating directly to foreign trade. Certainly the apparent *de facto* barriers in Eastern countries to imports of goods already produced domestically will depress the level of trade. Likewise, the geographic administrations (*upravlenia*) in the ministries of foreign trade make it much easier to affect the geographic structure of trade in Eastern economies. On the commodity composition of trade, it is easier for Eastern governments to convey policies concerning individual decisions on imports and exports, but there are also much stronger constraints on realization of those policies. There is, for example, a well-known set of policies designed to increase machinery and equipment exports, but potential foreign purchasers ultimately decide how effective those policies are. On the import side, the requirements of the economy, which indirectly arise out of many decisions (by planners and others) unrelated to foreign trade, ultimately play a major role in determining the import mix.[36]

POLICIES WITHIN THE SYSTEM ON OTHER OUTCOMES

Policies primarily directed at domestic economic activity may influence foreign-trade outcomes. Three such policies are the relatively strong Eastern preference for industrial production, different preferences on personal income distribution, and different preferences concerning the rate of investment.

Several economists have recently suggested theories that treat the total level of industrial goods output as a public good, that is, a source of utility to policymakers.[37] This certainly seems a useful assumption for modeling policy formation in many countries, particularly Eastern countries. For whatever reason—nationalism, externalities associated with an industrial society, or simply a desire to imitate—one of the hallmarks of central planning in Eastern Europe and the Soviet Union has been a massive drive to *industrialize*. In the literature on economic performance in general and foreign trade in particular, the share of industrial products in GNP and particularly machinery and equipment in exports take on a life of their own, independent of the products included in those categories.

Industrial production is a public good in some Western and probably all Eastern economies, but the latter may show a relatively stronger preference for it. Historically, the group with the power to plan in Eastern countries has represented the industrial interests, or the potential industrial part of society. Consequently, it has placed a much higher utility on industrial production than the somewhat more representative government of market economy.

Policies reflecting this preference will result in a relatively lower level of trade than otherwise, owing to the relatively high level of protection of industrial production. They would also reduce the share of industrial products in imports over what it would otherwise have been. Should the preference for industrial production drive the level of that production above what the domestic market can absorb, the products should spill out as exports, increasing the proportion of industrial products in exports. This raises special issues concerning the geographical structure of trade.

This preference for industrial products has a real cost in terms of private goods foregone (see figure 2). The curve AD represents the

FIGURE 2
Hypothetical National Income-Industrial
Production Trade Off

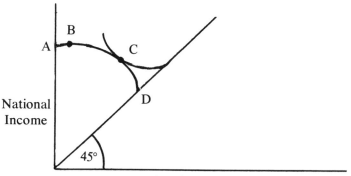

Industrial Production

SOURCE: Adopted from C.A. Cooper and B.F. Massell, "Towards a General Theory of Customs Unions for Developing Countries," *Journal of Political Economy* 73 (October 1965): 465.

trade-off between national income and the level of industrial production. In the area from A to B, increases in industrial production increase national income as the country specializes in products in which it has a comparative advantage. From point B on to D, the level of industrial production can only be increased by substituting domestic production for relatively cheaper imports; and national income falls to point D, where it is equal to the level of industrial production. (Where there is no preference for industrial production, the policymaker would move his economy to point B.) Of course, one could argue that while Eastern countries are further down the national-income industrial production curve than, *ceteris paribus*, Western economies, they still don't know the real costs of their decisions in terms of national income. In fact, the price system in the centrally planned economies hides the costs of protection and, therefore, may act as a special inducement towards protection.

Both Johnson and Cooper-Massel have shown how the costs of protection can be minimized through bilateral trade agreements; their results have obvious applicability to Eastern countries. If two countries have a preference for industrial production but no preference for specific products, then they can sign a bilateral agreement allowing each to specialize in the particular industrial products in which they have a comparative advantage. This would decrease the private goods costs of industrial production, because they moved to lower-cost products and possibly because of economies of scale.

This seems an accurate description of the CMEA countries. They share a very strong preference for industrial production, particularly investment goods, and are at a comparative disadvantage in their production costs compared to world markets. They negotiate bilateral agreements that allow them to maintain the level of industrial production in their individual countries, yet they specialize in the production of those industrial products in which they have some comparative advantage within CMEA. They expect economies of scale to occur because of specialization and take that into account in their calculations of the "effectiveness" of specialization.

Income distributions among individuals tend to be more equal in Eastern than in Western economies.[38] This seems to be a consequence of both systemic characteristics and policy. The system of property ownership guarantees that, unlike Western economies, most property incomes in Eastern economies accrue to the state. On the other hand, Eastern states may have somewhat stronger policies designed to take the tails off income distribution by taxing away all nonproperty rents and quasi-rents, including, for example, rents for human capital. These differences in the personal distribution of income will probably affect the demands for all goods, which in turn will affect potential exports and imports and possibly the level of trade. The demand for luxury cars, long trips abroad, and antiques may be lower in the Eastern economy; on the other hand, the demand for modest automobiles, short sojourns within the country, basic furniture, and food may be higher. This may have an affect on the composition of trade at the gross level (i.e., autos vs. food). It is not obvious what the effect will be on the level of trade, since shifts in demands for final products will have an indirect impact on the demand for imports and supply of exports.[39]

In Eastern economies, planners may differ from consumers by placing a greater premium on future vs. present comsumption., thus pushing up the investment ratio. As a result, a higher proportion of GNP going to machine-building, equipment and non-private construction should serve to restructure imports toward machinery, equipment, and investment-related intermediate products, and away from consumption goods. Exports may also be restructured in the same direction, if, for example, increased machinery and equipment production generate changes in comparative costs through economies of scale.

The upward pressure on the demand for imported investment goods may be particularly pronounced in the early years of industrialization, where characteristically the Eastern planners push up the investment/GNP ratio faster than productive capacity in machine building expands.[40] Such a demand may also temporarily raise the level of trade above what it would be in a market economy where investment/GNP ratios rise less rapidly. This special effect aside, there should be no long-term impact of the high I/GNP ratio on the level of trade since machine-building capacity can eventually catch up.

Appendix
Computation of the Confidence Bands
Reported in Table 2

The formula for computing a confidence band in a multiple regression is:*

(1) $\hat{Y}_o - s_f t_{n-k,\lambda/2} \leq Y_o \leq \hat{Y}_o + s_f t_{n-k,\lambda/2}$

(2) $s_f^2 = s^2(1+1/n) + (\underline{X}_o - \bar{X})s^2 (X'X)^{-1} (\underline{X}_o - \bar{X})$, where:

$\hat{Y}_o$	=	the predicted value of Y.
Y_o	=	the actual value of Y.
$t_{n-k,\lambda/2}$	=	the value of t at n-k degrees of freedom and a probability level of $\lambda/2$.

---

*Jan Kmenta, *Elements of Econometrics* (New York: Macmillan, 1971), pp. 374-76.

s^2 = estimate of the variance.

n = sample size.

$s^2(X'X)^{-1}$ = estimate of variance-covariance matrix.

X_o = vector of independent variables used in the prediction.

$\overline{X}$ = vector of average values for the independent variables.

s_f^2 = estimate of the variance of the forecast error.

If all of the independent variables used in the prediction are equal to the respective means of the independent variables in the sample, the $(X_o - \overline{X})$ is zero and $s_f^2 = s^2(1+1/n)$, which is approximated by s^2 for large samples.

The confidence bands in tables 2 and 3 were computed under the assumption that $s_f^2 = s^2$; that is, under the assumption that $(X_o - X) = 0$ and that $t_{n-k, \lambda/2} = 2.0$ (actually 1.96 for Broner and Pryor and 2.2 for van Brabant). The s_f's which are additive in log-log space are multiplicative in anti-log-anti-log space; thus, after computing $s_f t_{n-k, \lambda/2}$, either add and subtract that from the log of predicted trade or take the anti-log of $s_f t_{n-k, \lambda/2}$ and multiply and divide predicted trade by that number.

TABLE 4

Estimated Upper and Lower Bound Ratios for 95%
Confidence Bands on Predicted Trade

Study	Standard Error of Estimate (SEE)	Upper and Lower 95% Confidence Bands*	
Table 2:			
Pryor 1955A	.22	.64	1.56
van Brabant			
1955	.15	.74	1.35
1965	.20	.67	1.45
Broner 1970	1.03	.13	7.80
Table 3:			
van Brabant			
1965			
Machinery and Equipment	.089	.84	1.19
Manufactured Consumer Goods	.153	.74	1.36

*These are anti-log ($\pm$ 2 $\times$ SEE).

Finally, predicted trade in table 1 is in the denominator, so the entire procedure must be reversed when operating on those ratios. I chose to take the anti-logs, then divided and multiplied (simultaneously reducing all ratios by 10% in table 2, by 13% for machinery and equipment in table 3, and by 17% for manufactured consumer goods in table 3 to correct for the price differences discussed in the text). For tables 2 and 3 the ratios were computed on the basis of the reported standard errors are presented in table 4.

As an example of the computations in table 2, the band given for Czechoslovakia for Pryor 1955a is .26 = (.9 × .45/1.56) and .63 = (.9 × .45/.64).

Discussion
Frederic L. Pryor

It is important to explore the differences in the trade patterns of nations with different economic systems if we wish to understand some major economic and political forces underlying East European trade planning. In his interesting paper, Edward Hewett builds a convincing case for the necessity of exercising caution in interpreting the existing econometric evidence on these differences. He then attempts to outline how the foreign-trade outcomes of East Europe should be analyzed.

The subject can be approached in two ways. One can build a formal model of trade decisionmaking in centrally planned economies (CPEs), from which to derive a series of propositions about the expected patterns of trade. Or one can attempt a more informal approach by listing the major influences that might account for differences in trade patterns between the two economic systems and then using bits and pieces of evidence to intuitively assess their relative importance. The first approach represents a major undertaking that would undoubtedly require data that are unavailable. *Faute de meilleur*, Hewett tackles the subject using the more informal approach; despite the limitations of this tactic, I find myself in general agreement with most of his major points.

His most important message is how little we actually know about many aspects of East European foreign trade. Although I am convinced that careful econometric testing would show that their foreign trade is, other things being equal, lower than trade in a market economy[1], his calculations in tables 1 and 2 are useful. Further, his summary of the available literature on the composition of trade suggests that much work remains to be done. The comprehensive analyses of the comparative advantage of the Soviet Union (by Steven Rosefielde) and of Bulgaria (by Gur Ofer) point toward the beginning of an understanding of this commodity composition problem.

In the latter part of his paper, Hewett focuses primarily on relatively aggregative aspects of exports and imports. His list of factors influencing the pattern of CMEA trade gives rise to occasional doubts. For instance, some of his factors, e.g., the impact of greater investment ratios or more equal distributions of income, may be relatively unimportant. And perhaps he could have emphasized more the impact of the clumsy bilateral trade negotiation system, not to mention the peculiar biases of CPEs in their choice of industrial technologies that have, in turn, influenced the commodity patterns of trade. It might also have been instructive to focus more intensively on the various kinds of risks faced by central planners and the manner in which these have influenced trade flows.

In trying to develop some propositions about East European foreign-trade behavior, Hewett separates factors attributable to their environment (natural resources, climate, level of economic development, and other factors Marxists include in "the forces of production"), to their economic systems and the policies determining this system (hereafter labeled systems factors), and to their policies to keep the system in operation (hereafter called policy factors). Each set of factors deserves brief comment.

Environmental Factors

Hewett suggests that natural resources and climatic conditions play an important role in determining the volume and composition of a CPE's trade, but he does not tell us exactly how one might analyze these factors quantitatively. Theoretical arguments can be made that the presence of such resources decreases the volume of trade (by decreasing the necessity to import) or increases the volume (by increasing the availability of products to be easily sold on the world market). One possible method of extricating oneself from such a tangle is to take advantage of some historical data. In a brief note I wrote some years ago,[2] I investigated whether the relatively lower volume of trade in Eastern Europe in the 1950s could be attributed to resource factors that were reflected in their trade in the differences in volume of trade, *ceteris paribus*, in Eastern as contrasted with Western Europe; however, in comparison to this calculated "potential trade," there was considerable variation in the East European nations. To a certain extent, these differences carried over into the post-World War II period. Of course, it could be argued that East European trade was artificially high in the interwar period (in the same manner that some have argued the volume of foreign trade in pre-Castro Cuba was artificially high) but such a contention is difficult to support.

The question about the impact of the environment relates to the interesting results about Bulgaria that are presented by Gur Ofer in this volume. Although Bulgaria appears to be the only East European nation that has decided to specialize in agriculture, the climatic conditions of the country compared to the rest of Eastern Europe are obviously a major causal factor underlying this policy.

System

Most of Hewett's discussion concerns the impact of systemic or policy factors on the volume, composition, and direction of trade. Some of these points raise some difficulty in separating, but they are nevertheless sufficiently distinct to permit a tabular presentation, an exercise carried out in table 1.

The quantitative influence of the factors listed under "system" in table 1 may be tested in several ways. First, some matters can be explored by making detailed East-West comparisons. For instance, Hewett argues that the guarantee of a job for every worker has induced a greater protectionist feeling among the workers than in the West. One way to test this conjecture is to examine total domestic consumption and total imports of particular commodities for a group of countries in the East and in the West to see if, in practice, imports would bear a greater share in changes when dips in domestic consumption occur. I strongly suspect that Hewett has underestimated protectionist feelings among Western workers and that few differences would be found. Second, some systemic influences on the volume, composition, and direction of trade can be isolated by comparing trade patterns, particularly for specific goods or groupings of goods, of the more decentralized socialist nations, such as Hungary and Yugoslavia, with the more centralized nations, such as the GDR and Romania. And finally, still other systemic influences can be isolated by looking at patterns of trade before and after major systemic changes have been implemented. Such an exercise could probably be carried out only for Hungary (before and after 1968), the GDR (before the early 1960s and after the late 1960s) and, with less probability of success, Yugoslavia (before and after 1965) and Romania (before and after the late 1960s).

Some notion of the different specialization procedures within the CMEA can also be gained by comparing types (inter- and intrasectoral) of specialization patterns within CMEA and the EEC. Such an exercise is carried out for several product categories by Fallenbuchl in this volume and should be carried out on a much broader scale.

Policy

The quantitative influence of the factors listed under "policy" in table 1 can also be explored in several ways. As Hewett suggests,

TABLE 1
Foreign-Trade Influences Classified by Causal Factor and Impact

Foreign trade influence	Type of Causal factor		Impact on Foreign Trade		
	System factors	Policy factors	Volume	Composition	Direction
Strict assumptions about rationality, perfect knowledge, etc.					
Income distribution	X*	X		X	
Preference for investment over consumption		X		X	
Domestic industrial production as public good		X	X	X	X?
Preference for organizational forms	X		X	X?	X
Loosening above assumptions					
Ministerial autarky behavior	X		X	X?	
Workers' desires for protection		X	X	X?	
Uncertainties about terms of trade by central planners	X?		X	X?	X
Bias against long production runs		X	X	X	
Few specialized export prises	X		X?	X?	
Information barriers	X	X	X	X	X
Political factors		X	X	X	X
Special Intra-CMEA factors					
Desire to retain planning sovereignty		X	X	X	
Bilateralism	X	X	X	X	X
Lack of information about gains of trade	X		X	X	X?
Lack of comparative advantage in key industrial goods vis-à-vis West	(environmental)		X	X	X
Factors not emphasized by Hewett					
Distortions of CMEA prices	X		X	X	X
Bottleneck widening functions of imports	X		X	X	X
Poor quality goods			X	X	X
Poor sales techniques by East European foreign traders		X	X	X	X

*Evidence that the income distribution is strongly related to the type of economic system is presented in my *Property and Industrial Organization in Communist and Capitalist Nations* (Bloomington: Indiana University Press, 1973), pp. 320-22.

investigating these matters is more problematic because we face the same kinds of difficulties as other economists do in investigating the impact of individual preference functions on individual buying and selling behavior: namely, we have no measure of preferences other than observing what behavior is followed. However, the situation may not be completely hopeless since East European policymakers often announce changes in their preferences in various types of policy speeches or in the publication of various types of plans. Although in terms of explicitness, especially with regard to foreign trade, these documents often leave much to be desired, they seem an unexploited source of useful information. More particularly, confrontation between plan goals and plan realities tell us a good deal about systemic impediments for realizing certain preferences. Such research should be carried out not only at high levels of aggregation but also at more disaggregative levels if data are available. The deviations from past trends, which can be linked to particular policy changes, give an important clue to the impact of previous policy preferences.

A major problem in carrying out the lines of research I propose is setting out the *ceteris paribus* conditions. That is, this type of analysis must be made using multivariate statistical techniques which permit us to hold a variety of causal variables constant, e.g., business cycle conditions and number of years since promulgation of the five year plan. Dummy variables can be used to designate known changes in policy or system. Or, more specifically, we might have the types of equations which Vanous uses (in his contribution to the volume) to investigate intra-CMEA trade, supplemented by additional variables designating the particular changes we are investigating.

A second major problem of such research is the necessity to examine East European trade at a much greater level of disaggregation than heretofore. Only by comparing trade in relatively small commodity groups might we be able to extract some useful information about the role of economies of scale, ministerial autarky, and similar matters that Hewett mentions. Unfortunately, such research requires both trade and production data that are often difficult to obtain for individual East European nations.

To conclude, Hewett raises several interesting problems and makes valid points about problems of interpreting existing economic analyses of East European trade. Although some of the problems he discusses are unresolvable by empirical testing, others can be examined in a systematic fashion. Such research would have to be quite different from most of the quantitative analyses on East-West trade that have been carried out up to now. A new set of "generational" studies offers exciting prospects for obtaining some vitally needed information on the determinants of the volume, structure, and direction of East European trade.

Arpad Abonyi, Ivan J. Sylvain, and
James A. Caporaso

Political Economy Perspectives on Integration

A Comment on Integration Theories

Arpad Abonyi and Ivan J. Sylvain

Research on CMEA has suffered from a lack of communication between political scientists and economists. To be sure, analyses in both disciplines have been forced to recognize the close interconnection of politics and economics in the evolution of the region and its societies. Both have found it necessary to draw on each other's variables, but in a primarily ad hoc fashion. An interdisciplinary dialogue is necessary to provide a better understanding. As part of such a dialogue, we will review the two main political science theories of integration as they have been applied to CMEA. We will then add considerations drawn from developmental studies and suggest adjusting "integration" theory to a more generally applicable framework.

In the study of international integration, the underlying purpose of political scientists has been to articulate the conditions for achieving international peace.[1] As a result, they have been preoccupied with world order and the primary agent of war, the nation-state, concentrating their analyses on the *noncoercive* processes that circumscribe its ability to wage war and the circumstances under which its sovereignty is voluntarily superseded by higher forms of human community.[2] Political scientists view the emergence of such a community as a multidimensional phenomenon that subsumes what economists usually understand as integration, i.e., approaching relatively equal scarcities through trade creation and diversion. This economic dimension is intertwined with social and political aspects.

On the social plane, this phenomenon includes the evolution of increasingly common values and attitudes directed toward creating a new identity. Although there has been little common agreement on an acceptable definition of the political dimension of this phenomenon, the concept has been tied to the emergence of international authority in such a community either through policy coordination,[3] collective decisionmaking,[4] progressive forms of institutionalization,[5] or the emergence of nationalism at the international level.[6] The various processes in these dimensions are said to produce international peace as a by-product of primary concern with collective welfare gains. The phenomenon of integration, then, is viewed as implicitly beneficial, not only because it permits the creation of a security community—where differences are resolved through peaceful means, usually with institutionalized procedures and without resort to large-scale physical force[7]—but also because it is produced by interaction, which by and large is also rewarding to participants.

Although multidimensional in scope, the study of integration in political science is characterized by an almost exclusive focus derived from the West European experience. This serves as a major impediment to comparative analyses in general and studies of the CMEA in particular. This focus resulted from the formulation of neo-functional and transactions-communications analyses in the mid-1950s to explain the emergence of what appeared to be a movement toward a higher form of human community in Western Europe. Until now, these two approaches have dominated the analytical literature on Third World and CMEA integration,[8] but they have failed to recognize and incorporate regional political and economic conditions.

These two approaches try to articulate how a higher form of human community is realized and the form it will take. For instance, neofunctionalism stresses that cooperation in functional economic sectors will be fostered in a technically complex world. As welfare gains become more evident to participants, cooperation will spill over to other economic sectors. As technical cooperation schemes impinge on one another, policy coordination is necessary to ensure equitable distribution of costs and benefits among participants. According to neofunctionalism, such policy coordination requires the establishment of institutional arrangements at the international level. The greater the spillover, the more complex the task of policy coordination becomes. In order to make this coordination effective, more decisionmaking authority is transferred from national to supranational levels. Finally, the supranational authority will supposedly usurp the power of the nation-state and the loyalty of its citizens, who now look toward this new supranational organization for material benefits and political guidance.

Alternatively, communications-transactions analysis envisages the emergence of pluralistic or amalgamated security communities. Such communities are formed through social communication—increased trade, tourism, letter or telephone contacts—between participating societies, depending on the degree to which their capabilities permit responsiveness to one another. This communication, if mutually rewarding, increases the intensity and frequency of common experiences between societies. It thereby enhances the probability of a new community through social learning. The formation of community between two or more societies means the adoption of common values and habits and sharing the rewarding experiences that culminate in a cohesive feeling of togetherness and a sense of common identity.

The emergence of human communities depends on a common set of assumptions in both conceptual frameworks. First, these communities develop in a pluralistic political environment.[9] This environment permits—even encourages—individuals and groups independently to seek maximization of their goals and values.[10] Second, welfare gains are critically important in forming these new values and are achieved through market liberalization of trade.[11] Third, the existence of an industrialized, technologically oriented economy is a prerequisite for maximizing gains.[12] Moreover, high technology areas require increased cooperation. Fourth, integration is a voluntary, noncoercive process in which individuals or groups deliberately or consciously decide to cooperate in pursuit of reciprocal benefits.[13] Fifth, the nation-state is viewed as an impediment to achieving these benefits, not the least of which is international peace.[14] Finally, and not illogically, integration is assumed to be a "good" thing.

There are shortcomings in advocating integration as a peaceful solution for the world. Neo-functionalist and communications-transactions explanations share the ethnocentrism of Western scholars who attempt to define what the world should be in terms of what the West has become.[15] These theories stress the expansion of already stable, developed societies, rather than answering questions about those experiencing disruptions occasioned by fundamental structural change.

This unidimensional outlook, presupposing that all such schemes are characterized by the same causes and similar political and economic conditions, gained special currency with the modicum of success enjoyed by the EEC in its achievement of a security community. As such, it has had a profound influence on the application of political science integration theory to other regions of the world. This West European experience has become an example to be emulated on the euphoric premise that it would "contribute to world peace by creating ever-expanding cooperation, eventually spilling over into controversy-laden fields which threaten us directly with thermonuclear destruction."[16] With this in mind, students (especially of the neofunctional school) earnestly applied their framework in order to prove that the West European type of integration could work in all regions. This made for less-than-adequate comparative research; instead of explaining what conditions and purposes were endogenous to other regions, these analyses were undertaken in light of what conditions and purposes ought to exist in order to follow the West European pattern. Instead of fundamentally amending frameworks to include regional diversity, the situation was adapted to paradigms based on the experience of West Europe.

The Haas-Schmitter study of the Latin American Free Trade Association (LAFTA) is probably the best example of this.[17] Because certain variables contained in their neo-functional framework did not appear to explain integration of the LAFTA region, they substituted "functional equivalents" to take the place of the missing variables and thus rationalize what is actually an inherent weakness in the framework. Such patchwork changes leave the theoretical foundations largely intact. They may make neo-functionalism and communications-transactions analyses good tools for making comparisons, but they do not make them adequate for explaining the direction of processes found in developing regions.

A research outlook, which uncritically accepts the assumptions of these theories, has also shaped studies on the CMEA. Descriptive studies have been preoccupied with what integation "should" be and what it "should" be leading toward—usually the EEC notion of integration with a relatively decentralized type of market and subsystem autonomy for economic actors. The best example of this form of analysis is Werner Feld's "The Utility of the EEC Experience for Eastern Europe." Feld's purpose is to determine what utility, if any, the experience of EEC poses for "bridging the gap between the two halves of Europe and on the transformation of economic and political systems of the People's Democracies."[18] This type of analysis cannot explain the developmentally oriented political and economic forces that sustain Eastern Europe. It can only advocate what should be changed in order to emulate the EEC. This point of view has also crept into the works of other political scientists who have investigated the CMEA.[19] Even analytical reviews, such as Roger Kanet's, stay within the logic, value orientation, and methodological parameters of these theories, without suggesting new dimensions called for by the political and economic differences in the region.[20] On the whole, then, political scientists have treated the CMEA as an abberation, a limiting case, that does not possess the requisites for a West European type of integration.

Regional differences, in CMEA as well as Third World integration strategies, should not be dismissed so easily. First, instead of pluralistic-industrialized polities, the CMEA consists of mobilization regimes seeking to restructure society and to create a modern technological economy. In this respect, it resembles Third World areas more than Western Europe. As such, its objectives should be viewed as developmental strategies for pursuing industrial and technological progress—ones conditioned by the use of command planning methods within the region.

The type of regional strategy adopted by the CMEA has been shaped by qualitative differences that challenge the assumptions of Western frameworks. In place of pluralism, centrally controlled social change has been emphasized. Political control is extended to the economy by using the command planning system which deliberately restricts market forces. Through mobilizing extensive resources, command planning has created parallel, heavy industrial bases in all CMEA countries. This system has by and large limited regional cooperation to bilateral exchanges designed to level off domestic surpluses and deficiencies. Combined with an absence of market forces, this drive for establishing technological development de-emphasizes concern for welfare gains, which also characterize Third World regional strategies.[21]

In contrast to the assumptions of neo-functional and communications-transactions analysis, integration is not necessarily a "good thing" for all participants. Relatively equal distributions of values and attributes within integrating regions cannot be assumed.[22] To a degree, asymmetries are part of any integrative relationship because no two participants possess identical endowments. Favorable endowments offer some members increased leverage over others. There is no assurance that this leverage will be used equally to distribute gains and developmental priorities. In the CMEA, wide divergence among members with regard to levels of technology, industrial and military capability, size of internal markets, and relative resource endowment lead to inequality within the region. This asymmetry has led to dominance by and dependence on the Soviet Union.

Inequalities in the region have been exacerbated and maintained by the original Soviet imposition of centrally planned, parallel industrial development on mainly resource-poor countries. This development model has led to a particular pattern of regional trade. East European countries primarily dispose of their low technology, noncompetitive machinery surpluses on the large Soviet market. In return, they receive indispensable raw materials required for industrialization.[23] The Soviet Union, however, by and large does not depend on East European inputs to sustain development; its huge size—combined with directed, parallel, individual development—means that it regionally dominates absolute output in each economic sector.[24] A natural outgrowth of command planning is bilateralism. Because trade requires coordination of national production plans, negotiations are carried on bilaterally; each East European country's agents must deal with the Soviets separately.[25]

One result of these intra-regional imbalances is entrenchment of Soviet hegemony. The industrial growth of smaller CMEA members becomes tied to expanding extraction of Soviet raw materials, in return for which they must expand exports of machinery and other manufactures to the Soviet market and, despite tight funds, invest in Soviet resource development. Furthermore, bilateral negotiations place each East European nation in a disadvantageous bargaining position. This creates a situation in which the economies of the East European members of CMEA are conditioned by the development and policies of the USSR.[26] This relationship is asymmetrical, through which the Soviet Union is able to exert a major influence on the behavior of national political elites and on the economic decisions in the rest of the CMEA to meet its own needs and purposes. Because the reverse is not true—that is, East European members of CMEA do not have this same influence over the Soviet Union—this results in a relationship that can be characterized as *dependence*.[27]

The inequality of interstate relations within the CMEA has prompted some analysts to conclude that the organization may act as a vehicle for eventual Soviet absorption of East European socialist states.[28] In other words, creation of a higher form of international Leninist community may ultimately mean fusion with the "federal" structures of the USSR. The predictive merit of such arguments is open to debate. Nevertheless, they call into question the accepted Western doctrine that integration is necessarily a good thing.

In sum, qualitative differences in CMEA and the Third World mean that these theories need to be amended to include a wider range of variables and different outcomes. The notion of interdependence provides for such an expanded perspective. Using this general category, suggested by Caporaso,[29] qualitative differences may be combined with the conditions assumed by neo-functional and communications-transactions analyses to form common ranges of variables for study. These would include: conflict-cooperation; coercion-voluntarism; levels of industrialization; degree of autonomy in political and economic systems; stage of nation-building; stage of social transformation; marketization-planning; and symmetry-asymmetry in such attributes as resource endowment and potential. Interdependence can vary along all these dimensions, producing regional integration as one possible outcome.

Utilizing this more general formulation, one can establish the context of interdependence in any region. A particular configuration of variables characterizing a given region entails certain goals and outcomes which would not necessarily apply elsewhere. In the CMEA dependencies, inequalities and critical problems of change associated with intensive development create a structure that conditions ensuing regional goals, behavior, and institutions. While the economic goals are primarily developmental, they are overlapped by the political requirement to build an international Leninist community according to norms formulated largely by the dominant regional actor. These norms can affect elite behavior by circumscribing decisionmaking and policy options at the national level.

The technical, economic, and political necessity of region-wide command planning requires the emergence of regional institutional networks. The CMEA organizations created in response to this need require some transfer of national sovereignty to be effective. Yet, even where this stops short of supranationalism, the logic of regional plan coordination means that at minimum all CMEA members must adapt their institutions to relatively homogenous administrative norms. The extent of such conformity and any transfer of sovereignty to CMEA institutions depends critically on the East European state's links with the Soviet Union and the strength of the challenge posed by intensive development given political constraints.

To conclude: while interdependence may not be a definitive new concept for the study of CMEA, it can be useful for characterizing relationships which up to now have been inadequately addressed by the dominant integration theories in the field. We suggest that both political scientists and economists devote more attention to consideration of political-economic dependence and development in CMEA "integration."

Can Integration in Eastern and Western Europe Be Compared?

James A. Caporaso

On the face of it, the historical, political, and socio-economic conditions surrounding integration efforts in the CMEA are markedly different from those surrounding the counterpart process in the European Economic Community (EEC). The CMEA was born in 1949 as the beginnings of the Cold War were taking shape and as Europe began its process of fragmentation between East and West. The EEC was born into the "post-industrial society" atmosphere of the late 1950s and owed a great deal to the general economic boom Western Europe enjoyed during the previous decade. At the political level, the EEC was viewed as a pact among equals which, despite obvious differences among the member-states in terms of size, economic strength, and political leverage, had strong institutional safeguards built into the Rome Treaty to protect the weaker members. More importantly, the community system was based on consensus among member-states, extensive interactions among partners, persuasion, horse trades, and compromises. No state would be pushed into a supranational direction against its will. This contrasts sharply with CMEA's experience, where the sheer physical size, military power, and political-economic resources of the Soviet Union dominate and where institutional safeguards and correctives are not ensured in the decisionmaking procedures.

If there are sharp differences between the EEC and the CMEA in terms of the symmetry among their members, there are even more pronounced differences regarding the social, economic, and political "background" characteristics that condition and shape the process of integration. In Western Europe, the environment in which integration began was marked by a high level of pluralism in the social structure, a substantial amount of autonomy on the part of associated groups, markets which were at least partially if not predominantly private, a decline in ideology among key social groups, and an accomplished level of industrialization among all participant nation-states. On the other hand, the CMEA was characterized by democratic centralism, the subordination of social relations to a hierarchical structure, uneven industrialization, and asymmetric benefits ensuing from the process of integration.

The Western European environment was, therefore, seen as somewhat unique in that its integration process was based on the existence of background factors that were not shared with Eastern Europe. The three most important factors were:

1. *Social pluralism:* Society is broken up into a large number of fairly autonomous, private interest groups seeking to maximize social welfare.

2. *Separation of politics from economics:* This separation, or decoupling of political and nonpolitical interests, allowed for the initial depoliticization of a task area (e.g., tariff harmonization or standardization of transportation laws). Within this limited sector, states could cooperate without raising the political hackles of government officials.

3. *Post-industrial political culture:* There was a value system which can best be summed up as the "end of ideology." This phrase acts as a synopsis for a more elaborate description of a political culture where primordial sentiments, such as religious divisions and ethnic attachment, have waned and where important secular divisions, such as class warfare, have all but disappeared. This worldview leads to a bloodless social theory in which calculations of interest and instrumental rationality dominate the nonrational forces of nationalism, group loyalty, national fears, and power-political considerations. Of course, the domain of high politics, with its grandeur and incontestable prerogative of wielding ultimate power, was recognized. De Gaulle was recognized as a symbol incarnate (to use a somewhat contradictory expression) who, in one stroke, could bring the entire process of economic integration to a screeching halt. However, high politics belonged to a separate domain, moved in different, nonintersecting orbits, and did not mingle with economics on a day-to-day basis. This "two-world" assumption was elevated into a position of major importance for economic integration with the introduction of the separability assumption. That is, integration could begin to take root in non-controversial sectors and, once established there, it would spread to other more politically important sectors. The political would gradually succumb to the economic: "federalism à la carte" or "by installments."

One can see that the list of obstacles to a unified theory of integration is substantial. It includes differences that are purely descriptive as well as differences in the laws themselves. As a result, the fields of Western European and Eastern European integration took shape separately without knowledge of what the other was doing. When the same theory is used, it is criticized for assuming conditions that do not exist.[30] Consequently, scholars have tended to analyze separately developments in Western and Eastern Europe, from the perspective of their disciplines or sub-fields.[31]

Despite some obvious negative results of this bifurcated development, such as the fragmentation of our research efforts and the retarded cumulation of knowledge, there is an unmistakable appeal in "going it alone." The importance of power and coercion in the CMEA cannot be denied. Clearly, these variables ought to be represented in a theory of integration in Eastern Europe. We should applaud efforts that urge a partial paradigmatic shift away from an analysis of the maximization and distribution of the economic pie determined under conditions of rough symmetry or at least equity, toward a situation where the size and content of the economic pie are disproportionately determined by one actor, where bargaining conditions are extremely asymmetrical, and where, far from institutionally safeguarding small country rights, they are often trampled. Such a shift would focus our attention on distributional issues, resurrect the old question of "who gets what, when, and how," make us sensitive to asymmetries in the relations among nations, and reintroduce power and influence as inescapably important concepts. This is all to the good.

Although this "two-worlds" view is attractive in many respects, it can be criticized along both factual and methodological lines. Factually, we must recognize that, legalisms aside, the EEC was never composed of equals. Franco-German dominance was always implicitly recognized, although the limits to which they could exploit their superior positions were also very real. By the same token, the movement toward integration in Western Europe was not totally due to the maturing of forces within domestic society. Scholars such as Stanley Hoffman and Alting von Geusau[32] recognized the importance of external factors in Western European integration. Conversely, the CMEA is not held together purely by coercion. For example, Marer argues that "the catalyst providing CMEA its integration momentum in recent years has been Soviet willingness to supply a growing volume of energy and raw materials to Eastern Europe."[33]

Let me now shift to the more fundamental methodological question: What are the arguments justifying distinctive theories to explain the "same" process in two different arenas of application? For brevity, let me summarize the methodological claim of the "two-worlds" position as follows: the conditioning situation of integration in Western Europe is very different from that in Eastern Europe. Consequently, the causal structures of integration are themselves distinctive.

The methodological position of the "two-worlds" school results in unnecessary obstacles to the comparative study of regional integration. First, it is a mistake to treat either descriptive differences or parameter differences (i.e., relations among variables) between Western and Eastern Europe as a justification for a qualitatively different theory. Second, the "two-worlds" argument confuses the process of integration per se with any of its several modes of accomplishment (e.g., voluntary exchange, coercion, normative cohesion).

The existence of descriptive differences between Eastern and Western Europe poses no obstacle to a comparative study of integration. Observations that "pluralism is pronounced in Western Europe but not Eastern Europe" or that "coercion is present in the CMEA but not in the EEC" merely record observations that indicate variation in our independent variables. Differences in the conditioning situation, which determine how the variables will be related, provides a more serious obstacle to a unified theory. One methodological response has been to fashion a separate theory to accommodate the two situations. Is this the only methodological response? I think not. One could allow all the factors mentioned as part of the conditioning situation in both arenas to enter the theory as variables rather than as external limiting conditions. The resulting theory would read roughly as follows: "To the extent that societies possess autonomous interest groups, advanced levels of industrialization, a rational, profit-maximizing orientation toward the market, etc., they will also experience voluntary integration. To the extent that societies possess low scores on these variables, they will not experience voluntary integration." According to this approach, low observed scores for any or all of the conditioning factors do not invalidate the theory. They merely work against the growth of integration—quite a different thing.

My second criticism is simply this: it is a mistake to confuse the process of integration with one of the mechanisms that might bring it about. It is, for example, unduly restrictive to limit the process of integration to a system of voluntary exchange and contractual arrangements entered into by free individuals and groups. There are three general bases of social order which, in varying proportions, can provide a momentum toward integration: exchange, power, or sentiment (or culture). The disciplines of economics, politics, and sociology-anthropology have emerged around these social bases and each has a spokesman: Locke, Hobbes, and Durkheim. The EEC is a complicated horsetrade; it is principally an exchange system. The CMEA is more heavily based on the exercise of power and coercion to maintain the solidarity of relations. However, if voluntary exchange and its associated symptoms are seen in an instrumental capacity rather than as the *raison d'être* of integration per se, it fosters a more comparative viewpoint.

Perhaps the better part of wisdom would be to recognize the differences between the historical experiences of CMEA and the EEC and, adding the specialization of knowledge among area scholars, conclude that separate roads are likely to be followed. Despite the appeal of this argument, I should like to make a few proposals.

The first order of business is to make it clear, on conceptual grounds, just what the general category is that we are studying. Second, in a more methodological vein, a unified theory of integration will have to be a contextual theory—one that incorporates regionally specific variables. This is the only way to bridge the great diversity among regional systems with the need for general theory. As a corollary, I would argue for the progressive conversion of constants into variables as the way to acquire more generality.

Concerning the first suggestion, let me make a concrete proposal. The concept of integration, having developed in the liberal West, has connotations of both voluntarism and systemic transformation, i.e., integration includes structures. This limits the scope of its application. A more useful general category would be "the comparative study of regional interdependence among nation-states." This category is free to vary in the amount of conflict and cooperation, symmetry-asymmetry, coercion-voluntarism, level of industrialization, autonomy of subsystems, the rule of the state, and systemic transformation, of which regional integration is one possible outcome.

This approach is attractive because it does not define the class of things to be studied in terms of context-specific properties. The definers are general and abstract, allowing for comparison. Moreover, it follows a "minimum definition" strategy proposed by Sartori,[34] leaving many interesting variables free to vary rather than logically entailing them as part of the definition. That is a strategy that favors the development of theory by translating the parameters of the "two-worlds" view into variables in a "one-world" view. By doing this we have the variation we need to evaluate or, if possible, rigorously test hypotheses whose terms are constant within regional settings but vary across them (e.g., industrialization, amount of dominance, central vs. market economies). Since these terms vary little within settings, they cannot be tested except by moving outside a single setting. Now we can assert, without risk of circularity, that "high levels of asymmetry between nations should lead to negative perceptions of interdependence among the smaller or weaker members."

Finally, once the focus is on interdependence, a rich vein of concepts can be tapped: symmetry, asymmetry, sensitivity, vulnerability, etc. Once the question of interdependence is raised, it is natural to ask who depends on whom, for what, with what intensity, and with what available substitutes. And we return to those important questions so brilliantly posed by Albert Hirschman over three decades ago in *National Power and the Structure of Foreign Trade*.[35]

Thomas A. Wolf

On the Adjustment
of Centrally Planned
Economies to External
Economic Disturbances

Continued growth of East-West economic interdependence has made
the centrally planned economies (CPEs) of Eastern Europe and the
Soviet Union increasingly sensitive to economic conditions in the
West. Recent disturbances emanating from the West that can be considered exogenous to the CPEs include rapid inflation, sudden and
substantial changes in the terms of trade, severe recession in Western
industrialized countries, and the collapse of the Bretton Woods system of fixed exchange rates. These disturbances have led to considerable discussion of the implications for CMEA integration and for the
future development of East-West economic relations.[1]

This paper seeks to develop an analytical framework within which
the differing responses to exogenous disturbances of different CPEs
can be examined. This framework is most applicable to these countries' relations with the nonsocialist world and does not take into account effects on intra-CMEA economic relations (e.g., the growth of
East-West commerce and its effect on integration and the effects of
intra-CMEA foreign-trade price revisions based on moving averages
of recent years' world market prices).

A decade ago, Holzman demonstrated the absence of most "traditional" (i.e., market economy) balance-of-payments adjustment
mechanisms in CPEs, and Hoeffding's case study of the rapid Soviet
adjustment to external imbalance caused by massive grain purchases
from the West in 1963-64 illustrated the peculiarities of the Soviet-type
foreign trade system.[2] Discussants of those papers stressed the "very

The author is particularly grateful to the discussants of this earlier paper, Josef C.
Brada and Mordechai Kreinin, and to Peter Kenen, Paul Marer, and J. Michael Montias
for criticisms of that manuscript. Helpful comments were also received from Marton
Tardos and Urzsula Plowiec.

severe limits" of applying the "conventional 'Western' analytical apparatus" to the foreign trade of CPEs.[3] This study will seek to demonstrate, however, that several modern Western analytical approaches (but not necessarily the actual mechanisms or the behavioral models themselves) are useful in examining the recent external economic shocks to CPEs and the short-run policy options available to CPE policymakers to deal with their effects.

There are several reasons for renewed attention to balance-of-payments adjustment in CPEs. First, the CMEA countries find themselves in a policy environment quite different from that of the 1950s or early 1960s. East-West trade has grown in relative importance; and in contrast to the earlier period, CPEs today have considerable access to Western credit to finance hard-currency trade deficits. With the constraint of balanced hard-currency trade removed, the internal-external balance tradeoff for the CPEs is now more complex. We would like to have a simple framework for analyzing the more varied policy combinations now open to these countries in the event of external economic shocks.

Second, in the past decade, some CMEA countries (particularly Hungary and Poland) have undertaken significant foreign-trade reforms aimed at creating a link between world market and domestic prices, decentralizing economic decisionmaking, and improving efficiency. These countries may now be considered "modified" CPEs (MCPEs), which incorporate features of both market economies (MEs) and CPEs. These modifications, however, have meant a greater vulnerability of these economies to various external shocks, notably Western inflation and changing terms of trade. To better understand the distinctive macro-economic problems and policy options created by foreign-trade reform aimed at improving micro-economic efficiency, we need a consistent framework for analyzing balance-of-payments adjustment and policies for internal balance in both CPEs and MCPEs.

Third, the Western literature is frequently vague or contradictory regarding the relationships in a CPE among exogenous disturbances, the official foreign exchange rate, the so-called "price-equalization" subsidy or tax (*Preisausgleich*) paid to (by) foreign-trade organizations, the domestic money supply, and real output and domestic expenditure. For example, some writers have suggested that changes in the exchange rate, and hence changes in the "price-equalization" subsidies, can affect the domestic monetary equilibrium, while others stress the neutrality of exchange rate changes. The current ambiguity concerning the interaction of these variables needs to be removed before realistic behavioral models of CPE balance-of-payments adjustment can be carefully formulated.

Rather than hypothesize a particular behavioral model of the CPE and the MCPE in adjusting to external disturbances, this paper has a more modest objective: the development of a consistent framework for external and internal balance analysis. This framework draws on the three principal Western "approaches" to balance-of-payments analysis: the "elasticities," "absorption," and "monetary" models. It should be noted, however, that these approaches are used here more in their definitional than in their behavioral forms. The next step is to develop behavioral theories of CPE and MCPE balance-of-payments adjustment, which would permit us to predict the response of such economies to external economic disturbances.[4] Hopefully, the development of a consistent analytical framework will aid in the formulation of such models.

In several papers, Holzman correctly emphasized the "real" channels by which adverse economic shocks are transmitted within the CPE. In particular, it was suggested that the most direct effects will be on output and real absorption, with probably only negligible employment effects.[5] The problem of possible inflationary pressures resulting from induced increases in households' money holdings was considered, but not generally evaluated as significant. In this paper, the development of a balance-of-payments accounting framework relating changes in net international reserves, the money supply, and domestic credit creation inevitably results in a prominent place being given to the domestic money supply. Therefore, when analyzing the response to a specific external shock we will be interested, *inter alia,* in the implications for the stock of money. The objective is to establish precisely under what circumstances the CPE or MCPE authorities will have to be concerned about the accumulation of "excess" household money holdings as the result of external disturbances.

With respect to their trade with the nonsocialist world, CMEA countries are considered in this paper as partially analogous to the "small open economies" (SOEs) of Western international economic theory.[6] To be sure, most CMEA countries are not "open" in the sense that their domestic prices for goods and assets are determined (or even significantly influenced) through international trade and capital flows. But they are assumed to be similar to SOEs in that for most products they are assumed to be pricetakers on the world market. This paper will show how a framework for analyzing the response of the standard market-type SOE to external economic disturbances is applicable, with various modifications, to CPEs and MCPEs. (The assumption that CMEA countries are pricetakers in East-West trade is controversial. In this paper, this issue is only relevant when considering the price elasticities of these countries' import demands and export supplies. The assumption that they are pricetakers merely simplifies the analysis.)

We will also examine in some detail the "price-equalization" subsidy (tax) of the conventional CPE, the mechanism by which the CPE is kept from being an "open" economy. Although "price equalization" has been analyzed by others, there is a serious lack of consensus about its role in the macro-economic adjustment process of the CPE. Our analysis will permit the "price-equalization" mechanism to emerge from ambiguity and to assume a clearly defined role in balance-of-payments analysis of the CPE. We will also examine the internal-external balance dilemmas that policymakers in the conventional CPE face as the result of external economic disturbances. The distinctive internal-external balance problems and policy options that appear in MCPEs, as a result of eliminating "price-equalization" on all or some traded goods, will then be discussed.

External Economic Disturbances and the Small Open Economy

Different approaches can be used to analyze the balance-of-payments impact of exogenous disturbances on the SOE. Using the so-called "elasticities" approach, in the Bickerdike-Robinson-Metzler tradition,[7] the behavioral equations for export supply and import demand depend on single money prices rather than on relative prices and real income or expenditure. This approach is reasonable if it is also assumed that some nominal quantity (such as the money supply, income, absorption, the price level, or the price of nontraded goods) is being held constant, so that relative prices or the real value of one of the fixed nominal quantities are changing.[8] To find the impact on the SOE's balance of trade in foreign currency (B_T^*) of external price changes and exogenous changes in the SOE's exports, we differentiate B_T^* with respect to $P_x^*, P_m^*,$ and $Q_x,$ representing the foreign currency price indices for home's exports and imports and its quantity exports respectively.[9] Simplifying, we obtain:[10]

$$dB_T^* = V_x^*\left[\hat{P}_m^*\left[t^{*-1}(\epsilon_x + 1) - d^*(\eta_m + 1)\right] + \hat{Q}_x\right], \qquad [1]$$

where an "$\hat{\ }$" indicates the proportionate change in a variable, V_x^* and V_m^* are the foreign currency value of home's exports $(P_x^*Q_x)$ and imports $(P_m^*Q_m)$ respectively, d^* is V_m^*/V_x^*, t^* is $\hat{P}_m^*/\hat{P}_x^*$, and ϵ_x and η_m are the price elasticities of home's supply of exports and demand for imports respectively. The change in home's net barter terms of trade will be $\gtrless 0$ as $t^{*-1} \gtrless 1.00$.[11]

Take the case in which there is no exogenous change in exports $(\hat{Q}_x = 0)$, but there is external price inflation. The change in home's trade balance will be $\gtrless 0$ as $t^{*-1}(\epsilon_x + 1) \gtrless d^*(\eta_m + 1)$. Even if there is no change in the terms of trade ($t^* = 1.00$), home could still experience a deterioration in its trade balance if its trade elasticities are close to zero and its initial ratio of imports to exports is large enough. (This arithmetical curiosity is often overlooked in discussions of the impact of external price movements on a country's trade balance.) Note that in this case, however, if import demand is elastic ($\eta_m < -1.00$) and the export supply response is not perverse, home is assured of an improvement in its balance-of-trade regardless of its initial trade imbalance. The point is that we cannot draw simple conclusions about changes in the trade balance based solely on terms of trade trends, but must also consider the price elasticities of export supply and import demand as well as the initial trade balance.

Another approach to balance-of-payments analysis is the so-called "absorption" approach, in which a change in the trade balance is equivalent to the difference between the change in money income and domestic expenditure (or absorption). An excess of domestic income over absorption is often referred to as hoarding. In this approach, the change in the balance of trade is the identity:

$$dB_T = dY - dZ = dH, \tag{2}$$

where B_T is the trade balance in domestic prices, Y and Z are money income and absorption respectively, and H is hoarding. Deterioration in the trade balance means that expenditure has risen relative to income (i.e., a net reduction in domestic hoarding). Again assuming external inflation, which under fixed exchange rates is transmitted domestically, the trade balance deteriorates only if the increase in money absorption ($dZ_d + dZ_f$) is greater than the increase in money value of domestic output ($dZ_d + dZ_d^*$), where Z_d and Z_f represent domestic expenditure on domestic and foreign production respectively, and Z_d^* denotes foreign expenditure on domestic output. This approach emphasizes the various effects of external disturbances on output and expenditure decisions rather than the direct response of traded goods to changes in prices.[12]

Third is the so-called "monetary" approach. For simplicity, assume the central bank constitutes home's entire monetary system. (This, incidentally, is a very realistic assumption in the CPE, in which all or virtually all central and commercial banking functions are carried out by the state bank, or "monobank.")[13] The domestic money supply (M) equals the difference between the central bank's assets and its non-monetary liabilities (or government deposits):

$$M = F + L - D_g,$$

where F is the domestic currency value of the bank's net international reserves (assets minus liabilities to foreigners), L is the bank's loans to the government and private sectors, and D_g represents government deposits. Rearranging, focusing on changes in these variables, and ignoring capital flows unrelated to the financing of trade,

$$B_T = dF = dM - (dL - dD_g).$$ [3]

Visualized in this manner, a negative trade balance represents net domestic credit creation $(dL - dD_g)$ in excess of additions to the money supply, indicating that the excess of actual over desired cash balances is "leaking" abroad through an excess of absorption over income financed by a reduction in home's net international reserves. Deterioration in the trade balance $(dB_T < 0)$ simply indicates an increase in net leakage (which is another way of saying a reduction in hoarding). Rather than focusing on output and expenditure changes, this approach stresses the impact on the balance-of-payments of the demand for money and domestic credit creation.[14]

At first glance, these approaches may not seem very relevant to an understanding of CPEs. But to take the "elasticities" approach, observe that price elasticities in foreign trade are not fundamentally predicated on the existence of a market economy. Rather, to speak of quantities of imports and exports responding to price changes in "elasticity" terms is simply a shorthand way of describing the aggregate response of importers and exporters. If traders are profit maximizing private firms rather than state trading companies, the aggregate elasticities may be more "stable" (at a given initial price) over time; but whether they are is an empirical rather than a theoretical question. Thus, just as it is sometimes convenient in analyzing ME balance-of-payments adjustments to speak in terms of elasticities, it will also be useful for CPEs and MCPEs.

Similarly, what meaning does an "absorption" approach have in CPEs, in which domestic prices are determined primarily by internal economic priorities and fiscal balancing rather than by world market prices? For economies with "price-equalization" subsidies, we would not expect [2] to necessarily hold, as we could have, for example, a deterioration in the trade balance without any change in domestic hoarding at domestic prices. Or what relevance does the "monetary" approach have, particularly to CPEs in which the money plan serves to "validate" the real plan and in which discrepancies between desired and actual money balances can scarcely be thought to affect the trade balance (as is alleged in the monetarist view of the ME)? The monetary approach also suggests a built-in corrective mechanism for balance-of-trade deficits. Unless the monetary authorities continue to create more money than desired, a trade deficit will cease. These approaches are nevertheless extremely useful in their definitional form in developing a framework for CPE and MCPE balance-of-payments analysis, although the Keynesian or monetarist behavioral models, which usually accompany any discussion of these approaches, are far less applicable to CPEs.

The SOE, with fixed exchange rates, is commonly pictured as helpless in the face of external inflation. Prachowny has shown, however, that given no change in the terms of trade and flexibility of nontraded goods prices, a SOE can offset external inflation by revaluing its currency while maintaining a zero trade balance.[15] In our case, in which we want to allow for the possibility of initial trade imbalance, for changes in the terms of trade, and for the inflexibility of nontraded goods prices in the short run, we obtain the following expression by differentiating B_T^* with respect to the exchange rate e (domestic currency price of foreign currency):[16]

$$dB_T^* = V_x^* \, \hat{e}(\epsilon_x - d^*\eta_m). \qquad [4]$$

Now assume the authorities set (a) a target dB_T^*, which will be a function of current holdings of international reserves and expectations regarding the country's ability to increase its international liabilities and (b) a target change in the domestic price level (P), where P is defined as:

$$P = P_n w_n + P_x w_x + P_m w_m,$$

where P_n, P_x, and P_m denote the domestic price index for nontraded goods, exports, and imports respectively, and w_n, w_x, and w_m represent their corresponding weights in the overall price index. In the ME, $P_t = eP_t^*$, where subscript t denotes tradeables. Consequently, $\hat{P}_t = \hat{e} + \hat{P}_t^*$. Assuming inflexibility of nontraded goods prices $(dP_n = 0)$ and constant weights,

$$dP = (\hat{e} + \hat{P}_x^*) \, P_x w_x + (\hat{e} + \hat{P}_m^*) \, P_m w_m. \qquad [5]$$

Adding [1] and [4], we can use this combined expression and [5] to solve simultaneously for that $\hat{e}$ which will allow realization of target $dB_T^* = f$ and target $dP = k$:

$$(k - \hat{P}_m^*[(P_x w_x/t^*) + P_m w_m])/ (P_x w_x + P_m w_m)$$

$$= (f - V_x^* \, \hat{P}_m^*[\, (1/t^*) \, (\epsilon_x + 1) - d^*(\eta_m + 1)])/V_x^*(\epsilon_x - d^*\eta_m)$$

$$= \hat{e}. \qquad [6]$$

We would not, in general, expect these expressions to be equal. Consequently, under the above assumptions, there is in general no unique exchange rate change for the market-type SOE which will guarantee satisfaction of both balance-of-trade and domestic inflation targets. If the initial trade balance is zero $(d^* = 1.00)$, if there is no change in the terms of trade ($t^* = 1.00$), and if authorities set the target changes in the trade balance and domestic price level equal to zero ($dB_T^* = dP = 0$), however, [6] yields $\hat{e} = -\hat{P}_m^*$. In other words, only under these restrictive circumstances could external inflation be exactly offset by an equal percentage revaluation, while at the same time preserving a zero trade balance.[17]

The Effects of "Price-Equalization" in Centrally Planned Economies

The CPE is characterized by a state monopoly over foreign trade. Export and import transactions are carried out by foreign-trade organizations, hereafter lumped together as the Ministry for Foreign Trade (MFT). Foreign exchange is held only by the central bank (the monobank). Assuming that all East-West trade is transacted in foreign ("hard") currencies, the hard-currency trade balance in a given period is reflected by the change in the net international-reserve position of the central bank. When exporting for convertible currencies, the MFT must turn over its foreign exchange proceeds to the central bank in return for an increase in its domestic currency deposit at the bank. The size of the deposit increase equals the foreign exchange proceeds multiplied by the official exchange rate (e), otherwise known as the *valuta* value of its exports. Similarly, in order to import from the West, the MFT must purchase the necessary foreign exchange from the central bank at the official exchange rate. The MFT pays for the foreign exchange by drawing down its deposit with the central bank by the *valuta* equivalent of the foreign currencies purchased.

While its foreign exchange transactions with the central bank are reflected in *valuta* values (foreign currency price times the official exchange rate), the MFT is paid (pays) in domestic prices for imports it sells to (for exports it purchases from) domestic enterprises. In importing, the MFT's deposits with the central bank fall by the *valuta* equivalent of foreign exchange purchased but rise by the value of its sales to domestic enterprises evaluated at domestic import prices. In exporting, the MFT's central bank deposits rise by the *valuta* equivalent of foreign exchange sold but fall by the value of its purchases from domestic enterprises evaluated at domestic export prices.[18]

In a CPE, domestic prices are normally fixed for considerable periods. Likewise, the official exchange rate is adjusted only infrequently. Consequently, the *valuta* (primed) values of exports or imports will only incidentally be equal to their (unprimed) domestic values. In general, the MFT will experience a net change in its domestic-currency deposits at the central bank as a consequence of its foreign-trade activities. Defining π as the "profits" of the MFT that arise from this discrepancy between *valuta* and domestic price values, we have more formally:[19]

$$\pi = Q_m(P_m - P_m^*e) + Q_x(P_x^*e - P_x)$$

$$= Q_m(P_m - P_m') + Q_x(P_x' - P_x)$$

$$= \pi_m + \pi_x, \tag{7}$$

where the primed variables represent *valuta* values, and π_m and π_x are the net profits arising from price discrepancies in importing and exporting respectively.[20]

For the CPE, we may imagine the following relationships between domestic and foreign currency prices:

$$P_m/P_m^* = \alpha_m e; \ P_x/P_x^* = \alpha_x e; \ \text{and} \ \beta = \alpha_m/\alpha_x, \tag{8}$$

where $\alpha_t > 1.00 \ (t = m,x)$ indicates an implicit exchange rate (based on purchasing-power-parity) greater than the official rate, and β is a measure of the relative overvaluation (vis-à-vis the world market) of home importables against exportables at domestic prices. In the Soviet Union, this relative overvaluation has historically been considerable; Kostinsky and Treml estimated (implicitly) β as equal to 1.83 in 1959 and 1.81 in 1966.[21]

Utilizing [8], expression [7] can also be written as:

$$\pi = eV_x^*[d^*(\beta\alpha_x - 1) + (1 - \alpha_x)]. \tag{9}$$

Non-zero net profits (losses) can emerge under varying situations. For example, even if $\beta = 1.00$, there can still be net profits (losses) if the implicit exchange rate is different from the official exchange rate ($\alpha_x \neq 1.00$) and trade is initially unbalanced ($d^* \neq 1.00$). It is incorrect, however, to conclude that net profits (losses) can occur only if trade is imbalanced.[22] As [9] indicates, if $\beta \neq 1.00$, π will be equal to zero *only* if the initial trade balance (d^*) is equal to $[(\alpha_x - 1)/(\beta\alpha_x - 1)]$. We would therefore expect, in general, a net profit (loss) when $\beta \neq 1.00$. (Note also that $d\pi/d\beta > 0$. This can be understood intuitively in terms of [7]. The larger is β, the larger is P_m/P_m^* relative to P_x/P_x^*, and hence the greater [smaller] the MFT's profits [losses] on imports relative to its net profit on exports.)

For the CPE, for which we assume that domestic prices are fixed in the short run, we can obtain the response of these price discrepancy profits (losses) and the trade balance (denominated in domestic prices) to exogenous disturbances by differentiating π and B_T respectively with respect to P_m^*, P_x^*, and Q_x:

$$dπ = V_x^* e \left[\hat{P}_m^* \ (t^{*-1}[ε_x(1 - α_x) + 1] - d^*[η_m(1 - α_m) + 1] \right.$$
$$\left. + \hat{Q}_x \ (1 - α_x) \right] \tag{10a}$$

$$dB_T = V_x \left[\hat{P}_m^*(ε_x/t^* - dη_m) + \hat{Q}_x \right], \tag{10b}$$

where V_x, V_m, and d are the value of exports, imports, and the trade balance respectively, evaluated at domestic prices.

Expression [7] can also be rearranged:

$$π = (V_m - V_x) + e(V_x^* - V_m^*). \tag{11}$$

If we make the usual assumption that changes in the official exchange rate in a CPE have no direct effect on internal or external prices or quantities traded, then an exchange rate change can only affect overall MFT profits (losses) if trade is initially unbalanced in terms of foreign currency.[23] Holzman cites the Soviet economist Aizenberg, who suggests that the 1936 ruble devaluation was intended to improve the efficiency of foreign-trade managers.[24] The USSR was apparently running hard-currency trade surpluses in 1934 and 1935;[25] hence, by [11] we would have expected $dπ/de > 0$. Perhaps more significantly, we see from [7] that devaluation would result in $dπ_x > 0$ and $dπ_m < 0$. Overall MFT profits would have increased because of devaluation, but the ruble at this time was apparently overvalued ($α_t > 1.00$). Consequently, the devaluation would have reduced MFT losses on exports and profits on imports, which Holzman suggests in a CPE could be expected to spur foreign-trade managers to increased efficiency.[26]

Ames suggests that in general if $π \neq 0$, then $dπ/de \neq 0$.[27] However, whether $dπ/de \neq 0$ depends on whether $B_f^* \neq 0$. After defining $π$ in terms of an expression similar to [9], Ames differentiates $π$ with respect to e while treating $α_x$ and $α_m$ as parameters. Yet from [8] it is evident that $α_t$ is a function of e, P_t, and P_t^*; and when the exchange rate alone is modified, $α_t$ changes proportionately in the opposite direction ($\hat{α}_t = -\hat{e}$) because changes in the official exchange rate have no effect on domestic or foreign prices.

MFT profits (losses) are reflected in an initial net increase (decrease) in MFT deposits at the central bank. This net change can be analytically divided into the change in MFT deposits resulting from foreign exchange transactions with the central bank (dD_f', the prime indicating that these are *valuta* values) and changes in MFT deposits resulting from transactions with domestic enterprises (dD_f) evaluated at domestic prices.[28] The former deposit change (dD_f') appears on the central bank's balance sheet as the change in its liabilities which offsets the change in the *valuta* value of the central bank's holdings of net international reserves (i.e., $dD_f' = dF'$). The latter change in deposits (dD_f) is offset by a change in domestic enterprise deposits ($-dD_e$) at the central bank. Regardless of the particular configuration of

$dD'_f + dD_f$ occurring in a given period, the treasury in a CPE will exactly offset the MFT's profits (losses) on price discrepancies by so-called "price-equalization" taxes (subsidies). Abstracting from MFT commissions and other sources of revenue that could increase its deposit balances at the central bank, the price-equalization mechanism would leave MFT balances unchanged at the end of the period. Where S is the net price-equalization subsidy,

$$S = -\pi = -(dD'_f + dD_f).$$ [12]

Because the price-equalization mechanism is automatic, the circumstances under which MFT profits (losses) will occur and the impact of exchange rate changes on these profits (losses) also holds for the subsidies, where $dS/d\pi = -1.00$.

Balance-of-Payments Analysis in the Centrally Planned Economy

Having clarified the role of price-equalization subsidies, we proceed to develop a simplified framework for analyzing the impact of external disturbances in such an economy. The initial (pre-subsidy or tax) change in MFT deposits at the central bank $(dD'_f + dD_f)$ is equal to the *valuta* equivalent of the change in the central bank's net international reserves less the initial change in domestic enterprise deposits $(dF' - dD_e)$. From [12], we therefore have $\pi = -S = dF' - dD_e$.

Under varying circumstances, part or all of the change in enterprise deposits may be passed to households in the form of changes in household currency (and savings deposit) holdings. For the time being, it is convenient to ignore the important distinction between enterprise "money" and household "money." We will combine the two as M, where dM_o is equal to the *initial* change in domestic enterprise deposits (dD_e).[29] In general, the government may partially or totally offset any changes in the domestic money supply with fiscal or monetary policy. Where T_{eh} and L_e represent treasury taxes on enterprises and households (combined, for simplicity) and central bank loans to enterprises respectively,

$$\pi = dF' - dM_o = dF' - dM - dT_{eh} + dL_e.$$ [13]

Any change in the treasury's budget surplus (dT) will be used to increase its deposits (dD_t) with or pay off loans (dL_t) from the central bank. Recalling that the net treasury subsidy to the MFT (S) equals $-\pi$, $dT = \pi + dT_{eh} = dD_t - dL_t$. Solving for π, substituting in [13], and rearranging:

$$dF' = B'_T = dM - (dL - dD_t),$$ [14]

where $dL = dL_t + dL_e$. This expression is analogous to [3] for the ME: a negative trade balance (in *valuta* terms) represents *net* domestic credit creation $(dL - dD_t)$ in excess of increments to the domestic money supply. Regardless of government policy with respect to the domestic money supply, the "monetary" identity [14] does describe the *valuta* trade balance of the CPE. The important difference, of course, is that in the CPE, changes in the money supply and credit outstanding tend to passively reflect the authorities' particular response to exogenous shocks, whereas in a ME, these changes could be expected to influence foreign trade directly.

From [11], $\pi = -B_T + B'_T$, and rearranging we have:

$$
\begin{aligned}
B'_T &= B_T + \pi \\
&= (V_x - V_m) + \pi \\
&= (Z^*_d - Z_f) + \pi \\
&= (Z_d + Z^*_d) - (Z_d + Z_f) + \pi \\
&= Y - Z + \pi \\
&= H + \pi.
\end{aligned}
\tag{15}
$$

For a CPE, the difference between a "monetary" and "absorption" definition of the trade balance is simply the MFT's net profit on price discrepancies. Policymakers will look at foreign currency or *valuta* values when concerned with the trade balance (hence B'_T), but they must evaluate changes in domestic expenditure and hoarding in terms of the domestic prices actually paid. Furthermore, by analogy with the ME, if the CPE is characterized by equilibrium in the expenditure and monetary sectors, the *valuta* trade surplus (deficit) will equal the government's budget surplus (deficit). In practice, however, these sectors may often be characterized by disequilibrium, and consequently this one-to-one correspondence may not exist.[30]

We turn next to identifying those situations in which changes in price-equalization subsidies are and are not associated with insulation of the domestic economy from external disturbances. For simplicity, assume that the CPE planned its foreign trade such that $B^*_T = B'_T = 0$. Consider that the only external disturbance is an unexpected increase in the foreign currency price of imports $(\hat{P}^*_m > 0; \ \hat{P}^*_x = \hat{Q}^*_x = 0)$. First, take the case in which the authorities are unwilling to permit any change in planned real-trade flows, and are able and willing to run down the country's stock of net international reserves to pay for the increased import bill. Implicitly, the CPE's price elasticity of import demand is zero; and using [1], [7], and [10a]:

$$
dB^*_T = -V^*_m \hat{P}^*_m \text{ and } dB'_T = -V'_m \hat{P}^*_m < 0
$$
$$
d\pi = -e V^*_m \hat{P}^*_m \text{ or } d\pi = -V'_m \hat{P}^*_m < 0
$$
$$
dB_T = dB'_T - d\pi = 0,
$$

TABLE 1

Illustrative Changes in CPE Central Bank Balance Sheet, Given an External Economic Disturbance

Assumptions: $\hat{P}_m^* > 0$, $\hat{P}_x^* = \hat{Q}_x = \epsilon_x = \eta_m = dB_T = 0$.

Assets	Liabilities
$dF' = dB_T'\ (= -V_m'\ \hat{P}_m^*) < 0$	$dD_f' = dB_T'(= -V_m'\ \hat{P}_m^*) < 0$
Alternative A	$dD_t = dB_T' < 0$
	$dD_f' = (-dB_T') > 0$
Alternative B	$dD_{eh} = dB_T' < 0$
	$dD_f' = (-dB_T') > 0$
Alternative C $dL_t = (-dB_T') > 0$	$dD_f' = (-dB_T') > 0$

where the changes in variables indicate differences from planned values. Observe that $dB_T = 0$ because, by assumption, domestic traded good prices and real-trade flows are unchanged.

The treasury has three basic ways to finance its increased subsidies to (reduced tax revenue from) the MFT to offset the increase in MFT losses (fall in profits). Under alternative A, it could simply draw down its deposit balance at the central bank (see table 1 for T-accounts for the three alternatives). The net change in government deposits would then equal $d\pi$, and [14] becomes $dF' = dB_T' = dD_t$ (negative) because there has been no change in the domestic money supply or gross domestic credit outstanding. Under alternative B, the treasury could attempt to tax enterprises and households by an amount equal to $d\pi$, using the proceeds to finance the unplanned reduction in MFT balances. Expression [14] would become $dF' = dB_T' = dM$. It is unlikely that the authorities would pursue this option, however, because a reduction in the money supply might lead to an unnecessary reduction in domestic absorption and, if inventories are held constant, to a fall in output. In any event, the trade balance in domestic prices (B_T) would not differ from the plan. Finally, the treasury could subsidize the fall in MFT profits by borrowing from the central bank. Expression [14] now becomes $dF' = dB_T' = -dL_t$. The basic point is that because the government has chosen to reduce its net international reserves by an amount equal to the increase in import costs, it is perfectly able to maintain the planned level of real domestic absorption by following either the first or third alternative.

A second extreme response might be for the planners to instruct the MFT to reduce imports by just enough to keep the *valuta* balance at zero. Implicitly, the price elasticity of import demand in this case is -1.00. Using [1], [7], [8], [10a], and [10b],

$$dB_T^* = dB_T' = 0$$
$$d\pi = -V_m' \, \hat{P}_m^* \alpha_m = -V_m \hat{P}_m^* < 0$$
$$dB_T = V_m \hat{P}_m^* > 0.$$

In this case, net MFT profits decline: while MFT *valuta* expenditures remain as planned, the fall in real imports causes the value of MFT imports at unchanged domestic prices (hence, the value of sales to enterprises) to decline. This is reflected in a positive trade balance in domestic prices and an initial increase in the deposits of domestic enterprises. It is important whether the reduced real imports are consumer or producer goods. If the former, the initial increase in enterprise deposits will be offset by an equal decline in retail sales, and the resultant increase in money supply will represent enlarged household money holdings. If the latter, Holzman's foreign-trade bottleneck multiplier comes into play, with a possible fall in output and in bonus incomes, although the latter might be somewhat offset by unplanned wage increases as enterprises seek to offset the reduced supplies of intermediate goods by hiring more or higher skilled labor.[31]

Again the treasury has three basic alternatives for financing the required increased subsidy to (reduced tax revenue from) the MFT. But assuming the treasury maintains constant deposits at the central bank, it can subsidize the decline in MFT profits either by borrowing from the central bank or by reducing other domestic expenditures or raising taxes. Assuming for illustrative purposes that non-priority consumer goods bear the whole burden of the cutback, and if the treasury borrows, [14] becomes:

$$dF' = dB_T' = dM - dL = 0.$$

The trade balance in domestic prices improves, however, because of the decline in real imports and unchanged real exports:

$$dB_T = -dZ_f = -dZ.$$

The government has, in effect, forced an increase in hoarding. This might be a risky alternative, however, as households would now have higher-than-planned cash balances; and to the extent that they are unwilling to hold higher cash balances, their additional spending would create inflationary pressures (although open inflation might only occur in, say, the collective-farm produce or black markets).

An alternative policy in this second case would be for the government to follow a policy of increasing taxes on individuals and reducing other government expenditures or transfer payments. (Raising taxes might be difficult, however, because direct income taxes are only a minor source of revenue in CPEs, and raising turnover taxes would upset retail price stability.) Assuming only a fiscal response, [14] becomes: $dF' = dB'_T = 0$, and $dB_T = -dZ_f$ as before. The result is equivalent to the first policy except that the source of possible inflationary pressures ($dM > 0$) is removed. Regardless of how the increased subsidies to the MFT are financed, the government's unwillingness or inability to draw down its net international reserves requires a fall in real absorption. Even when household currency holdings increase, spending of the excess balances may result in the planned level of money expenditure and income, but real absorption must still decline. The possible disincentive effects of the fall in real absorption may trigger a decline in output (and possibly in exports).[32] It is more complex when the foregone imports are producer goods.

A third extreme policy response would be to maintain the planned flow of real imports but to direct domestic output from domestic absorption to exports (if possible) by an amount sufficient to pay for the increase in the import bill. Implicitly, the price elasticity of import demand is zero. This situation, along with Holzman's discussion of Soviet foreign-trade behavior in the 1930s,[33] is a specific instance of the more general case when a CPE, intent on maintaining the planned flow of real imports and balanced trade, becomes preoccupied with its terms of trade. Assume that $\eta_m = B^*_T = dB^*_T = 0$, that planners are able to divert domestic production (or inventories) to export, and that they can sell any such quantity at given world market prices. Expression [1] in this case gives:

$$dB^*_T = 0 = V^*_x \hat{P}^*_m \left[t^{*-1} (\epsilon_x + 1) - 1 \right]$$

and

$$\epsilon_x = t^* - 1.$$

In the case at hand, $t^* = \infty$ (only external *import* prices increase), so ϵ_x approaches infinity. If both $\hat{P}^*_x$ and $\hat{P}^*_m$ are positive but the terms of trade deteriorate, $t^* > 1.00$ and $\epsilon_x > 0$. In the 1930s, Soviet terms of trade deteriorated because export prices fell proportionately more than import prices ($0 < t^* < 1.00$) and, as Holzman pointed out,[34] the Soviet price elasticity of export supply was (seemingly perversely) negative. When exports are increased, the results for the trade balance and domestic absorption are not fundamentally different from the case in which imports are reduced. Real absorption must fall (unless exports are taken exclusively out of inventories, a possibility suggested by Hoeffding),[35] but in this case it falls because $dZ_d < 0$

(offset by $dZ_d^* > 0$) rather than $dZ_f < 0$. If the increase in exports includes some producer goods diverted from the domestic economy, output could also decline.

These illustrative cases indicate that whether the exogenous disturbance has a direct effect on the domestic money supply in a CPE with fixed domestic prices depends on whether the disturbance or the policy response gives rise to changes in *real* trade flows; in other words, to $dB_T \neq 0$. Whether the change in money supply persists depends on the monetary and fiscal policies of the government. Whether output is affected depends on the composition of the changed real-trade flows and on the possible incentive effects of changes in real absorption. Whether the disturbance gives rise to increased inflationary pressure, then, depends on all of these factors.

Pryor cites some evidence that in the 1950s at least one CPE used MFT profit maximization as a criterion for foreign trade decisionmaking.[36] In this connection, it is interesting to examine the consequences of planners seeking to minimize the adverse external trade balance effects of exogenous disturbances not by directly regulating trade flows, but by setting a limit to the amount by which the treasury would subsidize any deterioration in MFT profits. For example, assume that unplanned $\hat{P}_m^* > 0$ but that $\hat{P}_x^* = \hat{Q}_x = 0$. The maximum *valuta* trade balance deterioration under such circumstances would be $dB_T' = d\pi = -V_m' \hat{P}_m^*$ (i.e., assumes $\eta_m = 0$). The authorities might authorize increased subsidies (reduced taxes) of $\gamma(V_m' \hat{P}_m^*)$, where $0 \leq \gamma \leq 1.00$. Setting the general expression for $d\pi$ in [10a] equal to $\gamma(-V_m' \hat{P}_m^*)$, assuming finite ϵ_x, and solving for η_m gives $\eta_m = (\gamma-1)/(1-\alpha_m)$. If $\alpha_m > 1.00$ (typical in a CPE) and $\gamma < 1.00$, the implicit price elasticity of import demand will be perversely positive. This is because the MFT, to minimize the reduction in net profits (which reduction will not be entirely offset by a treasury subsidy), would in this case *increase* its quantity of imports purchased in order to compensate for their increased foreign currency price (see [7]). In general, therefore, by following such an *indirect* strategy and assuming the MFT is permitted such leeway (unlikely), the planners could not necessarily expect to achieve a specific trade balance target.

Finally, this framework enables us to address the issue of adoption of the "correct" exchange rate by the CPE. Ames suggests that "even though the exchange rate may not affect the trade program itself (as it would in a market economy), it can still play a definite role in determining the impact of the trade program upon the money supply and hence upon domestic monetary equilibrium."[37] This result is surprising, given the conventional assumptions that the exchange rate in a CPE has no direct effect on quantities traded or the foreign and domestic currency prices of traded goods.

Consider the case in which the net MFT profits are negative. By [15], this means that the trade balance in domestic prices must be algebraically larger than the *valuta* trade balance; but it could be greater, equal to, or less than zero. Now, $B_T \gtreqless 0$ means an initial $dM \gtreqless 0$, but any dM may in theory be partially or totally offset by monetary or fiscal policy. The net subsidy to the MFT can, as we have seen, be financed through some combination of a reduction in treasury deposits and an increase in treasury borrowing at the central bank, an increase in tax revenue from and reduction in transfer payments to households or enterprises, or a reduction in government expenditures. Why these measures should necessarily give rise to inflationary pressures (particularly if the net MFT profit is planned), as Ames and Holzman suggest, is not clear.[38]

Furthermore, it is not evident that the "inflationary problem," if it exists, would be removed by setting a "correct" exchange rate.[39] Revaluation or devaluation will affect the *valuta* values of the CPE's net international reserves and trade balance, but the trade balance in domestic prices will not be directly affected (because $\hat{\alpha}_t = -\hat{e}$), and thus neither will the money supply. In theory, the change in MFT profits caused by the change in exchange rate could be offset simply by, say, treasury borrowing at the central bank that need not influence either the money supply or domestic spending. It seems reasonable to conclude that domestic inflationary pressures will be determined by monetary, fiscal, and wage policies, and not by manipulations of the exchange rate.

Internal vs. External Balance in the Centrally Planned Economy

Let us assume that, regardless of external disturbances, the CPE is able to maintain full employment (although not necessarily maximum possible output); and by means of price controls and appropriate monetary and fiscal policies, the government ensures no open or repressed inflation.[40] In theory, a CPE could neutralize possible inflationary effects of exogenous disturbances through appropriate monetary and fiscal policies. This leaves two principal macro-targets (in the stationary state): the level of (or change in) net international reserves and the level of real domestic absorption.[41] Given an exogenous disturbance, policymakers have two instruments at their disposal to try to achieve both targets: direct controls over exports and imports respectively. As we have seen, changes in the exchange rate cannot be expected to directly affect either the trade balance or absorption.

With initially balanced trade, and assuming away invisible transactions and capital flows unrelated to financing trade, the change in net international reserves (dF^*) equals the change in the trade balance, dB_T^*. Recalling [1]:

$$dF^* = dB_T^* = V_x^* \left[\hat{P}_m^* t^{*-1} \|(\epsilon_x + 1) - d^* (\eta_m + 1)] + \hat{Q}_x \right] \quad [16]$$

Defining real absorption as Z/P: $d(Z/P) = dZ/P$, when dP is set at zero. Recalling that $dZ = dZ_d + dZ_f$, and postulating $Z_d = Z_d(Z_d^*, M)$, where we assume $dZ_d/dZ_d^* = -1.00$ and $dZ_d/dM = \lambda$, $(0 \le \lambda \le 1.00)$:

$$dZ = -dZ_d^* + \lambda dM + dZ_f$$
$$= -dB_T + \lambda(dF' + dL - dD_t).$$

If we assume that the authorities only engage in credit creation $(dL - dD_t)$ sufficient to finance an unplanned *valuta* trade deficit (i.e., no unplanned change in money supply is permitted), $dZ = -dB_T$. Recalling [10b]:

$$d(Z/P) = -V_x[\hat{P}_m^*(\epsilon_x/t^* - d\eta_m) + \hat{Q}_x] P^{-1}. \quad [17]$$

Given the authorities' targets for the change in reserves and real absorption, [16] and [17] can be solved simultaneously for ϵ_x and η_m, given exogenous $\hat{P}_m^*$, $\hat{P}_x^*$, and $\hat{Q}_x$ and predetermined V_x^*, V_x, P, d, and d^*. In actuality, of course, the authorities would solve for dQ_x and dQ_m, their control variables (from which we might derive the implicit elasticities).

If the government's ability to eliminate any initial unplanned increase in money supply arising from a possible $dB_T > 0$ is imperfect, then the safest course in avoiding inflationary pressures would be to place the entire adjustment burden, if possible, on the external *valuta* trade balance (i.e., on the country's net reserve position). Indeed, given two CPEs equally affected by, say, a deterioration in the terms of trade, the country with the greater possibilities for drawing on foreign exchange reserves or borrowing from abroad will be better off in being able to maintain the level of real absorption and to restrain domestic inflationary pressures. In cases in which the *valuta* trade balance is kept at zero but the changes in the real volume of exports and imports are in the same direction, real absorption changes will depend not only on the substitutability among traded goods in domestic consumption, but also on the value of β (i.e., the relative overvaluation of importables vis-à-vis exportables).

Internal vs. External Balance in the
Modified Centrally Planned Economy

Among the cornerstones of the New Economic Mechanism (NEM) introduced in Hungary in 1968 were increased enterprise autonomy and a thoroughgoing price reform. These changes were combined with a new system for directly linking domestic and foreign-trade prices and the decisionmaking of Hungarian production enterprises. The new price system consisted of three product categories: freely priced, fixed priced, and limited price flexibility. The proportion of 1968 turn-over consisting of free price products was estimated at 28% for raw materials and basic intermediate goods, 78% for processed producers' goods, 10% for agricultural products, and 23% for consumer goods.[42] According to Csikos-Nagy, the degree to which the newly established prices were based on nonsocialist world market prices depended on the relative importance for Hungary of East-West trade in the product in question. (For example, agricultural prices were largely based on domestic costs, prices in the ferrous metallurgical sector on intra-CMEA foreign-trade prices, and the prices of textile products on the world market.)[43] At the outset of the 1971-75 planning period, it was expected that by 1975 about 50% of consumer goods turnover would be subject to "free" prices (and hence sensitive to external prices).[44] It was envisoned that short-term external price fluctuations could be neutralized by enterprises by means of self-financing "reserve funds for price differences."[45] In 1968, it was expected that the overall price level might rise by 1 to 2% annually, primarily because of anticipated price increases for technology and capital goods imported from the West.[46]

The link between foreign and domestic prices was based on the introduction of *de jure* uniform foreign-trade price coefficients (e_c). Henceforth, dollar payments and proceeds in foreign trade would be converted for trading enterprises at 60 forints/dollar, and payments and proceeds in intra-CMEA foreign trade would be converted at 40 forints/transferable ruble. The uniform e_c for the dollar area was presumably based on the average forint cost of producing (through export) one dollar's worth of foreign exchange. The actual average cost at that time has been estimated at roughly 72 forints/dollar, however, with the marginal rate even higher.[47] That the dollar e_c was substantially below the marginal (and the average) rate is indicated by the fact that approximately three-fourths of the value of Hungarian exports to the West in 1968 had to be subsidized.[48]

Between 1968 and 1971, import and export subsidies were negotiated in advance for each enterprise. In the 1971-75 period, some progress was made toward *de facto* uniformity of foreign-trade price coefficients (for each currency area) by determining in advance (for roughly three-quarters of all enterprises) the amount of subsidy at the sub-branch rather than enterprise level. In theory, the subsidies were to decline each year in order to spur resource allocation into more efficient activities.[49]

In addition to establishing a direct linkage between foreign currency and domestic prices for a number of products, the 1968 reform also provided for the introduction of a customs tariff, both as a device for reducing direct controls over imports and as a bargaining instrument in Hungary's GATT accession negotiations. GATT membership has several implications for the attempt to insulate the economy from external disturbances. First, a uniform turnover tax should be imposed on both domestic production and imports of the same product. Consequently, just as "bound"tariffs should not be used for "variable-levy" purposes when foreign prices of imports fall, so the turnover tax should not be reduced when external prices rise, unless domestic production is similarly treated. A second implication is that the GATT member is not supposed to increase export subsidies to offset the trade balance effects of revaluation initiated for price stability purposes.[50]

We shall consider an economy such as Hungary after 1968 as a "modified" centrally planned economy (MCPE). The MCPE eliminates detailed central planning of outputs and trade and abolishes the automatic "price-equalization" subsidies or taxes on an important subset of traded goods. (In contrast with Hungary, the direct linkage of domestic and foreign currency prices for traded goods in Poland has been concentrated, for the most part, on exports.[51] Other CMEA countries have yet to move in this direction.) In general, the MCPE has two sets of traded goods: type A which is still subject to price-equalization, and type B for which there is now an organic relationship between domestic and foreign currency prices. Predetermined subsidies and taxes on B-goods may still exist ($\alpha_t \neq 1.00$), but changes in foreign-currency prices or the exchange rate (or e_c in the Hungarian case) will now cause changes in domestic prices because α_t is a constant ($\hat{P}_{tB} = \hat{P}^*_{tB} + \hat{e}$; see [8]).

Institutional arrangements for foreign trade in a MCPE may vary. The MFT (or industrial ministries) may still trade the A-goods. It may also trade B-goods on a commission basis for domestic production enterprises. Some enterprises or combines may conduct foreign trade on their own account, in both A- and B-products. Enterprises make their trading decisions on a basis of comparing domestic prices and domestic with foreign prices with the intention of maximizing some measure of enterprise profits, value added, and so forth. A CPE may have adopted various "export-efficiency indices" to guide the micro-planning of the commodity and geographic composition of its foreign trade. Nevertheless, if this attempt at rationalization is not accompanied by at least partial elimination of the price-equalization mechanism, the economy is not a MCPE. A MCPE, in its concern with moving toward an internal price structure more in line with external relative prices, may also *periodically* allow for administered changes in the prices of various A-products. Given changes in foreign currency prices, therefore, the MCPE may no longer even continuously set $\hat{\alpha}_{tA} = -\hat{P}_{tA}^*$ (complete price equalization: see [8]). Rather, it may periodically change domestic prices of A-traded goods by $dP_{tA} = \theta dP_{tA}^*$, where $0 \leqslant \theta \leqslant 1.00$.

For the MCPE, each balance of trade (*valuta* and domestic currency) has two balances, subscripted A and B for the two sets of goods:

$$B_T' = B_{TA}' + B_{TB}' = dM - (dL - dD_t)$$

and

$$B_T = B_{TA} + B_{TB} = H.$$

Assuming, for simplicity, that price-equalization is completely eliminated on B-goods ($\alpha_{tB} = 1.00$), we see from [15] that

$$B_T' = B_{TA} + \pi_A + B_{TB} = H + \pi_A. \qquad [18]$$

Expression [18] converges to the identity $(B_T' = H)$ as the value of trade subject to price-equalization goes to zero.

Assuming that the MCPE, like the CPE, will employ whatever measures are necessary to maintain full employment (whatever the efficiency costs), MCPE policymakers could be preoccupied with setting three additional policy targets in the face of external economic disturbances: dF^*, dP, and $d(Z/P)$. To achieve these targets, the policymakers have at their disposal (in addition to fiscal and monetary policies) three policy instruments: direct controls over the prices of exportables and importables of A-goods (θ_{xA}, θ_{mA}) and the exchange rate (e). In the following expressions, the targets are shown as functions of these variables and the parameters ϵ_{xA}, η_{mA}, ϵ_{xB}, and η_{mB}. The latter, which are now relative price elasticities, are parameters because import and export decisions are now being made by enterprises on a basis of price, value added, or profit calculations.

$$dF^* = dF_A^*(e, \epsilon_{xA}, \eta_{mA}) + dF_B^*(e, \epsilon_{xB}, \eta_{mB}) \qquad [19]$$

$$dP = dP_A(\theta_{xA}, \theta_{mA}) + dP_B(e) \qquad [20]$$

$$d(Z/P) = dZ_A(e, \epsilon_{xA}, \eta_{mA}) + dZ_B(e, \epsilon_{xB}, \eta_{mB}) \qquad [21]$$

In [20], dP_B is a function of only the exchange rate (along with exogenous foreign currency prices). More specifically, because $P_t = eP_t^*\alpha_t$, $dP_t = P_t^* e d\alpha_t + P_t^*\alpha_t\, de + e\alpha_t dP_t^*$. For B-goods, α_t is a constant (here assumed equal to 1.00); hence, dP_t changes only with changes in e and P_t^*. Expression [20] implicitly assumes unchanged nontraded goods prices and unchanged weights for all nontraded and traded goods in the price index.[52]

In the event of external disturbances, the MCPE has several alternative internal-external balance strategies available. One strategy is to follow a so-called "active" exchange rate policy, making periodic changes in the exchange rate to achieve the price level target. As an extreme case, assume that authorities are unwilling to tolerate any change in either the overall price level or the price index for A-goods $(dP = dP_A = 0)$. The authorities would solve [20] for $\hat{e} = -\hat{P}^*_{tB}$. In other words, for complete internal price stability, the authorities should revalue the home currency by the same proportion as the inflation in the weighted external price level for B-goods. But now the system [19]-[21] is overdetermined; only by chance would this exchange rate change yield all of the targeted figures. To ensure that all the targets are met, the authorities would have to reimpose direct quantitative controls on at least some traded goods.

It is commonly believed in Hungary that if the terms of trade are deteriorating, revaluation is insufficient to achieve overall price stability.[53] From [20], we see that this is not strictly so. The proponents of that point of view appear to be assuming that with external inflation and deterioration of the terms of trade, the currency would never be revalued by more than the percentage increase in export prices. Our formulation, on the other hand, would suggest revaluation (when, for example, $dP = dP_A = 0$) by $\hat{P}^*_{tB}$, which is the weighted value of external export and import inflation for B-goods. If the terms of trade are deteriorating, the domestic currency would be revalued by a greater proportion than the increase in export prices. This might worsen the trade balance, but it *would* give overall price stability.

An active exchange rate policy in a MCPE has several implications. First, the weights w_{mB} and w_{xB} will determine the relative impact of changes in the terms of trade on the exchange rate. Second, the net effect on the overall external trade balance will be determined by (1) the initial response of the trade balance to the external disturbance(s); (2) the further effect of, say, revaluation on the trade balance; and (3) the possible adoption of direct trade controls. If the authorities target some "acceptable" change in the overall hard currency trade balance, these direct trade controls become in fact *residual* "balancing" instruments. Of course, direct controls also play this role in the CPE; but for a MCPE faced with external inflation, revaluation could lead to further trade balance deterioration, and the balancing pressures may therefore be quantitatively greater than in a CPE.[54] Finally, while a MCPE can find an exchange rate change to hold the price level constant, this does not ensure price stability for all individual traded goods. The foreign currency price index for B-tradeables, $\hat{P}^*_{tB}$, is a weighted average reflecting varying degrees of inflation for individual importables and exportables. With a given exchange rate change applying uniformly to all B-goods, some B-traded goods will be subject to increased domestic prices, others to reduced internal prices.

A second strategy is to follow a completely inactive exchange rate policy, but still without price controls on B-goods. While the authorities might, as before, set a target value for dP_A, the change in the overall price level would now be out of their control, since dP_B would solely depend upon dP^*_{Bt}. Direct trade controls would again have to be used as balancing instruments.

A third strategy might combine an inactive exchange rate policy with the introduction of direct price controls over B-goods. In effect, this would probably mean the reintroduction of price-equalization in the B sector, although it might not be complete. Now dP_B would be a function of θ_{xB} and θ_{mB}. At least two basic variants of this policy would be possible. One would simply reintroduce price-equalization at the frontier, so to speak, in order to completely insulate domestic enterprise decisionmaking from external factors. All trading entities might once again have their real trade planned, as in the conventional CPE. In this case, ϵ_{xA}, η_{mA}, ϵ_{xB}, and η_{mB} would cease being parametric to the authorities and would become additional policy instruments (i.e., a return to the CPE).

A second variant would allow changes in foreign currency prices to play an informative role for domestic enterprises, while at the same time controlling the domestic price level through price-equalization subsidies. As suggested by Wojciechowski, this could be achieved by forcing domestic enterprises to buy imports and sell exports at *valuta* prices *(eP$_t^*$)*, which would be allowed to impinge directly on their value-added or profit criteria. Domestic factory prices would be kept constant, however, by subsidizing these enterprises for any losses incurred when selling or buying traded goods at domestic prices, which in general would differ from *valuta* prices. Alternatively, the separate system of factory prices could be abolished, and consumer goods prices could be maintained by manipulating turnover taxes.[55] Under this variant, despite price-equalization, the "elasticities" would continue to be parameters from the standpoint of the authorities.

A fourth strategy might be to avoid reintroduction of price-equalization in the B sector, but to reintroduce direct trade controls. Yet another possibility would be to influence B-sector trade in the desired direction (say, toward reduced imports and increased exports) through fiscal and monetary policy. Profit-oriented MCPE firms would be expected to be sensitive to changes in tax rates and to the availability and terms of short-term credit extended to support foreign-trade activities.

Two or more of these strategies could, of course, be combined. Only a more disaggregated model could adequately handle several of the more sophisticated strategies and suggest the probable micro- and macro-effects of their variants.

Summary and Conclusions

This paper has developed a simple framework for analyzing the short-run macro-adjustments of CMEA countries (or, more specifically, both conventional CPEs and MCPEs) to external disturbances in their East-West trade. This framework draws directly on the several major approaches currently used by Western economists to analyze balance-of-payments adjustments of market-type economies.

Despite the obvious difference in trade actors, we observed that the hard-currency balance-of-payments response of CPEs or MCPEs to external economic disturbances (inflation, changes in the terms of trade, exogenous reduction in exports) can be conveniently summarized in an elasticities framework similar to that frequently used in a market economy context. Indeed, the elasticities approach might be considered more applicable in the CPE and MCPE than in the market economy context because the prices of nontraded goods in these economies are typically fixed in the short run so that changes in the foreign currency prices for exports and imports do result in a change in the relative price of traded and nontraded goods. In CPEs (and to some extent in MCPEs), however, this is probably of little behavioral importance. For the most part, short-run foreign-trade decisions are not made on the basis of precise comparisons between foreign currency and domestic prices. (Over a longer time horizon, using various trade-efficiency indices may, however, have this result.) In any event, the elasticities approach is a useful way in which to characterize, *ex post,* the response of the trade balance to external disturbances in CPEs and MCPEs. For example, calculation of a "perverse" (positive) price elasticity of import demand suggests trade behavior of both theoretical and policy interest. Of course, we then want to characterize more precisely this behavior and its determinants.

In the process of developing the overall framework, it was necessary to remove the ambiguity surrounding the role of price-equalization subsidies in the balance-of-payments adjustment of CPEs and MCPEs. Once the actual role of the price-equalization mechanism was identified, it was integrated into a balance-of-payments national income accounting framework which draws directly on the definitional forms of the so-called "absorption" and "monetary" approaches to balance-of-payments analysis.

Changes in price-equalization subsidies (taxes) *per se* are unlikely to affect the domestic money supply or real variables such as output or expenditure. On the contrary, the price-equalization mechanism is passive and simply compensates for differences between the *valuta* and domestic price values of exports and imports. Changes in such discrepancies may come about through changes in the official exchange rate, modifications in foreign currency or domestic prices for traded goods, or changes in real-trade flows.

If there has been no change in real-trade flows, the authorities should be able to offset or "finance" any change in price equalization subsidies by means of direct credit transactions between the treasury and the central bank. Consequently, the domestic money supply and real variables remain unaffected. If, on the other hand, real-trade flows have changed, the money supply (at least initially) and real variables will be affected, regardless of how the treasury offsets the change in subsidies. Which money supply (domestic enterprise or household) is affected, and for how long, depends on the precise composition of the altered trade flows (producer or consumer goods) and the particular manner in which the treasury seeks to finance the change in subsidies. In some cases, one method of financing increased subsidies may be less inflationary than another, although a definitive answer awaits formulation of specific behavioral models and empirical testing. The effects on real output and expenditure also depend not only on the composition of the altered trade flows, but in some cases also on the method of offsetting the subsidies.

In the event of exogenous disturbances, the CPE can directly affect its external (hard-currency balance-of-trade) and internal (real absorption) targets by direct controls on real imports and exports. The linking of domestic and foreign-currency prices for some subset of traded goods (B-goods) and the elimination of centrally planned trade in the MCPE, undertaken to stimulate micro-economic efficiency, complicates the authorities' attempts to achieve certain external and internal macro-balance goals. Prices are still controlled in one sector (A-goods), but control is lost in the other (B-goods). Domestic prices of the latter will respond to changes in the exchange rate (or in the foreign-trade price coefficient), however, and it becomes an additional policy instrument. In contrast to the CPE, the MCPE has several available internal-external balance strategies including, in the case of external inflation, an "active" exchange rate policy (revaluation), some domestic (open) inflation, reintroduction of price equalization subsidies for B-goods combined with direct centralized controls, the reestablishment of price-equalization without direct controls, or monetary and fiscal policies to indirectly influence enterprise foreign-trade decisions. Clearly, the MCPE is not faced with the necessity of reverting entirely to the CPE with *de facto* direct-trade controls and automatic price-equalization for all traded goods. For some time, deterioration in both the external and internal balances may be tolerable, although at some point such deterioration may lead to significant recentralization.

This paper has been confined to outlining a framework within which balance-of-payments and internal-external balance analysis of CPEs and MCPEs might be conducted. It has undoubtedly raised more questions than it has answered. There are three important limitations of the study, which are really topics for future research. First, the framework should be extended to account for CPE and MCPE trade with other socialist countries, trade that is conducted primarily on a bilaterally balanced basis and not in hard currencies. Second, we would like to move from a taxonomy of possible responses by central planners, enterprises, and households to the development of behavioral models. Third, such models will need to be empirically tested, drawing on the rich experience of these economies with external shocks (as well as intra-CMEA economic disturbances) in the early 1970s.

Discussion
Josef C. Brada

Wolf's approach to the balance-of-payments mechanism in CPEs emphasizes monetary channels and basic macro-economic accounting relationships. It is taxonomic in that it focuses on the consequences for financial aggregates, such as the CPE's foreign exchange reserves and domestic money supply, of various changes in trade flows and alternative policy responses to such changes. This approach is presented as a complement to Holzman's work which focuses on the real consequences of external disturbances for output, employment, consumption, etc.[1]

Wolf's analysis is important for two reasons. First, he focuses attention on an important though relatively neglected and error-ridden aspect of the CPE economy. Second, and more important, his definitive treatment of the first-round monetary consequences of foreign trade provides the basis for an integrative approach to CPE adjustment mechanisms which parallels the newer approaches to the study of adjustment mechanisms in market economies.

In the literature, the trend has been away from the old elasticities approach, which viewed the balance-of-payments as a reflection of the market for foreign exchange, and toward a greater emphasis of the interactions between the foreign sector and the domestic economy. That is, the response of the economy to changes in the balance-of-payments is seen through the workings of a macro-economic model. An exogenous external shock to a market economy makes its initial impact on domestic output and employment felt through changes in domestic demand and supply or by changes in the domestic money supply occasioned by such a shock. The ultimate consequences of the external disturbance, in terms of both the balance-of-payments and domestic variables, are deduced from a macro-economic model, be it Keynesian, monetarist, or an alternative type.

The CPE, however, is not driven by demand, but by supply. Consequently, as Holzman has shown, the macro-economic adjustments observed in the market economy will not occur in a CPE; instead, they will be sterilized by revisions in the plan.[2] Output will, of course, change in response to altered trade flows, but not by the traditional foreign-trade multiplier. Rather, output changes will be determined by what Holzman calls the foreign-trade bottleneck multiplier. This type of analysis, however, deals with only the first-round impact on the domestic economy. To be sure, Holzman does discuss some possible second-round effects, but the framework for his discussion is heuristic. Similarly, Wolf precisely captures the first-round monetary consequences of changes in trade but, like Holzman, he is forced to rely on a heuristic approach or on analogies to the macro-economics of a market economy to explain the ultimate consequence of a change in trade flows.

There is, of course, a reason why these two first-rate economists abandon their analysis at the doorstep of the domestic economy. Simply put, we do not have an acceptable macro-economic model of a CPE. Consequently, an analysis that synthesizes the real and monetary consequences of an external disturbance on a CPE cannot be carried out.

In an attempt to move beyond what has been accomplished, I turn to the presentation of a macro-economic model which, I believe, sufficiently captures the essence of a CPE to permit a synthesis of the Holzman and Wolf contributions. The reader is cautioned that the key word is "essence." Many vital interrelationships and behavioral relations are missing. But since the model is sufficiently novel and complex, presenting only the essential variables and relationships has the advantage of highlighting the main implications in a manner that can be readily followed and understood.

Much like the traditional Keynesian model, the proposed model has four sectors. However, to reflect the unique features of the CPE, it differs in that, of the four markets—labor, goods, money, and bonds—only the first two are retained. The bond market is discarded entirely; in its stead are two money markets because there are really two separate and distinct media of payment in a CPE. One is cash, which consumers receive as wages, bonuses, and transfers and which can be used to purchase consumer goods and services. The second is enterprise deposits at the state bank, used only for inter-enterprise payments and for transactions between enterprises and the treasury. Cash may not be used for inter-enterprise payments or for consumer purchases of producers goods.

The second distinctive feature of this model is the element of disequilibrium. In a traditional market economy, prices are assumed to adjust so that markets are cleared; such an assumption obviously cannot be made in the case of a CPE. Prices generally are fixed, and the difference between desired and actual commodity or money flows can persist until economic agents act to bring their desired market behavior into line with actual market conditions. Since such adjustments may take considerable time, we assume that the four markets may be in disequilibrium.

The variables of the model are:

N = employment (man-years)
Y = output
C = nominal or desired consumption
C_A = actual or realized consumption
I = investment
M = imports
X = exports
M_s = supply of cash (currency units)
P = planned output
w = wage rate (currency units/man-year)

Unless otherwise indicated above, the variables are measured in domestic currency units per year. Because prices in a CPE remain fixed for relatively long periods, no distinction is made between real and nominal values of the variables denominated in money terms.

Turning to a description of the model itself, we first consider the labor market.[3] The demand for labor by state enterprises, N_D, is given by $N_D = N_D(P)$. The supply of labor is given by

$$N = N(w, E_C),$$ [1]

where E_c is the excess demand for cash by households as defined by [9] or [10]. We assume that $N_w > 0$ and $N_{E_C} > 0$. That is, either an increase in wages or an increase in household demand for cash will lead to greater supplies of labor. At the given level of wages, we assume that there is an excess demand for labor. Consequently, [1] describes not only labor supplied in the economy, but also the actual level of employment.

Because Holzman stressed the consequences of trade in intermediates on output and Wolf stressed the consequences of trade in final goods on household cash holdings, a version of the goods market must be formulated to deal with each case. If we are concerned with trade in final goods, then the demand for goods consists of consumption, investment, and exports, while the supply is equal to domestic production plus imports. The goods market is assumed to be in a state of disequilibrium characterized by excess demand for goods. Thus,

$$E_G = C + I + X - Y - M, \qquad [2]$$

where E_G is the excess demand in the goods market. Since we are dealing with trade in final goods only,

$$Y = Y(N). \qquad [3]$$

In the case of trade in intermediate goods, the excess demand for goods is:

$$E_G = C + I - Y. \qquad [4]$$

The level of output is:

$$Y = Y(N, X, M), \qquad [5]$$

where $Y_N > 0$, $Y_X < 0$, and $Y_M > 0$.

For both cases, we assume that the levels of imports and exports as well as the volume of investment are policy variables determined by the planners. The level of desired consumption, C, however, is determined by the level of disposable income:[4]

$$C = C(Y). \qquad [6]$$

However, [6] cannot be interpreted in exactly the same fashion as its counterpart in the Keynesian macro-model because the goods and cash markets are in disequilibrium in a CPE. As a result, the response of desired consumption to disposable income is asymmetric. If disposable income falls, given an excess demand for goods and excess cash holdings by households, there will be no decline in the desired level of consumption. On the other hand, an increase in disposable income under the postulated conditions will go toward increased demand for consumer goods. Thus, $C_Y = 0$ for decreases in disposable income and 1 for increases.

Like the goods market, the cash market is characterized by disequilibrium in that households have cash balances in excess of desired levels. For simplicity, we assume that the demand for cash consists only of a transactions demand. However, household demand for cash does not depend on the desired level of household consumption expenditures, but rather on the actual level of such expenditures as given by

$$C_A = Y + M - I - X, \qquad [7]$$

where trade flows consist of final goods, and

$$C_A = Y - I, \qquad [8]$$

where trade flows are comprised of intermediate goods. Letting k be the reciprocal of the velocity of cash circulation, the excess demand for cash, E_c, can be expressed as

$$E_c = k\ (Y + M - I - X) - M_s \qquad [9]$$

for trade in final goods, and

$$E_c = k\ (Y - I) - M_s \qquad [10]$$

for trade in intermediate goods.

The last market is the market for enterprise deposits. The demand for such deposits depends on the level of output, wages, and investment. Letting S_E represent the supply of such deposits, the excess demand for enterprise deposits, E_E, is given by:

$$E_E = D(Y, w, I) - S_E. \qquad [11]$$

Since by Walras's Law the sum of the four excess demands must be zero, we can eliminate one of the markets and use the remaining three to solve for the behavioral characteristics of the CPE macro-economic model. We proceed by eliminating the market for enterprise deposits and forming a system of three equations in three unknowns, N, E_G, and E_C. In the case of trade in final goods, we use [1], [2], and [9] to obtain:

$$F_1 = N - N(w, E_c) = 0, \qquad [12]$$

$$F_2 = C + I - X - M - Y - E_G = 0, \qquad [13]$$

$$F_3 = k(Y - M - I - X) - M_s - E_C = 0. \qquad [14]$$

In the case of trade in intermediate goods, [1], [4], and [10] yield:

$$G_1 = N - N(w, E_c) = 0, \qquad [15]$$

$$G_2 = C + I - Y - E_G = 0, \qquad [16]$$

$$G_3 = k(Y - I) - M_s - E_C = 0. \qquad [17]$$

The response of the endogenous variables, N, E_G, and E_C, to changes in the exogenous variables may be obtained as follows. First we define

$$\Delta = \begin{vmatrix} \dfrac{\partial F_1}{\partial N} & \dfrac{\partial F_1}{\partial E_G} & \dfrac{\partial F_1}{\partial E_C} \\[2ex] \dfrac{\partial F_2}{\partial N} & \dfrac{\partial F_2}{\partial E_G} & \dfrac{\partial F_2}{\partial E_C} \\[2ex] \dfrac{\partial F_3}{\partial N} & \dfrac{\partial F_3}{\partial E_G} & \dfrac{\partial F_3}{\partial E_C} \end{vmatrix} \qquad [18]$$

and

$$\Delta = \begin{vmatrix} 1 & 0 & -N_{E_C} \\ C_Y Y_N - Y_N & -1 & 0 \\ k Y_N & 0 & -1 \end{vmatrix} \qquad [19]$$

which yields $\Delta = 1 - k Y_N N_{E_C}$. Because Y_N and N_{E_C} are both positive, the sign of Δ would appear to be indeterminate. However, an appeal to the dynamic properties of the model enables us to show that the dynamic stability of the model requires that $1 - k Y_N N_{E_C}$ be positive.[5] Intuitively, stability requires that an increase in the supply of cash result in a situation characterized by a lower level of output and employment. However, an increase in cash supply reduces the excess demand for cash, thus lowering employment by N_{E_C}, output by $Y_N N_{E_C}$, and the demand for cash by $k Y_N N_{E_C}$. If the reduction in demand is greater than one, excess cash holdings must continue to increase and output must fall perpetually. Consequently, if we assume that our model is dynamically stable, Δ is positive. Finally, Δ for [15] through [17] can be obtained in an analogous fashion and, in this particular case, is identical to the Δ obtained by means of [19] and [20].

The effect of changes in an exogenous variable on the endogenous variable is obtained by differentiating the equations and by using Cramer's Rule. For example, changes in the level of investment are obtained by differentiating [12] through [14] with respect to I, yielding:

$$\partial F_1 / \partial I = 0, \quad \partial F_2 / \partial I = 1, \quad \partial F_3 / \partial I = -k.$$

Substituting these derivatives into Δ, we obtain:

$$dN/dI = -1/\Delta \begin{vmatrix} 0 & 0 & -N_{E_C} \\ 1 & -1 & 0 \\ -k & 0 & -1 \end{vmatrix} = -kN_{E_C}/\Delta, \qquad [20]$$

and thus $dN/dI < 0$.

Changes in exports and imports of intermediates and final goods have similar effects on domestic equilibrium (see table 1). However,

TABLE 1

Responses of Endogenous Variables to Changes in
Exogenous Variables

	*Response of endogenous variable**			
$Z = $ *Exogenous variable*	dN/dZ	dE_G/dZ	dE_C/d_Z	dY/dZ
Exports of final goods (X)	−	+	−	−
Imports of final goods (M)	+	−	+	+
Exports of intermediate goods (X)	−	+/0	−	−
Imports of intermediate goods (M)	+	0/−	+	+
Money supply (M_S)	−	+/0	−	−
Investment (I)	−	+	−	−

*Where two signs are displayed, the upper sign is for the case where $dZ > 0$, and the lower sign is for the case where $dZ < 0$.

the relative magnitudes of the impact multipliers and the mechanism through which changes in trade make their effect felt on the domestic economy differ. In the case of final goods, for example, a decrease of such imports leads to an increase in cash balances held by households and a reduction in labor supply with the ultimate fall in income, given by:

$$dY/dM = -kN_{E_C}/\Delta. \qquad [21]$$

In the case of imports of intermediate goods, a decline in imports leads to a change in income of:

$$dY/dM = Y_M - Y_M Y_N N_{E_C}/\Delta \qquad [22]$$

The first term is the import bottleneck effect, indicating the decline in output attributable to reduced availability of intermediate goods. However, because output falls, consumers experience an increase in their holdings of cash and, responding by reducing their supply of labor, cause a reduction of output given by the second term. Similarly, if imports of intermediates increase, cash balances decrease and the supply of labor increases.

Our analysis indicates that the full consequences of changes in trade flows involve both monetary and real mechanisms, and that the general equilibrium framework proposed here is of some assistance in indicating what these mechanisms are. Moreover, the asymmetries discovered between the impacts of positive and negative changes in certain variables suggest that changes in the commodity structure of trade may be an important policy variable in a CPE seeking to achieve a certain level of domestic disequilibrium in the face of changes in the total volume of exports and imports occasioned by external disturbances.

It is also evident from table 1 that there are policy options to offset the domestic consequences of changes in imports and exports. However, there is no guarantee that the planners will follow such policies. It may well be that they prefer to allow the markets to move farther from equilibrium rather than to undertake changes in the level of investment or some monetary reform.

In closing, it should be stressed that this model is a minimalist approach to the macro-economics of the CPE. Within the confines of this comment, we have merely attempted to demonstrate that both Holzman's and Wolf's analyses are required for a full understanding of the consequences of external disequilibrium for the CPE. Certainly a more comprehensive model would include taxes, government expenditures, some explanation of the impact of central plans on economic activity, and other features commonly associated with the CPE. Nevertheless, this more limited model highlights the main elements of balance-of-payments adjustment under central planning and underscores the need for a better understanding of the role of money in the macro-economics of the CPE.

PART III
ISSUES IN
CMEA INTEGRATION

Lawrence J. Brainard

CMEA Financial System and Integration

The financial system is one of three component parts of the foreign-trade mechanism of the CMEA. Together with the systems of trading and pricing, the financial system is often described as the weakest link in the structure of CMEA cooperation.[1] A corollary of this widely accepted point of view is that essential changes in the financial system, such as partial or full convertibility, will help spur integration.

The goals of this paper are (1) to assess whether the CMEA financial system acts to hinder integration, and (2) to assess how proposed changes in the financial system would promote progress toward integration. Problems of CMEA foreign trading and pricing are discussed briefly to point out the role played by the financial system.

The CMEA financial system consists of the mechanism of financial payments and receipts associated with international commercial activities among CMEA members. The principal aspects examined are: the currency in which they are denominated; conversions between domestic and foreign currencies (foreign exchange rates and convertibility); and the role of the two CMEA banks, the International Bank for Economic Cooperation (IBEC) and the International Investment Bank (IIB). Intra-CMEA financial flows are characterized by a dual structure: some flows are denominated in convertible currencies (CC) and others in transferable rubles (TR). In recent years, the CC component of flows among CMEA members has grown in importance. The volume of mutual trade settled in CC in 1974-75 is estimated at some 10% of the total. The share of CC transactions in the lending activity of IBEC and IIB is much larger.

The views expressed here are the sole responsibility of the author, and they should not be considered as reflecting the official position or endorsement of his employer. The author acknowledges helpful comments from J. M. van Brabant, M. Allen, A. Zwass, F. Holzman, and M. Lavigne.

CMEA Trading and Pricing

With the exception of some CC trade, external trading among CMEA countries is based on bilateralism and structural bilateralism. CMEA countries attempt to balance bilaterally both overall trade and trade by broad commodity group (e.g., machinery).[2] Bilateral trading acts to reduce uncertainty associated with central planning. This obvious advantage to planners accounts for the fact that there has been little change in CMEA trading relations (despite much talk about the desirability of multilateral trade) since the mid-1960s, when it was analyzed in detail by the Hungarian economist Sandor Ausch.[3] Since about 1970, rising rates of inflation in the West coupled with an expanded volume of East-West trade have introduced new elements in CMEA mutual trade. The traditional CMEA trading practices have not been able to adjust fully to new requirements posed by the increased economic fluctuations in world markets. Partial accommodation was made by expanding the share of mutual trade settled in CC which was outside the framework of bilateral trading and TR settlements.

CMEA pricing is best described as a special pricing system without clearly defined rules of price formation. In principle, CMEA foreign-trade prices are based on world market prices (wmp) of a previous period adjusted to remove monopolistic and business cycle influences. Prior to 1975, wmp's of a five-year period were used during the subsequent five years. Beginning in 1976, prices were to be adjusted annually based on changes in a moving average of world prices in the preceding five years. Actual prices, however, deviate significantly from world prices in both systematic and unsystematic ways.[4] An interesting description of the pricing system was made by Rezso Nyers, former member of the Political Committee of the Hungarian Socialist Workers [Communist] Party:

> A source of significant problems is the fact that the trend of departure from the average world-market prices is just as strong as the trend of following the world-market prices. Since within the CMEA there is no established special system of preferences, mutual concessions during trading negotiations have been provided mostly in the form of bilateral price agreements that for very many products depart from the pricing principle in the case of both export and import. As a result, the prices of specific products show a very wide dispersion, parallel with the principle that the average value of the commodities exchanged must be equal. Although this situation temporarily enhances smooth foreign trade, in the long run it makes every country interested in a rigid structure of foreign trade.[5]

The rigid structure of foreign trade is both the cause and effect of this situation, in which actual TR prices do not reflect the terms on which an individual good may be bought or sold within the CMEA.

As a result, the TR price of a given export good of one country may frequently vary 20% or more depending on the country to which it is exported.[6] The actual return to the exporting country's economy depends on what goods are in turn imported from the buying countries. TR prices do not reflect a common denominator of value. The gains to a given country from exporting or importing particular goods cannot be measured by the TR prices used;[7] the gains depend on the outcome of the bilateral bartering of goods during trade negotiations.[8] One consequence of the system of bilateral trading and pricing is that TR balances earned by running a trade surplus with one country usually undergo a significant depreciation when used to purchase goods from another CMEA country and, therefore, are seldom used for this purpose.[9] There is little incentive for any CMEA country to acquire and hold TR balances, since the future value of such sums would depend on the uncertain outcome of bilateral bargaining with CMEA members.[10]

The CMEA Banks' Role in the Financial System

An examination of the activity of IBEC and IIB provides a useful introduction to the CMEA financial system. An analysis of these banks' financial statements will show the dual structure of CMEA financial flows and the role of the TR in CMEA trade.[11]

International Bank for Economic Cooperation

IBEC began operations on January 1, 1964, and with its founding the TR was created. Although some expected that the bank would help facilitate multilateral trade among its members, it has so far been impossible to achieve this goal.[12] Trading continues to be bilateral. In fact, bilateral balancing continues to be facilitated by a special set of accounts at IBEC in which all bilateral commodity trade and payments are recorded.[13] Multilateral trade in recent years has amounted to no more than 1.5% of total CMEA turnover.[14]

One month after its founding, IBEC began deposit and payments operations in CC. In 1966, the CC equivalent of TR 30 million was added to the bank's capital stock, and in 1971-72 this amount was raised to TR 60 million.[15] IBEC's CC operations are similar to but less comprehensive than those of any Western bank: the taking and placing of short-term deposits, long-term lending up to seven years (to both socialist and nonsocialist banks), and long-term borrowings from

TABLE 1
IBEC Balance Sheet, 1969 and 1976
(million TR)

	January 1, 1969			January 1, 1976		
	Total	In CC	CC as percent of total	Total	In CC	CC as percent of total
ASSETS						
Liquid assets						
a. cash and current account	11.6	11.6	100.0	32.0	28.0	87.5
b. time deposits	303.6	303.6	100.0	1745.0	1745.0	100.0
Credits outstanding	351.4	23.3	6.6	1481.8	527.1	35.5
Other	3.2	3.0	93.8	47.4	5.5	11.5
Total assets	669.9	341.5	51.0	3306.4	2305.6	69.7
LIABILITIES						
Capital						
a. paid up	89.7	30.0	33.4	120.2	60.1	50.0
b. reserve	1.6	1.6	100.0	55.3	24.2	43.8
Deposits received						
a. current	121.1	3.4	2.8	426.7	20.0	4.7
b. time	452.6	301.6	66.6	2175.5	1772.6	81.5
Loans received	—	—	—	411.4	411.4	100.0
Other liabilities	3.3	3.3	100.0	92.5	—	0.0
Net profit	1.6	1.6	100.0	24.7	17.3	71.5
Total liabilities	669.9	341.5	51.0	3306.4	2305.6	69.7

SOURCE: Jozef M. P. van Brabant, *East European Cooperation: The Role of Money and Finance* (New York: Praeger, 1977), p. 150.

NOTE: Deposits are generally short term (less than one year); credits outstanding and loans received are usually long term (more than one year). The 1976 CC balance sheet is estimated using the IBEC Annual Report and van Brabant's CC estimates for 1975.

Western banks. The payments and receipts associated with commercial activity in CC among CMEA members are not handled by IBEC but by means of accounts of each country's foreign-trade bank in the West.

The CC portion of IBEC's balance sheet is not published, but sufficient information is available to reconstruct it. Using estimates made by van Brabant, IBEC's overall balance sheet totals rose 4.9 times between 1969 and 1976; the CC totals rose 6.8 times, increasing from 51% to 70% of the combined TR and CC total (see table 1). TR credits outstanding rose from TR 328 million to TR 955 million (or 2.9 times); TR time deposits received by IBEC went up from TR 151 million to TR 403 million (or 2.7 times).

It may seem paradoxical that only 30% of IBEC's balance sheet represent TR entries, given that some 60% of the member countries' foreign trade is with each other. The efforts by member countries to balance their trade bilaterally mean that in spite of a rising volume of trade settled in TR, members avoid accumulating current or time deposits at IBEC by running a trade surplus. A trade surplus would cause the automatic granting of a credit by the bank to the deficit country. Hence the pursuit of bilateral balancing in trade acts to limit the potential expansion of deposit and credit operations in TR. It should be emphasized, however, that IBEC's balance sheet reflects only its banking activities (deposit and credit) and only at year-end. The bank also acts as the clearinghouse for all TR payments and receipts associated with trade and noncommercial transactions. Given their short- term nature, TR credits outstanding at year-end are only a modest proportion (about one-third since 1971) of total TR credits granted during the course of the year. And total TR credit volume during a year has only represented some 5 to 8% of total settlements in TR.[16]

CMEA countries also seek bilateral balancing because the nominal interest received on TR deposits accumulated by running trade surpluses does not represent a claim on any particular CMEA member and is, therefore, not easily transformed into goods. Hence, countries do not view TR deposits as an asset desirable for reserve accumulation. These reasons limit IBEC's TR lending activity. There is very little that IBEC can do about this because its credit activity in TR depends on CMEA trading practices; that is, it cannot pursue an independent credit policy.[17]

The growth of IBEC's CC activities has been impressive. At the end of 1975, its $3,045 million CC balance sheet total would have made it the 195th largest bank in the world, approximately equal in size to the Paris-based Eurobank, largest of the Soviet-owned Western banks.[18] Most of the bank's CC activity is in the taking and placing of short-term deposits. Since 1970, long-term lending (up to seven years) has expanded rapidly, accounting for over a fifth of total CC assets in 1976. Deposits and loans received by IBEC come largely from Western banks; deposits and loans placed by the bank go predominantly to the foreign-trade banks of member countries.

IBEC's CC activities appear primarily to have helped to finance its members' trade with the West. There is little evidence on the role played by IBEC in financing intra-CMEA CC trade. The share of CC as a percentage of intra-CMEA trade in 1974-75 may be estimated at between 5 and 10% in value terms.[19] This estimate is based on published Hungarian data (see table 2) and on a preliminary analysis of 1975-76 Hungarian data, which for the first time allow the estimation of Hungary's CC trade with individual socialist countries.[20]

TABLE 2
Hungarian Hard Currency Settlements
with Socialist Countries, 1971-75
(million $US)

Year	Imports	Percent of total socialist imports	Exports	Percent of total socialist exports	Balance
1971	54.0	2.9	37.7	2.3	-16.4
1972	63.2	3.2	48.9	2.2	-14.3
1973	111.2	4.8	197.2	6.9	86.0
1974	260.2	8.6	341.1	10.3	80.9
1975	232.3	5.1	398.2	9.4	165.9
1971-75	720.9		1,023.1		302.2

SOURCE: *Statisztikai Havi Kozlemenyek,* various issues.
NOTE: Excludes Yugoslavia; imports valued at contract price (from CMEA yearbook), exports valued f.o.b.

It appears that there are significant differences among CMEA countries in the use of CC in mutual trade. About one-fifth of Hungarian-Romanian trade in 1975 was denominated in CC, while an insignificant volume of Hungarian-Czechoslovak trade was in CC. Hungarian CC trade with the Soviet Union, Poland, and the GDR was substantial, though it accounted for a smaller share of total trade than was true with Romania. Although some portion of the CC trade may represent above-plan deliveries of "hard goods" (high quality goods that could be sold easily in Western markets), the size of the CC trade would suggest that contracts must have been made at the same time that the annual trade plans were concluded. Further, there appears to be no pattern of bilateral balancing as is true for TR trade: the bulk of Hungarian exports represent direct sales, while imports tend to involve Western middlemen.

The rising importance of CC trade since 1970 reflects several factors. One is a general tightening of the CMEA market for goods in excess demand in recent years, caused in part by world inflation and the resulting changes in relative prices of raw materials compared with manufactured goods. Sales of such goods in excess of the quotas and for TR prices agreed upon in 1970 for the 1971-75 plan period were probably settled for the most part in CC rather than in TR. Another factor is the rising share of CC components—inputs and investments—in the cost of goods traded within the CMEA; countries seek to receive a certain percentage of the price of such exports in CC.

It is possible that the use of CC prices does not at the same time involve actual settlement in CC (i.e., actual CC payments through Western bank accounts of the member countries' foreign-trade banks), but rather an obligation to repay the CC import at some future date. If this were the case, then the significance of CC trade would be that current wmp's replace TR prices with bilateral balancing of these trade flows over several years. While there are likely elements of bilateralism in CC trade, the Hungarian data in table 2 show sizable CC surpluses since 1973. This implies that bilateral balancing is not evident, and the data available for 1975 do not reveal a balancing of CC trade on a country-by-country basis.

It may be assumed that, with its substantial CC activities, IBEC plays some role in intra-CMEA CC trade financing. The relevant issue, however, is whether the rising importance of CC trade is a factor promoting integration.

International Investment Bank

The IIB began operations on January 1, 1971, with authority to make long-term loans for investment projects in both TR and CC. At the end of 1975, paid-up capital totaled TR 369.2 million, of which 30% was in CC. About two-thirds of the bank's end-1975 total assets and liabilities (TR 942.6 million) were in CC.[21]

Judging by statements appearing in Soviet and East European sources, IIB's activities have fallen short of initial expectations.[22] The reasons are simple. In contrast to IBEC, whose TR credits are granted automatically as a result of imbalances in CMEA countries' commercial payments and receipts in trade with other members, IIB may grant TR credits only after the delivery of projected capital goods to be imported by the borrowing country has been arranged, i.e., after the borrower has negotiated the delivery and price with the supplying countries.

As a rule, a potential supplying country will be willing to export goods against IIB credit only if it can also arrange imports of capital goods for its projects, also using IIB credits. In other words, each country seeks to balance exports supplied on credit with imports on credit. A borrowing country must seek, through a series of bilateral negotiations with other CMEA countries, to obtain pledges for the delivery of the goods it desires to import—a cumbersome procedure made especially difficult by the exporter's insistence on counterbalancing imports and the problem of determining a mutually acceptable price. IIB's TR credits are, therefore, purely technical in nature because they are not arranged until the actual commodity deliveries have been decided upon. The essential problem is that IIB's TR capital does not represent real resources but only commitments by the members to supply capital goods up to the value of their TR capital shares of the bank. The nature of these commitments is only very general, so that negotiations for future deliveries of capital goods for projects to be financed by IIB are complex and drawn out.[23] It is not surprising, therefore, that the bulk of IIB's activity has been in CC.

At the end of 1975, IIB total credit commitments were TR 2,885 million for 40 projects.[24] Two credits for the Orenburg gas pipeline totaling TR 2,379 million accounted for 82.5% of total commitments. The average size of the remaining 39 projects was TR 13 million. At the end of 1974, it was reported that 87.4% of total commitments (amounting to TR 2,361 million) were in CC.[25] Included in this figure is the first credit of TR 1,890 million to the Orenburg project. During 1975, TR 523.7 million in new loan commitments were made, including the second Orenburg project credit of TR 489 million.[26] Although no data are available on CC commitments as of end-1975, it is likely that the share was 80 to 90% of total commitments.

IIB credit commitments in CC are largely funded from borrowings on Western capital markets. During 1975-76, $1,020 million in loans were raised in the Eurodollar market in three syndications.[27] Although IIB has had to pay slightly higher rates for Eurodollar loans than do the foreign-trade banks of CMEA countries, these same banks are helped by relieving them of the burden of raising the needed funding themselves.[28] IIB, therefore, plays a major role in raising the needed hard currency for the realization of joint integration projects.

Although IIB has failed to develop lending in TR as originally envisioned, it may be seen as playing a significant role in the process of CMEA integration, primarily by virtue of its activity in CC.[29] In this regard, however, the CC lending could just as easily have been done by expanding the role of the IBEC. The goal toward which IIB is uniquely oriented—the expansion of TR project lending—is still far from fulfilled. But as was true for the IBEC, the lack of effectiveness of IIB's TR banking activities is not a problem whose solution the banks themselves could find, but derives from the CMEA systems of trading and pricing. From this follows the tentative conclusion that reforming the two banks' structures or policies would do little to change the situation. Further evidence is reached when one looks at the issue of currency convertibility.

Exchange Rates and Convertibility

The issue of convertibility is frequently discussed in connection with CMEA integration on the assumption that full or partial convertibility of the TR is a necessary precondition for, or would at least promote, fuller integration. In his comment (p. 142), Mark Allen very helpfully distinguishes 24 different kinds of convertibility, depending on whether the conversion is into goods ("goods convertibility") or into other currencies ("financial convertibility"), the currency converted, and who has the right to make such conversion (resident individuals or enterprises or nonresidents). In addition, one may distinguish whether conversions are related to mutual payments (i.e., flows of goods and services) or are for accounting purposes (e.g., calculations concerning specialization agreements and capital contributions to CMEA joint enterprises). Two broad types of convertibility are examined below: (1) the convertibility between the TR and the national currencies of the CMEA countries; and (2) the convertibility of the TR into goods in the CMEA market. Other aspects of convertibility (e.g., the financial convertibility of the TR or national currencies into CC) are not discussed.[30]

CMEA National Currencies and the TR

Although CMEA national currencies are not used for settlement of foreign trade, there are purposes for which conversions are necessary between a country's domestic currency and the TR or other CMEA currencies. Examples include tourism, other invisible transactions, and the financing and operation of joint CMEA investment projects and CMEA international economic organizations (IEO). Several types of exchange rates are currently used for these purposes. So-called noncommercial exchange rates are used for converting invisible transactions. Such conversions involve cash or savings deposits of individuals. Noncommercial rates are also used for other conversions (described below). So-called internal commercial rates or coefficients are applied in the activities of multilateral CMEA institutions, economic organizations, and joint projects. Some CMEA countries also apply these rates for internal uses such as the conversion of TR receipts and payments into domestic currency. The scope of application of the internal commercial exchange rates in multilateral affairs is limited since most commercial payments are already denominated in TR.

Since 1956, noncommercial payments have been cleared by first converting payment flows denominated in national currencies into Soviet rubles using the agreed-upon noncommercial rates. These sums are translated into TR by multiplying by a coefficient (currently 2.3). Since 1964, the resulting balances have been cleared multilaterally through IBEC, though bilateral accounts are still maintained. During 1956-63, clearing was performed bilaterally. Noncommercial exchange rates are based on purchasing power comparisons calculated by using the cost of a standard market basket of consumer goods and services for a hypothetical diplomat's family of four. The current coefficient (2.3) is supposed to reflect the relationship of Soviet consumer prices and Soviet TR prices of the same or similar items. The two-stage conversion process (conversion into rubles and then into TR) apparently reflects the desire to avoid having to set separate coefficients relating each country's consumer prices to that country's TR prices (which may not be necessarily identical to Soviet TR prices for the market basket).[31]

The noncommercial foreign exchange rates were modified effective January 1, 1975. In principle, they are to be changed whenever there is a significant shift in relative consumer price levels.[32] The conversion coefficient may also be modified because of changes in the Soviet consumer price level relative to TR prices. There has been no mention of whether the coefficient will be adjusted on a periodic basis in line with the expected annual adjustment in TR prices, although there was apparently no change in the rate in 1976. If Soviet consumer prices rise less than TR prices and the coefficient is not adjusted downward to reflect this, it would penalize countries enjoying a surplus on their noncommercial accounts. It has been agreed, however, that any surcharge or discount applied on a bilateral basis will not exceed 10% of the multilaterally agreed-upon rates.[33] This would appear to limit the possibilities of unilateral adjustments in the rates and suggests that more frequent changes in the mutually agreed-upon rates are likely.

The noncommercial payments system faces the same problems of any comparisons based on standardized market baskets. There are significant variations in the type and quality of items included in the comparisons, and the weighting of items in the market basket may not adequately represent the actual pattern of noncommercial payments. Bulgaria, for example, has claimed in the mid-1960s that the market basket undervalued the tourist services it actually provided.[34] Despite these problems, the system appears to work, and if needed, more frequent adjustments in the relative rates could probably be made without difficulty. Thus, as far as noncommercial payments are concerned, a certain measure of convertibility between CMEA national currencies and the TR has been achieved. It could be possible to gradually expand the limits currently applied to the exchanges of individual tourists and the overall limits specified in the annual bilateral trade agreements.[35]

The introduction and use of internal commercial exchange rates between CMEA currencies and the TR, however, have encountered major difficulties. Initial agreement on internal commercial rates was reached in October 1973,[36] but so far these rates have been applied for multilateral purposes on only a very limited scale.[37] The various rates were said to be calculated by comparing domestic producer prices (excluding turnover tax) with the TR prices of that portion of each country's social product that represents exportable goods (excluding construction, transportation, domestic trade, and other services).[38]

The need for internal commercial exchange rates is explained by the growing number of multilateral CMEA institutions, economic organizations, and joint projects. The functioning of these multilateral endeavors would be facilitated by a set of exchange rates for converting domestic currencies into TR. In order to recognize and profit by situations of comparative advantage, however, domestic prices in each country must also bear some relation to real opportunity cost. Otherwise, the conversions into TR would preserve an inappropriate structure of relative prices and hence have limited usefulness for purposes of comparison or aggregation. Many of the difficulties encountered in the introduction of the internal commercial rates derive from irrational domestic price structures of CMEA countries.

Up to now, conversions between domestic currencies and the TR have been made by disaggregating the joint investment project or operation into its various cost components. Each physical item was "translated" into TR by using its existing TR price.[39] Wage costs were converted into TR by means of the noncommercial exchange rate. The result was a series of ad hoc coefficients for each activity or project for each CMEA country. It is hoped that the use of a single set of exchange rates will make such complicated calculations unnecessary. The chief stumbling blocks are the wide divergencies in domestic producer prices in CMEA countries and the annual adjustments in TR prices initiated in 1975.

The new TR pricing policy has made necessary the recomputation of the 1973 rates, and changes were to have been introduced at the end of 1976.[40] Presumably, annual rate adjustments will have to be made in line with the new CMEA pricing policy. The other problem concerning domestic producer price structures is more difficult. The single rates chosen reflect the average relationship between a country's domestic prices and TR prices. The ratio of domestic and TR prices for a specific branch of industry or type of service or commodity will differ considerably, as a rule, from the average internal commercial rate; and the nature of the differences will vary from country to country. For example, the structure of producer prices is significantly and (what is more important) arbitrarily different from country to country.[41] If commercial rates were applied, these deviations would create a disincentive for one and an incentive for another country to take part in a joint project. The only way around this problem at present is to use various ad hoc coefficients for individual joint undertakings on a case-by-case basis.

Recommended financing and accounting principles of the work of the various CMEA organizations were outlined during 1975 in the publication of model statutes.[42] International organizations include IEOs (referred to as *mezhdunarodnye khozyaistvennye organizatsii*) that operate on the basis of *khozraschet*, such as joint enterprises, associations, and scientific research organizations, and other international organizations (*mezhdunarodnye ekonomicheskie organizatsii*) that are financed by the budgetary contributions of CMEA countries. The latter are involved primarily in planning and coordination activities in various sectors. The IEOs have received considerable attention, as they represent a key institutional form of cooperation in the integration process; so a closer look at their financial organization is warranted.

The basic capital of the IEO is determined in the national currency of the country in which it is located. The basic capital is also valued in TR for fixing the contributions of the participating countries. Contributions to the IEO's financial working capital are to be made in TR, CC, and the national currency of the host country (which presumably applies only to the host country), depending on where and for what purpose expenditures will be made. Fixed capital is to be contributed in the form of goods (e.g., equipment, buildings) valued in TR. It is apparently not possible, or at least very difficult, to make fixed capital contributions in TR.[43] In addition to problems of capital valuation, books are kept in the local currency for local purchases and sales, in TR for purchases and sales from other CMEA countries, and in CC for transactions with nonsocialist countries. It is frequently uncertain which currency and which price is applicable to any given transaction, e.g., a TR price (there may be multiple TR prices or none at all), the domestic wholesale or retail price, or an ad hoc price. There are many unsolved questions about the imposition of turnover taxes, rents on land, payment for natural resources, and the taxation of the wage bill. Where conversions are necessary between the local currency and TR, the rates of exchange are decided "by agreement among the competent organs of the participating countries, taking into account the possibility of applying the Agreement of CMEA Member Countries about the Introduction of Mutually Agreed Rates or Coefficients of National Currencies in Relation to the Collective Currency (the Transferable Ruble) and among Each Other of October 19, 1973." In other words, the internal commercial exchange rates may be used, or special ad hoc exchange rates may be agreed upon. In actual practice, the internal commercial rates are rarely used; and because of the difficulty of determining prices and costs, the expansion of IEOs organized as joint enterprises selling their products has been hindered.

Although recommended financial and accounting procedures of the IEO have been spelled out, it appears that the introduction of internal commercial exchange rates will not help much to improve the convertibility between TR and CMEA national currencies. Even if the internal commercial rates are chosen for use by an IEO, complicated and time-consuming calculations must still be carried out in order to determine this. The complicated procedures for setting rates and accounting will act to weaken the interest of some countries in participating in IEOs or in making the most out of them once they exist. It is difficult to see how this situation can change much unless CMEA countries agree to unify their systems of setting domestic prices. It can be expected that the number of IEOs will continue to grow, but the problems mentioned above will act to slow the process and may weaken the efficient operation of this institutional form of cooperation.[44] It will be particularly difficult to expand the activity of IEOs organized as joint enterprises to manufacture and sell a given range of products. For these reasons, IEO activity may tend to be focused more on planning and coordination rather than on manufacturing.

A related issue should also be mentioned. Proposals for production specialization among CMEA countries should, in principle, contain comparisons of production costs, and the conversion of each country's costs into a standard unit (e.g., the TR) would greatly facilitate such comparisons. This approach, however, is not used in practice. In fact, there does not appear to be any agreed-upon methodology for analyzing and comparing specialization opportunities. CMEA countries have developed various ways to calculate indices showing the efficiency of importing and exporting goods that may be subject to specialization agreements.[45] But the specific formulas used differ from country to country.[46] As a result, such calculations are so far not used on a multilateral basis.

The topic of CMEA specialization also raises a number of interesting issues, particularly those related to pricing. Specialization, for example, tends to be concentrated on finished products rather than on components, both because ministries and firms are primarily interested in final output due to the nature of the plan targets they receive (it is easier to fulfill the targets by focusing on final output rather than components or spare parts) and because world prices for component parts are not known or do not exist.[47]

In summary, convertibility between the TR and CMEA national currencies has been achieved, but only on a very limited scale. The relative success of the noncommercial exchange rates derives from the homogeneous nature of the transactions for which they are used and the fact that these transactions take place in markets where converted monies may freely purchase available consumer goods or services.[48] It is important to note, however, that cooperation in the field of services has a relatively limited role in the integration process. The scope of cooperation in various fields of industry is much more important for the goal of furthering CMEA integration. It remains to be seen whether the internal commercial and ad hoc exchange rates will be able to function adequately, given the basic problems posed by the CMEA and foreign-trade price systems.

Convertibility of the TR into Goods within CMEA

Nonconvertibility of the TR into goods is frequently regarded as the key defect of the CMEA financial system. That it is an important problem is obvious. However, the basic cause of the problem lies not in the financial system itself, but in the nature of centrally planned economies (CPE) and in the bilateralism that characterizes their mutual trading relationships. The following discussion provides evidence for the conclusion that financial reforms cannot by themselves achieve convertibility of the TR into goods; it does not attempt to give a comprehensive analysis of the many issues surrounding TR convertibility.[49]

The convertibility of the TR into goods within CMEA would mean that the owner of TR financial resources may, on demand, use them to purchase goods from other CMEA countries. By definition, this means multilateral trade, which is insignificant in CMEA's TR trade. Multilateralism is an exceedingly important issue in examining the prospects for CMEA integration, but is not essentially a financial problem. The allocation of goods in CMEA is based on plans and directives, not financial instruments. The introduction of greater multilateral trade must be approached by modifying the CMEA system of planning and bilateral trading.[50]

It has been suggested that TR convertibility into goods may be approached by first introducing full or limited convertibility of the TR into CC.[51] It is argued that if TR financial resources were convertible into CC and thus into goods in world markets, this would encourage greater convertibility of the TR into goods within CMEA. Countries, for example, would have an incentive to supply high quality goods as an alternative to covering a deficit with CC payments.

With some 5 to 10% settled in CC, CMEA mutual trade is already partially on a convertible basis. It would be possible to redenominate this CC trade in TR by creating a unit called "convertible transferable ruble." This would result in a partially convertible TR only in a formal and meaningless sense because nothing but the name of the currency unit would be changed. Furthermore, it does not appear likely that the share of CC trade in CMEA mutual trade can be increased much from the present level. Efforts will be made to reduce unplanned CC trans-actions to reduce the uncertainty associated with such sales. They will likely be included within future bilateral trade agreements so that needs that must be met by imports can be balanced by planned ex-ports. There may, however, be an increase in barter deals with prices based on current wmp's as opposed to TR prices.

Hungary and the Soviet Union signed such an agreement in 1976 outside the quotas set in the 1976-80 five-year plan. The agreement calls for balanced deliveries of Soviet crude oil, gasoline, cotton, lumber, and cellulose for Hungarian wheat, maize, and beef.[52] To the extent that CC trade within CMEA is based on similar barter ar-rangements, the significance is merely that the traditional pricing for-mula for CMEA has been discarded for a certain portion of mutual trade. In other respects, the principle of bilateralism still prevails. CC trade within CMEA which does not represent bilateral balancing may be viewed as multilateral trade. The preliminary analysis of Hunga-rian foreign-trade data for 1975-76[53] indicates that such unbalanced trade appears to be a major portion of Hungary's CC trade with CMEA, though it still would be a relatively modest portion of Hun-gary's total CMEA trade. Judging by the difficulties experienced by CMEA countries in converting a portion of the TR trade into CC, the potential for multilateral CC trade within CMEA is limited.

In September 1973, the IBEC put into practice an agreement whereby 10% of a country's deficit balance over a given limit on its current account at the bank would be converted into CC or gold.[54] The results have not been encouraging. When countries approached the limit, they arranged special purpose TR loans and used part of the proceeds to reduce their deficit position on current account. Another effect was to make countries reluctant to import goods if it would lead to a deficit position in bilateral trade, i.e., if it increased some coun-tries' interest in maintaining strict bilateral balance, thus discouraging the expansion of trade by making bilateral trading more rigid.[55] And with the change in TR prices in 1975, some of the countries which previously had credit balances are now faced with deficits, and their interest in the scheme has waned. There is little likelihood that the 10% limit could be gradually increased as a way to expand TR convertibility.

The basic problem with this and other proposals for limited convertibility of the TR is that their introduction would almost certainly limit the interest of potential deficit countries in expanding trade. Otherwise, at least one country (e.g., the Soviet Union) would have to agree to run trade deficits with the others, settling the deficit in CC—a possibility that can easily be ruled out because no CMEA country enjoys a surfeit of CC.[56]

There is the possibility that TR convertibility into goods can be approached by efforts to bring the quality and technical standards of CMEA goods up to the levels of Western goods and to increase their availability. If achieved, this would be tantamount to multilateralism, since CMEA and Western goods would be interchangeable and there would be no need for bilateral trading. It is sufficient to note that convertibility in this case would accompany multilateral trading, and there would be no need for the TR since the national CMEA currencies would themselves be convertible.

The conclusion is simply that the convertibility of the TR into goods or CC is not feasible until multilateral trade of some form can be achieved. And reforms in the CMEA financial system will not change matters because they cannot influence the system within which trading takes place.

Conclusions

The analysis of the CMEA financial system has pointed to the dual structure of financial flows (in TR and CC). The CC financial subsystem appears to operate with considerable success: possibilities for the two CMEA banks to develop activities in CC are being utilized, and some of these activities support progress toward integration. The shortcomings of the TR subsystem stand in sharp contrast.

The future expansion of CC activities by the CMEA banks will be limited by the amount of borrowing in Western capital markets which IIB and IBEC desire or are able to make. IBEC financing in CC for CMEA members is concentrated in the shorter maturities (six months and less) as are the borrowings from the Eurodollar market. The bulk of Eurodollar transactions is concentrated in these maturities, and the overall market volume is enormous. It is unlikely that significant difficulties will be encountered by IBEC in obtaining short-term loans. Long-term borrowings also appear possible; although given IIB's orientation to long-term borrowing, IBEC may wish to restrict such borrowing to avoid competition.

As was noted, IBEC's CC lending primarily supports East-West trade expansion and is not directly relevant to CMEA integration. CC lending by IIB, however, is of considerable importance to integration. All IIB loans from Western banks have up to now carried floating rates of interest with final maturities of five to seven years. It is not likely that substantial borrowings can be made in Western bond markets due to lack of interest on the part of traditional bond purchasers and IIB's apparent reluctance to meet disclosure regulations required for access to the principle bond markets of the US and Germany.[57] Thus, IIB's CC lending will largely be limited by what it can raise in loans from Western banks. The amounts could be substantial, perhaps as much as $1 billion in annual volume. But there is obviously a limit, and a heavy volume of borrowing would tend to push up interest rates, which IIB may wish to avoid.

The shortcomings of the TR financial subsystem stand as a major barrier to CMEA integration. Yet the removal of barriers to integration posed by the CMEA foreign-trade mechanism cannot be achieved by means of changes in the financial system.[58] And here we encounter a basic contradiction in the concept of CMEA integration. The goal of multilateral trading and the benefits that would derive from it conflict with the self-interest of each country's policymakers in preserving the present system of trading and pricing. This is because the prospective future benefits of moving to multilateral trade are outweighed by the real or assumed costs such a move would entail. Bilateralism is still a basic interest of all countries for a variety of reasons: the lack of quality goods, the desires to avoid increased uncertainty in the planning process, and the need to expand manufactured exports. CMEA countries would find it difficult to trade multilaterally unless their current structures of production and export (which are similar in many ways) are altered in line with comparative advantages of the CMEA area.

Without basic changes in pricing and trading, CMEA cooperation will continue to be based on a system of barter, with only limited monetary elements present.[59] Under these conditions, CMEA joint planning and coordination, which is viewed as a key element of the current stage of integration,[60] will be complicated by the difficulties of determining mutual long-term advantage. Thus, there will likely be continued reliance on administrative or scientific-technical rather than economic criteria in CMEA decisionmaking.[61] But the stability and usefulness of long-term cooperation agreements depend on the maintenance of mutual interest. This will be difficult to achieve without effective economic calculations and incentives.

One conclusion, therefore, is that progress toward a more effective CMEA financial system depends on factors that significantly reduce the benefits of maintaining or reduce the cost of changing the present systems of planning, trading, and pricing. The limited success achieved by various efforts at economic reform within CMEA during the past decade would suggest that changes will be slow in coming. There remains the question, however, of whether the rapid expansion of CMEA trade and financial ties with Western countries since 1970 may change the costs and benefits of reform.

Some CMEA countries may seek continued close interdependence with Western markets as the most feasible and attractive way of increasing long-term productivity growth. The Western systems of trading, pricing, and financing would not likely pose a barrier to the greater integration of a CMEA country with the international economy. The major barriers would be on the other side: limits to what can be wisely borrowed from Western capital markets; inadequate standards of CMEA goods; servicing and marketing, which frequently fall short of competitive standards that must be met; and the irrational systems of domestic prices and other systemic obstacles that stand in the way of efforts to use effectively such new forms of technical transfer as joint ventures.

The removal or lessening of many of these barriers can be approached by means of domestic rather than CMEA-wide reforms. Poland and Hungary, for example, are attempting to increase the efficiency of their foreign trade by involving enterprises in decision-making and by reforming their system of pricing to forge a closer link between domestic and foreign prices. Greater interdependence with the West may intensify pressures for needed economic reforms. Yet, at the same time, other potential problems may be created or intensified—problems caused by continued price and business cycle instability in Western markets which makes planning doubly difficult, the unexpectedly rapid rise in indebtedness to the West, and the shifts in terms of trade. These factors tend to generate pressures for tighter central control of foreign trade.[62] It remains to be seen whether pressure for reform or tighter control will prevail.

Discussion
Franklyn D. Holzman

Dr. Brainard's assignment was to discuss the relationships between the CMEA financial system and integration, and he has covered the topic admirably. His discussion of the relationships between national CMEA currencies and the transferable ruble (TR) is very informative. These relationships have always been shrouded in some mystery. Their significance lies not in commodity trade *per se*, where bilateral balance between CMEA nations is largely achieved, and in world prices, but in the netherworld of financial relations that result from invisibles (so-called noncommercial transactions), joint investment projects, and international economic organizations (IEOs). Coefficients relating national currencies and TRs are necessary for unit of account purposes (since world prices apparently are not used here) and also to finance imbalances.

Brainard feels that some success (i.e., some convertibility) has been achieved in noncommercial exchanges. He attributes this to the homogeneity of the services exchanged (e.g., tourism) and the existence of limited commodity convertibility in these markets. On the other hand, each joint investment project and each IEO is unique, and great difficulties are encountered in making satisfactory financial arrangements. This, he feels, substantially impedes integration.

To return to noncommercial exchanges, I would argue that homogeneity of services is not a sufficient condition for convertibility. It is also necessary for the nations to be roughly in medium or long-run payments equilibrium on invisibles. This requires taking account of demand as well as supply conditions and exchange rates which will, in fact, yield a balance on invisible accounts—a condition that cannot be taken for granted.

My only dissatisfaction is with Brainard's discussion on the convertibility of the TR into goods and into convertible currencies (CC). This section is somewhat unsatisfactory not because Brainard doesn't understand the issues, but because causes and effects of inconvertibility are not always laid out clearly and logically.

In a Western context, inconvertibility and bilateralism result when a nation is in serious balance-of-payments trouble; multilateralism and currency convertibility, on the other hand, reflect a sound balance-of-payments situation or adequate reserves. The CMEA picture is more complex. Pure balance-of-payments problems are part of the picture. Just as fundamental, however, are problems related to central planning.

Inconvertibility in CMEA stems from central planning with direct controls and from the goals and priorities of the Soviet bloc authorities which keep them from introducing radical economic reforms. Two important consequences of central planning with direct controls are: (1) foreigners are not allowed to make unplanned purchases, particularly of intermediate products, because of the disruptive effects these would have on the plan; and (2) the lack of free markets, the exorbitant use of discriminatory sales taxes and subsidies, and marxist ideology combine to produce what are usually termed ''irrational'' prices. Commodity inconvertibility is due primarily to (1), namely, the unwillingness of central planners to see their short-run plans disrupted by unplanned exports. This is perfectly rational, given such planning, since the sum of iterated losses from every 100 rubles worth of disruption could be many times as great.

It is important to note that commodity inconvertibility is specific to Soviet bloc economies, but not to their currencies. While it is true that foreign importers with TRs, rubles, zlotys, or what have you cannot easily convert their currencies into Soviet bloc goods, the same applies to dollars, pounds, and gold. That is to say, Gossnab brooks no interference with its planned commodity flows, although the pressures for allowing exceptions would be greater for dollar than TR purchases.

The various Eastern currencies are all inconvertible into each other because, in the first instance, exchange rates can have no meaning when they equate irrational price systems. This is one reason why the exchange rates serve no function in intra-CMEA trade. The TR is inconvertible into each of the Eastern currencies partly because the particular set of price relatives which it reflects also cannot be meaningfully equated to the irrational East European prices. Inconvertibility as a result of irrational prices is aggravated by commodity inconvertibility: no Eastern nation will willingly buy or hold the currency of another because of the difficulties of using such currencies to buy goods. This, in fact, goes a long way toward explaining the rigid bilateral balancing of trade which takes place. The TR is even less desirable than national currencies since, while in theory the TR can be spent in any CMEA nation, in fact it has no real home.

The TR is inconvertible into hard currencies partly because of its commodity inconvertibility. It might be argued that dollars also have commodity inconvertibility in CMEA. The difference is that the dollar has commodity as well as currency convertibility throughout the rest of the trading world, whereas the TR has neither.[1]

What factors other than commodity inconvertibility and irrational prices are responsible for currency inconvertibility? Could CMEA national currencies and the TR achieve currency convertibility without commodity convertibility? It would be possible, but it would require large reserves of hard currency and strong balance-of-payments positions vis-à-vis Western hard-currency nations. Given these conditions, foreigners would be willing to move freely between TRs and hard currency, and IBEC would be willing to allow its members to freely buy hard currencies with TRs; that is, it would allow what might be termed resident convertibility. While it is possible for the TR to achieve currency convertibility in this manner, it is highly unlikely. The major factor behind commodity convertibility, namely central planning with direct controls, is also a basic cause of the hard-currency balance-of-payments difficulties with which CMEA is perennially faced. While I cannot discuss this in detail here, central planning is largely responsible for the relatively low quality of CMEA exportables (as mentioned by Brainard), problems in selling and marketing lag in technology, tautness in the economy which leads to pressures to overimport and underexport, inability to effectively devalue a currency, and so forth.[2]

What would it take to eliminate commodity and currency inconvertibility, and why aren't these steps taken by the CMEA nations? Briefly, the substitution of decentralized planning for direct control planning would eliminate commodity inconvertibility virtually by definition. It would also eventually provide necessary, though not sufficient, conditions for currency convertibility. That is, currency convertibility at the very least requires decentralized planning with its rational internal prices which would be organically related to world prices. (These statements cannot be proved here, but if the previous analysis is correct, they follow logically.) When one considers the consequences of such radical reforms, it immediately becomes clear why more progress toward convertibility and multilateralism has not been made. Such reforms would lead to a large reduction in intrabloc trade, something the USSR is not likely to contemplate with equanimity; imported inflation; foreign-trade-generated fluctuations in unemployment; and, as Brainard puts it, "increased uncertainty in the planning process."

These are a few of the economic consequences of radical reforms which are inconsistent with higher priority domestic goals. I agree with Brainard that one cannot be optimistic regarding the possibility of radical reforms because of their purely domestic political implications, an opinion most Western students share. Without such reforms, I cannot believe that either commodity or currency convertibility can be achieved. And, as Brainard argues, without convertibility, integration will be seriously impeded through bilateralism and through difficulties in assessing the possibilities of greater production specialization. In other words, CMEA lacks an effective medium of exchange and a usable unit of account, leaving it on square one.

Discussion

Mark Allen

I have no disagreement with Brainard's excellent description of the CMEA banks. Rather, my comments refer specifically to the section on convertibility. This is a complicated subject where the issues can best be grasped if the terms are properly defined. In particular, it is important to be clear at all times about whether convertibility is into another currency or into goods, who is to have the right to make the conversion, and which currency is being referred to. In the case of the currencies of the East European countries, the possible combinations give at least 24 different kinds of convertibility.

The first distinction is between commodity convertibility and financial convertibility. By commodity convertibility, we refer to the freedom of conversion of the currency into goods or, in other words, the freedom of the holder of money to spend it on the things he wants. Financial convertibility means the freedom to exchange holdings of one currency for another.

The second useful distinction is whether the convertibility of an East European currency into goods or other currencies is to apply to goods and other currencies in Eastern Europe or in the West. The two distinctions give four forms of convertibility for an East European currency: into East European goods, into other East European currencies, into West European goods, and into West European currencies.

The third distinction refers to who has the right to enjoy the convertibility of his holdings, the resident holder or the nonresident holder. Combined with the previously described forms, this gives eight possible varieties of convertibility.

Finally, there is the question of which currency is to be made convertible. There appear to be three relevant currencies: the transferable ruble (TR) used in intra-CMEA settlements and two kinds of domestic currency, consumer money in the form of cash and savings deposits and enterprise money that exists only on enterprises' bank balances. The 3 currencies combined with 8 varieties of convertibility give 24 possible kinds of convertibility to talk about. Brainard's paper moves from one form of convertibility to another, without making the change in subject clear.

The key problem for currency convertibility in Eastern Europe is the question of commodity convertibility. Since most other currencies in the world have a high degree of commodity convertibility, its general absence in Eastern Europe is the distinguishing feature of East European inconvertibility. The evidence shows that some degree of financial convertibility has been easiest to introduce where a large measure of commodity convertibility exists.[1]

Commodity convertibility means that the holder of money can use this money to purchase goods. In other words, there is a market in which the holder of money has command over goods. The degree of such command differs for each of the three currencies under consideration. In every East European country, the holder of consumer money (cash) can use his holdings to purchase available consumer goods. For consumer goods there is a market, at least from the demand side, irrespective of whether supply or prices respond to demand. Because consumers' money is already convertible into commodities to some extent, the greatest progress has been made in introducing some degree of financial convertibility for this currency.

Enterprise money in most East European countries is extremely inconvertible into goods. The theory and practice of centrally planned economies show that money does not command goods within the enterprise sector. If an enterprise obtains a good, this is not because it has spent money from its bank account, but because it has been allocated that good by the plan. The plan is the motive force, and the money flows are merely a response to what has already been decided. Commodity convertibility in the enterprise sphere can only arise if enterprises are allowed to use their money holdings to purchase what they want. Commodity convertibility is restricted as long as the planners preempt and allocate goods. Thus, the introduction of commodity convertibility in the enterprise sphere depends on the development of some form of market in this area.

The third currency under consideration is the TR. There is clearly potential for commodity convertibility here, and potential for an international market. Individual countries bargain about quantities to trade with each other at given prices without any intervention by a supranational allocation authority. Such an arrangement could be a real market where the holders of TR balances could purchase what they want. However, because of the well-known pricing problems, with the distinction between hard goods and soft goods, foreign-trade transactions within the CMEA become essentially bilateral barter. The supplying country will accept other goods in exchange for its exports, but normally no TRs. Accumulations of TRs are thus involuntary, because the money has little command over goods or, in other words, little commodity convertibility.

Financial convertibility has gone farthest for consumer money. All East European countries allow holders of both Western currencies and other East European currencies to convert holdings into their domestic cash currency. With this they can enter the domestic consumer goods market. Limits are almost invariably placed on the exchange since unlimited rights of conversion might disrupt the domestic consumer goods market, as happened when East Germany and Poland introduced unlimited convertibility as an experiment. The Prague Agreement of February 8, 1963, on noncommercial payments was relatively simple to conclude because it allowed a limited linking of a number of already existing markets.

The introduction of similar financial convertibility between the enterprise currencies of each country or between that of one country and Western currencies founders on the absence of domestic markets for producer goods and on the lack of discretion of enterprise managers about the use of their money holdings. Similarly, the problem of the financial convertibility of the TR into Western currencies will be virtually solved once relative TR prices on the CMEA market reflect supply and demand conditions and the holder of the currency can freely convert it into goods. Thus, by a somewhat different route, I find myself in agreement with Brainard's conclusion "that the convertibility of the transferable ruble into convertible currency is not feasible until multilateral trade of some form can be achieved."

Discussion
Adam Zwass

The inconvertibility of the CMEA countries' currencies is a real obstacle to East-West economic relations. I agree with Holzman that inconvertibility, and central planning as a major factor behind it, is a "basic cause of the hard-currency balance-of-payments difficulties with which CMEA is perennially faced." This also is the cause of the increasing indebtedness of the CMEA countries vis-à-vis the West.

In addition to the factors cited by Holzman, there remains the separation (full or partial) of the producing enterprises from the external market and from the competition of the world markets and therefore from the impact of technical progress. Under these conditions, the planned economies are not able to develop their exports service and marketing according to the demands of Western importers. The convertibility and the factors associated with it, namely the autonomous pricing and unrealistic exchange rates, exclude accurate calculations of trading options based on the principle of comparative cost advantages.

difficult because CMEA countries cannot use the facilities of these institutions and their currencies cannot function as a means of settlements in East-West trade.

Poland and Hungary proposed to improve the trade with CMEA and Western countries by perfecting IBEC activities by moving away gradually from inconvertibility. These countries thought that under CMEA conditions the most practical way would be first to achieve a partial convertibility of the TR, liabilities, and assets into CC, beginning in steps from 10%, then 20%, and so on. After some time, they could expand toward full convertibility, following the practice of the European Payments Union (EPU).

After ten years of negotiations, an agreement was achieved on September 1, 1973, to make the TR partially convertible on a temporary, experimental basis. The agreement includes, however, only some of the IBEC members who assumed that "with the experience thus gained it will be possible to extend the circle of the participants and to gradually increase the scope of convertibility."[1] However, this undertaking was not crowned with success.

The long, unfruitful discussions and the above-mentioned unsuccessful agreement suggest that convertibility of the common CMEA currency will confront insurmountable obstacles because the basic concept behind the attempt is faulty. After all, it was not the clearing unit of the EPU, but the national currencies of its members that achieved, after long-lasting efforts, convertibility. Moreover, there is no precedent of an artificial CC of any other integration group.

In the CMEA integration group of planned economies, where countries are at different economic levels, the obstacles to convertibility are greater than anywhere else. The impediments resulting from the systemic preconditions are multiplied by the obstacles that stem from the immaturity of the integration of the IMF but would also contribute by making available their own CCs to the IMF and its members. This proposal does not mean that the CMEA countries would have to accept Article VIII from the beginning of their membership in the IMF, only that one of the preconditions of membership would have to be the guaranteed achievement of full convertibility within an agreed-upon period.

To be sure, the association with the Bretton Woods institutions is first and foremost a political problem for each country. But it cannot be excluded that the example of Romania will be followed by some or all CMEA countries.

Zbigniew M. Fallenbuchl

Industrial Policy and Economic Integration in CMEA and EEC

Western observers of CMEA integration are often tempted to make superficial comparisons of that economic grouping with the European Economic Community (EEC). It seems to be a part of conventional wisdom to point out that the absence of supranational authorities of the sort that exist in Western Europe is a serious barrier to East European integration. It is also suggested that the EEC has been successful because its integration process depends on the operation of market forces, which is strengthened by the removal of tariff obstacles to trade, and that the centrally planned socialist economies cannot have the same results unless they introduce a certain degree of marketization to their economies.[1]

The process of integration can be defined as a process of creating economic dependence that is complementary under the two systems.[2] This paper examines only one aspect of integration. It attempts to draw attention to some factors of "industrial policy" which can stand in the way of successfully carrying out multinational efforts to promote industrial integration.

Most advanced countries have "industrial policies [which] are concerned with promoting industrial growth and efficiency" by "fostering conditions propitious to free competition, as well as by stimulating improvements in management performance, in manpower adaptability and mobility, in the diffusion and application of new technologies, and in industrial structures."[3] Selective and structurally oriented national industrial policies tend to limit the operation of market forces. They

The author wishes to acknowledge a grant from the Canada Council in support of research on which this paper has been based. A substantial revision was made as the result of extensive and exceptionally careful and generous editorial guidance provided by Professors J. M. Montias and Paul Marer, and comments expressed by the discussants at the Conference.

may involve measures to encourage structural changes in the branch composition and geographic distribution of industry, in the size of firms and the degree of concentration, and in the organization of investment, production, research and development, marketing, and other activities.[4]

These factors are often overlooked when West European integration is discussed, although they tend to affect the industrial structures of the member countries and the speed and extent to which these structures become more complementary. In Eastern Europe, the industrialization drive of the 1950s and early 1960s was based mainly on national industrial policies, and it has created certain industrial structures. This is an area where some valid comparisons between the two communities can be made and the role of supranational authorities and market forces, or the impact of their absence, can be examined.

National Industrial Policies

In the EEC, there was a transitional period from 1958 to 1968. The stress was on the removal of the commercial obstacles to trade, increased factor mobility, and coordination of national monetary and budgetary policies. The basic assumption was that the removal of commercial policy obstacles to trade would lead to nondiscriminatory transactions, depending purely on differences in costs and prices or quality, irrespective of the national origin of the suppliers and buyers. The enlargement of the markets would, under these conditions, create gains from economies of scale and specialization and stimulate competition that would invigorate economic activity and increase efficiency of production and trade. The removal of these barriers was, therefore, accepted as the end of the transitional period for the six original members and the beginning of a new phase during which EEC countries were expected to move "from cooperation to integration" with the locking of exchange rates and possibly the establishment of a common currency, as well as the centralization of policymaking at the community level in several important fields.[5]

A 1970 European Commission memorandum states that "considerable progress in liberalization has certainly been achieved between the six countries, but their six markets taken as a whole are far from resembling a single market" and that "the different price levels for similar products in the different member countries bear sufficient witness to this."[6] Among the reasons given, some can be regarded as relatively unimportant temporary imperfections, such as insufficient knowledge on the part of consumers, insufficient adaptation of products of one country to the tastes and habits of another, the discriminatory price policies, and collective agreements. More importantly, however, the removal of institutional obstacles required agreements among the governments of the member-states. These included differences in technical and legal requirements connected with industrial standards, legal provisions concerning safety and health, and protection of the consumers. In effect, a producer was sometimes forced to produce six different articles to meet the requirements of all member countries. Another obstacle was the existence of public contracts, which are usually reserved principally for national producers. By 1970, still less than 1% of public contracts was made with firms in other member countries, or approximately the same percentage as that of contracts with third countries. This situation was judged by the Commission as "certainly not normal for a single market."[7]

Even greater difficulty was created by the existence of national industrial policies in member countries. The objective of these policies was an increase in industrial efficiency and an improved competitive position which should lead to export expansion. In practice, however, the policy was also used to preserve existing inefficiencies and low productivity and to shelter domestic industry against foreign competition. It became a serious barrier to trade and integration.

There are two broad areas in which this situation may occur:

1. Support for declining industrial sectors, which are often concentrated in particular regions of a country, may serve to perpetuate inefficiencies in industrial operation and in the allocation of resources if it does not effectively provide for a transitional adjustment process to new conditions permitting self-sustained operation.

2. If support for the development of certain technologically advanced industries, motivated in the past by noneconomic considerations, is prolonged beyond a start-up phase, it may represent an artificial bolstering of industrial operations that would otherwise not be viable.[8]

In France, where the role of the state in economic life is greater than in other EEC countries, the list of sectors that have been the main beneficiaries includes the agricultural and food industries, the electronics industry, the aeronautical industry, shipbuilding, iron and steel, and textiles.[9] In the mid-1960s, there was a significant change in the priority for subsidization. In the preceding years, large amounts of resources had been allocated to sectors with slow growth prospects to assist in their restructuring and to facilitate the transfer of labor to other activities. As a corollary to aiding the problem industries, rapidly expanding sectors experienced difficulty in obtaining resources. Under the fifth (1966-70) and sixth (1971-75) plans, more support was provided for the dynamic sectors, mechanical engineering, organic chemistry (including plastics and man-made fibers), and electrical and electronic engineering.[10] The objective was to expand industries with the greatest growth potential and to improve their competitive position rather than to aid some over-expanded problem industries. The recent recession has frustrated the fulfillment of this objective, and government aid has been directed, above all, to industries with large labor forces to prevent further increase in unemployment: construction, steel, shipbuilding, aeronautics, and pulp and paper.[11]

Germany, although the most market-oriented among the EEC members, has also been applying an active structural policy. A similar shift in emphasis took place in that country during the 1960s. At first, the support was mainly granted to facilitate adaptation of problem industries, such as coal and iron ore mining and shipbuilding, as well as to develop structurally weak regions (Berlin and areas near the Soviet zone; special areas with a one-sided industrial structure, including the hard coal mining regions of the Ruhr and the Saar; and rural areas in which unprofitable farming predominates and there is a lack of industrial employment opportunities). Later, attention was concentrated on the development of the advanced technology industries and others that were regarded as important for general economic progress, when such industries could not expand or progress fast enough without government help.[12]

National industrial policies provide a shelter for a part of industrial output against the impact of the removal of commercial policy obstacles. The result is the same irrespective of whether they are designed to assist some problem industries, to slow down their decline and to facilitate their adjustment to the changed circumstances, or to provide support for advanced technology industries and industries that are regarded as essential for the future development of the country. Although in the latter case, the "infant industry argument" may often be advanced in their defense, in both cases the solution of the problem is applied on a national rather than a supranational level.

When the same industries are protected as problem industries or aided as advanced technology industries, the industrial structures of member countries become more competitive than complementary. In addition, national industrial policies reduce industrial interpenetration by making international productive cooperation and mergers with firms located in other countries of the community less attractive.

The removal of tariffs increased competition, enlarged markets, and provided a stimulus for reorganization of firms. Increases in the scale of operations became possible and even necessary. There was an acceleration in the movement toward concentration within each West European economy, but regrouping among firms across national borders was rather limited.[13] This was the result of the readiness of national governments to provide aid for restructuring industries to help them compete with industries in other countries rather than to assist them in effecting international cooperation and mergers with their EEC partners. Between 1961 and 1969, both production cooperation agreements and mergers with firms outside the community (particularly with US firms) were more numerous than with firms in other EEC countries. Out of 6,150 production agreements that took place in Western Europe during that period, 2,797 were made with firms outside the community, 2,352 were between firms of the same country, and 1,001 were between the firms in different EEC countries. During the same period, there were 2,938 mergers, including 1,861 between firms of the same country, 820 with firms outside EEC, and 257 with firms in other countries belonging to the community.[14] But international mergers and long-term production agreements create more permanent links between the national industrial structures and play an important role in increasing their complementarity. The lack of a strong tendency for mergers and agreements between the firms in different EEC countries, therefore, had an adverse effect on the progress of integration.

The impact of the removal of tariffs was also limited by the fact that in many industries, particularly those with new advanced technology, price competition was replaced by competition in research and development and investments that are necessary to put even more technologically advanced products on the market.[15] To the extent that the product innovations rather than price reductions are used to enlarge market share, government subsidies and preferential purchasing have been necessary to sustain the independent national firms in various nations in Western Europe.[16]

In order to establish or expand the advanced technology industries in face of strong American and Japanese competition, a number of European states developed the so-called "national champions" during the 1960s as the promoters of technological progress and innovations. Although some West European collaborative efforts have taken place among these enterprises, most of these efforts were formulated by the governments' nationalistic policies. This tendency has been particularly strong when state-owned enterprises participated; such enterprises "are concerned mainly with national issues." As a result, "difficult as the problems of collaboration and mergers might be in the privately owned enterprises, . . . it has been a bit more difficult when the stockholders of the enterprise were the several states and the managers were the servants of their respective states."[17]

It is difficult to estimate the full impact of national industrial policies on the process of integration. The following statement by the Commission of the European Communities to the Council of Ministers in 1970 should, however, be noted:

It is industries serving the private consumers which have most benefited from the customs union. Experience has shown that industries
which make use of the major new technologies do not feel the same
benefit of the customs union inasmuch as—since their development depends on public funds and orders—they cannot so easily break out of
the national market.

Initiated in the field of coal and steel, economic integration became
general in 1958 in semblance only. In practice it is limited to trade in
widely used products, in certain capital goods and organization of the
agricultural markets. It has not sufficient impact yet on the structure of
industry and on advanced technology industries.[18]

As the result of the operation of various aspects of national industrial policies, the existence of national champions, public contracts
and state-owned enterprises, and a shift from price to technological
competition (particularly strong in the most dynamic industries), the
powers of the supranational authorities and the ability of market
forces to effect integration have been seriously limited.

National industrial policies in Western Europe have many
similarities with such features of East European development as (1)
the "parallel industrial structures," or a tendency to create industrial
structures which are competitive rather than complementary; (2) the
well-known policy of "self-perpetuation of industrial structures,"
which involves the maintenance of inefficient enterprises and
branches of industry; and (3) the building up of the so-called progressive industries regardless of cost or dynamic-comparative-advantage
considerations because they are considered "carriers of technological
progress." These similarities are usually overlooked. Although they
are important, it is necessary to remember the basic systemic difference. In the West, the government structural industrial policies operate within the overall internally and internationally competitive
framework; and the industrial policy obstacles to trade and integration
cannot, therefore, isolate the domestic economies and shelter the national champions against foreign and domestic competition as effectively as in the centrally planned economies (CPE).

The "parallel industrial structures" were created in Eastern Europe
in the 1950s in imitation of the Soviet industrialization policy and the
Soviet industrial structure, irrespective of the national factor endowment and the scale of domestic market.[19] This tendency was noticed
in the mid-1950s by Imre Nagy, who complained that the East European countries competed with identical exports in the Western markets and had the same products to offer one another.[20] It did not
hamper the trade between Eastern Europe and the Soviet Union because the latter was willing to import large quantities of machines,
which were often identical to those domestically produced, in ex-

change for raw materials which the East European countries required in rapidly increasing quantities. As a result, a "radial" pattern of trade appeared within the CMEA: every East European country trades, above all, with the Soviet Union.[21]

The "self-perpetuation of industrial structures" resulted in an almost automatic tendency for the expansion of once-established enterprises and industries, irrespective of the impact of such decisions on the overall efficiency, capital intensity, or raw materials intensity of production. Its danger was stressed in connection with economic reforms of the late 1960s.[22]

During the late 1960s, it also became accepted that a strategy of economic development should not ignore new technological developments.[23] Some industries were established in East European countries because they were regarded as progressive. During the early stage of industrialization, heavy industry, particularly iron and steel, were considered as such. More recently, such industries as engineering, electro-technical, electronic, data-processing, plastics, man-made fiber, and some other "new branches" of the chemical industry have been regarded as absolutely necessary for the modernization, automation, and "chemicalization" of economic processes.[24] Many of these industries produce an excessively large variety of products required to meet domestic requirements, creating autarkic tendencies.[25]

In effect, these East European policies led to the creation of inefficient firms and industries, support for the "problem industries," and priority for advanced technology industries. Their impact on the progress of integration has been similar to that of national industrial policies in Western Europe.

International Agreements as a Tool for the Advancement of Integration

At the end of the 1960s, there was strong dissatisfaction with the progress of integration in each of the two economic groupings. In the early 1970s, both adopted new programs of action designed to stimulate the process. With the end of the transitional period in 1968, the EEC entered a new phase. During the transitional period, the removal of tariffs was the main tool for the advancement of integration, and the market forces were relied upon to effect the necessary adjustments. One of the main tasks of the supranational authorities was to ensure competition. However, because the national industrial policy barriers were strong and almost untouched by the process, the progress that was achieved by this mechanism was more limited than expected, and its effect on various sectors of the economy was uneven.

Since the end of the transitional period, international agreements have become the main tool for the advancement of integration. This is basically the same mechanism that has been used to effect integration since the establishment of the CMEA. In order to eliminate the obstacles created by national industrial policies, the Commission of the European Communities has attempted to formulate and implement supranational industrial policy, without which it would not be possible to advance beyond "the stage of a customs union and a common agricultural policy." The objective was the creation of "a European industrial fabric" which would provide "an unshakeable foundation for the economic and ultimately political unity of Western Europe, continued economic expansion and a reasonable degree of technological independence in relation to other major trading nations."[26] The program of action included the promotion of the advanced technology industries at a European scale; joint programs for technological progress; dissemination of technological knowledge; promotion of "European-scale" firms by international mergers; elimination of national bias in public sector purchasing in member-states; creation of EEC-wide business incentives; removal of technical, legal, and financial obstacles to trade; and a common approach to help "problem industries."

A common industrial policy was not envisaged by the Treaty of Rome, although several of its provisions could be interpreted as authorizing such a policy. The Commission's proposals were built on this basis and an understanding that the extension of the treaty in this direction was an absolute necessity.

Although there was a general agreement among the members that a common industrial policy was an essential part of the mechanism for further integration, the adoption of new measures in this field required consultations and negotiations between the Commission and member governments. Considerations of national interest proved to be a serious obstacle. In this field, which still remains the least developed area of community activity, "the ratio of draft directives to those adopted is, to say the least, extremely high."[27] An example of the delays that are inherent in the integration process can be provided from the field of technological cooperation. In 1967, seven areas were already designated for joint action: data processing, telecommunications, metallurgy, new transport technology, environmental control, meteorology, and oceanography. It was not, however, until 1971 that joint projects were finally agreed upon.[28] The agreement on a wider program was approved by the Paris Summit Meeting in 1972 and the Copenhagen Summit Meeting in 1973. Finally, in January 1974, the Council adopted "an outline program in the field of science and technology," which accepted the importance of the coordination of national policies in this field and the joint implementation of projects of interest to the community and presented a work program and timetable for their implementation.[29]

The Commission's 1970 proposal in the field of "industrial policy" underwent substantial changes during the preparatory work of a special study group and the Permanent Representatives' Committee. The action program was mentioned in the final communiqué of the Paris Summit and was adopted at the Copenhagen Summit. It consisted of a schedule for action in connection with the elimination of technical barriers to trade, the opening up of public contracts, the removal of fiscal and legal barriers opposing rapprochement between companies, and the setting of deadlines for a series of measures on sectoral industrial policy.[30]

On July 15, 1974, the Council adopted a resolution concerning collaboration in data processing. The resolution aimed at the establishment of a "European" industry in this field by the beginning of the 1980s and instructed the Commission to present some concrete proposals for collaboration. The first five proposals were submitted by the Council in March 1975. They involved encouragement and financial support for specialization and coordination in research and development and in the production of various components. On December 19, 1974, the Council adopted a resolution which established a permanent procedure of cooperation and consultation among the public authorities of member countries in matters concerning industrial policy in aeronautics.[31] Progress has been very slow. The lengthy negotiations and "horse trading" among representatives of member countries seem to have produced a general feeling of frustration and a decline of morale among the European civil servants in the Directorate-General III (Industrial Policy) who have been in charge of creating an industrial policy for the community.[32]

An example of the difficulties involved can be provided by recent negotiations concerning the Jet (Joint European Torus), an experimental thermonuclear project that is the first step toward a joint fusion energy program. The project was presented to the nine members in 1975. All countries agreed on its importance, but they have been unable to agree on its location. An independent committee of experts recommended Ispra in Italy. Germany, France, and Britain all wanted it in their own national research centers. A compromise emerged: the project would be located in Britain (Culham), Germany would provide the project leader, France would obtain subcontracting work, and Ispra would get some other compensatory community research. It was expected that research ministers would approve the compromise in Brussels in March 1977. But France objected to the proposed management structure and voting procedure. The smaller countries suspected that the French proposals would exclude them from the decisionmaking. They were also prepared to vote against the British location because of some unrelated issues (farm prices and fishery) and supported the German site. Voting did not take place, and the meeting was adjourned without setting another date. In the meantime, the community has been losing its world lead in fusion research, and 15 out of the 50 Jet scientists have left.[33]

For a student of the CMEA, the picture is familiar. The process of negotiations and "horse trading" has been discussed by Michael Kaser, J.M. Montias, and others.[34] A mixture of conflicting national interests, domestic politics of the party leaders, and vested interests of industrial enterprises and foreign-trade organizations create similar obstacles under the centrally planned socialist system in Eastern Europe as under the mixed system in Western Europe.

The first attempt to formulate a multinational industrial policy in Eastern Europe had very little success. It took four years to reach agreement on a set of policies designed to effect the shift from the coordination of trade, which had been the essence of CMEA during the 1950s, to the coordination of production. Every country wanted a "progressive" industrial structure and wished to continue priority development of the engineering, iron and steel, and chemical industries. None wanted to accept the role of the supplier of raw materials and foodstuffs, or even to specialize in manufactured consumption goods. A compromise was reached in the form of a document, "The Principles of International Socialist Division of Labor," which was discussed at the 19th session in 1961 and agreed upon at the party leaders and chiefs of state conference in June 1962. The program stated that "in the world socialist economic system favorable conditions exist not only for consistent and planned deepening of the division of labor among countries but also for the creation of a rational complex of interlinked and complementary sectors of national economy" and that every country should be able to create "a multisector structure of the national economy."[35] This combination of international specialization with each country's comprehensive and complex development was to be achieved by a continuation of industrial development with specialization in certain products within each branch of industry.[36]

It was hard to reach agreement on this compromise, but it was even more difficult to implement the policy of intra-sector specialization. A Polish economist observed that "every socialist country accepts the wisdom of specialization" but "the difficulties appear when it comes to making actual specialization agreements . . . [because] all socialist countries select, as a rule, the same, or similar directions of specialization."[37]

In 1967, the CMEA Executive Committee adopted a set of measures aimed at the improvement of preparation and realization of specialization projects.[38] The number of sectoral standing commissions and international organizations was increased to stimulate specialization and cooperation within sectors. They were responsible for about 2,500 specialization recommendations—mainly in the engineering and electro-technical industries—during the first ten years of activity.[39] Despite these efforts, by the end of the 1960s trade in those commodities which were subject to specialization agreements represented only 10% of CMEA trade.[40]

The existing methods of effecting specialization agreements came under severe criticism: the specialization recommendations were not compulsory; they concerned mainly those projects that were already produced and final products rather than component parts; they did not include cooperation in research and development; the agreements were signed by state organs that were not operating on the basis of economic calculations; and economic units often did not participate in the preparation of specialization tasks. The selection of particular products for specialization, their excessively wide range, and the acceptance of specialization proposals without a careful economic analysis ''led to the specialization along the lines of least efforts . . . [and] the acceptance of the existing situation, without solving important problems of cooperation in this field.''[41] There was also criticism of lengthy discussions and slow work within various CMEA bodies.[42]

The introduction of the Comprehensive Program in 1971 was an attempt to move from ''cooperation to integration.'' As such, it corresponded to the end of the transitional period in the EEC. The program was again a compromise adopted after lengthy negotiations.[43] It included measures to accelerate the development of the multinational industrial policy, joint forecasting, coordination of the long-run perspective plans and the five-year plans, strengthening of specialization agreements, and joint planning of individual branches of industry and production lines.[44]

Specialization agreements now include all stages, from the division of tasks in research and development to the allocation of production and distribution. Preference is given to agreements concerning specialization and cooperation in component parts and semi-finished products. Increasingly, the agreements are made between the economic units of member countries rather than between governments. Moreover, the agreements are made at the preparation stage of national plans and should be related to the long-run and five-year plans and the areas of national specialization. The process, however, is still lengthy, bureaucratic, and burdened by many obstacles (e.g., the basic problem of the quality of the products delivered under specialization agreements and their timely deliveries). Complicated regulations, including penalties for nonfulfillment of agreements, are expected to "gradually liquidate the existing parallelism in production of individual products in the CMEA member countries . . . [and] help to prevent starting new parallel production."[45]

The 29th session (1975) accepted the proposal concerning the preparation of the so-called "directional programs of coordination" for the most important sectors for periods from 10 to 15 years. These programs were the main topic of discussion at the 30th session (1976). They include: (1) the supply of energy, fuels, and industrial raw materials; (2) bilateral and multilateral coordination of the development of engineering industry on the basis of specialization and cooperation of production; (3) cooperation in agriculture and in the food industry; and (4) satisfaction of demand for manufactured consumption goods. Only a limited number of the most important tasks are included in the program, and the resources for their implementation must be secured in the national economic plans.[46]

Differences in the Pattern of Integration

At present, programs for further integration in both Western and Eastern Europe depend on international agreements. There are, however, two essential differences. First, the Soviet Union is the main supplier of fuels and raw materials and the main customer for many manufactured products, particularly machinery and equipment, produced by the newly established or greatly expanded industries in Eastern Europe. As such, the Soviet Union can exert considerable economic pressure to ensure a greater degree of complementarity of the industrial structure in order to improve the quality of products it imports, their modernity, and lower prices resulting from long runs of production. Political pressure can also be applied at the conferences of party leaders and during the bilateral talks that always precede formal Council meetings.[47]

The role of the US in Western Europe is different. Although the US exerted pressure to encourage economic integration in Western Europe for political reasons, it is not, like the Soviet Union, a member of the grouping. It cannot be expected to support a European industrial policy based on administrative measures which has as its main objective closing the technological gap and making Western Europe more competitive with Japan and the US.[48] While the American multinational corporations have been investing in the region and have established their subsidiaries in the EEC, particularly in advanced technology industries, the East European countries have been investing in the Soviet Union in primary-product exploitation.[49]

Because the Soviet Union can use economic and political pressure to promote integration, greater progress can be expected in the CMEA than in the EEC, whatever the degree of inefficiency such integration may involve. The CMEA countries may achieve a very high share of intra-bloc trade as the result of arbitrary decisions by the central planners which are incorporated into international agreements with the micro-efficiency considerations completely ignored. For CPEs, therefore, it is necessary to distinguish between the degree of integration, which can be measured by trade statistics, and "efficient integration." It is possible to enforce a higher level of integration and industrialization than would be achieved on the basis of micro-efficiency considerations. In both cases, there would be an adverse effect on national income.

The second difference is a relatively limited number of industries that are subject to national policies in the EEC, where the majority of economic activity is determined or at least seriously affected by the operation of market forces. In the CMEA, six years after the Comprehensive Program was adopted, those parts of the program that envisaged a greater role for financial and economic measures (as distinguished from administrative) have been behind schedule and have been deemphasized. The emphasis is now on administrative measures, such as coordination of national plans; joint forecasting; technological cooperation; joint planning in some sectors and types of production; and joint investments, particularly in fuels, raw materials, and some resource-intensive industries.[50] It is particularly difficult to use these methods in those sectors producing for the consumers' market, and joint ventures in that sector are particularly difficult without the operation of market signals.

In this sector, market forces operate strongly in the EEC, and the common market has been more successful here than in some basic advanced technology industries. On the other hand, in the CMEA countries, the administrative methods are easier to apply in a few high priority sectors. They may, therefore, succeed in accelerating the process of integration in some basic and advanced technology industries.

Some interesting differences can, therefore, be expected in the pattern of integration. To a certain extent, this pattern has already been established. Because of the differences between intra-CMEA and world prices, the share of intra-bloc exports may be biased differently from one year to another and from one group of commodities to another (see table 1).[51] There is also the problem of converting CMEA currencies into dollars and the degree of reliability of national statistical data reported to UN agencies. The picture presented by the table can, however, be accepted as fairly accurate.

TABLE 1

Average Share of Intrabloc Exports of the EEC and CMEA
by Major Commodity Groups, 1971-73

Commodity Group	EEC Share	CMEA Share	EEC Share as % of CMEA Share
Food, beverages, and tobacco (SITC 0 and 1)	66.9	46.3	144.5
Minerals, fuels, lubricants, and related materials (SITC 3)	63.9	46.7	136.8
Crude materials, excluding fuels, oils and fats (SITC 2 and 4)	67.5	46.2	146.1
Chemical products (SITC 5)	47.8	60.0	79.7
Machinery and equipment (SITC 7)	43.5	74.8	58.2
Other manufactured goods (SITC 6 and 8)	54.3	61.9	87.7
All groups (SITC 0-9)	51.7	59.6	86.7

SOURCES: Calculations based on statistics from UNCTAD, *Handbook of International Trade and Development Statistics* (New York, 1969); UN, *Yearbook of International Trade Statistics 1970-71* (New York, 1973): idem, *Yearbook of International Trade Statistics 1974,* vols. 1 and 2 (New York, 1975).

NOTE: EEC includes the nine present members, although three new members joined as of January 1, 1973.

If the average of the intra-bloc shares for 1971-73 are compared with all SITC commodity groups taken together, the EEC share represents 86.7% of the CMEA share. In three groups, however (food, beverages, and tobacco; minerals, fuels, and lubricants; and other raw materials), the EEC share is considerably above the CMEA share. In machinery and equipment, it is only 58.2% as large and in chemicals 79.7%. Price distortions may have some affect on the shares in some groups. Nevertheless, they would probably not explain the full extent of the difference.

It would, of course, be an oversimplification to assume that the greater share of intra-bloc export in the CMEA in machines, equipment, and chemicals reflects the adverse impact of national industrial policies and difficulties encountered in evolving a European policy within the EEC and a relative advantage in achieving integration by administrative methods in the CMEA. The EEC intra-bloc export shares exceed those of the CMEA in the so-called "hard commodities" area, where CMEA countries are usually able to find Western markets. These commodities are exported to pay for the necessary import of machines and equipment that are needed for the rapid development and modernization of the economies.[52] On the other hand, the export of machines and equipment to non-CMEA markets has usually been difficult not only because of commercial policy and psychological barriers, but because of the low quality and lack of technological sophistication of the products and special problems in marketing, servicing, supply of parts, and limited credit. For this reason, the intra-bloc share of this group usually tends to increase more rapidly than planned, while the plans for export to non-CMEA markets are underfulfilled.[53] Moreover, the EEC countries are important exporters of these commodities. They have "outgrown" the European market and need other markets.

It is, however, possible that the differences in the share of intra-bloc export are at least partly affected by the differences in the working of the integration mechanism. This mechanism seems to work better with respect to different types of products in each of the two groupings. The removal of the commercial policy barriers in the EEC and the common agricultural policy were particularly beneficial for integration with respect to foodstuffs. Here, the intra-EEC share of export represents 144.5% of the intra-CMEA share. There was probably a similarly strong effect in the two groups of raw materials in which the intra-EEC share is 146.1% (crude materials) and 136.8% (minerals, fuels, etc.) of the CMEA share. On the other hand, national industrial policies and the difficulties encountered in the evolution of a common industrial policy tend to create particularly strong obstacles for integration with respect to machines and equipment and, perhaps, some chemicals.

In the CMEA, the machine and chemical industries are priority sectors. Pressures from CMEA bodies and from the Soviet Union are probably particularly strong in this field. These industries are rapidly expanding, and at least some newly created productive capacities are built subject to multilateral and bilateral agreements (in the electrical and machine industry 27 multilateral specialization agreements and 180 bilateral specialization agreements were signed during the period 1968-75, a much greater number than in any other field).[54] They may also be affected by the coordination of national plans, joint planning in selected branches, and, more recently, joint investments. All these methods are effective only in a few priority sectors selected by the planners.

Some Evidence from the Steel Industry

Comparisons of the degree of complementarity in the industrial structure between the two groupings are difficult. Disaggregated data on production are scarce. They are expressed in value terms and are, therefore, distorted by price discrepancies. However, UN statistics on the steel industry are provided in physical units and are free from the price bias. As one of the basic industries, it is usually subject to national policies. Attempts have been made in both EEC and CMEA to replace these national policies with a regional multinational policy and to create an integrated regional industry.

The steel industry in Western Europe provides the best example of the inability of supranational authorities and market forces to increase complementarity of the industrial structure. This industry has been subject to the activity of supranational authorities and integration policies since 1951. At present, every member country is still determined to maintain an independent national steel industry and is trying to increase its competitiveness by restructuring with the help of public funds. It has been pointed out that "illusions that the creation of European Coal and Steel Community would overcome national identity and bring about pan-European specialization were quickly exploded."[55] In the opinion of at least some observers, the High Authority has not been able to develop supranational planning as expected, and it has had a relatively small impact on the long-run development of European coal and steel industries.[56] Although the degree of concentration has increased in member countries, with the encouragement and assistance of the High Authority and national governments, there is little evidence of a marked increase in international specialization, and the composition of the final output of the national industries has changed very little.[57]

During the 1970s, rapid technological progress in the steel industry, as well as some overcapacity in member countries, forced some structural changes, agreements, planning, mergers, rationalization, and regrouping.[58] Particularly important were such developments as an increase in the optimum size and a change in the optimum location to coastal areas. There was, therefore, an exceptionally good opportunity for an integrated international approach. This opportunity was, however, wasted.

> The instinct of most countries to retain a nationally controlled steel industry prevented any serious approach to a pan-European solution. The extent and direction of adjustments to the new situation were determined largely in the context of the national political process. The result was that the steel industries became no less autarkic than in the past. Their increases in efficiency were largely constrained by what could be achieved inside each national economy.[59]

A similar situation exists in the CMEA region. All East European countries established or expanded their steel industries during the industrialization drive of the early 1950s. In 1960, the metallurgical industry employed somewhat similar shares of the total industrial labor force in all East European countries: 5.0% in Bulgaria, 6.1% in Poland, 6.4% in GDR, 7.2% in Romania, 7.4% in Hungary, and 8.4% in Czechoslovakia. The range was actually slightly smaller than in the EEC, where it varied from 4.6% in Italy to 8.7% in the Federal Republic of Germany.[60]

In every East European country, attempts were made to establish as wide a product mix as necessary to meet domestic demand. This policy resulted in the creation of competitive rather than complementary productive capacities, which later seriously hampered attempts to develop specialization in the steel industry. Moreover, these parallel developments were responsible for similar shortages and surpluses that were appearing at the same time in every country, aggravating the overall shortage of certain products in the CMEA market or reducing the export prices of those products which those countries were attempting to export outside CMEA markets. It was only as the result of consultations within "Intermetal" (Organization for Cooperation in the Iron and Steel Industry established in 1964) and under the impact of the structure of deliveries to the Soviet Union that some restructuring was effected and "productive capacities were, to a certain extent, changed from competitive to partly complementary."[61]

While the range of the employment shares in metallurgy was even narrower in 1970 than in 1960 (5.7% in Bulgaria, 5.8% in Poland, 6.3% in GDR, 6.7% in Hungary, 6.8% in Romania, and 8.4% in Czechoslovakia), it widened considerably by 1973 (2.4% in Bulgaria, 5.7% in Poland, 6.1% in Romania, 7.0% in Hungary, 7.2% in GDR, and 8.6% in Czechoslovakia). In 1970, the range was already wider than in the EEC (4.6% in Italy and 7.5% in Germany), and the disparity became even wider in 1973 (4.8% in Italy and 7.2% in Germany).[62] However, employment shares are affected by differences in the productivity of labor, so the tendency for the CMEA range to increase and the EEC range to decline cannot be accepted as sufficient evidence that the degree of complementarity increased in the former and declined in the latter. In table 2, statistical comparisons are made among five EEC countries (original six without Luxemburg) and seven CMEA countries, both groups taken as blocs. Part A presents average shares of (1) crude steel in the total output of crude and finished steel products, and (2) groups of finished steel products. Part B presents coefficients of variation ($\frac{\sigma}{\bar{x}}$) for these sectors of the steel industry. A low numerical value of the index implies relatively similar percentage shares of product groups in the total output of finished steel products in the member countries of the bloc (i.e., a high degree of similarity in the structure of that industry). A high numerical value implies relatively big differences in the percentage shares (i.e., a high degree of complementarity).

TABLE 2

The Structure of Steel Production: EEC (Five) and CMEA (Seven)

Year	Crude Steel as % of Crude and Finished Steel (1)		Strips (2)		Plates (3)		Sheets (4)		Heavy Sections (5)		Light Sections (6)		Wire Rods (7)		Other Products (8)		Index of Coefficients of Variations (9)	
	EEC	CMEA	EEC	CMEA	EEC	CMEA	EEC	CMEA	EEC	CMEA	EEC	CMEA	EEC	CMEA	EEC	CMEA	EEC	CMEA
A. Average Shares ($\bar{x}$)																		
1954	55.56	57.24	6.64	3.93	16.78	10.67	18.04	7.97	5.42	13.67	24.84	25.64	9.62	13.69	18.66	24.43		
1960	54.38	59.00	6.18	3.83	15.22	14.86	24.50	8.20	4.46	16.36	21.64	24.46	9.42	11.50	18.58	20.80		
1965	55.40	55.81	5.90	5.10	14.70	20.03	28.12	12.10	5.42	16.39	20.70	24.79	9.36	7.77	15.80	13.83		
1970	55.24	58.40	5.97	5.31	15.64	21.59	29.12	12.20	5.42	13.60	21.32	20.60	8.82	9.53	14.06	17.17		
1974	54.46	56.89	5.00	5.11	17.26	26.50	29.88	10.81	5.44	13.40	18.64	17.94	9.16	9.90	14.62	16.37		
B. Coefficients of Variation ($\frac{\sigma}{x}$)																		
1954	.04	.04	.15	.74	.55	.49	.38	.51	.60	.40	.42	.27	.10	1.14	.28	.47	.35	.57
1960	.04	.03	.31	.63	.47	.52	.47	.27	.66	.51	.50	.28	.16	.99	.26	.52	.40	.53
1965	.02	.16	.30	.78	.25	.52	.54	.42	.59	.51	.44	.48	.30	.30	.22	.54	.33	.51
1970	.01	.04	.30	.73	.26	.34	.37	.42	.65	.62	.36	.37	.30	.22	.22	.38	.35	.44
1974	.02	.07	.46	.91	.37	.35	.35	.59	.77	.61	.50	.38	.34	.27	.43	.20	.46	.47

SOURCES: Calculations based on data originally expressed in thousands of tons. UN, *The European Steel Market in 1957* (Geneva, 1958), pp. 12, 13; idem', *The European Steel Market in 1958* (Geneva, 1959), pp. 44-45; idem', *The European Steel Market in 1961* (Geneva, 1962), pp. 64, 65; GUS, *Rocznik statystyczny przemyslu 1975* (Warsaw, 1975), pp. 234-35.

*Index of variation: average coefficients of variations (columns 2 to 8).

The average of the coefficients of variation for groups of finished steel products for each bloc (columns 2-8) is used as an index of overall complementarity in the two regions (column 9). The difference in the industrial structure may be affected by a number of factors that are independent from the influence of industrial integration: differences in the factor endowment of member countries and in their level of development; differences in the development of the steel industry in individual countries; the extent to which the steel industries of member countries compete in markets outside the region; and so on. At a lower level of development, a country would produce only a limited range of products, and an advanced country would have a diversified industrial structure. Similarly, a newly established steel industry would probably have a different structure than an old established one. If the members of a group are important exporters of steel to the third countries, they may have a more similar industrial structure than if they traded only among themselves. There should, therefore, be some differences in the degree of complementarity within the steel industry between the two regions. But when integration measures are applied and nothing else changes, each region can be expected to develop a more complementary structure than it had before.

The degree of disaggregation shown in the table is rather low. It may not be sufficient to discover the full extent of product specialization that can take place *within* the product groups. However, comparative data are available only at this level of disaggregation. There may also be an uneven degree of accuracy of basic data, and the quality may differ from one country to another and from one bloc to another.

Keeping in mind the above qualifications, it is possible to make some observations about the shares of crude and finished steel:

1. During 1954-74, crude steel represented a somewhat higher proportion of the total output of crude and finished products in the CMEA than in the EEC countries. This is probably related to the difference in the level of development of the steel industry in the two blocs, as a higher proportion of finished products is usually associated with a higher level of advancement.

2. There was no change in the degree of complementarity of the EEC countries between 1954 and 1960. Subsequently, these countries became less complementary.

3. The CMEA countries have not exhibited a definite long-term trend, although they became somewhat more complementary in 1974. The changing pattern is probably related to the rapid expansion of the steel industry in Eastern Europe in the form of the addition of relatively large units of productive capacity in various sectors of the industry.

4. The two blocs had the same degree of complementarity at the beginning of the period in 1954. CMEA countries were slightly less complementary than EEC countries in 1960 but more complementary in 1965, 1970, and 1974.

Comparing the structure of finished steel products in the two blocs suggests the following:

1. The relative shares of various product groups change considerably from one year to another in both regions. Coefficients of variation fluctuate more widely over time in CMEA than in EEC countries with respect to all product groups, except "strips" and "plates" (columns 2 and 3). Again, this may be a result of the rapid expansion with uneven growth of various sectors and the lumpiness of the process.

2. In 1954, the degree of overall complementarity of the structure of finished steel products, as measured by the index of coefficients of variation (column 9), was substantially higher in the CMEA than in the EEC. This could be the result of more uneven development of the steel industry in the former region. The difference between the two blocs in the numerical value of the index, however, declined and almost disappeared in 1974.

3. In the EEC countries, there was an increase in the degree of complementarity between 1954 and 1960, i.e., an early period of operation of the ECSC, and a decline in 1965 and in 1970, with a considerable improvement in 1974.

4. In the CMEA countries, the degree of overall complementarity of the structure of the output of finished products declined until 1970 with a reversal in 1974.

It seems, therefore, that the structure of the output of finished steel products in both economic groupings gradually became more competitive between 1954 and 1970 and that the trend reversed during the early 1970s. The decline in the degree of complementarity in the CMEA from the extremely high 1954 level can perhaps be regarded as inevitable during the period of rapid economic development, based on high investment ratios and a relatively high steel-intensive pattern of domestic production. With rapidly growing domestic demand for steel, greater opportunities were probably created for the expansion of various sectors of the steel industry to serve domestic needs. Despite the decline in the degree of complementarity, CMEA countries were not in a position any worse than the EEC countries in 1974. The absence of supranational authorities and the lack of market forces do not seem to lead to different results. It is possible, therefore, that the differences in the mechanism of integration may be less important than some basically similar national policies with respect to this particular industry.

The relatively high degree of complementarity in the structure of

TABLE 3

Finished Steel Products: Ratios of Export to Total Output
(thousands of tons)

CMEA		1966	1974	EEC			1966	1974
Bulgaria	Export	592*	669	Belgium	Export		9,063	14,257‡
	Output	1,251*	2,240	and Luxembourg	Output		11,084	15,959‡
	% Ratio	47.32	29.87		% Ratio		81.77	89.34
Czechoslovakia	Export	2,455	280	France	Export		6,248	8,598
	Output	7,590	9,087		Output		15,822	21,897
	% Ratio	32.35	3.08		% Ratio		39.49	39.27
GDR	Export	341†	1,334	Germany, FR	Export		9,674	19,702
	Output	3,075†	3,875		Output		27,281	43,163
	% Ratio	11.09	34.43		% Ratio		35.46	45.65
Hungary	Export	874	717	Italy	Export		2,114	4,303
	Output	2,556	2,928		Output		11,349	20,091
	% Ratio	34.19	24.49		% Ratio		18.63	21.42
Poland	Export	1,443	1,408	Netherlands	Export		2,134	3,102
	Output	7,939	10,914		Output		2,599	5,151
	% Ratio	18.18	12.90		% Ratio		82.11	60.22
Romania	Export	943	1,388					
	Output	3,816	5,833					
	% Ratio	24.71	23.80					
USSR	Export	6,970	5,809					
	Output	77,634	95,885					
	% Ratio	8.98	6.06					

SOURCES: UN, *Quarterly Bulletin of Steel Statistics for Europe* 21:1 (1970), 23, 4 (1972), 24:4 (1974); idem, *Statistics of World Trade in Steel 1974* (New York: United Nations, 1975); GUS, *Rocznik statystyki miedzynarodowej 1973* [Yearbook of international statistics] (Warsaw, 1973); idem, *Rocznik statystyczny przemyslu* [Statistical yearbook of industry 1975] (Warsaw, 1975).

* 1969   † 1967   ‡ 1972

TABLE 4
Export of Steel (Semifinished and Finished) to Other Bloc Countries

A. Average Size of Product Groups

Year	Ingots & Semis		Railway Track Material		Heavy & Light Sections		Wire Rods		Strip		Plates & Sheets		Steel Tubes & Fittings		Wire		Tinplate		Wheels Tyres & Axles		Index at variation	
	EEC	CMEA	EEC	CMEA	EEC	CMEA	EEC	CMEA	EEC	CMEA	EEC	CMEA	EEC	CMEA	EEC	CMEA	EEC	CMEA	EEC	CMEA	EEC	CMEA
1950	9.10	8.33	9.62	13.47	25.34	26.93	4.48	4.70	4.94	3.00	12.28	13.73	26.38	8.80	2.72	1.63	3.20	.00	1.94	4.40		
1958	29.46	13.37	1.54	10.63	22.14	18.23	6.94	.93	6.56	.67	26.20	33.50	3.38	19.00	.72	.93	3.00	.23	.04	2.53		
1969	20.10	7.60	.82	1.50	25.04	31.21	6.48	3.37	4.30	2.09	30.22	34.14	8.54	17.63	1.24	.39	2.08	.84	.04	.51		
1974	22.74	4.86	.86	2.10	21.64	35.92	6.16	7.02	4.70	3.26	27.52	31.18	13.00	13.42	1.56	.78	1.68	.52	.06	.90		

B. Coefficients of Variation $\left(\frac{\sigma}{\chi}\right)$

Year	Ingots & Semis		Railway Track Material		Heavy & Light Sections		Wire Rods		Strip		Plates & Sheets		Steel Tubes & Fittings		Wire		Tinplate		Wheels Tyres & Axles		Index at variation	
	EEC	CMEA	EEC	CMEA	EEC	CMEA	EEC	CMEA	EEC	CMEA	EEC	CMEA	EEC	CMEA	EEC	CMEA	EEC	CMEA	EEC	CMEA	EEC	CMEA
1950	.74	1.48	1.00	1.31	.74	.44	.72	.31	.69	1.40	.67	.05	1.41	.39	1.11	.02	1.48	.00	1.47	.61	1.00	.60
1958	.63	.96	1.58	.09	.59	.63	.63	1.55	.65	.23	.07	.77	.69	.69	.85	1.38	.84	1.76	2.24	.84	.88	.89
1969	.53	1.35	.79	1.49	.52	.38	.71	.73	.64	.92	.17	.45	.57	.92	.49	1.16	.85	2.00	1.37	1.52	.66	1.09
1974	.46	.77	1.13	1.28	.54	.37	.83	.41	.28	.98	.23	.29	.67	.79	.60	1.55	.61	1.64	1.49	.61	.68	.87

SOURCES: Calculations based on data originally expressed in thousands of tons. UN, *Statistics of World Trade in Steel 1913–59* (Geneva, 1961); idem, *Statistics of World Trade in Steel in 1969* (New York, 1970); idem, *Statistics of World Trade in Steel in 1974* (New York, 1975).

NOTE: CMEA: 1950 and 1958, 3 countries (Czechoslovakia, Poland, USSR); 1969, 7 countries (GDR 1967); 1974, 6 countries (excluding Romania).

production of finished steel products in CMEA countries does not seem to have much impact on the involvement in foreign trade. Table 3 compares the export-output ratios in this industry in the two economic groupings. Between the late 1960s and the early 1970s in all CMEA countries, except GDR, these ratios declined. They increased in all EEC countries except France, where they remained approximately stable, and the Netherlands, where they declined. In 1974, the export-output ratios were substantially lower in the CMEA countries than in the EEC. It appears that the earlier autarkic tendencies have not yet been eliminated in the CMEA. On the other hand, the EEC countries have been expanding their production for export more rapidly than for the domestic market.

Table 4 presents the average size of product groups in the intra-bloc trade (part A) and coefficients of variation (part B), as well as an index of variations (average of the coefficients of variation). Again, the degree of disaggregation is relatively low and cannot show specialization within the commodity groups. Moreover, the reliability of data may not be the same for all countries. Comparisons between the two regions, therefore, should be made with caution.

In 1950, the EEC started with a higher degree of complementarity of exports than the four CMEA countries listed. The latter were quite competitive at that time. While the EEC structure of exports became more similar in 1958 and in 1969, however, the CMEA structure became more complementary. In both regions, the trend was reversed in 1974. Except for 1954, the CMEA countries appear to have a higher degree of complementarity in the product structure of the intra-bloc trade than that found in the EEC countries.

A tentative conclusion is that, although the CMEA countries tend to export a smaller share of their total output of semi-finished and finished steel than do EEC countries, a larger part of their trade in this area is directed to other members of the region and both their production structure and the structure of their intra-bloc exports have a higher degree of complementarity. The structure of intra-bloc trade in steel products in EEC countries became less complementary by the middle of the 1970s than it was in 1950, while in CMEA countries it became more complementary.

The evidence from developments in the steel industry in EEC seems to support the view that those sectors that are subject to national industrial policies have not fully benefited from the removal of tariff obstacles and that it is not easy to implement the regional industrial policy and a complementary industrial structure even when there are some well-established supranational authorities. This is not, therefore, an important difference between EEC and CMEA.

Discussion

Carl H. McMillan

Professor Fallenbuchl draws our attention to the impact national industrialization strategies have had on the processes of integration in Western and in Eastern Europe. His central concern is with an hypothesis that might be formulated as follows: We can expect to find less divergence between Western and Eastern Europe in their relative progress toward regional economic integration in those sectors where national industrial policies are known to have played an especially strong role. He proceeds to investigate this hypothesis by describing and comparing national industrial policies and the efforts to harmonize them through inter-governmental agreements. He then focuses on the steel industry, which he feels provides a particularly apt example, and adds a quantitative dimension to the institutional evidence assembled.

The hypothesis is based on the assumption that the removal of artificial national barriers to the interplay of market forces constitutes an easier route to integration than the harmonization of national economic and social policies. In John Pinder's terminology,[1] "negative" integration is more readily achieveable than "positive" integration, since the automaticity and anonymity of the market, when available, provide a more effective mechanism for integration than the conscious, and inevitably highly politicized, coordination of national policies. Therefore, measures to reduce or remove tariff barriers to intra-regional trade are likely to have a more immediate and consequential impact on the integrative process than efforts to coordinate sectoral development strategies at the regional level through inter-governmental agreement.

According to this view, in comparison with Western Europe, integration in Eastern Europe would appear to suffer a dual handicap. To the extent that national planning has been substituted for market forces, Eastern Europe lacks recourse to negative means of integration. Lacking the supranational competence of the European Commission, the CMEA cannot dispose of comparable mechanisms to advance the process of positive integration. This leads to the prediction that while the process of integration will lag generally in Eastern Europe, the divergence will be less significant in those sectors where market forces have played a lesser role in both East and West, and which have been the focus of particular efforts in the East to coordinate national planning. Moreover, with the first, "negative" phase of West European integration completed, one would expect the problems faced by regional authorities in the two parts of Europe to be increasingly similar.

Fallenbuchl points out that in important sectors of industry, national economic policies have severely circumscribed market forces in Western Europe; so that even with the establishment of a customs union, powerful nontariff barriers to regional trade have remained. At the same time, national policies have tended to limit the effective competence of Brussels in these areas. In sum, national policies have limited both market forces and supranational authority in some sectors of West European industry. Here, differences between the institutional environments for integration in Eastern and Western Europe are less apparent. On the Eastern side, national policies have similarly fostered parallel industrial development and have obstructed efforts to introduce a planned pattern of industrial specialization among members.

Fallenbuchl provides us with an informative account of institutional and policy developments in the two regions. In so doing, he draws a number of parallels that contribute very much to the interest of his paper. These parallels serve to remind us that, despite systemic differences, the two regional organizations reflect the increasingly mixed nature of the economies that they span.

In his discussion of the processes of integration in Western Europe, Fallenbuchl emphasizes agreements at the national level and tends to discount the importance of long-term contractual agreements between firms within the region. Like regional trade ties, he regards these as having been adversely affected by national industrial policies, and quotes EEC data covering the period 1961-69 which show that intra-regional production agreements and mergers were overshadowed by agreements with other national firms or with firms outside the community. Others, however, have taken a more positive view of the integrative effect of intra-EEC cooperation at the enterprise level, and scattered evidence suggests an upturn in this activity in the early 1970s.[2]

The specialization in production and trade resulting from such relationships tends to occur within industrial sectors, as participating firms concentrate production on a narrower range of intermediate or final products and exchange them under the terms of inter-firm trade agreements. While the major aim of such arrangements is to reap economies in production, they can also be viewed as an accommodation tothe non-tariff barriers to regional trade, which Fallenbuchl stresses.[3] The industrial policies of member-states which encourage the growth of national champions also lead them ultimately to extend their horizons beyond national boundaries and thus indirectly foster transnational business collaboration. On the other hand, efforts of supranational actors at the regional level to maintain the competitiveness of regional markets may, by impeding transnational mergers, have a disintegrative impact. Therefore, at both the national and regional levels, the impact of sectoral policies on the process of regional integration through inter-firm cooperation would appear to warrant more complex analysis.

Regardless of how much integrative significance one attaches to such inter-firm relationships, they have been consciously emulated in Eastern Europe. Since the adoption of the 1971 Comprehensive Program, CMEA policies have encouraged the establishment of direct international links between operational, as opposed to administrative, economic institutions in member countries in order to speed up the process of regional specialization.[4] This new regional policy emphasis can also be regarded as having run into serious obstacles—some rooted in special conditions obtaining in Eastern Europe, others analogous to the national policy obstacles to regional inter-firm links that Fallenbuchl sees in Western Europe. Parallels might be drawn, for example, between the East European experience and the thesis cited by Fallenbuchl that Western European experience has shown collaboration between state enterprises to be inherently more difficult to achieve than between private firms.

In the concluding section of his paper, Fallenbuchl undertakes some comparisons of the structure of production and trade in the steel industry in the two regions. He selects steel as the focal industry because it has been subject in both regions to intensive national industrial policies as well as to attempts "to replace these national policies by a regional multinational policy, and to create an integrated regional industry." While careful to point out the limitations of the measures he uses, Fallenbuchl reaches the conclusion that national industrial policies have indeed tended to offset any institutional advantages enjoyed by the EEC over the CMEA in terms of mechanisms for negative and positive integration. On the contrary, in the one sector analyzed in any detail, the author paradoxically finds more statistical evidence of CMEA than of EEC integration.

Fallenbuchl's central thesis may well be valid. Certainly it matches the contemporary mood of skepticism, if not pessimism, with regard to the continued progress of West European integration, and the current tendency to take a second, more appreciative look at the accomplishments of the CMEA. Nevertheless, I would regard the evidence which he assembles as inadequate to support his conclusions.

The empirical investigation of a hypothesis of such scope is an ambitious task and necessarily raises a host of conceptual as well as technical problems. The paper focuses on the effects of differences in the institutional mechanisms for integration in the two regional systems. However, there are other important determinants of the comparative structures of production and trade in the two regions at any point in time. The two differ importantly in endowment and distribution of productive resources, in national and regional economic and political objectives, in the timing of the processes of their development and integration, and in the structure of their membership. To pursue the last briefly, a major difference noted by Fallenbuchl is the inclusion of a dominant actor on the Eastern side. But is the presence of the USSR an integrative factor as he suggests, or is the asymmetry that it imposes on regional structures not likely to have a significant divisive impact as well? In sum, can a simple comparison of the regional patterns of production and trade in the two groupings, based on the statistical measures used, tell us very much about the effects of institutional differences or similarities?

The case is further weakened by its reliance on evidence from only one sector. Moreover, the definition of integration introduced at the outset (the "process of creating economic dependence that is complementary") is not sufficiently rigorous to serve as an adequate reference point for the analysis. "Dependence" and "complementarity" are both ambiguous, and their relationships to specialization in production and in trade are not clearly developed in the paper. As a result, measures such as the share of intra-bloc exports or the coefficient of variation among members in production shares are not firmly grounded in a single, well-defined concept of integration.[5]

Moreover, complementarity and competitiveness are functions of the level of aggregation at which the statistical investigation is conducted. Fallenbuchl mentions this, but his analysis does not effectively cope with the problem. What he interprets as increased competitiveness may in fact conceal a trend toward greater specialization within commodity groups. He finds, for example, that country shares of intra-bloc trade in major groups of steel products become more similar over time for the EEC countries and less varied than the corresponding shares for the CMEA countries at most points in time investigated. However, given the level of aggregation maintained and the statistical measures employed, Fallenbuchl appears to be overlooking important patterns of intra-industry specialization that have emerged as a result of the removal of trade barriers under the ECSC.[6]

Whether or not the central hypothesis gains much support from the statistical analysis, it remains an interesting and important one. There have been all too few attempts to contrast the effectiveness of policies and instruments for regional integration in different contexts. Fallenbuchl's sectoral approach to the problem and his concern for both its institutional and quantitative dimensions establish useful precedents for further comparative studies in regional integration.

Jan Vaňous

An Econometric Model of Intra-CMEA Foreign Trade

This paper presents the results of an attempt to build an econometric model of intra-CMEA foreign trade.[1] It is a seven-country, four-commodity model, containing 56 equations (28 for exports and 28 for imports) and 24 identities. All nontrade variables and foreign-trade prices (ftp's) are assumed to be exogenous. The model uses the so-called "reservoir" or "pool" approach, in which exports are not distinguished by country of destination and imports are not distinguished by country of origin.

Trade flows are modeled separately for "hard" goods (raw materials and food) and "soft" goods (machinery and industrial consumer goods). Hard goods are readily salable on the world market without substantial price concessions from current world market prices (wmp's). Soft goods, when salable at all, require significant price concessions to compensate for their relatively lower quality in comparison with Western manufactures. Trade in hard goods has been characterized by persistent excess demand, trade in soft goods by excess supply. Consequently, exports of hard goods are modeled as supply-determined and imports of soft goods as demand-determined.

The principal explanatory variables in demand and supply equations are domestic activity, relative prices, bilateral balancing, and dummy variables. Rationing equations typically contain the total volume of intra-CMEA trade in a particular commodity group and sup-

In writing this paper, I benefited from numerous discussions with Professors John M. Montias and Paul Marer. Professor Herbert S. Levine of the University of Pennsylvania read the first draft and suggested several revisions. I also benefited from comments and suggestions by Professor Lawrence R. Klein of the University of Pennsylvania, Professor Edward Hewett of the University of Texas at Austin, Dr. Jozef M. van Brabant of the United Nations in New York, and participants in the Bloomington conference.

ply- or demand-pressure variables as key explanatory variables. Domestic activity variables are included to test the sensitivity of trade flows to changes in domestic economic activity (industrial and agricultural output, investment rate, retail sales of consumer goods). The presence of relative prices is justified by the belief that central planners make trade decisions that take into account (probably incorrect) relative prices as scarcity signals. Bilateral balancing variables (lagged exports and imports) are included to test the proposition that commodity trade is balanced on a bilateral basis and to introduce a trade-balancing mechanism into the model. Dummy variables represent temporary shifts in functional relationships due to other exogenous factors. Supply- and demand-pressure variables are used as proxies for the unknown scarcity prices.

We are interested in discovering whether the intra-CMEA trade flows behave in a systematic fashion and what their most important explanatory variables are. If successful, the model could be used as linking equations for a set of national econometric models of CMEA economies. In view of the rising importance of the foreign-trade sector and the increasing participation of CMEA economies in world trade, the construction of such a set of models is necessary to understand their functioning and to predict their future economic performance. Interest in analysis of Soviet and East European foreign trade should move away from the construction of untestable theories and theorizing without measurement. The results presented below indicate that the validity of at least one widely accepted theory—that the foreign-trade sector in centrally planned economies (CPEs) plays the role of a "buffer" in the economy and the concurrent assumption that relative prices play no significant role as a determinant of trade flows—has to be seriously questioned.

This paper discusses the principal characteristics of the foreign-trade sector and the behavior of central planners with respect to foreign trade. It then presents and explains the model and briefly describes the data used in its construction. A summary section follows, which discusses the empirical results of the model and offers a few suggestions for improvement.

The Foreign-Trade Sector and the Nature of Intra-CMEA Trade

Institutional Background

The foreign trade of CPEs is characterized by:
1. State foreign-trade monopoly.
2. Centralized planning and centralized decision of major foreign-trade activities.

3. Virtually complete separation of the domestic market from the world market and consequent separation of domestic prices from ftp's.

4. Use of disequilibrium and non-scarcity ftp's divergent from wmp's, and consequent extensive use of quantitative restrictions on imports and exports in intra-CMEA trade.

5. Strong tendencies toward bilateral balancing of total trade and trade in each commodity group in the absence of the usual mechanism for balancing trade based on adjustable exchange rates and flexible prices.

6. Absence of meaningful exchange rates between national devisa currencies and the transferable ruble (TR), and between national devisa currencies and domestic currencies.

7. Importance of political considerations in foreign-trade decisions.

In particular, foreign-trade corporations carry out fairly detailed orders received from the Ministry of Foreign Trade, which receives orders from the Central Planning Board. Foreign-trade corporations export and import commodities at ftp's, but they buy from and sell to production and internal trade enterprises at domestic wholesale prices, which are typically unrelated to ftp's. The resulting transactional losses or extraordinary profits are offset by subsidies from or taxes to a "price equalization" fund, which is a part of the government budget. Production and internal trade enterprises make no significant foreign-trade decisions. They do not know and typically do not care about actual transactional ftp's or their domestic currency equivalents. Consequently, export-supply and import-demand functions are not functions of decentralized units, but rather of central planners. Under these circumstances, the model of intra-CMEA trade presented below concentrates on the behavior of central planners and omits the analysis of the interaction between central planners and decentralized units with respect to the foreign-trade sector.

Pricing

Since ftp's in intra-CMEA trade can be modeled independently of foreign-trade flows, they are assumed to be exogenous to the model. They are primarily a vehicle for the distribution of gains from trade rather than signals of relative scarcities on the CMEA market. According to rather vague CMEA rules for price formation in effect until 1975, intra-CMEA ftp's were based on lagged averages of wmp's, revised periodically (every five years) and purged of various negative influences of capitalist markets, such as monopoly influences, temporary speculative trends, and short-term and cyclical influences.[2]

It is generally accepted that intra-CMEA price levels and relative price ratios deviate significantly and systematically from wmp's. Hard goods have historically been underpriced in relation to soft goods compared to the relative prices of these goods on the world market. There are several explanations for this: (1) the special CMEA price rule introduced in the early 1950s; (2) the presence of a seller's market in CMEA; (3) unrealistic exchange rates; (4) the transportation rule; and (5) the use of commodity bilateralism.[3]

The persistent bias in the intra-CMEA ftp structure, favoring exports of manufactures to exports of raw materials and food, has led to strong substitution effects in the structure of intra-CMEA trade. The bias in the CMEA ftp structure has encouraged intra-CMEA trade in manufactures and discouraged trade in raw materials and food.[4] This was reinforced by the possibility that CMEA countries could divert their exports of raw materials and food to markets of capitalist countries, while trying to sell their manufactures, particularly machinery, within CMEA. Simultaneously, CMEA countries (except the USSR) have tried to import Western machinery products, while demanding ever-increasing amounts of fuels, raw materials, and food from within CMEA. This has led to the well-known conflict between net importers of hard goods—Czechoslovakia, East Germany, Hungary, and Poland—and net exporters of these goods—the USSR, Bulgaria, and Romania. The USSR has particularly felt this pressure.

In its trade with other CMEA countries, the USSR decides to export certain amounts of raw materials.[5] Given these amounts and intra-CMEA ftp's, there are corresponding amounts of imports of manufactures that the USSR is willing to accept. Unlike the standard trade model, in which the small country determines the volume of trade, in this case it is the large country that does so. It follows that trade in raw materials between the USSR and the rest of CMEA is supply-determined, while trade in manufactures is demand-determined. The same assumption is made about trade between small East European countries on the grounds that a rational central planner will attempt to avoid exporting hard goods to a market in which they are relatively underpriced and will try to limit imports of soft goods from a market in which they are relatively overpriced.

The Balancing Mechanism

In the short run, central planners have two direct intervention tools to eliminate a deficit in the balance-of-trade: export drives and quantitative restrictions on imports. Both tend to involve soft goods; because of strong bilateral tendencies in intra-CMEA trade, exports of soft goods can be generally increased only if imports are increased. Similarly, imports can be lowered only if exports are lowered. Thus, the net result, if any, is likely to be negligible.

In the long run, balanced trade is achieved through a special form of quantitative restrictions on trade, namely bilateral balancing of trade flows by commodity groups (except food). In intra-CMEA trade, bilateral balancing is generally applied by two commodity groups—hard and soft goods—and typically on the margin only, i.e., to increases in trade.[6] Perfect bilateral balancing on the margin guarantees the maintenance of the trade balance at the original level. Even if not applied perfectly, such as when it is applied only to a fraction of the margin, bilateral balancing will have a stabilizing effect on the size of the trade balance. Imbalances in overall trade flows must be eliminated in the long run through special trade arrangements (ad hoc trade deals) between partner countries.[7]

The Model

Identifying Demand and Supply Functions

Any model of intra-CMEA trade must be a disequilibrium model because the quantity traded in the market will not satisfy the demand and supply schedules simultaneously. The disequilibrium nature of the market is taken into account by separating the sample of observations into demand and supply regimes so that each schedule may be appropriately fitted against the observed quantity for the sample points falling within its regime.

There are several methods for finding the optimal separation of the sample into demand and supply regimes. The directional method assumes that the direction of the price change is an indicator of the status of the market. An increase (decrease) in the relative price of a good implies the presence of excess demand (supply). The quantitative method also assumes that the amount of the price change is directly proportional to the amount of excess demand. In the absence of any information on how prices are set and how they are related to the excess-demand or excess-supply status of the market, the maximum likelihood method can be used to find the optimal sample separation.[8]

Since the direction of the movement of intra-CMEA ftp's cannot be assumed to indicate the status of the particular market in view of how intra-CMEA ftp's are set, only the last method could possibly be used to identify demand and supply functions. Unfortunately, likelihood functions are frequently not well behaved and do not converge to a global maximum, and efficient computational algorithms are not available. Since an exhaustive search over all possible separations was infeasible because of its cost, it was necessary to develop a new separation technique.

The separation technique chosen for the model was:

$$Q_{it}^d \gtreqless Q_{it}^s \text{ , if } \frac{P_{it}^{CMEA} \times QA_{it}^{CMEA}}{P_t^{CMEA} / P_t^{world}} \lesseqgtr P_{it}^{world}$$

for manufacturers ($i=1,4$; $t=1,2,...,T$)

$$\text{if}^4 \quad \frac{P_{it}^{CMEA}}{P_t^{CMEA} / P_t^{world}} \lesseqgtr P_{it}^{world}$$

for primary goods ($i=2,3$; $t=1,2,...,T$) [1]

Subscript i denotes the commodity group, P_t represents the overall price level, and P_{it} represents the price of commodity i in year t. QA_{it}^{CMEA} represents the quality-adjustment factor for CMEA commodity i in year t. This sample-separation technique is the price-differential method. The commodity is assumed to be in excess supply if its absolute intra-CMEA ftp exceeds the wmp and in excess demand if it is below the wmp (at official exchange rates). In this technique, all CMEA ftp's are adjusted for the overvaluation of the TR, arising from the difference between the average intra-CMEA ftp and the average wmp level, as represented by the ratio (P_t^{CMEA}/P_t^{world}). Otherwise, at times all CMEA prices exceeded wmp's, leading to the incorrect conclusion that markets for all commodities in CMEA were characterized by a state of excess demand.

The rationale for the price-differential method is the assumption that a rational planner making decisions with respect to the territorial pattern of trade will attempt to export a given commodity to a market in which it is relatively overpriced and import a given commodity from a market in which it is relatively underpriced. This is a simplified view that cannot take into account "tied" sales of bundles of goods containing both soft and hard components, different degrees of "hardness" or "softness" within each commodity group, etc. As a first approximation, however, it should be a fairly realistic description of how central planners in CMEA countries behave.

According to calculation [1] for each country's intra-CMEA trade by four different commodity groups, during 1960-74 the intra-CMEA market for machinery and industrial consumer goods was in a state of persistent excess supply and raw materials and food were in persistent excess demand. In the case of manufactures, the average rate of quality adjustment QA_{it}^{CMEA} was assumed to be 1.33.[9] The separation technique was not sensitive to different assumptions about the size of the quality-adjustment factor for different countries. Specifically, the assumption of lower adjustment factors for the more developed CMEA countries (Czechoslovakia, East Germany, and Hungary) and higher adjustment factors for the rest of CMEA, in view of its lower level of economic development and quality of output of manufactures, had no effect on the results of sample separation.

It is possible that some observations in the above markets fell into an atypical status of the particular market, i.e., excess supply for hard goods or excess demand for soft goods, and the separation technique did not pick them up. The error committed by assuming either perfect supply or demand determination will lead to biased estimates of parameters of the supply and the demand function, although this bias should be small since it is proportional to the number of incorrectly placed observations in a sample. As a result, the estimated demand and supply functions will be somewhat less price-elastic than the true functions.

The Import-Demand Function

CMEA countries are characterized by different degrees of sophistication in their foreign-trade planning methods.[10] Under a general model of a CMEA country's central planner, it is postulated that the planner's demand function is of the following general form:

$$\frac{MIJE_t^d}{PMIJE_t} = MIJE^d \, [AVIJ_t, \, DPMIJ_t, \, (PMIJE_t/PIJ_t), \, (PMIJE_t/\overline{PIJ}_t),$$
$$(PMIJE_t/PMIJM_t), \, (PMIJE_t/PMLJE_t), \, XIJE_t/PXIJE_t)$$

or

$$(XIJE_{t-1}/PXIJE_{t-1}), \, (XLJE_t/PXLJE_t)$$

or

$$(XLJE_{t-1}/PXLJE_{t-1})]$$

$$(I,L=1,2,3,4; \, I \neq L; \, J=B,C,G,H,P,R,U), \hspace{2cm} [2]$$

where $MIJE_t^d$ is the demand of central planners in country J for imports of commodity I from CMEA (E = Eastern Europe) in year t; $PMIJE_t$ is the import price of commodity I imported by country J from within CMEA; $AVIJ_t$ is the activity variable relevant for the use or consumption of commodity I in country J (such as the investment rate determining the volume of desired machinery imports and retail sales of consumer goods determining the volume of imports of industrial consumer goods); $DPMIJ_t$ is the indicator of demand pressure for imports of commodity I in country J; PIJ_t and $\overline{PIJ}_t$ are the actual domestic wholesale and scarcity (shadow) prices of commodity I in country J; $PMIJM_t$ is the import price of commodity I imported by country J from an alternative market (M = MDCs); and $XIJE_t$ and $PXIJE_t$ are exports of commodity I by country J to CMEA and their prices. Thus, it is suggested that the demand for imports is a function of three groups of variables: (1) domestic activity, (2) demand pressure and relative prices, and (3) bilateral balancing, represented by the current and lagged exports of commodities I and L.

Naturally, it is neither believed that all variables included in [2] influence central planners' demand at all times in all countries, nor is it empirically possible to test the significance of all explanatory variables. First, central planners' demand for imports of commodity *I* must be influenced by the trend in the activity variable requiring imports of commodity *I*. For example, the investment pattern may be such that a constant fraction of investment goods has to be imported.

Central planners are also likely to look at the relative cost of an imported commodity, unless they operate in a completely primitive manner. Ideally, they should compare the relative cost of the imported commodity to its cost if domestically produced (measured at scarcity prices), i.e., the ratio $(PMIJE/\overline{PIJ}_t)$. Since scarcity price $\overline{PIJ}_t$ may not be known to them, they may substitute the actual domestic wholesale price PIJ_t. However, there are two reasons for excluding either type of the relative price variable from [2]. First, observations on PIJ_t are difficult to obtain, and observations on $\overline{PIJ}_t$ are impossible to obtain for CMEA countries. Second, even if these could be obtained, there is reason to believe *a priori* that relative price elasticities with respect to these two types of relative price variables are low because of the nature of imports in CPEs. Central planners in CMEA countries are inclined to import only complementary goods, not substitutes that would compete with relatively expensive domestically produced goods. If the bulk of imports is complementary goods, their domestic scarcity price $\overline{PIJ}$ is very high or infinite. Then the ratio $(PMIJE_t/\overline{PIJ}_t)$ approaches zero, and the relative price variable may be excluded.

If we are not able to obtain observations on the relative scarcity price ratio $(PMIJE_t/\overline{PIJ}_t)$ and if we have reason to believe that some imports are substitute rather than complementary goods, then we should use a proxy for the domestic pressure to import to replace the effect of the excluded variable $\overline{PIJ}_t$. Variable $DPMIJ_t$ might, for example, relate the trend (short-run, long-run, or both) in variable $AVIJ_t$ to the trend in domestic output of commodity *I* in country *J*, i.e., OIJ_t. The simplest version of a short-run proxy may be:

$$DPSMIJ_t = (AVIJ_t/AVIJ_{t-1}) - (OIJ_t/OIJ_{t-1}) \qquad [3]$$

and

$$DPMIJ_t = (AVIJ_t - OIJ_t) \qquad [4]$$

for the long-run pressure. Either type of demand-pressure variable should be correlated with the domestic scarcity price $\overline{PIJ}_t$, and their variation should help to explain the cyclical aspects of imports of commodity *I* by country *J*.

The remaining relative prices that may influence demand for imports of commodity I by country J from CMEA are the import price of good I relative to its import price from another market (such as from MDCs), i.e., $(PMIJE_t/PMIJM_t)$, and the import price of good I relative to the import price of good L $(I \neq L)$, i.e., $(PMIJE_t/PMLJE_t)$. The inclusion of the former variable in [2] is justified if the products obtained from the two markets, i.e., from within CMEA and from the West, are substitutable. Since any commodity purchased from a CMEA country can also be purchased on the world market (in MDCs), its inclusion as an explanatory variable is certainly warranted. The latter relative price variable should be included if we believe that central planners exhibit some flexibility in their import decisions and compare relative import prices of major commodity categories of imports.

Finally, the application of some form of bilateral balancing on the margin in intra-CMEA trade justifies the inclusion of either current or lagged export variables in import-demand equations. The choice of these variables as proxies for bilateral balancing depends on whether the balancing is simultaneous or whether it takes place with a one-year lag. The presence of these variables in trade equations ensures that imports do not "explode," but grow steadily without creating significant trade imbalances. No argument is made here that the balancing mechanism operates uniformly vis-à-vis the CMEA partners jointly. Rather, the interpretation of coefficients attached to the proxies for bilateral balancing by commodity groups is that they represent an *average* degree of bilateral balancing on the margin.

Since bilateral balancing by commodity groups is not applied with perfect regularity, some trade imbalances have to be settled through a different type of mechanism, such as special trade deals. Furthermore, development credits are occasionally granted to a particular CMEA country, in which case the deficit of the debtor and the surplus of the creditor may be larger than usual. At other times, a certain CMEA country may be asked to repay accumulated debts (deficits) by increasing its exports and creating a special surplus. This part of the balancing mechanism can only be explained by dummy variables.

The Export-Supply Function

The concept of a supply function for central planners is more problematic. On the one hand, central planners are monopolists, and monopoly does not have a supply function; it chooses a point of supply on the demand curve that maximizes profit for the monopolist, a point determined by the elasticity of the demand curve. On the other hand, central planners who rely primarily on material balances for resource allocation must have some sort of a supply function indicating how much of a particular commodity they are willing to export in order to be able to import. The most general form such a supply function takes is:

$$\frac{XIJE_t^x}{PXIJE_t} = XIJE^x \, [OIJ_t, \, SPXIJ_t, \, (PXIJE_t/PIJ_t), \, (PXIJE_t/\overline{PIJ}_t),$$

$$(PXIJE_t/PXIJM_t), \, PXIJE_t/PXILE_t), \, (MIJE_t/PMIJE_t)$$

or

$$(MIJE_{t-1}/PMIJE_{t-1}), \, (MLJE_t/PMLJE_t)$$

or

$$(MLJE_{t-1}/PMLJE_{t-1})]$$

$$(I, \, L = 1,2,3,4; \, I \neq L; \, J = B,C,G,H,P,R,U). \tag{5}$$

The most prominent variable in the central planners' supply function of commodity I is its domestic output in country J, OIJ_t (e.g., in the case of raw-material exports, this would be the domestic output of raw materials). This is natural to postulate in view of the importance of material balances in the planning procedure.

Since it is believed that central planners take into account the relative profitability of an exported commodity, although probably incorrectly calculated, various relative price variables are included in the export-supply function. In view of the lack of information on the domestic scarcity and wholesale prices, $\overline{PIJ}_t$ and PIJ_t, respectively, we have to concentrate on the CMEA export price of good I relative to its export price to MDCs, i.e., $(PXIJE_t/PXIJM_t)$, and the export price of good I relative to the export price of good L $(I \neq L)$, i.e., $(PXIJE_t/PXLJE_t)$. Export-supply pressure variables are identical with demand-pressure variables defined by [3] and [4], except they are defined with the opposite sign.

The reason for including either current or lagged imports of commodity I or L in [5] is the same as for including current or lagged exports in central planners' import-demand function [2]. In particular, the willingness of central planners to export a hard commodity will depend on the amount of hard commodities they are able to import during the current year or were able to import last year. Thus, current or lagged imports of commodity I or L serve as a proxy for bilateral balancing by commodity groups on the margin.

The Rationing Equations

In this model of intra-CMEA foreign trade, two classes of commodities are distinguished: hard and soft goods. Hard goods (raw materials and food) are modeled as supply-determined, while soft goods (machinery and industrial consumer goods) are modeled as demand-determined. We assume that we have no observations generated by central planners' supply functions for exports of machinery and industrial consumer goods, and no observations generated by their demand for imports of raw materials and food.

All exports of hard goods go into two artificially created pools: one for raw materials and one for food. The size of each pool, according to our assumptions, is always smaller than the sum of aggregate values of either kind of hard goods demanded by all CMEA countries. The size of the pools of soft goods—one for machinery and one for industrial consumer goods—determined as a sum of the aggregate values of these goods demanded by CMEA countries from within CMEA, is always smaller than what CMEA countries are willing to supply. Hence, hard goods have to be rationed on the import side and soft goods on the export side. Consequently, a trade model of any CMEA country with the rest of CMEA consists of two import-demand equations (one for machinery and one for industrial consumer goods), two export-supply equations (one for fuels and raw materials and one for food), and four rationing equations (two for exports of soft goods and two for imports of hard goods). Finally, there are two identities: one for total imports and one for total exports.

The rationing equations for exports and imports are assumed to take the following form respectively:

$$XIJE_t = a_0 + [b_1 + b_2SPIJ_t + b_3SPSIJ_t](MIEE_t - MIJE_t)$$
$$(I=1,4),$$ [6]

and

$$MIJE_t = c_0 + [d_1 + d_2DPIJ_t + d_3DPSIJ_t](XIEE_t - XIJE_t)$$
$$(I=2,3).$$ [7]

Variables $SPIJ_t$ and $DPIJ_t$ represent the relative (long-run) export- and import-demand pressure in the case of commodity I in country J; $SPSIJ_t$ and $DPSIJ_t$ represent the short-run export-supply and import-demand pressure in the same case; and $MJEE_t$ and $XJEE_t$ are total intra-CMEA imports and exports of commodity I respectively.

While it is assumed that an increase in (desired) demand for hard goods or an increase in (desired) supply of soft goods by a particular CMEA country will have no effect on the size of the pools of goods, the above rationing procedure is flexible enough to allow country shares to vary over time. This variability depends on the "relative import-demand pressure in country J in comparison with other CMEA countries" in the case of hard goods, and on the "relative export-supply pressure in country J in comparison with other CMEA countries" in the case of soft goods. The inclusion of the short-run export-supply pressure variable in [6] and of the short-run import-demand pressure variable in [7] is justified on the grounds that in some (although probably exceptional) cases, exporters of soft goods and importers of hard goods may increase their respective export or import shares during bilateral bargaining sessions by pleading with importers of soft goods ("we have an ample supply of soft goods, but no hard goods available for exports") or with exporters of hard goods ("we have a short-run shortage of raw materials and unless you help us we will have to cut down our production").

Typical relative export-supply and import-demand pressure variables have the form:

$$SPIJ_t = OIJ_t - OIE_t \qquad [8]$$
$$(I=1,4)$$

and

$$DPIJ_t = AVIJ_t - AVIE_t \qquad [9]$$
$$(I=2,3)$$

respectively, where OIE_t is the output of industry I in all CMEA countries excluding country J, and $AVIE_t$ is the activity variable relevant to the use or consumption of good I in all CMEA countries excluding country J.

A natural question is whether this type of rationing scheme has any corresponding real-world process. One of the officially declared aims of CMEA is the equalization of levels of economic development in different CMEA countries. This can be achieved if the relatively less-developed CMEA countries catch up with the relatively more developed countries. When bilateral bargaining sessions take place, the faster growing, relatively less-developed CMEA countries will argue that they should be allowed to increase their exports of soft goods (manufactures) faster than they increase their imports from the more developed CMEA countries. At the same time, since their overall industrial growth rate exceeds that of the more developed CMEA countries, their raw material needs are growing faster. They will also argue that they should be allowed to increase their imports of raw materials at a rate greater than the rate at which they increase their exports. The USSR, of course, is one less-developed CMEA country for which this does not hold because it is willing to incur a relative loss in its trade with Eastern Europe. This can be viewed as the "empire maintenance costs settled through merchandise trade." The argument of faster growth to support demand for a greater share in intra-CMEA imports of hard goods is probably not equally effective in all bilateral bargaining sessions. In [6] and [7], coefficients b_2 and d_2 thus represent weighted averages of b_2's and d_2's achieved in different bilateral bargaining sessions.

Short-run export-supply and import-demand pressure variables are included in both [6] and [7] to test for the possibility that the rationing system used within CMEA is even more flexible and allows for an extraordinary increase in exports of soft goods and imports of hard goods when a country is experiencing temporary economic problems.

Two types of rationing procedures can be used: consistent and inconsistent. The former guarantees that export and import quantities balance on the overall CMEA level. But consistent rationing procedures typically render the results for one country meaningless because they compute export and import shares of the largest country, in this case the USSR, as a residual. The rationing procedure chosen here is not consistent: it does not guarantee automatic equivalence of exports and imports at the overall CMEA level. However, consistency can be achieved easily be setting up an ad hoc procedure allocating the discrepancy between intra-CMEA exports and imports in proportion to each country's exports or imports.

All commodities are rationed in the form of absolute values rather than shares.

Specification of the Model

The structure of the intra-CMEA trade model is as follows:

Trade in Machinery and Equipment (CTN I)

Demand: $M1JE_t = M1JE^d[IMJ_t; X1JE_{t-1}; (PM1EE_t/PM2EE_t)$ or $(PM1EE_t/P1WA_t)]$

Rationing: $X1JE_t = X1JE[(M1EE_t - M1JE_t); SP1J_t]$

Trade in Fuels and Raw Materials (CTN II)

Supply: $(X2JE_t/PX2JE_t) = X2JE^s[OI2J_t; (PX2JE_t/P2W_t)$ and/or $(PX2JE_t/PX1EE_t)]$

Rationing: $M2JE_t = M2JE[(X2EE_t - X2JE_t); DP2J_t; DPS2J_t]$

Trade in Food and Raw Materials for Food (CTN III)

Supply: $(X3JE_t/PX3JE_t) = X3JE^s[OAGJ_t$ or $OACJ_t$ or $OI3J_t;$ $(PX3JE_t/P3W_t); (M2JE_{t-1}/PM2JE_{t-1})]$

Rationing: $M3JE_t = M3JE[(X3EE_t - X3JE_t); DP3GJ_t; T]$

Trade in Industrial Consumer Goods (CTN IV)

Demand: $(M4JE_t/PM4JE_t) = M4JE^d[CRSJ_t, (PM4JE_t/P4WA_t)$ or $(PM4JE_t/PM2EE_t); (CRSJ_t - OI4J_t)]$

Rationing: $X4JE_t = X4JE[(M4EE_t - M4JE_t); SP4J_t; SPS4J_t;$ $(OI4J_t - CRSJ_t)]$

All equations are estimated on the basis of 15 observations (1960-74). Typically, a demand or supply equation contains a domestic activity variable, a relative price variable, a bilateral-balancing variable, and possibly a dummy variable in cases where a temporary shift in the function is suspected due to the influence of known or suspected factors. Rationing equations typically contain the total volume of exports or imports in a particular commodity category for the whole CMEA, with both short-run and long-run supply- and demand-pressure variables as their key explanatory variables. All explanatory variables are assumed to be exogenous, and the model is constructed so that the simultaneity problem is minimized.

Due to the scarcity and low degree of reliability of data on ftp's of CMEA countries, both in their trade with CMEA and with MDCs, certain simplifying assumptions were necessary.

In the import-demand equations for machinery, machinery imports are measured in current prices on the grounds that there was only a small change in the CMEA prices of these goods—about 5% increase over a 15 year period, which is not statistically significant. Since at the same time all machinery import price indices for different CMEA countries seemed to move in a similar fashion, in the actual specification of the model it was assumed that $PM1JE_t = PM1EE_t = 1$ for $t = 1,2, \ldots , 15$, where $PM1EE_t$ is the import (= export) price index for machinery for CMEA. Two relative price variables were included in the import-demand equations for machinery, namely the import price of CMEA machinery relative to the import price of CMEA raw materials, $(PM1EE_t/PM2EE_t)$, and the import price of CMEA machinery relative to the wmp of machinery, $(PM1EE_t/P1WA_t)$. In the case of the former, the import price index for CMEA raw materials, $PM2EE_t$, was chosen in preference to the actual import price index of country J, $PM2JE_t$, to avoid construction of seven separate import price indices for raw-material imports of each country J from within CMEA. In the case of the latter, an index of wmp's of machinery, $P1WA_t$, was substituted for the actual import price indices of machinery imported by country J from the West (MDCs), $PM1JM_t$. While $PM1JM_t$ better reflects the opportunity cost of imports of machinery, information on this type of price index was too scarce and unreliable to be used in the actual empirical estimation of the trade model.

In the export-supply equations for raw materials, similar simplifying assumptions were made. In the absence of reliable information on the export prices of raw materials for individual CMEA countries in their trade with the West, instead of using variable $PX2JM_t$, wmp's of raw materials, $P2W_t$, were chosen. Corresponding to the assumption that $PM1JE_t = PM1EE_t = 1$ for $t = 1,2, \ldots , 15$, and since $PM1EE_t = PX1EE_t$ by definition, it was also assumed that $PX1JE_t = PX1EE_t = 1$ for $t = 1,2, \ldots , 15$.

In the export-supply equations for food, several activity variables were tried because of a generally weak relationship between domestic output of food and its exports. Instead of food-export prices of CMEA countries in their trade with the West, $PX3JM_t$, wmp of food, $P3W_t$, was used. This was done because of the lack and poor quality of data on the variable $PX3JM_t$.

In the case of the import-demand equations for industrial consumer goods, the variable $P4WA_t$, wmp of industrial consumer goods, replaced $PM4JM_t$, country J's import prices for industrial consumer goods from MDCs. This was done for the same reason as in the case of machinery imports where $P1WA_t$ replaced $PM1JM_t$.

Economic theory does not indicate the correct functional form of demand and supply functions. Two standard forms, linear and log-linear functions, were estimated in each case. The log-linear function is considered preferable because it constrains all elasticities to be constant, a desirable property in the long-run. All rationing equations are linear because this form proved to be empirically superior to any alternative form.

Description and Sources of the Data

Commodity Coverage and Unit of Measurement

In accordance with the 1962 CMEA Trade Nomenclature (CTN), each country's trade is broken down into four major commodity classes:

1. Industrial machinery and equipment, including arms (CTN I = CTN 1).
2. Fuels and non-food raw materials (CTN II = CTN 2+3+4+5).
3. Food and raw materials for food (CTN III = CTN 6+7+8).
4. Industrial consumer goods (CTN IV = CTN 9).

The sample period is 1960 through 1974, extended to 1959, whenever the estimation of an export or import relationship involves a lagged trade variable.

All data on trade flows are measured in million SDR.[11]

Sources of the Data

The building of the econometric model required data on four groups of variables:

1. Export and import flows in intra-CMEA trade.
2. Intra-CMEA ftp's.
3. Activity variables of CMEA countries.
4. World market prices.

The data on export and import flows in intra-CMEA trade in current prices were taken from the author's work with Project CMEA-FORTRAM.[12] The data on intra-CMEA ftp's were reconstructed for the author's Ph.D. thesis.[13] The data on domestic activity variables were obtained from various issues of national statistical yearbooks of the CMEA countries or the *CMEA Statistical Yearbook* published by the CMEA Secretariat in Moscow. The data on world market prices were obtained from various issues of UN publications on world trade.[14]

Estimating the Model: Empirical Results

In virtually all equations, the explanatory variables are significant at the 95% level and in many cases at the 99% level. The regression fits (represented by the R^2 statistics) are very high, and the standard errors of regression are quite low. As expected, t-values and R^2 statistics are higher and standard errors are lower for rationing equations than for export-supply and import-demand equations. The volume of overall intra-CMEA trade in a particular commodity is an extremely powerful explanatory variable for determining the amount of imports of hard goods and exports of soft goods rationed to a particular CMEA country.

As far as the quality of parameter estimates by commodity groups is concerned, the best results were obtained for trade in machinery products, followed by trade in industrial consumer goods, fuels and raw materials, and food. This is not surprising in view of the fact that trade in raw materials (especially in food) exhibits greater fluctuations and has been subject to greater price changes than trade in manufactures.

As expected, the most powerful explanatory variables in import-demand and export-supply equations are domestic activity (or quantity) variables. Relative prices play a role in the case of exports and imports of some commodities and some countries, and this warrants further work in trying to introduce relative prices into the model. At the moment, the evidence is not sufficiently conclusive, but it seems to tilt in favor of including relative prices as explanatory variables. While activity variables always have the correct sign and are almost always highly significant, in several cases the relative price variables had the correct sign but were not sufficiently significant. I chose to retain them as explanatory variables on two grounds. First, if one believes in the role of relative prices as determinants of intra-CMEA trade flows, it is better to have some estimate of relative price elasticity than none at all. Second, over time, the significance of relative price variables is going to increase because of changes in the mechanism of formation of ftp's in CMEA economies. This will lead to greater variability in sample observations of relative prices from 1975 on.

The pattern of estimates of activity and relative price elasticities is discussed in greater detail below. In general, the *a priori* expectation was that the relatively more developed CMEA countries, with more sophisticated methods of planning and management of the foreign-trade sector (Czechoslovakia, East Germany, Hungary), should exhibit a pattern of greater sensitivity of trade flows with respect to relative prices. No such clear pattern was observed. There are several possible explanations. First, the relative price data are highly tentative and subject to a significant margin of error. Second, the data do not reflect the opportunity cost as closely as desired, primarily due to the absence of information on prices in East-West trade. Third, and probably most significant, the relatively less-developed CMEA countries (Bulgaria, Poland, Romania, and the USSR), which are also more primitive in their planning and management methods, had a stronger hand in bilateral bargaining sessions because they were net exporters of hard goods (Poland excepted) throughout the period under study. Thus, they could force the relatively more developed CMEA countries into trade deals with very little attention paid to accounting prices.

As far as the bilateral balancing by commodity groups is concerned, it was often impossible to establish its existence at all or only at the cost of forcing either activity or relative price variables to become completely insignificant or to change sign. Under these circumstances, the bilateral-balancing variable was excluded from the regression and the activity and relative price variables were retained. Interestingly, bilateral balancing by commodity groups, when its existence could be established, turned out not to be simultaneous, i.e., a current increase in exports matched fully or in part by a current increase in imports and vice versa, but had a one-year lag. This means that a particular country's imports of soft goods in year t depend on how much of these goods it was allowed to export in year t-1; and its exports of hard goods in year t depend on how much it was able to import of them in year t-1. This is somewhat surprising for it has generally been assumed that bilateral balancing by commodity groups occurred without any lags. On the other hand, it is not unwelcome from a modeling point of view, for it greatly simplifies the specification and solution of the overall model and makes it less urgent to use simultaneous-equation estimation techniques rather than OLS for its estimation.

The failure to establish the practice of bilateral balancing by commodity groups on the margin (except for machinery trade and in some supply equations for food exports) is not all that surprising. Trade of

CMEA countries with the USSR, which accounted for about one-half to two-thirds of their intra-CMEA trade during the period studied, was extremely unbalanced by commodity groups. Since the USSR probably does not even practice bilateral balancing on the margin with its CMEA partners, the verification of the hypothesis of bilateral balancing on the margin through a test vis-à-vis all CMEA countries is unsatisfactory and inconclusive. This hypothesis can be properly tested only in a model in which all bilateral trade flows are modeled separately, or at least where the USSR is separated. Increased data requirements and the fact that the size of the model would double made a proper test of bilateral balancing infeasible at this stage.

Trade in Machinery and Equipment

The equations for trade in machinery and equipment are the most satisfactory. All regressions have a very good fit (R^2 of 0.99 or above) and very low standard errors of estimate. In all CMEA countries, the demand for imports of machinery is sensitive to the rate of machinery investment. The machinery import elasticities with respect to investment are below unity, mainly in the range 0.45-0.90 (except in the case of East Germany for which the absence of bilateral balancing causes the investment elasticity to be well above one). In general, the increased importance of bilateral balancing causes the elasticity of machinery imports with respect to investment to decline.

The demand for machinery imports is also sensitive to the relative price of machinery with respect to raw materials in all CMEA countries but Poland. Except for Czechoslovakia, these elasticities are well above unity and significant. This indicates that a 1% increase in the price of raw materials relative to machinery will result in more than a 1% increase in demand for machinery imports from CMEA countries. The price sensitivity with respect to machinery import prices on the world market (in MDCs) was also tested. It could be established for all countries except Poland and Romania. Except for Bulgaria, for which is elasticity is one, these elasticities are in the 0.4-0.6 range only and not as significant as in the case of the former relative price variable. This would lead one to conclude that central planners in CMEA countries are more inclined to watch the development in the relative-price ratio of machinery to raw materials on the CMEA market when making their decisions, rather than to look at the comparative trends in machinery prices within CMEA and on the world market (or, rather, in East-West trade).

Bilateral balancing in machinery trade seems to occur with a one-year lag, and its existence could not be established for East Germany and Romania. It is a significant factor for machinery trade of the remaining five CMEA countries only. An attempt to model simultaneous bilateral balancing, i.e., current imports responding to current exports, yielded results significantly inferior to an assumption of a one-year lag.

The rationing equations show that exports of machinery in all countries but one depend on a country's long-term relative-supply pressure for exports and on total intra-CMEA imports of machinery. Only for Hungary does the relative supply-pressure variable have an incorrect sign. In the case of the USSR, its share in intra-CMEA machinery exports is steadily falling. The cause of this, captured by a time trend, is its willingness to maintain alone a high share of exports of hard goods in its trade with other CMEA countries. The coefficient attached to variable $Z1J_t$ represents the average share of country J in intra-CMEA exports of machinery. Since the variable $SP1J_t * Z1J_t$ is a dimensionless number, comparisons of the coefficients attached to it for different countries are not possible.

Trade in Fuels and Raw Materials

Equations for trade in fuels and raw materials are quite satisfactory, especially for the rationing of imports. Supply of exports of fuels and raw materials is primarily dependent on domestic output and to some degree on relative prices. With the exception of Bulgaria and Romania, for which the elasticity of exports with respect to domestic output is in the 0.1-0.3 range, output elasticities for CMEA countries are in the 0.7-1.3 range. Again, there is no systematic pattern, except that the relatively less-developed CMEA countries with a large food-export sector and a limited raw-material base have a very low output elasticity of exports. The Soviet supply elasticity of exports of 1.20 is of particular interest because it implies a growing strain of export deliveries to Eastern Europe on Soviet raw-material resources.

The sensitivity of raw-material exports to relative prices could only be established for Czechoslovakia and Poland. In all other cases, relative price variables are not significant or have an incorrect sign, in which case they were not retained in the regression.

Bilateral balancing, either simultaneous or with a one-year lag, could not be established for any country. This may suggest that the general belief among Western economists that intra-CMEA trade in fuels and raw materials is subject to fairly rigid bilateral balancing may not be quite correct. However, it is more likely that the failure to establish bilateral balancing in trade in fuels and raw materials is due to the use of an inappropriate test. While it is probably required in intra-CMEA Six trade, it is likely to be absent in their trade with the USSR. In order to test for this possibility, it will be necessary to increase the size of the intra-CMEA trade model and separate the Soviet trade from intra-CMEA Six trade.

Rationing equations for imports of fuels and raw materials offer significantly superior results to those obtained in the estimation of export-supply equations. R^2 statistics indicate an excellent fit (typically around 0.99), while standard errors are quite low. Imports of fuels and raw materials depend typically on a country's long-term relative-demand pressure for imports and on total intra-CMEA exports of fuels and raw materials. East Germany and Poland are two exceptions: their imports are sensitive only to short-term demand pressure for imports of fuels and raw materials.

Trade in Foodstuffs and Raw Materials for Food

Equations for trade in food are not as satisfactory as those in the rest of the model. Problems were encountered in modeling the supply of exports of food. This was to be expected in view of the fact that intra-CMEA trade in food involves considerable re-exporting of food raw materials purchased from the West (particularly Soviet resales of grain), food obtained from other socialist countries (such as recent East German re-exports of Cuban sugar), and special barter deals that increase a country's food imports and exports at the same time. The fact that, especially in the 1970s, an increased portion of trade in food and food raw materials involved intra-CMEA trade in hard currency and at wmp's rather than ruble trade at intra-CMEA ftp's further complicates the modeling. Moreover, the absence of data on stocks of food commodities in CMEA countries prevents the specification of any but the simplest trade equations. As a result, it is not possible to present a set of fairly similar supply equations for exports but only specifications for the different countries.

Dependence of food exports on a variable representing agricultural or food output was hard to establish even though three different activity variables were tried: gross output of agriculture, output of cereals, and gross output of food industry. Even lagging the output variable by one period did not improve the significance of output as a determinant of food exports. Only in the case of the USSR did this step prove useful.

The relative price of food within CMEA in comparison with the wmp of food seems to have some influence on food exports of Bulgaria, Czechoslovakia, and East Germany. Czechoslovakia and East Germany, however, export only small amounts of food. Thus, among the four significant food exporters within CMEA (Bulgaria, Hungary, Romania, and the USSR), only the Bulgarian relative-price elasticity is of interest.

The presence of bilateral balancing in intra-CMEA food trade could not be established for the same reason as noted for fuel and raw-material exports. However, three countries—Bulgaria, Hungary, and Romania—pay for some of their fuel and raw material imports (which come primarily from the USSR) with food exports. This is a case of bilateral balancing of two groups of hard commodities. Bulgarian and Hungarian current exports of food are best explained by their lagged imports of fuels and raw materials. This relationship is so strong in the case of Hungary that no additional significant explanatory variable could be found. Bulgaria and Hungary, two main CMEA food export-ers, are thus locked into an almost completely inflexible position. No matter what happens to the agricultural harvest, they are obliged to export food to CMEA (primarily to the USSR) in payment for their imports of fuels and raw materials. Thus, the supply slack caused by a bad harvest must be taken up by domestic consumption, exports to the rest of the world, or both. In the case of Bulgaria and Hungary, both substantial net importers of raw materials primarily from the USSR, a 1% increase in imports of raw materials last year leads to an increase of about 0.95-1.10% in exports of food during the current year. In the case of Romania, which is a small net importer of raw materials from CMEA countries, the above elasticity is much smaller, about 0.15-0.25.

Rationing equations for imports of food give somewhat better re-sults. Imports by a particular CMEA country typically depend on its long-term relative-demand pressure for imports of food and on total intra-CMEA exports of food. Bulgaria and Romania are exceptions, their import shares appearing to be constant in the long run. Other unknown exogenous factors, the effects of which are captured by a time trend, steadily lower the import shares of Czechoslovakia, East Germany, and Hungary in intra-CMEA food trade. The hypothesis of long-term relative-demand pressure for imports of food is especially appropriate for the USSR which, contrary to common belief, has be-come by far the largest importer of food within CMEA.

Trade in Industrial Consumer Goods

The equations for trade in industrial consumer goods are the second most satisfactory group in the model. The demand for imports of in-dustrial consumer goods depends primarily on domestic retail sales. With the exception of Bulgaria and Romania (for which the elasticity of demand for imports of industrial consumer goods with respect to domestic retail sales is in the 0.8-0.9 range), these elasticities are well above unity. For Czechoslovakia and East Germany, they are well above 2; and for Hungary, the retail sales elasticity is about 1.7. All three countries are characterized by relatively greater sensitivity of central planners to consumer needs than in the less-developed CMEA countries. The Polish elasticity of 1.2-1.3 is lower than expected in view of the policy of Polish central planners toward greater concern for consumer needs since 1970. It implies that the improvement in the supply of consumer goods on the Polish market is primarily due to its greater domestic production than to increased imports.

Bulgarian, East German, Polish, and Soviet imports of industrial consumer goods are also dependent on their relative price either with respect to CMEA raw material prices or wmp's of industrial consumer goods. The former elasticities are generally greater and more significant than the latter. This would imply that central planners, as in their import decisions concerning machinery and equipment, are more likely to look at the exchange relationship between industrial consumer goods and raw materials (representing the bulk of primary goods) within CMEA than at the comparative prices of industrial consumer goods within CMEA and on the world market. In all four cases, the elasticity exceeds unity. This implies that a 1% increase in intra-CMEA raw material prices relative to the prices of industrial consumer goods will lead to a greater than 1% increase in imports of industrial consumer goods in the above four countries.

Equations for the rationing of exports of industrial consumer goods show the general dependence of exports on overall intra-CMEA imports of industrial consumer goods. The long-term relative-supply pressure for exports of industrial consumer goods seems to play a role for Bulgaria, Czechoslovakia, East Germany, and Poland. In a modified form (as the difference between the domestic output of industrial consumer goods and retail sales to consumers), it also influences exports of industrial consumer goods by Czechoslovakia and the USSR.

Bulgarian and Hungarian export shares in intra-CMEA trade are also influenced by the short-term supply pressure. The Romanian export share is relatively stable over time and appears to be insensitive to any variable. Bulgarian export share is steadily declining over time due to the impact of an unknown exogenous factor, the effect of which is captured by a time trend.

The demand of Czechoslovakia and East Germany for imports of industrial consumer goods also depends on the variable representing domestic pressure for their imports. This is defined as the difference between indices of the domestic retail sales of all consumer goods and the domestic output of industrial consumer goods. No bilateral balancing in trade in industrial consumer goods could be empirically established. This is undoubtedly the result of the extremely unbalanced trade of CMEA Six with the USSR in this category. Thus, an additional test of the presence of bilateral balancing in this category will have to be made when intra-CMEA Six trade is separated from trade with the USSR and modeled independently.

Suggestions for Improving the Model

The model could be improved in several respects. First, further work on the introduction of relative prices, possibly with respect to domestic wholesale prices, is desirable. Ftp's in East-West trade instead of wmp's should be used as measures of the opportunity cost of intra-CMEA trade.

Second, the balancing mechanism requires further investigation. The first step should be to separate intra-CMEA Six trade and trade of CMEA Six with the USSR, in view of the different degree of structural bilateralism applied in these two trades.

Third, further commodity disaggregation is desirable according to the degree of hardness of commodity groups. Thus, arms should be separated from machinery; fuels, iron and steel, and chemicals should be separated from CTN group II; and grain should be separated from other food.

Fourth, the optimality of the price-differential method of sample separation should be tested, especially after improved data on ftp's in intra-CMEA and East-West trade become available.

Appendix
Equations of the Model and Notation

Description of Equations

Two types of equations are presented in the model: linear (Lin) and log-log transformation in natural logarithms (Ln-Ln). The latter constrains all elasticities to be constant over time.

The dependent variable in all rationing equations is measured in current prices. Demand for imports of machinery and equipment is also measured in current prices, in view of the negligible price increase during 1960-74. The remaining dependent variables (supply of exports of fuels and raw materials, supply of food and raw materials for food, and demand for imports of industrial consumer goods) are measured in constant 1960 prices. All activity indices have a base $1960 = 100$.

Notation

$CRSJ$ = index of retail sales to consumers in country J.
$D..$ or $D.. - ..$ = dummy variable (with a value of 1) for year .. or for period from year .. to year .., e.g., $D60\text{-}64$ is a dummy variable for years 1960 through 1964.

$DP2J_t$ = $OIJ_t - \{[OIE_t - (M2JE_{1960}/M2EE_{1960}) \times OIJ_t]/[1-(M2JE_{1960}/M2EE_{1960})]\}$

= long-term relative demand pressure for imports of fuels and raw materials in country *J*.

$DPS2J_t$ = $[(OIJ_t/OIJ_{t-1}) - (OJ2J_t/OI2J_{t-1})] \times 100$

= short-term demand pressure for imports of fuels and raw materials in country *J*.

$DP3GJ_t$ = $OAGJ_t - \{[OAGE_t - (M3JE_{1960}/M3EE_{1960}) \times OAGJ_t]/[1-(M3JE_{1960}/M3EE_{1960})]\}$

= long-term relative demand pressure for imports of food.

IMJ = index of investment in machinery in country *J*.

$M3UM$ = imports of food by the USSR from MDCs.

$MJEE$ = intra-CMEA imports of commodity *I*.

$MIJE$ = imports of commodity *I* by country *J* from CMEA countries.

$OACJ$ = index of output of cereals in country *J*.

$OAGE_t$ = $\Sigma_{J=B}^{U}$ $OAGJ_t \times (M3JE_{1960}/M3EE_{1960})$ = index of gross output of agriculture in all CMEA countries.

$OAGJ$ = index of gross output of agriculture in country *J*.

OIE_t = $\Sigma_{J=B}^{U}$ $OIJ_t \times (M2JE_{1960}/M2EE_{1960})$ = index of gross output of industry in all CMEA countries.

OIJ = index of gross output of industry in country *J*.

$OI1E_t$ = $\Sigma_{J=B}^{U}$ $OI1J_t \times (X1JE_{1960}/X1EE_{1960})$ = index of gross output of machinery industry in all CMEA countries.

$OI4E_t$ = $\Sigma_{J=B}^{U}$ $OI4J_t \times (X4JE_{1960}/X4EE_{1960})$ = index of gross output of consumer goods industries in all CMEA countries.

$OI1J$ = index of gross output of machinery industry in country *J*.

$OI2J$ = index of gross output of raw-materials industries in country *J*.

$OI3J$ = index of gross output of food industry in country *J*.

$OI4J$ = index of gross output of consumer goods industries in country *J*.

PIW = index of prices of commodity *I* on the world market $(I=2,3)$.

$PIWA$ = index of prices of commodity I on the world market ($I = 1,4$).

$PMIJE$ = index of prices of commodity I imported by country J from CMEA countries ($PM1JE = PM1EE = 1$ at all times).

$PM3UM$ = index of prices of food imported by the USSR from MDCs.

$PXIJE$ = index of prices of commodity I exported by country J to CMEA countries ($PX1JE = PX1EE = 1$ at all times).

$SP1J_t$ = $OI1J_t - \{[OI1E_t - (X1JE_{1960}/X1EE_{1960}) \times OI1J_t]/ [1-(X1JE_{1960}/X1EE_{1960})]\}$

  = long-term relative supply pressure for exports of machinery.

$SP4J_t$ = $OI4J_t - \{[OI4E_t - (X4JE_{1960}/X4EE_{1960}) \times OI4J_t]/ [1 - (X4JE_{1960}/X4EE_{1960})]\}$

  = long-term relative supply pressure for exports of industrial consumer goods.

$SPS4J_t$ = $[(OI4J_t/OI4J_{t-1}) \times (CRSJ_t/CRSJ_{t-1})] \times 100$

  = short-term supply pressure for exports of industrial consumer goods.

$XIEE$ = intra-CMEA exports of commodity I.

$XIJE$ = exports of commodity I by country J to CMEA countries.

$XIJE$ = exports of commodity I by country J to CMEA countries.

T or = time trend (1960 = 1) or time trend starting from year . .
$T .. - ..$ to year . . , e.g., $T70\text{-}74$ is time trend with 1970 = 1 and 1974 = 5.

Numbers in parentheses under regression coefficients are the corresponding t-statistics. Numbers in parentheses next to regression coefficients in the "dummy variable" column are the respective years to which the dummy variable applies. Mean is the mean of the dependent variable. R^2 is the coefficient of determination which measures the goodness of fit. *SEE* is the standard error of estimate of the regression. *D-W* is the Durbin-Watson statistic for measuring serial correlation of residuals.

TABLE A-1
Demand Equations for Imports
of Machinery and Equipment ($M1JE^d$)

Equation Number	Country J	Type of Equation	Constant Term	IMJ_t	$X1JE_{t-1}$	$(PM1EE_t \times 100/PM2EE_t)$
(1a)	B	Lin	394.0	0.8782	0.7098	−2.5324
			(1.03)	(2.22)	(3.89)	(0.62)
(1b)	B	Ln-Ln	7.3413	0.4530	0.2058	—
			(4.21)	(2.28)	(1.54)	
(1c)	B	Ln-Ln	9.0623	0.5932	0.2141	−1.5481
			(2.83)	(2.19)	(1.37)	(1.97)
(2a)	C	Ln-Ln	3.2233	0.6107	0.6688	−0.9420
			(2.54)	(5.14)	(7.22)	(3.28)
(2b)	C	Ln-Ln	2.2834	0.4348	0.6810	—
			(1.50)	(2.91)	(6.21)	
(3a)	G	Ln-Ln	5.3876	1.9439	−0.0825	−1.7335
			(2.08)	(6.76)	(0.34)	(3.38)
(3b)	G	Lin	1291.0	8.3701	0.1339	−19.4412
			(2.75)	(5.75)	(1.00)	(3.91)
(3c)	G	Ln-Ln	−0.2804	1.3364	0.3153	—
			(0.11)	(4.77)	(1.04)	
(4a)	H	Lin	540.0	2.8213	0.1266	−6.1056
			(3.13)	(6.07)	(0.99)	(3.49)
(4b)	H	Ln-Ln	5.1303	0.8667	0.2663	−1.1054
			(3.01)	(5.68)	(2.14)	(2.90)
(4c)	H	Ln-Ln	3.4801	0.8992	0.1463	—
			(1.64)	(4.88)	(0.87)	
(5a)	P	Lin	10.1	1.5942	0.5111	0.5542
			(0.03)	(4.02)	(3.92)	(0.17)
(5b)	P	Ln-Ln	2.2701	0.4368	0.4883	−0.2490
			(1.12)	(3.47)	(4.28)	(0.55)
(6a)	R	Ln-Ln	2.9387	0.9411	−0.0434	−0.4650
			(1.97)	(9.14)	(0.51)	(1.46)
(6b)	R	Ln-Ln	8.7211	0.6496	0.1452	−1.5546
			(3.35)	(3.22)	(0.83)	(2.64)
(6c)	R	Ln-Ln	3.7842	0.4358	0.2612	—
			(1.39)	(1.87)	(1.24)	
(7a)	U	Lin	3639.4	17.4175	—	−41.2288
			(5.45)	(37.48)		(6.22)
(7b)	U	Ln-Ln	7.3562	0.9163	0.2309	−1.2877
			(5.17)	(2.79)	(0.88)	(4.34)
(7c)	U	Ln-Ln	3.7339	0.2768	0.6442	—
			(2.43)	(0.65)	(1.84)	

Equation Number	$(PM\,\backslash EE_i \times 100/P\,\backslash WA_i)$	Dummy Variable		Mean	R^2	SEE	D-W
(1a)	—	− 103.8 (3.48)	(69-70)	614.6	0.9900	34.8	1.99
(1b)	− 1.0172 (2.67)	− 0.1223 (1.94)	(69-70)	6.3165	0.9834	0.072	1.43
(1c)	—	− 0.1413 (2.07)	(69-70)	6.3165	0.9795	0.080	1.00
(2a)	—	—		6.5395	0.9913	0.045	1.33
(2b)	− 0.5772 (2.14)	—		6.5395	0.9879	0.053	1.66
(3a)	—	—		6.6151	0.9966	0.039	1.94
(3b)	—	—		877.2	0.9940	44.4	1.41
(3c)	− 0.4749 (1.17)	—		6.6151	0.9938	0.053	1.39
(4a)	—	− 100.1 (2.98)	(70)	475.5	0.9900	26.2	2.92
(4b)	—	0.1839 (2.78)	(70)	6.0665	0.9887	0.057	2.55
(4c)	− 0.6354 (1.61)	—		6.0665	0.9760	0.080	1.63
(5a)	—	—		836.0	0.9933	40.2	2.34
(5b)	—	—		6.6055	0.9908	0.056	1.79
(6a)	—	0.0671 (6.49)	(60-64)	5.8457	0.9936	0.040	1.58
(6b)	—	—		5.8457	0.9668	0.088	1.32
(6c)	− 0.3706 (0.69)	—		5.8457	0.9481	0.110	1.17
(7a)	—	—		2781.4	0.9918	110.9	2.08
(7b)	—	—		7.8536	0.9923	0.041	2.15
(7c)	− 0.4463 (1.65)	—		7.8536	0.9832	0.060	1.70

TABLE A-2

Rationing Equations for Exports of Machinery and Equipment ($X1J/E$)

Equation Number	Country J	Type of Equation	Constant Term	$Z1J_t = 0.01^* \times$ ($M1EE_t\text{-}M1JE_t$)	$SP.1J_t^* \times Z1J_t$	$T^* \times Z1J_t$	Dummy Variable	Mean	R^2	SEE	D-W
(8)	B	Lin	-120.9 (3.91)	7.3705 (9.34)	0.00686 (4.90)	—	—	418.3	0.9973	17.6	0.77
(9)	C	Lin	77.5 (1.61)	20.8540 (15.75)	0.02732 (3.47)	—	-105.7 (68) (3.55)	1201.8	0.9970	27.9	2.03
(10)	G	Lin	-162.1 (2.15)	31.8496 (17.82)	0.02825 (3.64)	—	169.5 (60-61) (4.86)	1597.3	0.9986	27.3	2.49
(11)	H	Lin	60.6 (3.87)	7.4843 (21.02)	-0.00643 (1.94)	—	71.8 (72-74) (4.43)	559.6	0.9988	10.4	2.33
(12)	P	Lin	-189.4 (4.61)	17.6706 (16.99)	0.00530 (1.36)	—	88.8 (69) (2.95)	884.9	0.9975	28.2	1.45
(13)	R	Lin	14.6 (1.30)	2.7036 (10.63)	0.00300 (7.30)	—	78.5 (73) (8.15)	231.2	0.9973	8.3	2.13
(14a)	U	Lin	78.1 (0.78)	47.6882 (11.24)	-0.04886 (1.68)	—	—	1836.9	0.9951	59.9	1.53
(14b)	U	Lin	-500.4 (2.16)	83.0725 (6.07)	0.08225 (1.51)	-2.8794 (2.67)	—	1836.9	0.9970	48.8	2.15

TABLE A-3
Supply Equations for Exports of Fuels and Raw Materials ($X2JE^s/PX2JE$)

Equation Number	Country J	Type of Equation	Constant Term	$OI2J_i$	$PX2JE_i^* \times 100/P2W_i$	$PX2JE_i^* \times 100/PX1EE_i$	Dummy Variable	Mean	R^2	SEE	D-W
(15a)	B	Lin	98.1 (2.78)	0.2787 (6.51)	0.2462 (0.84)	—	—	187.7	0.8033	14.1	1.05
(15b)	B	Ln-Ln	3.3856 (4.88)	0.3133 (6.46)	0.0346 (0.29)	—	—	5.2230	0.7974	0.077	0.99
(16a)	C	Ln-Ln	-8.1712 (2.28)	1.1269 (8.72)	0.3158 (1.96)	1.6124 (3.01)	—	6.2513	0.9535	0.055	1.00
(16b)	C	Ln-Ln	-2.0156 (1.06)	0.9035 (13.33)	—	0.8222 (2.09)	—	6.2513	0.9372	0.061	1.07
(17a)	G	Lin	145.1 (4.94)	2.8715 (14.58)	—	—	159.3 (73-74) (7.00)	605.2	0.9770	25.5	1.38
(17b)	G	Ln-Ln	2.7944 (9.59)	0.7114 (12.09)	—	—	0.2137 (73-74) (4.84)	6.3775	0.9624	0.050	1.12
(18)	H	Ln-Ln	-5.9122 (1.38)	1.3285 (10.24)	0.2106 (1.13)	0.7758 (1.10)	—	5.3006	0.9554	0.076	1.87
(19a)	P	Ln-Ln	-4.9083 (3.27)	0.9081 (22.63)	0.1446 (2.15)	1.2650 (4.98)	—	6.1981	0.9912	0.030	1.42
(19b)	P	Ln-Ln	-2.4791 (2.20)	0.8389 (30.67)	—	0.9543 (4.01)	—	6.1981	0.9875	0.034	1.49
(20a)	R	Lin	261.2 (24.12)	0.1881 (5.34)	—	—	—	313.4	0.6867	18.1	1.01
(20b)	R	Ln-Ln	3.6403 (1.41)	0.1094 (1.87)	—	0.3234 (0.53)	—	5.7430	0.5758	0.067	0.99
(21)	U	Ln-Ln	1.6741 (3.54)	1.1994 (27.10)	0.0527 (0.85)	—	—	8.0826	0.9928	0.035	1.55

TABLE A-4
Rationing Equations for Imports of Fuels and Raw Materials (M2JE)

Equation Number	Country J	Type of Equation	Constant Term	$Z2J_t = 0.01^* \times (X2EE_t{\cdot}X2JE_t)$	$DP2J_t^* \times Z2J_t$	$DPS2J_t^* \times Z2J_t$	Dummy Variable	Mean	R^2	SEE	D-W
(22)	B	Lin	-59.3 (0.90)	7.4502 (4.23)	0.03441 (4.16)	—	58.3 (66-69) (7.01)	472.3	0.9971	14.0	1.65
(23)	C	Lin	-234.9 (2.47)	24.8575 (9.08)	0.05271 (2.33)	—	—	909.9	0.9936	24.2	2.75
(24a)	G	Lin	411.1 (2.20)	17.5433 (3.23)	0.00223 (0.05)	—	174.4 (74) (2.18)	1276.2	0.9739	51.2	0.89
(24b)	G	Lin	392.9 (9.48)	17.6660 (20.87)	—	0.9871 (3.03)	222.0 (74) (4.46)	1276.2	0.9858	37.8	1.48
(25)	H	Lin	-180.3 (7.80)	15.4198 (28.81)	0.00833 (1.20)	—	43.1 (71) (4.56)	635.4	0.9989	8.7	2.39
(26a)	P	Lin	-299.5 (4.18)	21.6047 (12.56)	-0.00242 (0.09)	—	64.9 (70) (1.44)	789.9	0.9878	40.0	0.65
(26b)	P	Lin	-174.4 (3.20)	18.1855 (13.23)	—	0.9359 (2.63)	94.4 (70) (2.73)	789.9	0.9925	31.3	1.10
(27)	R	Lin	151.7 (3.94)	3.3553 (3.32)	0.00276 (1.15)	—	38.3 (64) (2.53)	345.4	0.9689	14.2	1.68
(28)	U	Lin	245.9 (7.78)	31.5517 (18.25)	0.42043 (6.05)	—	—	1082.8	0.9915	24.1	1.94

TABLE A-5

Supply Equations for Exports of Food and Food Raw Materials ($X3JE^s/PX3JE$)

Equation number	Country J	Type of equation	Constant term	$OAGJ_t$	$OACJ_t$	$OI3J_t$	$PX3JE^*_t \times 100/P3W_t$	$M2JE_{t-1}/PM2JE_{t-1}$	Other variables	Mean	R^2	SEE	D-W
(29a)	B	Ln-Ln	3.6488 (2.22)	—	0.3101 (1.64)	—	0.5574 (2.05)	0.9319 (8.64)	—	5.8678	0.9825	0.073	1.73
(29b)	B	Ln-Ln	-4.7276 (2.24)	0.5180 (1.18)	—	—	0.6145 (2.19)	0.8996 (5.88)	—	5.8678	0.9807	0.077	1.60
(30a)	C	Lin	-33.0 (0.80)	—	0.1142 (0.90)	—	0.6007 (1.77)	—	9.81 T70-74 (3.67)	39.8	0.7795	5.8	2.89
(30b)	C	Ln-Ln	-4.8172 (1.15)	—	0.3886 (1.18)	—	1.4462 (2.06)	—	0.2507 T70-74 (3.63)	3.6526	0.7540	0.140	2.75
(30c)	C	Ln-Ln	-5.7819 (0.96)	0.5278 (0.89)	—	—	1.5163 (1.82)	—	0.2721 T70-74 (3.83)	3.6526	0.7416	0.143	2.62
(31a)	G	Lin	-0.7 (0.05)	—	—	—	0.1515 (1.12)	—	7.98 T70-74 (8.41)	20.5	0.9606	2.6	1.86
(31b)	G	Ln-Ln	-1.9633 (0.48)	—	—	—	1.0044 (1.11)	—	0.3688 T70-74 (4.65)	2.8808	0.8780	0.198	1.60
(32a)	H	Ln-Ln	-1.8494 (19.79)	—	—	—	—	1.1079 (75.74)	—	5.2147	0.9977	0.023	2.35

Table A-5—*Continued*

(32b)	H	Ln-Ln	-2.3227 (2.62)	—	—	0.2702 (0.88)	0.0156 (0.15)	0.9576 (5.67)	—	5.2147	0.9979	0.024	2.05
(33a)	P	Lin	-33.1 (1.19)	—	—	0.6825 (2.74)	—	—	2.9726 ($OI3P_t$-) (2.03) $OI3P_{t-1}$	81.9	0.7814	18.6	2.42
(33b)	P	Ln-Ln	-3.1105 (1.81)	—	—	1.4671 (4.10)	—	—	22.3802 ($OI3P_t$- (1.83) $OI3P_{t-1}$)	4.3167	0.6922	0.262	2.51
(34a)	R	Ln-Ln	1.0476 (2.03)	—	0.4575 (2.93)	—	—	0.2256 (2.34)	—	4.5765	0.8118	0.065	1.75
(34b)	R	Ln-Ln	0.6350 (0.45)	0.5075 (2.46)	—	—	0.1309 (0.62)	0.1527 (1.06)	—	4.5765	0.7922	0.071	1.72
(35a)	U	Lin	310.9 (3.83)	2.3887 (t-1)- (3.39)	—	—	—	—	-0.2862 ($M3UM_t/$) (5.93) $PM3UM_t$	505.6	0.7570	44.3	1.80
(35b)	U	Ln-Ln	2.1640 (0.72)	0.7898 (t-1)- (2.78)	—	—	—	—	-0.1477 ($M3UM_t/$ (3.85) $PM3UM_t$)	6.2126	0.7118	0.103	1.87

TABLE A-6

Rationing Equations for Imports of Food and Food Raw Materials (M3JE)

Equation Number	Country J	Type of Equation	Constant Term	$Z3J_t = 0.01^* \times$ $(X3EE_t \cdot X3JE_t)$	$DP3GJ_t^* \times Z3J_t$	$T^* \times Z3J_t$	Dummy Variable	Mean	R^2	SEE	D-W
(36a)	B	Lin	-8.1 (0.49)	3.4220 (1.88)	0.01880 (0.33)	—	—	27.7	0.2989	13.5	1.47
(36b)	B	Lin	-6.5 (0.52)	3.2633 (2.61)	—	—	-32.1(69) (3.04)	27.7	0.5998'	10.2	1.84
(37a)	C	Lin	219.0 (12.98)	4.0121 (3.42)	0.15642 (1.78)	—	-51.2(61) (2.95)	266.1	0.7406	15.2	0.99
(37b)	C	Lin	98.5 (1.60)	17.6510 (2.48)	—	-0.5345 (1.90)	-44.3(61) (2.71)	266.1	0.7481	15.0	1.42
(38a)	G	Lin	321.9 (6.76)	-1.3125 (0.27)	-0.27729 (1.94)	—	—	351.1	0.4399	36.6	1.33
(38b)	G	Lin	-103.0 (1.30)	47.5302 (5.29)	-0.29742 (3.93)	-1.9492 (5.66)	—	351.1	0.8569	19.3	3.18
(39a)	H	Lin	-2.0 (0.13)	4.9495 (3.32)	-0.10361 (1.46)	—	—	49.2	0.4880	12.5	2.02
(39b)	H	Lin	-76.8 (1.95)	14.5866 (2.95)	-0.12055 (1.88)	-0.3501 (2.03)	—	49.2	0.6272	11.2	1.92
(40)	P	Lin	-83.6 (4.50)	18.0706 (10.39)	-0.23007 (2.52)	—	—	125.4	0.9183	17.3	2.89
(41a)	R	Lin	-12.3 (0.79)	2.9111 (1.89)	-0.00358 (0.11)	—	—	23.8	0.4658	11.4	2.18
(41b)	R	Lin	-23.3 (3.79)	3.5455 (7.69)	—	—	36.6(64) (5.77)	23.8	0.8583	5.9	1.34
(42)	U	Lin	-97.9 (8.64)	73.4079 (43.96)	-0.22140 (3.14)	—	—	510.6	0.9967	15.0	2.49

TABLE A-7
Demand Equations for Imports of Industrial Consumer Goods (*M4JE*^{d}/*PM4JE*)

Equation Number	Country J	Type of Equation	Constant Term	$CRSJ_t$	$PM4JE^*_t \times$ $100/P4WA_t$	$PM4JE^*_t \times$ $100/PM2EE_t$	$CRSJ\text{-}OI4J_t$	Mean	R^2	SEE	D-W
(43a)	B	Ln-Ln	11.8197 (1.69)	0.8145 (2.53)	—	-2.5799 (2.15)	—	4.3227	0.9316	0.148	1.64
(43b)	B	Ln-Ln	5.6656 (1.10)	0.8544 (2.31)	-1.2910 (1.73)	—	—	4.3227	0.9242	0.156	1.33
(44a)	C	Lin	-179.7 (1.98)	2.6949 (7.31)	-0.3482 (0.42)	—	1.1968 (1.67)	135.2	0.9748	12.9	1.75
(44b)	C	Lin	-191.8 (1.76)	2.7199 (6.84)	—	-0.2552 (0.22)	1.1143 (1.63)	135.2	0.9745	13.0	1.75
(44c)	C	Ln-Ln	-6.6682 (10.32)	2.3264 (17.72)	—	—	—	4.7658	0.9603	0.116	1.39
(45a)	G	Lin	-0.9 (0.01)	3.0652 (14.16)	—	-2.3936 (1.90)	0.8636 (2.10)	120.3	0.9717	12.2	2.07
(45b)	G	Lin	-97.9 (0.85)	2.8095 (7.91)	-1.1554 (1.34)	—	1.1506 (3.05)	120.3	0.9677	13.1	2.04
(45c)	G	Ln-Ln	2.2519 (0.44)	2.7198 (12.88)	—	-2.3172 (1.97)	—	4.6714	0.9361	0.134	1.26
(45d)	G	Ln-Ln	-1.6048 (0.35)	2.2143 (6.74)	-0.9779 (1.37)	—	—	4.6714	0.9269	0.143	1.19
(46a)	H	Ln-Ln	-4.4361 (12.42)	1.7288 (24.46)	—	—	—	4.2829	0.9787	0.082	1.59
(46b)	H	Lin	-17.1 (0.32)	0.8065 (11.88)	-0.3242 (0.70)	—	—	82.7	0.9711	7.9	2.02

(47a)	P	Lin	258.9 (1.19)	0.8616 (2.44)	−2.7666 (1.48)	—	—	158.6	0.9454	18.3	1.26
(47b)	P	Lin	217.8 (0.88)	1.1920 (6.52)	—	−2.6684 (1.12)	—	158.6	0.9417	18.9	1.35
(47c)	P	Ln-Ln	1.2828 (0.26)	1.2179 (3.99)	0.5492 (0.71)	—	—	4.9716	0.9316	0.127	1.47
(47d)	P	Ln-Ln	4.9912 (0.72)	1.2599 (6.74)	—	−1.4010 (1.04)	—	4.9716	0.9347	0.124	1.54
(48)	R	Ln-Ln	−0.6834 (2.01)	0.8882 (13.70)	—	—	—	3.9643	0.9352	0.088	2.03
(49a)	U	Lin	1464.3 (0.84)	11.1248 (18.96)	—	−19.5056 (1.11)	—	1373.5	0.9702	109.7	1.06
(49b)	U	Ln-Ln	10.7031 (1.42)	1.4447 (16.20)	—	−3.3710 (1.47)	—	7.1265	0.9613	0.102	1.02

TABLE A-8

Rationing Equations for Exports of Industrial Consumer Goods (X4JE)

Equation Number	Country J	Type of Equation	Constant Term	$Z4J_t = 0.01^* \times (M4EE_t, M4JE_t)$	$SP4J_t^* \times Z4J_t$	$SPS4J_t^* \times Z4J_t$	$(OI4J_t-CRSJ_t)^* \times Z4J_t$	Dummy Variable	Mean	R^2	SEE	D-W
(50a)	B	Lin	48.7 (1.05)	6.4490 (1.64)	0.01541 (0.61)	—	—	—	181.4	0.9036	24.1	0.62
(50b)	B	Lin	-44.6 (1.52)	18.9016 (5.84)	0.08382 (5.08)	0.1309 (3.56)	—	$-1.1862 (T^* \times Z4B_t)$ (5.27)	181.4	0.9825	11.2	2.06
(51a)	C	Lin	96.3 (1.85)	14.8222 (3.12)	0.00071 (0.02)	—	—	—	355.1	0.9078	37.4	0.74
(51b)	C	Lin	165.6 (4.27)	8.3727 (2.36)	0.08772 (2.42)	—	0.2024 (4.01)	—	355.1	0.9625	24.9	1.98
(52)	G	Lin	-27.3 (1.38)	30.5302 (19.98)	0.04114 (4.70)	—	—	61.9 (63-64) (5.27)	479.2	0.9944	14.7	1.75
(53a)	H	Lin	-26.5 (1.99)	17.1067 (18.60)	0.01117 (0.42)	—	—	—	285.1	0.9829	18.9	1.55
(53b)	H	Lin	-27.3 (2.83)	17.1637 (34.27)	—	0.0837 (3.11)	—	—	285.1	0.9904	14.2	1.97
(54)	P	Lin	-93.2 (5.97)	21.6636 (16.47)	0.02054 (2.60)	—	—	-50.3 (71-72) (4.93)	298.2	0.9967	11.5	1.15
(55a)	R	Lin	-64.3 (3.39)	11.4225 (7.78)	0.00133 (0.59)	—	—	—	150.8	0.9777	15.9	1.76
(55b)	R	Lin	-73.5 (7.11)	12.2298 (23.53)	—	—	—	—	150.8	0.9771	15.5	1.79
(56a)	U	Lin	22.6 (2.02)	16.5918 (7.01)	-0.15313 (2.50)	—	—	—	136.1	0.9448	15.4	0.67
(56b)	U	Lin	59.4 (4.35)	9.3379 (2.89)	—	—	0.1452 (2.59)	63.4 (74) (5.49)	136.1	0.9837	8.7	0.64

Discussion
Jozef M. van Brabant

In spite of substantial progress during the past decade or so, our empirical knowledge and understanding of CPE foreign-trade behavior is still remarkably sketchy. Anyone with enough courage to embark on a research project that seeks to combine economic theory and policy with extensive empirical information into an econometric study of the CPEs should be congratulated. Mr. Vanous's study belongs to this category, and his modeling and testing of intra-CMEA trade commands respect. I shall limit my observations to three topics: the theory underlying the model of intra-CMEA trade, the relevance of the model to intra-CMEA relations, and the insights that may be gained from the estimated equations.

The Theory of Centrally Planned Foreign Trade

Without attempting to encompass all of the special features of the CMEA market, Vanous builds an interesting framework of supply and demand determinants that probably play a crucial role in East European trade. These determinants, which are central in the modeling and testing of regional trade behavior, rely almost exclusively on the fact that intra-CMEA prices are inconsistent with domestic relative costs and wmp's. Such discrepancies should normally lead to substitution between trade and domestic activities or between alternative trade partners. Owing to the special features of the CMEA market, however, such shifts are constrained, and the countries concerned have to embrace another mechanism to contain the opportunity cost of trading with CMEA. In the CMEA, the USSR stands to gain or to lose the most—unlike in conventional trade models in which the small country determines the volume of trade. Given this and the fact that the USSR exports mostly hard goods and imports mostly soft goods, Vanous argues that regional trade in raw materials and foodstuffs is supply-determined while regional trade in manufactured products is demand-determined.

Theoretically, it is problematical to specify continuous demand and supply functions when there is only one supplier of exports and only one purchaser of imports, i.e., the central planner who does not optimize trade. It is even more difficult to visualize such smooth functions in the case of bilateral monopoly, which is rather typical for the CMEA region with its nearly perfect separation of markets. However,

---

The views expressed here are mine and do not imply any opinion whatsoever on the part of the United Nations Secretariat in New York.

let us take for granted that such continous functions exist, at least for the observed sample of trade flows; otherwise, the exercise would not be possible.[1]

The Relevance of the Model for Intra-CMEA Trade

In this section, some of the pivotal assumptions of the trade model will be investigated. When appropriate, I shall amplify the evidence or suggest some shortcomings of the *a priori* formulations.

The Selection of Hard and Soft Goods

If none of the commodity markets is in equilibrium—a somewhat artificial assumption[2]—one can avoid the strenuous identification problems inherent in estimating demand and supply functions. The selection of the goods that belong to either the sellers' or buyers' market is, then, crucial.

In the absence of firm knowledge about price-setting criteria and on how prices are related to market imbalances, Vanous develops the price-differential method. If the relative price of a commodity is higher on the CMEA market than on the world market, suitably normalized for the discrepancy in the general price level and quality differentials, then it is considered a soft good and vice versa. This is decidedly simplistic. In particular, relatively overpriced goods are always soft and relatively underpriced ones are always hard. Other factors that may influence price-setting without entailing potential substitution cannot be accommodated, although it is precisely those factors that are crucial in determining the nature of the CMEA market for a number of products. Thus, the reported practice of tied sales cannot be accommodated. A related case concerns excess demand for (excess supply of) products that are priced well above (well below) wmp's. For various reasons (e.g., security of supply), the CPEs may decide not to switch markets.[3]

Regardless of these objections, one should note that hard and soft goods are identified on the basis of the rather vague evidence and allusions frequently aired in the East European literature concerning the approximate magnitude of CMEA-ROW price ratios, rather than according to the price test. The possible errors resulting from this shortcut will be dealt with below.

The Role of Prices in the Model

CMEA and world prices are assumed to be exogenous. Moreover, intra-CMEA prices are assumed to be uniform across countries, at least in order to determine what is soft and hard. While this vastly simplifies the computational burden and makes for a simple specification, it is likely not to hold in all cases.

Perhaps the most important feature of the CMEA world is the bilateral setting of actual trade prices. One important consequence is that prices are not uniform and that price heterogeneity differs markedly between commodities.[4] In this context, it would have been interesting to follow up on a hypothesis first suggested in the mid-1960s,[5] which has been gaining currency in the East European professional literature:[6] Intra-CMEA export prices are a function of domestic wholesale prices, especially for manufactured products.

Considering CMEA price practices—as distinct from abstract principles—it would have been useful to specify a regional price-formation mechanism, although admittedly this would not have been a straightforward task. At any rate, the inclusion of a price mechanism tailored according to official CMEA price-setting principles would be naive, unless there were conclusive proof that current CMEA prices are indeed a linear combination of some past wmp's.

Balancing Mechanism

Another important feature of CMEA bilateralism is the imposition of constraints by commodity groups on the imbalances that partners are willing to sustain in some bilateral relations. In the absence of price-induced adjustments, CPEs must seek balanced trade by direct policy measures, which are in fact embedded in their bilateral trade system. Vanous argues that the CPEs will maintain balanced trade by imposing constraints on the imbalances of additional trade in specific commodity groups. Assuming that hard and soft goods can be identified with the familiar four CTN groups, I find it hard to believe that balancing takes place on the margin only or even typically;[7] it is also implausible that this mechanism operates more or less in the same way for all CMEA partners.[8]

A case is made for detaching the USSR from the rest of CMEA, chiefly because only the USSR can afford to maintain large imbalances in trade in soft and hard goods. From a close analysis of the shifts in the commodity composition of bilateral trade of the seven CMEA countries, it would seem plausible that balancing policies differ substantially even if the USSR is dealt with separately. Without allowing for the re-examination of the state of imbalance of all trade by commodity group and partner, it would seem difficult to explain the large shifts in the composition of regional imports of the developed CPEs and of regional exports of the less-developed ones.

Specification and Estimation of the Model
The Data Base

The only serious reservation I have with respect to the data relates to the various price indices. UN price indices are probably not very relevant for intra-CMEA practices. It would have been more appropriate to use price indices of the CPEs' trade with nonsocialist countries whenever such data are available or can be reconstructed. The use of uniform intra-CMEA price indices, as argued above, is inadequate because actual prices are set bilaterally.

Official or reconstructed price indices are variously adjusted to obtain comparable coverage. Indices for manufactured goods are adjusted uniformly for the presumed quality differences. This adjustment is probably too severe for some countries and insufficient for others, for it is intuitively difficult to subscribe to the notion that whatever average quality inferiority was apparently identified in 1963 applies to all CPEs. Second, since the average quality adjustment factor should be larger than one for all CPEs, most observations are probably correctly identified as soft and hard. However, the magnitude of the quality adjustment factor for individual CPEs may crucially affect the estimated price elasticity parameter, and hence its statistical significance.

Similar observations pertain to the crucial 1963 price ratios, which are probably not fully representative for CMEA trade. The sources used do not enable Vanous to cover each CPE's trade with CMEA in a particular commodity group,[9] which may entail several serious problems. If the price ratios used differ significantly from the real ones, as seems likely,[10] the present method of rejecting or accepting a price variable when no significant t-ratios can be found may be misleading. In any case, some sensitivity tests might have been fruitful for assessing the robustness of some of the major assumptions underlying the econometric model.

The CMEA Trade Model

Given the severe constraints on data availability, Vanous's model specification is adequate and permits interesting, yet in some instances preliminary, conclusions.

SPECIFICATION PROBLEMS

In evaluating the reported statistical results, it is important to draw attention to the possible problems of using ordinary least-squares (OLS) in the case of measurement errors. To the extent that there are systematic measurement errors in the identification of what is soft and what is hard, the estimated coefficients and related statistics should be interpreted with caution.

Vanous's data might be subject to two such problems: First, commodities found to be generally soft may not be soft in each year and for each country. Second, not every product of a particular commodity group identified as soft or hard will have the same characteristic. The first case would require rejecting some observations from the sample, which one is probably reluctant to do considering the already limited degrees of freedom. The second, however, is more disturbing. If a commodity group consists of soft and hard goods (i.e., not every product passes the price test with the same result as the whole does), then each equation consists of a true demand (supply) portion and a rationed demand (supply) portion. Estimating the relationship between total trade of the bundle and the demand (supply) determinants only will lead to (1) biased coefficients unless all variables and error terms are independent, (2) larger variances than desired, (3) serial correlation, or (4) difficulties in comparing the estimates for the seven CPEs if the soft-hard composition of the commodity groups differs for the various CPEs.

It is admittedly difficult to evaluate even approximately the share of trade by commodity group that is genuinely soft or hard. As a crude gauge, I compared Hungarian unit values in CMEA trade with those in trade with other countries after adjustment for estimated price level differences. For each commodity group, I found several "wrongly priced" goods amounting to more than a negligible share of trade. If the price separation rule is to be the criterion to identify soft and hard goods, it would seem advisable to disaggregate the commodity groups, especially CTN2 and CTN3.

BILATERAL BALANCING

A bilateral balancing variable is included in the equations, and its explanatory power is discussed at some length. But this variable is not quite what it is claimed to be. Rather than testing the balancing of increases in bilateral trade, the model as specified is only capable of showing relationships between the elasticity of current imports (exports) with respect to current or lagged exports (imports) of the same or a competing commodity group.[11] A close correlation does not necessarily confirm the use of structural bilateral policies. There is an intrinsic difference between bilateral balancing at the aggregate level and structural bilateralism at the level of broad commodity groups. Since bilateral balancing is said to be widely practiced, testing a regional constraint on overall trade could provide some evidence of this balancing practice. At the commodity group level, however, there is no rationale for strict balancing in each instance.

The evidence found in a few relations that current exports (imports) depend on previous year's imports (exports) of the same or the competing commodity group is of more than passing interest, but its significance should not be overemphasized. In particular, this finding is insufficient evidence to reject the working hypothesis that structural bilateralism constrains intra-CMEA trade.

DEMAND AND SUPPLY PRESSURE

The specification of the rationing equations includes short-term pressures, which typically originate on account of unbalanced growth in the given economy, and long-term pressures, which stem from shifts in the growth of domestic activity aggregates in the given country relative to those for the rest of CMEA. In view of the available data, this specification is probably adequate. In some instances, however, it might be interesting to redefine the pressure variables. Short-term pressure is assumed to stem from differences in growth rates of industrial output of machinery production[12] and the domestic variable that is directly bearing on the trade equation. This implies that if growth rates are the same, there is no pressure, although significant shifts in the composition of the aggregate variables may alter the pressure for trade. Similar observations can be made for the long-term pressure specification, which is the difference between two index numbers and, therefore, lacks a dimension. This is difficult to rationalize in economic terms. The test could perhaps be improved by using growth rates in conjunction with an indicator of the activity level at which these rates occur.

Empirical Results and Their Interpretation

Vanous's best equations are those for imports of machinery and consumer manufactures. The estimated rationing equations are much more difficult to interpret because the most powerful exogenous variable, rationed overall imports or exports, exhausts much of the variation of the dependent variable; and there is probably strong multicollinearity between the overall trade variable and the adjusted pressure variable.

The estimated coefficients and associated statistics suggest that relative prices, as defined here, are probably not as important as theory tends to suggest; in the case of foodstuffs and consumer durables they seem to play a marginal role, if any. But judgment must be reserved since not all of the equations are correctly specified.

Though Vanous had undoubtedly good reason to specify many dummy variables, their use in some cases is odd. Whenever a dummy variable is introduced for one or two observations, it presumably attempts to take care of excessive estimated errors for the observations in question. Also, in the case of foodstuff exports by the GDR, the equation states essentially that exports were constant until 1970 when they started to be positively correlated with time. Clearly the country is not in a position to continue trading along this kinked curve, and the equation is therefore of limited value for forecasting purposes.

In many cases, the results do not corroborate the expectation that the more developed CPEs should exhibit greater price consciousness, although I suspect for different reasons than those given. First, it would be surprising to obtain a different result when the USSR is included, since this CPE has, until recently, been the least active in forcing the terms of trade in its favor. Second, it would seem naive to suggest that "the increased importance of bilateral balancing causes the elasticity of machinery imports with respect to investment to decline." If anything, the causality should be more differentiated: increased industrialization results in a low import elasticity for machinery in the developing CPEs and exerts pressure for exports, thereby increasing the apparent elasticity in the smaller developed CPEs.

It is not surprising that the presence of bilateral balancing in CTN2 could not be established. With the USSR included, one would not expect strict balancing to take place. Even if dealt with separately, one would not expect balancing to occur, for CTN2 comprises a great diversity of products, some of which are really soft or are competing with other groups.

The reason for the relatively poor fit of the foodstuff equations is undoubtedly complex. However, dollar trade is not mainly responsible for this; until recently, the dollar share in intra-CMEA trade was very small. In the case of Hungary, for example, it appears that this share, in most cases, is significantly larger than the foodstuff component.

Conclusions

These observations do not, of course, negate the value of Vanous's work. His equations are far superior to other econometric work about the CMEA and form a solid basis for further research.

I am well aware that not all of my suggestions can be implemented at this time. Data paucity precludes vastly expanding the present trade model, though for some CPEs further refinements could be introduced. To the extent that the theory underlying soft and hard goods is to be upheld, it would be valuable to test the separation of trade flows in more detail. Given that the price-differential criterion is the tool that classifies markets, it remains to be proven that the CTN categories can always be identified with soft and hard goods. Prices form perhaps the weakest link in the current specification and testing of the model. Refinements of the price variable and a further disaggregation of trade into nine categories with the USSR treated separately would be highly desirable.

Discussion

Zdeněk Drábek

I must admit to being worried when I first heard about Mr. Vanous's ambition to build an econometric model of intra-CMEA trade. In many respects, his task was much more difficult than those faced by econometricians in building comparable models for Western countries. While theory represents an absolutely crucial part of any econometric model, we have been hampered by the lack of a testable theoretical framework concerning the trade of the centrally planned economies (CPEs). On the other hand, published East European data have serious gaps and have often been criticized as unreliable, even to a greater extent than data available for developed market economies. The degree of aggregation in specifying the model had to be greater than desired in order to keep the model within manageable limits for a single researcher.

Vanous's effort is remarkable and his results quite encouraging. He has presented a theoretical model that is both testable and realistic because it incorporates many of the known basic features of trade under central planning. He has rebuilt time series of trade data by collecting a vast amount of information, ensuring comparability of the data, disaggregating into four commodity groups, and providing estimates of data needed but not published. His results are interesting, even though they represent only the beginning of econometric work on trade of CPEs. Perhaps the most important finding is the significant test of the hypothesis that planners are sensitive to relative foreign-trade prices (ftp's).

I agree fully that intra-CMEA trade should be analyzed in the general disequilibrium framework. In spite of recent measures to introduce greater flexibility of ftp's and to reduce the large divergence between intrabloc and world prices, the ruling prices clearly cannot be regarded as "market clearing prices." Some economists argue, however, that such prices could be compared to prices existing under conditions of repressed inflation. Theories that treat such prices in the general equilibrium framework by employing an alternative *modus operandi* of the market clearing procedure are not, in my view, suitable because they create even more practical problems for empirical testing.[1] It may be useful to point out that studies applying the disequilibrium approach now appear more frequently even in Eastern Europe.[2]

The problem with disequilibrium models is that they involve a separation and identification of supply and demand schedules. In this respect, Vanous suggests a new method that identifies trade in raw materials and food as supply-determined and trade in manufactures as demand-determined by means of the "price-differential method." The logic of the method is based on two fundamental assumptions concerning planners' behavior. First, production and internal trade organizations are assumed to make no significant foreign-trade decisions. Import-demand and export-supply functions are, therefore, those of central planners. Interactions between planners and the "periphery" (decentralized units) are specifically excluded. Second, a rational central planner will be sensitive to relative ftp's or, more specifically, to the degree of over- or underpricing of goods within the CMEA in relation to world market prices (wmp's).

While the role of planners' decisions is undoubtedly crucial in the highly centralized model to which Vanous refers, the role of the "periphery" should not be entirely disregarded. Clearly, planners do not make their decisions independently of domestic producers and consumers; they take into account information about, for example, production potential or input requirements, which is provided by the "periphery." Moreover, it may be argued that what the planners want to trade will generally depend on what the "periphery" will provide for exports and demand as imports. True, the decentralized units may not know or even care about actual transactional ftp's or domestic currency equivalents. However, if, as a result of their behavior, domestic shortages or surpluses of commodities appear, the planners will call on foreign trade for rescue.

The existence of disequilibrium markets is attributed to the fact that USSR (and other raw material and food supplying countries) could gain more if their trade were conducted at world prices. For example, an excess demand for a commodity group is supposed to arise in the CMEA market if the ftp is lower than wmp after adjusting for the quality factor. But why would planners try to import commodities from other CMEA countries if such commodities are over-priced in relation to world prices? Why would they try to export relatively under-priced commodities to CMEA countries? To answer these questions, Vanous assumes that planners will be sensitive to the foreign price differences. In other words, the planners will try to maximize foreign-exchange earnings from exports and minimize payments for imports in terms of foreign currency. The domestic cost of earning a unit of foreign currency does not seem to affect the planners' decisions. But if the planners are so rational as to be sensitive to relative ftp's, perhaps they should be also sensitive to domestic relative prices.[3] Vanous dismisses this possibility by claiming that the relative price elasticity of the planners with respect to domestic wholesale or scarcity prices is very low, since a typical CPE usually imports complementary commodities.

I would not see any difficulty with this interpretation if intra-CMEA trade were conducted according to Kravis's theory.[4] The theory states that countries' desire to trade depends on the presence of a scarce factor that provides a national advantage for each country (e.g., a scarce natural resource, know-how, monopoly). But if the trade is indeed conducted according to the principle of comparative costs, as suggested in the model, the evidence that, for example, the USSR has a comparative advantage in raw materials is inconclusive. In fact, Rosefielde's study suggests that there has been a movement away from the Heckscher-Ohlin rationality of Soviet trade in time, probably as capital accumulation proceeded and techniques of production changed.[5]

The Kravis theory does not seem to be the approach adopted in the model, since domestic (scarcity) prices are used as explanatory variables in export-supply and import-demand functions. In such a case, it can be shown that food and raw material supplying countries will still gain from trade with other CMEA countries, provided that relative ftp's are not discriminatory in comparison to relative prices that would prevail in the food and raw material supplying country (e.g., the USSR) under autarky. With reference to the diagram below:

> Let the USSR have comparative advantage in raw materials and Eastern Europe in manufactures. The autarky position can be determined by point T on the PPF where the highest indifference curve touches the PPF. The USSR will, therefore, benefit from trade with Eastern Europe if foreign trade prices (BX, B′Y) fix its production point on PPF (such as B′) to the right of T′. Under these circumstances, it will produce more raw materials and food and export part in exchange for manufacturers from Eastern Europe. The production point will be on PPF and ftp will be tangent to the higher indifference curve.

> If we were to include world prices in this model, the intra-CMEA trade could be treated as trade within a customs union which is facing the world price line steeper than BX (=B′Y). The Soviet Union will gain from a preferential trade arrangement with other Eastern European countries although not so much as it would if the trade was conducted under world prices.

But what if planners decide on the basis of domestic prices that are not true scarcity prices? If the planners realize their mistake, they will most likely want (1) to reduce what they considered their comparative advantage exports (food and raw materials in this case), (2) to change domestic prices, or (3) to share their costs with their trade partners. In fact, all these phenomena can be frequently observed in CMEA practice.

I would argue that domestic prices do matter for two reasons: (1) domestic prices (and plans) affect the behavior of domestic producers and consumers, which will typically lead to unplanned shortages and surpluses of commodities; and (2) even if imports are complementary,

Production Possibilities and Comparative Advantage

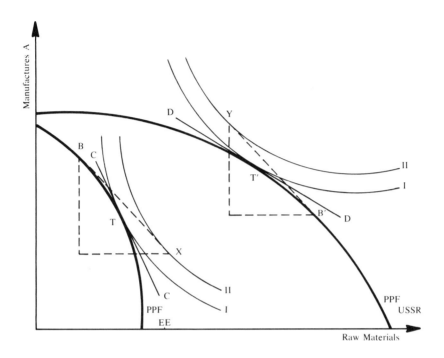

the planners may wish to use imports (and exports) to pressure domestic producers to use domestic and imported resources more efficiently. In this respect, the demand pressure indicator as a proxy for domestic scarcity price variable is not completely satisfactory since such pressures may arise due to wrong signals received by the ''periphery'' (e.g., domestic prices, inconsistent plans, inefficiencies, etc.). Therefore, the emphasis on the difference between ftp's and world prices (price-differential method) could be misplaced.

There is another reason why the comparison between world prices and ftp's in intra-CMEA trade is not theoretically ideal, although it can be used as an approximation together with domestic prices to identify the price bias in intra-CMEA trade. In particular, the criterion of world prices does not take into account the special trading arrangements that may make CMEA trade economically attractive to individual CMEA member countries. For example, using the familiar customs union type of analysis, the actual gains from trade will depend on the level of initial tariffs (or equivalent measures of CPEs), on the terms of trade that must include special trading arrangements among CMEA member countries (e.g., the benefits assigned by planners to increased stability of trade supplies provided by long-term trade agreements, methods of payment, savings on excessive trade promotion, gains from diversion of trade subject to quantitative restrictions in the West). The gains will also depend on domestic consumption in each country within the area after forming the preferential trading area.

In fact, there are already some indications that domestic final demand and technology in the CMEA are different from those implicit in the application of world prices. In my own study, I have made a calculation of the absorption of natural resource products (i.e., raw materials and food), on both the level of production and final demand. The results point to a greater domestic absorption of natural resource products in relation to comparable market economies.[6]

In view of all that has been said above, it seems that excess demand for and excess supply of particular commodities in intra-CMEA trade cannot arise only from gains (or losses) to be derived from trade with the rest of the world, but also from decisions (of the planners and the "periphery") based on domestic prices. On the one hand, the production points under autarky are fixed in terms of domestic prices. On the other, the structure of output generated through the intra-CMEA trade is fixed in foreign-trade prices by definition. At the same time, domestic prices are characterized by (1) different price levels between wholesale and retail prices and, indeed, between prices of manufacturers and agricultural procurement prices; and (2) different price relatives as compared to world prices. It is conceivable, therefore, that unless the domestic and foreign-price relatives are identical among CMEA countries, the difference in domestic price formation may itself lead to the biases in the intra-CMEA trade described by Vanous.

On the empirical side, Vanous had to rely on secondary sources and estimates of ftp's that may lead to some degree of error in identifying "hard" and "soft" commodities. For the same reason, it would be advisable to further disaggregate the commodity groups. To the list of statistical shortcomings, which he himself notes, I would only add the relatively high degree of serial correlation of regression residuals and, in some cases, low levels of t-ratios. For example, out of his 56 equations, the serial correlation in 4 of them should be considered too high for comfort, and serial correlation in 14 of them lies within critical points at 95% significance. This could either be due to the defects of the available data or to the misspecification of the model. In view of the presence of serial correlation, I wonder whether a procedure of normalized equations would not eliminate at least part of the problem. On the other hand, the time series are too short at present, and I feel that this econometric improvement on his OLS method may be rather limited.

PART IV
INDIVIDUAL COUNTRY
PERSPECTIVES

Theodore Shabad

Soviet Regional Policy and CMEA Integration

Until recently, one of the most evident features of Soviet regional policy was the effort to implement developmental strategies for the western and eastern regions of the USSR with little consideration of foreign markets or investment sources. The regional policy of the Soviet Union has become closely interwoven with CMEA integration. "Integration" means, first and foremost, more joint planning of output and decisions on the location of new capacity in relation to total demand within CMEA rather than with regard to national demand only. Second, integration implies as a corollary that a larger share of any particular output (e.g., wood, oil) crosses national borders. Much of what is described in this essay suggests that such integration tendencies are at work for the USSR, at least in the energy and raw material sectors.

The increasing foreign trade and the growing interdependence of the USSR and Eastern Europe with respect to the development of joint projects have expanded the role of CMEA markets and investments in Soviet locational decisions. This paper will document the linkage between CMEA integration and Soviet regional policy in the European USSR by examining the pull of the CMEA market on industrial development in the western borderlands and seacoasts and by noting some joint investments. The investigation of the CMEA contribution to the development of the Soviet east, which also helps meet the resource needs of these countries, will focus on specific joint projects in resource exploitation or transport construction.

With the elimination of forced labor as a mass institution, Soviet planners were confronted with a new situation. Economic devices, such as regional wage increments, proved inadequate to attract settlers to Siberia. Workers could be recruited for short contractual periods, but few settled permanently because of inferior living and working conditions. The provision of adequate living conditions matching those in the European regions would require a large investment in social infrastructure in addition to the huge outlays already being invested in productive capacity. Across-the-board economic development and settlement of the eastern regions have never been carried out in practice, and recent writers have described the old aspirations of uniform distribution as "mechanistic."[1]

The relative inertia of existing population patterns and the growing scarcity of industrial labor have become increasingly accepted by Soviet planners. It is no longer unusual to find statements similar to one recently advanced by a labor-resource specialist: "If the redistribution of population is impossible, consideration should be given to making changes in the originally planned volumes and proportions of the economy in light of the actual labor-resource factor."[2] As a result of this more realistic approach to labor availability and technological improvements in Soviet transportation (modernization of railroads, greater use of oil and gas pipelines, the proposed long-distance transfer of Siberian electric power to the European regions), Siberia is being viewed increasingly as a source of fuels, energy, and raw materials for the industrialized western regions of the Soviet Union. Development within Siberia is focused on power-intensive industries (e.g., aluminum and some chemicals) as well as resource-oriented processing activities. Over the objections of pro-Siberian enthusiasts, investment in the eastern regions is assigned primarily to resource-oriented development while most investment in manufacturing, especially labor-oriented activities, is being channeled into the established industrial regions of the European USSR.

This trend has been accentuated by the Soviet Union's growing involvement in foreign economic relations, both within the framework of CMEA and within the context of the world economy at large. The resource potential in Siberia has become an asset in Soviet dealings with countries dependent on raw-material imports, especially against a background of rising world prices for energy and raw materials. The Soviet Union is seeking to speed Siberian resource development, both for domestic use and for export, by enlisting financial resources from abroad and paying back with the product of the completed resource projects.

Another aspect of the Soviet Union's involvement in foreign economic relations has been the focus on the development of border regions and seacoasts. Historically and by virtue of national security considerations, the Soviet Union has been essentially a self-sufficient, continental economy, with key industries favoring safe interior locations. The increasing Soviet outward orientation, associated with the CMEA economic integration program unveiled in 1971 and with expanding East-West commerce, has made planners aware of the advantages of peripheral economic development, which in many cases involved economically undeveloped regions with surplus labor resources. Soviet writers have begun to talk about the attractiveness of seaboard location[3] and about maritime-oriented economic systems in the USSR.[4] A particular focus of border-region development has been the western frontier, which adjoins the East European countries. The nascent emphasis on seacoast development is particularly evident in the Black Sea, the Baltic Sea, and the Pacific coast of the Soviet Far East.

No longer are regions and local production centers being evaluated merely in terms of their contribution to the Soviet economy and their spatial interaction with other Soviet regions and centers. Regional functions are also being assessed in terms of their contribution to foreign trade or, in Marxist terminology, the international division of labor.[5] The eastern regions are being viewed as sources of fuels, energy, and industrial raw materials, not only for the expanding manufacturing economy of the European USSR, but also for the CMEA partners and the industrially developed nations of the West. Border and seaboard regions serve both as transit areas handling commodity flows between foreign countries and the Soviet interior and, increasingly, as the sites of industrial activities interacting with the Soviet interior and other countries.

There are serious difficulties in separating CMEA-oriented activities from the impact of East-West commerce and foreign trade. Moreover, many new industrial activities in the western periphery of the USSR were developed to meet local domestic needs more than to supply CMEA markets. However, an effort will be made to limit this discussion to intrabloc relations in keeping with the basic theme of the volume.

This relationship and its impact on industrial location can be discussed from two points of view: (1) the effects of CMEA integration within particular industries; and (2) the impact of integration on particular regions of the Soviet Union. The topics that will be examined within the framework of individual industries are the sources of raw materials that the Soviet Union is increasingly providing to East European countries; the location of joint projects, which are becoming a common form of CMEA integration; and the arrangements to improve transportation between East European countries and the often distant Soviet sources of raw materials. A distinction will be made between Soviet border regions, which are being integrated with the East European economies in a variety of linkages, and more distant resource areas of the Soviet interior, whose role is limited to the provision of raw materials. The following discussion will take the sectoral approach, with emphasis on primary raw-material oriented industries and energy sources.

Fuels and Energy

Because of the dependence of East European countries on deliveries of fuels and energy from the Soviet Union, these economic sectors are among the most significant aspects of CMEA integration. In view of the relatively good supply of solid fuels in Eastern Europe, these have not played an important part in integration. By far, the most important Soviet fuel export to the CMEA countries has been crude oil. In the future, deliveries of natural gas and electric power are expected to play an increasingly larger role as the Soviet Union seeks to divert a larger portion of its oil exports to the West to earn more hard-currency revenue. Through a radical modification of its national fuels policy, the Soviet Union expects to free more oil resources for export to meet its commitments to the East European countries and to increase its shipments to the West.

After a long reliance on coal, the USSR went through a virtual revolution in fuel use in the last quarter century by reorienting its economy to greater reliance on oil and natural gas. In the national fuels budget, coal use declined from 66% in 1950 to 27.2% in 1978, while the use of oil rose from 17.4 to 45.7% and natural gas from 2.3 to 24.6%. This shift to hydrocarbons is now beginning to slow because of the higher price of oil on the world market since 1973 and because of a realization that hydrocarbons are generally a scarcer resource than solid fuels. Domestic oil consumption is planned to increase at a lower rate in the Soviet Union, making more oil available for export. Domestic savings are to be achieved by more effective use of available oil supplies. Presently, about 50% of the oil is used for motor fuels and petrochemical feedstocks, and the rest is burned in oil-fired power stations.[6] Through improved refining technology, such as catalytic cracking and hydrocracking, the residual fuel oil share for use in power stations is to be reduced. More electricity is to be generated by coal-burning stations, especially those using low-grade, stripmined lignite, and by hydroelectric stations and nuclear power plants. All these structural shifts are reflected in CMEA integration programs.

Oil

The impact of changing Soviet fuels policy is evident in the pattern of Soviet oil deliveries to East European countries (except Romania). The percentage of the five importing countries (Bulgaria, Czechoslovakia, East Germany, Hungary, and Poland) in combined net Soviet exports of crude oil and products rose rapidly until 1973 while world prices were low and the general scarcity of hydrocarbons compared with solid fuels had not yet become an issue. Since 1973, while Soviet deliveries to the five countries have continued to rise in absolute terms, their percentage in Soviet exports has slowly declined, from 53.4% in 1973 to 48.4% in 1976. Thereafter, the Soviet Union imposed secrecy on the physical volume of oil exports.

After the center of Soviet oil production shifted from the Caucasus to the Volga-Urals, the CMEA partners joined in building the so-called Friendship oil pipeline system to reduce the transport cost of Soviet crude oil moving to East European refineries (see map). The pipeline, in contrast to later projects, did not involve capital transfers or worker assignments across borders. It was jointly planned, and each participating country was responsible for building segments within its national territory. When the first string was completed in 1964, the pipeline carried 8.3 million tons of oil and, after the completion of a second string in 1974, oil movements through the system rose to 50 million tons. Since 1970, the rapidly growing West Siberian oil-producing region has also been feeding crude oil into the Friendship system,[7] as has the Mangyshlak oilfield (with high-paraffin oil) on the northeast shore of the Caspian Sea.[8] As a result, the Friendship system, which supplies most of the crude oil exported to Poland, East Germany, Czechoslovakia, and Hungary, carries a mixture of crudes. Soviet shipments to Bulgaria have been moving chiefly by tanker from Black Sea terminals (Novorossiysk, Tuapse, and Odessa).[9]

Soviet writers have suggested that it may be more economical over the long run to reduce crude oil exports to the East European countries and to trade more in refined products, with greater concentration of production and specialization in refineries situated in western border regions and at seaboard locations. About 90% of all Soviet oil shipments to Eastern Europe is now in the form of crude oil. Out of total net Soviet exports of refined products of 36.2 million tons in 1975, only 8.6 million, or 24%, moved to Eastern Europe and other communist countries.[10] In contrast to crude oil, refined products tend to move mainly by rail. Refined products for Eastern Europe originate mainly in Central European Russia and the Volga-Urals, where most of the Soviet refining capacity is concentrated. Thus, refinery development near the western border is designed to reduce expensive rail hauls of oil products from interior locations.

The first western refinery began operation at Novopolotsk in Belorussia in 1963, followed by one at Kremenchug on the Dnieper River in the Ukraine in 1966.[11] A second Belorussian refinery opened in 1975 at Mozyr', at the point where the Friendship pipeline system

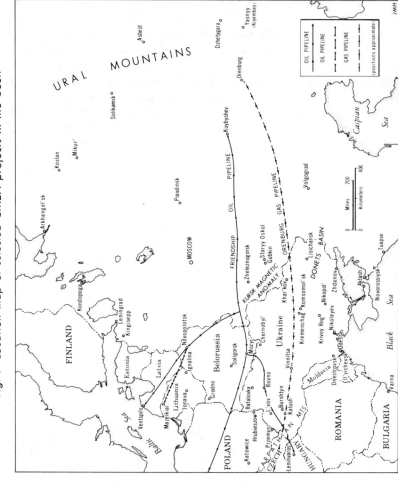

Fig. 1 Location map of selected CMEA projects in the USSR

splits into branches going west through Poland to East Germany and southwest to Czechoslovakia and Hungary.[12] The most recent completion was the Lisichansk refinery in the Donets Basin.[13] As part of a continued program of western refinery construction serving both the western regions of the Soviet Union and the CMEA market, a refining complex is rising at Mazeikiai in Lithuania. The Lithuanian refinery has been designed specifically for the East European market, particularly Poland. Under an agreement signed in 1974, Polish workers have laid an extension of the Friendship pipeline system from Novopolotsk to Mazeikiai, a distance of 275 miles. The refinery, under construction since 1971, is scheduled to start operating in 1980.[14] The Soviet ninth five-year plan (1971-75) called for the start of construction on one more western refinery, at Vinnitsa in the Ukraine,[15] but the project appears to have been shelved. Instead, the following five-year plan (1976-80) scheduled construction of another Ukrainian refinery in the Zaporozh'ye area.[16] The long-term trend appears to be the expansion of Soviet refining capacity in the western regions, using crude oil transmitted by pipelines from the expanding West Siberian fields, with the ultimate objective of producing more refined products for export while stabilizing or even reducing the international flow of crude oil.

Natural Gas

Compared with oil, natural gas has been a relatively late starter in Soviet foreign trade, just as the entire natural gas industry has been a relatively recent development in the Soviet Union. Large-scale exports began only in 1966 when an old pipeline linking the Carpathian gas fields around Dashava in the western Ukraine with Poland was converted to a wider diameter, tripling the capacity from 300 million to one billion cubic meters a year. The so-called Brotherhood pipeline from the Soviet Union to Czechoslovakia opened in 1967, with a branch extending into Austria the following year. These three countries were the only importers of Soviet natural gas until 1973, when a second pipeline was completed through Czechoslovakia to supply gas to West and East Germany. Bulgaria began to receive gas in 1974 through a pipeline across Romania and Hungary was connected to the Czechoslovak transmission system in 1975.

The Soviet Union is a significant importer of natural gas. Imports from Afghanistan, which began in 1967, are now running at an annual rate of nearly 3 billion cubic meters; and imports from Iran, which started in 1970, reached a level of 10 billion cubic meters a year, before dropping off due to the Iranian revolution of 1978-79. The Soviet Union was actually a net importer of gas from 1970 through 1973 until the completion of the second Brotherhood pipeline resulted in a doubling of exports in 1974.

Early Soviet exports originated in the Ukraine, first in the Carpathian fields of the western Ukraine and, after 1970, in the large Shebelinka field near Khar'kov in the eastern Ukraine. Soviet gas production potential was greatly enhanced with the discovery and development of vast reserves in the Central Asian republics of Uzbekistan and Turkmenia as well as in West Siberia. Both regions were distinguished by great distances from consuming centers and by hostile environments. For the development of these fields, the Soviet Union turned to the West for long-term deals involving Western deliveries of steel pipe and other equipment and Soviet payback in natural gas. Agreements were signed with Austria, West Germany, Italy, and France.

A direct gas transmission system from the West Siberian fields to the western Ukraine was completed in 1977. To ensure a steady flow for export to Western Europe, some of the depleted Carpathian fields were being converted to gas-storage reservoirs. Flows to the West were to be further expanded in the 1980s under a multilateral agreement signed in 1975 involving additional importation of Iranian gas into the Soviet Union and equivalent deliveries of Soviet gas to West Germany, France, and Austria. The Soviet Union thus sought to assure Iranian supplies for the Caucasus and the eastern Ukraine, making Soviet supplies available for export to Western Europe.[17] But the project has been tabled as a result of the Iranian revolution.

CMEA integration in the natural gas industry focused on the Orenburg field in the southern Urals and the joint construction of a 1,700-mile pipeline to the western border of the Soviet Union. In a new form of joint development the 56-inch line was divided into segments, each of which was built by a participating CMEA country as a complete turn-key job. (More than 20,000 East European construction workers participated in this project).[18] The pipeline, with a total capacity of 28 billion cubic meters a year, was completed in 1978 and will supply a total gas volume of 15.5 billion cubic meters a year in payback over a 12-year period to Eastern Europe. The Orenburg deposit, discovered in the late 1960s, contains natural gas with a high sulfur content and natural gas liquids which are separated as byproducts before the gas is pumped into pipelines. The field was developed in stages, each with a capacity of 15 billion cubic meters of gas, about 400,000 tons of recovered sulfur, and over one million tons of gas liquids. The first stage went into operation in February 1974 and the second in September 1975. Total production in 1976 was 31.4 billion cubic meters of natural gas (10% of the Soviet total gas output), 680,000 tons of sulfur, and 2.5 million tons of natural gas liquids (mainly propane and butane).[19] The third stage, designed to yield ethane and helium as additional byproducts, went on stream in late

1978 in time for the inauguration of the CMEA pipeline. In the meantime, the output of the Orenburg field has been feeding into the domestic Soviet gas-transmission network.

Coal and Coke

Coal plays a relatively minor role in the Soviet contribution to CMEA integration in the fuels and energy sphere. While total net oil exports in the mid-1970s represented 25% of Soviet production, net coal exports made up only 2.3% of national output. Coal shipments consist mainly of anthracite and high-grade coking coal and, together with coke, have been flowing to East European countries poorly supplied with high-grade coals, particularly Bulgaria and East Germany. Soviet exports have been balanced to some extent by imports from Poland, Eastern Europe's pre-eminent coal exporter, which supplies some of the Soviet Union's fuel-short western border areas. Poland imports about one million tons of very high-grade Soviet coking coal.

Soviet coal shipments represent significant portions of the needs of Bulgaria and East Germany, whose resources are limited largely to brown coal or lignite. In 1977, Bulgaria produced only 287,000 tons of high-grade coal and imported 6.3 million tons, 6 million of which came from the Soviet Union. East Germany, whose imports were equal to those of Bulgaria, obtained 4 million tons from the Soviet Union and the rest from Poland. Virtually all Soviet coal and coke shipments originate in the Donets Basin of the eastern Ukraine, with some shipments to Bulgaria using the Black Sea route. Although the Donets Basin is the Soviet Union's leading coal producer, accounting for 29% of all Soviet coal in 1978, its potential for expansion is limited by difficult mining geology and high costs. Any substantial export increase would have to be met by the much longer hauls of high-grade coal from the Kuznetsk Basin in southern Siberia, either directly for export or to compensate for any rise in coal shipments from the Donets Basin.

Electric Power

Among the fuel and energy industries, the production of electricity probably offers the best opportunities for genuine long-term integration among the CMEA partners, with the Soviet Union providing the largest export. Interconnections between the national electricity grids provide the capability for peak-load transfers to take advantage of differences in time zones. The interconnected national power systems of Czechoslovakia, East Germany, Hungary, and Poland were joined in 1962 to the L'vov electricity system of the western Ukraine to form the international "Peace" power grid, which was joined in 1963 by Romania and in 1967 by Bulgaria.[20] In addition, a separate direct intertie was completed in 1972 between a large central electric station at Dnestrovsk in Soviet Moldavia and Bulgaria across Romania.[21] In 1977, a 400-kilovolt line linking these areas carried 4 billion kilowatt-hours of electricity, which represents 30% of the Moldavia power output and 14% of Bulgaria's electric consumption.

Soviet electricity transfers also represent a significant input in the Hungarian economy, whose electric power importation of 4.5 billion kilowatt-hours in 1975 represented 16% of total Hungarian consumption. Although total Soviet electric power exports to Eastern Europe doubled in the first half of the 1970s, from 4.6 billion kilowatt-hours in 1970 to 10 billion in 1977, transfers are still limited by the inadequate carrying capacity of transmission lines, which operate mainly at 220 kilovolts, with only a few trunk lines. In an effort to increase the power transfers, the first of a proposed network of high-voltage interties was built in 1978 between the Soviet Union and Hungary at 750 kilovolts. The Soviet-Hungarian intertie is an extension of a domestic Soviet 750-kilovolt line completed in 1975 between the Donets Basin and Vinnitsa in the western Ukraine, a distance of 470 miles. Under a joint CMEA project, the line was extended from Vinnitsa to the Hungarian electric power grid at Albertirsa, 30 miles southeast of Budapest. It was a 140 million ruble agreement signed by all East European members of CMEA except Romania. Under the terms of the project, the Soviet Union and Hungary built their own national segments of the transmission line, and other CMEA partners supplied equipment and materials in proportion to the benefit they would ultimately derive. The first Soviet section between Vinnitsa and the Khodorov substation near L'vov, a distance of 225 miles, was completed in early 1977,[22] and the entire line, including the difficult construction segment across the Carpathian Mountains, was completed in late 1978. It is expected to carry 6.4 billion kilowatt-hours of electricity, or two-thirds of total Soviet exports to Eastern Europe as of 1975. Additional 750 kilovolt international interties have been proposed between the Soviet Union, Romania, and Bulgaria and between the USSR and Poland under a coordinated electric power development plan running until 1990.[23]

Until the construction of the high-voltage interconnection within the Ukraine, Soviet electric power exports, except for the Moldavian-Bulgarian intertie, originated in the L'vov power system of the western Ukraine. The L'vov system generated about 20 billion kilowatt-hours a year in the mid-1970s and exported roughly 30%. Most of the electricity in the system is generated by the Burshtyn station, which began producing power in the summer of 1965 and reached its designed capacity of 2.4 million kilowatts at the end of 1969. It was one of the largest Soviet power producing centers at the time. .

The new 750-kilovolt interconnection, aside from raising the capacity for intra-CMEA electricity transfers, will also connect the "Peace" power grid with the unified Soviet domestic grid beyond the L'vov system, thus enhancing maneuverability of power transfers. In the Ukraine, for example, three-fourths of the electric power is generated by stations in the eastern Donets-Dnieper economic region.

Under the new energy policy, which applies to the Soviet Union and CMEA countries, further increases in electric generating capacity will be based mainly on lignite-fired and nuclear power stations for base-load requirements and on hydroelectric stations and pumped-storage facilities to cover peak loads. The Soviet contribution, in the absence of large fossil fuel reserves or hydroelectric potential in the western regions, will be mainly in nuclear power. A major expansion program is under way, with much of the nuclear generating capacity being installed in the western border regions.[24] In the Ukraine, the first major nuclear station, with an ultimate designed capacity of 4 million kilowatts, began operating in 1977 at Chernobyl' north of Kiev, with the first of four proposed 1 million kilowatt reactors, followed by a second in 1978. Other stations were under construction at Rafalovka, north of Rovno, on the main Kiev-Warsaw rail line, and near Nikolayev in the southern Ukraine. The start of construction on a fourth, the Aktash lagoon of the eastern Crimea, was announced in early 1977.[25] Projected nuclear station sites in the Ukraine include Khmel'nitskiy, Rozhnyatov in the Carpathian foothills west of Ivano-Frankovsk, and Tuzly on the Black Sea southwest of Odessa. In Lithuania, the projected 6 million kilowatt Ignalina nuclear station at Sneckus has been specifically earmarked for interconnection with the CMEA power network.[26] Over the longer term, if technological advance makes it economically feasible to transfer large blocks of electricity from Siberia to the European USSR at extra-high voltages, the combined CMEA power transmission network may benefit from such additional power supplies together with the entire European part of the Soviet Union.

Ores and Metals

Iron and Steel

In view of the limitations of the East European raw material base, iron ore represents by far the largest Soviet input. Because of inadequate blast-furnace capacity in Eastern Europe and a large supply of scrap metal for the steel industry, crude steel production has been running far ahead of pig-iron production, and the Soviet Union has been obliged to supplement East European production with pig-iron shipments. Fabricated steel products also represent a significant element in intra-CMEA trade, with an effort to foster specialization in particular rolled steel products.

In view of the significance of the Soviet iron-ore supply, integration efforts focus especially on this aspect of the industry, with the Soviet Union's CMEA partners joining in iron-ore and ferroalloy projects under agreements signed in 1974.[27] Since the early postwar period, Soviet ore shipments have increased to 32.4 million tons in 1970 and 36.1 million tons in 1977. Domestic ore production in East European countries totaled only 3.7 million tons in 1977. Over 60% of all ore shipments from the Soviet Union went to Poland and Czechoslovakia, the two principal iron and steel producers.

In contrast to fuel and energy supplies, which originate to a large extent in the distant West Siberian gas and oil fields, Soviet ore shipments cover much shorter hauls. In a marked exception to the usual eastern resource concentration, most of the iron-ore resources occur in the European section in proximity to CMEA partners. Most of the ore shipments to Eastern Europe originate in the Krivoy Rog district, which in 1978 produced about 110 million tons of ore, or 45% of total Soviet output. But in recent years, an increasing volume of ore exports has been coming from the Kursk Magnetic Anomaly, which in 1978 yielded about 40 million tons of ore, or 16% of national production.

In view of the increasing needs for Soviet ore in Eastern Europe, in 1974 the CMEA nations agreed to develop additional production capacity in both the Ukraine and the KMA district to increase ore deliveries by 25% by 1980, or about 48 million tons compared with 38 million in 1975. Much of the emphasis is on the preparation of iron pellets, a compact iron concentrate that enhances the efficiency of blast-furnace operation. In the Ukraine, an additional pelletizing capacity of 20 million tons will be added under the CMEA agreement. In early 1976, the Ukraine produced 18 million tons of pellets, so the proposed capacity additions would raise the total to 38 million tons by 1980.[28] Substantial expansions in pelletizing capacities are also underway in the KMA district. The first stage of the new Zheleznogorsk pelletizer, with a capacity of 3.1 million tons, began operations in late 1976 with a major contribution by Bulgarian workers. The additional annual shipments from these ore projects will total 9 million tons.[29]

The increased ore flows to Eastern Europe are made particularly necessary by the construction of a large new iron and steel plant at Katowice, Poland, with an ultimate designed capacity of 9 million tons of steel. The first stage of the complex was inaugurated in late

1976. In connection with growing ore traffic from the Soviet Union to Poland, plans have been announced for building a new rail line. The proposed northern route between the KMA district and Katowice would cross the Soviet-Polish border at Vladimir-Volynskiy/ Hrubieszow and would use the Soviet broad gauge along the entire route to eliminate the time-consuming practice of trans-shipment at border stations.

While increasing the need for ore supplies, the Katowice plant will improve Poland's pig-iron situation and reduce the shipments of pig-iron from the Soviet Union, amounting to 1.5 million tons a year, or 35% of all Soviet pig-iron deliveries to Eastern Europe. However, pig-iron exports will still be required, particularly to East Germany, where the gap between pig-iron production (2.6 million tons in 1977) and steel output (6.9 million tons) has been particularly pronounced.

The 1974 agreement of CMEA partners in the iron and steel industry also provided for joint development of additional ferroalloy capacity in the Soviet Union, particularly at the Nikopol' center in the Ukraine and at the distant new producing complex of Yermak in northeast Kazakhstan. The Yermak ferroalloys plant, adjoining the lignite-fired 2.4 million kilowatt Yermak thermal power station, was inaugurated in 1968 and reached a capacity of about 250,000 tons by 1975. Under the CMEA arrangement, it is being expanded by the addition of 50,000 ton electric furnaces that will raise capacity to about 600,000 by 1980. The first six furnaces, with a combined capacity of 300,000 tons of ferrosilicon, went into operation in 1979.[30] The Nikopol' ferroalloys plant, which originally went into operation in 1966, is situated in the heart of the Soviet Union's principal manganese mining district (over 70% of total Soviet ferroalloy exports, which went mainly to Czechoslovakia and Romania); and the increasing flow from the joint investment projects at Nikopol' and Yermak is designed to upgrade the quality of East European steel. The added deliveries will total 200,000 tons a year.

Over the long term, the Soviet Union wants to slow the ever-increasing shipments of raw materials to the East European iron and steel industry and to base integration to a greater extent on specialization in semifinished steel products to reduce the long hauls of large volumes of low-value ores. In accordance with this policy, there are plans for the construction of a huge iron and steel complex in the KMA district, with a projected capacity of 10 to 12 million tons of steel, serving mainly the CMEA market. But the project has been delayed while the Soviet Union gives priority to the construction of a smaller steel plant using a new technology. The plant, using the so-called direct conversion process with a first-stage capacity of 1.8 million tons of steel, is being built with West German financial and technical assistance at Staryy Oskol. The process bypasses the blast furnace stage of conventional iron and steel production and smelts pellets with a high iron content directly in steel furnaces. It thus eliminates the entire pig-iron stage and the need for coke. There are tentative plans to follow up the direct-conversion plant with the large conventional CMEA plant.[31] The first-stage design of the larger plant, also in the Staryy Oskol area, includes two 5,000 cubic meter blast furnaces with a combined capacity of 8 million tons of pig-iron and three basic oxygen converters with a capacity of 9 million tons of steel. Staryy Oskol, with a population of 50,000 in 1970, has been envisaged as one of the largest iron and steel centers of the Soviet Union by 1990; it reached a population of 115,000 in 1979.

The need for the CMEA-oriented steel plant is regarded as particularly urgent in view of the long hauls now involved in some Soviet steel exports to Eastern Europe. Although close to 75% of all iron and steel exports originated in the Ukraine and Central Russia, relatively close to the western border, there were instances of excessively long hauls in the early 1970s.[32] For example, East Germany, by far the leading importer of Soviet steel products (42% of total product exports in 1977), obtained more than one-half of its supplies from the Urals, West Siberia, and Kazakhstan, involving hauls of 3,000 to 4,000 kilometers. A Soviet writer commented that "it would probably make more sense to have a larger portion of iron and steel shipments originate in the European portion of the USSR, particularly when it comes to shipments destined for East Germany."[33]

Aluminum

The Soviet role in CMEA integration involves a variety of nonferrous metals, among which aluminum accounts for more than one-half by weight. Because of the production of particular metals in some East European countries, the nonferrous trade flows are somewhat complex, with the Soviet Union in the position of importer in some cases. In the case of zinc and lead, for example, Soviet exports go mainly to East Germany and Czechoslovakia while Poland ships zinc to the Soviet Union. Unlike zinc and lead, which the Soviet Union exports mainly to Eastern Europe, copper moves largely outside the CMEA market, where Czechoslovakia and Hungary are the principal importers.

In aluminum, however, the Soviet Union has a pre-eminent position, mainly because of the availability of vast resources of low-cost hydroelectric power, which is the principal cost element in the aluminum industry. The locational attraction of the great waterpower resources of south central Siberia outweighs a general shortage of high-grade aluminum ores in the Soviet Union, an unusual situation for a country that is generally regarded as a potential source of a wide range of raw materials. In the mid-1970s, as much as 40% of the Soviet production of aluminum metal is estimated to have been derived from imported raw materials, either bauxite, the ore, or alumina, an intermediate product.[34]

One source of raw materials has been Hungary, which, as one of the major bauxite producers, has the raw-material base for an aluminum industry but not the required cheap electric power resources. Until 1955, Hungary supplied bauxite to the Soviet aluminum industry. After a hiatus of about ten years, in which Hungary used the bauxite to build up a domestic alumina and aluminum industry and to supply aluminum industries in East Germany and Czechoslovakia, a new Soviet-Hungarian aluminum arrangement went into effect. Under the accord, Hungary was to supply alumina to a Soviet plant opened in 1959 at Volgograd and to receive aluminum in return. Alumina and aluminum shipments were to be in the ratio of 2:1 because it takes two tons of alumina to make one ton of aluminum. In practice, however, the Soviet Union has been importing Hungarian alumina far in excess of the equivalent aluminum exports. The gap has been widening, particularly since 1972, apparently reflecting the increasing Soviet need for imports of aluminum raw materials. Under the original agreement with Hungary, the exchange for 1975 was to involve 240,000 tons of alumina and 120,000 tons of aluminum.[35] Actual deliveries in 1975 were 405,000 tons of alumina and 102,000 tons of aluminum, or a ratio of 4:1. The agreement, originally concluded for the period 1967-80, was extended until 1985.

The Soviet Union made a similar arrangement with Yugoslavia, which, though not a full member, participates in CMEA activities. Yugoslavia has been an increasingly important supplier of bauxite to the Soviet Union since 1965, with shipments reaching 947,000 tons in 1975, or 42% of Yugoslav production.[36] Under the new agreement, the Soviet Union is to obtain alumina from a large Yugoslav plant built at Zvornik with Soviet technical assistance, with total shipments of 5.7 million tons of alumina over the ten-year period 1976-85. These shipments, averaging 570,000 tons a year, would exceed the Hungarian contribution and make Yugoslavia the principal foreign source of alumina for the Soviet aluminum industry.

Asbestos

In the realm of building materials and other nonmetallics, including cement, window glass, and refractories, one of the principal CMEA integration efforts focuses on the development of additional asbestos capacity in the Soviet Union, which rivals Canada as an important producer of the mineral fiber. Soviet production of asbestos in 1975 is estimated at about 2.5 million tons, including very low-grade short fibers suitable only as fillers in such products as floor tile, plastics, and asphalt. Because of high world demand, based on the growth of the construction industry in industrial countries, asbestos, including some of the short fibers known as refuse, represents a significant earner of foreign exchange for the Soviet Union. Shipments to East European members of CMEA rose from 38% of total Soviet asbestos exports in 1970 to 43% in 1975, cutting into potential exports to the West.

Demand for Soviet asbestos rose in the first half of the 1970s in Poland, Romania, and Hungary, with an expansion of production of asbestos-cement building materials. This accounted for a 77% growth in Soviet exports to Eastern Europe compared with a 48% increase in shipments to other countries.

By far the largest reserves and production of asbestos in the Soviet Union are associated with the Urals deposit of Asbest (the former Bazhenovo) near Sverdlovsk, which now accounts for 75 to 80% of Soviet output. Since the mid-1960s, two other asbestos sites have been developed: at Dzhetygara, in the Urals section of northwest Kazakhstan, where production in 1975 was close to 600,000 tons, and at Ak-Dovurak, in the Tuva Autonomous Republic of southern Siberia, where 1975 output was 65,000 tons.

Development of a fourth major deposit, the Kiyembay site of the southern Urals in Orenburg Oblast, began in 1961. The following year the mining town of Yasnyy was founded on the project site and by 1970 has a population of 15,900. But with limited Soviet investment allocation, the project dragged on and came to a virtual standstill. In this context, in 1973 the CMEA partners agreed on joint development of the Kiyembay deposit. Under the agreement, the six East European members are contributing equipment and supplies valued at 100 million rubles for the development of the mine and construction of the mill, with their shares to be paid back with asbestos shipments. The mill, with a designed capacity of 500,000 tons, is to be completed in two 250,000 ton stages: the first opened in 1979 and the second is due in 1981. Reserves of asbestos rock are said to be adequate for at least 40 years of production.[37]

Under the 1973 agreement, the Soviet Union is committed to pay back the CMEA investment with total annual shipments of 180,000 tons, or 36% of the total output, over the 12-year period 1980-91. These shipments would represent a 70% rise over the asbestos exports to Eastern Europe in 1975. Poland is contributing the largest credit—30 million devisa rubles, or about 28% of the total—and will take an equivalent share of asbestos—50,000 tons—reflecting rapidly growing needs.[38]

Chemicals

CMEA integration in the chemical industry has relied significantly on Soviet resources, involving both bulk commodities like chemical raw materials and fertilizers and hydrocarbon-based petrochemicals such as thermoplastics (polyethylene and polypropylene), which in addition to a gas or petroleum base also require large energy inputs.

Phosphates

Exports of phosphatic raw materials have consisted mainly of apatite concentrate, a high-grade material from the Kola Peninsula, used in the manufacture of superphosphate. Shipments reached a peak of 6.6 million tons in 1973 (50% of Soviet apatite output), with about 70% going to East European countries. Because of growing domestic demand and the need for conserving the high-grade, but limited apatite reserves, Soviet exports declined in the mid-1970s to 5.8 million tons in 1975, or 38% of Soviet output.[39] The Soviet Union has sought to make use of lower-grade phosphate rock, notably the Karatau deposit in southern Kazakhstan. The 1971 program for CMEA integration envisaged the joint development of the Karatau resources, but thus far they have been developed largely outside of the multinational framework.

On a more limited scale, the CMEA nations joined in the modernization of a phosphate rock complex at Kingisepp (Leningrad Oblast), where the output had been limited to low-nutrient ground rock. With credit from the East European nations (except Romania), the local rock, in combination with apatite from the Kola Peninsula, served as the basis for an ammonium phosphate complex via the sulfuric acid route. A first section opened in 1973 and the second in late 1975.[40]

Potash

Although the Soviet Union has been historically a leading potash producer from mines in the Solikamsk-Berezniki area of the Urals, CMEA needs were largely met by East German potash until the development of a second potash mining district at Soligorsk in Belorussia. Three mining complexes were completed at Soligorsk in the 1960s with investment from Poland, the largest consumer of potash in Eastern Europe. Since 1970, almost 30% of the potash output of Soligorsk has moved to Poland. The Belorussian potash deposits, though of lower grade than the Urals ore, have thus become a significant export industry of the Soviet Union because of proximity to Eastern Europe.

The development of the Belorussian potash deposit greatly stimulated Soviet exports. In 1965, before production at Soligorsk reached full capacity, exports represented only 14.5% of Soviet production. In the mid-1970s, as much as 35% of Soviet output was exported. Poland now meets more than 60% of its needs from the Belorussian mines.

Nitrogen Fertilizers

On the western border of the Soviet Union, the construction of natural-gas pipelines from interior fields has given rise to important nitrogen fertilizer complexes. Gas transmission from the Carpathian fields in the Dashava district, later supplemented by pipelines from other regions, led to the construction of nitrogen fertilizer plants at Jonava, Lithuania; Grodno, Belorussia; and Rovno, Ukraine. The Grodno plant produced 1.5 million tons of fertilizer (in standard units of 20.5% nitrogen nutrient) in 1975 and is slated to double its capacity, thus becoming one of the largest nitrogen fertilizer complexes in the USSR.[41] Both the Jonava and Rovno plants have upgraded their output from simple ammonium nitrate to higher-analysis fertilizers.[42] In general, the tendency in Soviet manufacture and export of chemical fertilizers has been to upgrade simple products with low nutrient content to higher-analysis products.

Petrochemicals

In the petrochemical field, CMEA integration aims at specialization based on feedstocks derived from Soviet oil both at Soviet and at East European petrochemical plants. Probably the best example of such interlinkages is the so-called olefin complex involving Hungary and the Soviet Union. Olefins are a class of hydrocarbons that include ethylene, an important building block in the chemical industry. Under the 1975 arrangement, the Hungarian petrochemical plant at Leninvaros extracts ethylene and another olefin, propylene, from Soviet oil brought in by the Friendship-2 pipeline. Surplus olefins are then shipped to the Soviet chemical plant at Kalush in the western Ukraine. The shipments include 130,000 tons of ethylene which moves by rail tank cars. At Kalush, the ethylene is combined with locally produced chlorine to produce ethylene chloride, an intermediate product in the manufacture of the widely used resin polyvinyl chloride (PVC). One-fourth of the PVC produced at Kalush is earmarked for export, mostly to Hungary. Indeed, Soviet trade figures show a marked jump in resin exports to Hungary, from 9,500 tons in

1974 to 32,200 tons in 1975. The Kalush PVC complex, based on Hungarian feedstocks, has a capacity of 250,000 tons, virtually doubling Soviet production.[43]

Forest Products

Vast forest resources are the key factor in the role the USSR plays in CMEA integration in the forest industries, but a lag in the development of processing has accounted for an excessively large share of roundwood and sawnwood in Soviet exports and relatively limited exports of woodpulp, paper, and paperboard. Moreover, these processed products tend to be of low grade, such as newsprint, while high-grade pulp and paper products continue to be imported by the Soviet Union, mostly from Finland.

The largest share of Soviet exports of roundwood has been going to Japan (sawtimber) and Finland (pulp wood). In 1977, only 17% of roundwood exports went to Eastern Europe, with Hungary and East Germany the principal importers (three-fourths of all Soviet shipments to Eastern Europe). Most of the roundwood shipments to the CMEA countries originate in northern European Russia and move through the ports of Arkhangel'sk and Leningrad.

Bulgaria, which has furnished labor for many Soviet development projects, has had a special arrangement in the forest sector since the late 1960s, with Bulgarian loggers felling timber in the Komi ASSR of northern Russia for shipment to Bulgaria. In connection with the logging project, Soviet roundwood exports to Bulgaria jumped sixfold, from 65,000 tons in 1965 to 400,000 tons a year in the late 1970s, while sawnwood shipments doubled during the same period.

In the case of sawnwood, a larger share of Soviet exports—37% in 1977—moves to Eastern Europe, with East Germany and Hungary the principal importers. Most of the sawnwood exports originate in northern European Russia, but Siberia is beginning to play a more important role as the European forest areas become depleted and logging activities move eastward. In the ten-year period 1965-75, the northern Russian share in Soviet sawnwood production declined from 16.5 to 15.9% while the Siberian share rose from 26 to 28%. In contrast to roundwood, some areas of Siberia are considered an economical source of sawnwood for Eastern Europe. Transport costs are twice as high from Siberia, but production costs are lower, according to Soviet cost calculations, so that the combined delivered cost of sawnwood from West Siberia is actually said to be lower than from North European Russia (though not from East Siberia).[44]

In view of the Soviet Union's huge domestic demand for paper and paperboard and the historical lag of wood-processing industries, these processed products play a negligible role in CMEA integration. Net Soviet exports of all paper in 1977 represented only 3.1% of Soviet production, and in the case of paperboard, net exports were 6.6% of output. The principal exceptions were newsprint and woodpulp.

Soviet newsprint exports in 1977 constituted 23% of total production, accounting for virtually all the newsprint used in Bulgaria and Hungary, and for 20 to 30% of the newsprint needs of East Germany, Poland, and Romania. Because of the market-oriented location of paper mills in general and newsprint mills in particular, Soviet newsprint production is concentrated in the European part of the country within reasonable transport distances of Eastern Europe.

Of particular interest are the evolving relations between the Soviet Union and its CMEA partners in the woodpulp field. Of all the wood-processing industries, pulp production has been most responsive to the growing eastward shift of Soviet logging activities to Siberia. The Siberian share in the industry increased from 10% in 1965 to more than 20% in 1975.[45] The principal Siberian producer is the Bratsk complex, which began operations in 1967 and reached a pulp-manufacturing capacity of 1 million tons in 1976.

The eastward trend in woodpulp production is assuming significance in the context of CMEA integration. Soviet net pulp exports in 1977 were relatively small in relation to production, amounting to 480,000 tons or 6.4% of total output. Exports of 680,000 tons, of which 63% moved to Eastern Europe, were balanced to some extent by imports from Scandinavia, particularly Finland. However, the Soviet Union has been a major source of pulp for some East European countries, supplying as much as 44% of the needs of Hungary, 30% of Bulgaria's, 15% of Poland's, and 12% of East Germany's.[46]

Because of increasing East European demand and the high cost of developing additional capacity in the Soviet Union, the CMEA countries (except Czechoslovakia) agreed in 1972 to supply construction workers, building materials, machinery, and consumer goods for the joint construction of a large pulp-making complex at Ust'-Ilimsk on the Angara River in East Siberia, where a hydroelectric station was under construction. The first stage of the Ust'-Ilimsk pulp complex, with an ultimate capacity of 500,000 tons, is now scheduled for 1980, a slippage of two years beyond the original deadline.[47] This project is the largest in the Soviet wood-products industry during the current five-year plan (1976-80) and is absorbing one-fourth of all Soviet investment allocated to the pulp and paper industry, with annual allocations averaging 250 million rubles.[48] The total East European contribution amounts to 328 million rubles and is to be paid back with shipments of woodpulp.[49] Soviet planners have pointed out that the deliveries of pulp to Eastern Europe over distances of 3,500 miles will place an additional burden on the Soviet transport system. "It would seem legitimate for the participating countries to invest jointly in the development of transport facilities associated with these long wood-pulp hauls," one Soviet author suggested.[50]

Conclusion

This survey of selected industrial sectors suggests that CMEA integration linkages have involved the development of the western Soviet regions, adjoining the borders of Eastern Europe, and of more distant areas distinguished by a wealth of resources. The complex interrelationships in manufacturing, particularly machine-building, were outside the scope of the discussion.

The eastward shift in resource development within the CMEA context is associated generally with the disparity that exists within the Soviet Union between the populated and economically developed western regions and the presence of most of the natural resources in the eastern regions. The joint CMEA projects in the eastern regions represent only a part of the development that is essential for Soviet domestic needs as the need for energy and raw materials increases. Siberia is viewed as a resource reservoir for the western regions and, by extension, for the Soviet Union's allies in Eastern Europe.

Both the European regions of the Soviet Union and the countries of Eastern Europe are thus looking to the east for supplies of oil and natural gas from West Siberia, for shipments of high-grade coking coals and steam coals from the Kuznetsk Basin, and for the provision of electric power from the low-cost Siberian sources of hydroelectricity and lignite-fired thermal power complexes. With the gradual depletion of the North Russian forests and the growing demand for wood products, Siberia is also beginning to play a more significant role in the forest industries.

Of particular interest, however, has been the development of CMEA linkages in the Soviet border regions, involving the western Ukraine, Moldavia, Belorussia, and Lithuania. Industrialization of these regions has been fostered in recent years both by the presence of surplus labor and, particularly, by proximity to the East European partners. Examples of close integration in the western border areas may be found in the establishment of the Peace electricity grid, the construction of oil refineries and petrochemical complexes, the iron and steel industry, and the expansion of chemical activities.

The CMEA electric power network will reach more deeply into the Soviet Union because of the completion of the 750-kilovolt transmission line between the Donets Basin and Hungary. In the longer term, the international grid will also receive increasing support from large nuclear power stations near the Soviet western border. The petrochemical development is designed to shift gradually from the Soviet provision of crude oil via the Friendship pipeline system to a greater interchange of semifinished or finished products between the Soviet Union and Eastern Europe. A start has been made by the interesting olefin exchange involving the Hungarian petrochemical center of Leninvaros and the west Ukrainian chemical complex of Kalush.

An exception to the general resource situation in the Soviet Union, iron-ore reserves are concentrated in the west. This feature will enhance the role of the western regions of the Soviet Union in CMEA integration in the iron and steel industry. Thus far, the trend still involves iron-ore shipments from the Krivoy Rog area and, increasingly, from the expanding ore district of the Kursk Magnetic Anomaly in central European Russia. But the long-term aim, as in the petrochemical industry, is to slow the ever-increasing flow of raw materials in favor of an interchange of semifinished and finished products. The long-planned iron and steel complex in the Staryy Oskol area of the KMA would be a step in that direction.

Closely associated with the development of the western regions is the increasing attention being given to seaboard development. Although this aspect is being fostered to a large degree by the growing interchange between the Soviet Union and the world economy—the construction of oil-export tanker terminals at Novorossiysk and at Ventspils and the building of chemical port terminals at Yuzhnyy (near Odessa) and Ventspils—the new seaward orientation also has a bearing on CMEA linkages. In the Baltic Sea, a growing volume of shipments to Poland and East Germany use the maritime route to ease the burden on the overloaded rail system. In the Black Sea, the growing traffic between the Soviet Union and Bulgaria is using an unusual three-decker rail ferry system between Il'yichevsk, the outer port of Odessa, and Varna, put in operation in 1978.[51]

The long-term outlook for CMEA integration would thus appear to involve not only the much discussed development of Soviet resources at distant Siberian sites, but also increasing interplay between Eastern Europe and the western regions of the Soviet Union, both overland and by sea.

This survey of the regional effects of Soviet-CMEA foreign trade and joint investment projects documents the thesis that Soviet regional policies have become closely linked to CMEA integration. Substantial evidence exists that the pull of the CMEA market and the flow of CMEA commodity credits have significantly altered the pattern of Soviet industrial location and regional development.

Discussion
Robert N. Taaffe

Theodore Shabad has provided a useful listing of East European investments in the exploitation of Soviet natural resources and the impact of the East European market on the development of Soviet regions, particularly in the western borderlands. Much of this evidence could be used to provide insights into such complex questions as the interrelationships of Soviet regional policies and CMEA objectives or the theory and practice of regional development in the USSR. Apart from documenting the impressive recent gains in industrial investment, Shabad makes little effort to derive policy or methodological implications from his inventory. An evident preoccupation with the specific locational details of resource and industrial sites contrasts sharply with his neglect of comparative costs, location theory, and major unresolved methodological and practical issues of regional development in the Soviet Union.

Shabad raises a basic regional issue in his reference to the growth of diversified industrialization in the West in response to the proximity of the CMEA market. By contrast, a resource-oriented path of development is pursued in Siberia and the Far East to meet expanded domestic and CMEA demands. The questions of relative investment problems in these areas (henceforth the East and the West) are far more complex than Shabad suggests. My comments will focus on the problems in development planning in the East and West. This is the most significant and persistent issue in Soviet regional planning and is of considerable importance for the entire CMEA bloc inasmuch as the joint investments in the regions of the USSR should continue to expand significantly.

The actors in this protracted game of locational decisionmaking have been the regional advocates, the sectoral planners in Moscow and the centralized research institutes, and the Party leadership, which has assumed the dominant role in arbitrating conflicts within and among these groups. Characteristically, the Party and regionally oriented research institutes, such as the Council for the Study of Productive Forces of Gosplan, have tended to support major investment programs designed to utilize the resources of the East. The opposition, often including Ukrainian planners and many sectoral ministries, usually has pointed out the difficulties of implementing many of these programs and often has succeeded in scaling down their national priority in favor of the intensification of development in the West.[1] In addition, many costly water-diversion, transport, and metallurgical projects in the East have been deferred for decades, in part as a result of the arguments of the regional and sectoral advocates of investment in the West. The resolution of this conflict is impeded by serious limitations in the available data, mechanisms, and methodologies of regional planning in the USSR. Many of the planning devices tend to encourage development in Siberia, although they have not been able to diminish significantly the pre-eminence of the West.

An accurate assessment of the effectiveness of investment in the regions of the USSR is a particularly complex task because of some serious methodological and data problems. The difficulties associated with the Soviet use of differential coefficients of normative investment effectiveness for industrial sectors are magnified substantially by the use of differing compensatory norms of investment effectiveness for construction in ten regions, four climatic zones, and even one seismic zone. The net result is that competitive regional disadvantages caused by high relative costs for construction or the installation of machinery often are mitigated by an arbitrary planning device, and Siberian investment opportunities in particular are made to appear more attractive in economic calculations.[2]

The evaluation of transport costs from Siberia to the western regions of the USSR or to other CMEA countries is also quite tenuous; Soviet freight tariffs usually are not used in economic calculations because of their substantial and highly variable regional and modal deviations from costs. In addition, the formidable task of estimating the costs of movement and investments in transport facilities often yields results that reflect ministerial preferences and are of uncertain utility in spatial decisionmaking.[3] Artificially low transport costs frequently have been used to justify specific projects in Siberia. The costs associated with the long-distance flow of Siberian goods to the CMEA market are of more concern to the Soviet Union than its East European trading partners inasmuch as the basic contractual foreign-trade prices do not include transport costs and each country bears the costs for movement within its borders. However, prices for inter-CMEA trade for bulk commodities with low unit values normally include "half-freight" charges. This involves adding one-half the transport rate from the hypothetical world supplier to the specific CMEA market to the contractual inter-CMEA foreign-trade price (with a second adjustment for trade between noncontiguous CMEA countries).[4] In contrast to even rudimentary notions of spatial efficiency, this freight-pricing system enables a CMEA country to reduce its transport outlays by importing a bulk commodity from a Siberian source 6,000 miles away rather than by obtaining the same commodity by a 200-mile haul from a contiguous West European country. As a rule, the transport costs the USSR bears for Siberian exports to CMEA nations appear to be substantially in excess of that portion of the world transport charges added to the contractual foreign-trade prices. Apparently, the USSR believes that the diverse benefits of development in Siberia outweigh the extra construction, production, and transport costs which this locational strategy often incurs. By contrast, the growth of industries in the western borderlands and seacoasts which process raw materials and energy resources for export of higher value products represents a Soviet effort to minimize its transport costs and maximize commodity trade revenues.

In one sense, the CMEA countries would tend to be indifferent to Soviet locational choices because of the procedures for the allocation of transport costs and because the commodity repayments are based on the magnitude of the credits regardless of the investment efficiency of the specific regional development. On the other hand, the CMEA evaluations of the investment and trade opportunity costs of joint participation in Soviet resource exploitation projects, among other things, presumably consider many locational problems. For example, an assessment would be made of the costs of tying up massive investment credits at low interest in expensive and long-term industrial and transport developments in Soviet regions, and the problems induced by a growing need for a large-scale influx of CMEA labor to construct joint projects. Thus, the CMEA partners of the USSR also have a strong interest in the regional aspects of Soviet development planning.

The general guidelines for regional development in the USSR are based on relative factor endowments and do not provide planners with answers to a complex question such as the optimal level and structure of regional development and interregional or international trade. Nor do they address subsets of this problem such as the extent to which resources should be processed locally or shipped interregionally (or internationally) for processing; the detailed elaboration of comparative regional advantage; the degree to which local productive and social infrastructures should be developed to support specialized activities; and the balancing of considerations of economic efficiency, regional equity, political and defense objectives, and environmental protection in regional decisionmaking. Soviet scholars have turned their attention to these problems and have made progress toward clarifying them, usually in the process of developing analytical frameworks for the investigation of spatial or regional problems. On the other hand, the planning system has made only modest advances in incorporating these concepts or methods into comparative regional analysis or in handling the complexities of regional planning in general.

The issues raised in the East-West locational controversy point out some of the problems of regional and spatial planning that are relevant to an understanding of the difficult task of linking Soviet regional development to CMEA objectives. One of the most evident problems is the limited role assigned to regional planning in the Soviet Union. The strong orientation of the USSR toward centralized, sectorally focused planning has led to the dominance of the center in locational decisionmaking and the frequent neglect of external economies and diseconomies. The union republics devote most of their planning efforts to the compilation of a republican plan and a set of diverse planning balances, both derived primarily by combining the ministerial sectoral plans for enterprises within the territorial jurisdiction of individual republics. In these endeavors, the planning commissions of the union republics rely essentially on information supplied by ministries. This information often arrives too late to be used for the scrutiny of major projects and is structured to support ministerial preferences rather than independent regional assessment. The central ministries usually win conflicts with regional groups by noting that ministerial decisions reflect national rather than provincial interests. The limited access of regional planners to national data and central decisionmakers makes it difficult to present a successful counterargument, in the accepted language of discourse for this type of debate, that the ministerial decisions reflect a "narrow-departmental" approach.

Most of the union republics are not meaningful regions for economic administration (nor are the states in the US) because they have been delimited on the basis of ethnic criteria. This problem is particularly apparent in the Russian Republic, which occupies 76% of Soviet territory, or one-eighth of the land area of the world, but which constitutes a single planning region. Even the modest effort of 1961 to provide administrative functions for the 19 statistical regions of Gosplan, including 10 regions in RSFSR, only lasted until 1969 when the regional planning commissions were abolished. The national economic plan includes a section describing the goals for industrial development of the regions of the Russian Republic with special sections on the East and some of its subregions. But as Pavlenko has pointed out, the industrial ministries of the USSR are not assigned responsibility for the fulfillment of the regional aspects of the plan.[5]

Another serious problem is the failure of sectoral plans to consider the interrelationships of a wide range of economic, social, and environmental variables apparently because the methodological, informational, and computing problems would be increased exponentially when locational planning is placed in a complex regional framework. An impressive amount of applied and theoretical work in the Soviet Union has been directed toward this problem and some important gains have been made. For example, a multitude of ad hoc special regions have been used to plan the local impact of major investment projects. On a broader scale, the concern for the measurement and assessment of intraregional linkages has led to the use in certain instances of a form of spatial organization referred to as territorial productive complexes. These entities represent a spatially and technologically related set of industrial activities, usually focused on the complex utilization of fuels, hydropower resources, or raw materials in pioneer regions, as well as other infrastructural elements. Among the most important industrial complexes in the current plan are those based on West Siberian petroleum and natural gas, East Siberian hydropower, ores and forests (including the CMEA cellulose project cited by Shabad), and the resource-exploitation developments scheduled for the area served by the Baikal-Amur Magistral. The delimitation of these complexes factilitates the concentration of industrial investment in areal units, which are considerably more meaningful than the sprawling political-administrative divisions of Siberia.

The most ambitious innovation has been the formulation of a long-term plan for the location of sectoral activities and regional development in the 1971-80 period, which was used to draw up the ninth five-year plan (1971-75). As with so much of the work in this field, this long-term locational plan was excessively ambitious and was subject to attacks for the crudity of its methods and the limited utility of its prognoses.[6] Nonetheless, another long-term projection, which provides locational guidelines for the current five-year plan, has been devised for the 1976-90 period. However, it does not appear that the state of the art of regional forecasting in the USSR (or anywhere else) has advanced to a point where accurate predictions can be made or where notions of optimality in a complex regional setting can be determined in planning goals.

By contrast, suboptimal quantitative approaches to the distribution of certain sectoral activities have provided an operational form for a portion of the oft-quoted socialist principles of location, which embody a combination of Weberian-type transport minimization objectives for industrial locations, regional equity considerations, and defense motives. Linear and non-linear programming methods have not only been effective practical approaches to the first of these objectives but they have also been expanded into production-transportation models to deal with broader locational problems. Moreover, the frequent use of the objective function of maximizing consumption has transcended the limitation of the narrow, least-cost approach in the socialist principles.

From a regional perspective the widespread compilation of input-output tables for union republics and economic regions, particularly for the years 1966 and 1972, has been accompanied by work on inter-regional input-output tables. However, the well-documented limitations of input-output analysis in general are magnified substantially in the inter-regional variants, particularly when inter-regional supply coefficients have to be estimated.

The normative programming approaches that have attempted to reconcile sectoral and regional interests are exciting intellectual ventures, although their practical applications are rather limited. For example, Albegov has approached this problem with a parametric non-linear programming model in which the parameter is the capacity of particular plants in specific points (including a zero-capacity possibility), and the cost-minimization objective function includes a measure of external economies at different sites.[7]

The mathematical economists at the Siberian Institute of Economics and the Organization of Industrial Production are in the forefront of quantitative regional analysis. Aganbegyan, Granberg, and others have applied a series of optimal, multi-sectoral, and multi-regional models to the study of the East-West locational problem for 16 general commodities.[8] They rely on a modified version of a method devised by the Hungarian economists, Kornai and Liptak, in which the objective function is the maximization of consumption, subject to the constraints of national capital investment limitations, obligatory inter-regional deliveries, and the requirement of equal levels of life in the eastern and western zones. Game-iterative procedures and shadow-price magnitudes are used to shift investments between zones and create inter-zonal commodity flows until no further gains in national consumption are possible. Among the conclusions was that Siberian resources must play a crucial role in Soviet development, a finding they certainly would extend to the entire CMEA bloc. The Siberian group also has applied the decomposition rule of Danzig and Wolfe to problems involving optimization in regional subsets subject to constraints of national capital investment funds and inter-regional trade. A far-reaching implication drawn from this approach is that an optimal national plan could be derived from optimal regional plans subject to national constraints, which indeed would be a drastic departure from existing planning practices.

A recent advance in programming methodology in the U.S. and Western Europe (and which almost certainly will be used by the Siberian group) is the burgeoning growth of multi-objective programming models, such as hierarchical and interactive programming, which treat a number of objective functions.[9] In interactive programming, for example, trade-offs between objective functions are made with the aid of payoff tables to obtain "best-compromise" solutions. The multi-objective approaches give every indication of becoming one of the most powerful analytical tools for the investigation of the characteristics and multiple goals of regional development.

At present, the practical utility of rigorous analytical approaches in Soviet regional decisionmaking is seriously restricted by the complexity of regional problems in general and the specific difficulties of inadequate information, including the existing price system, unresolved methodological questions, limitations in computer capacity, and the intricacy of the task of incorporating important noneconomic variables. Thus, relatively few answers to the pressing problems of development in the regions of the USSR, the East-West locational dilemma, or the evaluation of joint Soviet-CMEA projects are provided by current regional planning practices and methodologies. As in the past, joint CMEA investment will be located in scattered projects of resource exploitation. This will help meet complementary resource and capital needs, but substantial benefits would be gained if these projects were selected by valid investment and locational criteria and if they were encompassed in comprehensive and well-conceived regional plans. The limitations in the Soviet approach to spatial and regional planning seriously inhibit the introduction of broad CMEA collaboration in this process and the consequent enhancement of bloc integration.

Philip Hanson

Impact of Western Technology: The Soviet Mineral Fertilizer Industry

The rapid growth of Soviet imports of advanced machinery and know-how over the past two decades has been widely discussed. In the 1970s, many commentators associated it with Soviet-US détente. Some argued that in the late 1960s or early 1970s there was a major Politburo decision to trade political concessions (if necessary) for improved commercial access to Western technology.[1] Whether or not the link with détente is as close and conscious as this, the growth of hard-currency machinery imports has been substantial—from $310 million in 1960 to $4 billion in 1975 in current prices, a volume increase of about 430%.[2] There has also been a clear, though unquantifiable, increase in Soviet license and know-how purchases in association with plant imports and in pure licensing deals. This high marginal propensity to import Western know-how and capital goods is one reason why the share of total trade turnover with the rest of CMEA has tended to fall—a phenomenon which even in the first half of the 1970s could not be attributed entirely to Western inflation.

What are the consequences of this growth for the Soviet economy and for CMEA integration? Are we witnessing a historical turn to the West that reflects some new and increasing economic dependence on the commercial acquisition of Western technology? Will this rapid growth of technology imports, which other CMEA countries also display, tend to weaken intra-CMEA economic links? This paper will examine the interplay of technology imports from the West and domestic inputs in the recent development of one Soviet industry and will assess the impact of these imports on the Soviet economy.

The author is grateful to all those who participated in the discussion of an earlier draft of this paper at the Bloomington conference, especially Robert Campbell, Michael Dohan, Eugene Zaleski, and the editors for suggesting several amendments and clarifications incorporated in this revised text.

A.C. Sutton's historical study of the Soviet acquisition of Western technology[3] concludes that there has been virtually no successful indigenous Soviet innovation in the production of non-military items: almost all Soviet civilian technological change has been the result of "borrowing" from the West by copying, importing, "reverse engineering," scaling-up, and so on.[4] Sutton's evidence is detailed and persuasive. But if Soviet civilian technological change—which was clearly massive between 1917 and 1976—has always been overwhelmingly dependent on the West, in what sense can this dependence have significantly increased since the 1950s?

As a framework for this case study, the following propositions are presented:

1. It is generally accepted that all countries "borrow" from one another; the spread of technical knowledge and of new products and processes is an international process.

2. Late-developing countries, from Russia and Japan to Brazil and Mexico, tend to make few major innovations; their technological change is primarily a result of adaptation and diffusion from more advanced countries—at least until they reach a comparable level of economic development and technological sophistication.

3. The process of "borrowing" foreign technology, if it is to go beyond an enclave of foreign-managed enterprises, requires indigenous research and development (R&D) inputs and technical and management skills. Their development takes time and entails cost. Some technical knowledge is virtually free; some is patented or secret and must be bought. Almost all applications of technical knowledge entail costs.

4. Diffusion from abroad takes place through a variety of channels. Some have either small or zero implications for trade (screening foreign technical journals; buying individual machines, materials, or components and reverse engineering them; direct observation by visiting scientists and technologists; industrial espionage). These channels can be used even between countries that deal with one another "at arm's length," as was the case with Russia and the West in the late 1940s and early 1950s, though they could be greatly restricted by a blockade and a severing of diplomatic relations. Other methods of technology transfer, such as substantial plant and machinery imports, technological cooperation, license deals, and turn-key projects, are vulnerable to commercial and foreign policies and cannot be used effectively without a certain level of inter-governmental affability and regular commercial contact. International technology transfer of the first sort can be termed "non-negotiable transfer." This political distinction corresponds closely to the economic distinction made between disembodied and embodied diffusion. (The embodied-

disembodied distinction is made with respect to technical change. A technology may be diffused by the sale of machinery in which it is embodied or in a disembodied or "naked" form, as when licenses, designs, etc. are sold.)

5. Generally speaking, non-negotiable transfer requires greater domestic R&D, design engineering, and other "technology sector" inputs in the recipient country than negotiable transfer.

6. Soviet specialist discussion since about 1960 suggests a growing awareness of the economic merits of negotiable transfer. This appears increasingly to have influenced Soviet policy. The Fiat Tolyatti agreement (1966) was the most conspicuous, but by no means the first, manifestation of this (e.g., a specialist foreign-trade organization to deal in licenses and know-how was set up early in 1962). The growing preference for negotiable transfer may correspond to a historical, worldwide tendency for the cost-effectiveness of negotiable transfer to increase relative to that of non-negotiable transfer. Such a trend might be postulated in view of the rapid growth since World War II in the number of products and processes and their technical complexity, and the observation that R&D costs in at least some fields have been rising in relation to their economic returns. The costs of non-negotiable transfer, with its greater requirement of indigenous inputs, would in that case have been rising relative to the costs of negotiable transfer. There is circumstantial evidence of this in rapid growth since World War II of international licensing and joint ventures and of multinational firms, which have had a major role in diffusing technology within the developed West. Soviet specialists, planners, and policymakers have been impressed and have learned from it.[5]

7. The constraints of the hard-currency balance-of-payments, however, have limited the absolute size and growth of negotiable transfer from the West. Even in 1975-76, Western machinery comprised no more than 6% of total Soviet machinery investment.[6] There has been a moderate but by no means steady rise in this figure from around 2 to 2.5% in the mid-1950s.

8. The direct contribution of negotiable transfer from the West to Soviet output would presumably come chiefly in the form of increased output from given inputs resulting from the improved technology embodied in imported hardware or transmitted by know-how sales.[7] As this hardware is such a small part of the increments to Soviet capital stock, it is arithmetically impossible for this direct effect to be large in relation to Soviet national income. It may be of considerable consequence in particular branches, e.g., a merchant marine fleet, a sophisticated chemical industry, and a modest automobile industry, but many branches receive very small quantities of Western plant. In general, the flow of such inputs, in relation to all inputs into the Soviet economy, is small.

9. Indirect effects can, however, be substantial. They would come from (a) increases in productivity attributable to new or improved intermediate or capital goods made on imported plant; (b) the diffusion to domestically built machines of technology embodied in imported machines (i.e., the reverse engineering, adaptation, and scaling-up analyzed by Sutton); and (c) the "ripple" or feedback effect of imported technology on domestic technology in the production of components and materials for a product made with the imported technology (e.g., on steel, rubber, and plastic components for the Zhiguli cars at Tolyatti).

It is clear that the direct effects of technology imports from the West cannot be large in relation to Soviet national income. (This conclusion need not, of course, hold for the East European countries, which have a much higher ratio of trade to GNP.) Moreover, some have argued in favor of the view that the Soviet economic system will be relatively poor at utilizing effectively, diffusing rapidly, and responding promptly to imported technology.[8] On the other hand, there are campaigns and other forms of pressure on an administrative economy where routine operation is prone to inertia. All of this must be considered in the broad historical context of the massive technological transformation that has occurred since the 1920s and of some tentative econometric estimates that support the view that the total impact of negotiable technology transfer from the West is, in fact, quite large.

Though tentative and subject to some obvious provisos, estimates support the hypothesis that the total—and therefore the indirect—effects of technology import in the Soviet economy have been large. The principal purpose of this study is to see whether a detailed analysis of one branch of industry also supports this view. A secondary purpose is to examine the extent to which the Soviet planners have used other CMEA sources of plant and know-how, and whether the resort to Western technology was at the expense of CMEA integration. This picture of CMEA aspects, however, is sketchy, and conclusions about them must be provisional.

The chemical sector is the clearest example of a major branch of Soviet production in which large-scale purchases of machinery and know-how from the West have made a significant contribution to growth and technical change during the past two decades. Within the chemical sector, the manufacture of mineral fertilizers has been strongly affected by imported technology. It is also an important and politically sensitive field of production. Soviet policymakers have seen the manufacture of mineral fertilizers as a key element in the drive to transform agriculture in order to improve Soviet food supplies.

Soviet Policies in the Mineral
Fertilizer Industry, 1960-80

To raise Soviet crop production and yields sharply, it was necessary not merely to produce more of the existing fertilizers at the beginning of the "chemicalization" drive in 1958, but to produce new and more efficient kinds of fertilizer. To explain the technology import issues, it is necessary to begin with a review of the nature of mineral fertilizers.

The nutrients needed to support plant growth are fixed nitrogen (N), phosphorus (P_2O_5), and potassium (K_2O), supplied artificially in intensive agriculture. Nitrogenous, phosphate, and potash fertilizers can deliver these nutrients in a variety of ways. It is normally advantageous to deliver them in substances with a high nutrient content (concentration) or with the major nutrients combined in one fertilizer or both. The second is often referred to in the West as a "complex" fertilizer.

Complex fertilizers include both physical mixtures and chemical compounds of nutrients. They are variously referred to as "compound," "mixed," "composite," or "polynutrient" fertilizers. In this paper, "compound" will refer to chemically compounded fertilizers, and "mixed" will refer to physical mixtures of separately manufactured single-nutrient fertilizers. Complex fertilizers are appropriate for application at planting time, with nitrogenous fertilizers applied later. Their nutrient content is varied substantially according to requirements and can be expressed in a nitrogen:phosphorous:potassium (N:P:K) ratio, e.g., 1:1.5:1. They may also be manufactured to include valuable trace elements, such as boron.

Nitrogen is especially important to the growth of "high quality" foods such as fruit and vegetables, so that rising real incomes tend to shift the balance of the nutrients applied in favor of nitrogenous fertilizers. The nutrient ratio in application in US agriculture in 1965 (N:P:K) was about 5:4:3. About a third of the nitrogen was applied in complex fertilizers at that time in the US, and as much as 80% of phosphorus and 87% of potassium were applied in complex form.[9]

Soviet development of concentrated and complex fertilizers lagged well behind that of Western Europe and North America at the end of the 1950s. Indeed, compound fertilizers were not produced at all in 1960, and production of mixed fertilizers was very small. The main aims of subsequent Soviet policy, therefore, were to increase the supply of the more concentrated forms of the three primary nutrients and of complex fertilizers containing two or three of these nutrients. This meant increasing production, since there was no case for choosing substantial imports.

The extent to which fertilizers are internationally traded varies.

Nitrogenous and phosphate fertilizers are relatively widely produced and little traded: 21 and 17% of 1973-74 world consumption, respectively, entered world trade. This reflects the balance of locational factors that favor production near the market rather than near the source of primary materials (usually naphtha, coke oven gas, or natural gas, in the case of nitrogenous fertilizer; apatite in the case of phosphates). The production of potash fertilizers, on the other hand, tends to be located near the relatively few major deposits of brines and sylvinite ore, and 62% of 1973-74 world consumption was traded.[10] Since the USSR has large reserves of all the main raw materials and is a major exporter of apatite, it is probably reasonable for it to seek self-sufficiency in fertilizers. It would be extremely difficult to demonstrate this point conclusively, given the lack of comparability between established Soviet and non-Soviet costs and prices and given the detailed data that would be needed. The above considerations, however, suggest that imports of mineral fertilizers would be justifiable only as a stopgap arrangement or for logistical reasons to agricultural areas closer to foreign than to domestic sources of supply, of which the Soviet Far East would appear to be the only likely instance.

The main technical requirements of the drive to improve fertilizer output were as follows: To increase nitrogenous fertilizer production, a major expansion of ammonia output was required, since nitrogenous fertilizer production is based on ammonia as an intermediate. Nitrogenous fertilizers are normally produced in integrated complexes that include an ammonia plant. Processes using natural gas as the feedstock were particularly desired, in view of the rapidly increasing exploitation of natural gas deposits. Within the group of nitrogenous fertilizers, rapid growth was sought in the output of types with a high concentration of nitrogen, notably urea, and in complex fertilizers containing nitrogen.

The degree of sophistication of the different processes varies. In ammonia production, for example, technical change has sharply increased optimal plant size during the past 15 years.[11] Requirements for tanks, tubes, compressors, etc. in large ammonia plants are critical, with narrow tolerances. The technology for making ammonium nitrate and ammonium sulphate, on the other hand, is relatively simple and well-established.

Within phosphate fertilizers, a major change in product-mix was needed in order to increase the output of those with a high concentration of phosphorus. In practice, this meant an intended shift from an output-mix dominated by single superphoshate (18-21% P_2O_5 content typically made by phosphoric acid treatment of phosphate rock, and rather confusingly referred to in the Soviet Union as double superphosphate) and monoammonium phosphate (MAP, or ''ammophos").[12] A Soviet study of the early 1960s concluded that in the development of complex fertilizers containing phosphates priority should be given to processes using phosphoric acid and nitric acid treatment.[13] In the 1970s, the impossibility of continuing to rely on the very high-grade Kola apatite and the need to use more lower-grade phosphate rock at Kara-Tau, Kingisepp, and Chilisaisk have posed some special problems.[14]

Potash fertilizers appear to have presented rather different technological problems. They are produced close to a small number of major brines and sylvinite ore deposits: in the USSR, production is mainly at integrated mining and processing complexes at Berezniki and Solikamsk in Perm *oblast* on the Kama River, and at Soligorsk in Belorussia. Processing is a relatively simple "cooking" procedure, usually adapted to suit the particular characteristics of local deposits. The main development problems appear to have been with mining operations rather than with fertilizer production.[15]

Other technological requirements were increased granulating capacity, the production of special "hopper"-type railway wagons for transport, and the provision of special-purpose mechanical warehouses with loading and mixing equipment for district- or farm-level storage and mixing. (Local mixing of nutrients to produce composite fertilizers with a nutrient-mix adapted to particular local soil and crop requirements is an established arrangement in the US; retailers commonly use small-scale bulk-blending machines to produce mixtures of granulated fertilizers for local farms. In Western Europe, on the other hand, complex fertilizers are usually produced in factories and delivered ready-made. This difference is the result of locational factors: in the US, extensive crop-growing areas are situated at a distance from the main locations of fertilizer raw materials and feedstocks. To what extent the Soviet planners should follow the American pattern, especially in view of the poor Soviet transport system, is not clear.)

Organizational rather than narrow technological changes were (and still are) required in the agricultural-chemical advisory services to farms that are provided by both the USSR Ministry of Agriculture and Soyuzselkhoztekhnika and in transport services where the latter created bottlenecks to fertilizer supply.[16] More broadly, the whole program required improvements in training and changes in the attitudes of agricultural workers and planners. As with all technical change, questions of incentives, of economic organization, and, ultimately, of social and cultural norms were involved.

In brief, at the beginning of the chemicalization drive in 1958, Soviet policymakers wanted to introduce a whole new range of products and processes. In 1960, the Soviet Union produced no compound fertilizers, no triple superphosphate, and only 104,000 tons of urea and 136,000 tons of liquid ammonia.[17] Total capacity in 1960 was around 17 million tons per annum (tpa). In 1958, it was probably about 14 million tpa. The 1959-65 seven-year plan referred to a target of 100 million tons total fertilizer output by 1970; in 1963, Khrushchev subsequently modified this to 80 million tons. This was to be achieved by extending capacity at existing plants by 20 million tpa and building 55 new plants (28 for nitrogenous fertilizers, 19 for phosphate, 6 for potash, and 2 for phosphate rock).[18] As far as longer-run targets were concerned, the 20-year program called for a 130 million tpa capacity in 1980.

A near-autarkic policy for developing the industry was conceivable: the USSR has all the necessary raw materials and could presumably develop the processing units by combining domestic R&D with "non-negotiable technology transfer" from the West. An authoritative textbook on the chemical industry describes the whole heavy inorganic branch as ". . . highly traditional. The technologies are well understood and largely in the public domain."[19]

Such a program would, however, have been more costly than one that exploited potential gains from trade. Such gains might conceivably have been found within CMEA from relative-cost differences in the production of either fertilizer plant or fertilizers—differences that might have been apparent in 1960 or which might have been deliberately created by a CMEA specialization program. Some use of CMEA cooperation has, in fact, been made. But the major apparent source of gains from trade was in the transfer of technology from the West; this has, in fact, entailed a major commercial ("negotiable") transfer of technology via plant and know-how contracts.

The justification for this is that some tricky production technology is involved. For example, basic technical problems in the production of urea were not solved in the West until the 1950s. The maximum size of ammonia plants (often the optimum size) has been rising rapidly since the early 1960s. In 1977, about half of the world's ammonia output was from Kellogg-designed plants. These sophisticated developments may not constitute technological changes of the very largest kind in that they require writing university-level textbooks, but their economic impact is nonetheless considerable. And they were occurring in an area where Soviet applied research and development, as well as production, were particularly backward.[20] The potential gains from trade through the import of Western machinery and know-how must have appeared particularly great in this field.

TABLE 1
The Growth of Soviet Production and Deliveries to Agriculture of Mineral Fertilizers, 1950-80
(in million tons)

	1 New capacity installed*	2 Total* end-year capacity	3 Total production*	4 Total production†	5 Deliveries to agriculture*	6 Deliveries to agriculture†	7 Deliveries to agri. in kg./hectare†	8 For comparison, Italy†	9 Grain yields‡	10 For comparison, Italy‡
1950	NA	NA	5.5	1.2	5.4			(c.60)	7.9	20.5
1955	NA	NA	9.7	NA	NA				8.4	18.1
1960	NA	(17)	13.9	3.3	11.4	2.6			10.9	21.7
1961	c.0.3	17.3	15.3		12.1					22.0
1962	c.0.5	17.8	17.3		13.6					21.0
1963	7.4	25.2	19.9		16.0					22.2
1964	c.8.0	33.2	25.5		22.0					23.8
1965	7.1	40.3	31.3	7.4	27.1	6.3	28.5	55§	9.5	23.8
1966	3.4	43.7	35.9		30.5				13.7	26.0
1967	3.1	46.8	40.1		33.7				12.1	25.1
1968	5.2	52.0	43.5	10.2	37.5				14.0	26.5
1969	11.4	63.4	45.9	10.8	38.8				13.2	27.3
1970	9.8	73.2	55.4	13.1	45.6	10.4	47.0	76	15.6	29.3
1971	3.0	76.2	61.4	14.7	50.5	11.5	51.4		15.4	29.4
1972	7.4	83.6	66.0	15.9	54.8	12.5	55.9		14.0	30.0
1973	8.9	92.5	72.3	17.4	60.0	13.8	60.9		17.6	
1974	c.7.0	99.5	80.3	19.3	63.9	14.6	63.8#		15.4	
1975	11.7	111.2	90.2	22.0	75.4		78		(c.10.8)	
1976 plan			115.0	NA	NA					
1980			138.0	55+	115.0					

SOURCES: **Column 1:** *Pravda* annual plan fulfilment reports:: 1961 and 1962 figures inferred from *Narkhoz*, 1969, p. 498, and *Pravda*, January 26, 1963, p. 2. **Column 2:** The 1960 figure is the lowest two-digit figure consistent with output not exceeding estimated capacity in any subsequent year. The rest of column 2 is derived by adding column 1 figures cumulatively. 10 FYP target for capacity increase is 55.4 million tpa (*Ekon gaz.*, 1976, no. 21, p. 1). **Column 3:** R.A. Clarke, *Soviet Economic Facts* (London: Macmillan, 1972), p. 63: *Narkhoz* 1973, p. 272: *USSR in Figures for 1974* (Moscow, 1975), p. 85; *Pravda*, February 1, 1976, and December 14, 1975. The 1976 plan figure is from Moscow II radio, December 31, 1975 (BBC SWB SU/W865/A/13) and is markedly higher than the 94.5 million target given in *Pravda*, December 3, 1975. **Column 4:** *Narkhoz* 1969, p. 212: *Narkhoz* 1973, p. 272: *USSR in Figures*. **Column 5:** Clarke, p. 109: *Narkhoz* 1973, p. 421, *USSR in Figures for 1974*, p. 123: Kosygin report to 25th Party Congress, *Pravda*, March 2, 1976, p. 5; *Planovoe khozyaistvo*, 1976, no. 1, p. 7; L.A. Kostandov, *Khimicheskaya promyshlennost'k XXV s''ezdu KPSS* (Moscow, 1976), p. 17. **Column 6:** *SSSR v tsifrakh v 1971 g.*, p. 119; *Narkhoz* 1973, p. 424; *USSR in Figures for 1974*, p. 123. **Column 7:** *Narkhoz* 1973, p. 424: estimate for 1974 derived from *USSR in Figures for 1974*, p. 123; 1975 figure from Kostandov, p. 17. **Column 8:** Eurostats, *Agricultural Statistics 1974*, no. 3, p. 132. For 1955, an estimate derived from UN FAO, *An Annual Review of World Fertiliser Production and Consumption, 1955, 1956*, and arable area figures from Eurostats, *Agricultural Statistics*, 1974, no. 2. **Column 9:** *Narkhoz* 1973, p. 351; *USSR in Figures for 1974*, p. 105: for 1975 estimate from harvest figure of 140 million tons. **Column 10:** Eurostats, *Agricultural Statistics*, 1974, no. 2, pp. 110-11 (cereals including rice).

*In standard units of fertilizers.

†In 100% nutrients.

‡Centners per hectare.

§1965-66.

1970-71.

#Estimated on the assumption that total arable land (the area by which fertilizer deliveries appear to be divided to give per hectare figures) was 229 million hectare in 1974. Sown area that year was 217 million hectare.

The Growth of the Soviet Mineral Fertilizer Industry, 1960-80

On the whole, the growth of mineral fertilizer output and capacity has been rapid, and so has the transformation of the product-mix. In terms of total output, the drive to expand this industry has been successful. The 1980 output of 138 million tons (excluding 5 million tons of feed additives for livestock) in the tenth five-year plan actually exceeds Khrushchev's original 1980 target in his 20-year program—the only published major product target of which this can be said. It is true that the 1980 target is a taut one and may be underfulfilled, but it does not represent a wildly implausible growth between 1975 and 1980. In other words, it reflects the rapid growth actually achieved between the late 1950s and the mid-1970s.

Fluctuations in capacity installed follow a five-year plan cycle.

Production rose fairly closely behind estimated installed capacity, generally at 80% of end-year capacity (see table 1). (The estimates of total installed capacity are supported by a Soviet reference to a total capacity of 47 million tons in 1968, whether at the beginning or end of the year is unclear.)[21] Deliveries to agriculture, in turn, rose steadily, but again with a lag behind production.

The rising rate of deliveries per hectare, finally, contributed to the generally upward, though fluctuating, movement of crop yields per hectare. Until the early 1960s, in fact, mineral fertilizer supplies were concentrated on technical crops. Thereafter, the proportion going to grain was stepped up.

TABLE 2

Selected Changes in the Structure of Soviet Fertilizer
Output in Terms of Nutrients, 1965-80 Plan
(in percentages)

	1965	1970	1975	1980 Plan
Percent of nitrogenous fertilizer output				
Urea	17.2	27.3	25.9	27.1
Complex	1.3	5.0	10.7	19.3
*Percent of phosphate fertilizer output**				
Triple superphosphate	6.7	21.8	16.5	21.6
Monoammomium phosphate (MAP)	—	3.6	28.6	30.1
Complex†	2.7	7.9	10.4	30.2
(of which, identified as NPK)	1.2	3.5	4.3	17.6

SOURCE: V. M. Borisov, in *Khimiya v sel'skom khozyaistvo,* no. 6 (1976), pp. 7-13.

*Excluding ground rock phosphate and feed phosphates.
†Soviet sources report MAP as a complex fertilizer; this is not the usual Western classification.

TABLE 3
Levels of Fertilizer Deliveries to Agriculture, USSR
and Western Europe, circa 1971
(kg. per hectare, in nutrients)

	USSR 1971	Federal Republic of Germany 1970-71	France 1970-71	Italy 1970-71
Nitrogenous	23.5	84	44	34
Phosphate	11.1	68	56	29
Potash	12.6	88	43	13
Total	51.4	238	143	76
of which, complex	(3)*	122	92	33

SOURCES: *Narkhoz*, 1973, pp. 424-28; Eurostat, *Agricultural Statistics*, no. 3 (1974), pp. 116, 132.

*Approximate.

In addition to this rapid overall growth, there has been a rapid rise in the share of fertilizer output represented by the more sophisticated and cost-effective types of fertilizer to which the planners had assigned priority (see table 2). In this sense, there have been qualitative as well as quantitative gains.

At the beginning of the 1970s, Soviet utilization of chemical fertilizers still lagged behind Western levels (see table 3 and columns relating to Italy in table 1; Italian figures are introduced for comparison with a medium-developed Western country). As the 1980 target figures indicate, further rapid growth was planned during the 1970s.

The Role of Technology Imports

Broadly speaking, Soviet policy has been to make extensive use of Western plant and know-how imports in developing nitrogenous (especially ammonia) and compound fertilizer production and to rely largely on domestic plant for phosphate and potash fertilizers. Plant imports have been overwhelmingly from the West, but there have also been imports of relatively small-scale ammonia plant from Czechoslovakia, lines for producing granulated fertilizers from the GDR, some Hungarian equipment, and sulphuric acid plant (particularly important as an intermediate in phosphates) in substantial quantities from Poland. The East European contribution appears to be in well-established and relatively simple technologies. If the Polish contribution is excluded, plant imports from Eastern Europe seem to have been small compared with the import of Western plant. It has not, however, been possible in this study to measure the East European contribution with any precision.

None of this information can be obtained from the Soviet foreign-trade statistics: they do not disaggregate import data within the CTN (1971 edition) 3-digit category 150 (equipment for the chemical industry) by country and give little detail in the breakdown of total imports from all trade partners. The pattern has to be reconstructed from Western press reports and industry sources, which give a fairly full and detailed picture of Western plant contracts.*

The procedures used in this study to identify and quantify the role of imported plant are as follows:

1. Comparisons were made of total known capacities of imported plant, 1960-75, with growth in Soviet capacity or output of the relevant product during the same period.

2. For 1971-75 only, a compilation of Soviet plant and "shop" start-up data has been derived from Soviet radio broadcast sources, using the convenient *BBC Summary of World Broadcasts, Weekly Economic Report* series. This gives a detailed listing of the new and reconstructed plants and subunits coming on stream. It is definitely not comprehensive, and capacity data are frequently not included; but comparison of this material with import data shows vividly how imported plants fit into the range and type of new units that are *not* imports from the West.

3. A good deal of supplementary information has been obtained from Soviet press articles and specialist literature.

There is a sequence of steps in assessing the impact of imported technology. First, it is necessary to establish, as far as possible, how much of each major kind of fertilizer is or has recently been produced on imported plant (see pp. 264-73). Second, the net contribution to agricultural output of the fertilizer produced on imported plant is estimated (see pp. 273-75). Third, the extent of domestic diffusion of commercially imported technology is assessed (see pp. 276-77). No attempt has been made to quantify the "ripple" effect on domestic technology, even though it may be significant, because we lack substantial information.

How should one then proceed to measure impact? Let us begin by referring back to points 8 and 9 above, where a classification of direct and indirect impacts is put forward. In the remainder of this paper we shall ignore type (c) indirect impact, for lack of quantifiable information, and attempt to measure direct plus other types of indirect im-

---

*A detailed tabulation of Soviet purchases of Western machinery for the manufacture of mineral fertilizers during 1960-76, showing date of contract, capacity, supplier, and Soviet destination, is available upon request from the author.

pact. The measurement is, in fact, highly speculative and approximate because of data problems, but the principles involved are clear.

When superior technology is imported and utilized in an economy, it affects production functions (shifting given isoquants inwards toward the origin) in one or more lines of production. In other words, it makes domestic resources more productive than they would otherwise have been. This is true simply by definition of the term "superior technology." A "technology" in this sense is a set of production techniques that are known and can be applied in practice. From the point of view of the country importing a technology, it is not important whether the technology in question is new or long-established in other countries. If the importing country was not previously able to apply it, the import of the technology can be seen as a move to a new isoquant.

The ideal situation in which to measure such a change would be one in which the economy in question was characterized by scarcity prices and resource allocation that was efficient in a static sense. If no other changes were occurring and if one could identify a point at which the full direct-plus-indirect impact had been achieved, measurement would be easy. The impact (in terms of the rate of output per unit of time) would be the total change in the rate of output between the period before utilization of the new technology and the period following the full achievement of its impact. If other changes were also occurring, this comparative statics approach would have to include an allowance for changes in quantities of inputs and perhaps for other technical and price changes but could still yield a measure in terms of a net growth of output at market prices. As long as the direct and indirect impact of the technology is restricted to a relatively small part of the economy, this should in principle be fairly simple.

The direct impact is part of the output coming directly from the imported hardware. It is that part that is attributable to the superior technology embodied in the hardware, i.e., output over and above that which would have been produced by the same quantity of inputs using the pre-existing domestically established technology. If the product in question is a producer good, this increased output would be associated with "downstream" increases in the outputs of other goods for which it served as an intermediate or investment good. These would not need to be considered separately, however, in our hypothetical "textbook" economy because these effects would already be expressed in the market value of the producer good in question.

The indirect effects that need to be separately considered are listed under point 9 above. These would again be changes in output at market prices, net of the cost of inputs, and attributable to (a) any improved quality in producer goods produced on the imported hardware and (b) the embodiment of the imported technology in domestically built capital goods (i.e., diffusion). (In any economy in which the allocation of resources—including the utilization of existing domestic know-how—was efficient, there could be no "ripple" effect.)

In any economy, these measurements are hard to make. In the Soviet case, the non-scarcity nature of established prices is a particular obstacle, and data on Soviet mineral fertilizer prices are not readily available. The approach used here, therefore, is to focus on the "downstream" impact on crop output of increased fertilizer supplies. This is used, first of all, as a proxy measure of direct impact. It requires an estimate of (a) the output of fertilizer nutrients on imported fertilizer plant that is attributable to the superior technology of that plant, i.e., over and above what the same inputs would produce with indigenous technology, and (b) an estimate of the impact on crop output of that fertilizer output, net of cooperating inputs in agriculture. Both estimates rely on sketchy and ill-explained Soviet data and agronomic calculations and are, therefore, necessarily speculative.

What about type (a) indirect impact? In the case of complex fertilizers, the imported plant and its embodied technology produced an improved product new to the USSR, whose properties include an increase in agricultural productivity compared with the use of single-nutrient fertilizers. This is an indirect effect of technology transfer. Using crude and approximate calculations (p. 272), some attempt is made to allow for this effect, but the estimates telescopes it and the more straightforward direct impact in one figure. Ideally, a similar indirect impact should be allowed for in nitrogenous fertilizers insofar as Western plant facilitated the supply of fertilizers with a higher concentration of nitrogen, but this point has been neglected for lack of quantitative information.

As for type (b) indirect impact—diffusion—I have had to make do with a small, arbitrary upward adjustment of the crop impact figure to reflect the apparent success in diffusing technologies embodied in imported Western phosphoric and complex fertilizer plant. Other possible spillover benefits to other branches of the chemical industry, as well as the ripple effect, are simply neglected here. This is hardly satisfactory, but at least it militates against any overestimate of the total impact.

The Pattern of Technology Imports

Table 4 gives a schematic picture of some major fertilizer industry products and intermediates. It is not meant to be comprehensive, nor does it depict vertical process linkages. Broadly speaking, products

TABLE 4
The Pattern of Plant Imports for the Soviet Mineral Fertilizer Industry, 1960-76

Type of Fertilizer	Materials and Intermediates	Intermediates and Products	Intermediates and Products	Intermediates and Products
N fertilizers	ammonia (major Mk_w) nitric acid (limited Mk_w) sulphuric acid (major Mk_E)	urea (major Mk_w) ammonium nitrate (D) ammonium sulphate (D)		
P fertilizers	apatite ore, phosphorites (D)	sulphuric acid (major Mk_E) phosphoric acid (limited Mk_w)	single super-phosphate (D) monoammonium phosphate (D) triple super-phosphate (D)	complex fertilizers (major Mk_w)
K fertilizers	potassium salts, sylvinite ore mining (D)	potassium sulphate (D) potassium chloride (D)		

Mk_w = plant imports from the West.

Mk_E = plant imports from Eastern Europe.

D = wholly or predominantly domestically built plant.

and intermediates on the left are located earlier and those on the right located later in the production process, but a great many additions and complications would have to be introduced to give a proper picture. (Liquid ammonia, for example, is used directly as a fertilizer, so "ammonia" is not solely an intermediate.) The table does, however, give a broad idea of where the technology imports "fit in."

Ammonia and urea constitute one of the two main areas where imported plant has been concentrated (the other is compound fertilizers). The chairman of the foreign-trade organization responsible for chemical plant imports, V/O Tekhmashimport, has claimed that 50% of Soviet ammonia and 62% of Soviet urea production was from imported plant (the reference is probably to 1973).[22]

Total capacity ordered from the West to mid-1976 was about 13.1 million tpa of ammonia and 3.0 million tpa of urea. This capacity is planned to be on stream by the end of 1980. In addition, 0.8 million tpa of Czechoslovak-built ammonia capacity were ordered in the mid-1960s, and apparently more Czech plant is on order for 1976-80. I estimate that total installed ammonia capacity planned for 1980 is probably not more than 24 million tpa.[23] It appears, therefore, that Western-built plant will, if anything, become increasingly important in the next few years.

This policy of relying on Western plant is based on the very high savings obtained by the Kellogg and Chemico large-plant processes, the high cost and difficulty for Soviet or East European design engineers and manufacturers to replicate such plant, and the existence of competing Western contractors able to supply the plants. The terms of the deals, especially those with Toyo, are obviously important here. The Soviets are covering the cost of purchases from Toyo and Creusot Loire in part by parallel agreements with other Japanese and French firms to purchase ammonia. There is, therefore, an element of product payback, although it does not involve counterpurchase by the plant contractors themselves.

These gains from trade arise from a technology transfer based in large part on the detailed design engineering expertise of specialist plant contractors such as the Japanese Toyo Engineering Corporation and the French Creusot Loire Enterprises. The fundamental technology underlying the plant design is contained in the ICI-Kellogg and Chemico ammonia processes, but it is probable that the Russians are buying the more empirical and experience-based (and less readily communicable) expertise of the specialist contractors as well as detailed design work from Kellogg and Chemico.[24] In some of the contracts, Soviet organizations participated in design, assembly work, or both, presumably as a learning process. It is possible that the continued reliance on imported large ammonia plants is also in part the result of weaknesses in Soviet metallurgy and metal-working which preclude, for the time being, domestic production of adequate tanks and tubes—a problem similar to that which is holding up Soviet production of wide-diameter pipes for gas trunk pipelines, leading to extremely expensive imports of this product. The relevant skills, know-how, and manufacturing capacity probably exist in the USSR but are pre-empted by the defense sector and not readily extended outside it.

There appear to have been two rounds of ammonia-plant ordering. The first was in the early and mid-1960s and involved several contractors. From 1969 to 1976, there was a rapid succession of orders for plants, nearly all of 1,360 tons per day (tpd) or 450,000 tpa. These orders were to three contractors—Toyo, Creusot Loire, and Chemico—and embodied two basic ammonia processes—Kellogg and Chemico. Within this second round, Toyo secured the overwhelming bulk of the contracts. When the USSR began to order these units, they were among the largest and most advanced units on order anywhere, and they are still at the top end of the range of plant-size in the West.

The supply side of the ammonia plant market is oligopolistic. The oligopolists in question appear to be competing rather than colluding. It must be presumed, therefore, that none of the sellers has been able to extract from the USSR much of the "producer's surplus" represented by the net return on these plants. The values of many of these contracts have been reported in the Western press: for a total of 11.3 million tpa ammonia capacity (mostly 1970-76), reported costs are $1.4 to $1.9 billion. Total costs of all reported ammonia plant deals might have been $1.6 to $2.2 billion at early 1970 prices. This is almost certainly a modest amount in relation to the returns on ammonia plant.

Similar conditions apply to urea plant. It is clear, however, that reliance on the West is less than total: the review of 1971-75 broadcasts turned up four instances—at Chirchik, Ionava, Grodno, and Rustavi—of new or reconstructed plants coming on stream that do not appear to have been imports. At Gorlovka, a Czech-built urea plant is being installed. Expenditure on Western urea plants has been less than on ammonia plant. The two 450,000 tpa plants ordered in 1976 were reported to have cost $100 million; the cost at 1978 prices of the total capacity ordered from the West could be about $0.3 billion.

Other nitrogenous fertilizers and intermediates require relatively simple, established processes. Here, the planners appear to have relied on domestic and, in the case of sulphuric acid, Polish plant, and know-how. The only major exception seems to be an order in 1975 for a large nitric acid plant from France. But in general, domestically built machinery is installed. The radio reports for 1971-75 refer to at least ten new ammonium nitrate units coming on stream, all apparently Soviet-designed and built. They include 1,400 tpd granulated ammonium nitrate units. There were also at least six new, domestically built nitric acid plants. Storage, handling, and pipeline transport of nitrogenous fertilizers, on the other hand, are related activities in which there has been resort to Western technology. The cost of the Black Sea-Tolyatti ammonia pipeline in the Occidental Petroleum deal was reported at $301 million.

In *phosphate* fertilizer production, phosphoric acid is the key intermediate for producing concentrated (e.g., triple superphosphate) and complex fertilizers. The Western phosphoric acid plants imported in the 1960s were of 160, 170, and 330 tpd P_2O_5 capacities. Soviet producers have subsequently mastered the production of plants of this size, and domestic plant has been substituted for imports. Certainly the plants reported on stream at Dzhambul in 1971 and at Samarkand in 1975 do not appear to have been imports. But continuing design improvements in the West have led to plants of 600-1,000 tpd P_2O_5, and there are reports that the Russians are interested in buying such plants.[25] It is also possible that in phosphorus production, the 50 MW furnaces bought from Uhde in the 1960s aided subsequent increases (beyond 50 MW) in the size of Soviet-built phosphorus furnaces.

The most publicized use of East European plant and technology—the use of Polish sulphuric acid plant—is most clearly related to phosphate fertilizers. Sulphuric acid has a variety of uses, but most of the plants bought from Poland appear to have been installed at phosphate fertilizer works where they supply phosphoric acid, single superphosphate, or both. Polish sulphuric acid technology is traditionally considered to be relatively strong. In the chemical industry, Polish sulphuric acid plant is considered to be about five years behind West German plant, but quite respectable. Poland has recently obtained a sulphuric acid plant contract in West Germany by tendering at a low price.

The rapid development of triple superphosphate and monoammonium phosphate production appears to have been essentially on the basis of Soviet-built machinery. Here, the radio reports supply a flood of detail for the ninth five-year plan period. Triple superphosphates production has been developed at a number of non-ferrous metals enterprises, and there are at least four locations involved for which there is no record of any Western plant deliveries. The start-up of monammonium phosphate plants in this period was reported for Krasnoperekopsk, Tselinograd, Samarkand, Dzhambul, Sumy, Almalyk, Kingisepp, Gomel, and Voskresensk. These all appear to be "indigenous" developments. Again, the technologies involved are relatively simple.

For *potash* fertilizers, some use has been made of Western mining and granulating equipment, but the increase in output between 1971 and 1975 from about 14 million tons to at least 19 million tons[26] and the increase in capacity of at least 4.4 million tpa[27] must be attributed almost entirely to indigenous inputs. In this area of production, Soviet technology seems to be quite strong, partly because it was developed specifically to fit the particular location and composition of the very large Soviet ore and brine deposits.

It is interesting that the Soviet Union has sold a license in a related field to a US joint venture company formed by the National Steel Corporation and Earth Sciences Corporation. This is a $1 million license for an alunite processing plant, based on Soviet technology, to be built at Hawesville, Kentucky. The plant will produce both alumina and potash of sulphate.[28]

The Soviet output and capacity data should also include mixed as well as compound fertilizers, at least if the mixing is done at a chemical plant rather than by distributors using bulk-blending machines on granular single-nutrient fertilizers. Unfortunately, the balance of compound and mixed fertilizers in the total is not known.

What is clear is that the imported plants were for a time the only source of compound fertilizers and virtually the only source of complex fertilizers. In 1973, 74% of complex fertilizer production was said to be on imported plant.[29] If the comparison of imported capacity and estimated output for 1975 is comparable with this figure, the share of indigenous capacity appears to have risen from 26% of output in 1973 to 34% in 1975. With the proviso that MAP complicates the issue somewhat, this is an apparent instance of successful domestic diffusion of imported technology. The detailed engineering and manufacturing requirements for complex fertilizer plants are less critical (with wider tolerances) than for large ammonia plant, and this may go a long way toward explaining diffusion in one case and its absence in the other.

Meanwhile, it is sufficient to note that the review of broadcast reports for 1971-75 produced a number of complex fertilizer plants on stream or under construction. Unspecified volumes of diammonium hydrogen phosphate were produced at Dzhambul at the beginning of 1971; another complex fertilizer plant was said to be in operation there in 1973.[30] An 80,000 tpa monopotassium phosphate unit went into operation at Gomel in 1973;[31] at Rovno, a 2,064,000 tpa unit, apparently for complex fertilizers, went on stream in December 1975;[32] and at Ionava a 500,000 tpa complex fertilizer plant was reported in operation in October 1975.[33] A total of at least another 7.5

million tpa complex fertilizer capacity is apparently under construction at Ionava, Dorogobuzh, Kokhtla-Yarve, Novyi Rozdol, and
Cherepovets. And at Almalyk, an 853,000 tpa unit that went on
stream in 1974 may be producing complex fertilizer in the Western
sense, or may be producing only monoammonium phosphate.

A Western-import content can be traced for only one of these projects, the one at the Ionava nitrogenous fertilizer works. It is said that
this will be the largest granulated-complex fertilizer plant when fully
operational: an additional 500,000 tpa capacity was apparently still
under construction at the end of 1975. Equipment was said to be
supplied from Soviet, Czechoslovak, Hungarian, and Japanese factories.[34] It is possible, but not certain, that the Japanese plant is an
ammonia unit ordered in 1975 rather than complex fertilizer machinery as such. In general, the recent development of complex fertilizer capacity seems to have been based on Soviet plant and machinery. However, the recent order to Potasse et Engrais Chimique
for seven liquid fertilizer plants is probably part of a further round of
technology acquisition in the field of liquid complex fertilizers. They
will presumably be used to make ammonia polyphosphate liquid
complex fertilizer (or fertilizer ingredients) and may use polyphos-
phoric acid imported as part of the Occidental Petroleum deal.

Those mid-1960s contracts that were definitely for complex fertilizer plant and for which values were reported totaled $26.5 million
for 4,754,000 tpa capacity. From this, a guesstimate of about $48 mil-
lion for the total 1960s import bill for 8,556,000 tpa capacity can be
derived, at early 1970s prices.

The total cost of fertilizer plant contracts placed in the West from
1960 to mid-1976, at early 1970s prices, appears to be at least $2.4
billion (it could be $3 billion and possibly as much as $4 billion).
These figures are based on the total-cost figures suggested above for
ammonia plant, urea plant, and ammonia pipeline and the (mid-1960s)
cost of complex fertilizer plant, together with those other contract
figures that have been reported: $17.6 million for phosphorus furnaces
and triple superphosphate drying equipment (potash sector); $6.8 mil-
lion for potash mining equipment (potash sector); $7.2 million for the
1976 liquid-fertilizer plant contract, and $10.7 million for other items.

Outside the nitrogenous fertilizer group, the reported contract
figures relate mainly to the middle or late 1960s. These might need to
be raised by as much as a quarter to correspond to early 1970s prices,
but any such adjustments are too small to affect a total rounded to
two significant digits. There are a number of contracts for which cost
data are not available, and several for which the exact coverage of the
value data is unclear; hence, there is a wide range in the estimates of
the total import bill. Since most of the large and costly ammonia

plants ordered are not yet on stream, the cost of the capacity that was actually on stream before the end of 1975 was considerably less—in the range of $1 billion to $2.6 billion and most probably $2 billion.

Effects on Agricultural Output

The productivity increases in agriculture that are attributable to the supply of fertilizers produced on imported plant are considerable. In the early 1970s, Soviet agricultural specialists estimated that, on the average, the application of an extra ton of mineral fertilizer to grain crops increased the harvest by 1.2 tons. In relation to the weight of nutrients applied, this was a response rate of about 5:1.[35] A later estimate by the All-Union Institute of Fertilizers and Agro-soil Culture ascribes an increment of 5.5 billion rubles of agricultural output to the increment in fertilizer supplies to agriculture between 1970 and 1975. This is said to be a gross measure; net of the cost of cooperating agricultural inputs, the growth in output is put at 3.4 billion rubles. This appears to be broadly compatible with a 5:1 response rate. Allowing for variations in weather, it does not appear to give a picture that is exaggerated in comparison with the aggregate historical data.[36]

Unexplained Soviet estimates of this kind must be treated cautiously. Still, fertilizer deliveries to Soviet agriculture have been quite modest by West European standards, while at the same time the rate of application to crops has been rising sharply (see table 1). Both points apply with particular force to the key crop—grain—for which the volume of nutrients applied per hectare was 29 kg. in 1970 and 42 kg. in 1974.[37] So a pronounced incremental impact of fertilizer supplies on agricultural output is to be expected.

An increase of 30 million tons between 1970 and 1975 in the annual rate of supply of fertilizers (in standard units) to agriculture is credited, therefore, with a substantial net effect on agricultural output. If we relate this effect to 1974—not to 1975 because of adverse weather conditions—it is equivalent to 5.2% of Soviet-style national income originating in agriculture as measured in Soviet official statistics at current wholesale prices.[38] This 30 million tons represents about 40% of fertilizer supply in 1975. The estimate of the net effect of this increase is at least *prima facie* plausible. If it is approximately correct, it follows that the mid-1970s supply of fertilizer coming from Western-made plant can also be credited with a substantial net contribution to agricultural output.

In 1973, imported plant accounted for 50% of ammonia, 62% of urea, and 74% of complex fertilizer production.[39] Of this, not more than 15% of ammonia and a probably smaller percentage of urea would be from Czechoslovakia plant; the rest would be from plant imported from the West. By 1975, the share of Western plant in total output of ammonia may have risen somewhat, with the commissioning of five big 1,360 tpd imported ammonia plants between 1973 and the end of 1975.[40] On the other hand, the share of Western plant in complex fertilizer production[41] may have fallen slightly by 1975— perhaps to around 66%. It is also evident that at least a small proportion of phosphate and potash fertilizer output comes from imported Western plant.

A very rough estimate, then, is that in 1975 the percentages of fertilizer output that came from imported Western plant were of the following order: nitrogenous, 40; phosphate, 5; potash, 5; complex, 65. The balance of nutrients supplied at about this date (N:P:K) was 1.0:0.7:1.0.[42] So about 19% of nutrient supply can be ascribed to Western plant if complex fertilizers are excluded. Of the total supply, probably about 5 to 10% was in the form of compound fertilizers, if MAP is omitted (cf. tables 1 and 3). Local mixing of granular single-nutrient fertilizers may have meant that total application in complex form was larger. As already noted, complex fertilizers, whether compound or mixed, are more efficient in application than single-nutrient fertilizers. In the USSR, they are believed to give at least a 10% saving in agricultural production costs per unit of output.[43] Therefore, they merit some extra weighting in the total, insofar as the impact of fertilizers on output net of the cost of cooperating units is considered. The effect of complex fertilizers is a type (a) indirect effect of technology import since it stems from an improved product made on imported plant. For practical reasons, however, it is easier to assess it jointly with the direct impact.

In assessing the technology-import effect for complex fertilizers, double-counting must be avoided. These fertilizers are derived from single-nutrient fertilizers; they therefore absorb some of the output of ammonia, etc. and are included in the figures of total nutrients supplied to agriculture. To allow for the substantial Western-plant output of complex fertilizers, therefore, it seems reasonable to make a small upward adjustment of the Western plant share in nutrient supply—say, to 25%.

The outcome of these admittedly crude calculations, then, is that in the mid-1970s about 3.25% of the value of net agricultural output (or about 4.5% of gross crop output at 1965 prices) could be attributed to the application of fertilizers produced on imported Western plant. Again, this measure is net of the cost of inputs cooperating with the fertilizer in agriculture and must be regarded as tentative in view of its reliance on the unexplained Soviet estimate (see p. 273). It is expressed in relation to net agricultural output as conventionally valued in Soviet national income accounting. On this basis, it is equivalent to just under 1% of Soviet net material product in 1975. It is widely accepted, however, that agricultural output is undervalued relative to nonagricultural output in Soviet national income statistics; if all output were valued at scarcity prices, agriculture's share would be greater. On the other hand, if we want to relate the impact to the more comprehensive Western-style measure of national output, for which GNP at factor cost would be appropriate, the aggregate would probably be somewhat larger. In fact, a recent authoritative Western estimate puts agriculture's sectoral share of Soviet 1970 GNP at factor cost at 20.4%—almost identical with agriculture's share of NMP in Soviet official statistics.[44] Since the impact figure is a guesstimate, it is sufficient to conclude that it is 1% of mid-1970s Soviet GNP.

This represents the gross contribution of imported technology combined with cooperating domestic inputs in the fertilizer industry. What would the net figure be; i.e., how much less fertilizer would have been produced in the absence of the technology embodied in the imported hardware? The difference appears to be large. The technology embodied in the imported plant typically has a very large impact on labor and material costs per unit of output without the imported plant itself constituting a very large share of total capital costs. Thus, I estimate, for example, that the 1,360 tpd ammonia unit supplied by Toyo for the Cherepovets chemical works (planned to become the main source of complex fertilizers for the whole non-Black Earth zone of the RSFSR) accounts for about 15 to 20% of the total equipment investment cost of the project and around 5% of the project's projected capital cost.[45] The equipment elements in the total investment cost of a large ammonia plant in the USSR appears to be about 20 to 25%.

Yet such plants bring enormous savings. The minister of the Chemical Industry has stated that 1974 production costs of ammonia at the similar (Kellogg process) 1,360 tpd Nevinnomyssk plant were only a third of those on existing types of plant, and labor productivity was seven times higher.[46] Soviet broadcasts refer to output being raised sixfold and electricity consumption being cut to one-fourteenth by the similar plant at Severodonetsk,[47] and to a projected 90% cut in the labor force at the ammonia plant under construction at the Novokemerovskii works.[48] A cautious judgment would be that the net impact was equivalent to at least half a percentage point of GNP; Soviet 1975 GNP in 1973 US dollars has been estimated by the Central Intelligence Agency at about $736 billion.[49] One-half of 1% of GNP in 1973 US prices is, therefore, $3.7 billion.

Diffusion

The other effect of negotiable technology transfer is diffusion. To assess with any precision the Soviet performance in replicating, in domestically built fertilizer plant and machinery, new technologies embodied in imported Western plant would require both a wealth of technical detail and expertise. Even if these obstacles were removed, there would still be the conceptually difficult problem of assessing the separate contributions of the imported technologies and the Soviet development, design, and other engineering inputs that would necessarily be involved in any successful diffusion.

Some plant imports from the West are intended for several sub-branches of the fertilizer industry, which suggests the likelihood of some spin-off by way of diffusion even in, say, potash production. The preceding discussion, however, suggests that the main areas of diffusion are ammonia, urea, and compound fertilizer plant and, perhaps, phosphoric acid plant.

The continuing resort to foreign contractors for ammonia and urea plant and the lack of evidence of Soviet-built large plants in this field suggest that there has not been substantial diffusion there. Soviet-built phosphoric acid plant may have benefited from technology embodied in 1960s imports, but Soviet design engineers do not appear to have been able to go beyond the plant sizes common in the West in the mid-1960s. This appears — at least from this cursory consideration — to be a case where there was not enough diffusion to close the technology gap in an area of fairly rapid change.

The major instance of successful diffusion appears to be compound fertilizer plant. If we tentatively assume that the domestically built compound fertilizer capacity that was on stream by 1975 was about 4 million tpa, this would seem to be a moderate spin-off from the imports of around 8.6 million tpa capacity.

Both the scale of this domestic development and its precise relationship to the imported plant are highly uncertain, however. It is intriguing that the 207,000 tpa propane fertilizer plant ordered for Vinnitsa and reported in the Soviet press as going on stream in late 1968 is described as a "pilot plant." Pravda stated that it will be followed by plants of the same type at Odessa and Konstantinovka.[50] These would presumably be Soviet-built and scaled to a larger size.

I have been unable to find reports of these plants coming on stream. They may have done so, but it is striking that the 80,000 tpa plant at Gomel', which came on stream in 1973, was referred to in 1971 as the largest complex fertilizer plant in the USSR.[51]

Numerous explanations of these apparent inconsistencies are possible, but they suggest caution in assessing Soviet diffusion of complex-fertilizer technology. The main difficulty, apart from the lack of detailed information, is that the term "complex fertilizer" covers a range of products of differing characteristics whose manufacturing processes differ in technical sophistication. Nonetheless, there has been at least some successful diffusion of imported complex fertilizer technology, and there may well be a good deal more by 1980 as plants now under construction come on stream.

For the time being, there is no satisfactory basis for even a crude quantitative assessment of the indirect impact of technology imports via diffusion, either for complex fertilizers in particular or for mineral fertilizers in general. One might hazard the guess that, on the whole, domestic diffusion of these technologies has been less rapid than the planners may have hoped. At the same time, there is enough evidence of diffusion to make it clear that the total impact of technology imports is somewhat larger than the sum of the direct plus type (a) indirect effects. Thus, a conservative estimate of total net impact of mineral fertilizer technology imports from the West comes out, very tentatively, at about $4 billion a year, expressed as an increment to mid-1970s GNP at 1973 US prices.

Implications for CMEA

Eastern Europe has apparently contributed little to the "chemicalization" of Soviet agriculture. This is despite the fact that at the start of the chemicalization drive, Czechoslovakia and the GDR had, in general, more sophisticated chemical industries than the USSR. More information from East European sources is needed to verify this impression, but it is an impression that emerges very clearly from both Western and Soviet sources.

Broadly speaking, the Soviet planners turned to the West for the latest technology in more sophisticated processes. For the rest, it appears that they tended to rely mainly on their own domestic suppliers. They did, however, make use of a substantial volume of Polish sulphuric acid plant, lesser quantities of Czechoslovak ammonia plant, and some East German and Hungarian machinery. At least some supplies of this kind are planned to continue in 1976-80. Apparently 27 Polish sulphuric acid plants were delivered to the USSR in 1963-75, and another 23 are to be delivered in 1976-80.[52]

It seems reasonable to assume that the Soviet planners did not spend hard currency to import plant and know-how they could have bought within CMEA. Eastern Europe has weaknesses in fertilizer technology and a reliance on imported Western know-how that are broadly comparable with those of the USSR.[53] However, there was some scope for CMEA cooperation in developing the Soviet fertilizer industry,and some use has been made of it. Whether the Soviet planners made efficient choices between domestically made and East European fertilizer plant and know-how is a question which I can raise but not answer.

Intra-CMEA transactions may have certain costs specific to themselves and absent from East-West transactions, arising out of the cumbersome nature of national bureaucracies and the generally poor quality of their manufactures. The Soviets evidently had a high rate of time preference as far as the expansion of their fertilizer industry was concerned, and this may have been a particularly powerful factor in their preference for Western sources of supply. Even where an East European country may have had the capacity to supply fertilizer plant of an acceptable quality level, it may have been unable to supply the plant quickly enough to satisfy Soviet planners.

On the whole, systematic intra-CMEA cooperation does not seem to have played a significant part. When the Minister of the Chemical Industry, reviewing the industry's aims and problems in the mid-1970s, deals with CMEA cooperation, he talks of chemical products, not chemical plant. The only reference to fertilizers in this context is to Soviet exports of potash fertilizers and materials for them, which is described as a Soviet export to other CMEA countries under CMEA specialization arrangements. This appears to refer mainly to apatite concentrate, traditionally exported in large quantities to non-CMEA countries. When the Minister speaks of plant imports and product payback deals, on the other hand, the examples seem to be nearly all with Western partners.[54] Some bilateral cooperation is apparently in effect between Bulgaria and the USSR, which includes Bulgarian participation in plant construction at Kingisepp, with repayment at least partly in product (26,000 tpa of MAP), but this may be an isolated instance.[55]

Conclusions

Case studies tend to be rather inconclusive, except about the particular case being studied. The Soviet mineral fertilizer industry probably employs less than three-quarters of a million people and is a small part of the Soviet economy. It has undoubtedly received an above-average share of machinery and know-how imports from the West, and cannot be regarded as representative of the Soviet economy in general.

The evidence is, however, that the total economic impact of technology imports has been considerable. An import bill of almost $4 billion (at early 1970s prices) over 15 years, of which not more than $2.6 billion has yet been converted into plant in operation, has yielded an annual return in the mid-1970s which we have put at around 0.5% of national income or about $4 billion at US 1973 prices. This is admittedly a crude guesstimate and could easily be disputed. Moreover, in principle, it is not a true cost-benefit assessment because the cost is in world market prices and the benefit is derived from data in established ruble prices and expressed in US factor cost. What is required, ideally, is a measure of both costs and benefits in terms of prices reflecting Soviet resource costs and scarcities. (On the cost side, this would measure the opportunity cost of the exports needed to pay for the plant and know-how imports.) But even this estimate is enough to indicate that the rate of return on these technology imports is very high—almost certainly much higher than the rate of return on domestic investment embodying indigenous technology.

This need not mean that the Soviet economic system has performed well in utilizing and diffusing imported technologies. That could only be judged from comparisons with other countries—and even then it might be hard to identify the performance of the "system." There are many reasons for doubting that the technology has been well utilized. We know that storage and application of fertilizers on Soviet farms is often extremely inefficient. We know that the mix of nutrients produced by the industry is still far from what is wanted, with phosphates underproduced relative to potash. One can point to delays in plant construction, quality defects in the fertilizers produced, and so on. And we have seen that imported technologies have certainly not all been rapidly diffused in domestically built plant.

At the same time, though, there are numerous instances of plants completed ahead of time and some examples of successful diffusion. And the quantitative evidence shows that, in this case, most plan targets have been reached, and the quantity and quality of fertilizers delivered to agriculture have risen enormously. Perhaps pressure from above (there were decrees on various aspects of the industry's development in 1968, 1973, and 1976) does, by and large, get results in precisely those priority areas where it is applied.

The apparently high impact of technology imports in this instance exemplified the powerful effect of new technology on output in any economy, and the particular high impact it will have in previously neglected lines of production in which there is a large technological backlog. This is clearly the case with both Soviet agriculture and the Soviet chemical industry, and one would not expect such proportionally large results if corresponding quantities of Western machinery and know-how were imported across the whole spectrum of Soviet production.

Green and Levine have given evidence that, at present rates of importation of Western plant, the rate of return on these imports is generally high.[56] This study tends to reinforce this view. If this is correct, hard-currency borrowing is highly advantageous for the USSR. On the other hand, it seems likely that the rate of return is especially high in the case of imported fertilizer plant. The rate of return on other current imports of Western equipment is probably less striking, though still high; and a substantial increase in the rate of importation of Western machinery (in relation to Soviet investment) would probably be associated with a fall in this rate of return, as in a movement along a marginal efficiency of capital schedule.

Even where the rate of return is high, it need not follow that the Soviet Union is catching up with Western technology levels. This largely depends on whether there is a continuing rapid evolution of the technology in question. The evidence from a major team project on Soviet technology levels at Birmingham University shows that in a number of major and broadly representative areas of industrial technology, the USSR did not appear to be reducing its technology gap vis-à-vis the West between the mid-1950s and the early 1970s.[57] It remains to be seen whether the intensification of negotiable technology transfer from the West in the 1970s will alter this situation.

Even with these qualifications, however, it is easy to see that Western technology can exercise a strong magnetic affect on Soviet trade, and on the trade of the East European countries, tending to pull the CMEA countries away from intra-CMEA dealings. In this case, the import of Western technology seems to be a continuing rather than a once-for-all process, at least in the rapidly evolving ammonia and urea fields; and the acquisition of Western technology has given no obvious stimulus to intra-CMEA transactions. The hard-currency balance-of-payments, however, still sets severe limitations to this diversion of trade to the West.

Discussion

Robert W. Campbell

Professor Hanson provides a concrete way of answering questions that are central to debates about technology transfer. First, his paper gives a quantitative answer to the impact of East-West technology transfer in generating resource savings and output increments for the Soviet economy. Second, he seeks to differentiate between the direct impact of transfer and the question of long-run effects through diffusion, though he doesn't pursue this matter nearly so far or so concretely. He provides some interesting factual material on the question of "integration"; i.e., given a decision to seek technology transfer, what choice is made between acquiring foreign technology from some country within the group and going outside the group to take advantage of a possibly higher level of technology. Concrete case studies like this one always appeal to me. Admittedly, any such case is only one example; but as this one shows, case studies suggest what the issues are and what kind of answers may be found when we dig into the empirical referents of such abstractions as "gains from technology transfer."

Hanson's paper provides a good example of how prices affect foreign-trade composition and direction, a question with which an earlier panel and a paper by Rosefielde were concerned. Decisions to import advanced technology embodied in capital goods rest on some kind of effectiveness calculation, that is, on the comparison of two variants, A and B. Variant A involves carrying on without importation of technology. Variant B involves putting additional resources into agriculture via the indirect route of exporting goods to buy fertilizer plant. Under variant A, agricultural output remains unaffected; under B there is a net increment in output because of the extra fertilizer used. Hanson has been able to find some numbers on which to base his estimate of the economic effect of this import decision because Soviet decisionmakers have already made some such calculation in which prices *do* count, and have revealed to us some of the economic magnitudes they found.

Hanson did not quite finish his reconstruction of the Soviet calculation to the point of showing the payoff in the usual Soviet "effectiveness" terms. He estimates a total expenditure on import of $2.7 to $4 billion, which creates an increment to Soviet GNP of .50%, but he doesn't translate this into a ruble rate of return on the domestic opportunity cost. At this point, he must have run out of the old envelopes on the backs of which I gather he does his calculations as a substitute for computer analyses. In preparing my comments, I pulled a discarded envelope out of my wastebasket and finished off the calculation. GNP in the mid-1970s was about 400 billion rubles; so .50% of GNP is 2 billion rubles. The ruble cost to import the chemical plant could be estimated as exports of about 2 billion rubles, if we use the general range of ratios which researchers have found for the relationship of foreign to domestic prices for exported goods. This investment thus has a pay-out-period of one year, or a 100% return.

This conclusion has all kinds of interesting and alarming implications. For one thing, credit extended to the socialist countries would appear to be a very great gift. I believe the estimate of their current level of indebtedness circa 1978 is about $50 billion, and a 100% return to their capital stock would be a bonus of $50 billion in annual output in perpetuity. That calculation involves only loans, and when the volume of imports of technologically advanced equipment is expanded to include those paid for by exports, this means an extraordinary boost to the socialist economies. It also raises the question of how those economies could possibly have a debt service problem. If opening up their economies to trade and net investment from abroad has provided so great a spur to output growth, this gives point to the question of whether what the West gets in return is worth what is given them. Maybe we should ask for more in return or be the dog in the manger and refuse to let them garner that surplus.

I am not sure, however, that we can really accept the premise and its corollaries. Grossman earlier raised the issue of how accurate the calculations of the socialist planners are in making foreign-trade decisions. Perhaps the large gain Hanson has calculated by accepting some Soviet-produced numbers does not exist in fact, but simply embodies a distorted estimate that Soviet foreign-trade decisionmakers have made to justify this policy. The technology import calculations may be done to justify a decision taken on other grounds, rather than actually to generate a decision.

Gur Ofer

Growth Strategy, Specialization in Agriculture, and Trade: Bulgaria and Eastern Europe

Contrary to what the image of their growth strategy may appear to be, socialist countries (SOC)—especially those less developed—employ a larger proportion of their labor force in agriculture than do equally developed market economies (ME).[1] Likewise, despite a very rapid industrialization drive at growth rates much higher than in most MEs at comparable levels of development, the urban sectors in those countries are relatively smaller (as measured by the proportion of the population residing in cities) than in corresponding MEs. The apparent contradiction is resolved by showing that part of the urban deficiency in SOC is due to an abnormally low level of economic activity and employment in the service industries, mostly located in cities. The other part results from the choice of production techniques: much more highly capital-intensive techniques in manufacturing and much more highly labor-intensive ones in agriculture than in MEs. The rationale offered for this policy, at least during the early stages of industrialization, is the high costs of (1) the capital needed for urban infrastructure and (2) moving large numbers of people from the countryside to the cities. Such a strategy of economizing on urbanization and of deviating from the apparently efficient location of labor and capital is much more suitable for the less-developed SOC (except Czechoslovakia, East Germany, and to some extent Hungary) with an overconcentration of people in rural areas and agriculture and a large initial deficiency in urban infrastructure.

A question left unanswered is to what extent such a growth strategy is indeed the optimal one. An important aspect of this question is whether the policy implications of such a strategy with respect to the agricultural sector are optimal; that is, can a country avoid a severe loss in total factor productivity in agriculture by substituting labor for capital (and other out-of-agriculture inputs) as if along a given isoquant? Since modernization of agriculture is strongly embodied in capital and market inputs, there seems to be a general agreement that the answer is negative.[2] Indeed, because of the "neglect of agriculture," which is a recognized part of the "socialist growth strategy," there developed a general shortage of agricultural products—food and nonfood raw materials—in the socialist bloc. That shortage manifested itself in the inclusion of agricultural products within the category of so-called "hard" goods and resulted in a growing dependency of East European countries on agricultural imports, first from the Soviet Union and later from outside the bloc. The growing worldwide scarcity in products of agricultural (A) crops in recent years aggravated the already severe hard-currency problems of SOC. Neglect of agriculture can certainly be identified as a serious mistake in structural planning; this may also have important political repercussions on both East-West and Soviet Union-Eastern Europe relations.

What seems to be a collective mistake of all SOC (or of CMEA) would be a particularly serious error for countries with a potential (and historical) comparative advantage in A-products. They could plan to meet the developing shortages in farm products. It would seem reasonable that if one country was willing to diverge from the typical socialist industrialization strategy by specializing in A-origin products within CMEA, it could enjoy economic gains that would, with less sacrifice and effort, allow for a higher rate of growth. While in the Western world the debate between the two basic growth strategies—specialization in the production and export of primary products vs. specialization in manufacturing cum import-substitution—may still be unsettled, it seems plausible that within a semi-autarkic group of countries zealously pursuing the second strategy, one or two countries adopting the first could flourish.

While working on the industrial structure of SOC, certain characteristics of Bulgaria's internal structure and of its foreign trade indicated a trend towards a strategy of more production and trade of A-origin products than all other SOC, especially the less-developed ones and particularly Romania.[3] The differences between the Bulgarian and Romanian strategies are quite in accord with their different approaches towards CMEA. While Romania, in the name of the orthodox growth strategy of self-propelled, all-around industrialization, has limited its relations and level of cooperation with CMEA, Bulgaria's increased in an apparent effort to go along with some of the demands made by the more developed SOC to specialize according to its relative advantage.[4]

This paper will try to identify whether or not there was an effort by any less-developed SOC to "swim against the stream" in its trade and internal production structure and priorities, especially with respect to the A-sector, and to try to evaluate the economic consequences of such a policy.

Pressures For and Against Specialization in A-Products Within CMEA

The structure and direction of trade among SOC are determined by a host of factors, the most important being: (1) the ideologically determined growth strategy; (2) the level of economic development of individual countries and the disparity among them; (3) the economic and political dominance of the Soviet Union; and (4) natural endowments, terms of trade, and the degree of access to trade with other countries. The last pair of factors are at least partly dependent on the other factors. Likewise, the structure and direction of trade of SOC change over time in response to changes in these factors.

Most of the ex-ante ideological factors seem to work against specializing in A-trade or, for that matter, in A-production.[5] According to the strategy of socialist growth, agriculture should supply the food and industrial raw materials essential to satisfy the minimum needs of the population and spare its extra resources to help in the industrial drive. Active development of agriculture would absorb scarce resources needed for industrial development, which has little need of A-raw materials because of its concentration on engineering and other branches of heavy industry. Moreover, economic development through agriculture, even if collectivized, is politically dangerous because it postpones the growth of an ideologically conscious proletariat. Collectivization itself, clearly considered an ideological necessity, may also contribute to difficulties in making agriculture a productive fast-growing sector.

There is much debate in the West on whether, and to what extent, "autarky" is one of the elements of socialist growth strategy. It seems quite clear that while a certain degree of autarky is either a norm or a consequence of this strategy, it has always been legitimate or even desirable for SOC to export surplus agricultural products to acquire the machinery necessary to support the industrialization drive. The conflict created between the low priority accorded to agriculture in domestic production and the need for A-goods to pay for imported machinery is resolved by reducing urban consumption of A-goods, by putting more pressure on agriculture to increase sales (procurements) to the public sector, or by sporadic efforts to increase A-production for export purposes in the short run.[6] The eventual increase in industrial production, it is believed, will preempt the need for such exports in the long run.[7]

The ex-ante ideological and strategic bias against agriculture has contributed much to the developing scarcity of A-products in the CMEA group. This scarcity has been strongly reinforced by two ex-post developments: (1) the failure of the agricultural sector to develop even at the minimum rates that had been planned, and (2) the higher-than-expected rate of increase in the consumption of the local food (and light industry products) since 1953-55. Part of the gaps have been closed by gradually according a higher priority status to the A-sector and part by increasing imports.

The ideological bias against the A-sector and against systematic long-run specialization in A-products stands in direct conflict with the initial structure of comparative advantages of the East European SOC: the socialist bloc was made up of countries with a wide range of development levels which raised the potential for growth via indus-trialization along different paths, thus working for an intensive "socialist division of labor." According to this efficient division, the less-developed members that were naturally better endowed for A-production would follow a more "classical" industrialization process—with higher levels of A-production and specialization and higher emphasis on light industry—to the benefit of all the countries of the bloc. While the ideological bias made such a strategy more difficult to follow, it increased substantially the potential gains to any country that would adopt it.[8]

The important difference, in the socialist context, between extrac-tive raw materials (metals, energy sources) on the one side and A-origin products on the other (that together make the primary goods sector) must be emphasized. While, according to the general theory of economic development, the relevant distinction is between primary production and manufacturing, according to socialist theory, extrac-tive industries are an important part of heavy industry—the leader of the industrialization drive.[9] In this respect, on the socialist ideological spectrum, these industries are not on the same side as agriculture. If, after years of intensive efforts by all SOC to develop their own raw material base, they relaxed this approach to a degree, it is partly be-cause of the exorbitant costs and partly because of the readiness of the Soviet Union to shoulder much of the burden.[10] In the following discussion, we shall concentrate only on trade in products of A-origin which, like raw materials, are scarce but which, unlike them, do not enjoy a higher ideological status.

The dominance of Soviet economic and political power within the bloc has created a structure of intra-CMEA trade that is different from that implied by Eastern Europe's emulation of Soviet growth strategy. First, the Soviet Union's huge endowment of natural re-sources and its willingness to supply them to its clients allowed the latter to limit raw material developments to levels lower than those required by their ambitious heavy industrial development plans. Until recently, this was also true with respect to food and other A-products, but the Soviet Union's ambitious plans to increase its own food consumption and its failure to meet these plans have contributed to the aggravation of the A-products shortage in the bloc as a whole.[11] Furthermore, Soviet reparations demands during the late 1940s and early 1950s and its unsatiated demand for machinery may have pushed the more developed SOC towards a concentration in machine-building above the levels warranted by strict adherence to socialist growth strategy.[12] This may have increased the relative glut in the production of basic machines, which is another point in favor of specializing in A-products.

The slow pace of technological advances in the machine-building industries of the more developed SOC also contributed to the relative glut for East European machinery. The failure of these countries to advance fast enough to new technologies—to more sophisticated types of equipment—and thus to leave the market of more ordinary equipment to less-developed members, is no less responsible for turning machines into "soft" goods than the latter's eagerness to create a machine-building sector of their own at early stages of development.[13]

These ideological and economic factors have created two categories of goods within the CMEA, "soft" and "hard," with A-origin products included in the latter. Had the relative prices between the two groups been scarcity prices, economic pressures would have pushed the whole bloc toward the production of hard goods. But actual price differences between soft and hard goods discouraged specialization in the right direction. Studies for periods after the mid-1950s show that, compared with world market prices (wmp's) or with CMEA production costs, hard goods have been underpriced, most severely the A-goods among them.[14] Wrong prices not only discourage specialization in A-goods, but actually outweigh all the pressures working in the opposite direction. In a situation where prices cannot move freely to balance demand and supply, substitutes to price mechanisms develop. The most important substitute mechanism is bilateral balancing: "package deals" in which hard goods sales are balanced against hard goods purchases, and tying arrangements under which a hard goods buyer also has to buy a certain amount of soft goods, i.e., machinery and equipment, at high prices.[15] The problem with such an arrangement is that the only way to gain in trade from A-specialization within the bloc is to produce and export soft goods in a quantity large enough to go along with available hard goods or sale; this may push the production structure in the opposite direction from that suggested by A-food specialization. Other, indirect compensations for the seller of hard goods—such as aid extensions—are also possible and are in effect being used.

In our discussion up to now, all the arguments in favor of and against A-specialization assumed a closed socialist market. One partial solution to the relative scarcity of primary goods and the relative abundance of machinery in the bloc is to increase trade with less-developed countries (LDC). This policy has been pursued to some extent, but it cannot solve the main food problems (grain, fodder, fresh produce, dairy products), except for the tropical varieties. This is probably one issue the Romanians considered when they insisted on the inclusion of the Asian SOC within CMEA during the CMEA debates in the early 1960s.[16]

The technological backwardness of much machine-building and other industrial activities, even in the more developed SOC, seems to be the major factor that prevents CMEA from solving its structural imbalance through trade with the West.[17] Moreover, it significantly worsens the situation. The failure of SOC to develop industrial products marketable in the West increased the pressure to market them inside the bloc, which in turn put pressure on the less-developed members to abstain from "parallel industrial development." It deprived the bloc of hard-currency revenues that could alleviate the shortage in primary goods. On the other hand, this technological failure encouraged the less-developed SOC to seek better and more advanced equipment in the West and to pay for it with primary goods of A-origin, thus increasing the excess supply for machinery and reducing the already short supply of primary goods within CMEA.[18] Clearly the CMEA's trade price structure encouraged such behavior. But, paradoxically, it also yielded potential payoffs for a strategy of specialization in A-products (and other primary goods), either for the exports to the West or to acquire a better bargaining position within CMEA.

So, with the single important exception of the distorted CMEA trade price structure, economic conditions seem to favor specialization in A-products as a consequence of the socialist growth strategy adopted and of other ideological and political considerations. To make this conclusion more realistic, let us define A-specialization. We must first recognize a whole range of possible strategies between the two (unrealistic) extremes of intensive, self-propelled autarkic industrialization and a high degree of specialization in agriculture with little industrial effort.[19] We take it for granted that industrialization is necessary for modern growth, certainly an indispensable part of socialist growth strategy, and that an eventual development to a status of net importer of agricultural and other primary goods is realistic. The real question separates into three elements, only partly mutually dependent: (1) the time-frame of the structural changes in production and trade; (2) the sequence of development of the various manufacturing industries; and (3) the degree of dependence on trade. A few relevant variations may be mentioned. To an almost completely autarkic industrialization drive directed primarily toward heavy industry (the Soviet model), one may juxtapose a strategy where the same goal—fast development of industrial self-sufficiency—is achieved by a short period of intensive importation of machines and equipment paid for by surplus A-products accumulated by various short-run ad hoc methods (the model of at least some SOC during 1946-53, and Romania during the late 1950s and early 1960s).[20] Both models are different from a growth strategy that plans for a longer period of net exportation of A-goods and a somewhat slower industrialization drive. An essential part of this latter strategy is the development of a long-range production capability in the A-sector.

Our hypothesis is that Bulgaria inside CMEA and Yugoslavia outside it have indeed chosen this last path, while the other SOC did not. However, the proof of such a hypothesis (that is, the identification of the policies as well as their consequences) is not simple. If this strategy is really better than the other two variants, it should show up in the overall economic performance of the countries pursuing it, all other things being equal. Many factors enter into the determination of the overall performance of each economy; the particular variant of the growth strategy chosen, though important, is only one factor. Among the other factors is the different pattern of trade relations with the West. The relative disadvantage of a strategy of extremely rapid industrialization (as pursued by Romania) may be compensated for by the fact that this strategy is accomplished to a large extent with Western equipment—contrary to Bulgaria which may have chosen the other path but is pursuing it to a much larger degree within CMEA. Even the identification of A-specialization policies may be hampered by the "package deal" phenomenon described above; this might force a country like Bulgaria to produce machinery to accompany its inter-CMEA A-exports.

Two points need to be stressed before turning to an empirical testing of these propositions. First, the general effort in recent years by all SOC to compensate for past neglect in agriculture may blur the picture of a single country that has long directed special efforts toward agriculture. Second, since 1973, the rapid rise of energy and other primary production prices has benefited SOC. SOC may have suffered in the past from investing too much in raw-material production, so that the most orthodox socialist growth strategy is now "paying off." The largest gainers are the Soviet Union, Poland, and Romania. In order not to obscure our argument and the data with consequences of recent changes in world conditions and the CMEA countries, the empirical part of this study is confined to the 1950-70 response to them.

Trade Structure and Growth Strategy:
A Comparative Analysis

Two main differences in the pattern of trade of SOC and MEs are dealt with in the literature. One is the autarkic phenomenon; that is, the ratios of trade volumes to GNP in SOC are below "normal" rates for MEs for comparable levels of development and size of population.[21] The second difference is in the commodity structure of SOC, which is our main interest here.[22]

The "normal" pattern of the trade structure of MEs, compared to that of SOC, is estimated by the following equations:

$$[E_i, I_i, F_i] = \alpha + \beta (ln Y) + \delta ln N + u \qquad [1a]$$

$$[E_i, I_i, F_i] = a + b(ln Y) + c(ln Y)^2 + d ln N + u, \qquad [1b]$$

where E_i, I_i, F_i are the proportions of defined commodity groups in total exports, imports, and net trade, respectively. These proportions are to be explained by the level of economic development as measured by GNP per capita (Y) and by country size as measured by size of the population (N). The particular functional form [1b] is taken from Chenery and Syrquin.[23] The rationale for the inclusion of two Y terms is to allow for a decline in the rates of change as per capita GNP grows (and even for a change in the sign of the Y coefficient) as indeed has been observed in many processes of structural change.[24] The commodity groups investigated here are: A, trade in agricultural and forestry products,[25] and M, machinery and transport equipment and armaments.[26] In addition, some references are made to trade in total manufactures (non-A) and to non-machinery (other) manufactures (OM). The proportions of EA and EM are computed from total exports identified by commodity groups (and defined usually as fob) and IA and IM from total imports identified alike (and defined usually for MEs as cif).[27] FA and FM, the net trade proportions, are defined as $F_i = RE_i - I_i$, where R is the ratio of total exports to total imports.[28] Because of different definitions of imports and exports, the values of FA and FM are biased; and these equations can only be used to show trends of change. The E, I, and F variables correspond to two quite different concepts of specialization. The E and I variables measure the degree of overall specialization; that is, specialization that takes place both *inter* and *intra* the defined commodity groups. The F variables, on the other hand, measure only the degree of specialization between entire commodity groups since any commodity exchange within a given group is netted out in the computation of F_i for that group. If interest is focused on "industrialization" and the relative size of the manufacturing vs. agricultural sectors, the F concept of specialization is relevant. The E concept is relevant when policies toward agriculture and total economic performance are of interest. Still, the F concept may conceal information about specialization even in terms of its own concept: the same F can result from high or low volume of trade in the relevant commodity group.[29] Clearly one has to assign higher specialization marks to the first case. In the second, the relative impact of such specialization is very limited. One thus has to examine the F values in conjunction with those of E and I.

The sample is composed of 18 countries, including most European countries, the US, Canada, and Japan. We have not included less-developed countries in Asia and Africa because their per capita GNP and structure are not within the SOC range. We have not included any Latin American countries because of the lack of data for some and because of the very specific primary-intensive export structure of others. Originally, we used two series of GNP per capita, one based on official exchange rates (Y_1) and the other on purchasing power parities (Y_2).[30] The results are based on the latter, which generally give better estimates.

Equations were estimated for 1950, 1960, and 1970, first separately for each year and then by pooling all the observations and adding two dummy variables, D_{50} and D_{60}, to differentiate (by raising or lowering the intercepts of the functions) between each year's trade structure.

Some of the estimated equations are presented in table 1. Almost all of them have highly significant Y and N coefficients. Only for trade in machinery do the equations without $(lnY)^2$, [1a], give more significant Y coefficients than those of [1b]. Hence, we added results of those equations to the table. The general results are expected: as the level of development rises, the share of A-imports rises and the share of A-exports falls, thus bringing about an even steeper fall in net A-exports. Trade proportions in machinery (and, of course, in industrial goods) are changing in exactly opposite directions to those in A-trade. We also find that the larger the country, the smaller the proportions of A-exports and net exports, and the larger those of M, which is according to well-established international trade theory.[31]

On the basis of the above "normal" pattern, the *actual* trade structure of SOC was compared to that *estimated* from the normal equations. These comparisons are made in two ways. First, they are made for each SOC where its trade structure, for three dates, and its deviations [Δ] from the normal pattern [1b] is estimated from table 2.[32]

Second, they are made collectively for all SOC by estimating trade

TABLE 1

Trade Structure and Economic Development: Regression Results
for 18 Market Economies, 1950, 1960, 1970

Year	Trade variable	Constant (1)	lnY_2 (2)	$(lnY_2)^2$ (3)	lnN (4)	R^2 (5)
1950	EA	1129.75	−312.46	23.16	−16.50	0.63
		2.55	−2.32	2.27	−4.38	
	EM	−201.72	51.27	−3.17	5.31	0.70
		−1.20	1.00	−0.82	3.71	
	EM	−65.16	9.56		5.02	0.68
		−3.90	3.97		3.67	
	IA	−716.60	225.70	−17.36	13.08	0.85
		−3.83	3.96	−4.01	8.20	
	IM	365.43	−102.75	7.75	−5.59	0.70
		2.97	−2.74	2.73	−5.33	
	FA	1797.62	−541.95	41.41	−21.13	0.75
		3.99	−3.96	3.99	−5.52	
	FM	−425.85	109.59	−7.51	11.05	0.75
		−1.80	1.52	−1.37	5.48	
1960	EA	1599.42	−434.32	30.59	−11.57	0.63
		2.82	−2.63	2.55	−3.83	
	EM	−517.15	137.55	−9.06	6.91	0.72
		−1.68	1.54	−1.39	4.22	
	EM	−91.17	13.13		6.27	0.68
		−3.60	3.67		3.87	
	IA	−542.56	165.31	−12.28	7.77	0.74
		−2.31	2.42	−2.47	6.21	
	IM	606.70	−162.23	11.59	−6.93	0.69
		2.45	−2.25	2.21	−5.24	
	FA	1533.46	−447.24	33.07	−14.02	0.61
		2.56	−2.57	2.61	−4.39	
	FM	−775.61	194.45	−12.84	14.75	0.78
		−1.64	1.41	−1.28	5.83	
1970	EA	1274.73	−322.25	20.99	−6.45	0.58
		1.79	−1.66	1.59	−2.95	
	EM	−335.73	81.65	−4.43	6.79	0.83
		−0.85	0.71	−0.57	5.25	
	EM	−118.15	16.72		6.58	0.82
		−4.83	5.09		5.43	
	IA	−897.92	253.74	−17.68	5.07	0.85
		−4.51	4.67	−4.77	8.26	
	IM	1843.61	−496.25	33.91	−3.56	0.40
		2.87	−2.83	2.84	−1.80	
	FA	1569.62	−431.56	29.92	−9.05	0.65
		2.58	−2.60	2.65	−4.83	
	FM	−2020.84	523.19	−34.32	11.23	0.73
		−2.52	2.39	−2.30	4.55	

Table 1—*Continued.*

SOURCES: **GNP per capita—1960:** Based on Abram Bergson's worksheets (explained in detail in Abram Bergson, "Development Under Two Systems: Comparative Productivity Growth Since 1950," *World Politics* 13 [July 1971]: 611-13). Estimates for Spain and Finland were made on the basis of UN, *Yearbook of National Accounts Statistics.* **GNP per capita—other years:** MEs and Yugoslavia: UN, *Yearbook of National Accounts Statistics,* based on growth rates for GNP per capita given in various years; Socialist countries: based on growth rates given by Thad P. Alton, "Economic Growth and Resource Allocation in Eastern Europe," in JEC-1974, p. 270 (all Y_2 data are expressed in US dollars 1964). **Population—MEs and Yugoslavia:** UN, *Demographic Yearbook,* various years; International Bank for Reconstruction and Development, *World Tables 1971;* and statistical yearbooks of individual countries. SOC: Paul F. Myers, "Population and Labor Force in Eastern Europe: 1950 to 1966," in JEC-1974, p. 424. **Trade data—MEs and Yugoslavia:** UN, *Yearbook of International Trade Statistics,* various years; SOC: 1950, 1960; Marer, *Soviet and East European Foreign Trade,* pp. 45-59; 1960, 1970, Council for Mutual Economic Assistance, *Statistical Yearbook* (Moscow: CMEA, 1975), pp. 327-32.

NOTE: Definition of terms: Y—GNP per capita; N—population (mid-year) based on purchasing power parities; E—proportion in total exports; and I—proportion in total imports. *EA, IA*—goods originated in agriculture and forestry; for MEs and Yugoslavia including revised SITC categories 0, 1, 2 *less* 27, 28, and 4; for Socialist countries including CTN categories 5, 6, 7, 8 (Paul Marer, *Soviet and East European Foreign Trade 1946-1969* [Bloomington: Indiana University Press, 1972], pp. 312, 318, 324-25). *EM, IM*—machinery, transportation equipment, and armaments: revised SITC categories, 7, 95; CTN category 1. Inconsistencies between SITC and CTN for the above categories are mainly due to the exclusion of household appliances in SOC from machinery production, and some ambiguity about the inclusion of armaments in the available SOC statistics in category 1 (see John M. Montias, "The Structure of Comecon Trade and the Prospects for East-West Exchanges," in JEC-1974, pp. 662-680). The exclusion of household appliances biases downwards SOC trade in M and possible SOC M exports. *FA, FM,* and *FOM* are the proportions of net exports in total imports and are computed as $F_i = RE_i - I_i$, where R is exports/imports.

Another inconsistency between MEs (and Yugoslavia) and SOC arises from the fact that the former trade data are mostly fob for imports and cif for exports, while SOC data are mostly fob, which makes R systematically higher for SOC. For this reason, F deviations for individual SOC are calculated on the basis of E and I equations.

The MEs sample includes 18 countries; all European countries with the exception of Switzerland, Turkey, the US, Canada, and Japan. SOC include all East European countries except Albania (for lack of data), the USSR (because of its large size there is no meaning to estimates of normal trade pattern for it), and Yugoslavia.

TABLE 2

Trade Structure of Socialist Countries and Deviations
from "Normal" Structure of Economies, 1950-70

Trade in A-goods

			Czecho-slovakia (1)	East Germany* (2)	Hungary (3)	Poland (4)	Bulgaria (5)	Romania (6)	Yugo-slavia† (7)	SD (8)
1950	EA	Act.	15.4	6.8	38.6	28.1	88.0	54.7	54.5	
		Δ	-19.2	-22.8	-4.8	1.2	24.3	9.7	4.5	17.4
	IA	Act.	60.7	33.0	41.7	31.9	13.9	22.4	41.3	
		Δ	13.0	-22.1	-3.8	-26.6	-20.6	-25.5	-3.9	7.4
	FA	Act.	-43.6	-27.2	-7.4	-5.2	63.5	25.2	-15.7	
		Δ	-34.3	2.5	-0.5	27.7	42.0	33.9	6.0	(17.7)
1960	EA	Act.	10.4	5.9	27.4	23.0	56.4	35.9	45.3	
		Δ	-17.7	-19.0	-8.4	-3.3	5.7	-4.2	-0.6	14.6
	IA	Act.	37.1	39.2	29.2	33.9	16.7	18.4	26.4	
		Δ	6.1	5.2	-2.5	-6.0	-11.4	-16.5	-7.3	6.0
	FA	Act.	-26.0	-33.2	-4.0	-13.4	34.6	21.5	1.7	
		Δ	-24.9	-24.4	-5.2	3.1	16.6	11.8	6.9	(18.1)
1970	EA	Act.	7.3	7.4	26.7	15.9	43.4	26.8	25.7	
		Δ	-13.8	-13.5	-3.6	-11.3	7.2	-6.2	-1.6	10.6
	IA	Act.	24.1	28.1	24.4	21.4	15.9	15.4	16.5	
		Δ	0.6	2.3	0.2	-7.7	-6.3	-10.3	-10.9	2.3
	FA	Act.	-16.6	-21.7	0.7	-5.8	31.4	9.8	1.6	
		Δ	-14.8	-15.1	-4.1	-3.4	14.1	4.5	10.0	(9.1)

Trade in Machinery

(7)	1950	EM	Act.	20.3	28.0	20.7	7.8	0.0	4.2	1.6	6.6
(8)			Δ	6.1	15.3	13.3	−5.0	0.4	−1.5	−2.4	
(9)		IM	Act.	0.7	5.5	17.4	32.4	37.2	37.1	31.8	4.9
(10)			Δ	10.5	−3.3	4.2	24.8	18.2	24.1	17.4	
(11)		FM	Act.	15.3	18.6	1.0	−25.0	−37.2	−33.5	−31.1	(9.3)
(12)			Δ	−4.4	16.5	7.6	−29.6	−17.8	25.4	−18.5	
(7)	1960	EM	Act.	45.7	49.0	38.6	28.3	12.9	16.7	16.5	7.9
(8)			Δ	23.9	26.5	24.8	8.9	7.5	5.0	7.6	
(9)		IM	Act.	21.7	12.7	28.5	27.1	43.9	33.6	35.9	6.4
(10)			Δ	0.2	−6.8	4.5	9.7	14.5	10.3	10.7	
(11)		FM	Act.	26.7	36.8	7.0	−1.9	−32.2	−15.1	−25.7	(12.5)
(12)			Δ	25.1	33.6	18.3	−1.8	−7.8	−4.8	−6.0	
(7)	1970	EM	Act.	50.4	51.7	32.6	38.5	29.0	22.8	22.7	6.3
(8)			Δ	24.1	26.1	16.5	17.6	17.4	6.7	2.9	
(9)		IM	Act.	33.4	34.2	30.9	36.2	40.6	40.3	33.3	9.6
(10)			Δ	13.0	15.9	9.3	15.4	14.8	15.2	13.1	
(11)		FM	Act.	18.5	14.9	−0.3	1.5	−9.0	−18.9	−20.1	(12.0)
(12)			Δ	11.8	8.9	6.2	1.8	4.2	−8.9	−11.4	

Net Trade in Other Manufacturing (FOM)

(13)	1950	Actual	39.3	−5.4	−4.7	25.2	−38.3	−4.7	−6.2	⋮
(14)		Δ	38.7	−19.0	−7.1	1.9	−24.2	−8.5	12.5	⋮
(15)	1960	Actual	5.3	−2.6	−11.0	4.3	−11.4	4.6	−14.0	⋮
(16)		Δ	−0.2	−9.2	−13.1	−1.3	−8.8	−7.0	−0.9	⋮
(17)	1970	Actual	1.1	1.8	−6.4	2.3	−13.4	3.1	−23.5	⋮
(18)		Δ	3.0	6.2	−2.1	1.6	−18.3	4.4	1.4	⋮

Table 2—Continued.

SOURCES: See sources to table 1.

NOTE: EA and IA and FA (REA−◯IA) are the proportions of exports and imports and net exports of agricultural originated goods; IEM, IM, and FM are corresponding proportions of trade in machinery and FOM (= −FA −FM) is the proportion of net exports of other, non-machinery manufacturing goods. The exact definitions are given in table 4. The deviations for E_i and I_i are from regressions presented in table 1, equations [1b]. The F_i deviations for each country are computed from the E_i and I_i deviations according to the formula $F_i = RE_i − I_i$, where R is the ratio of total exports to total imports for each country. SD in column 8 is the standard deviation of the estimate of the above equation, SD. Figures in parentheses are from FM equations in table 1.

In this table, we show results of estimates of equations [2b] and [3b] (estimated while excluding the observation for Yugoslavia). Some of the coefficients of S in equation [2b] are in column 8 of table 2 (ignore the rest of table 4 at this point). The estimates shown are based on individual equations for 1950 and combined ones for 1960 and 1970. Nineteen-fifty was separated out because at that time neither the industrial structure nor the trade structure of SOC reflected fully the new economic system. In the 1960-70 equations, we also added a dummy variable, D_{60}, for the 1960 observation to account for shifts over time in the trade environment of both SOC and MEs. The data on the trade structure in SOC are based on CMEA's classification of commodities (CTN) which for the relevant categories dealt with here seem to be very similar to the SITC classification. (The A-proportions are composed by CTN categories, 5, 6, 7, 8 and the M-proportions by category 1. (For a comparison of the various trade classifications, see Marer, *Soviet and East European Foreign Trade*, pp. 5-11, 308-41.) SOC data, however, are given fob for both imports and exports; thus the SOC R (=exports/imports) are usually higher. For this reason (and those mentioned above), we estimate SOC net trade deviations from the deviations observed in the relevant export and import equations. Per capita GNP for the SOC is made consistent with the two series used for the MEs (see details in notes to tables 1 and 4). In each case, the SOC deviations in tables 1 and 2 can be compared with the standard error of estimate of the corresponding equation (column 8).

*In 1950, EA, IA, and FA do not include trade in "raw materials" of vegetable and animal origin. With these inclusions, I assume, FA will be negative.

†Based on SITC classification and on exports fob and imports cif, as contrasted with fob for other SOC. The exceptionally small R of Yugoslavia (even by ME standards) causes some peculiar results, especially with respect to FOM.

equations based on observations of all SOC and non-SOC countries that also contain, in addition to the variables included in equations [1], specific variables to identify the deviant trade pattern of SOC. The equations are of the form:

$$[E_i \, I_i] = \alpha + \beta lnY + (\delta(lnY)^2) + \delta lnN + S + u \qquad [2ab]$$

$$[E_i \, I_i] = a + blnY + (c(lnY)^2) + dlnN + S + b'SlnY + u, [3ab]$$

where S is a dummy variable of "being a SOC" and $SlnY$ is an interaction variable allowing for the pattern of change of trade structure with respect to Y.

The main results on SOC trade deviations are as follows:

1. The proportions of A-exports (EA) are below normal levels in SOC during most periods, in many instances by wide margins, especially for Czechoslovakia and East Germany (table 2, lines 2). Even traditionally heavy A-exporting countries like Poland, Romania, and Yugoslavia are often below the norm and are never above it after 1950. Of all SOC, only Bulgaria shows a consistent positive EA deviation during the entire 1950-70 period. Since most other less-developed SOC (Poland, Romania, and Yugoslavia) have a much larger population than Bulgaria, the normal level of EA estimated for them is lower at each level of GNP per capita; the differences in actual EA proportions between Bulgaria and the other countries are thus much more extreme (compare table 2, lines 2 with lines 1).

2. Most countries compensate for the low proportion of A-exports by low, sometimes even lower, proportions of A-imports (table 2, lines 4). As a general rule, and together with the findings on EA, this demonstrates that SOC trade in A-goods is even lower than their general participation in trade. Whatever the degree of relative autarky in SOC, the autarkic approach with respect to the A-sector is stricter. Formerly A-exporting countries especially seem to have diverted their A-goods to domestic consumption and, to compensate, reduced imports drastically (see the high IA and EA negative deviations of Hungary, Poland, Romania, and Yugoslavia). Although in this respect Bulgaria also reduced its A-imports, it did so to a lesser degree than did Romania, its peer in GNP per capita.

3. The deviations of the net-export proportions (FA) are usually either negative or, if positive, are based on negative deviations of both EA and IA proportions. Czechoslovakia, East Germany, and, in most years, Hungary have negative FA deviations,[33] while Poland, Romania, Yugoslavia, and Bulgaria have positive ones. Except for Bulgaria, however, these positive values are always (except for 1950) based on negative EA and IA deviations. Only in the case of Bulgaria,

which has the *highest FA deviations* among SOC, is it based on posi-ive ΔEA's and negative ΔIA's. The latter, however, is lower (in abso-lute value) than similar deviations of Poland and Romania.

4. SOC deviations in trade in machinery and equipment (M) (part b, table 2) are as expected: both the more developed SOC, which by 1950 already had positive EM deviations, and the less-developed ones, which started with very low EM proportions (and negative de-viations), increased the proportions of EM above those warranted by the growth in their GNP per capita levels, thus creating positive EM deviations. The deviations reached magnitudes several times larger than the corresponding standard deviations: in Czechoslovakia, East Germany, and Hungary, this was the case by 1960; in Poland and Bulgaria, large positive EM deviations developed a few years later. Bulgaria is again in a special position: starting from the lowest level of EM, by 1960 it had built up a positive deviation equal to that of all other less-developed SOC; by 1970 it far surpassed both Romania and Yugoslavia in EM and ΔEM and reached a ΔEM figure equal to those of Hungary and Poland.[34]

5. In contrast to A-goods, SOC have higher than normal propor-tions of machinery imports. With few exceptions, including Czecho-slovakia and East Germany until 1960, all countries have positive ΔIM figures that are no less than one standard deviation of the normal estimates, and in many cases much higher. This active trade clearly indicates a higher degree of general specialization in machinery. As to the particular specialization in M versus other commodity groups, a pattern begins (in 1950) with large net M-exports (lines 11 and 12) and large positive deviations for the developed SOC while the less-developed SOC have large M-imports and large negative deviations. Over time, the number of SOC with positive FM deviations includes Hungary by 1960 (or before) and Poland and Bulgaria by 1970; only Romania within CMEA and Yugoslavia without show negative values of ΔFM. This pattern is similar to a "normal" trade and development process, but is moving much faster than warranted by the growth of GNP per capita; hence, the large MF deviations—negative in the be-ginning and positive at the end.

6. By 1960, most SOC developed a negative deviation in net exports of other manufactures (including raw materials, semi-manufactures, and light nonfood manufactures). Most of these deviations were elim-inated by 1970, largely as a result of increasing net exports of light industrial goods (mostly in the case of the more developed SOC), but also to some extent by renewed measures to reduce imports and in-crease exports of raw materials. The latter was a reaction to the developing scarcity of raw materials in the bloc and (for Romania and Poland) represented their efforts to increase exports to the West.

Here, too, Bulgaria stands apart as the only country that substantially increased its negative deviation of other manufacturing (OM) between 1960 (or before) and 1970. Bulgaria was able to keep its M-exports at high levels on the one hand and its large (net) exports of A on the other.[35]

7. These typical SOC deviations are also found for the entire group of SOC (see table 4, column 8). Here it is *assumed* that the only way SOC can differ from MEs is in the intercept levels of the estimated functions (as in equation [2] above) and not in their slopes (as in equation [3]). Given this assumption, at least since 1960 SOC as a group had a (most probably significant) negative FA deviation of 7.3 points. It was made up from a large, and significant, negative ΔEA deviation and a much smaller nonsignificant ΔIA one. Correspondingly, we find a large positive ΔFM deviation of 10.2 points made up of a large positive deviation in machinery exports and a smaller, though also significant and positive, deviation in machinery imports.[36]

The composition of SOC FA and FM residuals—the former made up of two negative import and export residuals and the latter of two positive ones—also indicates that SOC specialize to a lesser degree than normal in A-goods and to a higher degree than normal in M-goods.

8. As for most individual SOC, the collective SOC deviations in 1950 also show higher than normal net exports of A-goods and net imports of machinery. The former deviation is made up entirely of an extremely lower than normal level of imports of A-goods and the latter mainly of heavy imports of machinery. This specific 1950 pattern reflects traditional pre-socialist trade patterns, Soviet reparations demands, severe austerity in the field of consumption, and initial industrialization attempts.

9. On the basis of some further calculations, it can be shown that SOC are net importers not only of A-goods but also of non-machinery industrial goods, non-A raw materials included (OM). The net exports of industrial goods are equal by definition, when imports equal exports, to -FA and the net exports of non-machinery industrial goods: FOM = $-FA - FM$. From results for the S coefficients (table 4, column 8) we can calculate FOM to be -5.7 in 1950 and -2.9 points in 1960 and 1970.[37] The deficit shown is most likely made up of positive net exports in consumer manufactures and a larger deficit in raw materials.[38]

10. In equations [3] we test the hypothesis that there are interactions between the effects of the socialist system and the levels of GNP per capita in shaping the special SOC trade patterns. This indeed proves to be the case for at least some of the trade groups, some of the time (see table 4).[39] For example, the SOC deviations in the im-

TABLE 3

Trade Structure Pattern of Socialist and Market Economies
(regressions based on equations [2b] and [3b]

	Coefficients	Constant	lnY_2	$(lnY_2)^2$	lnN	SOC	$S \times Y$	D_{60}	R^2
1950	EA	1405.67	-392.65	29.00	-17.5	-2.39			0.65
		3.44	3.14	3.05	-4.89	-0.3			
	EA	1176.61	-326.60	24.24	-16.80	259.77	-41.64		0.72
		3.00	-2.74	2.68	-5.06	2.04	-2.06		
	IA	-791.49	246.42	-18.74	12.53	-13.66			0.71
		3.26	3.32	3.31	5.88	-2.56			
	IA	-623.37	197.95	-15.25	12.00	-206.08	30.56		0.80
		-2.87	3.00	-3.04	6.53	-2.92	2.73		
	EM	-264.12	69.68	-4.51	5.20	4.71			0.64
		-1.57	1.36	-1.15	3.53	1.27			
	EM	-212.29	54.73	-3.43	5.04	-54.61	9.42		0.66
		-1.21	1.03	-0.85	3.40	-0.96	1.04		
	IM	484.81	-137.13	10.19	-5.48	10.29			0.56
		2.57	-2.38	2.32	-3.31	2.48			
	IM	337.93	-94.78	7.14	-5.01	178.39	-26.70		0.73
		2.13	-1.96	1.95	-3.73	3.46	-3.27		
1960-70	EA	917.66	-228.84	15.03	-8.63	-9.56		2.78	0.59
		3.13	-2.75	2.54	-4.95	-2.05		0.69	
	EA	844.58	-209.24	13.73	-8.63	72.30	-11.78	2.05	0.60
		2.81	-2.46	2.28	-4.95	0.95	-1.08	0.50	
	IA	-487.47	140.04	-10.06	5.99	-2.26		7.52	0.67
		-3.50	3.61	-3.66	7.36	-1.04		4.02	

IA	-382.40	114.28	-8.35	5.98	-109.89	15.49	8.48	0.74
	-3.05	3.22	-3.33	8.23	-3.47	3.40	5.00	
EM	-287.36	64.66	-3.37	6.42	18.25		0.64	0.77
	-1.65	1.31	-0.96	6.20	6.60		0.27	
EM	-189.57	38.43	-1.62	6.42	-91.31	15.77	1.62	0.80
	-1.13	0.81	-0.48	6.61	-2.16	2.59	0.71	
IM	675.29	-177.89	12.39	-4.69	7.99		-5.38	0.45
	3.42	-3.17	3.12	-3.99	2.55		-1.99	
IM	640.28	-168.50	11.77	-4.69	47.21	-5.64	-5.73	0.46
	3.15	-2.92	2.89	-3.97	0.92	-0.76	-2.08	

SOURCE: See sources to table 1.

NOTE: For the definitions of the variables, see note to table 2. The deviations of E_i and I_i of individual SOC are from regressions based on equation [2a] as presented in table 3 and in which SOC, except Yugoslavia (see note †) participated as observers. The FA and FM deviations are computed on the basis of the E_i and I_i deviations using the formula $F_i = RE_i - I_i$. The SOC coefficients given in column 8 are the general SOC vertical deviations of all socialist countries as a group from the normal-market economy line (equation 2a); SD (column 9) is the standard deviations of the estimates of the relevant equations. The figures in the second line of each entry are the t values of the coefficients.

*See note (*) in table 2.

†See note (†) in table 2. The deviations of Yugoslavia are derived from equations similar to those described above, except Yugoslavia's observations are also included in the regressions.

TABLE 4

Deviations of Trade Structure of Socialist Countries from Normal Trade Pattern, 1950-70

			Czecho-slovakia (1)	East Germany (2)	Hungary (3)	Poland (4)	Bulgaria (5)	Romania (6)	Yugoslavia (7)	S (8)	SD (9)
(1)	1950	ΔEA	-14.6	18.8	-2.4	4.7	21.7	9.4	2.2	-2.4 -0.3	17.1
(2)		ΔIA	25.5	-8.4	10.0	-12.3	-4.9	-16.0	9.9	-13.7 -2.6	10.2
(3)		ΔFA	-41.7	-7.8	-12.1	16.8	24.0	24.2	-8.9	11.3	..
(4)		ΔEM	0.7	10.1	8.3	-9.9	-3.5	5.7	-5.0	4.7 1.3	7.1
(5)		ΔIM	-13.3	-13.1	6.0	14.5	5.5	12.1	3.8	10.3 2.5	7.9
(6)		ΔFM	13.8	21.8	1.4	-23.9	-8.6	-7.1	-6.2	-5.6	..
(1)	1960	ΔEA	-8.9	-13.0	-4.7	-2.9	10.8	-1.6	2.2	-9.6 -2.1	12.4
(2)		ΔIA	8.0	8.3	1.9	0.8	-6.2	-9.8	0.1	-2.3 -1.0	5.8
(3)		ΔFA	-17.4	-21.4	-6.2	-3.4	16.0	8.0	1.3	-7.3	..
(4)		ΔEM	5.7	9.5	9.9	-5.1	-7.0	-9.0	-5.0	18.2 6.6	7.4
(5)		ΔIM	-5.6	-13.6	-3.0	-0.7	5.7	-0.3	-0.5	8.0 2.5	8.4
(6)		ΔFM	11.6	23.2	12.1	-3.8	-12.1	-9.7	-2.6	10.2	..
(1)	1970	ΔEA	-6.7	-5.5	5.7	-2.0	17.7	7.2	8.6	9.6 2.1	12.4

(2) ΔIA	5.0	6.7	4.0	−6.1	−3.5	−9.1	−7.3	−2.3	−1.0	5.8
(3) ΔFA	−11.9	−11.9	1.4	8.1	22.8	15.9	12.3	−7.3		..
(4) ΔEM	6.1	8.0	−2.4	−1.2	−1.9	−12.5	−13.9	18.2	8.0	7.4
(5) ΔIM	−0.8	1.8	−3.2	6.8	4.8	8.2	2.0	6.6		8.4
(6) ΔFM	7.1	5.8	0.9	−8.0	−6.9	−20.0	−10.1	2.5	10.2	..

Sources from Table 3.

port proportions of A-goods (ΔIA) in 1960-70 are positively related to income; that is, the more developed countries among SOC are becoming heavy importers of A-goods (much above normal) to a larger extent than in less-developed SOC (see the SY coefficient at 15.49 in the relevant [3a] equation). Without discussing every case of income dependency, let us point to the most significant result. Because of income dependency of either import or export deviations of SOC, there is always a strong interaction between the net-export SOC deviations of both A and M and GNP per capita. The more developed SOC show larger positive FM and larger negative FA deviations than the less-developed SOC. Such a deviant pattern of trade creates the impression of a higher level of A-goods vs. M-goods specialization between countries of different levels of GNP per capita among SOC than among MEs. This impression is to a large extent artificial. First, much of the abnormal A to M specialization results from the suppression of trade in A-goods among SOC. Second, much of deviational structure does not result from trade among the East European SOC included in the analysis but from their trade with the Soviet Union, which, despite its position as one of the most developed SOC, is willing to play a role of a net exporter of A-goods and raw materials and net importer of machines and equipment.[40]

The final step of the comparative analysis is to estimate the deviations of the trade patterns of individual SOC from the normal SOC pattern, as established by equations [2] and [3] (see table 5 for trade residuals). In all cases where the coefficients of $SlnY$ were significantly different from zero, the residuals are based on equation [3b]. When this was not the case, the residuals are estimated from equation [2b]. The net-trade proportions and residuals are computed from the best version of the E and I equations (with or without $SlnY$).[41] The residuals for individual SOC are based on regressions in which the same individual SOC participate as observations. This underestimates somewhat the magnitudes of the "pure" residuals on regressions in which the investigated country does not participate.

The findings concentrate mainly on the peculiarities of the trade structure of Bulgaria, which here show up even more clearly than when compared to the normal pattern (compare column 5 in tables 4 and 5):

1. Bulgaria is clearly a consistent exporter and net exporter of A-goods in proportions much higher than other SOC. This is true even in 1950 when, as a group, all SOC exported larger than normal proportions of A-goods. Only then did any other SOC come close to it: Romania as only a deviant *net* exporter (ΔFA) of A-goods, and this because it reduced A-imports more drastically than did Bulgaria. In 1960, Bulgaria is the only country with positive EA and FA residuals.

TABLE 5
Deviations of Trade Structure of Socialist Countries from Normal Socialist Trade Pattern, 1950-70

		Equat. used (0)	Czecho-slovakia (1)	East Germany* (2)	Hungary (3)	Poland (4)	Bulgaria (5)	Romania (6)	Yugo-slavia† (7)	SD (8)
(1)	1950	ΔEA	3b	6.7	−12.9	−1.7	5.3	5.6	−3.1	−9.1	15.8
(2)		ΔIA	3b	9.9	−12.7	9.4	−12.7	6.9	−0.8	16.3	8.7
(3)		ΔFA		−2.5	1.6	−10.9	17.7	−2.0	−1.9	−20.6	:
(4)		ΔEM	3b	−4.1	8.8	8.1	−10.1	0.1	−2.9	−1.7	7.0
(5)		ΔIM	3b	0.6	−9.3	−5.6	14.9	−4.8	4.1	−3.9	6.4
(6)		ΔFM		−5.2	16.7	12.8	−24.5	4.9	−6.6	3.1	:
(7)		ΔFOM		7.7	−18.3	−1.9	6.8	−2.9	8.5	17.5	:
(1)	1960	ΔEA	2b	−8.9	−13.0	−4.7	−2.9	10.8	−1.6	2.2	12.4
(2)		ΔIA	3b	3.6	5.5	4.5	4.8	−1.1	−3.1	5.8	5.2
(3)		ΔFA		−13.0	−18.6	−8.8	−7.4	10.9	1.3	−4.4	:
(4)		ΔEM	3b	1.2	6.6	12.5	−1.1	−0.0	−2.3	1.5	6.9
(5)		ΔIM	2b	−5.6	−13.6	−3.0	−0.7	5.7	−0.3	−0.5	8.4
(6)		ΔFM		6.9	20.3	14.5	−0.3	−5.7	−2.3	1.4	:
(7)		ΔFOM		6.1	−1.7	−5.7	7.7	−5.2	1.0	3.0	:
(1)	1970	ΔEA	2b	−6.7	−5.5	5.7	2.0	17.7	7.2	8.6	12.4
(2)		ΔIA	3b	−3.2	0.3	2.6	−5.3	−2.7	−7.4	−7.9	5.2
(3)		ΔFA		−3.7	−5.5	2.8	7.3	22.0	14.2	12.9	:
(4)		ΔEM	3b	−2.4	1.5	−3.8	−0.5	−1.0	−10.8	−14.7	6.9
(5)		ΔIM	2b	−0.8	1.8	−3.2	6.8	4.8	8.2	2.0	8.4
(6)		ΔFM		−1.7	−0.4	−0.4	−7.3	−5.9	−18.4	−10.5	:
(7)		ΔFOM		5.4	5.9	−2.4	0.0	−16.1	4.2	−2.4	:

NOTE: The definitions are as in table 2 (see note), and the deviations are estimated in the same manner as in table 4, only here the E_i and I_i deviations are estimated from the *best equations* in each case (column 0). The equations are presented in table 3. SD (column 8) are standard deviations of estimates of the relevant equations.

*See note (*), table 2. †See note (†), table 4.

2. Bulgaria is much more in line with the rest of SOC in respect to the trade proportions of M. In all years they are about normal; the sign of the deviation depends on whether one looks at table 4 or 5. Only in 1970 does an important difference appear between Bulgaria on the one hand and Romania and Yugoslavia on the other: while Bulgaria manages to keep its machinery exports at normal socialist levels, Romania and Yugoslavia fall behind and develop relatively large negative exports and net export deviations. In the case of Romania, higher than normal M-import residuals (even above the high SOC levels) also contribute to the M net export negative deviation. The growing difference between Bulgaria and Romania is a result of Romania adopting a separatist policy since the late 1950s, reducing its relative level of trade with CMEA and turning more and more to the West.

3. Being a deviant net exporter of A-goods, Bulgaria is, of course, also a deviant net importer of all industrial goods; since its M-trade is lately "normal" by SOC standards (it was in deficit in 1960), all the abnormal deficit in industrial goods trade is concentrated in non-machinery goods. An examination of the breakdown of its trade in industrial goods, other than machinery, seems to indicate that the entire deficit concentrates in materials and raw materials and none of it in light industry.[42] The trade deficit in light industry, if it exists, is compensated by a surplus in the food industry and does not raise any serious problem. However, the trade deficit in raw materials has recently become more serious and may endanger Bulgaria's economic position, especially when compared with other less-developed SOC with higher exports and smaller deficits in this category, as do Romania, Poland, and Yugoslavia (a net exporter of materials). This tendency (specific to Bulgaria and abnormal even by socialist standards) to concentrate on M within heavy industry results from a poor natural endowment which raises the cost that must be paid for the development of the country's raw-material industries to exorbitant levels. But it may have resulted also from the nature of CMEA's trade, which ties together soft and hard goods in package deals. It may have encouraged Bulgaria to use the development of hard-goods producing sectors, like agriculture and processing industry, not only to help finance imports of machinery for industrialization purposes, but also as a bait to promote sales of locally manufactured machinery. This is, in any case, the only way to realize the advantages of A-exports in trade with CMEA countries, i.e., to compensate for the low prices received for them by the relatively high prices received for machinery.

Bulgaria's exceptional trade structure is probably best underlined by the fact that it is responsible to a large extent for the significant interaction between GNP per capita and the specific trade pattern of SOC. When the Bulgarian observation is excluded, the *SlnY* coefficients drop both in their magnitudes and their levels of significance.

A few comments should be made on the principle of comparative advantage in the analysis and phenomena described above. No explicit variables, in addition to income and size, were to take care of differences between countries in natural endowment and environment. This omission results largely from difficulties in defining such variables that will be independent from the phenomena they have to explain and that will represent real natural conditions rather than induced and developed ones. Furthermore, most East European countries had been known historically (prior to World War II) as having a comparative advantage in agriculture, as the granary of (Western) Europe.[43] So if a specific "natural advantage" variable had been included in the equations, we would have probably found that the trade pattern of SOC is even further removed from the "normal" pattern than was here estimated. SOC had chosen a growth strategy which they believed to be superior and which deliberately sacrificed the natural advantage in agriculture.

The main point in this paper is that there is a case for a country among SOC to specialize in A-goods. Clearly, we would both advocate and expect that this would be the country with the strongest natural advantage in agriculture; thus, we are not surprised to find that it happens to be Bulgaria. The main argument is not to re-establish that well-known fact, but that Bulgaria had decided to exploit it, and by so doing, it deviated to some extent from the typical East European socialist growth pattern.

The Deviant Pattern of Bulgaria's Agricultural Policies and Its Economic Performance

According to information on the comparative performance of agriculture in East European SOC during 1950-70, Bulgaria has the best record. This is true with respect to indexes of total output, output per unit of land or per worker (or both), and the share of investment devoted to agriculture and modernization measures. However, in the late 1960s, this relatively good performance was upset: while most other SOC finally directed greater efforts to improve their agriculture, a relative retreat took place in Bulgaria. Recent records, however, seem to point to a renewal of past trends.

During 1950-72, Bulgaria's agricultural output and gross and net product grew at the highest rates in Eastern Europe. Output, for example, grew at 4.1% per annum compared with 3.8% in Yugoslavia,

3.4% in Romania, and less than 3% in all other countries.[44] The difference in performance, while not dramatic, is still significant. (Over a period of 22 years, the difference between 4 and 3.5% annual growth rate accumulates to a total growth difference of about 20%.) This record is even more impressive if the last five years are dropped, or if the base year is moved back to World War II normal levels. The comparatively best relative record was shown by Bulgaria between 1955 and 1965, when its A-output grew at rates of 7.3 (1955-60) and 5.2% (1960-65), with only Yugoslavia coming close in the first period. These findings hold also with respect to each of the two main subdivisions of agriculture: crops and animal products.[45] The early 1960s is particularly crucial because it coincides with the important intra-CMEA debates on cooperation.

A small relative increase in agricultural land vis-à-vis other SOC explains some of Bulgaria's record;[46] most of it, however, is explained by the fastest rates of growth in the bloc in product (output and gross or net product) per unit of land,[47] with the exception of Yugoslavia. This is also true for crops and animal products. The highest growth rates are also found in yields of grains, wheat, potatoes, sugarbeets, milk (per cow), and many other products.[48] Similar results were obtained for the period from the early 1960s to the early 1970s.[49] Lesser achievements were obtained for meat and egg yields. Bulgaria's better achievements in terms of output per unit of land and yields can be explained in some cases by relatively low initial levels; but already in the early 1950s its output per unit of land was quite close to the average in the region (it surpassed it by 1970), and its crop output much above that average. In all these cases, as well as in animal output per unit of land—in which the initial relative level was indeed low—Bulgaria's initial levels were still much higher than those of the other less-developed SOC.[50]

When we examine inputs in agriculture, Bulgaria moved intensively at the highest rates of change in East Europe: it had the fastest decline of labor force employed in agriculture and, in most cases, the highest rates of growth of external inputs and investment. During 1950-72, agricultural labor declined in Bulgaria at 3% per year. Similar rates of decline occurred only in the more developed SOC, while those in Poland (-0.1), Romania, and Yugoslavia (-1.8) were much lower.[51] This exodus of unemployed or underemployed labor was compensated by the highest rates of growth of external inputs, its agriculture, almost the highest when calculated, per unit of land or per worker; Bulgaria had the highest proportion of total investment devoted to agriculture during the entire period.[52] This makes the share of total productive capital devoted to agriculture the highest in the region (except for that of Poland);[53] the growth rate of depreciation during 1950-72 was also the highest in the region. Bulgaria's advances in the use of tractors and fertilizers are also very impressive, probably the highest in the region from 1950 (or prewar) to 1970. Only during the last years have other countries advanced faster in these areas.[54] In any case, Bulgaria is using tractors and fertilizers at higher levels per unit of land than do Romania and Yugoslavia and, in the case of tractors, Poland.

This appears to suggest a different economic policy toward agriculture in Bulgaria than the labor-intensive, capital-saving technology employed in all other SOC and especially in those less-developed; communist Bulgaria had apparently decided to change the input relations in its agriculture and to modernize it—at least relative to other SOC.

The results in terms of labor productivity in agriculture are clear: as land and commercial inputs and investment per worker were all growing at the fastest rates in the region, so did output per worker. During 1950-72, it increased at an annual rate of 7.2%, with Hungary in second place with 5.8%. During 1960-70, Bulgaria's rate reached 8.6%, which was more than 3 percentage points above any other country. Similar figures are obtained for gross and net product.[55] The superior Bulgarian performance is even more pronounced according to the UN study that covers 1950-67. It estimates that the Bulgarian growth rates of labor productivity were, for net output, more than twice as high as in any other East European country.[56] While agricultural labor productivity in Romania and Yugoslavia stayed during 1950-55 to 1971-72 at about one-half and two-thirds, respectively, of the region's average level and Poland's dropped from one and a half times the region's average down to the average, labor productivity in Bulgaria moved from about 70% of the region's average to above the level.[57]

Bulgaria's product share originating in agriculture is higher than its share of labor engaged in agriculture. Series in both constant and current prices show that the share of agriculture (including forestry) in any total product measure of the national economy (GNP, NMP, and the like) is the largest in East Europe.[58] In terms of agricultural employment, it moved from first place in 1950 to either third or fourth place, depending on the source of the data.[59] This is another manifestation of the relatively ''modern'' structure of Bulgarian agriculture, especially as compared to the agricultural sectors of Romania, Yugoslavia, and Poland.

The final productivity test is output per unit of combined inputs and figures that are difficult to estimate. Using Alton's separate estimates for changes in labor and capital productivity for 1960-72 and subperiods thereof, assuming that land does not contribute to *changes* in productivity and weighing capital and labor 30% and 70% respectively, we obtain the following figures for annual growth rates of total product per unit of combined inputs during 1960-72 and 1960-65:[60]

	1960-72	*1960-65*		*1960-72*	*1960-65*
Bulgaria	2.5	4.8	Hungary	2.3	5.1
Czechoslovakia	1.9	-3.4	Poland	0.3	0.5
East Germany	2.2	0.9	Romania	1.7	0.3

Bulgaria ranks first in the 1960-72 and second in the 1960-65 period. Our guess is that for 1950-72 the *relative* record of Bulgaria would have been even better.

A country's potential export capability of A-products may be measured roughly by the levels of per capita production. The translation of potential into actual exports depends on the efficiency of the procurement system, the degree of control on and allowed level of domestic consumption, and the level of development of processing industries that enhance the value-added of A-exports. With full collectivization and high levels of concentration and centralization of Bulgarian agriculture, its procurement system should be at least as efficient as other SOC.[61] Furthermore, there is no reason to assume that Bulgaria allows a more lavish consumption of A-products than do the other SOC.

During 1950-72, Bulgaria achieved the highest rates of growth of agricultural output per capita:[62] 3.3% per annum (2.8 in crops and 4.1 in animal products). Yugoslavia was second with 2.7 (2.4 and 3.0) and Romania third with 2.3 (1.9 and 2.9).

During 1950-55, Bulgaria's A-output per capita was a mere 2% above the region's average; during the prewar period, it was about 10% above average. By 1966-70, per capita output was more than 20% above average. At that time, only Hungary matched this level, while Romania and Yugoslavia stayed at below 90% of the average. Moreover, from 1950-55 to 1966-70, Romania and Yugoslavia improved their relative positions only very slightly, if at all.[63] Bulgaria's advantage in per capita output comes from its level of crop production: 134% of the average in 1950-55 and 159% in 1966-70 (152 in 1971-72) which, in both periods, was far above second-place Hungary. On the other hand, its initial relative level of animal products per capita was only 72%, slightly above Romania and Yugoslavia. In this field, too, Bulgaria moved up to 91% of the average, 10 to 20 points above Romania and Yugoslavia. With Bulgaria's relatively lower level of per capita income and meat consumption, by East European standards, this may be considered high enough to allow for net export of animal products, which is indeed the case.

If we assume that the Bulgarian people can be (or have been) brought to consume food and A-originated goods at average East European production per capita levels of crops and at 75% of that level for animal products (which is still above the 1970 levels of Romania and Yugoslavia), it may be able to export on a net basis about one-third of its crop products and one-sixth of its animal products. Bulgaria is situated more favorably than, say, Poland, which has serious procurement problems because its agriculture is not collectivized and because its average A-product per capita has declined over time.

On examination of Bulgaria's production and foreign-trade *trends*, it is clear that the growth rate of A-exports (and net exports) during 1950-70 by far outpaced the growth in agricultural production, that the growing potential surplus could cover only a small part of the increased net exports, and that the growth of the food processing industries and other light-industrial consumers of A-products had to contribute to increase the local value of these products.[64]

Bulgaria, of course, has had its fair share of problems connected with running agriculture under communism. These problems range from consequences of forced collectivization, unprofitable state farms, poor incentives, or shifting policies toward private plots, planning problems, and frequent organizational changes, labor shortage, and the like.[65] In effect, the apparent slowdown in the growth of agricultural output during the late 1960s seems to be connected with these problems, as well as with efforts to increase the production and the relative share of meat and dairy products and of feed crops.[66] Until the mid-1960s, growing fruit and vegetables—the main Bulgarian exports—and raising livestock were carried out in large proportions by private or (mainly) semi-private activities within and outside the cooperatives. By then, Bulgarian authorities seem to have been convinced that modernization of agriculture, so necessary to keep production of exports and local supplies, could only be achieved by a major centralization and "industrialization" of agricultural production. Hence, a move was made to create very large, specialized agricultural-industrial units (agro-industrial complexes or later industrial-agricultural complexes) to deal with large-scale specialized production, processing, and sales—often directly for exports. This form of large-scale agricultural organization is the most advanced in Eastern Europe.

While it is not clear whether Bulgaria has managed to overcome the problem of the transition period, it is quite clear that it remains Bulgaria's policy that the export of A-goods play a major role in industrialization and growth. Export needs are offered as a justification for the organizational changes mentioned above, allegedly a prerequisite for bringing Bulgarian agriculture to international standards in terms of quality, supply punctuality, and profitability.

Conclusions

Did Bulgaria have a different industrialization pattern than the other, less-developed SOC? Like all other SOC, Bulgaria put most of its effort into industrialization and succeeded, together with Romania, in achieving exceptionally high growth rates of industrial production.[67] Starting from the lowest level in the bloc, Bulgaria still has a somewhat smaller industrial sector than other SOC (when the share is measured in current prices)[68] and a very close share to that of other SOC, except Czechoslovakia and East Germany (when the shares are calculated on the basis of constant prices).[69] In contrast to agriculture, Bulgaria employs a higher share of its labor in industry than Romania and Poland, another indication of the more balanced allocation of capital and labor among the different branches of the economy.[70] More important, however, is the internal structure of industry, especially the reasonable balance between heavy industry (group A) and light, or consumer-goods industries (group B). Like other SOC, Bulgaria maintains a higher rate of growth in heavy than in light industry; but, starting from very unorthodox proportions in 1950, with about 40% of total industrial output and less than a third of all employees in manufacturing,[71] Bulgaria had to try harder to close the gap. Still, in 1970, Bulgaria's group A made up only 55% of industrial production—the lowest in the bloc by a considerable margin—compared with shares of 70% in Romania, 65% in Poland and Hungary, 62% in Czechoslovakia, and 70% in the Soviet Union and East Germany. The proportion is still going up—by 1974 it reached 58.3%—but it has a long way to go to reach the "typical" socialist proportion between 65 and 75%.[72] The same is true with respect to the proportion of the industrial labor force employed in heavy industry: Bulgaria is the only country in the bloc with less than 50%.[73] While having more ground to cover, Bulgaria seems to have taken it with a longer breath.

While it is not clear where or when Bulgaria will stop shifting toward more heavy industry, it is clear that this has been a long-range plan making use of Bulgaria's comparative advantage in agricultural goods. To accomplish this, under the unfavorable conditions of underdeveloped and collectivized agriculture, a somewhat different approach was needed.

Did this strategy pay off? Many factors contribute to a final outcome reflected in the growth rate of GNP or GNP per capita. But in terms of growth rates of consumption per capita, Bulgaria probably did better compared to other CMEA countries, a fact that may indicate a more efficient use of its investments.[74] Beyond the common explanation that less-developed countries tend to grow faster, it is not possible to give differential marks. It seems safe to assume, however, that within a socialist system Bulgaria did not do anything very wrong. An alternative strategy of concentrating more on heavy industry, especially in developing its own raw material base, at the expense of agriculture would have brought less favorable results, other things being equal.[75]

Discussion

Jan Vaňous

Professor Ofer's paper is an interesting exercise that raises an important question: "Did Bulgarian economic strategy differ from the standard socialist strategy by stressing the development of agriculture to a much greater degree than the rest of the socialist bloc?" Inevitably, two additional questions have to be discussed. First, did Bulgarian central planners foresee the development of shortages of agricultural goods within the CMEA and deliberately choose to diverge from the standard socialist industrialization strategy stressing manufacturing-import-substitution economic policy, expecting that the strategy of "swimming against the stream" would bring special benefits to Bulgaria? Second, did Bulgaria in fact benefit from its special policies with respect to agriculture?

Professor Ofer establishes that Bulgarian growth strategy was indeed different from other East European countries. He proves it by relying primarily on evidence from Bulgarian export and import structure, showing that Bulgaria has been a significant net exporter of agricultural goods in proportions much higher than other socialist countries. Although I do not doubt this conclusion, I have some doubts about the magnitude of the difference in agricultural export and import shares between Bulgaria and other East European countries. The essence of Professor Ofer's work is an empirical test of trade share deviations from the "normal trade structure" based on a particular equation specification:

$$[E_i, I_i, F_i] = a + b(lnY) + c(lnY)^2 + dlnN + u,$$

where E_i, I_i, and F_i are the proportions of defined commodity groups in total exports, imports, and net trade; Y is GNP per capita; N is population; and u is the residual term.

Although the above formulation has been suggested by two respected development economists, Chenery and Syrquin, I fail to understand the reasoning behind this equation when it comes to agricultural goods. This specification was bound to show very high positive deviation in the case of Bulgaria as far as the share of exports of agricultural products and their net exports are concerned, and very high negative deviation in its imports of agricultural products. A brief look at the pattern of deviations in agricultural trade shares in the seven East European countries studied reveals that these deviations are highly correlated with climatic and soil conditions. By excluding the area of arable land, climate, and soil quality from the equation, the pattern of deviations presented was bound to occur. Under the circumstances, it is no longer possible to say that these deviations are solely a result of a particular growth policy rather than, in part, a result of the specification of the equation for normal agricultural trade of a group of market (and socialist) economies.

In the Koopmans-Montias framework, which postulates outcome $= f$ (environment, system, policies), Professor Ofer has presented a model in which the set of environmental variables is incomplete, and the deviations from "normal behavior" (which in fact is no longer normal) are attributed to the impact of economic system, its policies, or both. This certainly weakens the empirical test of the proposition of special Bulgarian policies with respect to agriculture in the overall Bulgarian growth and industrialization strategy.

Granted the somewhat limited power of the above test to show the degree of deviation from "normal behavior" due to the impact of Bulgarian policies, Professor Ofer's model could still be of considerable value. Unfortunately, he makes the same mistake that Western researchers of East European trade have made for years: He computes commodity shares in total trade by dividing trade flow in a given commodity group by total trade as reported by East European countries. This procedure produces commodity shares of little economic meaning.

East European trade statistics are very different when compared to Western trade statistics. Due to different price levels (and different qualities of products) in different geographic and commodity markets, East Europeans report trade totals as sums of "apples and oranges pound for pound." In fact, they complicate matters even more because "some oranges have much thicker skins than others, and some apples are rotten." My own research indicates that in 1960 and 1970 the overall CMEA price level exceeded the world market price (wmp) level by about 33% and 23% respectively. After adjusting for the distortion in overall price levels, intra-CMEA prices of food in 1960 and 1970 were well below wmp's, by 20% and 26% respectively. With different commodity structures of trade and different allocation of exports and imports to different geographic markets, use of raw trade data with no adjustment for price distortions renders empirical results questionable. To illustrate the problem, I have recomputed the shares of food exports in total exports, adjusting for distortions in intra-CMEA prices, for six CMEA countries. These shares, based on valuation of all trade at wmp's, are presented in table 1.

TABLE 1
Share of Food Exports in Total Exports for
Six CMEA Countries, 1960-70
(in percentages)

Country	Year	Unadjusted Share of Food Exports in Total Exports	Adjusted Share of Food Exports in Total Exports	Ratio of Adjusted to Unadjusted Share
Bulgaria	1960	38.2	43.7	1.14
	1970	35.3	43.1	1.22
Czechoslovakia	1960	5.3	6.6	1.25
	1970	3.9	5.0	1.28
East Germany	1960	3.5	4.5	1.29
	1970	4.8	6.2	1.29
Hungary	1960	20.6	25.2	1.22
	1970	21.8	26.9	1.23
Poland	1960	18.1	21.1	1.17
	1970	13.1	16.0	1.22
Romania	1960	20.8	23.1	1.11
	1970	16.1	18.6	1.16

SOURCE: Author's calculation from Data Bank of Project CMEA-LINK, University of Pennsylvania.

The impact of the above adjustment on Professor Ofer's results is straightforward. Adjusted share of food exports in total exports is higher for all countries, and, consequently, the correctly estimated impact of socialist system (table 3, column 8 in Professor Ofer's paper) would be smaller. Adjusted share of machinery exports (and imports) in total exports (imports) will be smaller for all countries, thus weakening the impact of economic system on the share again. The direction of the adustment depends on whether the commodity in question is relatively overpriced (machinery and industrial consumer goods) or underpriced (raw materials and food) within the CMEA in comparison with the world market. The larger the unadjusted share of manufactures in total exports and imports, the larger the relative upward adjustment in the case of the share of underpriced goods, and the larger the downward adjustment in the case of the share of over-priced goods. In addition, the relative size of the adjustment also depends on the importance of CMEA trade in a country's trade: the greater the importance of CMEA, the greater the relative adjustment necessary.

In the case of food exports, Professor Ofer underestimated food export shares for Czechoslovakia and East Germany to a greater degree than for Bulgaria, thus artificially strengthening the desired conclusion. Coupled with problems involved in the specification of his equation for "normal" agricultural trade structure, which exhibits bias in the same direction, i.e., against CMEA countries north of Bulgaria, the doubts about the *degree* to which Bulgarian agricultural policies were indeed a strategy of "swimming against the stream" are increased.

Concerning the second question raised at the beginning of this comment, Professor Ofer seems to agree that Bulgaria's agricultural policy was indeed deliberate and was initiated by Bulgarian planners on their own initiative. I do not agree with this conclusion, especially in view of the results obtained in my model of intra-CMEA foreign trade.

There are three less-developed CMEA countries that could have chosen the agricultural oriented growth strategy: Bulgaria, Poland, and Romania. There is also one medium-developed country: Hungary. In the late 1950s and early 1960s, when intra-CMEA foreign-trade prices began to diverge increasingly from wmp's, there was increased pressure for bilateral balancing of trade in soft goods (machinery and industrial consumer goods) and hard goods (raw materials and food). Poland and Romania, with substantial raw material resources of their own, were able to increase their raw material supplies to CMEA to cover to some degree (Poland) or almost completely (Romania) increases in imports. Bulgaria and Hungary, both without a significant raw material base of their own, were not able to do so.

The persistent agricultural problems in Poland ruled out a possibility of exacting increased food supplies from Poland to other CMEA countries in order to cover a greater portion of its raw material deficits, but pressure was applied on the three remaining countries to cover their deficits by surpluses in food deliveries. Romania, upset by this pressure that perpetuated its status of a less-developed CMEA economy, reacted angrily in 1965. It began to reduce the share of CMEA in its trade and orient itself increasingly on trade with MDCs and LDCs. Bulgaria and Hungary—both less economically and politically independent of the USSR, the key supplier of raw materials to CMEA countries—had no choice but to agree to cover some portion of increases in raw material imports by increases in exports of agricultural goods, especially food. This conclusion is supported by my estimates of elasticities of food supply to CMEA countries with respect to imports of raw materials from CMEA (lagged by one year), which are 0.93 for Bulgaria and 1.11 for Hungary. The corresponding elasticity for Romania is only 0.23 and zero for Poland. This means that, for Bulgaria and Hungary, an increase in imports of raw materials last year has to be covered by about 0.9-1.1% increase in food exports during the current year. We can then hardly speak of Bulgarian initiative as far as its special policy with respect to the development of the agricultural sector is concerned: rather, we should speak of CMEA or USSR "economic dictate."

There is some evidence that Bulgaria was not particularly pleased about the imposed trend. In 1966, an attempt was made to change the development strategy and follow the Romanian pattern. In that year, one year after the beginning of Romanian "revolt against the CMEA," Bulgaria sharply increased its trade with the West, reducing the relative importance of CMEA countries. However, within a year, Bulgaria was "brought in line" by outside pressure and returned to the previous pattern of trade.

As far as the final question is concerned, i.e., whether Bulgaria benefited from its special policies with respect to agriculture, Professor Ofer concludes that the answer is not certain; but it seems safe to assume that, within the socialist bloc, Bulgaria at least did not do something wrong. I agree, and in fact it does not surprise me that one does not see any extraordinary gains as could be expected from the theoretical case made for specialization in agricultural goods. It is true that economic theory would lead us to predict that, within a semi-autarkic group of countries following manufacturing-import-substitution strategies, the presence of a country willing to diverge from this strategy and specialize in the production of goods of agricultural origin might bring special benefits to the country in question. In order for this to occur, there must be a free-market scarcity pricing of goods traded within the bloc; and this condition certainly has not been satisfied within the CMEA. If, however, the recent tendency toward a more rational system of foreign-trade prices within the CMEA continues, and intra-CMEA prices of food gradually approach wmp's, Bulgaria may yet benefit from the special growth strategy chosen.

These remarks by no means negate Professor Ofer's work. Rather, they stress the necessity of improvement of econometric specifications of his model as well as improvement in the quality of the data used in his study. Only then will it be possible to estimate correctly the impact of an economic system or its policies on the development strategy with respect to agriculture. Whether the special Bulgarian growth strategy, stressing the development of agriculture, was a result of preferences of Bulgarian planners or more or less imposed from outside is still subject to further discussion. The evidence cited in support of the latter hypothesis is preliminary, and further work is required in order to consider it sufficiently conclusive.

Discussion
Mark Allen

Bulgaria's relative emphasis on agriculture in its growth strategy is well known to those familiar with internal developments in that country in the 1950s and 1960s. Ofer confirms this observation by a completely different technique: a comparative econometric analysis of the trade structures of the socialist countries. This comment will summarize the changes in the Bulgarian growth strategy during the period 1950-70. The start of a conscious emphasis on agriculture can be dated to 1956-58.

Montias has described the main elements of Bulgaria's development strategy in the 1950s.[1] In outline, this was to expand exports of raw materials in order to provide funds to import the machinery necessary for industrialization. In the early 1950s, Bulgaria concentrated on expanding the production of its extractive industries, particularly lead and zinc mining. By 1955, 20.7% of Bulgarian exports consisted of fuels, ores, and metals (mainly ores) compared to only 9.2% in 1950.[2] The second part of the development strategy consisted of establishing industries to process domestically extracted raw materials, a policy of "valorification." Thus, the next step was to establish refineries for lead and zinc ore and to export the metals in refined form. Following this, processes were established to incorporate the metals in products which in turn were exported, such as, in Bulgaria's case, batteries. However, such a policy of valorification meant that potential hard goods exports were being converted into soft goods exports whose sales were more difficult to expand. The exportable surplus of fuels, ores, and metals thus fell rapidly to 8.4% of exports in 1960.

Had this policy continued, Bulgaria, as a small, rapidly industrializing country, would have suffered a balance-of-payments constraint on its growth. The shift in emphasis to agricultural production and exports in the second half of the 1950s allowed both the flow of necessary machinery imports to continue through the 1960s and, as is argued below, promoted industrialization.

The event that signaled the change in agricultural policy is subject to some dispute. Bulgarian sources attribute the change in policy to the decisions of the April 1956 Plenum of the Central Committee of the Bulgarian Communist Party which followed closely upon the 20th Congress of the CPSU. However, it seems probable that the Bulgarian Great Leap Forward, which started in late 1958, also had a significant impact. Since this period was perhaps the most fascinating in Bulgaria's postwar development, it merits a digression.

In October 1958, a movement was announced to fulfill the third five-year plan (1958-62) in three to four years. The same month, Chervenkov, then deputy prime minister, led a delegation to China, which was then in the middle of its Great Leap Forward. On his return to Bulgaria, enthusiastic articles on China's experiment appeared in the press, and the merger of Bulgaria's collective farms into larger units was announced. The name "Great Leap Forward" was adopted, party and government leaders pledged themselves to do 30 to 40 days' manual labor a year, and in December it was announced that Botevgrad County had been turned into a giant commune. Agricultural production in 1959 was going to double the 1958 level and triple it in 1960. Less than two months after the campaign started, the Chinese elements began to be played down. It was denied that communes had been established, and the name "Great Leap Forward" was replaced by that of "Movement for the Accelerated Development of the National Economy."

While the Great Leap Forward failed to achieve the overambitious targets set, it represented a turning point in Bulgarian policy. Among its achievements were to bring about a sharp increase in agricultural production and to wipe out unemployment and hidden unemployment. The mass mobilization campaigns served, as in China, to organize these labor resources both to carry out capital construction projects in agriculture and to increase the volume of fieldwork, the additional labor having a small but still positive marginal return. The effect of the Great Leap Forward on investment in agriculture was extraordinary. In 1952, such investment constituted only 13.7% of all investment but, as in all socialist countries, this share rose in the next few years and reached 21.6% in 1956. In 1959, the share had risen 29.8% of all investment, or 90% of the level of investment in industry. By 1960, the share fell back slightly to 27.9%, still at a level virtually unprecedented in a socialist economy.

The end of the Great Leap Forward (although under a different name) in 1960 led to various changes in Bulgarian agricultural policy. Since the movement had eliminated hidden unemployment in agriculture, from that point any further increase in agricultural production had to come from intensive rather than extensive techniques. The high absolute level of investment in agriculture was maintained in the early 1960s and increased further from 1965. At the same time, there was a change in the attitude toward agricultural management. From 1960, agriculture ceased to be treated as an ideological subject in Bulgaria and became viewed as a technical matter. The leadership appears to have had a high regard for agricultural expertise and let the people who knew about farming get on with it without undue interference from the party hierarchy.

The increased emphasis on agriculture in the Bulgarian development strategy also had a favorable impact on industrial development. This paradox resembles one of Mao's "Ten Great Relationships": If you really want to increase the growth rate of industry, you must increase your investment in agriculture. There are two reasons why this emphasis on agriculture was probably higher than in industry: not only could the savings rate be increased, but the country found itself with a smaller volume of inefficient industries than it would otherwise have had. Second, it allowed an exploitation of the gains from foreign trade.

Bulgaria's foreign trade has concentrated on its CMEA partners. It has been characterized by a net surplus of hard goods exports and an enthusiastic adoption of CMEA specialization decisions. The persistence of the surplus of hard-goods exports was only made possible by the emphasis on agricultural production. The prices of hard goods in CMEA trade are below those dictated by supply and demand but, as Ofer points out, substitute forms of remuneration have emerged for hard-goods exports. In Bulgaria's case, it has in practice been able to tie hard-goods exports to sales of soft goods—in other words, the products of its industry. Thus, agricultural exports have implicitly subsidized industrial exports. Bulgaria's industrial exports have been helped both by this cross-subsidization and by CMEA industrial specialization agreements. Thanks, in part, to the captive markets created by such agreements, Bulgaria has never had difficulty in selling industrial goods within Eastern Europe. It is, therefore, wrong to see the system of CMEA specialization as one that necessarily hinders Balkan countries from industrializing.

Finally, one cannot regard agricultural trade as being the sole determinant of Bulgaria's successful growth. Bulgaria, for a variety of reasons, has received very favorable treatment from the USSR, receiving considerable credits from this source during the 1960s. However, it is worth emphasizing that the relative shift of emphasis to agriculture which occurred at the end of the 1950s led neither to lower overall growth rates nor to lower industrial growth rates, and probably allowed development to be pursued at a lower domestic resource cost than had agriculture been neglected.

John Michael Montias

Romania's Foreign Trade Between East and West

Nearly 20 years have elapsed since the rulers of Romania began to reorient its foreign trade toward the West. The political aspects of this move have been much studied, particularly in terms of Romania's periodically strained relations with the Soviet Union and with the latter's close allies in CMEA.[1] In this paper, I take a strictly behavioristic view of the direction of Romania's trade. I will not dwell on the public pronouncements, views, and opinions of Romanian officials but will try to make the statistics of trade and development *reveal* the basic policies of the government with respect to the direction of Romanian trade as well as the obstacles that stood in the way of these policies. I will try to show that the larger part of the fluctuations in the share of East and West in Romania's imports in the 1960s and early 1970s can be accounted for by economic factors—chiefly by the Romanians' willingness to seek credits in the West and by the availability of such credits, as well as by the country's capacity to earn convertible currencies (CC) through exports of raw materials and foodstuffs.

Not all data necessary for a thorough analysis of the economic aspects of Romania's policy shift are yet available. But enough have come to light in the last few years, particularly with regard to the commodity structure of trade with East and West, to launch a more systematic study than was possible a decade ago.[2] One aim of this paper is to update my earlier study and to present the fairly extensive new data that have been uncovered recently. Another is to test

I wish to acknowledge my debt to Jan Vanous for the use of his data on Romania and for his assistance on the econometric part of this paper. Vanous and I had many discussions on CMEA trade in general and Romanian trade in particular which influenced me in writing this paper. David Colesworthy kindly assisted me with the computational work.

hypotheses aimed at explaining the fluctuating share of the West in Romania's total imports of machinery in the period 1960-75. (Machinery accounts for the bulk of imports of manufactures from "advanced capitalist countries.") Before doing this, however, I will sketch the main lines of Romania's economic development in the 1960s and early 1970s along with the role played by foreign trade in this country's continuous progress toward industrialization.

Industrialization and Foreign Trade

According to official statistics, Romania's net material product (NMP) grew at an average rate of 9% per year both from 1960 to 1965 and from 1965 to 1973.[3] An index of GNP reconstructed by Thad Alton and his associates from sectoral data shows a growth rate of 5% per year in the first period and 6% in the second.[4] The sizable difference between the two measures is due in part to Alton's inclusion of slow-growing services excluded from official NMP and the greater weight given to the farm sector, which expanded at a very sluggish pace during this period. (The net output of agriculture was virtually constant from 1960 to 1970, then shot up by 9.8% per year from 1970 to 1973.) From 1960 to 1972, industry grew at 12.6% per year according to the official index of gross output and at 10% per year according to the reconstructed Alton index of value added in industry, with only a slight retardation between the first five and the last seven or eight years of the period.[5] According to official estimates, gross industrial output continued its rapid progress from 1973 to 1975 at rates slightly in excess of those recorded in the early 1970s (13.8% from 1973 to 1975 as against 11.8% from 1970 to 1972). The independent Alton measure of GNP, which is more sensitive to fluctuations in farm output than the official NMP, grew at a rate of 5.6% from 1973 to 1975, a shade below the performance of 1965-73. The growth rate of value added in industry was about the same, according to this measure, as in the preceding period.[6]

Foreign-trade turnover (imports plus exports) valued in current devisa prices kept pace with industrial output, rising by 11% per year from 1960 to 1972. No indexes of prices in Romanian trade have been released for this entire period. According to a unit-value index prepared by the Romanian Ministry of Foreign Trade, export prices rose and import prices dropped by about 3% from 1960 to 1966.[7] Hungarian export prices were more or less constant, and import prices rose by perhaps 1% per year from 1966 to 1972. The evolution of Romanian prices was probably much the same. For the entire period 1960 to 1972, therefore, it is unlikely that the growth of the current-value index of foreign trade significantly overstates the real momentum of the sector. From 1972 to 1975, however, prices rose rapidly in the world market and, from 1975 on, in the CMEA market as well. The increases in the current value of foreign trade were officially estimated at 38.9% in 1973, 38.3% in 1974, and 6.6% in 1975. When deflated by an index based on Hungarian indices for four commodity groups in trade with the dollar and ruble areas, aggregated according to the approximate shares of these groups and areas in Romanian imports and exports, these large percentage increases are reduced to 14% in 1973 (exports 17%, imports 10%), 12% in 1974 (exports 8%, imports 19%), and a bare 1% in 1975 (resulting from a 3% increase in exports and a 1.5% decline in imports). However approximative the price indexes on which these deflated figures are based, it is manifest that the growth rate of trade slackened appreciably in the period 1973-75 (from an average of 11.2% for total trade turnover from 1960 to 1972 in current prices, which remained fairly stable in the period, to 6.7% for the years 1972-1975). Imports in this more recent period probably did not keep up with industrial production.

In general, however, the forward momentum developed by the Romanian economy in the first half of the 1960s was maintained into the 1970s. As in the past, the economy was propelled by the rapid expansion of industry and construction which pulled the remaining sectors, with the exception of agriculture, in its wake. Only in the period 1971-74 did the large investments allotted to the farm sector in the 1960s begin to pay off.[8]

Growth, again as in the past, was pressed forward by high rates of capital accumulation officially estimated, in relation to NMP, at 25.5% in 1961-65, 29.5% in 1966-70, and 34.1% in 1971-75.[9] The fixed assets in industry rose by 12.7% and employment by 5% per year from 1966 to 1973. With any reasonable weights used to combine capital and labor, we find that total factor productivity increased by 4.5 to 5.5% per year if we use the official data on NMP arising in industry and by 2 to 2.5% if we use Alton's estimates. In either case, the growth of productivity was on a high level and showed but a slight retardation, compared to the performance of the early 1960s.[10] Real wages of employees in state enterprises and (nonagricultural) cooperatives, according to the official index (which is subject to some upward bias due to the use of an index of retail prices as a deflator that may underestimate the full extent of price increases in the retail market), rose by 3.6% per year in the period 1970 to 1975. This was on a par with the previous five years but below the record growth of 4.1% per year achieved in the period 1960-65.[11] The real incomes of collective farmers (from their work on the collective and on private plots) inched up by 1% per year in the period 1965 to 1975 according to recently released official estimates. The difference between the two periods reflects the significant improvement in farm performance of the early 1970s. It should also be kept in mind that the absolute population engaged in agriculture has been declining (at the rate of nearly 5% per year from 1970 to 1975, or nearly twice the rate of the 1960s), so that large numbers of ex-farmers are now acceding to the higher levels of living enjoyed by urban dwellers.

Dramatic changes have taken place in the commodity structure of Romania's foreign trade in the course of industrialization.[12] Until the early 1960s, Romania was a net exporter of raw materials and foodstuffs and a net importer of manufactures. By 1973, it was exporting a slightly larger volume of manufactures, including chemicals, than it was importing; but, like all East European members of CMEA, it was running a very large deficit in industrial raw materials. This deficit was mainly paid for with exports of processed and unprocessed agricultural products. It is instructive to examine this transformation in greater detail on the basis of the breakdown of trade into nine commodity groups according to the official CMEA nomenclature.

From 1960 to 1973, total imports and exports expanded at an average rate slightly in excess of 10% per year. Imports of fuels, mineral raw materials, and metals (group 2 of the CMEA nomenclature) during this same period increased (fairly regularly) at an average rate of 8.9%,[13] while exports rose (less regularly) at nearly half this rate (4.7% per year). Exports of petroleum products, which amounted to two-thirds of the value of these raw-material and semifabricated exports in 1960, had fallen to a third by 1972. They stagnated at or fell below 1960 levels until the price windfall of 1973.[14] In sum, the net deficit in the raw materials and metals group increased at a rate of over 4% per year from 1960 to 1973. Much the same evolution may be observed in the case of trade in raw materials used in light industry—group 5, including cotton, wool, leather hides, and sundry agricultural raw materials other than foodstuffs. The 1960 surplus was converted into a growing deficit, which rose at nearly 4% per year in the period 1960 to 1973. It is noteworthy that imports of raw materials for light industry increased at an average of 9.1% per year from 1960 to 1973, a rate only slightly inferior to the officially recorded rate of growth of light industry (group B) in the period.[15]

Exports of raw materials for the production of foodstuffs (group 7) increased irregularly, owing to fluctuation in harvest yields and in the size of animal herds. Over the entire period 1960 to 1973, they grew at an average rate of 5.5%, hitting a first peak in 1967 which was only surpassed in 1973.[16] Exports of processed foodstuffs (group 8) rose both more rapidly (11.5% per year) and much more steadily[17] than exports of raw materials for the production of foodstuffs. Even the high average rate of increase for this group was exceeded by the growth rate for exports of chemicals (19.5% per year), manufactured consumer goods (20.7% per year), and machinery and equipment (14.0%). Imports of manufactured goods expanded more slowly than exports, averaging about 9% per year for chemicals and consumer goods and 11% for both machinery and processed foodstuffs.

Since 1972-73, the net supply of hard goods (raw materials, semifabricates, and foodstuffs) turned from a trade surplus of about one billion lei ($166 million) to deficits of 538 million lei in 1974 and 1.5 billion lei in 1975 (roughly 340 and 980 million lei respectively at 1971 prices).[18] In this period, exports of raw materials for the foodstuff industry stagnated, fluctuating around 1 billion lei at 1971 prices; but processed foodstuffs, including meat and meat products, rose from less than 1 billion lei in 1972 to 2 billion in 1973 and 2.9 billion in 1974 (all at estimated 1971 prices). They then receded to 2.1 billion lei in 1975, a poor year for agriculture due to extensive floods. If it had not been for much higher exports of processed foodstuffs in these last years, the deficit in hard goods caused by steadily rising imports and declining exports of raw materials for heavy industry would have been much worse.

Over the last 15 years, the trends in trade and domestic production can be summarized very simply. By and large, domestic consumption expanded faster than domestic output for the products of the less rapidly growing sectors, including mining and agriculture; it expanded more slowly than output for the more rapidly growing sectors, including machine-building, chemicals, and manufactured consumer goods. The disparity between the two rates was much greater for consumer goods than for machines and chemicals in heavy demand in a period of overall rapid expansion. Manufactured foodstuffs represented an exception: their exports expanded at a rapid pace despite the under-average growth of their domestic output (6.4% per year from 1960 to 1974 according to the official index).

This exception notwithstanding, the generalization may be upheld that foreign trade has tended to reduce substantially the disparities in the growth of consumption in different sectors that would have occurred if domestic output had been the only source of supply. Insofar as these outcomes resulted from planning decisions, the strategy revealed by these observations consisted in importing enough raw materials and semifabricates as a supplement to domestic inputs to satisfy the needs of a very rapidly growing manufacturing industry, and in using exports of manufactured products to pay for as large a proportion of the import bill as possible. In the sphere of consumer goods, trade was used to smooth out exogenous fluctuations in supplies (particularly in foodstuffs) and, by keeping the rate of increase in household consumption lower than it would have been in the absence of trade, to generate resources for growth. The rapid growth of exports of foodstuffs in the face of sluggish progress in farm output was, of course, rendered possible by the steep investment rates that depressed the domestic consumption of foodstuffs and made them available for export.[19]

The Geographic Orientation of Romania's Trade

To implement the strategy of trade outlined above, a country must find partners willing to run accommodating surpluses or deficits in the appropriate commodity groups. For Romania, the choice of partners—and the possibilities of carrying out its strategy—was influenced by the following considerations:

1. The Romanians wanted to import equipment of the highest quality and of the most modern types, principally available in Western industrialized economies.

2. Their manufactures were not of sufficient quality to pay for more than a fraction of their imports from advanced Western countries.

3. They were less discriminating in their specifications concerning imported consumer goods and were, therefore, willing to import goods of mediocre quality from CMEA and their socialist partners.

4. Their possibilities of trading manufactured exports for raw-material imports with CMEA members other than the USSR were severely restricted by the efforts of their partners to accomplish the same ends.

5. Short- and medium-term commercial and private bank credits, long-term official credits (including IMF), and earnings from tourism facilitated Romanian imports from industrialized market economies (ME) and made it possible for Romania to run deficits in merchandise trade with these partners.

The data in table 1 show the geographic distribution of Romania's trade that took place after 1960. The most dramatic and politically significant change has been the rise in the share of "developed capitalist countries" (market developed countries or MDCs) in Romania's imports of machinery. In 1960, this share amounted to 25.7%, already up from 9.5% in 1958; in the period 1966 to 1973, it averaged 47.3%. If we consider that, in the early 1960s, machinery prices on the CMEA market were about 35% higher than in the world market and, judging by price trends in CMEA and world prices since that time, retained that edge throughout the period under consideration, the share of MDCs in total machinery imports valuated at comparable prices for East and West came to nearly a third in 1960 and averaged around a half in the period 1966-73.[20] This share fluctuated in the 1960s and 1970s for reasons explored below. For the time be-

TABLE 1
Romania's Exports to and Imports from Major Areas by Commodity Division (CTN) in 1960, 1966, 1971, and 1973
(millions of current devisa lei)

	Exports				Imports			
	1960	1966	1971	1973	1960	1966	1971	1973
Division I — Machinery to:								
CMEA	456	926	1,793	3,158	924	1,595	2,917	3,726
Other socialist	167	207	527	550	13	34	69	244
Developed capitalist	3	26	230	399	325	1,352	2,292	3,350
Developing countries	91	77	362	432	—	2	36	16
Total*	716	1,235	2,912	4,539	1,263	2,983	5,315	7,338
Division II — Raw materials and semifabricates to:								
CMEA	1,659	1,719	2,050	2,444	1,442	1,868	2,330	2,710
Other socialist	104	187	525	580	148	142	449	583
Developed capitalist	578	1,122	1,982	2,796	525	1,251	2,281	3,727
Developing countries	103	357	571	858	112	275	691	1,223
Total*	2,443	3,385	5,128	6,679	2,227	3,535	5,750	8,243
Division III — Foodstuffs to:								
CMEA	509	693	792	989	117	76	263	153
Other socialist	31	14	14	87	20	44	279	258
Developed capitalist	316	877	1,342	2,526	34	55	291	496
Developing countries	38	101	98	255	25	53	85	112
Total*	894	1,686	2,247	3,857	196	228	917	1,020

Division IV — Industrial
consumer goods to:

CMEA	210	648	1,413	1,784	157	308	333	347
Other socialist	5	19	43	n.a.	20	98	151	n.a.
Developed capitalist	19	104	716	1,460	23	113	123	217
Developing countries	15	40	148	n.a.	—	15	28	n.a.
Total*	249	811	2,320	3,500	201	533	634	817
Total, all groups	4,302	7,117	12,606	18,576	3,887	7,279	12,616	17,418

SOURCES: **1960 and 1966:** Ministerul Comerțului Exterior, *Dezvoltarea comerțului exterior al R. S. România 1960-1966*)Bucharest, 1967), pp. 45-55; **1971-1973:** official statistics.

NOTE: CMEA includes Bulgaria, Czechoslovakia, Hungary, Poland, Romania, and the USSR only. "Other socialist countries" are Albania, China, North Korea, North Vietnam, Mongolia, Yugoslavia, and Cuba. Advanced capitalist countries comprise all of non-socialist Europe plus the United States, Canada, Japan and Australia. Developing countries are all other countries not listed above, including New Zealand and Israel. A minor revision of the CMEA (CTN) classification took place in 1971. Figures availllable for both the old and the revised classifications for 1970 show that its effect was to raise exports of machinery by 1% qand imports by 2% at the expense of division II. Trade in foodstuffs (division III) was also increased by less than 1% as a result of the removal of tobacco from division II and its transfer to III. The data in the table for 1960 and 1966 correspond to the old and for 1971 and 1973 to the revised classification.

Trade with developed capitalist countries in 1973 is based on a breakdown that sppears to omit 603 million lei of exports to and 321 million lei of imports from these countries.

*Minor differences between sums for each year and their totals are due to rounding error.

ing, suffice it to note that the deficit with CMEA in trade in machinery at current devisa prices was not much greater in 1973 than it had been in the early 1960s (about 500 million lei). By contrast, the deficit in machinery trade with the MDCs rose from 322 million lei in 1960 (roughly $50 million at the old official rate of 6 lei to the dollar) to 3.4 billion lei in 1975 ($684 million at the new rate of 4.97 lei to the dollar). Credits extended to Romania by the MDCs, which are reflected in the large and increasing deficits in total trade with this area, greatly alleviated the burden the country would have had to bear if it had been compelled to run surpluses in other groups to pay for this equipment. (On average, from 1971 to 1973, the deficit in trade with the MDCs came to approximately half of Romania's deficit in the machinery group.) The large surpluses in machinery trade with other socialist countries (OSCs) and with the less-developed countries (LDCs), amounting to 722 million lei in 1973,[21] offset less than a fourth of the deficit in this division with the MDCs. It is doubtful, in any case, whether any significant fraction of these surpluses could have been used to offset deficits in hard currencies with the MDCs.

As noted earlier, the surplus in raw materials and semifabricates of the early 1960s turned into a sizable deficit in the 1970s. The turnaround occurred with both CMEA and the MDCs, but the shift was much more pronounced in the latter.[22] With CMEA, there was a surplus of 217 million lei in 1960 and a deficit of about 300 million lei in 1971 and 1973; with the MDCs, there was a tiny surplus of 53 million lei in 1960 and a large deficit amounting to almost 1 billion lei in 1973 and possibly even more in 1974 and 1975. Surpluses in foodstuffs and industrial consumer goods played a crucial role in bridging these gaps. With CMEA, the surplus in foodstuffs rose only moderately — from 392 million lei in 1960 to 836 million lei in 1973. With the MDCs, however, it leaped from 282 million lei in 1960 to slightly more than 1.9 billion lei in 1973 ($380 million at the new exchange rate of 4.97 lei to the dollar). The Romanian planners pushed exports of industrial consumer goods toward both East and West as vigorously as possible, holding their imports in this category from both areas to minimal levels. The surplus in trade in these goods, which had been negligible in 1960, rose to nearly 1.5 billion lei vis-à-vis CMEA and to 1.2 billion lei vis-à-vis the MDCs. Success in penetrating West European markets with consumer goods contrasts with Romania's mediocre performance — characteristic, however, of all less-developed socialist states — in promoting machinery exports to the developed West, the value of which amounted to hardly more than 10% of machinery imports from this group of countries in 1973. (This percentage was slightly higher than the USSR's and slightly lower than Poland's.)

The pattern of trade with the OSCs and LDCs is similiar in one important respect: Romania ran large surpluses in the machinery group throughout the 1960s and early 1970s in trade with both areas. But the methods of balancing this trade differed. The OSCs (chiefly accounted for by China and Yugoslavia) for the most part paid for Romanian machinery with foodstuffs and consumer goods. In some years, the LDCs balanced their accounts with Romania with raw-materials surpluses; but their deficit in total trade—generated by Romanian medium- to long-term credits—was so large in most years (amounting typically to a fourth of imports in the early 1970s) that, as an aggregate, they could afford to import a greater value of goods than they exported in any division. (Because exports of manufactures to LDCs must be lubricated with credits and because repayment is generally tied to bilateral accounts, the possibilities open to Romania of solving her trade and payments problems via exchanges with LDCs would seem rather limited.)[23] By contrast, credits to the OSCs, judging by the trade surpluses with these countries, only exceptionally rose above 10% of exports to these countries, at least in the 1970s. Trade with the Chinese People's Republic, for one, has been more or less balanced for a number of years. If we may judge from these figures, Romania seems to be more interested in cultivating the LDCs than her partners in the great socialist adventure. The motives for the preferential treatment of the LDCs with respect to credits would seem to lie at least as much in the political as in the economic realm.

The above analysis, divided into four major commodity groups and four areas, needs to be disaggregated further in at least two respects: (1) divisions II and III (raw materials, semifabricates, and foodstuffs) should be subdivided into four groups differing in their degree of processing or manufacture, with consequences for the direction of trade; and (2) the Soviet Union should be separated from the rest of CMEA because of the special place it holds in Romania's trade.

In division II (raw materials and semifabricates), the chemicals group (CTN 3) is of special interest. In 1960, Romania exported 72 million lei and imported 214 million lei of these goods. By 1973, exports had risen to nearly 1.4 billion lei and imports to 1.7 billion lei. In that same year, exports of chemicals to MDCs (negligible in 1960) came to 85% of their exports to CMEA (about 500 million lei). This expansion was made possible at least in part by imports from the West of technologically sophisticated equipment for the chemical industry. On the other hand, imports of chemicals from the MDCs were 2.8 times as large as from CMEA. The behavior of the chemicals group in Romanian foreign trade resembles that of the machinery group: in both cases, the Romanians have turned away from CMEA toward the West for the bulk of their supplies. But the two groups differ in that the Romanians have been far more successful in their efforts to boost exports of chemicals to the West than they have been for machinery products.

In division II, groups 2 and 5 may also be distinguished. Raw materials and semifabricates for heavy industry are covered chiefly in group 2 and raw materials for light industry (for textiles and footware) in group 5. Because heavy industry grew more rapidly than light industry, the deficit in group 2 rose faster, particularly in the 1960s, than the deficit in group 5. There was a small surplus in group 2 at the beginning of the 1960s which turned into a deficit in 1962, whereas in group 5 the deficit first appeared in 1970 and became significant only after 1972. Interestingly enough, in the crisis year 1975, the deficit in group 2 continued to increase (at least at current prices), while the deficit in group 5 was curtailed by nearly 1 billion lei. It is not known whether this curtailment was achieved by running down available stocks of cotton, wool, leather, and other raw materials used in light industry or by operating textile and other consumer goods industries below capacity.

Exports to CMEA in groups 2 and 5 were remarkably stable from 1960 to 1971, as if they had been set according to quota. Imports in group 2 from this area rose by 4.5% per year in the period and in group 5 by 1.3% per year. Exports to the MDCs in groups 2 and 5 grew rapidly from 1960 to 1971 (by 11.1 and 8.4% respectively), but imports rose even faster (by 16.8 and 9.7% respectively). The bulk of exports to the developed West in group 2 consisted of oil products, over 70% of which (reckoned by tonnage) was directed to the West in the early 1970s.[24]

In division III, group 7 represents raw materials for the food industry (cereals, fresh vegetables, and fruits), and group 8 covers processed foodstuffs, including meat. The MDCs accounted for the bulk of exports in group 7. Out of 2.5 billion lei of exports in group 8 in 1973, CMEA took 716 million and the MDCs took approximately 1.5 billion. The foodstuffs accruing to CMEA included a large share of canned products and processed foodstuffs; the West got most of the meat, butter, and eggs.[25] Groups 7 and 8 illustrate the general rule according to which raw products are more likely to be sold to the West and processed products to the East. By and large, the more highly manufactured a product happens to be, the harder it is to sell to the West.

Estimates of trade with the Soviet Union and the rest of CMEA broken down by nine commodity groups (CTN) are presented in table 2. The following points may be inferred:

1. Trade in manufactures (machinery and industrial consumer goods) with CMEA members other than the Soviet Union showed only a very small surplus in favor of Romania in 1973.

TABLE 2
Romania's Trade with the Soviet Union and with other CMEA Members in 1960, 1966, 1972, and 1973
(in millions of devisa lei)

TRADE WITH THE SOVIET UNION

Group	Exports				Imports			
	1960	*1966*	*1972*	*1973*	*1960*	*1966*	*1972*	*1973*
1 Machinery and equipment	158	478	898	1,055	429	949	1,437	1,530
2 Industrial raw materials and semifabricates	872		513	613	814		1,354	1,505
3 Chemicals	29	1,023	321	324	71	1,281	61	62
4 Building materials	64		82	72	9		15	24
5 Raw materials of agricultural origin other than foodstuffs	237	n.a.	270	226	148	128	196	203
6 Live animals	—	—	—	—	7	—	1	1
7 Raw materials for the food industry	78			98	53		—	—
		359	378			11	47	
8 Processed foodstuffs	93		102	343	6			29
9 Manufactured consumer goods	159	n.a.	1,305	1,389	60	67	92	95
Total†	1,689	2,631	3,869	4,120	1,596	2,437	3,203	3,449

TRADE WITH OTHER CMEA MEMBERS

Group*	Exports				Imports			
	1960	1966	1972	1973	1960	1966	1972	1973
1 Machinery and equipment	307	—	1,290	2,102	495	619	2,057	2,195
2 Industrial raw materials and semifabricates	287	537	520	573	270	403	528	612
3 Chemicals	40		162	171	63		174	181
4 Building materials	23		171	312	18		58	58
5 Raw materials of agricultural origin other than foodstuffs	107	n.a.	119	154	49	46	60	65
6 Live animals	—	—	—	—	1	—	—	1
7 Raw materials for the food industry	99	271	33	68	12	48	12	15
8 Processed foodstuffs	239	n.a.	386	480	39	165	85	106
9 Manufactured consumer goods	51		247	373	97		271	248
Total†	1,154	1,581	2,929	4,232	1,045	1,282	3,246	3,483

SOURCES and METHODS: **1960 and 1973**: Derived from percentages in *Ekonomicky casopis*, no. 9 (1975), p. 790; **1966 and 1972**: *Rumanian Press Survey*, no. 961, p. 10. Trade in consumer goods was estimated from *Comertul exterior al R. S. R. 1973*, pp. 108-16. Other data, Vanous, *Data Bank*.

*Group 1 is identical with division I in table 1; groups 2 through 5 are included in division II, groups 6 to 8 in division III, and group 9 in division IV.

†Minor differences between sums for each year and their totals are due to rounding error.

2. In that year, trade in machinery with the Soviet Union other than armaments was just about balanced (around 1.1 billion lei).[26]

3. The great surplus in manufactures ("soft goods") in Romanian trade with CMEA originated almost entirely in the surplus of manufactured consumer goods exported to the Soviet Union (1.3 billion lei) in 1973. Exports of these goods to the Soviet Union rose 8.7-fold from 1960 to 1973; imports rose by only 50%, remaining at negligible levels.

4. Trade with the USSR in raw materials and semifabricates (group 2) turned from a slight surplus in favor of Romania in 1960 to a deficit of nearly 900 million lei in 1973. The onset of this deficit may be traced to declining oil exports and rising imports of metallic ores, pig iron, and ferro-alloys.

5. The surplus in division II (groups 2 to 5) in trade with CMEA countries other than the Soviet Union came to 294 million lei in 1973, far short of the deficit with the Soviet Union in these groups (559 million lei).

6. Romania ran a surplus in foodstuffs (groups 7 and 8) with both the Soviet Union and other members of CMEA in all four years. In trade with the Soviet Union in 1973, this surplus was insufficient to offset the import surplus in groups 2 to 5, leaving a continued deficit of 149 million lei in "hard goods" (divisions II and III). The surplus earned from exports of foodstuffs to the other countries of CMEA, however, was so large that it more than offset the deficit in hard goods with the Soviet Union, leaving a positive balance in hard goods with CMEA as a whole equal to nearly 570 million lei. This positive balance, however, was appreciably smaller than in 1960.

The year 1973 was somewhat exceptional in that the overall balance of merchandise trade with both the Soviet Union and other CMEA nations showed very large surpluses (671 and 749 million lei respectively). In 1972, exports to CMEA as a whole exceeded imports by less than 400 million lei, and the surplus in hard goods with CMEA was some 100 million lei smaller than in 1973.[27] However, the main difference between the two years showed up in exports of Romanian machinery to CMEA members other than the USSR. These exports increased from 1.3 billion lei in 1972 to 2.1 billion lei in 1973, thus reducing the deficit in this group from 767 to 93 million lei. The available data allow us to infer that when Romania was faced with the necessity of repaying debts or to offset other negative items in its balance of payments with non-Soviet CMEA countries in 1973, it was able to do so mainly (i.e., to the extent of perhaps two-thirds) by increasing exports of soft goods to these countries, thus economizing on the hard goods needed to earn CCs in the West.

A Hypothesis on the Direction of Machinery Trade

In earlier works,[28] I advanced and tested a hypothesis in which the share of the West in a CMEA member's imports of manufactures significantly depended on two basic variables: (1) the deficit in each country's trade with the West (a proxy for its net invisible earnings from tourism and transportation plus its capital imports from the West) and (2) its overall surplus in hard goods (CTN divisions II and III). The available data supported the hypothesis, at least for the medium- and less-developed countries of CMEA. In this paper, I test the same hypothesis on Romanian machinery imports only, after adjustment on the data for broad price movements.[29] I also adjust the data in the base year 1960 by deflating imports from CMEA by the 35% reported difference in the levels of machinery and equipment prices in Romanian trade with CMEA and the "world market."[30] (The data used are shown in table 3.)

Before presenting the results, a few comments about my specifications are in order. I hypothesize that the decisions to import a piece of equipment from an MDC rather than from CMEA depends critically on Romania's capacity to earn hard currencies over and beyond its minimum raw-material or food requirements from the West.[31] The presumption here is that any CC earnings that are not earmarked for the *purchase* of raw materials or foodstuffs either from MDCs or LDCs are likely to be spent on machinery imports from an industrialized market economy, either within the calendar year in which these earnings accrue or in the following year (in the case of regressions where one-year lags are introduced). Note that if prices of machinery in the CMEA market for comparable quality were lower than in the West or if Romania were willing to sacrifice economic interests for the sake of CMEA solidarity, hard currency might conceivably be spent, instead, on the purchase of machinery made by fellow members of CMEA. Current earnings might also be added to foreign-exchange reserves with no discernible impact on the current or even the following year.

The dependent variable in my specification is the percentage of total machinery imports obtained from the MDCs, or $MACH^W/MACH^T$, where $MACH^W$ is the deflated value of machinery imports from MDCs and $MACH^T$ is the value of total machinery imports, adjusted not only for price changes, but for the initial disparity in prices between CMEA and the world market. My explanatory variables are (1) D^W, Romania's deficit in commodity trade with MDCs (a proxy for credits from the West and for tourist expenditures in hard currencies), and (2) S, Romania's hard-goods surplus vis-à-vis the world.

TABLE 3
Data Used in Regressions Explaining the Direction of Romania's Machinery Imports 1960-75
(in millions of devisa lei)

Year	Total Machinery Imports		% of Adjusted Machinery Imports for MDCs	Deficit in Trade with MDCs		Surplus in Hard goods	
	Actual	Adjusted		Actual	Deflated	Actual	Deflated
1960	1,263	1,024	31.7	8	8	572	572
1961	1,978	1,618	42.5	198	208	914	962
1962	2,450	2,061	42.4	386	424	1,062	1,167
1963	2,563	2,135	38.1	321	357	802	891
1964	2,749	2,254	35.4	466	548	1,002	1,179
1965	2,516	2,109	43.6	516	538	542	565
1966	2,983	2,568	52.6	641	704	1,145	1,258
1967	4,528	4,051	65.7	1,755	1,994	1,307	1,485
1968	4,511	3,892	60.4	902	1,048	1,117	1,520
1969	4,624	4,022	55.3	1,442	1,639	910	1,034
1970	4,655	3,939	46.5	1,115	1,199	119	128
1971	5,315	4,556	40.2	717	747	682	710
1972	6,670	5,748	52.0	996	1,006	968	978
1973	7,338	6,237	51.6	592	515	1,252	1,089
1974	8,698	6,869	49.1	2,242	1,410	−538	−339
1975	9,214	6,705	47.9	2,117	1,340	−1,500	−949

SOURCES: Actual machinery imports, deficits in trade with MDCs, and surpluses in hard goods are from the official statistical yearbooks of appropriate years. Imports of machinery from CMEA and from MDCs for 1960-66 are from Ministerul Comerțului Exterior, *Dezvoltarea comerțului exterior al R. S. România 1960-1966* (Bucharest, 1967), pp. 45-55. Data for subsequent years are based on Pawel Bozyk, "Economic Integration of Poland with the CMEA Countries and Economic Relations with the West," *Handel zagraniczny,* Special Issue (1973), p. 16. N. Suta, *Relațiile economice dintre țarile membre ale CAER* (Bucharest, 1975), pp. 80-81; and official statistics.

NOTE: Actual machinery imports from the entire world were adjusted as follows: Imports from CMEA in 1960 were scaled downwards by 35% (see n. 30). Data for 1961-66 were then deflated by a Romanian price index for machinery imported "from the West" and for the years 1967-73 by a Hungarian index of machinery import prices from CMEA. For the years 1974-75, Hungarian index numbers of prices of machinery imported from the ruble area were used as a deflator. Romanian price indices of "imports from the West" were used to deflate imports of machinery from all other areas (including OSCs) from 1960-66 and a Hungarian index of imports of machinery from "capitalist countries" for 1966-73. Data for 1974-75 for all areas were deflated by Hungarian price indices of imports of machinery "from the dollar area." Both the deficits with MDCs and the surpluses in hard goods were deflated with indices of *import* prices from the West (Romanian for the years 1960-66, Hungarian for 1967-75) to reflect changes in the purchasing power of actual or potential hard-currency accruals.

It is evident that $MACH^W$ in the numerator of the dependent variable is identically equal to

$$D^W + S^W + F_X^W - F_M^W + M_X^W,$$

where S^W is the surplus in hard goods with the MDCs, F_X^W and F_M^W represent exports and imports of manufactured consumer goods to and from the MDCs, and M_X^W stands for machinery exports to the MDCs. Are the results of the regression prejudiced by this underlying identity? First, we note that S is by no means identical with S^W. Possible increments in S might be accompanied by declines in S^W if Romania were obliged to increase its surplus or reduce its deficit in hard goods with CMEA, the LDCs, or the OSCs. This would happen if Romania's partners, particularly the Soviet Union, were bent on the elimination of exchanges of raw materials for soft goods (e.g., Romanian manufactured soft goods). The hypothesis that the sign of the coefficient of S will be positive and significant virtually rules out the above phenomenon as a significant possibility.

When $MACH^W$, the *absolute value* of deflated machinery imports from the MDCs, was regressed on D^W and S, the coefficient of D^W turned out to be larger than unity and the coefficient of S to be negative[32] (though not significant). R^2 for this specification equaled 54.3%, quite a bit less than in the case of our main regression [1] below. The wrong sign of S is due to the fact that this variable has been declining through time while $MACH^W$ has been rising at a high average rate. When time t was added as an explanatory variable, both the coefficients of S and of D^W were positive, but they fell short of significance at the 95% level of probability. The coefficient of t, as we would expect, was highly significant.

Dividing $MACH^W$ by total machinery imports and using the percentage ratio as the dependent variable in our main regression reduces the constraining effect of the identity chiefly affecting the numerator and eliminates most of the powerful time trend obscuring the effects of D^W and S on the direction of imports.

Another shortcoming of the specification is that the deficit-in-trade-with-MDCs variable, used as a proxy for tourist earnings and credits, is not independent of $MACH^W$ itself, since machinery imports from the West are generally purchased on credit. We have here a bias (in the direction of increasing the coefficient of D^W) that can only be eliminated by formulating the problem as a set of two or more simultaneous equations. Unfortunately, I could not find suitable exogenous variables that would have allowed me to construct a properly identified model for this purpose.

While the specification of the regression set forth below is not as "clean" as one would wish, I consider it adequate for a first stab at the problem of isolating the factors determining the direction of machinery imports.

The results of the regression corresponding to my basic specification are these:

$$M = 31.36 + 0.0137D^W + 0.00535S$$
$$\quad\;\;(10.79)\;\;(5.96)\quad\;\;(2.78) \tag{1}$$
$$R^2 = 0.75 \quad D\text{-}W = 1.96,$$

where M is the percentage of adjusted machinery imports originating in MDCs, D^W is the deflated deficit in trade with the MDCs, and S is the surplus in hard goods (raw materials and foodstuffs) vis-à-vis the world (both D^W and S being expressed in millions of devisa lei). The t-statistics, shown in parentheses, are all significant at the 95% probability level. The R^2 is quite high for a regression purporting to explain percentages. The Durbin-Watson statistic is satisfactory. Positive and negative residuals of actual time trend values do not show a clearly defined pattern that would suggest a serious misinterpretation of the equation.

The regression shows that, other things equal, an increase of 100 million lei in the overall deficit with the MDCs will be associated with a 1.37% increase in the share of MDCs in total machinery imports. Similarly, a 100 million lei increase in the surplus in hard goods will be associated with a 0.54% increase in this same share.

Was the impact of S and D^W on the provenance of machinery imports in the post-1965 years associated with the intensification of Romania's links with the West under Ceausescu? The introduction of a dummy variable for the years 1966-71 helps to answer this question:

$$M = 30.86 + 0.0093D^W + 0.0055S + 6.69DUM$$
$$\quad\;\;(11.7)\quad\;\;(3.05)\quad\quad\;\;(3.17)\quad\;\;(1.99)$$
$$R^2 = 0.82 \; D\text{-}W = 1.88 \tag{2}$$

The coefficient of the dummy variable, DUM, for the years 1966-75 falls just short of significance at the 95% probability level. The fact that R^2 is now a bit higher than in [1] should also be noted. The coefficient of D^W is lower than in [1] (though still clearly significant), while that of S is only a shade higher.

It may be objected that the latter-years dummy is a proxy for exports of manufactures to the MDCs, which increased greatly in the last decade or so. The insertion of this variable produces a fit that is not quite as good as [2] $(R^2 = 0.795$; the t-statistic of the coefficient of the new variable is only 1.63).

The introduction of a one-year lag in the explanatory variables D^W and S, denoted $D^W[1]$ and $S[1]$ respectively, causes a marked deterioration in the fit:

$$M = 35.58 + 0.0078D^W[1] + 0.0065S[1]$$
$$\quad (7.67) \qquad (2.3) \qquad\qquad (1.6)$$
$$R^2 = 0.39 \qquad D\text{-}W = 1.32 \tag{3}$$

However, a dummy variable for later years raises R^2 again to a respectable level:

$$M = 32.31 - 0.0014D^W[1] + 0.0078S[1] + 14.70DUM$$
$$\quad (9.27) \qquad (0.39) \qquad (2.65) \qquad\qquad (3.57)$$
$$R^2 = 0.704 \qquad D\text{-}W = 1.487 \tag{4}$$

The dummy variable for the years 1966-75 in this regression is so powerful that it obliterates the variable registering the lagged deficit in trade with the West. The coefficient of $S[1]$ is slightly higher (and even more significant) than the coefficient of $S[1]$ in [3].

The results of regression [4] again confirm that, in the last decade, the Romanians were more inclined, with a given potential for hard-currency earnings, to turn to the West for their machinery purchases than during the last years of Gheorghiu-Dej's rule.

Since equation [2] provides the best fit, I shall use it as the basis for my speculations on the effects of long-range changes in the explanatory variables on M, on the assumption that the positive impact of the dummy variable on M for the period 1966-75 was maintained in subsequent years.

On the basis of trade data for 1965-66 to 1971-72, when price changes were negligible, we may estimate that the deficit in raw materials (division II) has been growing at 25% per year and the surplus in foodstuffs (division III) at 5% per year. Projecting these figures from 1972 to 1980 yields approximately a value of S equal to -4,250 million lei. Using equation [2] and substituting this estimate for S, we infer that in order to maintain M at its 1975 level of 47.9%, D^W would have to go from 1,340 million lei in 1975 to 3,623 million lei, a compound rate of 22% per year. Considering that there has been virtually no growth in this deficit since the late 1960s, the chances that *net* credits and invisible earnings would rise sufficiently fast to support a gap of this magnitude by 1980 appear slim. Note also that if the surplus of foodstuffs rose by 3% per year instead of 5, other things equal, the overall deficit in trade with the MDCs would have to increase another 300 million lei to prevent the share of the West in machinery imports from declining.

Another way of predicting the hard-currency gap D^W is to forecast independently the numerator and the denominator of $MACH^W/MACH^T$. Total machinery imports in 1980 may be estimated in two steps. First, regress $MACH^T$ on total domestic investments in machinery at 1959 prices for 1960 to 1975.[33] Next, project $MACH^T$ to

1980 by assuming the same rate of growth in investments in machinery as in the period 1960-75. This yields a forecast of 13,986 million devisa lei in 1980. To maintain the share of imports from the MDCs at 47.9%, Romania would have to import 6,693 million lei of machinery and equipment from those countries. A regression of $MACH^W$ on S, D^W, and F_X^W for 1960-75 yields the following result:

$$MACH^W = -12.3 + 0.469S + 0.816D^W + 1.382F_X^W$$
$$(0.1) \quad (5.41) \quad (9.16) \quad (15.2)$$
$$R^2 = 0.977 \tag{5}$$

This equation is, of course, highly constrained by the accounting identity relating $MACH^W$ to S, D^W, F_X^W, F_M^W, and M_X^W; but this is not damaging, since the identity itself could be used as a basis for the projection. We now substitute into the right-hand side of [5] the value of S already used (-4,250 million lei) and a projection of F_X^W from the trend in the period 1965-72 (3,200 million lei). For $MACH^W$ we substitute 6,693 million lei. Solving for D^W gives an estimate of 2,812 million lei for the size of the deficit with MDCs in 1980 (compared to 3,623 million lei according to the method of direct estimation). A deficit with MDCs of this size would imply a growth rate in this variable of 15.9% per year from 1975 to 1980, which, while more manageable than the 22% per year predicted by the alternative method, may still be considered quite high in view of the past record. It should be kept in mind that the deficit in question must be net of any payments on principal and interest due from past loans. According to Chase Manhattan Bank estimates,[34] the total indebtedness of Romania to the West was $2.3 billion at the end of 1975. If yearly interest and repayments came to 15% of this sum, they would amount to $345 million or about 1.1 billion lei at the new rate of exchange. The servicing of Romania's debt, which, as these figures suggest, is already fairly heavy, is expected to become an even greater burden in the years 1978-80 when a number of loans will become due. Gross borrowings and invisible earnings would then have to rise more than I have estimated in order to provide the net accruals in hard currencies required to maintain the net share of the West in Romania's machinery purchases.

These exercises in projection assume that the forces determining the direction of trade in machinery will be the same in the second half of the 1970s as they were in the period 1960-75. This is unlikely given the drastic changes in world and CMEA prices that took place from 1973 to 1975. If, as is generally expected, CMEA prices from the mid-1970s on will be patterned more closely and with a smaller lag after world prices, then it may be that the "hard" and "soft" goods dichotomy will gradually disappear. It may become advantageous for

Romania to export raw materials and foodstuffs to CMEA members in exchange for machinery products. This would, other things being equal, reduce the share of the West in its machinery imports. But then again, the Soviet Union may be more willing than in the past to export raw materials to Romania in exchange for manufactured consumer goods, releasing Romanian materials and foodstuffs for sale to the West if so desired. This would have the reverse effect. The net impact of the new structure of CMEA prices is not easily predictable.

Even if we abstract from these possible structural changes, these simple-minded projections should not be taken too literally. They are mainly suggestive of the plausible long-term effects on the direction of trade in machinery products that alternative growth rates in our key variables might have. They chiefly throw in relief the pivotal role that farm exports have played and are likely to continue to play in Romania's industrialization and trade strategy. Given the widening gap between exports and imports of nonagricultural raw materials— an ineluctable consequence of the rapid growth of industry—net exports of farm products must rise fairly rapidly to moderate the resulting drain on CCs. Exports of manufactures to the West, which have enjoyed a remarkable growth in the last few years starting from a negligible level, can also moderate this drain. Doubtless the factories equipped with Western machinery and the technical cooperation between Romania and individual MDCs have facilitated exports of manufactures to the West and will continue to do so. The key question is whether agricultural exports *in toto*, exports of manufactures to the MDCs, and earnings from tourism can rise fast enough to prevent either an excessive and potentially hazardous increase in hard-currency liabilities or a reduction in purchases of manufactures from the West.

Romania's Strategy and Trade Options

So far, the argument has been developed that the fluctuating share of the developed market economies in Romania's imports of machinery and equipment has been conditioned by the country's capacity to generate exports of hard goods and tourist earnings and by its net imports of capital. Due in part to rising domestic requirements for raw materials and semifabricates and in part to difficulties in building up food exports in recent years, the share in question has generally remained below 50% (at comparable prices for imports from East and West). What changes in strategy would be required to raise it to significantly higher levels and thus lessen Romania's dependence on CMEA?

First, a more "intensive" industrialization policy would help, especially one that would stress investments aimed at reducing material inputs per unit of output at least on a par with investment in new plants designed to augment production capacities.

A typical feature of an "extensive" growth policy geared to increasing output at almost any cost is the maintenance in operation of old and obsolete plants with lower labor and material productivities than newly constructed capacities. The comparative neglect of investment in higher education and research and development personnel are also characteristic of such a policy, as Marvin Jackson points out in his survey of the Romanian economy.[35] True, Romania regularly invests more in the energy, fuels, and metallurgical sectors (as a fraction of total investments in industry) than any other member of CMEA, with the possible exception of the Soviet Union.[36] But a good deal of this goes to expand high-cost metallurgical output and to drill for oil at enormous depths under unfavorable conditions. One may question whether if some of these investments had been used to defray the expense of modernizing existing plants and reducing outlays on materials, the impact on net imports of raw materials and semifabricates would not have been more favorable than that which resulted from the output-focused policy actually adopted.

The farm sector may offer even greater possibilities of expanding hard-currency earnings at a greater rate than in the past. Agriculture received 16.7% of all investment funds in 1951-65, 15.6% in 1966-70, 14% in 1971-75, and is only slated to receive 11.6% in 1976-80.[37] Bulgaria, which, as Gur Ofer has shown in this volume, has opted for a strategy of modernizing its farm sector more rapidly than Romania, has traditionally invested a greater share of its total investments in agriculture than its northern neighbor.[38] In recent years, Romania has begun to make up the neglect of the 1950s and early 1960s by investing heavily in irrigation works for tomato and other vegetable growing; but there is a long way to go before opportunities for profitable investment in farming are exhausted. Perhaps the most backward sector of Romanian agriculture, relative to its unexploited position, is fruit-growing and viniculture. Output of fruit and grapes has been stagnating at or below 1938 levels for the last decade,[39] while Bulgaria has made major progress on this front. The investment required to make a decisive breakthrough in the output of fruit is relatively large and cannot be expected to yield benefits rapidly. But if the calculation of costs and returns were made in terms of the opportunity costs of the hard currencies that fruit exports could generate, I am confident they would be more profitable than some of the industrial investments that have been planned for 1976-80, when industry will absorb a greater percentage of all investments than in any previous period.

Romania also lags behind Bulgaria in the modernization of dairy farms. Milk yields in Romanian farms have been stagnating in recent years, while they have been increasing regularly in Bulgaria. To remedy the lack of forage in Romania, which seems to be the principal cause of the low milk yields, more resources would have to be invested in the extension of the irrigation network and more foodstuffs would have to be imported, a policy that should pay off in terms of increased exports of dairy products in the short run.

These suggestions are quite speculative in the absence of precise data on relative opportunity costs of domestic production. Even official accounting-costs data, which are rarely obtainable, may be misleading since they may not reflect comparative advantage accurately. It so happens, for example, that in the early 1970s exports of parallel lathes and of most ordinary types of production machinery appeared very profitable—they cost only 20 to 30 lei per dollar of foreign-exchange receipts—whereas fruit (costing 42 lei per dollar), wheat (34 lei in 1971), potatoes (59 lei per dollar), and textile garments (61 lei per dollar) appeared extremely unprofitable.[40] On the basis of such data, the planners may have been induced to curb exports of agricultural goods and textiles and to press exports of engineering goods. Yet the relative profitability of exporting these items might have looked quite different if costs had been fully expressive of relative scarcities. As Danescu points out, the reported calculations were made in terms of accounting costs per dollar earned and made no allowance for the opportunity costs of the imported or exportable raw materials and semifabricates incorporated into the goods exported. The costs of imported inputs alone represent 40% of the value of a 40-horsepower tractor and 21% of a diesel truck.[41] Capital costs, including interest charges, are likely to be grossly underestimated, not only at the machinery-production stage, but on the steel and other capital-intensive inputs that enter engineering products. These indirect costs are surely smaller, relative to total unit costs, in the production of fruit or potatoes.

Calculations of production costs in lei per dollar earned averaged over all markets may also miss the mark, inasmuch as these costs are known to be higher in exports to the West than to the East. The question of relevance here is the cost of the export goods necessary to import the machinery that would be best suited to Romanian needs, irrespective of origin.

The crux of the matter, in any case, may not be relative costs as they were recorded in 1970 or 1971 but the costs that would have obtained if investments had been efficiently apportioned among the different branches of the economy. It may be that production costs were high in agriculture just because the sector has suffered from suboptimal levels of investment. A reapportionment of funds between the machinery and the farm sectors might, after some time, produce very different relative costs of dollar- (or ruble-) earning exports.

In sum, crude calculations of relative profitability, geared to accounting costs that reflect neither static nor dynamic advantage, may merely reinforce the prejudice that many Romanian technocrats harbor in favor of exporting machinery products, with an eye to the emulation of industrialized countries.

Romania is now so far along in industrialization that its leaders cannot possibly be apprehensive of any return to agricultural specialization. Clearly, many manufactured items, including engineering products, do enjoy a comparative advantage after years of cost reductions made possible by the acquisition of greater skills by the labor force and as a result of technical progress. The only alternative that may be worth considering is whether marginal adjustments that would place greater stress on the production of farm products, which can be exported relatively easily to the West, might be in order. The question is whether the present all-out stress on the continued expansion of heavy industry may not further deepen Romania's dependence on CMEA, both as a ready market for the country's metal manufactures and as a principal source of the inputs that go into the making of these goods.

Discussion

Marvin R. Jackson

Professor Montias's paper points at matters beyond that country's development to the evolution of CMEA and East-West relations, economic and political. Two decades ago, Romania's reaction to attempted CMEA interference in her plans for "all around" industrialization led not only to her turn to the West for machinery and credits and, in due course, to a pioneering of East-West economic and political détente, but also to probable weakening of CMEA's attempt at greater specialization among its members. Subsequently, when other members of CMEA began to turn toward the West, and when Romania's behavior seemed less unorthodox, her policy conflict shifted from an ostensibly economic base to a political one, focused on the issue of Soviet domination of other socialist countries' domestic and foreign affairs. Should Romania be forced to return to greater economic dependence on CMEA or, better said, if her leaders choose this path rather than compromising their commitment to industrialization, would her economic growth be reduced by having less access to Western quality machinery and technology? Would her political independence also be compromised? Would this subsequently influence East-West relations or the future course of CMEA?

These questions acquire an urgent tone in view of Montias's analysis, since one must conclude from it that, unless Romania is willing to accelerate agricultural development, she is headed for greater economic dependence on CMEA. Slower growth in the West promises little growth of either Romania's tourist earnings or her exports of manufactured goods. Her past neglect of agriculture, only partially remedied in 1971-75, still leaves agricultural output and foreign trade subject to the caprice of the weather. Since at least 1965, the export surplus of foodstuffs has neatly conformed to fluctuations in gross agricultural production with some lag.[1] For example, in 1976 gross output increased 17.3%, followed by a jump in the foodstuff export surplus in 1977 of 75.8% in current prices. Then, gross output fell in 1977 by about 1%; preliminary reports on the 1978 harvest suggest no better performance.[2] Given the evident 1977 squeeze on domestic supplies and that summer's unprecedented strike of Jiu Valley coalminers over, among other complaints, food shortages, the 1978 export surplus of foodstuffs is likely to show a sharp reduction.

In the long run, Romanian foreign-trade planners may find agricultural exports more dependably available; nearly half of investments in agriculture in the present five-year plan are for schemes to reduce its vulnerability to flood and drought. But from 1980 to 1990, resources allocated to it are planned to result in a growth of output of only 1.6-2.3% a year, with most of the growth aimed at raising per capita animal products.[3] As development is now planned, the relative concern of foreign-trade planners for agriculture could even turn to the import side. Their tasks, even more than at present, will be centered on finding markets for manufactures, with an increasing accent on producer rather than consumer goods, and to find sources of raw materials. If they cannot fulfill these tasks through Western markets, the implied turn to the East would seem, at the least, an ironical turn of events. One might say that by having pursued too diligently the very strategy that once led to independence, Romania could end up once again in the arms of CMEA and the Soviet Union. Of course, this scenario would be an acid test of how much Romanian leaders value independence or see it as a means to other objectives. If the value of independence is as great as has seemed through past actions and current public pronouncements, would Romanian leaders place it in as much jeopardy as implied in Montias's paper? Or are they counting on an alternative either neglected or discounted by Montias? Could that alternative be Romania's trade with LDCs and possibly OSCs, an alternative "beyond either East or West"?

The third option for Romanian strategy is not overlooked by Montias. Rather, he considers it neither a viable source of CC earnings nor an important means to reduce Romania's hard goods deficit with MDCs. Still, Romania has emphasized this option since at least 1970 as part of a general alignment toward the Third World. Targets were set for a total LDC trade turnover of 25% in 1977-78 and 30% in 1980.[4] Policies stressing the primacy of so-called "cooperation" in trade, which appeals to LDCs, have been accompanied by changes in foreign-trade organization to complement them. Moreover, LDC trade is not without possible advantages. It lends serious support to Romania's Third World commitment. It better suits the Romanian style of foreign-trade organization than do the requirements of Western marketing.[5] But more than anything, it offers a chance to reduce dependence on both East and West.

The statistical record shows that the combined shares of LDCs and OSCs in Romanian trade changed insignificantly in the late 1960s and until 1974.[6] Their import shares did increase slightly, but their export shares fell in 1973, relatively more than that of CMEA in a year beginning the international price inflation and large increases in the MDC shares of both imports and exports. Perhaps Romania's trade with the Third World was, like that of CMEA, tied to price agreements, or perhaps imports and exports were diverted to MDCs. Shares of MDCs rose again in 1974, but this year the combined shares of LDCs and OSCs rose relatively even more, especially on the export side. Now CMEA shares plummeted. With the 1975 price adjustments in CMEA trade, its import share rose while that of MDCs fell; the combined LDC/OSC share remained constant. On the export side, the CMEA share rose, but far less than the MDC share fell; both were under pressure by another very large relative increase in the share of exports to LDCs and OSCs. By 1977, the CMEA shares averaged about their levels in 1973,[7] but the MDC share of exports fell to its 1970 level. The share of MDC imports fell to between 1965 and 1966 levels!

There remains the task of explaining the relative real and price-level changes at work in the shifts and to disaggregate them among commodity groups. Price and commodity-group by country-group data are available only up to 1975. Given the axis of Montias's analysis on the MDC share of Romanian machinery imports, a useful complement is a closer look at Romania's imports of industrial materials, a possible focus of her LDC trade. As shown in table 1, the CMEA share had declined steadily except for the movements in 1974 and 1975 when the

TABLE 1

Sources of Romanian Imports of Fuels and
Non-Food Raw Materials, 1960-1975
(percentages)

Year	CMEA	MDC	LDC	Other
1960	64.4	23.6	5.0	7.0
1961	62.1	21.8	8.8	4.9
1962	65.9	22.1	9.0	3.0
1963	62.5	24.4	9.0	4.1
1964	59.4	30.0	6.6	3.9
1965	55.6	32.4	8.1	3.8
1966	52.3	35.4	7.8	4.6
1967	48.4	38.3	8.1	5.3
1968	46.6	35.8	10.2	7.4
1969	42.6	40.1	12.3	5.0
1970	40.9	42.1	11.0	6.0
1971	41.0	39.8	11.7	7.5
1972	37.8	40.0	14.2	8.0
1973	32.6	45.5	14.7	7.2
1974	22.0	52.8	20.1	5.1
1975	29.1	42.1	22.2	6.6

SOURCE: Jan Vanous, *Project CMEA-FORTRAM Data Bank of Foreign Trade Flows and Balances of CMEA Countries 1950-1975* (Vancouver, University of British Columbia, 1977), pp. 219-27.

sharp dip and rise reflected the lagged rise of CMEA prices compared to world prices. The declining CMEA share up to 1970 was offset principally by a rising MDC share, a behavior that may be explained in terms of both availability to Romania of means of payment and, given the evolution of its trade organization to that date, the relative efficiency of importing through MDC intermediaries. After 1969, the MDC share grew only in 1973 and 1974, carried up by world price inflation and Romania's evident continued dependence on Western intermediaries and production sources. The LDC share rose in 1968, 1969, again in 1972, then in 1974, and only slightly in 1975. While parts of the MDC and LDC share increases in 1973 and 1974 reflect price rather than real changes, a recalculation after 1970 in constant 1970 foreign-trade prices shows them to be nearly identical to current price shares except for 1974.[8] It appears, then, that Romania's emphasis on LDC trade has brought a continued diversion of industrial material imports from CMEA but, up to 1975, it had not yet reduced the large share of imports from the MDCs.

Romania's declared interest in LDC trade has found an action counterpart. But how this trade might influence the analysis and projections in Montias's paper is less clear. The issues are: (1) has

Romania earned or can it be expected to earn CC balances from LDC trade, and (2) has this trade affected or can it be expected to affect the balance of hard goods exports to MDCs?

There are two evidences of possible Romanian CC earnings outside of its trade with MDCs. First, estimates of her total trade balance in CCs show different deficits than her total MDC trade. They were smaller in 1971, 1972, 1974 and 1975 by, respectively, about 16, 8, 8-14, and 24%, but in 1973, larger by 10-68%.[9] However, the differences cannot be attributed only to LDC trade, because Romania might have had CC trade with CMEA countries. Second, not all of Romania's trade with LDCs is conducted through known and formal bilateral clearing agreements. Romania had trade surpluses of 120, 145, and 268 million dollars in, respectively, 1973, 1974, and 1975 with LDC partners for whom no bilateral clearing agreement was recorded. Still an uncertain, but possibly large portion of them might have involved Romanian credit or (what amounts to the same thing) have been covered in cooperation projects.[10]

It remains to explore the impact of Romania's Third World trade on hard goods balances with MDCs. As Montias points out, Romania has commonly experienced net export balances of soft goods (machinery and consumer manufacturers) and net import balances of hard goods (industrial materials and foodstuffs) with LDCs and OSCs. Before the 1970s, the balances were insignificant compared to those with CMEA and the MDCs.[11] Since 1970, within the hard goods category, net exports of foodstuffs to LCDs have tended to be offset by net imports from OSCs.[12] Within the soft goods category, net exports of consumer manufactures to LDCs have been offset by net imports from OSCs. Combining LDC and OSC balances shows that, by and large, Romania has gained net imports of industrial raw materials in exchange for net machinery exports. Romania's desire for this exchange, as Montias points out, has evidently been so strong that, while still officially a less-developed country, it extends credits to other LDCs.

Of course, it is still unclear how Romania's shift to LDCs with her gains of hard goods for soft goods might have influenced trade with MDCs and, especially, this trade's hard goods balances. Table 1 suggests Romania's LDC trade has been a substitute for CMEA trade, not MDC trade. As imports of industrial materials were shifted from CMEA to LDCs, so was a package of soft goods exports.[13] Yet, if Romania had been intent, above all, on reducing CMEA trade dependence, without the LDC alternative her imports of industrial materials from MDCs would have been even greater.[14] No doubt, in such a case, MDC machinery imports would have had to be reduced. Instead, Romania's shift to LDCs provided imports of industrial materials for payment in soft goods, thus saving CC earnings for machinery imports from MDCs. The magnitude of CC savings can be roughly approximated as the ratio of net imports of hard goods from the Third World to Romania's commodity trade deficit with MDCs. The ratio averaged 37.5% for 1971-75, rose to a high of 63.1% in 1973, and then fell in 1974 to 30.2% and, in 1975, to only 19.2%, By this estimate, the CC savings are large. However, they may have been smaller in view of other more complex interactions between MDC and LDC trade. First, given that Romania's capacity to supply exports has been constrained, necessary exports to the Third World might have diverted hard goods exports away from MDCs.[15] Second, Romania's net import balances of industrial materials are offset by the hard goods import content of her machinery exports, a factor multiplied as long as additional credits flow to LDCs through her commodity trade surpluses. The hard goods import content is partly from Third World sources and partly from MDC sources, both machinery and materials.

Table 1 shows that Romania's increasing imports of industrial materials from Third World sources did not reduce the share of them imported from MDC during 1971-75. In fact, MDC shares rose in 1973 and 1974, both in current price terms and in real terms. But the share fell in 1975 to its 1970 level in current prices and to its 1969 level in real terms. Looking directly at the MDC hard goods balance shows that, compared to 1966-70/71, in 1970/71-75 the deficit in industrial materials grew much faster, while the surplus in foodstuffs grew at about the same rate. That is, turning to the Third World had not yet helped Romania reduce or even hold the line on the rate at which its hard goods balance with MDCs was turning from surplus to deficit.

The critical years in this case were 1973 and 1974, when the international price inflation upset Romanian planners' control over foreign trade and seemed to delay the implementation of her turn toward the Third World. While there is only one year's complete data in 1975 (a year complicated by inflation of CMEA prices), to show a turn from MDCs to LDCs, the overall reductions in MDC trade shares in 1976 and 1977 suggest that the policy has been continued. Will the reduced total MDC trade shares in 1976 and 1977 show up as reduced imports of industrial materials from MDCs while imports of MDC machinery are maintained? If so, will Romania's success stimulate similar shifts by other CMEA members who are now so hard pressed for supplies of industrial materials? Perhaps Romania will prove to have led the way to another realignment of CMEA, this time beyond the East or the West.

Discussion
Gregory Grossman

In the present paper, Professor Montias continues the masterful line of analysis relating Romania's foreign trade and her economic development with which we became acquainted in his *Economic Development in Communist Rumania* (1967) and which we have had further occasion to admire in a series of subsequent papers. In the empirical portion of the paper, he tests the general hypothesis that the *share* of Romania's machinery imports from the West (since 1960) can, in significant measure, be explained by broad foreign-trade variables such as Romania's deficit in total trade. Using four alternative equations, he finds the hypotheses borne out insofar as the record of the past is concerned.

The future is something else again, as the author recognizes. Since borrowing in the West—and, therefore, the deficit in total trade with the MDCs—is largely to finance machinery imports from the West, projection of these imports is highly dependent on estimates of the West's willingness to continue lending and Romania's readiness to continue borrowing. Second, hard-currency debt service has been growing sharply in magnitude since the end of the 1960s,[1] and its servicing is likely to be a substantial drain on Romania's hard-currency resources for some years to come. In other words, any formal projections of machinery imports from the West will have to take explicit account of debt service. Needless to say, the effect will be to reduce the share of machinery imports coming from the MDC.

This is only one respect in which Romania faces growing difficulty in its policy of relatively lesser economic dependence on the CMEA in general and on the Soviet Union in particular, a policy Romania launched in the late 1950s and pursued with considerable success since. The chief economic constraint to this policy in recent years has been the decline of her exportable surpluses of raw materials and semifabricates, and the appearance of a *net* import surplus in this commodity category in the later 1960s vis-à-vis the MDCs (and LDCs), as the paper points out. The question naturally suggests itself whether rising export surpluses of raw and processed foodstuffs could at least in part offset the deteriorating tendency on the side of nonagricultural raw materials and semifabricates. The possibility is more intriguing in that Romania's neighbors in Eastern Europe, Bulgaria, and Hungary seem to have had some success in pursuing deliberate policies of developing agricultural exports, the Bulgarian case being analyzed in depth by Professor Ofer in this volume. This question came in for some discussion at the Bloomington conference and has been addressed by Professor Montias in this version of his paper in the concluding section, "Romania's Strategy and Trade Options." Montias notes that Romania has not made as much of an effort as her neighbors to enhance agricultural production and exports, though lately there have been some signs of greater concern in this direction. He further speculates that the true (opportunity) cost situation in Romania may point in the direction of the profitability of greater food exports despite some (apparently spurious) calculations to the contrary mentioned in Romanian sources. The remainder of this comment will address itself to certain aspects of this problem.

Comparatively speaking, Romania's food exports are not very large. Because of the variety of prices at which the East European countries trade, it is desirable to bring the official statistics to a common price level. Thanks to the diligent efforts of Professor Jan Vanous and his kindness in sharing some of his computations, I am able to cite the following figures adjusted for price disparities. In 1975, the share of food and tobacco in total Bulgarian exports was 32.0%; in total Hungarian exports, 21.8%; and in total Romanian exports, 16.3%. While the bulk of Bulgarian food and tobacco exports went to other CMEA countries, 39% were sold to the MDCs (36.5% of total Hungarian exports to MDCs). In the case of Romania, as much as 53% of the food and tobacco exports went to the MDCs (24.8% of total exports to MDCs).[2]

Professor Vanous's figures on food exports can also be related to each country's population. Performing the division, we find that 1975 exports of food and tobacco to all destinations were as follows, in SDRs per capita: Bulgaria, 140; Hungary, 92; Romania, 34. Although Romania's *total* exports per capita were under one-half of those of the other two countries, the contrast is still rather striking. A comparison of food exports per person in agriculture would be even less favorable to Romania. To resort to a favorite Soviet euphemism, there would seem to be significant "internal reserves" in Romanian agriculture to be placed at the service of the balance-of-payments and industrialization.

Romania comes out even less favorably in the comparison if one bears in mind that it is a considerably more agrarian country than either Hungary or (even) Bulgaria and might, therefore, be expected to have larger exportable food surpluses on this score. Thus, we can cite the following data for 1976 (the first figure is the percent of economically active population accounted for by agriculture and forestry; the second figure is the percentage of the gross national product originating in agriculture and forestry): Hungary, 19.7, 20.9; Bulgaria, 25.8, 24.0; Romania, 36.8, 29.4.[3] These figures also suggest that average income produced in agriculture is considerably lower relative to that in the rest of the economy in Romania than in the other two countries, a contrast affected both by relative physical productivity per person and by local relative prices of agricultural and nonagricultural goods.

A more direct way of expressing the contrast in productivities is in terms of agricultural output per capita in comparable prices. Thus, Lazarcik found that on the average over the period 1971-75 (and, in parentheses, for 1976), Hungary's per capita agricultural output was 50(28)% higher than Romania's, and Bulgaria's was 34(19)% higher.[4] As stressed in Montias's paper, Romania's agricultural output was rising very rapidly in the early and middle 1970s; hence, as here shown, by 1976 the gaps between Romania and the other two countries were being rapidly reduced.

The increase in the exportable surplus is a function of both the growth of production and the urgency of domestic demand for food. Production growth in Eastern Europe is often in large measure associated with specific governmental policies. During the first half of the 1970s, the Romanian government seems to have taken some serious steps in this direction. Between 1970 and 1975, gross fixed investment in agriculture (including forestry), at current prices, increased some 42%, most of it in the last two years of the period; this was even slightly more than the corresponding increase in Bulgaria (40%), and much more in Hungary (17%). As a result, by 1975 all three countries were devoting almost the same percentage of total gross fixed investment to agriculture and forestry—13-14%, though still far behind the Soviet level of 21%.[5] In terms of mineral fertilizers applied per hectare, Romania has been reducing the lead of Bulgaria and, in 1975, reached two-thirds the Bulgarian level; but in terms of tractor horsepower per hectare, it was Bulgaria that was overtaking during the early 1970s.[6] (Any student of East European or Soviet agriculture would, however, immediately retort: how efficiently were fertilizers and tractors used?)

Parallel to these positive developments, a series of institutional changes were introduced between 1965 and 1976 that generally aimed to enhance peasant incentives. Perhaps most notable among these is the formation of "small groups" of peasants in a contractual relationship ("global accord") with the cooperative (collective) and with a remuneration in cash or in kind that is essentially a form of sharecropping.[7] One wonders to what extent the upsurge in agricultural output in the 1970s might be attributable to this institutional innovation (an arrangement similar to the "autonomous link" that has been successfully tried in the Soviet Union but was rejected for what appears to be primarily political reasons). In the meantime, peasant earnings from the cooperatives rose sharply and were practically transformed (as in the USSR) from residual incomes to guaranteed wages. Private-plot production was encouraged. Legislation at the end of 1975 prescribed that earnings from cooperatives not exceed rates of pay for similar work in the rest of the economy.[8] The 1975 law carries the suggestion that the authorities do not wish to stem the rapid flow of manpower from the village into nonagricultural pursuits or to diminish the size of the agricultural surplus by dint of growing consumption by the peasants themselves.

Nonetheless, all is not well in agricultural labor. There are underemployment and shortages, low level of skills, aging and feminization, and so forth. A 1970 law provided for the mobilization of local nonagricultural population at times of peak demand for labor (as perennially in the USSR).[9] In short, Romania, as do most other East European countries, has to contend at once with the many unfavorable legacies of its rural economy and the specific stresses imposed on it by rapid industrialization and communist auspices. But, then, according to an expert observer, even the vaunted Bulgarian agricultural system is plagued with considerable inefficiency.[10]

As Jackson shows, between 1965 and 1975, exports of food products from Romania tended to fluctuate and grow rather closely with total agricultural output,[11] while domestic consumption of agricultural products per capita rose by about 3.2% per year, or about two-thirds as fast as real disposable incomes.[12] On the other hand, long-term plans call for an optimistically high rate of increase in agricultural output per capita in 1976-80 (the highest in Eastern Europe), but then only about 0.5-2% per year per capita on the average between 1980 and 1990, depending on the rate of population increase.[13] Moreover, if the general experience of East European countries and the USSR is at all indicative, further appreciable increases in Romanian agricultural output will tend to come at substantially rising unit cost. Altogether, on the production side, the outlook for generating rapidly growing exportable surpluses does not seem to be too rosy (although higher degrees of processing of foodstuffs for exports may help the value of exports), not to mention the protectionist obstacles on the West European side.

But there is also the domestic demand problem. In the past, the income (or expenditure) elasticity of demand for food has been rather high, as just noted. In fact, between 1960 and 1975, retail sales of food rose almost exactly as much (measured at constant prices) as retail trade as a whole—an expenditure elasticity of demand only slightly above that found in nearly all other East European countries, the Soviet Union included. The share of meat and meat products in total retail sales rose from 5.8% in 1960, to 6.3% in 1970, to 7.6% in 1975.[14] At the same time, per capita consumption of meat is still very low, even by East European standards. In recent years, there has been a good deal of "tension" in the retail market in Romania, not the least in respect to meat and fruit and vegetables. In view of the clear determination on the part of Romanian authorities to continue the policy of extremely rapid industrialization, the inevitable implications for consumer money incomes, and the political difficulty of sharply rising food prices, one might expect the tension to continue. It will not be easy to balance domestic political and economic imperatives against balance-of-payment pressures—as indeed is the case in most other East European countries.[15]

One might ask, again referring to Ofer's contribution to this volume, why Romania in the late 1970s and 1980s could not embark on the same road of development via agricultural exports that Bulgaria has been travelling with apparent success for some time? Perhaps she could. But on the other side of the argument, one might mention the substantially lower per capita agricultural output of Romania and the deliberate policy of building economic independence on her much better endowment of mineral and forest resources. It may also be that the passage of time now works against Romania embarking on the Bulgarian strategy; the intensity of her consumers' expectations may by now have reached a point where diversion of high quality food to exports is politically more difficult than before. In the meantime, as Montias stresses, Romania has been relatively quite successful in selling manufactures, chiefly consumer goods, in Western markets.[16] Perhaps this success, too, will tempt the authorities to defer the hardest choices in regard to agriculture and the allocation of food supplies to domestic and external markets.

Andrzej Korbonski

Poland and the CMEA: Problems and Prospects

One way to study the interaction between a member country and the larger regional body is to produce a historical, chronological, and descriptive account. There is obviously nothing wrong with this approach; however, in the relationship between Poland and the Council for Mutual Economic Assistance (CMEA), the historical facts are essentially well-known and an annotated chronology of events is not likely to generate any strikingly new insights.[1]

Another possible approach is to study the relationship of Poland to CMEA in purely economic terms. By now, the basic statistical data on the volume, value, and composition of Poland's foreign trade are available, permitting not only a detailed analysis of the changes in the country's economic relations with the other CMEA members but also supplying an underpinning for the testing of some new and fashionable hypotheses such as the "dependency" theory.[2] While one cannot ignore the economic dimension of CMEA, the exclusive concentration on this aspect of the integrative processes in Eastern Europe provides only a partial explanation of Poland's attitude and its policy toward CMEA. Moreover, the recent interest in testing the dependency theory in the regional East European context has also been largely confined to economics, with political factors often being neglected.[3]

Still another alternative is to treat integrative behavior as a dependent variable and the national political system as an independent one. This approach takes into account both the political and economic factors, thus providing a more complete set of influences determining a country's policy vis-à-vis CMEA. The difficulty with this method, however, is that we lack reliable information regarding the whole question of decisionmaking in a country such as Poland and are forced to rely largely on impressions, intuition, and informed guesses.

Moreover, by concentrating on decisionmaking at the highest level, we tend to lose sight of the other components of the political and economic systems such as the party and government bureaucracy, the managers, and other pressure groups. Finally, this approach carries with it the integrative dilemma: are Poland's relations with CMEA determined primarily by economic or by political considerations, and if both play a role, which is more important?

The approach chosen here is the so-called revised neo-functionalist approach, based on a theoretical formulation most thoroughly elaborated by Joseph Nye.[4] Briefly, the framework is not concerned with the actual initiation of an integrative scheme, but with the forces and process mechanisms that are generated by the formation of a new organization and that influence political decisionmakers to move toward closer or looser integration. The elite response to these pressures depends on the strength of these forces—some created by the establishment of new institutions and some resulting from conscious policy decisions—and the strength of several conditions that, taken together, constitute the "integrative potential" of the region or country. Some of the conditions that Nye refers to as "structural" are determined by factors outside the integration process, while the "perceptual" conditions are said to be strongly influenced by the process of integration. Neither the process mechanisms nor the conditions remain constant, but undergo changes in the course of the integration process.

Nye's list of process mechanisms and integrative conditions contains the following:

Process Mechanisms
  Functional linkage of tasks
  Rising transactions
  Deliberate linkages and coalition formation
  Elite socialization
  Regional group formation
  Ideological-identitive appeal
  Involvement of external actors

Integrative Potential
  Structural Conditions
    Symmetry or economic equality of units
    Elite value complementarity
    Existence of pluralism (modern associational groups)
    Capacity of member-states to adapt and respond
  Perceptual Conditions
    Perceived equity of distribution of benefits
    Perceived external cogency
    Low (or exportable) visible costs

The main strength of the revised neo-functionalist framework lies in stressing the behavior, perceptions, and motives of political and economic actors: "Neo-functionalism takes self-interest for granted and relies on it for delineating actor perceptions."[5] The approach focuses on "bargaining style strategies" and on the process of organizational growth or decay rather than on the volume and rate of transactions.[6] Its major weakness is the basic assumption of the existence of the modern pluralistic-industrial member-states, which appears to limit its applicability to selected regions and countries.

It has been argued that the application of the various regional integration models to the study of economic integration in Eastern Europe has been inappropriate and has not provided any fresh insights: "The theories, as originally developed at least, assume market economy conditions and the rather free movement of capital, ideas, and people. These conditions do not exist in Eastern Europe, and theories based upon the assumption of their existence—even when modified—are not likely to result in fruitful analysis."[7] The neo-functionalist model in particular was seen as unsuited since the approach assumed "the existence of processes independent of the political elites—e.g., the development of regional pressure groups and cross-national coalition formation—which are not present in Eastern Europe."[8]

In a sense, this position touches on a much broader and more controversial issue of the propriety and utility of applying Western social science models, concepts, and paradigms to the study of Communist systems. By refusing to utilize "Western" theories and methodologies in "non-Western" societies, we are depriving ourselves of a sophisticated research tool.

In the case of CMEA integration, the advantages of the neo-functionalist framework outweigh its failings. The emergence of regional interest groups and the creation of cross-national coalitions have not been particularly strong in other cases of regional integration, and they did not greatly affect the ultimate outcome.[9] Moreover, as will be shown below, they have not been entirely absent in Eastern Europe. The same holds true for the presence of pressure groups within individual polities. On the other hand, the major advantage of the neo-functionalist framework—the emphasis on "enlightened self-interest" of various national actors—makes it especially attractive as an analytical tool for the study of economic integration in Eastern Europe in the 1970s, which witnessed the continued existence of divergent national interests articulated implicitly or explicitly by different countries in the region. For that reason, using this framework for the analysis of Poland's participation in economic integration in Eastern Europe is appropriate, even if some of the variables are not highly relevant in this particular case. The neo-functionalist model should be viewed simply as a tool for making comparisons. It enables one to ask questions about the possible consequences of several countries establishing some form of close economic cooperation.[10] Although it has been argued that regional integration theories may be obsolete in the West European context,[11] the neo-functionalist model should still be a useful tool of comparison in the rest of the world.

The main purpose of this paper is to analyze the relationship between Poland and the CMEA to reach some conclusions about the country's current and future integrative behavior. If the Soviet Union were excluded from CMEA, Poland would occupy a leading position in the organization, not only as the most populous country, but also as the largest producer of several key raw materials and other commodities such as coal, steel, copper, electricity, cement, and sulphuric acid, and of agricultural commodities such as wheat, rye, barley, potatoes, sugar, and meat. The picture would be somewhat different on a per capita basis that would show, with some exceptions, Poland ranking behind East Germany and Czechoslovakia.

Politically, Poland occupies a rather unique position as the most "liberal" country in the area. Since 1956, it has managed to maintain a fairly relaxed political system. Only in the relatively brief 1967-70 period did it revert to the harsher policies of an earlier era. As if to compensate, the period since 1971 has been marked by a return to the more liberal policies of the late 1950s. Poland clearly compares favorably in this respect with the rest of CMEA countries, with the possible exception of Hungary.

Since this paper discusses elite response to various forces pressing for Poland's closer or looser integration with CMEA, it is important to raise the question of possible internal or external limitations on the Polish elite's calculation of costs and benefits of integration. The question is whether decisionmakers freely made decisions or whether they operate under constraints that were clearly defined or loosely perceived.

The presence of the Soviet Union as an external actor whose weight is heavily felt in Polish decisionmaking needs no elaboration. Yet, in the past two decades, Polish leaders such as Gomulka and Gierek considered themselves not as agents of Moscow, but as leaders of Poland and the sole interpreters of the Polish national interest. While their perception of the need for closer or looser relations with CMEA may have been faulty at any given time, it reflected a Polish rather than a Soviet national interest.[12]

Functional Linkage of Tasks

Related to the concept of "spillover," the functional linkage of tasks includes both the perceived and the engineered linkages between certain policies and events in individual member countries and in the region as a whole. In other words, a decision or an event substantially affecting the situation in a given area of activity is likely to create an imbalance that necessitates further action—intended or unintended—in another area. In some cases, the chain reaction may ultimately lead to an increase or a decline in the level of cooperation.

To illustrate, once the decision was reached in the mid-1950s to broaden and deepen CMEA collaboration, it became clear that both "objective" factors (increasingly similar national industrial profiles, large differences in the levels of economic development, and significant differences in the natural resource endowments among individual countries) and "subjective" factors (autarkic tendencies and irrationalities in planning, pricing, investment, and other policies) would make such upgrading virtually impossible without drastic changes in the domestic and foreign economic policies of member countries. Thus, the newly ordered coordination of national economic plans required, among other things, institutionalization of joint consultations via the CMEA secretariat and the setting up or revitalization of various coordinating commissions. The desired increase in intra-CMEA trade necessitated a discussion and decisions regarding a CMEA-wide division of labor, an agreement on prices to be charged in that trade, and decisions on methods of settling outstanding balances. Expanded trade and specialization in turn gave further impetus to closer coordination of production plans.

Among additional results of the agreement to raise the level of integration in the region were the gradual introduction of CMEA industrial standards and the creation of several cartel-like enterprises, such as *Intermetal* and *Interchim,* designed to implement the details of various branch specialization agreements, to exchange scientific and technical information, and to coordinate joint research and development plans.[13] The establishment of two CMEA banks—the International Bank for Economic Cooperation (1964) and the International Investment Bank (1970)—were also linked to the decreed changes in the areas of planning, trade, and specialization.

While the decision to revitalize and strengthen CMEA could be said to have raised the level of integration, it also gave rise to disintegrative tendencies. The best known example was, of course, Romania's opposition to both the establishment of a supranational planning body and to the implementation of a far-reaching plan of industrial specialization.[14]

Poland, by and large, supported the early efforts of upgrading CMEA for political rather than economic reasons. The revival of CMEA coincided roughly with the bloodless 1956 "October Revolution" in Poland which brought Gomulka back to power. Initially, Gomulka tried to maintain a certain distance from the Soviet Union and the rest of the CMEA, but he soon realized that such a course would eventually result in Poland becoming largely isolated from other East European countries, which appeared too risky in the circumstances. By late 1957, he decided to return to the fold and, for all practical purposes, became one of Moscow's closest and most trusted allies until his removal in December 1970.[15] Hence, it is not surprising that, in contrast to Romania, Poland did not generally object to the strengthening of CMEA in the 1960s. Only in a few instances did it resist the implementation of Soviet-sponsored policies, such as Khrushchev's supranational planning agency or the institutionalization of CMEA-wide division of labor. In both cases, Poland's attitude tended to be shared by other member countries, and neither venture has shown much progress.

Again, in contrast to Romania's leaders, Gheorghiu-Dej and later Ceausescu, Gomulka was never able to establish full and absolute control over the party; and it may be assumed that had he decided to maintain Poland's relative autonomy vis-à-vis CMEA and the USSR (which he intended to do for a brief period following his return to power), he could not count on the undivided support of the party elite. In those conditions, the safest course was to follow the Soviet lead.

From an economic point of view, this decision could be questioned. Poland was the first East European country that attempted to reform and liberalize its economy in the late 1950s. The short-lived effort, terminating in the early 1960s, did not favor closer cooperation with CMEA, but aimed at opening the country to the West.[16] The atmosphere for such an opening was favorable, as illustrated by the first American loan to Poland in 1957 and by the granting of the most-favored-nation (MFN) status by the US in 1960. However, Gomulka's growing political conservatism at home prevented further significant expansion of trade with the West until later in the decade.

Rising Transactions

Increase in the volume of commercial transactions among members of a regional organization may be the result of growing collaboration, which in turn may provide a stimulus for further cooperation. Statistics show that intra-CMEA trade expanded rapidly between 1949 and 1953 but, apparently, not fast enough for the post-Stalin Soviet leadership, which was interested in larger trade and closer CMEA integration. The well-known campaign, launched by Khrushchev and aimed at tighter coordination of national plans and bloc-wide division of labor, was intended to contribute signally to the growth of CMEA trade by enlarging and diversifying the product mix of traded goods.

How did Poland's trade with CMEA develop during the past two decades? According to official data, trade with CMEA between 1956 and 1970 almost quadrupled while trade with the West tripled.[17] The situation changed drastically in 1971 when, following the removal of Gomulka, the regime re-ordered priorities and embarked on a major expansion of Poland's trade with the West. Between 1970 and 1975, trade with CMEA doubled while trade with the West quadrupled. Total trade in real terms increased in the same period by 86%, with exports rising by 66% and imports more than doubling.

As a result of the major expansion of Western trade by the Soviet Union, Poland, and other East European countries, both the Soviet Union and its allies created a new dilemma. The USSR had to choose between selling more oil and other scarce raw materials to the West by reorienting at least part of what it supplied to the rest of CMEA in return for modern technology, and maintaining its status as the leader of the Warsaw Pact alliance, which demanded that there be no drastic reorientation that would adversely affect the economic welfare of its junior partners. Any major cutback in Soviet deliveries to CMEA was bound to create a serious economic and, possibly, political crisis in such countries as Czechoslovakia, East Germany, and Hungary, which were particularly dependent on Soviet raw materials. Alternatively, if these countries could succeed in obtaining supplies elsewhere, either in the Third World or, worse still, in China, that would have been interpreted as the inability of the USSR to take care of its allies, with obvious adverse political implications.

The East European countries, including Poland, also found themselves in a difficult situation. Until relatively recently, their lives were fairly simple: they exported to the West whatever high quality goods they produced while treating the Soviet Union as a ready market (some say a dumping ground) for their lower quality products exported to pay for the necessary raw materials. The sharp global increase in the price of fuels and other key materials after 1973 and the simultaneous increase in trade between the USSR and the West had a major impact on the East European foreign-trade strategy. The smaller CMEA members increasingly faced the difficult choice of importing either Soviet raw materials or Western technology, finding that Moscow was apparently becoming less and less willing to accept their second-rate products as payment for oil and other scarce materials. In the next few years, the future of intra-CMEA trade will be determined to a significant degree by the expansion or reduction of East-West trade and the role played in it by the Soviet Union which, so far at least, has showed no signs of reorienting its trade to any large extent.[18]

Deliberate Linkages and Coalition Formation

On the basis of the experiences of regional integration schemes outside Eastern Europe, it has been claimed that coalitions of entrepreneurs, bureaucrats, and politicians might engineer "package deals" designed to strengthen integrative tendencies. In contrast to the type of linkages discussed earlier, which were derived primarily from functional requirements, this tendency is based not on technical prerequisites, but on ideological and political considerations that may originate with pressure groups, political leaders, or bureaucrats.[19]

Thus far, this variable has not shown much strength in CMEA countries, including Poland, mainly because of the nature of the communist political and economic systems. Throughout most of CMEA's history, economic elites, such as planners and enterprise managers, had little contact with each other. In centrally planned economies, foreign transactions were, as a rule, conducted by the Ministry of Foreign Trade through subordinated foreign-trade enterprises, and central planners and enterprise managers in the member countries frequently tended to compete with each other in both CMEA decisionmaking bodies and in foreign markets. While inter-industry and inter-enterprise cooperation has often been advocated by various CMEA commissions and councils, little progress has been achieved. The appearance of economic reforms in the mid- and late-1960s made such collaboration even more difficult because of growing divergencies in planning and management methods among CMEA members.

Bureaucratic alliance formation was just as unlikely. Elite socialization within the CMEA secretariat and the standing commissions has not progressed very far. Growing economic nationalism, which at times resembled the notorious "beggar my neighbor" policy of the inter-war period, made cooperation, trade agreements, and coalition formation increasingly harder to reach even before the expansion of East-West trade.[20]

The increase of trade with the West strengthened the centrifugal tendencies within CMEA in several ways. Instead of cooperating, foreign-trade enterprises and individual managers and officials in different countries tended to compete sharply with each other on both the import and export side. Thus far, at least, despite impressive institutional growth, CMEA has not formalized a common import policy that would have made it easier to obtain better terms from Western exporters. Conversely, individual East European countries competed in Western markets, underbidding each other to gain a foothold for their exports or to obtain better credit terms. The growing number of industrial cooperation agreements between West and East European enterprises provided a convincing testimony: it was often easier to reach an agreement between socialist and capitalist firms than between enterprises in different CMEA countries.[21]

If there was any coalition building at all, it was usually aimed at satisfying some particularistic, rather than collective, objective. Thus, in the late 1950s, Czechoslovakia and East Germany, the two most industrially advanced countries in CMEA, strongly supported industrial specialization on a CMEA-wide basis which, if approved, would have given them a privileged and dominant position in the Council, tending to freeze the existing production profiles. A few years later, Hungary and Poland pushed for partial or total convertibility of CMEA currencies because both tended to generate surpluses on their balances of payments vis-à-vis the rest of CMEA. The raw-material producing countries of Bulgaria and Romania at times formed a coalition against the more advanced countries, demanding improved terms of trade, investment capital for the development of new sources of raw materials, and other assistance to help close the gap in development levels among the CMEA countries.

Poland, although committed in principle to closer CMEA integration, has been just as concerned over the years about protecting its own interests as any other member of the Council. On several occasions, while lip service was being paid to the need for strengthening and improving economic integration, it was also clear that whatever CMEA policies Poland pursued or advocated, its position would benefit the country more than most of the other members. A few examples illustrate this point:

1. In 1956, Poland refused to honor its obligation to supply coal to Czechoslovakia and East Germany, creating a major crisis in both countries. Poland claimed that it could not deliver the promised amounts because of domestic needs.[22]

2. In 1965, Poland made a strong push for making CMEA currencies at least partially convertible. Poland was enjoying a surplus in its trade with CMEA in 1964 and hence could have increased its hard-currency reserves.[23]

3. In 1966, Poland supported changing the methods of industrial cooperation and specialization within CMEA, emphasizing inter-branch and inter-enterprise collaboration in preference to inter-governmental cooperation. It also preferred short-term over long-term specialization agreements. Poland has a lesser developed engineering

industry than several of its partners and, in addition, it was most advanced in some of the most capital-intensive and slowest growing industrial branches, such as coal mining, shipbuilding, and railroad equipment; it did not want to be saddled permanently with declining or slow growing industries.[24]

4. In the early 1970s, at a time when other CMEA countries were contributing to the development of new sources of raw materials in the Soviet Union, Poland asked the other member countries to provide investment capital for the development of newly discovered large brown coal deposits in Central Poland. The request was turned down, contributing to pressures to approach the West for the necessary credits.[25]

Elite Socialization

By the early 1970s, CMEA had developed an impressive institutionalized network that provided increased contacts among members of the national political, bureaucratic, and economic elites.[26] The question remains, however, whether these contacts generated a greater commitment to closer cooperation and gave birth to a feeling of collective identity. As Nye suggested, elite socialization is an important potential process force, especially when it impinges on those individuals and groups, such as bureaucrats and planners, that are bound to be particularly affected by even a partial transfer of national sovereignty to a regional decisionmaking body. Its influence on the process of integration (which may be positive or negative) is notoriously hard to measure and to evaluate.[27]

The strong impression derived from the literature and from talking to participants in the work of the CMEA is that elite socialization has not made significant headway in CMEA for several reasons. The political elites have often little in common in terms of shared values and perceptions except that they all belong to the ruling communist parties. This is as true for the top leadership as for the middle echelons, and is just as valid for internal as for international comparisons. The striking policy differences between the regimes of Novotny and Dubcek, Ulbricht and Honecker, or Gomulka and Gierek on a national basis, and between Bulgaria and Poland or Romania and Czechoslovakia with respect to their political systems, can be clearly seen and documented.

Similarly, the contrast between the various communist parties has been growing. The different traditional experiences and socialization patterns, the persistent (if not growing) contrasts in political cultures, and the different operational codes and varying degrees of exposure and reaction to Western influences have made it difficult to find a common language and identity, as shown by the frequent policy conflicts at various levels of CMEA's institutional structure.[28] Since there are signs that political infighting is becoming a permanent feature of communist bureaucracies, it may be speculated that reaching consensus within CMEA even on purely technical matters may become impossible in most cases.[29]

In the late 1950s, Poland was isolated from the rest of the CMEA, and it took the country a few years before it was received as a legitimate member of the socialist commonwealth, largely because Khrushchev proclaimed Gomulka and his program acceptable.[30] Under Brezhnev, Poland and Gomulka continued to occupy an important position in CMEA, although the Soviet leader did not help Gomulka when the latter was ousted in December 1970. Since neither Gierek nor his views on CMEA have been well-known to other East European leaders, it took him a while to become legitimized within CMEA, especially since the workers' riots on the Baltic coast, which triggered the Polish succession crisis and elevated Gierek to leadership, caused considerable uneasiness among some member countries. Nevertheless, the transition period did not last long, and Gierek soon became a full-fledged member of the alliance.

It is difficult to say whether this is true today. The events of June 1976, which resulted in the Gierek regime's yielding to workers' demands and suspending the contemplated rise in food prices, may have once again put Poland in a difficult position vis-à-vis the rest of the bloc. It can be assumed that many CMEA countries feared the possible demonstration effect on their own societies, especially considering the relatively benign attitude of the Polish regime toward the rioters and other political dissenters as compared with the tough stance taken by Czechoslovakia, East Germany, and Romania. Thus, it may be speculated that, in early 1977, the Polish ruling elite found itself roughly in the same situation as 20 years earlier, and that, except for Hungary, its relations with other CMEA members were not particularly close.

There is also an interesting similarity between the Soviet attitude toward Poland in 1956 and in 1976. In both years, Poland's economic situation was, to say the least, difficult; and in each case, the Soviet Union decided to aid the country by cancelling debts and providing hard-currency loans (in 1956) or by promising additional deliveries of foodstuffs and raw materials, some on credit (in 1976). In both cases, it may be assumed that the Soviet leadership was fearful of the area-wide impact if Poland's economic difficulties exploded into a major political crisis. It decided, therefore, to provide some economic aid, not unmindful of the leverage this provided for tying the country closer to the USSR.

The absence of socialization appears equally if not more valid for the economic elites. The uneven progress in economic reforms resulted in a growing socio-economic differentiation of CMEA members, each tending to follow its own path away from the traditional centralized model. Since the presence of central planning in the late 1950s and early 1960s did not contribute signally to a speed-up in cooperation, despite a high degree of uniformity in basic economic institutions and policies, it can be argued that the dismantling of the centralized system in some countries and its replacement by a "synthesis of plan and market" have created serious obstacles to the development of a collective CMEA identity. On the contrary, the pursuit of separate national economic policies by the reforming countries, which more often than not involved greater reliance and dependence on trade with the West, meant that the economic elites began to drift apart, probably even more so than their political and bureaucratic counterparts, thus reducing their commitment to collective action. The non-reforming countries also tended to pursue different policies despite a greater similarity in their economic models.

The expansion in the scope and volume of Poland's trade with the West was not likely to contribute to the strengthening of the process of elite socialization. On the contrary, a case can be made that the opposite was more likely to be true, especially if we perceive the increase in that trade as part of the overall rapprochement between East and West. From the Polish standpoint, it meant principally the growing influence of the international environment beyond the confines of CMEA, the Warsaw Treaty Organization, or the communist camp as a whole. This was reflected in increasing contacts between Polish and Western political, economic, professional, and academic elites at international meetings, bilateral or multilateral commissions, and professional conferences.[31]

Regional Group Formation

The creation of a regional integration scheme may give rise to the formation of nongovernmental groups designed to protect the interests of their members on the regional level. These associations may in time exert pressure on national elites in favor of integration.[32] It is clear that this process mechanism, weak to begin with in all regional economic organizations, has had little applicability to CMEA and Poland. Even the relevance of the concept of interest or pressure groups in communist societies is controversial; it is clear that its relevance to communist *regional* systems is even more doubtful. It follows that the impact of this particular force on Poland's attitude toward CMEA has been insignificant.

Ideological-Identitive Appeal

Has the CMEA developed an ideology or a sense of identity, and has this made it more or less attractive to a country such as Poland? A simple answer would most likely be negative, as nothing in the history of the Council would suggest that a sense of collective identity has actually taken root. The discussion of why this is so deserves a separate treatment, but there is little if any evidence of authentic or even symbolic attachment and loyalty to the organization on the part of its members.

However, in recent years, an interesting development has added a new dimension to what appeared to be a rather simple picture. To begin with, the institutionalization of CMEA proceeded apace, and it may be hypothesized that at least certain segments of its bureaucracy began to internalize some sense of identity with CMEA. This became quite visible in the mid- and late-1960s when the Common Market countries announced the imminent introduction of new trade restrictions directed against third countries. Such a move would have meant a major reduction of East European exports to Western Europe, and Poland began urging other CMEA members to close ranks behind the Council to present a united front against the European Economic Community (EEC) and to force the latter to grant concessions to CMEA. But the facade of unity began to crumble almost as soon as it was established.[33]

More recently, the spirit of détente, reflected in the series of East-West negotiations at various levels, appeared to have spilled over into CMEA. For example, after years of official non-recognition of the EEC, there was a rather sudden suggestion by the CMEA secretariat to open discussions with the Common Market Commission with a view to possible cooperation. The new approach was reflected in the February 1975 visit of EEC representatives to Moscow where they met with their CMEA counterparts.[34] A year later, in February 1976, CMEA presented EEC with a 15-article draft agreement that called on both organizations to grant each other MFN status and on EEC to grant generalized preference status to CMEA allowing some CMEA commodities to enter the Common Market duty-free.[35] In November 1976, EEC formally rejected the CMEA draft-agreement, suggesting instead an agreement for exchange of information and offering to sign bilateral trade agreements with individual CMEA members.[36] Of the CMEA countries, only Romania attempted to negotiate separately with the Common Market Commission, but there were indications that Poland and other East European countries were also interested in establishing closer relations with EEC.[37]

Thus, there is no evidence that CMEA has succeeded in developing an identity of its own to make it more attractive to member countries such as Poland. However, recent world developments may contribute to the emergence of a CMEA cohesion and identity. Individual East European countries may become gradually convinced of the continuing if not growing importance of economic blocs. Despite some serious problems, EEC has maintained its status as a major factor in the world economic order. The OPEC cartel has dominated the world's oil market, and its example was bound to be followed by other raw materials producing countries. The most recent moves by other developing countries in a variety of international arenas testify to the growing global belief in the efficacy of collective action. One may argue that all this was bound to induce Poland and other East European countries to seek closer integration with CMEA and that the latter would become a permanent fixture on the international economic scene.[38]

Involvement of External Actors

Active involvement of external actors has been a key factor in the process of integration in various parts of the world. In the case of CMEA, the most significant actor, which, in a sense, has been both external and internal, is the Soviet Union. It not only created the Council, but it guided the Council's destiny throughout most of its existence. Today the Soviet Union exerts a major influence on Council policy. However, it is also a matter of record that Moscow's involvement in CMEA affairs ran in cycles ranging from feverish activity to almost benign neglect.

The nature of the Soviet commitment to the economic integration of Eastern Europe may be open to question. With the expansion of East-West trade, the question remains whether the USSR is presently in favor of or against enlarged economic contacts between CMEA and the West. For a long time, one of the basic assumptions underlying Western perceptions of Soviet foreign economic policy was that the USSR was strongly opposed to any substantial increase in trade between Eastern and Western Europe and the US, and that CMEA was originally formed to divert East European trade from the West to the East.

There is some evidence that this assumption was valid for only a brief period after the war. Since the late 1950s, Moscow has tolerated a gradual increase in trade between some CMEA members and the capitalist world. Poland's growing trade with the United States, especially after the granting of MFN status, Romania's opening to the West in the mid-1960s, and the rather substantial volume of transactions between East and West Germany apparently encountered little opposition. One explanation of this passive attitude may be that even before the USSR was ready to enter the world markets, it was interested in acquiring modern technology from the West—an objective it was able to achieve in part through its junior partners re-exporting it either directly or in their own exports. Thus, Poland and other East European countries can be viewed as a channel or conduit through which Western licenses, know-how, components, and products could eventually reach the Soviet Union. Today, of course, the situation is much less complex. Not only has the Soviet Union become a major trading country in Western markets, but it has encouraged the smaller CMEA countries to expand trade with the non-Communist world, especially with raw-materials producing countries, thus reducing its own obligation to supply the scarce materials to its East European allies.

There is no doubt that Poland and most of the other CMEA members considered the Soviet connection a profitable one. While Poland was comparatively well endowed with natural resources, it was still heavily dependent on the USSR for the supply of key raw materials, such as iron ore and oil. At the same time, for many years the Soviet Union provided a useful market for some low quality Polish producer and consumer goods that helped to pay for the imports.

One may go even further and speculate that if over the years Poland has voiced support for CMEA, it was not so much because it was particularly enamored of the Council as an integrative mechanism, but because in practical terms it was a convenient instrument for ensuring a steady supply of Soviet material for Polish industry and a market for Polish products. Poland has been one of the strongest supporters of CMEA joint investment projects on Soviet territory that aimed at developing new sources of raw materials for export to CMEA to reassure the Soviet leaders of Poland's loyalty to Moscow at a time when the Gierek regime has embarked on a major expansion of trade with the West.[39] Many of these projects, of course, also make good economic sense in today's world.

The West, initially symbolized by the economically pre-eminent US and more recently by the Common Market, was the second key external actor in the region. A standard communist justification for the formation of CMEA in 1949 has been that it was a purely defensive measure designed to offset the effects of the strategic embargo imposed on the reluctant Western Europe by the US. In other words, since the East European countries were prevented from trading with the West, they had little choice but to turn inward and trade among themselves. Thus, the East Europeans postulated a kind of inverse relationship between CMEA and embargo; and if that argument is taken at face value, it implied that the gradual lifting of Western restrictions followed by an expansion of East-West trade was bound to weaken the fabric of CMEA.

Another recent Western policy may also have had an impact on CMEA, namely the EEC decision to conduct trade negotiations with third countries, including CMEA, centrally by the Common Market Commission rather than by the individual members of the community. It may be assumed that once this takes place, the East European countries will be in a relatively weaker bargaining position, thus forcing them, however reluctantly, to emulate the Common Market by making the CMEA secretariat the negotiating agent for the Council as a whole.[40] The expansion of the European Community from six to nine members may well have further contributed to this process. One of the new members—Great Britain—has long been a major trading partner of several CMEA countries, and its entry into EEC meant that its trade with Eastern Europe would become subject to EEC regulations.

Any curtailment of East-West trade would have grave consequences for Poland, probably more serious than for any other CMEA member. Leaving aside the question of Western credits, since 1971 Poland has become heavily dependent on imports of Western technology to modernize its industrial base.

The rapid expansion of Poland's trade with the West in the period 1970-75 indicates that Poland's balance-of-trade has changed from a surplus of 307 million devisa zlotys in 1970 to a deficit of 9,771 devisa zlotys in 1975, representing by far the largest individual trade deficit in CMEA outside the Soviet Union.[41] Until now, Poland has been relatively fortunate in being able to tap a series of large credits, in part granted for political reasons; but it is clear that if imports continue to increase at the present rate with exports lagging behind, these credits might soon be exhausted.[42] Moreover, the economic difficulties at home which culminated in the workers' riots of June 1976 apparently led Western bankers to re-examine the limits of Poland's ability to carry foreign debt.

The export obligation arising from the debt burden combined with continued Western stagflation, which in recent years was responsible for the slow growth in Polish exports to the West. There is the possibility that Poland is or will soon be forced to reorient its commercial relations back toward CMEA in general and the USSR in particular.

The influence of the various process mechanisms or forces on the political decisionmakers depends, on the one hand, on the strength of these mechanisms and, on the other, on the presence or absence of integrative conditions which add up to the "integrative potential" of the region.[43] When various integrative conditions are receptive to the influences generated by the integrative forces or mechanisms, there is a good chance for political decisionmakers to respond positively to those pressures. What follows is an examination of those conditions and of their influence on Poland's attitude and policy toward CMEA.

Symmetry or Economic Equality of Units

Without entering into the argument of whether economic inequality among partners—defined either in gross terms (total GNP) or in terms of per capita indicators—is or is not conducive to regional integration, it is clear that the sheer size of the Soviet Union and the character of its economy do influence the character and structure of CMEA.[44] The resulting asymmetry within CMEA may make the latter more attractive to a country such as Poland, whose relative size presents neither an obstacle nor an incentive to closer cooperation with CMEA members. It is by now conventional wisdom that the USSR has long been viewed by Poland and the other CMEA countries as an attractive market for their inferior products. One could make a case that had there been no Soviet Union in CMEA, it would have to be invented for the purpose of absorbing low quality goods unsalable on the world markets.

Elite Value Complementarity

Did the Polish political and economic elites hold similar views and exhibit similar attitudes as the other CMEA elites over the past 20 years? During the period 1956-66, the views and attitudes of East European elites became more and more differentiated, ranging from relatively conservative (Bulgaria, Czechoslovakia, East Germany, and Romania) to relatively liberal (Hungary and Poland). The growing lack of complementarity applied equally to the political and economic elites, and it reached its peak in the mid-1960s when several countries launched a program of reforms aimed at improving the performance of their respective economic systems.

The background and progress of economic reforms in most of Eastern Europe has by now been extensively analyzed in the literature.[45] The scope and depth of the reforms corresponded by and large to the overall value systems of the ruling elites and to the state of the economy, although there were also some interesting discrepancies among them. While the reforms in Bulgaria, East Germany, Hungary, and Romania were essentially congruent with the ideological makeup and outlook of the respective national elites, this was not quite the case in Czechoslovakia and Poland. In the former, fairly radical reforms were initiated by an essentially conservative Novotny regime, while the

basically moderate Gomulka regime in Poland made little if any attempt to revamp the economy, except at the very beginning and the
end of his tenure.

There are several reasons for the differences between the two countries. The conservative Czechoslovak regime was forced to adopt the
reforms as a result of growing domestic difficulties that culminated in
the serious economic crisis of 1963-64. A declining growth rate, a pe-
rennial labor shortage, and a significant decline in Czechoslovakia's
earlier pre-eminent position in CMEA were responsible for the decision to overhaul the economic system.

In contrast, in the mid-1960s, Poland did not face such problems.
Its rate of growth, although not spectacular, was not declining. Not
being as heavily dependent on foreign trade as its neighbors to the
west and the south, Poland did not encounter major balance-of-
payments problems. It had a labor surplus and its relative standing in
CMEA remained roughly unchanged, giving little cause for concern.
Hence, it can be argued that Poland had relatively few reasons to
undertake a major economic reform.[46]

Additional factors contributed to Poland's rigid stance on the economic front. There was an increasing political conservatism on the
domestic scene, manifested in the rapidly ascending role of the party
apparat at the expense of the experts and specialists. Whereas in the
late 1950s Polish economists such as Lange, Kalecki, and Brus represented the true avant-garde of pragmatically oriented reformists, a
few years later none of them exerted major influence on economic
policy. Party bureaucrats took over, whose main purpose appeared to
be to anticipate the wishes of Gomulka, who by that time seemed to
have lost touch with reality and whose economic views have not
changed for many a decade.[47] His well-known dislike of the intel-
ligentsia was eventually transferred to the political system as a whole,
with the result that in the second half of the 1960s, the country's economic system was being increasingly run by a small clique of the *apparatchiki*. The professional economists were removed from positions
of responsibility and either totally isolated or, in some instances, for-
bidden to teach and publish. Paradoxically, while banned or criticized
in their own country, they provided the intellectual and theoretical
underpinning for the far-reaching reforms in other CMEA countries,
especially Czechoslovakia and Hungary.[48]

Toward the end of his rule, Gomulka apparently concluded that the
time was ripe for a comprehensive reform of the Polish economy.
Assisted by a newly formed Economic Council, the Polish leader decided to seek Western investment credits for the development of
selected industrial branches that were to stimulate the growth of the
entire economy. This strategy was opposed by those who represented

branches not included among the preferred sectors.

Gomulka, although in favor of the reforms, believed that they required an accumulation of large domestic reserves; in 1970, he proposed a major increase in retail prices in order to generate such reserves. Despite the opposition of the Economic Council, Gomulka succeeded in having his way.[49] Poland entered the 1970s with the traditional planning apparatus largely intact, with emphasis on investment rather than consumption, refusing to expand its trade with the West.[50]

In the latter arena, the difference between Poland and the rest of CMEA reached its deepest point. Expansion of foreign trade, especially with the West, has been one of the most important albeit controversial features of economic reforms in Czechoslovakia and Hungary.[51] In fact, it was sometimes difficult to say which came first—increased trade with the capitalist world or economic liberalization at home. Whichever it was, both policies tended to reinforce each other: successful reforms stimulated larger trade whereas profitable trade with the West encouraged further reforms.

Even politically conservative countries such as Bulgaria, East Germany, and Romania, which pursued relatively modest reforms, tended to emphasize the growing importance of trade with the West, apparently confident in their ability to resist the political effects of closer economic contacts with the capitalist camp. Throughout most of the 1960s, Poland appeared alone in its determination not only largely to retain the status quo in the domestic economy, but also in its foreign economic relations. It was not until Gomulka's replacement by Gierek that the country's attitude toward trade with the West began to resemble that of other CMEA members.

The radical turnabout in Poland's foreign-trade strategy was accompanied by a change in its attitude toward CMEA. In this sense, the Gierek regime appeared to follow its predecessor in doubting CMEA's ability to aid Poland's economic development. The rapid expansion of trade with the West coupled with Poland's success in obtaining Western credits made CMEA less important and attractive as a source of investment goods and credits. The main attraction of the CMEA was its role as supplier of raw materials and market for manufactures.

The presence or absence of elite value complementarity, especially with regard to economic issues, has been one of the major factors responsible for different attitudes of East European elites toward CMEA. In the case of Poland, that attitude showed many changes over time, depending largely—although not exclusively—on the character and makeup of the ruling political elite at a given point in time.

Modern Associational Groups

According to Nye, "functionally specific" interest groups played a major part in strengthening integrative tendencies in Western Europe. They also supplied scarce information to the bureaucrats engaged in creating integrative mechanisms in many less-developed countries.[52]

During the early years of CMEA's existence, it was difficult—if not impossible—to talk seriously about pluralistic tendencies within individual member countries. Even today this characterization of East European societies is controversial.[53] However, in the early 1960s some professional and expert groups began to emerge in some of the countries, and they started to participate in the discussions and debates focused on the problem of economic and other reforms.[54]

As discussed above, the progressive bureaucratization of Poland's political, economic, and social elites throughout most of Gomulka's rule prevented the spontaneous emergence of vocal interest groups. In fact, professionalism and expertise were officially frowned on, and entry to positions of political and economic power was reserved either for trusted bureaucrats or for a group of sycophants who owed their careers to paying homage to the increasingly isolated and reactionary leader.

Initially, it appeared as if Gierek learned the lesson of Gomulka's demise; and during the first two or three years of his rule, a major effort was made to bring the experts back and to involve them in economic policymaking. The renewed emphasis on efficient and rational economic management, the stress put on education and expertise, and the general feeling of optimism gave rise to the gradual emergence and strengthening of some professional groups that hoped to play an increasingly active role in the running of the economy. But the euphoria did not last long, and a certain slowing down of the growth rate provided an excuse for the *apparatchiki* to stage a counterattack against the professionals. It became apparent that the network of formal and informal groupings was quite fragile, and the bureaucracy once again triumphed. Ironically, having gained the upper hand, the bureaucrats proceeded to commit the same errors as their predecessors by ordering a sharp increase in food prices in June 1976. Workers' riots followed. Although Gierek survived, the foundations of his regime were badly shaken and remain so to this day.

In contrast to Hungary and, to some extent, Czechoslovakia, interest groups in Poland never succeeded in becoming accepted as an important factor in political and economic decisionmaking. This was as true for professional groups as for labor unions and managers. With minor exceptions, none of these groups played a major role in policy formulation and implementation. Weakness of Polish pressure groups provides one explanation for the absence of significant economic reforms in that country and for the neglect of foreign trade during most of the 1960s.

The question of what role trade with and credits from the West should play in the economy turned out to be one of the most controversial features of East European economic reforms. The chief supporters of increased involvement favored the expansion of commercial relations for a variety of reasons: importation of modern technology, introduction of competition on the domestic market, and pressure exerted on the exporters to raise quality standards to make goods competitive on world markets. The opponents of reforms, especially the economic bureaucracy and most of the enterprise managers, disliked increased trade with the West because the planners and bureaucrats still harbored autarkic leanings; expanded trade complicated their plans by making their fulfillment dependent on the willingness of trading partners to deliver and buy the goods planned to be purchased and sold. Trade with the CMEA countries was difficult enough, but trade with the West was even more so because of the element of uncertainty in the form of fluctuating business conditions and world market prices over which the planners had no control.

The great majority of Polish managers, especially those whose task it would be to export, disliked the opening to the West for much the same reasons. They were simply not prepared to compete on foreign markets. It is not surprising, therefore, that by and large the Polish managers favored the continuation of the status quo.

Capacity of Member-States to Adapt and Respond

The capacity of member-states to adapt and respond to signals and pressures originating in the integrative process depends on two major factors: the willingness of members to act in concert with each other and their ability to do so. The former is to a large extent a matter of perception and will be discussed in the final part of this paper. The latter is largely a function of the elite's power to control the economy.

Under the traditional centralized system, East European political and economic decisionmakers exercised, at least in theory, a nearly total control of the political and economic systems. This was somewhat changed by the introduction of economic reforms, the main feature of which was decentralization and devolution of authority and responsibility. In practice, the regimes were no longer always able to coerce enterprises to adhere to a policy favored by the governments. To be sure, the latter still retained enough power to have their way, but it may be presumed that they were reluctant to use it too often lest it undermine the system of incentives on which reforms were based.[55]

The ability to adapt and respond was also affected in some CMEA countries, including Poland, by the gradual emergence of pluralistic tendencies and the resulting conflict between the "conservative" and "modern" or "progressive" groups. On the one hand, large segments of bureaucratic and managerial elite tended to oppose any change that might weaken their status and authority. On the other, various professional groups, in alliance with the younger elements of bureaucratic and entrepreneurial elites, favored greater rationalization and modernization of decisionmaking processes at all levels of society. As a result, in the last decade or so, any major decision taken by the top leadership was often hotly contested by the competing hierarchies, and the implementation of the final outcome has taken much longer. This was equally true for the final blueprint of the economic reforms as for the elite decision to support or resist closer cooperation with CMEA.

The growing problems in reaching agreement on major policy issues and on the ways and means of implementing the ultimate decisions were best illustrated by the effects of leadership succession, especially when the new leader was determined to undertake major changes in domestic and foreign policy. There is often a considerable time lag between personnel changes at the top and in the middle echelons of the political and bureaucratic elites. A reformist leader is frequently faced with a hostile middle-ranking bureaucracy whose resistance to change must eventually be broken, usually through a purge. This cannot be accomplished overnight; and in the interval, the changes and reforms can be (and often have been) delayed if not sabotaged by the *apparat*. Any decision favoring closer integration, such as giving greater authority to CMEA bureaucracy at the expense of national elites, would be hotly contested, just as any move toward greater decentralization in domestic decisionmaking would be strongly resisted by the central bureaucracy.

In October 1956, Gomulka succeeded in stacking the Politburo and the Council of Ministers with his followers, but it took him several years to purge the Central Committee and the party and government bureaucracy. It may be argued that, except for relatively brief periods, Gomulka was never able to establish total control over the party and the government, both of which were occupied with factional conflicts throughout the 1960s. This, among other reasons, explains his inability to deal with the crisis situation of December 1970.

Gierek faced a similar problem after 1970. It was relatively easy for him to purge the top echelons of the party and the government and to put experts into positions of responsibility. However, all this was done at a cost of antagonizing the ousted bureaucracy, which became a pressure group for the return to more orthodox policies. As long as the Polish economy performed satisfactorily, Gierek was able to keep the bureaucracy at bay. The impending economic crisis weakened his hand and opened the door for the return of the *apparatchiki,* who nevertheless were unable to reclaim all their previous power. Gierek found himself immobilized between two competing forces, the retreating experts and the advancing bureaucrats; and when another crisis appeared in June 1976, he could do no better than to bow to popular pressure.

It is clear that, except for some brief periods, Polish decisionmakers in the past two decades were unable to exert full control either over the polity or the economy. Thus, their capacity to adapt and respond to outside signals and stimuli was severely curtailed.

Perceived Equity of the Distribution of Benefits

The equity in the distribution of benefits is obviously a key condition governing the perception of the policymakers. It demonstrates whether their country is gaining or losing in the course of integration. What matters here is not the absolute or relative gain or loss, but whether it is perceived as such by the elites and the public.[56]

As with all other perceptual phenomena, the equality or inequality of gains derived from integration and distributed among the member countries lies in the eyes of national beholders. On the basis of my own impressions, I would argue that economic integration under CMEA auspices has been perceived by the Polish people at large and, I suspect, by sizable segments of various Polish elites, as a zero-sum game with the smaller CMEA partners, such as Poland, the losers and the Soviet Union the winner.

This attitude is likely to continue in the short run, as the memories of Stalinist exploitation of the former satellites remain vivid among some elements of East European societies. Since these memories have not yet been fully offset by the more recent Soviet subsidization of the East European imports of oil and other raw materials, CMEA continues to be popularly viewed as operating largely for the benefit of the USSR. It may take several years, possibly decades, for the new generation of East Europeans to accept the fact that the situation has changed and that CMEA has at worst benefited both the Soviet Union and its junior partners and at best favored the smaller East European countries.

Perceived External Cogency

For most of the CMEA's history, the political elites in the smaller East European countries saw the Council principally as the creation of the Soviet Union. In other words, they viewed it as a primarily political rather than as an economic integrative device benefiting the USSR which, they felt, was strong enough to coerce any recalcitrant member to tow the line. This perception was somewhat dissipated following Romania's challenge to the Soviet specialization *ukaz* in the early 1960s; and one may speculate that the East European countries no longer fully believed in strong Soviet commitment to CMEA and its willingness to use strong-arm tactics to achieve integration.

It may be assumed that the decline in the perceived external cogency contributed to the weakening of the CMEA's fabric. Initially, this might have been partly compensated by the perceived success of West European integration efforts that propelled some East European policymakers in the direction of closer cooperation, partly as a defensive measure vis-à-vis the EEC and partly in an attempt to emulate the Common Market.[57] Subsequently, the arrival of East-West détente accompanied by the partial lifting of the embargo and the availability of credits was perceived by most of the smaller East European countries as an invitation to expand economic relations with the West. Since the Soviet Union was also engaged in such trade, the Soviet policy was seen as granting an imprimatur for further expansion of trade with the West.

The arrival of détente coincided with Gierek's assumption of power in Poland. There is little doubt that the climate of East-West rapprochement made Gierek's decision to expand trade with and seek credits from the West considerably easier. While a similar decision by Ceausescu in the mid-1960s entailed the risk of antagonizing Moscow, that risk was largely absent in the Polish case. The hegemonial power in CMEA apparently no longer objected to the junior partners turning to the West. In Poland, the decision to establish closer economic relations with the West was also influenced by the fact that the CMEA, which was counted on earlier to help Poland's economic development, proved to be a major disappointment; and the prospects of its being able to supply the necessary capital and consumer goods in the near future did not appear promising.

Poland's initiative met with positive Western response. For both political and economic reasons, West Germany, France, and the US appeared only too willing to expand their trade with Poland and other East European countries and to grant extensive credits to cover the growing gap between imports and exports.[58] Altogether, Poland's indebtedness vis-à-vis the West rose from $1,158 million in 1971 to about $10,200 million at the end of 1976.[59] Still, regardless of Western receptivity, there is little doubt that the Soviet policy of "benign neglect" and the absence of external cogency to expand trade with the East most likely persuaded Gierek to seek closer relations with the capitalist world.

What about the future? Clearly, if the Soviet attitude were to change or if Polish policymakers were to sense the existence of external cogency to get once again closer to CMEA, Poland would most likely do so. However, it can be presumed that the same might happen if trade expansion with the West were to stop either as a result of a new policy imposed by the EEC or the US or because of continuing recession in the West. Poland might see the former policy in the same light as the embargo of Cold War days, and it could lead to the country's getting closer to CMEA. The latter situation has already resulted in several East European countries taking another look at their trade with the West and treating various CMEA projects more seriously than in the past.[60]

Low (or Exportable) Visible Costs

Throughout most of its history, East European integration has been fairly costly to most CMEA members, including Poland. At least during the Stalinist period, there were documented cases of Soviet exploitation of Poland, which was only partly made up by the so-called "loan forgiveness" granted by the USSR in 1956.[61] The politically motivated diversion of trade from West to East in the late 1940s and early 1950s also hurt Poland by depriving it of certain key imports, especially in the field of advanced technology. The already mentioned grandiose plan of CMEA specialization also involved major costs, at least in the short run, by forcing the various countries either to restructure their economies or to specialize in declining industries. Finally, the presence of the protected Soviet market gradually weakened the technical dynamism of East European exporters who had few incentives to upgrade the quality and modernity of their products. On the other hand, there were also some offsetting factors such as the continued Soviet willingness to supply its junior allies with substantial quantities of raw materials at prices below the world market level.

Conclusion

The preceding discussion attempted to analyze the relationship between Poland and CMEA in the period 1956-76. Specifically, an effort was made to determine whether that relationship was likely to get

TABLE 1
Poland's Integrative Potential

	Aggregate Judgment
Process mechanisms	*low-moderate*
Functional linkage of tasks	moderate-high
Rising transactions	moderate-high
Deliberate linkages and coalition formation	low
Elite socialization	low
Regional group formation	low
Ideological-identitive appeal	low-moderate
Involvement of external actors	moderate
Integrative potential	*low-moderate*
Structural conditions	*low-moderate*
Symmetry or economic equality of units	low-moderate
Elite value complementarity	low
Existence of pluralism	low-moderate
Capacity of member states to adapt and respond	moderate
Perceptual conditions	*low-moderate*
Perceived equity of benefits	low-moderate
Perceived external cogency	low-moderate
Low (or exportable) visible costs	low
Outcome of integrative process	*status quo*

closer in the future and whether the Polish economy would become more integrated with other CMEA members. The results of the investigation are summarized in table 1. The rankings attached to the various process forces and integrative conditions are derived from the foregoing discussion. They represent arbitrary and intuitive judgments which, although suspect, are not entirely devoid of plausibility. This applies especially to the predicted outcome of the integrative process which is seen, *ceteris paribus,* as the maintenance of the status quo.

Has Poland's past behavior vis-à-vis CMEA been typical of all or most East European countries? The answer is both yes and no. Poland's domestic political system appeared to be more volatile and unstable than that of its CMEA partners. In the past two decades, it went through three major internal upheavals (March 1968, December 1970, and June 1976) that resulted either in the removal or in the serious weakening of the top party leadership. Moreover, the country's relations with the West were probably closer than those of the rest of CMEA, including the Soviet Union. The performance of the economic system was generally uneven, ranging from impressive to mediocre.

These factors undoubtedly influenced Poland's attitude and policy toward CMEA, which tended to oscillate between strong support, indifference, and mild hostility, with indifference probably predominant. It may be speculated that membership in CMEA has neither benefited nor harmed the country to any large extent and that this was partly responsible for the lack of interest in closer integration, at least until the late 1970s. While both the industrially advanced countries in the region (Czechoslovakia and East Germany) and the least developed ones (Bulgaria and Romania) have derived some tangible advantages from CMEA, mostly in the early years of its existence, there is no evidence of Poland's benefiting greatly from its membership in the Council. Perhaps because of this, the Council has never been a major domestic political issue.

The political and economic developments in Poland and in the region at large neither favored nor deterred the country's getting closer to CMEA. Both the integrative forces and the integrative potential were shown to have been relatively weak, which did not augur well for any drastic positive change in Poland's attitude toward CMEA, at least in the immediate future. In the long run, however, the country's integrative behavior will be largely determined by exogenous forces in both East and West over which Poland has no control. This may well result in Poland seeking closer integration with the CMEA.

Discussion

Adam Zwass

It is the great merit of Korbonski's essay that it tests for the first time the applicability of Nye's method to analyze the relationships in CMEA. The CMEA integration group, however, is unique in its structure: one of its members possesses not only 70% of the total population and GNP of the group, but it also has enormous political influence on decisionmaking, an influence guided not by economic objectives alone. Moreover, because market-type economic relations are underdeveloped in this alliance, and prices in intra-CMEA trade are based not on internal CMEA, but on Western demand and supply conditions, there is no tool for measuring benefits or losses of commercial activities within the CMEA.

To study CMEA relationships with instruments designed for market-type integration groups is, therefore, very difficult. A methodology constitutes, however, only research direction. What is important is to establish whether the author succeeds in throwing new light on Poland's relationship with the CMEA.

Specific Comments

Korbonski stresses correctly that Poland occupies the top position after the Soviet Union in the CMEA as the most populous country and largest producer of several key raw materials and manufactured goods. The statistical data cited show the great progress achieved by Poland in its economic development during the last 15 years. However, the author's evaluation of Poland's political system as "fairly relaxed," with "harsher policies" having been implemented only in the relatively brief period of 1967-70, and his opinion that, "with the possible exception of Hungary," Poland is "by and large the most liberal country in the area" cannot be accepted without some qualification.

It is necessary to distinguish between the political system and the conditions under which political power is exercised. The system created and maintained by the Polish United Workers Party is not much more liberal than that found in several other CMEA countries. At the same time, it is beyond contention that the Polish people enjoy more liberties than the citizens of several other CMEA countries. This is, however, a consequence of the consistent resistance of the Polish people to a government based on the traditional Soviet model (as witnessed by the stand of the Polish workers in 1956 in Poznan, in 1970 on the Baltic coast, and in 1976 in Warsaw and in Radom), the resistance of the Polish peasants against collectivization, and the vocal opposition of the Church and the intellectuals against repressive excesses of the regime.

I disagree with Korbonski's explanation of why Gomulka turned conservative and back toward the Soviet Union, allegedly because Gomulka "has never been able to establish full and absolute control over the ruling party" as the Romanian leaders did, or that to maintain relative autonomy vis-à-vis CMEA and the USSR he could not count on the undivided support of the party elite. Gomulka's policies were based on his own deeply rooted conviction that CMEA cooperation was an indispensible tool in competition with capitalism. Until the end of the 1960s, this was the decisive factor in Gomulka's attitude toward the CMEA. Thus, while Korbonski implies that Gomulka's natural inclination was to be a liberal national communist leader who was forced by circumstances to turn conservative and closely ally with Russia, I contend that Gomulka's natural inclination was to be an internationally minded communist leader subservient to Russia who was forced by circumstances in 1956 to foster a liberal image.

Korbonski is right in stating that cooperation between enterprises in the CMEA has achieved little progress. But the statement, "throughout most of the CMEA history, economic elites, such as planners and enterprise managers, had little contact with each other," does not accurately reflect reality. For example, planners of the national planning boards have a steady contact with one another, through the CMEA planning bureau, the standing commissions, and innumerable working committees.

He is correct in stating that during the 1956-66 decade, "the views and attitudes of East European elites became more and more differentiated." But it is difficult to share the author's opinion "that Poland [in contrast, for example, with Czechoslovakia] had relatively few reasons to undertake a major economic reform." The low productivity rate, stagnating incomes, rising inventories and unfinished investment projects, weak incentives for the expansion of exports and overemphasis on import substitution, supply difficulties that led to the price increases in December 1970, and the rebellion on the coast were all significant reasons for a reform.

Unconvincing is the link extended between "increased trade with the capitalist world" and "economic liberalization at home," which Korbonski claims mutually reinforce each other. The intensification of trade with the West became necessary to acquire the tools of technical progress that were impossible to obtain under the conditions of the conservative steering model. Increasing trade with the West was, in this case, a substitute for an economic reform. This caused "even politically conservative countries, such as Bulgaria, East Germany, and Rumania, which pursued relatively modest reforms, . . . to emphasize the growing importance of trade with the West."

Korbonski's discussion of the existence of modern associational groups as playing a role in strengthening integrative tendencies manifests the poor adaptability of Nye's scheme to the analysis of the specific cooperation conditions in Eastern Europe. Interest groups cannot play a major role in planned economies in "strengthening integrative tendencies."

It is quite true that experts played a decreasing role during the final years of the Gomulka regime and that Gierek enlarged their influence. However, Korbonski's statement that, under Gierek, "a certain slowing down of the growth rate provided an excuse for the *apparatchiki* to stage a counterattack against the professionals" is not accurate: the growth rate in Poland during the 1971-76 period was steadily very high. For example, the increase of the official index of industrial production in 1976 was 10.7%, not untypical of growth rates in the earlier years under Gierek.

It is my view that the low capacity of the Polish decisionmakers to adapt and respond to outside signals resulted not from the fact that Gomulka, and later Gierek, were "never able to establish total control over the party and the government," but from the new situation with which they were confronted.

It was relatively easy to rule in the first years after the war, under the auspices of Stalin's authority, using drastic instruments of power. It was easier to manage the economy with the abundance of manpower, when the main problem was to satisfy the primary needs of the population. Now, the issue of quality and of technical progress is the vital problem of existence, and leaders are confronted with diversified needs of the population. Under present conditions, exercise of rule by the old methods becomes a handicap that can be removed not by a more efficient "party control," but by a comprehensive decentralization of decisionmaking.

On the perceived equity of distribution of benefits, it is true, as Korbonski observes, that the popular perception among the Polish (and other East European) people has been that the CMEA is "operating largely for the benefit of the USSR." It is also true that many Soviet citizens ascribe some of their country's difficulties to the aid the USSR extends to the People's Democracies in Eastern Europe and outside the region.

Be that as it may, it is certain that the Stalinist exploitation methods—exemplified by the Sovroms in Romania, the mixed Soviet-East German companies, and the artificially low prices of East European deliveries to the USSR—are no longer in operation. Furthermore, it is also true that the price of Soviet oil to Eastern Europe in 1976-77 was still cheaper by about one-third than world prices, even though the Soviet Union would encounter no difficulty in selling oil or other raw materials to the West while the smaller CMEA countries do not find it easy to sell their finished goods in Western markets.

But the East European perspective on these issues must also be considered. The Soviet Union supported the "just demands" of the oil countries (which, by the way, are perfect examples of "imperialist monopolies"). An enormous redistribution of world wealth followed, including very large losses for all East European countries.

The price of Soviet oil for the CMEA countries will probably reach the world level soon; it may already have done so by the time this appears in print. In the meantime, the difference is compensated— partly or fully, it is difficult to tell—by small-country participation in the financing of the large Soviet investment projects with cheap credits and manpower. These include the Orenburg pipeline, for which the smaller countries raised, via the International Investment Bank, a $600 million credit in the world financial markets in order to pay for the large-diameter pipes.

Moreover, any evaluation of the gains and losses in the complex of CMEA cooperation that would not account for the armaments problems and the price of participation in various "peace projects"—

projects quite removed from the interests of the smaller countries and representing power policy of the USSR—would offer a distorted picture. Of importance for the appreciation of the benefits and losses of cooperation within the CMEA is the realization that there is no workable alternative for the smaller countries to the present arrangements.

The Twists and Turns in Poland's Attitude Toward CMEA

Post-1956 Background

Under the leadership of Gomulka, beginning in October 1956 new paths of development were opened and welcomed enthusiastically by the population. In the first phase, social and economic policies were liberalized and Poland's accumulated debts with the Soviet Union were cancelled by the agreement of November 1956. An economic council, which proposed new ways and means of development, was established under the chairmanship of the world renowned economist Oskar Lange. An essential theme of their proposals was that enterprises should be allowed to develop their economic activities without interference by the central planners; central planning should be confined to work on long-term development concepts.

Meanwhile, the heavily impaired party machine had recovered and returned to its usual methods of administration. Gomulka, who had lost and regained power, was not willing to keep his promise to found the power of the state on self-management and parliamentary institutions more than on central party decisions. As soon as he was firmly established in power, the idea of independent decisionmaking by enterprises was abolished and the proposals thought up carefully by the economic reformers did not materialize.

Gomulka's Early Attitude Toward CMEA

In the late 1950s, Gomulka intended to revive the CMEA system established under Stalin a decade earlier. He also wanted to convince Khruschev of this idea. Gomulka saw the future for Poland in a close integration with the Eastern bloc. And his conviction grew with his successes in removing the liberals from competent positions in government. Economic integration was to form a potential both for defense and aggression in competing with the West. On November 6, 1962, Gomulka wrote in the party paper *Trybuna Ludu:* "The forms and intensity of CMEA-cooperation developed until now are inadequate for competition with capitalism." Gomulka was both the initiator and inspirer of the programmatic meetings of the CMEA-party leaders in May 1958, in June 1962, and in July 1963, which approved new principles of the international socialist division of labor, the coordination of the national economic plans, a multilateral system of payments between the CMEA-countries, and the establishment of the IBEC.

The Polish party leader not only advocated far-reaching forms of integration and cooperation within CMEA but he was also ready—more so than the other East European leaders—to subordinate national rights of sovereignty to an international executive body.

Poland's Attitude Toward the CMEA in the Early 1960s

At the end of the 1950s and at the beginning of the 1960s, when the control mechanisms of the CMEA were taking shape, Poland advocated not only an efficient CMEA executive with a strong influence on the national economies and with more emphasis on common planning, but also workable instruments of economic control (i.e., an efficient credit and settlement system, a realistic price system in intra-CMEA trade).

When preparing the agreement of October 22, 1963, concerning multilateral settlements in transferable rubles (TR) and the organization of the International Investment Bank, Poland advocated the creation of conditions for the evolution of the TR from a clearing unit to a convertible currency (CC) as a prerequisite of multilateral foreign trade. According to the Polish proposals, compulsory quotas were to be set only for raw materials and similar goods urgently needed to meet economic targets, while the exchange of other goods should be listed in aggregate amounts, thus allowing a free choice of goods within the total quotas as well as a wider range of suppliers in the whole CMEA area. The prices of these goods should be agreed upon by direct negotiations between the supplier and the consumer and be influenced by quality, fashion, and other market factors.

Poland's proposals met with stiff opposition not only from the Soviet Union, but also from Bulgaria and Romania. The agreement of October 1963, therefore, mentions only vaguely that "the Council of the IBEC will examine the possibilities of exchanging the transferable ruble into gold or convertible currencies." No progress has been achieved in this direction, however. In the first year of IBEC's operation, it was already evident that foreign trade within the Eastern bloc would remain bilateral. Only an insignificant share, 3% to 5% of total settlements, are carried out on a multilateral basis.[1]

Little progress has been achieved in the cooperation and specialization on the implementation of large projects through joint enterprises. Such a genuine jointly owned enterprise was realized only in the relatively small "Haldex" venture, a joint Hungarian-Polish enterprise created in 1959 to process coal byproducts. The second joint enterprise in the CMEA, a Polish-East German spinning mill, was created only in 1975, 16 years after the first one. The participation of the CMEA countries in the international division of labor remains unsatisfactory: the share of the CMEA countries in world trade, measured as a ratio of their share in the world export to their share in the world industrial production, diminished from 0.37 at 1950 to 0.33 at 1970. During the same period the EEC's ratio rose from 1.40 to 2.18.[2]

Gomulka's Second Attempt to Strengthen the CMEA

Faced with the collapse of the ambitious plans of the early 1960s, Gomulka tried once more to reinforce the CMEA activities in the latter part of the 1960s. At the end of 1967, the Committee for Cooperation with Foreign Countries, under the guidance of Jaroszewicz and the Polish group in the CMEA headquarters in Moscow, began to prepare new proposals. In mid-1968, the Polish Government presented to the CMEA Secretariat a lengthy memorandum which provided the impetus to the decision of the 23rd CMEA session (April 1969) to prepare the "Comprehensive Program."

The main points of the Polish memorandum were to enlarge multilateral trade (by liberalizing the exchange of industrial consumer goods), to intensify cooperation and specialization through perfecting the economic mechanisms by adjusting the prices of industrial goods traded in CMEA to the level of the world market, and to strengthen the credit system of the CMEA market by creating adequate facilities for financing joint investment projects. It was Gomulka's personal idea to create a collective CMEA currency with all monetary functions, including the function as a reserve unit, thus being able to function as a CC.

But not many of these proposals were included in the Comprehensive Program. The free exchange of goods without quantitative contingents was admitted only within a very limited scope, namely for deliveries over and above the scope of plan targets. Section seven of the Comprehensive Program mentions only vaguely the future role of the TR in world trade and omits effective measures which could make it at least partially convertible in the near future.

Gierek Between East and West

The continued role played by Jaroszewicz represents the continuity of Polish attitudes vis-à-vis the CMEA. As deputy prime minister, he represented Poland in the Executive Committee from 1962 until the departure of Gomulka in 1970. And as prime minister under Gierek, he has been the main strategist of Poland's policies in CMEA. But

Poland's attitudes toward the CMEA under Gierek have changed as a consequence of the very complicated situation he inherited and of the economic development policy he initiated. In order to survive, he had to improve the standard of living and modernize and push forward stagnating industrial growth. But in carrying out his ambitious development plans, he could rely neither on Eastern technology nor on finance.

He opened wide the borders for Western technology and credits. The eagerness with which the West was ready to finance Poland's economic upswing spurred the country's economic growth.

In the period 1971-75, GNP rose not by 38-39% as envisaged, but by 59.4%. At the same time, economic growth under Gierek has been more oriented toward heavy industry and was more investment-intensive than in the preceding period: the share of the "accumulation" (gross fixed investment and inventories) rose from 25.1% in 1970 to 35.1% in 1975 and the share of consumption diminished from 74.9% to 64.9%.[3]

The large investment projects were equipped with modern technology, imported mainly from the West (in 1975, imports from the West were 550% higher than 1970 and its share in total imports rose from 25.8% in 1970 to 49.3% in 1975).[4] The country was, however, in this short time not able to develop an export structure matching the needs of the Western markets: in 1975, exports to the West covered only 51.8% of imports, and in subsequent years the situation did not improve much.

Taking into account the 40% increase of real wages during 1971-75 and the price freeze for foodstuffs, the emphasis on heavy industry must cause an enormous discrepancy between demand and supply for consumer goods. This complicated the international situation and weakened the position Poland had in the Eastern bloc.

The rising dependence on the East must be compensated for with greater concessions to CMEA. Poland must accept the new cooperation strategy stipulated at the 29th CMEA session (June 1975), which concentrated the main investment projects of "common interest" on the territory of the Soviet Union with total costs during 1976-80 of 7.4 billion rubles (approximately $10 billion), in which the East European countries will participate with 3.4 billion rubles ($4.6 billion rubles),[5] and Poland with a credit of 500 million rubles ($675 million rubles)[6] as well as with 4,000 workers engaged in the construction of the Orenburg pipeline.

The concentration of the objects of "common interest" on Soviet territory was criticized at the 29th CMEA meeting not only by Romania, but, in somewhat milder terms, by the GDR. As can be inferred from the speech of the Polish premier, Jaroszewicz approved this policy. At the 30th meeting of CMEA in July 1976, he said: "We hold that the participation of the member-countries in the output and production of some raw materials and goods on Soviet territory is of considerable importance and are of the opinion that this truly international cooperation in which the Soviet Union plays the leading part, should continue and expand."[7]

Poland's earlier proposals for perfecting the economic instruments of cooperation, still vigorously advocated by Hungary, have not been implemented. This new policy of Poland will hardly please the Polish observers of the CMEA proceedings. It is generally known that Poland's request to engage the CMEA in the exploitation of Poland's large resources of energy, especially of its brown-coal deposits in Belchatow, was rejected.

Hence, Poland has been facing a difficult situation. Poland had to turn to American, West German, and other Western bankers for credits to start the development of the copper, coal-gassification, and other projects. At the same time, she must finance the investment of "CMEA joint projects," partially with credits borrowed through the International Investment Bank on the Western capital market.

The political and economic situation of Poland is precarious. The heavy debt has to be serviced, the supply of foodstuffs improved, and the artificially repressed inflation (price subventions on consumer goods constituted 23% of the state budget in 1975[8]) alleviated. The strengthening of Poland's position in the CMEA depends directly on solving these problems, but the outlook for this is not very promising, at least not in the near future.

Morris Bornstein

Comparing Romania and Poland: A Summary

I shall comment on the two papers by Professors Montias and Korbonski from a comparative viewpoint, discussing some important similarities and differences in their analyses of the foreign trade of Romania and Poland. This is not an easy task; the papers differ considerably in scope and method.

Montias's paper is much more narrowly focused on the level, commodity composition, and geographic direction of Romanian merchandise trade. First, it provides a detailed statistical picture of the evolution of trade levels and patterns based on official Romanian figures and Montias's estimates. Next, it presents an econometric analysis of Romania's machinery imports from the West. Montias finds that these depend on (1) Romania's exports of food and raw materials and (2) its trade deficit with industrialized capitalist market economies, which is taken as a proxy for the sum of Western credits and tourist expenditures in Romania. Finally, the paper examines possible changes in industrialization strategy which could redirect Romanian trade further from CMEA to the West.

In contrast, Korbonski's paper applies Joseph Nye's "revised neofunctionalist approach" to analyze factors affecting Poland's attitude toward East European integration in the CMEA. This framework includes seven "process mechanisms" generated by efforts at integration plus four "structural conditions" and three "perceptual conditions" that determine a country's "integrative potential." Korbonski reviews Polish experience from 1956 to 1976 in each of the 14 dimensions, examining political as well as economic aspects and trying to distinguish cause and effect. He concludes that Poland's potential for integration in CMEA is only "low-moderate" and that Poland's relationship to CMEA is not likely to change in the near future.

Although Montias and Korbonski differ substantially in subject matter, analytical framework, and research methods, a comparison of the two papers brings out a number of similarities in the foreign trade of Romania and Poland.

1. Both countries have ambitious industrialization programs calling for imports not only of machinery and equipment, but also of raw materials and semifabricates, in payment for which they export food and manufactured consumer goods.

2. To modernize their economies, both countries want to increase imports of machinery and technology from industrialized capitalist economies, but they find it difficult to pay for them by expanding their exports. The reasons for this include domestic requirements, commitments to CMEA partners upon which they remain dependent, and deficiencies of their manufactured products in regard to style, quality, packing, and service.

3. In both countries, agriculture is considered a "bottleneck" sector that fails to produce enough to meet domestic needs and to furnish adequate surpluses for export—to the world market and to the CMEA area, where processed foodstuffs are among the "hard goods" that provide a strong bargaining position in bilateral negotiations and earn payment in convertible Western currencies.

Yet, despite these common features, there are important differences between the two countries.

1. Soviet economic, political, and military influence is much greater in Poland than in Romania. Korbonski notes that the USSR has given Poland emergency aid during more than one crisis, and that Poland has supported some key Soviet initiatives in CMEA, such as joint investment projects in the USSR. In contrast, Romania has resisted proposals for closer integration in CMEA through supranational planning or comprehensive specialization agreements. It has sought to pursue an "independent" foreign (including economic) policy different from the USSR. In this respect, Montias chooses to label Romania's willingness to seek Western credits and their availability as "economic factors." But introducing a dummy variable intended to capture the effect of the intensification of Romania's links with the West under Ceausescu since 1966 significantly improves the fit of his regressions, causing him to conclude that "with a given potential for hard-currency earnings" Romania was more inclined to import machinery from the West than during the last years of the Gheorghiu-Dej regime.

2. The Romanian and Polish regimes differ markedly in the extent of their control, not only over their respective societies but over the ruling communist parties themselves. In Romania, the Ceausescu regime can follow a determined policy of limiting domestic consumption increases in order to release resources for investment and export. In

Poland, the Gierek regime's shaky position rests on a "social compact" with the workers that appears to give the latter an effective veto over significant changes in retail prices and wages. Thus, Romania is better able to pursue a strategy of industrial development involving exports of foodstuffs and manufactured consumer goods to finance imports of machinery, raw materials, and semifabricates. In turn, its greater independence from the USSR and its more secure domestic position have enabled the Romanian government to be much more innovative than the Polish government in the area of industrial cooperation arrangements with Western multinational corporations, which provide machinery and technology for production in Romania and marketing outlets in the West.

3. The (nonsocialist) less-developed countries (LDCs) of the Third World play a more important role in Romanian than in Polish foreign trade. According to official CMEA figures for 1975, LDCs accounted for 18.5% of total trade turnover (exports plus imports) of Romania, compared with only 6.5% for Poland. Although Romania's total trade turnover (with all areas) was less than half of Poland's, its exports, imports, and trade surplus with LDCs substantially exceeded Poland's.[1] However, Romania's potential for overcoming her trade and economic development problems through exchanges with LDCs is limited by the LDCs' ability to meet Romania's machinery requirements and by the inconvertibility of their currencies, which leads to bilateral settlements.

4. Although Romania has serious economic problems, they are similar in nature and degree to those of many rapidly developing countries. In contrast, Poland is much closer to the crisis stage. According to Chase Manhattan Bank calculations,[2] in 1975 the ratio of net hard-currency indebtedness (gross, or total, hard-currency indebtedness minus foreign exchange deposits in Western banks) to the value of hard-currency exports was 1.1 for Romania and 2.0 for Poland. Equally striking are more recent estimates that during 1976 Poland's gross indebtedness to the West rose 38% from $7.8 to $10.8 billion, while Romania's remained at $2.8 billion.[3] Thus, Romania is more likely than Poland to be able to meet debt service obligations without sacrificing badly needed imports or requiring refinancing of old credits.

Notes

Marer and Montias, "East European Integration"

1. The CMEA referred to, unless otherwise noted, includes only the USSR and the six East European countries of Bulgaria, Czechoslovakia, the German Democratic Republic (GDR), Hungary, Poland, and Romania although Mongolia (early 1960s), Cuba (early 1970s), and Vietnam (1978) joined the CMEA as full members. See the appendix for a discussion of CMEA membership and other types of affiliation.

2. Franklyn Holzman, "Soviet Foreign Trade Pricing and the Question of Discrimination," *Review of Economics and Statistics* (May 1962), pp. 134-47, reprinted in F. Holzman, *Foreign Trade Under Central Planning* (Cambridge, Mass.: Harvard University Press, 1974).

3. An externally erected barrier to extra-regional trade during the 1950s was the embargo imposed by the Western countries on trade with communist countries during the 1950s. See Nicolas Spulber, "East-West Trade and the Paradoxes of the Strategic Embargo," in *International Trade and Central Planning,* ed. Alan A. Brown and Egon Neuberger (Berkeley: University of California Press, 1968).

4. UN Economic Commission for Europe, "Note on the Projection of the Matrices of International Trade," *Economic Bulletin for Europe* 22:1 (1971).

5. Gerhard Fink, "Measuring Integration: A Diagnostic Scale, Applied to EEC, CMEA, and East-West Trade, 1938-1975," *Forschungsberichte,* no. 42 (Vienna: Wiener Institut fur International Wirtschaftsvergleiche, August 1977), p. 14.

6. How these and other considerations affect the level of CPE trade is elaborated in Alan A. Brown, "Towards a Theory of Centrally Planned Foreign Trade," in *International Trade and Central Planning.*

7. According to a refinement of this measure by using foreign-trade intensities as weights, a West German economist also concluded that CMEA integration tended to decline over the 1961-76 period. See Sabine Baufeldt and Franz Walter, "Once More Measuring Integration: A Diagnostic Scale Applied to EEC, CMEA, and East-West Trade," Wirtschaft 3/79 (September 1979):184-95.

8. For recent attempts to measure "trade creation" (among member countries) and "trade diversion" (away from nonmember countries) on the basis of such "gravity models," see Joseph Pelzman, "Trade Creation and Trade Diversion in the Council of Mutual Economic Assistance 1954-1970," *The American Economic Review* 67:4 (September 1977): 713-22, and Edward Hewett, "A Gravity Model of CMEA Trade," in *Quantitative and Analytical Studies in East-West Economic Relations,* ed. Josef Brada (Bloomington, Ind.: International Development Institute, 1976), pp. 1-15. Hewett's model estimates potential trade between two countries as a multiplicative function of the trade partners' GNPs and populations; the distance between them; and two sets of dummy variables, one to capture the impact on the level of trade if two countries

belong to the same economic union and another to test the proposition that CMEA countries have a lower level of trade, *ceteris paribus,* than do Western countries. Hewett found that, in 1970, a CMEA country's *total* exports were somewhere between one-tenth (USSR) and one-third (Bulgaria) of what they would be for other countries, but that the level of intra-CMEA trade was several times larger than what trade would be between a CMEA member and a nonmember country. Among the problems that make these results difficult to interpret, Hewett recognizes the drawback of using the more industrialized West European countries as a reference point for estimating hypothetical trade.

9. The comparative advantage is both "static" and "dynamic." Relative costs, and hence comparative advantage at any point in time, are affected by investments. But the prospects for lowering costs via investments are not the same for all sectors and for every commodity within a sector. According to neo-classical theory, given a fixed amount of investment funds to be allocated, the relative endowment of resources (including human capital and know-how) determines the commodities that stand the best chance of being exportable or at least of withstanding competition from foreign goods at home (in the absence of subsidies or barriers to trade). The alternative "new theory" of intra-industry trade, which is not based on these assumptions, is discussed on page 15.

10. When there is a wide gamut of goods that can be traded in A and B, which will actually be exploited by A—whether *x* or coal—and which by B—whether *y* or oil—will also be determined by the relative demands in the two countries. But, in general, resources must flow toward the industries producing the goods that have become relatively scarcer as a result of trade.

11. With respect to consumer prices, however, our impression is that substantial differences in relative prices, especially of industrial consumer goods, among the countries do persist. This provides opportunities for tourists within the bloc to engage in arbitrage. This practice is quite extensive between pairs of countries and for certain commodities, such as consumer products imported from the West.

12. Clues to subregional integration may be found if two or more CMEA countries are relatively strongly trade-dependent on each other. Calculations of standardized trade dependence within CMEA (which correct for differences among countries in the total values of trade flows and disregard country differences in the share of total trade conducted with CMEA) were made by Paul Marer, "Intra-COMECON Trade: Patterns of Standardized Trade Dependence," in *COMECON: Progress and Prospects* (Brussels: NATO Directorate of Economic Affairs, 1978). Focusing on the level of trade and disregarding changes in the trade structure (which must be analyzed to ascertain whether there is increased specialization), the main finding was that while the East European members of CMEA strongly bias their intrabloc trade toward certain partners, such as Bulgaria toward the USSR, the Soviet Union's trade is by far the least concentrated. "This may have to do with the size of the country—or with the special imperial position of the USSR which requires it to maintain a reasonably uniform degree of penetration into the economies of all of its East European client states, whereas the client states, from their perspective, have a much more diverse group of potential trading partners with which to cooperate closely or remain relatively aloof" (p. 81).

13. Romanian economist Julian Danescu points out that there has been a decline since 1960 in "excessive specialization" with CMEA by *branch* within the machine-building industry (e.g., machine tools, electro-technical equipment), but an increase in specialization by *types* of machines and subassemblies. He uses an index of specialization related to the "inequality" measure suggested here. See J. Danescu, *Optimizarea exportului de maşini şi utilaja al României în perspective anîlor 1975-1980* (Bucharest, 1973), p. 32. Recent work by Joseph Pelzman indicates that intra-industry specialization (at the three-digit CMEA trade nomenclature level) in Soviet-CMEA trade has grown from 26% in 1958 to a high of 31% in 1972. But these percentages are substantially lower than those found in intra-EC trade ("Soviet-COMECON Trade: The Question of Intra-Industry Specialization," *Weltwirtschaftliches Archiv* 114: 2: 299).

14. See, for instance, E. Ames and Y. A. Carson, "Production Bias as a Measure of

Economic Development," *Oxford Economic Papers*, no. 1 (1968), pp. 26-27.

15. Assar Lindbeck, "International Economic Integration: Comment," in *The International Allocation of Economic Activity*, ed. Bertil Ohlin, P. O. Hesselborn, P. M. Wijkman (London: The McMillan Press, 1977), pp. 218, 226.

16. Bela Balassa, "Effects of Commercial Policy on International Trade, the Location of Production, and Factor Movements," in *The International Allocation of Economic Activity*, p. 249.

17. Several empirical studies confirm that the reduction and eventual elimination of tariffs among the EC countries gave rise to intra-industry rather than inter-industry specialization. See Bela Balassa, "Trade Creation and Trade Diversion in the European Common Market: An Appraisal of the Evidence," *Manchester School* 44:2 (1974): 93-133. The point mentioned in the text can be found in Gary C. Hufbauer and John G. Chilas, "Specialization by Industrial Countries: Extent and Consequences," in *International Division of Labor*, ed. Herbert Giersch (Tubingen, 1974), p. 6. For earlier discussions of inter-industry trade, see Bela Balassa, *Trade Liberalization Among Industrial Countries* (New York, 1967) and Herbert Grubel, "The Theory of Intra-Industry Trade," in *Studies in International Economics*, ed. I. A. McDougall and R. H. Shape (Amsterdam, 1970).

18. For a recent model of intra-industry trade, see Paul Krugman, "Scale Economies, Product Differentiation, and the Pattern of Trade," (unpublished, 1978). The advantages are listed in Hufbauer and Chilas, "Specialization by Industrial Countries," p. 7. We are indebted to Paul Krugman for a discussion on the theory of intra-industry trade and bibliographical references.

19. For a more detailed discussion, see Franklyn Holzman, "Foreign Trade Behavior of Centrally Planned Economies," in *Industrialization in Two Systems: Essays in Honor of Alexander Gerschenkron*, ed. Henry Rosovsky (New York: John Wiley, 1966), pp. 237-63, reprinted in F. Holzman, *Foreign Trade Under Central Planning*, and Alan A. Brown and Egon Neuberger, "Foreign Trade of Centrally Planned Economies: An Introduction," in *International Trade and Central Planning*.

20. An excellent analysis of the history and consequences of bilateralism can be found in Géza Kozma, *Bilaterális mérlegegyensúly és külkereskedelmi hatékonyság* [Bilateral balancing and the efficiency of foreign trade] (Budapest: Közgazdasági és Jogi Könyvkiadó, 1976).

21. This analysis of partial and comprehensive reforms is based on Alan A. Brown and Paul Marer, "Foreign Trade in the East European Reforms," in *Plan and Market: Economic Reform in Eastern Europe*, ed. Morris Bornstein (New Haven: Yale University Press, 1973).

22. Neither can a valid claim be made, in our view, that calculations based on costs and prices, as conventionally used in East European discussions of foreign-trade planning, will yield better guidelines to these decisions than material balances. While material balances can identify "deficit" commodities, their output may be increased only at steeply rising, if not infinite, marginal cost. "Synthetic calculations," by contrast, implicitly assume constant costs of production.

23. Note that in the absence of direct contacts between potential consumers of *x* in the "deficit" country (A) and potential suppliers in the surplus country (B), there may be no information channel through which a producing enterprise in B can bring to the attention of its superiors that it has the capacity to produce the required demand for *y* (or some part of it). If approached by A, the superiors in B would have to be acquainted in detail with their subordinates' production capacities and be able to ascertain whether the necessary inputs can be made available for the extra production. If the search for the "surplus" happens to be more trouble than it is worth, no supply may be forthcoming, and A's demand will be frustrated.

24. Kálmán Pécsi, *A KGST termelési integrácio közgazdasági kérdései* [Economic issues of CMEA's production integration] (Budapest: Közgazdasági es Jogi Könyvkiadó, 1977), p. 318.

25. Ákos Balassa, "A gépipar szerkezete es a nemzetközi együttmüködés [The structure of machine building and international competition], *Közgazdasági Szemle* 2 (November 1964): 1277. After Hungary discontinued the production of railway freight

cars, on the basis of CMEA specialization recommendations, for years it had difficulties importing this product in adequate quantities from the countries that were to specialize in freight cars.

26. A recognition of this paradox supported the position of the architects of Hungary's comprehensive economic reforms. See Béla Csikós-Nagy, *Általános és szocialista árelmélet* [General and socialist price theory] (Budapest: Kossuth, 1968), p. 250.

27. Cited in J. M. Montias, *Economic Development in Communist Rumania* (Cambridge, Mass.: The M.I.T. Press, 1967), p. 217.

28. C. H. McMillan, "Some Thoughts on the Relationship Between Regional Integration in Eastern Europe and East-West Economic Relations," in *International Economics: Comparisons and Interdependencies,* ed. F. Levcik (Vienna: Springer-Verlag, 1978), pp. 184-85.

29. Ibid., p. 184.

30. Ibid., p. 185.

31. Ibid.

32. Martin J. Kohn, "Soviet-Eastern European Economic Relations, 1975-78," in *Soviet Economy in a Period of Transition* (Washington, D.C.: Joint Economic Committee, 1979).

33. Harry Trend, "Economic Integration and Plan Coordination Under COMECON," in *Eastern Europe's Uncertain Future,* ed. Robert R. King and James F. Brown (New York: Praeger, 1977).

34. J. Danescu, *Optimizarea exportului de maşini şi utilija,* pp. 29-32. In the early 1970s, CMEA specialization agreements on machines and equipment covered only a relatively small proportion of the total exports of these goods to CMEA partners (15% for Hungary, 19% for Czechoslovakia, 30% for Poland, 36% for the GDR, 41% for Bulgaria, and 37% for the Soviet Union), according to data in Danescu's study.

35. See Paul Marer, "Soviet Economic Policy in Eastern Europe," in *Reorientation and Commercial Relations of the Economies of Eastern Europe* (Washington, D.C.: Joint Economic Committee, 1974), and Kohn, "Soviet-East European Economic Relations."

36. The share of specialized products in the total 1974 exports of the individual CMEA countries was as follows: Bulgaria, 24.9%; GDR, 13.4%; Poland, 11.8%; Czechoslovakia, 11.5%; Hungary, 10.7% USSR, 6.1%; Romania, 5.2%. F. Levcik and J. Stankovsky, *Industrial Cooperation Between East and West* (White Plains, N.Y.: M.E. Sharpe, 1979), p. 14.

37. William F. Kolarik, "Statistical Abstract of East-West Trade Finance," in *Issues in East-West Commercial Relations* (Washington, D.C.: Joint Economic Committee, 1979), table 2.

38. See Paul Marer, "Western Multinational Corporations in Eastern Europe and CMEA Integration," in *Partners in East-West Economic Relations: The Determinants of Choice* (New York: Pergamon Press, 1979), and McMillan, "Regional Integration in Europe."

39. Paul Marer and Joseph C. Miller, "U.S. Participation in East-West Industrial Cooperation Agreements," *Journal of International Business Studies* (Fall-Winter 1977), pp. 17-27.

40. The illustration is based on a case study undertaken collaboratively by a team organized by Indiana University and a team from the Foreign Trade Research Institute of Poland's Ministry of Foreign Trade and Shipping, conducted during 1977-79. The findings will be published in *East-West Industrial Cooperation During the 1980s: Findings of a Joint US-Polish Project,* ed. Paul Marer and E. Tabaczynski (Bloomington, Ind.: International Development Institute, forthcoming).

41. Kálmán Pécsi, *A KGST termelési integrácio közgazdasági kérdései,* p. 345.

42. See Edward Hewett, *Foreign Trade Prices in the Council for Mutual Economic Assistance* (Cambridge, England: Cambridge University Press, 1974), and Paul Marer, *Postwar Pricing and Price Patterns in Socialist Foreign Trade* (Bloomington, Ind.: International Development Research Center, 1972).

43. We exclude from consideration here Mongolia, Cuba, and Vietnam, whose indus-

trialization is still at such an early stage that the problem of ensuring balanced industrial growth in the framework of CMEA specialization agreements probably does not yet pose an issue for these countries.

44. A case in point was the CMEA-sponsored division of labor between Hungary and Bulgaria whereby Hungary was to specialize in producing television sets and Bulgaria in radios. But the Bulgarians could not produce radios up to required standards, and Hungary resumed their production. Since then an agreement has been made that each country will only produce certain types of radio sets. This agreement, however, may only have formalized the failure to specialize.

45. Ivan Berend, "The Problem of Eastern European Economic Integration in a Historical Perspective," in *Foreign Trade in a Planned Economy*, ed. Imre Vajda and Mihály Simai (Cambridge, England: Cambridge University Press, 1971), esp. pp. 11-14.

46. Friedrich Levcik, "Migration and Employment of Foreign Workers in the CMEA Countries and Their Problems," in *East European Economies Post Helsinki* (Washington, D.C.: Joint Economic Committee, 1977). Sixty to seventy thousand Bulgarians, Poles, Hungarians and Yugoslavs work in the GDR (a significant number being sent for training purposes), several thousand Poles and Hungarians cross the border daily to find employment in Czechoslovakia, and the Soviet Union imports a few thousand workers from Eastern Europe to work on joint projects.

47. As Robert Mundell demonstrated in a classic article, exports of capital-intensive goods from a country with abundant capital to a country where labor is relatively plentiful are an effective substitute for exports of capital, when the latter for one reason or another are blocked. Robert Mundell, "International Trade and Factor Mobility," *The American Economic Review*, vol. 47 (1957).

48. William F. Kolarik, "Statistical Abstract."

49. Allen J. Lenz, "Potential 1980 and 1985 Hard Currency Debt of the USSR and Eastern Europe Under Selected Hypotheses," in *Issues in East-West Commercial Relations*.

50. An analysis of the prospects for CMEA integration in terms of centrifugal and centripetal forces can be found in Paul Marer, "Prospects for Integration in Eastern Europe: The Council for Mutual Economic Assistance," *International Organization*, 30:4 (1976), reprinted in *Political Development in Eastern Europe*, ed. Jan F. Triska and Paul M. Cocks (New York: Praeger, 1977).

51. Detailed proposals for simulated calculations on which to base efficient foreign-trade decisions can be found in Witold Trzeciakowski, *Indirect Management in a Centrally Planned Economy: System Constructions in Foreign Trade* (Amsterdam: North-Holland, 1978).

52. For more information about the evaluation of CMEA institutions, see Michael Kaser, *COMECON: Integration Problems of the Planned Economies* (London: Oxford University Press, 1967).

53. Harry Trend, "Economic Integration," p. 96.

54. "Complex Program for Further Intensification and Improvement of Co-operation and Development of Socialist Economic Integration of the COMECON Member Countries," in *Documents COMECON* (East Berlin, 1972), p. 13.

55. Marie Lavigne, "The Problem of the Multinational Socialist Enterprise," *The ACES Bulletin*, 18:1 (1975).

56. Heinrich Machowski, "International Economic Organizations within COMECON: Status, Problems, and Prospects," in *COMECON: Progress and Prospects*.

57. Ibid., pp. 194-95.

58. These and other financial issues are discussed in great detail in Jozef M. van Brabant, *East European Cooperation: The Role of Money and Finance* (New York: Praeger, 1977), and Adam Zwass, *Money, Banking and Credit in the Soviet Union and Eastern Europe* (White Plains, N.Y.: M. E. Sharpe, 1979).

Hewett, "Foreign Trade Outcomes"

1. For simplicity, the Soviet and East European countries will be referred to as "the East" or "Eastern countries."
2. This is also true in the Hungarian case. Recent wmp changes have created a massive problem for Eastern countries since, for political reasons, many of the relative price changes (particularly for oil, but also for other primary products) were absorbed by the state in order to maintain the appearance of price stability. The reforms had been intended as a mechanism to gradually bring domestic prices into line with relatively stable wmp's, and now, given the massive changes in world prices, the domestic/wmp correspondences are probably even farther away than before.
3. See Alan A. Brown, "Toward a Theory of Centrally Planned Foreign Trade," in *International Trade and Central Planning,* ed. Alan A. Brown and Egon Neuberger (Berkeley: University of California Press, 1968); Franklyn Holzman, "Foreign Trade Behavior of Centrally Planned Economies," in *Industrialization in Two Systems: Essays in Honor of Alexander Gerschenkron,* ed. H. Rosovsky (New York: John Wiley and Sons, 1968); Jozef M.P. van Brabant, *Bilateralism and Structural Bilateralism in Intra-CMEA Trade* (Rotterdam: Rotterdam University Press, 1973); and Peter J.D. Wiles, *Communist International Economics* (New York: Praeger, 1969).
4. At one point, van Brabant defined autarky as the assumption that "each CMEA [country] wishes to produce domestically a minimum proportion of the total domestic consumption of each good." Such a policy could mean either higher or lower imports than is typical of Western countries. See van Brabant, *Bilateralism and Structural Bilateralism,* p. 88.
5. Ibid., p. 78.
6. Ibid., pp. 71-72.
7. Wiles, *Communist International Economics,* p. 419.
8. Ibid., pp. 427-30.
9. While Brown ostensibly concerns himself with foreign-trade behavior in precisely the way I have defined it, most of his conclusions seem to surround the level of trade and the terms of trade, of which only the former is of concern here.
10. See, for example, Edward A. Hewett, "Prices and Resource Allocation in Intra-CMEA Trade," in *The Socialist Price Mechanism,* ed. A. Abouchar (Durham, N.C.: Duke University Press, 1977).
11. Assuming unadjusted total trade is 100, including 60 at inflated intra-CMEA prices, then adjusted trade is 88 if intra-CMEA prices are 20% above wmp's and 85 if they are 25% above wmp's.
12. van Brabant, *Bilateralism and Structural Bilateralism,* p. 77.
13. Ibid., p. 119.
14. Many authors have suggested such a proposition, either directly or indirectly, without seriously developing it as a set of hypotheses. For a brief outline of one way to approach this problem, see Edward A. Hewett, "Economic Systems and East-West Economic Relations," in *East-West Trade and Technology Transfer,* ed. Robert W. Campbell and Paul Marer (Bloomington, Ind.: International Development Research Center, 1974). See also Franklyn Holzman, "A Theory of Persistent Convertible Currency Deficits of Centrally Planned Economies" (Mimeographed, 1977).
15. van Brabant, *Bilateralism and Structural Bilateralism,* pp. 196-99, 243-49.
16. van Brabant was aware of this problem, but he did not attempt numerical corrections to his data. See ibid., p. 249.
17. Hewett, "Prices and Resource Allocation," p. 108. These two numbers are an average of the ratios 1968 CMEA foreign-trade prices/1968 wmp's and 1968 CMEA foreign-trade prices/1960-64 wmp's.
18. These are casual estimates, the only purpose being to establish orders of magnitude.
19. Although I did not calculate confidence bands for other years, the ratios of actual to predicted trade indicate that results for those years would be even more ambiguous than for 1965.
20. van Brabant, *Bilateralism and Structural Bilateralism,* pp. 73, 75.
21. Edward A. Hewett, "A Gravity Model of CMEA Trade," in *Quantitative and*

Analytical Studies in East-West Economic Relations, ed. Josef C. Brada (Bloomington, Ind.: International Development Research Center, 1976).

22. Dummy variables are a crude attempt at this, but the problem is that, for example, "central planning" is not a "yes or no" proposition.

23. Tjalling G. Koopmans and John M. Montias, "On the Description and Comparison of Economic Systems," in *Comparison of Economic Systems: Theoretical and Methodological Approaches,* ed. A. Eckstein (Berkeley: University of California Press, 1971). Much of the substance of the article reappears in John M. Montias, *The Structure of Economic Systems* (New Haven, Conn.: Yale University Press, 1976). The parts of the framework I am using are in both the article and the book, but I shall only refer to the article.

24. Koopmans and Montias, "The Comparison of Economic Systems," pp. 31-32.

25. Ibid., p. 33.

26. Ibid., pp. 33-34.

27. Hungary has such a rule informally, which occasioned a humorous (and presumably fictitious) story in *Figyelö.* The manager of a factory producing oars is bemoaning to his bookkeeper that "higher authorities" have ordered him to discontinue his exports to hard-currency markets because their forint/dollar ratio is too high. The costs are high because there are so many defective products. There are so many defective products because of poor materials and bad workmanship. The accountant's solution is simple: charge all the defective oars off against domestic production. It's only right since they are already passing some of those off on the domestic market, and then the forint/dollar ratio looks fine. Finally, this will make the cost of production for their domestic market oars so high that they can plead low profits and push through a price increase. *Figyelö,* May 11, 1977.

28. For a discussion of norms in this sense, see János Kornai, "A gazdasági viselkedés normái és a normák szerinti szabályozás [The norms of economic behavior and norm-related regulation]," *Közgazdasági szemle* 23:1 (January 1976): 1-14. Koopmans and Montias, "The Comparison of Economic Systems," give the same term a different meaning: "norms" to them are the criteria used to compare various systems' performance.

29. It seems to me that Kornai's way of describing a system through response functions and hierarchies of "real" and "control" spheres holds some promise toward "quantifying" a system. One could talk, for example, of system changes in terms of changes in response functions or changes in hierarchical relations among decisionmaking units. See János Kornai, *Anti-Equilibrium* (Amsterdam: North Holland, 1971), esp. parts I and II.

30. Nicholas Spulber, "The Role of the State in Economic Growth in Eastern Europe Since 1860," in *The State and Economic Growth,* ed. Hugh G.J. Aitkin (New York: Social Science Research Council, 1959).

31. John M. Montias, "Economic Nationalism in Eastern Europe: Forty Years of Continuity and Change," in *Eastern Europe in Transition,* ed. Kurt London (Baltimore: Johns Hopkins University Press, 1965).

32. Edward A. Hewett, *Foreign Trade Prices in the Council for Mutual Economic Relations* (Cambridge: Cambridge University Press, 1974), chapter 4.

33. For an elaboration of this point, see P.R. Lawrence and J.W. Lorsch, *Organization and Environment* (Cambridge, Mass.: Division of Research, Graduate School of Business Administration, Harvard University, 1967), and C. Perrow, *Organizational Analysis* (London: Tavistock Publications, 1970).

34. For a brief discussion of the Soviet case, see Joseph S. Berliner, "Prospects for Technological Progress," in US Congress, Joint Economic Committee, *Soviet Economy in a New Perspective* (Washington, D.C.: Government Printing Office, 1976).

35. Holzman, "Foreign Trade Behavior," pp. 142-43, and Brown, "Centrally Planned Foreign Trade," p. 68.

36. See Edward A. Hewett, "Most-Favored Nation Treatment in Trade Under Central Planning," *Slavic Review* 37:1 (March 1978): 27-30, for a more extensive discussion of these points.

37. Harry Johnson, "An Economic Theory of Protectionism, Tariff Bargaining, and

the Formation of Customs Unions," *Journal of Political Economy* 73:3 (June 1965): 256-83, and C.A. Cooper and B.F. Massell, "Towards a General Theory of Customs Unions for Developing Countries," *Journal of Political Economy* 73:4 (October 1965): 451-76.

38. Frederic L. Pryor, *Property and Industrial Organization in Communist and Capitalist Nations* (Bloomington: Indiana University Press, 1973), pp. 74-89, and Peter J.D. Wiles and Stefan Markowski, "Income Distribution Under Communism and Capitalism: Some Facts About Poland, the UK, the USA and the USSR," *Soviet Studies* 22:3 (January 1971): 345-69 and 22:4 (April 1971): 487-511.

39. Ferenc Kozma, *A két Europa gazdasági kapcsolatai és a szocialista nemzetközi együttmükodés* [The two Europe's economic relations and socialist international cooperation] (Budapest: Kossuth, 1970), has suggested that even though two countries may have quite similar resource endowments but socialist central planning rules in one and capitalist markets in the other, it may be that the socialist country will export less food and import less luxuries, choosing instead to feed all of its population well. His example is North and South Vietnam, where the North exported far less rice and imported far fewer luxuries than the South.

40. John M. Montias, "Socialist Industrialization and Trade in Machinery Products: An Analysis Based on the Experience of Bulgaria, Poland, and Rumania," in *International Trade and Central Planning*.

Pryor, "Discussion"

1. Readers interested in exploring such problems in a statistical fashion might want to know that GNP data in comparable dollars for all major countries of the world (except China) are given for 1970 by Irving B. Kravis, Alan W. Heston, and Robert Summers, "Real GDP *per Capita* for more than One Hundred Countries," *The Economic Journal* 88 (June 1978): 215-42; and Frederic L. Pryor, "Comparable G.N.P.'s *per Capita*: An Addendum," *Economic Journal* 89 (June 1979), forthcoming. Detailed and comparable trade data can be found in Paul Marer, *Soviet and East European Foreign Trade, 1946-1969* (Bloomington: Indiana University Press, 1972), the data bank on East European trade maintained by Jan Vanous, and standard international sources.

2. Frederic L. Pryor, "Discussion to Paper by Montias," in *International Trade and Central Planning,* ed. Alan A. Brown and Egon Neuberger (Berkeley: University of California Press, 1968), pp. 159-66.

Abonyi, Sylvain, and Caporaso, "International Integration Theories"

1. Werner Levi, "The Concept of Integration in the Research on Peace," *Background* 9 (August 1965): 114.

2. Ernst B. Haas, "The Study of Regional Integration: Reflections on the Joy and Anguish of Pretheorizing," in *Regional Integration: Theory and Research,* ed. Leon N. Lindberg and Stuart C. Scheingold (Cambridge, Mass.: Harvard University Press, 1971), p. 114.

3. Joseph S. Nye, *Peace in Parts* (Boston: Little, Brown, 1971), p. 59.

4. Leon N. Lindberg, "Political Integration as a Multidimensional Phenomenon Requiring Multivariate Measurement," in *Regional Integration, passim.*

5. Ernst B. Haas, *The Uniting of Europe* (Stanford, Calif.: Stanford University Press, 1958), p. 16.

6. Karl W. Deutsch, "Communications Theory and Political Integration," in *The Integration of Political Communities* ed. Philip E. Jacob and James V. Toscano (Philadelphia: J.B. Lippincott, 1964), pp. 46-74.

7. Karl Deutsch et al., *Political Community in the North Atlantic* (Princeton, N.J.: Princeton University Press, 1957), p. 5.

8. Regarding the CMEA, this has been thoroughly summarized and documented in Roger Kanet, "Integration Theory and the Study of East Europe," *International Studies Quarterly* 18 (September 1974): 379.

9. Haas, *Uniting of Europe,* p. 30; Charles C. Pentland, "Neofunctionalism," *The*

Year Book of World Affairs (1973), pp. 361, 362; and Deutsch, *Political Community*, pp. 6, 148-50.

10. Pentland, "Neofunctionalism," p. 362; and Deutsch, *Political Community*, p. 149.

11. Ernst B. Haas and Phillippe C. Schmitter, "Economics and Differential Patterns of Political Integration," in *International Political Communities: An Anthology* (Garden City, N.Y.: Doubleday, 1966), p. 264; Deutsch, *Political Community*, p. 141; idem, "Communications Theory," pp. 46-74; and idem, "Transaction Flows as Indicators of Political Cohesion," in *Integration of Political Communities*, pp. 75-97.

12. Haas, *Uniting of Europe*, pp. xxxv, xxxvi; and Deutsch, *Political Community*, pp. 137-40.

13. Haas, "Regional Integration," p. 4.

14. Haas, *Uniting of Europe*, p. 16; Haas and Schmitter, "Economics and Differential Patterns," pp. 265-66; and Deutsch, *Political Community*, pp. 129-30.

15. This "diffusion" of the Western approach has met progressively with more criticism, especially regarding development and underdevelopment. See, for example, Sidney Verba, "Some Dilemmas in Comparative Research," *World Politics* 20 (October 1967): 111-15; Henry Bernstein, *Underdevelopment and Development: The Third World Today* (Harmondsworth, England: Penguin Books, 1973), pp. 16-27; Ronald H. Chilcote and Joel C. Edelstein, eds., *Latin America: The Struggle with Dependency and Beyond* (Cambridge, Mass.: Schenkman Publishing Co., 1974), pp. 24-26; Lucien W. Pye, ed. *Political Science and Area Studies: Rivals or Partners* (Bloomington: Indiana University Press, 1975), pp. 6, 7.

16. Ernst B. Haas, "International Integration: The European and the Universal Process," in *International Political Communities*, p. 93. See also pp. 93-130 for further discussion.

17. Haas and Schmitter, "Economics and Differential Patterns, pp. 259-300.

18. Werner Feld, "The Utility of the EEC Experience for Eastern Europe," *Journal of Common Market Studies* 8 (March 1970): 236-61.

19. For example, see Olav L. Berthun and Terkel T. Nielson, "Comecon and EEC: A Comparative Study," *Res Publica* 10 (1968): 407-31; Charles F.G. Ransom, "Obstacles to the Liberalization of Relations Between EEC and Comecon," *Studies in Comparative Communism* 2 (July/October 1969): 61-78; Cal Clark, "The Foreign Trade as an Indicator of Political Integration in the Soviet Bloc," *International Studies Quarterly* 15 (September 1971): 259-95; idem, "The Study of East European Integration: Method Madness and Mundanity?" (Paper delivered at the International Studies Association Conference, St. Louis, Missouri, March 1974); and Michael P. Gehlen, "The Integrative Process in East Europe: A Theoretical Framework," *Journal of Politics* 30 (February 1972): 90-113.

20. Kanet, "Integration Theory," *passim.*

21. J.M.P. van Brabant, *Essays on Planning, Trade and Integration in Eastern Europe* (Rotterdam: Rotterdam University Press, 1974), pp. 43-63; and Michael Kaser, *Comecon: Integration Problems of the Planned Economies* (London: Oxford University Press, 1967), p. 29. For the Third World, see Tayser A. Jaber, "Relevance of Traditional Integration Theory to Less Developed Countries," *Journal of Common Market Studies* 9 (March 1971): 256; Hirashi Kitamura, "Economic Theory and the Economic Integration of Underdeveloped Regions," in *Latin American Economic Integration*, ed. Miguel Wionczek (N.Y.: Praeger Publishers, 1966), pp. 42-66; and Lynn Mytelka, "The Salience of Gains in Third World Integrative Systems," *World Politics* 25 (January 1973): 230.

22. See Mytelka, "Third World Integrative Systems," pp. 236-50; Stuart I. Fagan, *Central American Economic Integration: The Politics of Unequal Benefits*, Research Series no. 15 (Berkeley: Institute of International Studies, University of California, 1970), *passim*; and W. Andrew Axline, "Integration, Development and Dependence: The Politics of Regionalism in the Third World" (Paper presented to the Carribean Studies Association, St. Lucia, West Indies, January 1976), pp. 1-16.

23. Paul Marer, "The Political Economy of Soviet Relations with Eastern Europe," in *Testing Theories of Economic Imperialism*, ed. Steven J. Rosen and James R. Kurth (Lexington, Mass.: D.C. Heath, 1974), pp. 251-53.

24. Catherine Séranne, "Les situations d'inégalité au sein du Conseil D'Assistance Économique Mutûelle (COMECON),"*Études internationales* 2 (1971): 275.

25. Ibid., p. 275; van Brabant, *Essays on Planning,* p. 225; Marer, "Soviet Relations with Eastern Europe," p. 253.

26. Adapted from the definition of dependency offered by Theotonio Dos Santos, "The Structure of Dependence," in *Readings in U.S. Imperialism,* ed. Donald C. Hodges (Boston: Porter Sargent Publishers, 1971), p. 226.

27. For a discussion of this type of dependence, see James Caporaso, "Methodological Issues in the Measurement of Inequality Dependence and Exploitation," in *Testing Theories of Economic Imperialism,* ed. Steven J. Rosen and James R. Kurth (Lexington, Mass.: D.C. Heath, 1974), p. 91.

28. See Paul Marer, "Soviet Economic Policy in Eastern Europe," in Joint Economic Committee, *Reorientation and Commercial Relations of the Economies of Eastern Europe* (Washington, D.C.: US Government Printing Office, 1974), p. 160; Teresa Rakowska-Harmstone, "Socialist Internationalism: A New Stage," *Survey* 22 (Winter 1976): 38-54 and part 2 (Spring 1976), pp. 81-86; and F. Pindak, "Comecon's Program of Socialist Economic Integration," *Jahrbuch der wirtschaft osteuropas* 5 (1973): 435-53.

29. See James Caporaso's contribution below (p. 81).

30. Roger E. Kanet, "Integration Theory and the Study of Eastern Europe," *International Studies Quarterly* 18 (September 1974): 388.

31. See, for example, Arpad Abonyi and Ivan J. Sylvain, "Alternative Concepts for the Political Economy of CMEA Integration" (Paper presented at the Conference on Integration in Eastern Europe and East-West Trade, Bloomington, Ind., October 29-31, 1976).

32. Stanley Hoffman, "Obstinate or Obsolete? The Fate of the Nation-State and the Case of Western Europe," in *International Regionalism: Readings,* ed. Joseph F. Nye, Jr. (Boston: Little, Brown, 1968), pp. 177-230; and Frans A.M. Atting von Geusau, *Beyond the European Community: The Case of Political Unification* (Belguim: Heule Publishers, 1968).

33. Paul Marer, "Prospects for Integration in the Council for Mutual Economic Assistance (CMEA)," *International Organizations* 30 (Autumn 1976): 632.

34. Giovanni Sartori, "The Tower of Babel," in *Tower of Babel: On the Definition and Analysis of Concepts in the Social Sciences,* ed. Giovanni Sartori, Fred W. Riggs, and Henry Teune (International Studies Association, 1975), pp. 7-37.

35. Albert O. Hirschman, *National Power and the Structure of Foreign Trade* (Berkeley: University of California Press, 1945).

Wolf, "Adjustment of Centrally Planned Economies"

1. On the implications for CMEA integration, see Paul Marer, "Prospects for Integration in the Council for Mutual Economic Assistance (CMEA)," *International Organization* 30 (1976): 631-48. On the implications for East-West economic relations, see Christopher Saunders, "New Trends in the World Economy: Their Impact on East-West Relations," in *World Economy and East-West Trade,* ed. Franz Nemschak (New York: Springer, 1976), pp. 43-62; and Franz Nemschak, "The Economic Relationships Between East and West in the Light of Recent World Economic Trends" (Paper delivered at International Economic Association Conference on Economic Relations Between East and West, Dresden, June 29-July 3, 1976).

2. Franklyn D. Holzman, "Soviet Central Planning and Its Impact on Foreign Trade Behavior and Adjustment Mechanisms," and Oleg Hoeffding, "Recent Structural Changes and Balance-of-Payments Adjustments in Soviet Foreign Trade," in *International Trade and Central Planning,* ed. Alan A. Brown and E. Neuberger (Berkeley: University of California Press, 1968), pp. 280-305, 312-37.

3. Comments by Joseph S. Berliner and Gregory Grossman in *International Trade and Central Planning,* pp. 306-10, 340-46.

4. This point was stressed by Josef Brada and Mordechai Kreinin in their comments on the original version of this paper.

5. See Franklyn D. Holzman, *Foreign Trade Under Central Planning* (Cambridge, Mass.: Harvard University Press, 1974), chapters 4 and 5.

6. On the concept of the SOE, see Martin F.J. Prachowny, *Small Open Economies* (Lexington, Mass.: Lexington Books, 1975).

7. Rudiger Dornbusch, "Exchange Rates and Fiscal Policy in a Popular Model of International Trade," *American Economic Review* 65 (1975): 859-71.

8. Ibid.

9. The idea that the SOE might be subject to, say, an exogenous reduction in its exports at a given foreign currency price for exports might seem strange, considering that the SOE is assumed to be a price-taker on the world market. In a discussion of this paper, Herbert Levine made the observation, however, that SOEs such as CMEA countries may be considered for many products as "residual" suppliers to the world market; hence, they are both price *and* quantity takers.

10. Differentiate $B_T^* = P_x^* Q_x - P_m^* Q_m$ with respect to P_x^*, P_m^*, and Q_x. Define $\epsilon_x = \hat{Q}_x / \hat{P}_x$, which equals $\hat{Q}_x / \hat{P}_x^*$ because $\hat{P}_x = \hat{P}_x^* e$, where e is the fixed exchange rate. Similarly, $P_m = P_m^* e$ and $\eta_m = \hat{Q}_m / \hat{P}_m = \hat{Q}_m / \hat{P}_m^*$. Substitute ϵ_x and η_m in the expression for dB_T^* and simplify, using $d^* = V_m^* / V_x^*$ and $t^* = \hat{P}_m^* / \hat{P}_x^*$.

11. Note that t^{*-1} is not exactly the same as the percentage change in the net barter terms of trade, which would be $[d(P_x^*/P_m^*)]/(P_x^*/P_m^*)$.

12. For the classical statement of the absorption approach, see Sidney S. Alexander, "Effects of a Devaluation on a Trade Balance," *IMF Staff Papers* 2 (1952): 263-78, reprinted in *Readings in International Economics*, ed. Richard E. Caves and Harry G. Johnson (Homewood, Ill.: Richard D. Irwin, 1968), pp. 359-73.

13. George Garvy, *Money, Banking and Credit in Eastern Europe* (New York: Federal Reserve Bank of New York, 1966).

14. Harry G. Johnson, "The Monetary Approach to Balance-of-Payments Theory," *Journal of Financial and Quantitative Analysis* (March 1972), pp. 1555-72. For recent attempts to reconcile the different approaches to balance-of-payments analysis, see Harry G. Johnson, "Elasticity, Absorption, Keynesian Multiplier, Keynesian Policy, and Monetary Approaches to Devaluation Theory: A Simple Geometric Exposition," *American Economic Review* 66 (1976): 448-52; and Leland B. Yeager, *International Monetary Relations*, 2d ed. (New York: Harper and Row, 1976), chapter 9.

15. Prachowny, *Small Open Economies,* chapter 6.

16. Differentiate B_T^* with respect to e, recalling that $\epsilon_x = \hat{Q}_x / \hat{P}_x$ and $n_m = \hat{Q}_m / \hat{P}_m$. Also, $dP_x^*/de = dP_m^*/de = 0$, $dP_x/de = P_x^*$ and $dP_m/de = P_m^*$, because of small country assumptions, where $P_x = P_e^* e$ and $P_m = P_m^* e$.

17. There is actually a cross-product term when de and dP_T^* are non-negligible; thus, the condition for $dB_T^* = dP = 0$ under these circumstances is $\hat{e} = -[(dP_T^*/(P_T^* + dP_T^*)]$.

18. I am grateful to Josef Brada for some clarification on this subject.

19. For an early analysis of MFT profits and price-equalization, see Edward Ames, "The Exchange Rate in Soviet-Type Economies," *Review of Economics and Statistics* 35 (1953): 337-42. The classical analysis of price-equalization is F. Pryor, *The Communist Foreign Trade System* (Cambridge, Mass.: M.I.T. Press, 1963), pp. 101-105 and appendix F. See also P.J.D. Wiles, *Communist International Economics* (New York: Praeger, 1969), chapter 6.

20. The problems involved in attempting to estimate the size of these profits and losses (and the offsetting price-equalization subsidies and taxes) are discussed in Franklyn D. Holzman, "Some Financial Aspects of Soviet Foreign Trade," in Joint Economic Committee, *Comparisons of the United States and Soviet Economies,* part 2 (Washington, D.C.: Government Printing Office, 1959), pp. 427-43.

21. Barry L. Kostinsky and Vladimir G. Treml, *Foreign Trade Pricing in the Soviet Union: Exports and Imports in the 1966 Input-Output Table*, Foreign Economic Reports FER-no. 8 (Washington, D.C.: Department of Commerce, 1976), table 3.

22. Holzman, *Foreign Trade Under Central Planning*, p. 113, for example, seems to make unbalanced trade a condition for $\pi \neq 0$. Wiles, on the other hand, recognizes the possibility of $\pi \neq 0$ when $d^* = 1.00$ but $\beta \neq 1.00$, although his unconventional style and notation make his argument difficult to follow (Wiles, *Communist International Economics,* pp. 135-36).

23. See Pryor, *The Communist Foreign Trade System,* pp. 101-105.

24. Franklyn D. Holzman, "Review of I. Aizenberg, *Voprosy valiutuogo kursa rublia,*" *American Economic Review* 50 (1960): 481-83.

25. Holzman, *Foreign Trade Under Central Planning,* chapter 2.

26. Ibid., chapter 10.

27. Edward Ames, *Soviet Economic Processes* (Homewood, Ill.: Richard D. Irwin, 1965), pp. 211-13.

28. In an earlier version of this paper, I suggested that the MFT had both *valuta* and domestic currency deposits. I am grateful to Josef Brada for clarifying comments.

29. The importance of distinguishing between these two types of money was emphasized by Josef Brada in comments on the original manuscript.

30. This equilibrium condition can be derived by drawing up four identities: [(1) national product by expenditure; (2) national product by income, including enterprise income and turnover taxes; (3) enterprise investment; and (4) household consumption], substituting (3) and (4) into (1), setting (2) equal to (1), solving for the domestic currency trade balance (B_T), and remembering from expression [15] that $B'_T = B_T \ \pi$. I am grateful to Peter Kenen for stressing the analogy.

31. See Holzman, *Foreign Trade Under Central Planning,* chapters 4 and 5.

32. Brada emphasized this point in comments on the original manuscript.

33. Holzman, *Foreign Trade Under Central Planning,* chapter 4.

34. Ibid.

35. Hoeffding, "Recent Structural Changes."

36. Pryor, *Communist Foreign Trade System,* pp. 101-105.

37. Ames, "Exchange Rate in Soviet-Type Economies," p. 342.

38. Ibid., and Holzman, *Foreign Trade Under Central Planning,* pp. 112-13.

39. This is in contrast to the implications of the arguments in ibid.

40. That this is no easy task is demonstrated by Franklyn D. Holzman, "Soviet Inflationary Pressures, 1928-1957: Causes and Cures," *Quarterly Journal of Economics* 74 (1960): 167-88; and articles by Andrzej Brzeski and John M. Montias in *Money and Plan,* ed. Gregory Grossman (Berkeley: University of California Press, 1968).

41. In this and the following section, we assume for simplicity that any change in real trade flows will involve only consumer goods.

42. Bela Csikos-Nagy, "The New Hungarian Price System," in *Reform of the Economic Mechanism in Hungary,* ed. Istvan Friss (Budapest: Akademai Kiado, 1971), pp. 148-50.

43. Bela Csikos-Nagy, "Can the Accelerated Economic Growth Be Maintained?" *Acta Oeconomica* 12 (1974): 303.

44. Bela Csikos-Nagy, "Anti-Inflationary Policies: Debates and Experience in Hungary," in *Anti-Inflationary Policies: East and West* (Milan: CESES, 1975), p. 154.

45. Csikos-Nagy, "New Hungarian Price System," p. 153.

46. Csikos-Nagy, "Anti-Inflationary Policies," p. 152.

47. Alan A. Brown and Paul Marer, "Foreign Trade in the East European Reforms," in *Plan and Market,* ed. Morris Bornstein (New Haven: Yale University Press, 1973), pp. 153-99.

48. Ibid.

49. Zs. Esze, "The Modified System of Export Incentives for 1971-1975," *Acta Oeconomica* 8 (1972): 61-75.

50. Csikos-Nagy, "Can the Accelerated Economic Growth be Maintained?" p. 306.

51. Heinrich Machowski, "Poland," in *The New Economic Systems of Eastern Europe,* ed. Hans-Hermann Höhmann, Michael Kaser, and Karl C. Thalheim (Berkeley: University of California Press, 1975), p. 92.

52. Over short periods of time, this may be a reasonable procedure. Over a longer period or for large price changes, however, fixed weights could seriously bias overall price level calculations.

53. See, for example, Csikos-Nagy, "Can the Accelerated Economic Growth be Maintained?" pp. 306-307; and Istvan Hagelmayer, "Internal Effects of External Inflation and of the Deterioration in the Terms of Trade," *Közgazdasági Szemle,* no. 7/8 (1975), pp. 809-21, as translated for the author.

54. If the MCPE eschews direct trade controls, the authorities lose direct control over the level of the trade balance and real absorption and must, like the market economy, opt for some combination of an active exchange rate policy and monetary and fiscal policies to achieve both the internal and external balance targets.

55. Bronislaw Wojciechowski, "Comments," in *Anti-Inflationary Policies: East and West*, pp. 274-75. Wiles, in response to Wojciechowski's comments, is skeptical about whether such a policy combining centralized price controls with decentralized foreign-trade decisionmaking is feasible. See ibid., pp. 286-87.

Brada, "Discussion"

1. Franklyn D. Holzman, *Foreign Trade Under Central Planning* (Cambridge: Harvard University Press, 1974), chapters 4 and 5.

2. Ibid., esp. pp. 133-35.

3. It is assumed that the reader has sufficient knowledge of the CPE to recognize these stylized representations of the four markets and their behavior under disequilibrium. Good descriptions can be found in Franklyn D. Holzman, "Soviet Inflationary Pressures, 1929-1957: Causes and Cures," *Quarterly Journal of Economics* (May 1960), pp. 167-88, or J. Michael Montias, "Inflation and Growth: The Experience of Eastern Europe," in *Inflation and Growth in Latin America*, ed. Werner Baer and Isaac Kerstenetsky (Homewood, Ill.: Richard D. Irwin, 1964), pp. 216-50.

4. We are equating disposable income with total income. Even in the absence of direct and turnover taxes, such a procedure is questionable because households in CPEs do not receive income from rents and profits. However, a change in income may very well yield an equal change in disposable income, given the progressive nature of the bonus system. Since the model is concerned with the magnitudes of changes in total and disposable incomes rather than with absolute levels, the proposed formulation may not violate the facts unduly.

5. For the relationship between static and dynamic stability, see John R. Hicks, *Value and Capital*, 2d ed. (London: Oxford University Press, 1946), chapter 5 and pp. 335-37; and Paul A. Samuelson, "The Stability of Equilibrium: Comparative Statics and Dynamics," *Econometrica* 9 (1941): 97-120.

Brainard, "CMEA Financial System and Integration"

NOTE: Translations of articles appearing in the Joint Publication Research Services "Translations on East European Economic and Industrial Affairs" are identified by JPRS followed by the date and page number.

1. See, for example, Rezso Nyers, "The CMEA Countries on the Path of Economic Integration," *Kozgazdasagi Szemle*, no. 9 (September 1974) (JPRS, November 1, 1974, p. 9).

2. These practices are described fully in the literature. See Sandor Ausch, *Theory and Practices of CMEA Cooperation* (Budapest: Adakemiai Kiado, 1972), chapter 10. On structural bilateralism, see Jozef M. P. van Brabant, *Bilateralism and Structural Bilateralism in Intra-CMEA Trade* (Rotterdam: Rotterdam University Press, 1973).

3. Ausch, *Practices of CMEA Cooperation*.

4. For examples and analyses, see N. Mitrofanova, "Perspektivy dal'neishego sovershenstvovaniya vneshnetorgovykh tsen sotsialisticheskikh stran," *Planovae khozyaistvo*, no. 4 (1974), pp. 41-49; and Paul Marer, *Postwar Pricing and Price Patterns in Socialist Foreign Trade* (Bloomington, Ind.: International Development Research Center, 1972).

5. Nyers, "On the Path of Economic Integration," p. 11.

6. Eugeniusz Drabowski, *Rubel transferowy: -miedzynarodowa waluta krajow RWPG* (Warsaw: PWN, 1974), p. 65.

7. To estimate the real costs and returns to the national economy from foreign trade, the Soviet Union and other CMEA countries calculate "foreign trade equivalents" that measure the effective purchasing power of exports (by computing what the domestic cost of producing the imported goods obtained for exports would be) and the real costs

of imports (by calculating the domestic cost of producing the exports necessary to pay for the imports). These foreign-trade equivalents are computed for trade with each socialist country and are not aggregated across countries because they vary considerably from country to country. For a fuller discussion, see Lawrence J. Brainard, "Soviet Foreign Trade Planning," in *The Soviet Economy in a New Perspective*, ed. John P. Hardt (Washington, D.C.: Government Printing Office, 1976).

8. "[T]he *actual* value of the TR is fixed indirectly during the annual *bilateral* trade and payments negotiations with the result that it has in fact no uniform value and is not fully stable in time or at any given moment." Jozef M. P. van Brabant, "Multilateralism and the Emergence of a Capital Market in Eastern Europe," *Ost Europa wirtschaft*, no. 4 (1975), p. 275.

9. Drabowski, *Rubel transferowy*, pp. 66, 91.

10. "The collective currency [TR] is not a reserve currency, i.e., one which the CMEA countries would be interested accumulating as a reserve fund for transformation into needed goods." V.V. Kulikov, *Tovarnye otnosheniya v mirovom sotsialisticheskom khozyaistve* (Moscow: Moskovskogo Universiteta, 1972).

11. For a full discussion of the history and development of these banks, see Adam Zwass, *Monetary Cooperation Between East and West* (White Plains, N.Y.: International Arts and Sciences Press, 1975), chapter 3; and Jozef M. P. van Brabant, *East European Cooperation: The Role of Money and Finance* (New York: Praeger, 1977). Bilateral government-to-government credits are not discussed here because they are seldom associated with CMEA institutions or activities.

12. van Brabant, "Multilateralism," p. 274.

13. Ferenc Bartha, "Some Ideas on the Creation of a Multilateral Clearing System Among the Comecon Countries," *Soviet and East European Foreign Trade* 12 (Spring 1976): 22. The original article appeared in *Kulgazdasag*, no. 1 (1975).

14. Drabowski, *Rubel transferowy*, p. 26; and van Brabant, *East European Cooperation*, pp. 94-96.

15. Zwass, *Monetary Cooperation*, pp. 125, 131.

16. van Brabant, *East European Cooperation*, pp. 161-62.

17. Since credits are granted automatically, IBEC's TR crediting activity is of a technical rather than economic nature (van Brabant, "Multilateralism," p. 288). This is not true with regard to its activity in CC.

18. *The Banker* (London), June 1976, p. 679.

19. A similar estimate, 9%, is given by Marie Lavigne in "Espoirs et difficultes d'une intensification des echanges," *Le Monde Diplomatique* (September 1976), p. 9. The 10% estimate was quoted to the author by several Eastern European officials.

20. An analysis of this data is underway by J. P. van Brabant and C. Wittich of the United Nations. I rely here on data contained in an unpublished study by J. P. van Brabant, "Le rouble transferable et son role dans le commerce est-ouest" (May 1977), p. 24.

21. The largest item on the liability side of the balance sheet is TR 495.5 million in CC borrowings. See IIB 1975 Annual Report.

22. "Analysis has shown that in the functioning of this economic mechanism [IIB credits] obstacles are encountered from time to time. . . . For example, credits are not backed by goods in the necessary measure, are not able to be used opportunely, which weakens the economic interest in them." Yu. Konstantinov, "Valyutno-finansovoe sotrudnichestvo stran SEV," *Voprosy Ekonomiki*, no. 6 (1975), p. 88.

23. For a further discussion of the problems in giving real substance to the bank's capital, see van Brabant, *East European Cooperation*, pp. 203-10. The following remark of Hungary's deputy finance minister provides a further illustration: "The utilization of credits granted by IIB in transferable rubles is still difficult as the procedures to integrate such credits into the bilateral trade relationships between members have not been established yet." Imre Vincze, "Thoughts About the Promotion of the Multilateral Settlement of International Trade and the Enhancement of the Role of Common Currency within the CMEA," *Penzugyi Szemle* (June 1974), p. 64.

24. Karel Hajek, "Ve spolecnem zajmu," *Hospodarske Noviny*, no. 19 (1976), p. 11.

Other sources mention a total of 42 projects. A complete list of the projects financed is shown in van Brabant, *East European Cooperation,* pp. 234, 355-60.

25. Stefan Torma, "Rozvoj medzinarodnych investicnych uverovych vztahov v mechanizme socialistickej ekonomicky," *Finance a uver,* quarterly supplement, no. 1 (1976), p. 67. Total commitments for end-1974 are derived by subtracting new loan commitments in 1975 from total end-1975 commitments.

26. CMEA Secretariat, *Survey of CMEA Activities in 1975* (Moscow, 1976), p. 73. The first Orenburg credit was calculated by subtracting the second credit from the total reported in Hajek, "Ve spolecnym zajmu," p. 11. Financing arrangements for the Orenburg project call for all machinery, equipment, and pipe imported from the CMEA countries or the West to be financed at current interest rates (presumably the part financed by IIB). Additional bilateral government-to-government credits are provided by participating countries to the Soviet Union at 2% for 12 years after completion. These credits apparently cover the construction costs—labor, room and board, materials, etc. *Hospodarske noviny* (November 21, 1975), pp. 8-9.

27. *East-West Markets,* May 17, 1976, p. 10.

28. A $600 million syndication signed in June 1976 carried a nominal interest rate spread of 1⅜% above the London Interbank Rate (LIBOR). Additional fees, however, brought the real rate above an equivalent 1½% over LIBOR. CMEA countries were paying from 1¼% to 1½% over LIBOR at this time. IIB pays a higher rate because banks do not gain related commercial business from IIB by lending to it. Payments for goods imported from the West go through the accounts of the respective foreign trade banks rather than IIB.

29. "[IIB] is already serving effectively the realization of joint investments, primarily by supplying convertible foreign exchange for such investments." K. Botos, "Coordination of Investment Policies Within CMEA," *Kulgazdasag,* no. 12 (1974) (JPRS, January 31, 1975, p. 13).

30. On financial convertibility, see Peter Wiles, "On Purely Financial Convertibility," in *Banking, Money and Credit in Eastern Europe,* ed. Y. Laulan (Brussels: NATO Directorate of Economic Affairs, 1973), pp. 119-26. A detailed discussion of some of the issues examined here may be found in van Brabant, *East European Cooperation,* chapters 6-7.

31. For a complete analysis of CMEA noncommercial exchange rates, see van Brabant, *East European Cooperation,* chapter 6.

32. Imre Vincze, "Exchange Rates in CMEA's International Monetary System," *Figyelo,* May 26, 1976, p. 3 (JPRS, June 22, 1976, p. 6).

33. Ibid. In other words, two countries may decide to change the noncommercial rate between their currencies to a limit of 10%. Hungary and the Soviet Union have adjusted for bilateral purposes the agreed-upon rate of 14.75 forints per ruble to 16.23 forints per ruble, or 10%. Source to the State Bank of the USSR.

34. van Brabant, *East European Cooperation,* pp. 267-73.

35. Amounts CMEA tourists could exchange in the Soviet Union were approximately 30 rubles in March 1975. Michael Kaser, "IBEC and Comecon's Inflationary Gap," *International Currency Review* (March/April 1975), p. 48, table 2. The figure 300 rubles in the text on p. 49 appears to be a misprint.

36. Harriet Matejka, "Convertibility in East Europe," *Annales d'etudes internationaux,* no. 5 (1974), p. 176.

37. Vincze, "Exchange Rates" (JPRS, June 22, 1976, p. 5).

38. These rates are identical to internal shadow exchange rates to the TR used by many CMEA countries for converting TR receipts and expenditures of enterprises and foreign trading organizations into the domestic currency. Most countries also use various coefficients which translate TR prices into domestic producer prices for the purpose of fixing domestic price of imported machines. In the Soviet Union, 200 to 250 coefficients were set by the State Committee on Prices in 1967 for this purpose. For a discussion of how these are used, see Yu. Kormnov, *Spetsializatsiya i kooperatsiya proizvodstva stran SEV* (Moscow: Ekonomika, 1972), pp. 176 ff.

39. This is not as simple as it appears, since any given item might have a wide range of TR prices that could be chosen.

40. Interview material.
41. Vincze, "Exchange Rates" (JPRS, June 22, 1976, p. 5). An excellent discussion of these problems in the area of CMEA agricultural cooperation can be found in Yu. Kormnov and B. Frumkin, "Agrarno-promyshlennaya integratsiya stran-chlenov SEV," *Planovoe khozyaistvo*, no. 1 (1975), pp. 88-90.
42. "Primernye polozheniya o finansirovanii i osushestvlenii raschetov mezhduna rodnykh organizatsii zainteresovannykh stran-chlenov SEV" (Moscow: CMEA Secretariat, 1975). This material was surveyed by Yu. Konstantinov, "Finansy mezhduna rodnykh khozyaistvennykh organizatsii," *Ekonomicheskaya gazeta*, no. 40 (1975), p. 20.
43. The same holds for joint investment projects according to Vincze, "Thoughts," p. 60.
44. The international organizations operating on budgetary principles are to utilize noncommercial rates to make conversions between TR and national currencies. The major cost element in their activity is wages, and thus the need to make conversions between TR and national currencies is rather limited. There are a number of other issues associated with IEOs that have not been discussed here, namely the pricing of inputs and outputs, the legal status of IEOs, and their relation to CMEA countries' national plans. See, for example, J. Penkava, "Zdokonalovani cenove tvorby v procesu socialisticke ekonomicke integrace clenskych statu RVHP," *Finance a uver*, no. 10 (1975), pp. 649-56; V.A. Durnev, "Tvorba cen pri mezinarodni socialisticke kooperaci vyroby," *Finance a uver*, nos. 2 and 3 (1976), pp. 104-11, 175-78; Z. Knyzyak, "Elementy mezhdunarodnogo planirovaniya v natsionalnykh planakh khozyaistven-nogo razvitiya," *Planovoe khozyaistvo*, no. 8 (1975), pp. 27-29.
45. For a description of the methodology used in the Soviet Union, see V. Grinev, "Ekonomicheskaya effektivnost mezhdunarodnoi spetsializatsii i kooperirovaniya proizvodstva," *Planovoe khozyaistvo*, no. 2 (1974), pp. 82-88; and O.K. Rybakov, *Ekonomicheskaya effektivnost sotrudnichestva SSSR a socialisticheskimi stranami*, (Moscow: Mysl, 1975), chapter 5. Where mutual deliveries are unbalanced, a foreign exchange coefficient is used to convert the surplus or deficit into domestic currency in order to measure the cost or benefit to the economy. Because of the uncertainty as to what any surplus will be able to buy in goods, there are strong pressures to balance specialization trade. Kormnov, *Spetsializatsiya*, p. 63.
46. V. Grinev and V. Khromov, "Effektivnost mezhdunarodnoi spetsializatsii i kooperirovaniya proizvodstva," *Planovoe khozyaistvo*, no. 3 (1976), p. 119; and Rybakov, *Ekonomicheskaya*, p. 185.
47. Grinev and Khromov, "Effectivnost," p. 115.
48. See Mark Allen's comment for further elaboration of this point.
49. For a fuller discussion, see Franklyn D. Holzman, *Foreign Trade Under Central Planning* (Cambridge: Harvard University Press, 1974), pp. 139-63; and van Brabant, *East European Cooperation*, chapter 7, pp. 300-42.
50. For a discussion of prospects for multilateral CMEA trade, see Bartha, "Some Ideas," and van Brabant, *East European Cooperation*, pp. 302-14.
51. Bartha summarizes these proposals in "Some Ideas."
52. *East-West Markets*, April 19, 1976, p. 10.
53. See n. 20.
54. Stanislaw Raczkowski, "International Money of the Socialist Countries," *Oeconomica polona*, no. 3 (1975), p. 326; Drabowski, *Rubel transferowy*, pp. 104, 108, 123.
55. This information is derived from interviews in Warsaw and Budapest in August 1976.
56. G.G. Mazanov, *Mezhdunarodnye raschety stran-chlenov SEV* (Moscow: Iz-datelstvo Finansy, 1970), p. 108. If a scheme of partial convertibility were to be tied with the wider use of quota-free trade, as is sometimes suggested, the tightening of bilateralism would primarily focus its effects on mutual trade in "soft goods" (poorer quality goods which can be sold on Western markets only at substantial discounts). See Bartha, "Some Ideas," p. 25.
57. Hungary, for example, was able to float a DM 100 million issue in Germany by

publishing a three-page prospectus in *Handelsblatt* (August 29-30, 1975) containing detailed information on the balance-of-payments (though only with GATT members) and on international reserves. It is not clear what IIB would have to do to gain access to this market.

58. Many CMEA financial specialists who discuss possible financial reforms are careful to link them to changes in CMEA trading and pricing. See, for example, Drabowski, "Rubel transferowy," pp. 128-31; and Raczkowski, "International Money," p. 327. Raczkowski concludes: "One thing is beyond dispute, however, that without progress in the field of money, or without introduction of a more rational structure of domestic prices and exchange rates and without introduction of a real multilaterality of trade and payments among CMEA countries, no further progress in the economic integration of the socialist community can be achieved."

59. "[T]he cooperation of CMEA is not based on a monetary system but on the direct barter of commodities." Bela Csikos-Nagy, *Socialist Economic Policy* (New York: St. Martin's Press, 1973), p. 220.

60. See, for example, Yu. Shiryaev, "O tendentsiyakh ekonomicheskoi integratsii stran-chlenov SEV," *Planvoe khozyaistvo*, no. 6 (1975), pp. 34-36. For a discussion of problems associated with joint planning, see P. Litvyakov, "Sovmestnoe planirovanie: predposylki soderzhanie i printsipy," *Planovoe khozyaistvo*, no. 9 (1974), pp. 51-60.

61. "The reason for this is the fact that there is no uniform method of economic calculation of the benefits resulting from specialization and the related fact that there are no bases for making unequivocal assessments of these benefits." See J. Rutkowski, "Functions of World Price Forecasts in the Cooperation of CMEA Countries," *Gospodarka planowa*, no. 9 (1975) (JPRS, December 16, 1975, p. 2).

62. The dual nature of the impact of external pressures—for reform to give more flexibility, and for tighter centralized control—was noted by Alan A. Brown and Paul Marer, "Foreign Trade in the East European Reforms," in *Plan and Market: Economic Reforms in Eastern Europe*, ed. Morris Bornstein (New Haven, Conn.: Yale University Press, 1973), pp. 160-63, 190-91.

Holzman, "Discussion"

1. It is my view that the TR has less "moneyness" than any other financial instrument that pretends to be a currency. See Franklyn D. Holzman, "CMEA's Hard Currency Deficits and Ruble Convertibility" (Paper presented at the International Economic Association Conference on Economic Relations between Different Economic Systems, Dresden, June 29-July 3, 1976).

2. These matters are discussed in detail in Franklyn D. Holzman, *Foreign Trade Under Central Planning* (Cambridge, Mass.: Harvard University Press, 1974), pp. 225-29; and idem, "Theories of the Persistent Hard Currency Payments Pressures of Centrally Planned Economies" (Unpublished, 1976).

Allen, "Discussion"

1. Wiles discusses the possibility of "purely financial convertibility." Although this is an interesting concept, it seems more closely related to the issuing of short-term treasury bills by the country in question, rather than convertibility in the generally understood sense. See P. Wiles, "On Purely Financial Convertibility" in *Banking, Money, and Credit in Eastern Europe*, ed. Y. Laulan (Brussels, 1973).

Zwass, "Discussion"

1. S. Raczkowski, "International Money of the Socialist Countries," translation published in *Intergracja ekonomiczna krajow socjalistycznych*, ed. P. Bozyk (Warsaw: Ksiazka i Wiedza, 1974), p. 326. The participants in the September 1973 agreement were all CMEA countries except Romania, Cuba, and Mongolia.

Fallenbuchl, "Industrial Policy and Economic Integration"

1. In the late 1960s and early 1970s, two views that linked integration with economic reforms could be found in East European economic literature. The first view was that to move "from cooperation to integration," it was necessary to effect economic reforms that would increase the autonomy of individual enterprises and permit the operation of market forces. For example, J. Soldaczuk, "Integracja czynmikiem pogwsólpracy krajów RWPG" [Integration as a factor in increasing cooperation among the CMEA countries], in *Integracja ekonomiczna krajów socjalistycznych* [Economic integration among socialist countries], ed. P. Bozyk, 2d ed. (Warsaw, 1974), p. 47. For an example of Soviet criticism of the "market type of integration" and particularly of some views expressed by the Hungarian economists, see J. Belayev and L. Semionova, *Sotsialisticheskaia integratsia i mirovoe khoziaistvo* [Socialist integration and the world economy] (Moscow, 1972). The second argument was that the successful functioning of the reformed economies of the member countries required an enlarged market, which could be best provided by the acceleration of the process of integration. For example, J. Kleer, *Wzrost intensywny w krajach socjalistycznych* [An intensive pattern of growth in the socialist countries] (Warsaw, 1972), pp. 202-209.

2. This definition, modified by J.M. Montias, is close to that suggested by Z. Kamecki, "Pojęcia i typy intergracji gospodarczej" [Concepts and types of economic integration], *Ekonomista*, no. 1 (1967). For a brief statement of definitions and views on the nature of integration under the centrally planned socialist system, see Belayev and Semionova, *Socialist Integration and the World Economy*. For the author's definition, see Z. M. Fallenbuchl, "Integration economique en Europe de l'Est," *Revue d'études comparatives Est-Quest* 8:2 (1977): 7.

3. Organization for Economic Cooperation and Development, *The Aim and Instruments of Industrial Policy: A Comparative Study*, mimeographed (Paris: OECD, 1974), p. 7. These policies have been described in idem, *The Industrial Policies of 14 Member Countries* (Paris: OECD, 1971), and a series of subsequently published monographs on individual member countries.

4. OECD, *Instruments of Industry Policy*, p. 7-8.

5. B. Swann, *The Economics of the Common Market*, 3d ed. (Harmondsworth, England: Penguin, 1975), p. 195.

6. Commission of the European Communities, *Industrial Policy in the Community* (Brussels: EEC, 1970), p. 123.

7. Ibid., p. 124.

8. Ibid., p. 140.

9. Organization for Economic Cooperation and Development, *The Industrial Policy of France* (Paris: OECD, 1974), p. 124.

10. Ibid., pp. 124-25. Cf. Charles-Albert Michalet, "France," in *Big Business and the State: Changing Relations in Western Europe*, ed. R. Vernon (London: Macmillan, 1974), pp. 109, 112, 121.

11. "French Economy: Keeping Cool," *The Economist*, April 2, 1977, p. 86.

12. OECD, *The Industrial Policies of 14 Member Countries*, pp. 27-36; George H. Kuster, "Germany," in *Big Business and the State*, pp. 73-74.

13. Michalet, "France," p. 116.

14. Commission of the European Communities, *Bulletin of the European Communities*, no. 5 (1970), p. 30.

15. C. Freeman, *The Economics of Industrial Innovation* (Harmondsworth, England: Penguin, 1974), p. 127; H.G. Johnson, *Technology and Economic Interdependence* (London: Macmillan, 1975), pp. 37-38.

16. Freeman, *Economics of Industrial Innovation*, p. 138.

17. R. Vernon, "Enterprise and Government in Western Europe," in *Big Business and the State*, pp. 17-20.

18. Commission of the European Communities, *Industrial Policy in the Community*, pp. 8-9.

19. Z.M. Fallenbuchl, "The Communist Pattern of Industrialization," *Soviet Studies*, no. 4 (1970), pp. 458-84.

20. I. Nagy, *On Communism* (New York: Praeger, 1957), p. 189.

21. Z.M. Fallenbuchl, "The Commodity Composition of Intra-CMEA Trade and the Industrial Structure of the Member Countries," in NATO Directorate of Economic Affairs, *Comecon: Program and Perspectives* (Brussels: NATO, 1978), pp. 103-34.

22. J. Kleer, "Reformy gospodarcze w krajach socjalistycznych w latach 1960-ych" [Economic reforms in the socialist countries during the 1960s], *Ekonomista*, no. 1 (1973), p. 79; Z. M. Fallenbuchl, "Industrial Structure and the Intensive Pattern of Development in Poland," *Jahrbuch der wirtschaft osteuropas*, vol. 4 (1973).

23. L. Zacher, "Zewnętrzne aspekty polityki przemian strukturalnych w gospodarce" [The external aspects of structural changes in the economy], *Gospodarka planowa*, no. 12 (1969), p. 21; Z. M. Fallenbuchl, "Growth Through Trade in the Socialist Economies," in *Papers and Proceedings of the Conference on Current Problems of Socialist Economies*, ed. W.D.G. Hunter, mimeographed (Hamilton, Ontario: McMaster University, 1970).

24. P. Bozyk, *Korzyści z międzynarodowej specjalizacji* [Benefits of international specialization] (Warsaw, 1972), p. 193.

25. P. Bozyk, A. Czepurko, and S. Góra, *Prognozowanie rozwoju rynku RWPG* [On forecasting the development of the CMEA market] (Warsaw, 1972), p. 10.

26. Commission of the European Communities, *Industrial Policies in the Community*, p. 7.

27. Swann, *Economics of the Common Market*, pp. 211-12.

28. Ibid., p. 217.

29. Commission of the European Communities, "Council Resolutions of 14 January 1974 on an Outline Programme in the Field of Science and Technology," *Official Journal of the European Communities*, c 7/2 (January 29, 1974).

30. Commission of the European Communities, "Action Program on Industrial Policy," *Europe Documents*, no. 781 (January 3, 1974).

31. *Official Journal of the European Communities*, c-59 (March 13, 1975).

32. This was evident during personal interviews at the Commission of the European Communities in May 1975.

33. "Research: Fusion Confusion," *The Economist*, December 25, 1976, p. 32; and "Jet: Stalled Again," *The Economist*, April 2, 1977, p. 69.

34. M. Kaser, *Comecon: Integration Problems of the Planned Economies*, 2d ed. (London: Oxford University Press, 1967), pp. 92-129; J.M. Montias, "Background and Origins of the Rumanian Dispute with Comecon," *Soviet Studies* 16 (1964); and idem, "Obstacles to the Economic Integration of Eastern Europe," *Studies in Comparative Communism*, no. 3/4 (1969); E. Neuberger, "International Division of Labor in CMEA: Limited Regret Strategy," *American Economic Review* 54 (1964); H.W. Schaefer, *Comecon and the Politics of Integration* (New York: Praeger, 1972); Z.M. Fallenbuchl, "Eastern European Integration: Comecon," in *Reorientation and Commercial Relations of the Economies of Eastern Europe*, ed. J.P. Hardt (Washington, D.C.: JEC, 1974).

35. "Podstawowe zasady międzynarodowego socjalistycznego podziału pracy" [The principles of international socialist division of labor], in *Podstawowe dokumenty RWPG: organizacji wyspecjalizowanych* [Fundamental documents of CMEA and of specialized organizations], ed. B.W. Reutt (Warsaw, 1972), p. 71.

36. Fallenbuchl, "Eastern European Integration," pp. 89-90.

37. Z. Knyziak, "Zasada nakładów komparatywnych w rachunku ekonomicznym współpracy gospodarczej krajów socjalistycznych" [The principle of comparative costs in the economic calculations of the economic cooperation among the socialist countries], *Gospodarka planowa*, no. 3 (1970), p. 1.

38. "Efektywne przedsięwzięcia w zakresie polepszenia prac w dziedzinie specjalizacji i kooperacji produkcji, w szczególności w zakresie trybu przygotowywania, form prawnych i realizacji specjalizacji i kooperacji produkcji" [Effective measures to improve specialization and cooperation of production, particularly concerning preparation, legal forms, and realization of specialization and cooperation of production] (29th Meeting of the Executive Committee, May 15, 1967).

39. B.W. Reutt, "Problemy specjalizacji i kooperacji przemysłowej Polski z państwami RWPG" [Problems of specialization and cooperation between Poland and

the CMEA countries], *Handel zagraniczny,* no. 7 (1974), p. 284.

40. B.W. Reutt, "Formy planowych powiązań krajów RWPG" [The forms of the planned links among the CMEA countries], *Gospodarka planowa,* no. 9 (1968), p. 63.

41. Belayev and Semionova, *Socialist Integration,* p. 280.

42. J. Ptaszek, "Postępy współpracy" [The progress of cooperation], *Zycie gospodarcze,* no. 38 (1972), p. 5.

43. For detailed discussion of these negotiations and differences among the countries, see Schaefer, *The Politics of Integration.*

44. Fallenbuchl, "Eastern European Integration," pp. 96-104.

45. Reutt, "Problemy specjalizacji i kooperacji," p. 285.

46. K. Kerbin, "O koordynacji planów gospodarczych po XXX Sesji RWPG" [On coordination of economic plans after the thirtieth session of CMEA], *Handel zagraniczny,* no. 9 (1976), pp. 5-6.

47. Fallenbuchl, "Integration economique."

48. The need for a European industrial policy was supported by *Rapport sur la capacité concurrentielle de la Communeauté Européenne* (Brussels: EEC, 1971).

49. This point was stressed at the Bloomington Conference by Professor Marie Levigne.

50. See, for example, K. Olszewski, "5 lat Kompleksowego Programu Socjalistycznej Integracji" [Five years of the Comprehensive Program of Socialist Integration], *Handel zagraniczny,* no. 7 (1976), pp. 3-4; B. Diakin and A. Kupich, "Intergracyjne aspekty polityki economicznej w dziedzinie kształtowania struktur gospodarczych krajów RWPG" [The integration aspects of economic policy in the field of creating economic structures in the CMEA countries], *Gospodarka planowa,* 31, no. 5 (1976): 248-53; R. Nyers, *The CMEA Countries on the Road to Economic Integration* (Budapest: Hungarian Scientific Council for World Economy, 1975), pp. 11-15.

51. P. Marer, *Postwar Pricing and Price Patterns in Socialist Foreign Trade (1946-1971)* (Bloomington: Indiana University Press, 1972); E.A. Hewett, *Foreign Trade Prices in the Council for Mutual Economic Assistance* (London: Cambridge University Press, 1974).

52. J.M. Montias, *Economic Development in Communist Rumania* (Cambridge, Mass.: M.I.T. Press, 1967); and idem, "Socialist Industrialization and Trade in Machinery Products: An Analysis Based on the Experience of Bulgaria, Poland and Rumania," in *International Trade and Central Planning,* ed. A.A. Brown and E. Neuberger (Berkeley: University of California Press, 1968), pp. 130-59.

53. Z. M. Fallenbuchl, "Economic Developments," in *The Communist States in the Era of Détente 1971-1977,* ed. A. Bromke and D. Novak (Oakville, Ontario: Mosaic Press, 1978), pp. 245-74.

54. K. Derbin, "Rozwój kooperacji i specjalizacji produkcji pomiędzy Polską a krajami RWPG" [Expansion of cooperation and specialization in production between Poland and the CMEA countries], *Handel zagraniczny* 21:7 (1976): 5.

55. J.E.S. Hayward, "Steel," in *Big Business and the State,* p. 269.

56. Ibid., p. 270. Cf. P. Saint-Marc, *La France dans le CECA* (Paris: Colin, 1961), p. 197.

57. A. Cockerill, *The Steel Industry: International Comparisons of Industrial Structure and Performance* (London: Cambridge University Press, 1974), p. 150.

58. A. Shonfield, *Modern Capitalism* (London: Oxford University Press, 1969), pp. 255-59.

59. Hayward, "Steel," p. 257.

60. GUS, *Rocznik statystyczny przemyslu 1975* [Statistical yearbook of industry, 1975] (Warsaw, 1975), p. 396. In the CMEA countries, these figures include employment in ore mining.

61. J. Gwiaździński, *Hutnictwo żelaza i stali krajów RWPG* [Iron and steel metallurgy in the CMEA countries] (Warsaw, 1972), pp. 197-98.

62. GUS, *Rocznik statystyki międzynarowdowej 1973* [Yearbook of international statistics, 1973] (Warsaw, 1973), p. 121; and idem, *Rocznik statystyczny przemyslu 1972* [Statistical yearbook of industry, 1972] (Warsaw, 1972), pp. 472, 473.

McMillan, "Discussion"
1. John Pinder, "Comecon: An East European Common Market?" in *The People's Democracies after Prague: Soviet Hegemony, Nationalism, Regionalism*, ed. J. Lukaszewski (Bruges: Templhof, 1970).
2. Cf. Werner J. Feld, *Transnational Business Collaboration Among Common Market Countries: Its Implication for Political Integration* (New York: Praeger, 1970). Examples of inter-firm ties within the EEC are frequently provided in the *Economist*, with subsidiaries of firms outside the EEC (especially US firms) shown to play an important role in the creation of a regional web of inter-firm collaboration. See, for example, the *Economist* (London), September 13, 1975, p. 66, and August 14, 1966, pp. 66-67.
3. Coproduction agreements, for example, permit participating firms to specialize in the production of components while serving national markets for the end products from within.
4. See Marie Lavigne, *Le Comécon: Le programme du Comécon et l'intégration socialiste* (Paris: Editions Cujas, 1973), esp. section 2.6.
5. In a short discussion of inefficiency and integration (pp. 000-00), Fallenbuchl appears to equate integration with the volume of regional trade.
6. Cf. Bela Balassa, "Tariff Reductions and Trade in Manufactures among the Industrial Countries," *American Economic Review* 56 (1966): 466-73. Following Balassa's lead, Adler examined the pattern of specialization in the West European steel sector. Analyzing ten categories of steel products, he found no evidence of inter-industry specialization and a marked increase in intra-industry specialization in the ECSC over the period 1952-66. See Michael Adler, "Specialization in the European Coal and Steel Community," *Journal of Common Market Studies* 8 (1970): 175-91. As Fallenbuchl points out (p. 000), intra-branch specialization has been a conscious aim of the CMEA. In a study I made of the trade of the Soviet Union alone, I found for the period 1958-68 a lesser degree of intra-industry specialization in Soviet trade than in the trade of the EEC countries and even of the US. I also found less intra-industry specialization in Soviet trade with other CMEA countries than in total Soviet trade. See C.H. McMillan, "Soviet Specialization and Trade in Manufactures," *Soviet Studies* 24 (1973): 522-32.

Vanous, "Intra-CMEA Foreign Trade"
1. For purposes of this study, CMEA refers to the economies of Bulgaria, Czechoslovakia, East Germany, Hungary, Poland, Romania, and the USSR. This contribution is an abbreviated version of the original paper presented at the conference. A revised and substantially improved version of the model appears in Jan Vanous, "Econometric Model of World Trade of Member Countries of the Council for Mutual Economic Assistance" (Ph.D. diss., Department of Economics, Yale University, May 1979).
2. For a more detailed description of intra-CMEA price formation, see Edward A. Hewett, *Foreign Trade Prices in the Council for Mutual Economic Assistance* (London: Cambridge University Press, 1974), pp. 25-43; and Paul Marer, *Postwar Pricing and Price Patterns in Socialist Foreign Trade (1946-1971)* (Bloomington, Ind.: International Development Research Center, 1972), pp. 4-7.
3. Marer, *Postwar Pricing*, pp. 15-22.
4. Empirical evidence on this question is contained in Jan Vanous, *Project CMEA-FORTRAM Data Bank of Commodity Shares in Foreign Trade Flows of CMEA Countries, 1950-1975* (Vancouver: Project CMEA-FORTRAM, Department of Economics, University of British Columbia, November 1977), pp. 28-55.
5. This amount will be determined, with other factors, by political considerations. The USSR subsidizes Eastern Europe through merchandise trade, by selling underpriced primary goods in exchange for overpriced manufactures in order to secure the political allegiance of Eastern Europe and to acquire military security in this region. Alternatively, it can produce security by military investment at home or in Eastern Europe. The mix of the three factors of production in the USSR security production function depends on their relative cost.

6. Empirical evidence on this question is contained in Edward A. Hewett, "Prices and Resource Allocation in Intra-CMEA Trade" (Paper prepared for the conference on "The Consistency and Efficiency of the Socialist Price System," University of Toronto, March 8-9, 1974), pp. 23-39; and Marer, *Postwar Pricing*, pp. 8-36, 86-88.

7. Empirical evidence concerning bilateral balancing can be found in Vanous, *Commodity Shares in Foreign Trade Flows*, pp. 28-55. This practice results in converging commodity structure of the trade of all countries, using it as a balancing mechanism. On pp. 49-54, it can be seen that the hypothesis of bilateral balancing by commodity groups is more relevant to intra-CMEA Six trade than to the trade between them and the USSR.

8. These methods are described in Ray C. Fair and Dwight M. Jaffee, "Methods of Estimation for Markets in Disequilibrium," *Econometrica* (May 1972), pp. 497-514; and idem and Harry M. Kelejian, "Methods of Estimation for Markets in Disequilibrium: A Further Study," *Econometrica* (January 1974), pp. 177-90.

9. This average was based on Marer, *Postwar Pricing*, p. 41, where he calculates that, on the average, CMEA manufactures are sold on the world market (in the West) with 10-40% discount off the particular wmp. This means that in intra-CMEA trade, one has to take into account the relatively lower quality of CMEA manufactures in comparison with Western manufactures; and the quality adjustment factor, QA_{it}^{CMEA} ($i=1,4$), is calculated as $1/[(0.6 + 0.9)/2] = 1.33$.

10. See an extensive discussion of this subject in Hewett, *Foreign Trade Prices*, pp. 115-56.

11. The following conversion rate between SDR and TR was used for the entire period: SDR 1 = TR 0.9, i.e., SDR is defined as the pre-devaluation (December 1971) US dollar.

12. Jan Vanous, *Project CMEA-FORTRAM Data Bank of Foreign Trade Flows and Balances of CMEA Countries, 1950-1975* (Vancouver: Project CMEA-FORTRAM, Department of Economics, University of British Columbia, November 1977), pp. 34-43.

13. A detailed description appears in Jan Vanous, *Project CMEA-FORTRAM Data Bank of Foreign Trade Prices of CMEA Countries* (Vancouver: Project CMEA-FORTRAM, Department of Economics, University of British Columbia, forthcoming).

14. Copies of worksheets with unpublished time-series of these data are available from the author on request.

van Brabant, "Discussion"

1. I shall also eschew the problems related to shifts over time in these functions.

2. Some partial markets are probably subject to competitive pressure. Such observations belong simultaneously to the supply and demand functions.

3. Long-term planning and price stability on the basis of outdated wmp's might produce such a result.

4. For some details on price levels, see S. Ausch, *Theory and Practice of CMEA Cooperation* (Budapest: Akadémiai Kiadó, 1972), pp. 86ff; and N. Mitrofanova, "Perspektivy dal'neishego sovershenstvovaniia vneshnetorgovykh tsen sotsialisticheskikh stran," *Planovoe khoziaistvo* 4 (1974): 41ff.

5. S. Ausch and F. Bartha, "Theoretical Problems of CMEA Intertrade Prices," in *Socialist World Market Prices*, ed. T. Földi and T. Kiss (Budapest: Akadémiai Kiadó, 1969), pp. 117ff.

6. Mitrofanova, "Perspektivy dal'neishego," pp. 94ff; and M. Savov, *Sotsialisticheskata ikonomicheska integratsiia—vunshnoturgovski i tsenovi problemi* (Varna: Bakalov, 1975), pp. 216ff.

7. It might be useful to distinguish between regular trade agreements and supplementary protocols. The latter attempt to even out marginal supplies.

8. Vanous admittedly makes a strong case that balancing is not practiced uniformly by all CPEs. However, no attempt is made to test for differences.

9. Vanous derived these proportions from the data in Ausch, *CMEA Cooperation*, pp. 230-32, as reaggregated in Paul Marer, *Postwar Pricing and Price Patterns in Socialist Foreign Trade, 1946-1971* (Bloomington, Ind.: International Development Research Center, 1972), pp. 10, 86-88.

10. A recently published unit value index for Soviet exports (Savov, *Sotsialisticheskata ikonomicheska,* p. 216) shows significant differences from those reported in E.A. Hewett, *Foreign Trade Prices in the Council for Mutual Economic Assistance* (Cambridge, England: Cambridge University Press, 1974), pp. 70-71, Vanous's main source of information. An index constructed for Hungary also shows large differences. The results for Hungary are available from the author.

11. This applies to the double logarithmic equations only. In the linear equations, the coefficients should be close to one if balancing is practiced.

12. In several instances, the pressure variables are not really representative of the relevant commodity groups traded.

Drábek, "Discussion"

1. For an example of this approach applied to internal price systems in CPE, see R. Portes, "Macroeconomic Equilibrium Under Central Planning," Seminar Paper No. 40 (Stockholm: Institute for International Studies, September 1974).

2. See, for example, K. Dyba, "Odhad parametru poptávkové funkce na nerovnováznem trhu" [An estimate of parameters of demand function in a disequilibrium market], *Politická ekonomie* (Prague) 21 (December 1973): 1123-31.

3. F.D. Holzman, *Soviet Taxation* (Cambridge, Mass.: Harvard University Press, 1955), pp. 293-94.

4. I.B. Kravis, "Availability and Other Influences on the Commodity Composition of Trade," *Journal of Political Economy* 64 (1956).

5. See S. Rosefielde, "Factor Proportions and Economic Rationality in Soviet International Trade," *American Economic Review* 64 (September 1974).

6. Z. Drábek, "An Application of Input-Output Price Models in Inter-Country Comparisons" (Paper presented at the 7th International Input-Output Conference, Innsbruck, April 1979).

Shabad, "Soviet Policy and CMEA Integration"

1. A.A. Mints, "A Predictive Hypothesis of Economic Development in the European Part of the USSR," *Soviet Geography* (January 1976), pp. 4-5.

2. N.A. Salikova, "Methodological Problems in the Geography of Labor Resources," *Soviet Geography* (June 1977), pp. 396-402.

3. V.V. Pokshishevskiy, "Theoretical Aspects of Attracting Population to Seacoasts and the Measurement of That Attraction," *Soviet Geography* (March 1976), pp. 145-53.

4. O.N. Krivoruchko, "Maritime Economic Systems of the USSR," *Soviet Geography* (March 1976), pp. 153-59.

5. *Geografiya proizvoditel'nykh sil SSSR i mezhdunarodnoye ekonomicheskoye sotrudnichestvo* [Geography of the productive forces of the USSR and international economic collaboration] (Moscow: Mysl', 1976), p. 128.

6. A.N. Kosygin, "Speech at the 30th session of CMEA in Berlin, July 1976," *Ekonomicheskoye sotrudnichestvo stran-chlenov SEV* [Economic collaboration of CMEA member countries], no. 4 (1976), p. 12.

7. "News Notes," *Soviet Geography* (October 1970), p. 699; (November 1973), p. 604; (November 1976), p. 647.

8. *Soviet Geography* (March 1971), p. 177.

9. *Regional'nyye problemy ekonomicheskoy integratsii SSSR v sisteme stran SEV* [Regional problems of the economic integration of the USSR into the system of the CMEA countries] (Moscow: Nauka, 1975), p. 63.

10. Calculated from *Vneshnyaya torgovlya* [Foreign trade], no. 5 (1976), p. 6, which says that 74.2% of total Soviet crude oil exports of 93.1 million tons went to communist countries.

11. Theodore Shabad, *Basic Industrial Resources of the USSR* (New York: Columbia University Press, 1969), pp. 192, 203.

12. *Soviet Geography* (May 1975), pp. 343-44.

13. Ibid. (December 1976), pp. 719-20.

14. *Sovetskaya Litva,* February 15, 1976; December 14, 1978.

15. *Gosudarstvennyy pyatiletnyy plan razvitiya narodnogo khozyaystva SSSR na 1971-1975 gody* [The state five-year plan of economic development of the USSR for 1971-1975] (Moscow: Politizdat, 1972), p. 263.

16. *Pravda Ukrainy*, February 13, 1976.

17. *Geografiya proizvoditel'nykh sil*, p. 80.

18. In addition to direct CMEA investment, this project will be financed by a loan of 600 million Eurodollars to the International Investment Bank from a consortium headed by the Deutsche Bank of West Germany to purchase equipment from the West. The East European countries that must acquire commodities outside CMEA to meet their obligations to the joint project in the USSR must repay the International Investment Bank in hard currencies at Western interest rates. This procedure enables the Soviet Union to obtain Western equipment without an outlay of its own hard currency and, also, constitutes a type of interest subsidy to the USSR, which repays East European participants for these commodity credits at an interest rate of only 2 to 3%.

19. *Sovetskaya Rossiya*, January 3, 1977.

20. *Vneshnyaya torgovlya*, no. 4 (1974), p. 19.

21. *Soviet Geography* (January 1975), pp. 50-51; *Sovetskaya Moldaviya* (May 26, 1976).

22. *Pravda Ukrainy*, January 5, 1977.

23. *Ekonomicheskaya gazeta*, no. 6 (1977), p. 20.

24. Theodore Shabad, "Soviet Union Is Stepping up Expansion of Nuclear Power," *The New York Times*, January 14, 1977.

25. *Pravda Ukrainy*, January 4, 1977.

26. *Geografiya proizvoditel'nykh sil*, p. 86.

27. *Ekonomicheskoye sotrudnichestvo stran-chlenov SEV*, no. 4 (1976), p. 94.

28. *Pravda Ukrainy*, February 13, 1976; November 19, 1976; *Sotsialisticheskaya industriya*, January 5, 1977.

29. *Vneshnyaya torgovlya*, no. 12 (1976), p. 8.

30. *Kazakhstanskaya Pravda*, May 12, 1976; February 24, 1979; *Stroitel'naya gazeta*, January 1, 1977.

31. *Geografiya proizvoditel'nykh sil*, p. 95; *Sovetskaya Rossiya*, May 16, 1975; *Pravda*, October 9, 1975.

32. V. Shanina, "The Impact of the Transport Factor on the Location of Export Industries in the Comecon Countries," *Soviet Geography* (April 1975), pp. 262-70.

33. Ibid., p. 263.

34. Theodore Shabad, "Raw Material Problems of the Soviet Aluminum Industry," *Resources Policy* (December 1976), pp. 222-34; also *Soviet Economy in a New Perspective* (Papers submitted to the Joint Economic Committee, Congress of the United States) (Washington: Government Printing Office, 1976), pp. 661-74.

35. *Vneshnyaya torgovlya*, no. 3 (1975), p. 7.

36. Shabad, "Raw Material Problems," p. 232.

37. *Vneshnyaya torgovlya*, no. 9 (1974), p. 36.

38. *Ekonomicheskoye sotrudnichestvo stran-chlenov SEV*, no. 5 (1975), p. 83.

39. *Gudok*, March 30, 1976; *Vneshnyaya torgovlya SSSR v 1975*, statistical handbook, p. 71.

40. *Pravda*, December 29, 1973; *Stroitel'naya gazeta*, December 19, 1975.

41. *Sotsialisticheskaya industriya*, January 15, 1976; *Sovetskaya Belorussiya*, July 3, 1976.

42. *Pravda Ukrainy*, December 25, 1975; *Sovetskaya Litva*, October 28, 1975.

43. *Ekonomicheskaya gazeta*, no. 15 (1975); *Sotsialisticheskaya industriya*, February 2, 1975; *Planovoye khozyaystvo*, no. 6 (1975); *Vneshnyaya torgovlya SSSR v 1975*, statistical handbook, p. 78; *Statisticheskiy yezhegodnik stran-chlenov SEV* [Statistical yearbook of the CMEA member countries] (Moscow, 1976), p. 100.

44. *Regional'nyye problemy*, pp. 153, 156.

45. Theodore Shabad and Victor L. Mote, *Gateway to Siberian Resources* (New York: Halsted Press, 1977), p. 54.

46. Calculated from data in *Statisticheskiy yezhegodnik* and *Vneshnyaya torgovlya SSSR v 1975*.

47. *Ekonomicheskaya gazeta,* no. 5 (1977), p. 24.
48. *Lesnaya promyshlennost',* December 16, 1976.
49. *Regional'nyye problemy,* p. 159.
50. Shanina in *Soviet Geography,* April 1975, p. 265.
51. *Bakinskiy rabochiy,* January 4, 1977.

Taaffe, "Discussion"

1. Leslie Dienes, "Investment Priorities in Soviet Regions," *Annals of the Association of American Geographers* 62 (September 1972): 437-454.
2. Vsevolod Holubnychny, "Spatial Efficiency in the Soviet Economy," in *The Soviet Economy in Regional Perspective,* ed. V. Bandera and L. Melnyk (New York: Praeger, 1973), p. 26.
3. E.I. Popova, *Transportnyye zatraty v obshchestvennom proizvodstve* (Moscow: Nauka, 1972), pp. 95-169.
4. Edward Hewett, *Foreign Trade Prices in the Council for Mutual Economic Assistance* (Cambridge, England: Cambridge University Press, 1972), pp. 33-34.
5. V.F. Pavlenko, *Territorialnoe i otraslevoe planirovanie* (Moscow: Ekonomika, 1971).
6. A.G. Granberg, *Optimizatsiya territorialnykh proportsii narodnogo khoziastva* (Moscow: Ekonomika, 1973), pp. 27-31.
7. N.N. Nekrasov, *Regionalnaya ekonomika* (Moscow: Ekonomika, 1975), pp. 93-95.
8. A.K. Aganbegyan, Bagrinovskiy, and A. Granberg, *Sistema modeley narodnokhoziastvennogo planirovanika* (Moscow: Myse, 1972), pp. 286-98.
9. P. Nijkamp and P. Rietuld, "Multi-Objective Programming Models: New Ways in Regional Decision-Making," *Regional Science and Urban Economics* 6 (September 1976): 253-74; and M. Zeleny, *Linear Multi-Objective Programming* (Berlin: Springer-Verlag, 1974).

Hanson, "Impact of Western Technology"

1. This is argued with some force and in some detail by Peter Wiles in "On the Prevention of Technology Transfer," in *East-West Technological Cooperation,* ed. NATO Economic Directorate (Brussels: 1976), pp. 23-43. My own interpretation of the economic aspects of détente, which I have argued in "The Import of Western Technology" in *The Soviet Union Since the Fall of Khrushchev,* ed. Archie Brown and Michael Kaser (London: Macmillan, 1975), pp. 16-49, is rather different. I believe the change in Soviet policies to be more gradual.
2. Philip Hanson, "International Technology Transfer from the West to the USSR" in US Congress, Joint Economic Committee, *The Soviet Economy in a New Perspective* (Washington, D.C.: Government Printing Office, 1976), table 1.
3. A.C. Sutton, *Western Technology and Soviet Economic Development,* 3 vols. (Stanford, Calif.: The Hoover Institution, Stanford University, 1969-73).
4. Sutton distinguishes technological from technical change in the wider, economic sense, the latter embracing all changes that raise factor productivity. Technological change is the application to production of technical knowledge not previously applied in the USSR, resulting in the appearance and spread of products and processes not previously made or used in that country.
5. Political circumstances have helped Soviet policymakers to build closer economic links with the West. The main factors here are the strategic developments underlying détente (a more equal military balance between the superpowers, a shared desire for crisis management and the containment of military spending); the development of a more pragmatic and sophisticated style of leadership in the USSR; the inability of Western governments to adopt unified, rather than competitive, commercial policies towards the East; the strength of Western business lobbies; and the decline of anti-communism as a force in US domestic politics.
6. Hanson, "International Technology Transfer," table 1.
7. Similar effects could also come from (1) license and know-how purchases not

associated with significant plant purchases, (2) improved materials imported from the West, (3) imported products other than plant, and (4) materials capable of affecting productivity. "Pure" license deals are not numerous, and these factors in general seem likely to be minor compared with machinery imports. Wide-diameter pipe for oil and gas pipelines is, however, currently an important non-machinery item; it is of course a capital good.

8. I have set out these arguments, together with some anecdotal evidence for and against them, in "The Diffusion of Imported Technology in the USSR" in *East-West Technological Cooperation*.

9. A.V.G. Hahn, *The Petrochemical Industry* (New York: McGraw-Hill, 1970), p. 39.

10. UN FAO, *1974 World Fertilizer Review* (Rome, 1975).

11. For an account of the technological breakthroughs, see N.L. Dickinson, J.A. Finneran, and E. Solomon, "Single-Train Ammonia Plant: Is There a Limit on Size?" *European Chemical News*, Large Plant Supplement, September 29, 1967, pp. 100, 102. This account ascribes a major innovative role to the engineers of plant contracting firms. It also indicates that losses from not using experienced contractors could be very large because of delays in a complex and expensive series of inter-related construction and start-up sequences.

12. V.M. Bushuev, *Khimicheskaya industriya v svete reshenii XXIV s"ezda KPSS* (Moscow, 1974), pp. 34-45; and private communications from M.R. Freeman of the British Sulphur Corporation. MAP is a highly concentrated substance containing more than one nutrient (11% N, 52% P), but it is not normally used directly as a complex fertilizer because of the extreme imbalance between its N and P content; it has to have other materials mixed with it.

13. F.G. Margolis and T.P. Unanyants, *Proizvodstvo kompleksnykh udobrenii* (Moscow: Khimiya, 1968), p. 195.

14. M.R. Freeman, "Special Report on Phosphates," *Times* (London), May 10, 1976, p. 27.

15. See L.A. Kostandov, *Khimicheskaya promyshlennost' k XXV s"ezdu KPSS* (Moscow: Khimiya, 1976), p. 25; and P.M. Sudilovskii, "Kurs—na tekhnicheskoe perevooruzhenie," *Ekonomicheskaya gazeta*, no. 20 (1976), p. 6. Kostandov is the Minister of the Chemical Industry; Sudilovskii is the director of the Byeloruskalii production association, based at Soligorsk.

16. See the CPSU Central Committee and USSR Council of Ministers decree, "On measures for the further increase in efficiency of utilisation of mineral fertilisers, the reduction of losses during transportation, storage and application, and the improvement of agro-chemical services to *kolkhozy* and *sovkhozy*," *Sotsialisticheskaya industriya*, June 18, 1976, p. 1.

17. Bushuev, *Khimicheskaya industriya*.

18. UN FAO, *Annual Fertiliser Review, 1964* (Rome, 1965).

19. B.G. Reuben and M.L. Burstall, *The Chemical Economy* (London: Longman, 1973), p. 365.

20. R. Amann, "The Soviet Chemical Industry: Its Level of Modernity and Sophistication," CREES Discussion Paper RC/C11 (Birmingham, England: University of Birmingham, 1974).

21. *Pravda*, November 15, 1978, p. 2.

22. *Vneshnyaya torgovlya*, no. 10 (1974), p. 45.

23. This is a devious calculation that assumes that no "large" plant (0.4 million tpa or above) will be commissioned by end-1980 that is not of Western origin and that large plant output is close to capacity; both assumptions are in line with the evidence. It is based on reports that 1975 ammonia output was 12 million tons, of which about 2 million tons was from large plant and that the large plant share was to rise to 54% in 1980 (Kostandov, *Khimicheskaya promyshlennost'*, pp. 22, 78); and that 23 Western-built large plants are to be commissioned in 1976-80.

24. This, rather than research and development strength, is the typical specialty of chemical plant contractors in the West. Basic processes and designs stem mainly from the large research and development input of chemical companies. See C. Freeman, *The*

Economics of Industrial Innovation (Baltimore, Md.: Penguin, 1974), pp. 63-69. For a further analysis of the relations between plant contractors, process licensors, and CMEA purchasers, see Paul Marer, "US-CMEA Cooperation in the Chemical Industry," in *East-West European Economic Interactions: Workshop Papers*, ed. F. Nemschak, vol. 2 (New York: Springer-Verlag, 1977).

25. They were not included, however, in Kostandov's "shopping list," which he reeled off at a recent press conference in London. See *Financial Times*, April 9, 1976.
27. BBC SWB SU/W605/A/27 (1971); SY/W610/A17 (1971); SU/W834/A10 (1975).
28. *Soviet Business and Trade* 4 (February 4, 1976): 2.
29. *Vneshnyaya torgovlya*, no. 10 (1974), p. 45.
30. BBC SWB SU/W605/A/26 (1971); SU/W611/A/18 (1971); SU/W707/A/14 (1973).
31. BBC SWB SU/W619/A/14 (1971) and SU/W749/A/15 (1973).
32. BBC SWB SU/W865/A/15 (1975).
33. BBC SWB SU/W855/A/13 (1975).
34. Ibid; BBC SWB SU/834/A/10 (1975); SU/W839/A/11 (1975).
35. V. Manyakin in *Ekonomika sel'skogo khozyaistva*, no. 4 (1972), p. 41. A subsequent article by VASkhNIL academicians V. Pannikov and S. Skoropanov (*Sel'skaya zhizn'*, September 26, 1976, p. 2.) states that a 10:1 impact is to be expected under optimal soil, weather, and organizational conditions. The authors go on to imply that a 5:1 impact may be a realistic average expectation for the USSR as a whole.
36. L.A. Kostandov, *Khimicheskaya promyshlennost' k XXV s''ezdu KPSS* (Moscow: Khimiya, 1976), p. 18. Presumably this (1) is in agricultural wholesale prices and (2) allows for the influence of other factors, since bad weather made the 1975 harvest of most crops lower than that of 1970. Between two good harvest years, 1970 and 1973, we observe an increase of 35.7 million tons, 0.8 million tons, and 8.1 million tons in the grain, cotton, and sugar beet harvests, respectively, from a sown area enlarged by 4%. These were presumably the main elements in the 7 billion rubles increase in gross value of crop output at 1965 prices. Over the same period, the weight of mineral fertilizer nutrients supplied to agriculture rose by 3.4 million tons.
37. Derived from Manyakin, *Ekonomika sci'skogo khozyaistva*, table 1; *Narkhoz, 74*, p. 341; and *Vestnik statistiki*, no. 6 (1975), p. 95.
38. 3.4 billion rubles as a percentage of 65.2 billion rubles (*Narkhoz, 74*, p. 574).
39. *Vneshnyaya torgovlya*, no. 10 (1974), p. 45.
40. Kostandov, *Khimicheskaya*, pp. 21, 22.
41. Excluding monoammonium phosphate.
42. K.F. Vinogradov, "Kachestvu produktsii—bol'she vnimaniya'," *Khimicheskaya promyshlennost'*, no. 8 (1975), p. 565.
43. Saving about 0.3 man-days per hectare, compared with the equivalent nutrient volume of single-nutrient fertilizers, according to Margolis and Unanyants, *Proizvodstvo*, p. 6. For the mid-1970s, Pannikov and Skoropanov (Sel'skaya zhian') estimate a saving of more than 10% of production costs per unit of output from the substitution of complex for single-nutrient fertilizers.
44. R.V. Greenslade, "The Gross National Product of the USSR 1950-1975" in US Congress, Joint Economic Committee, *Soviet Economy in a New Perspective* (Washington, D.C.: Government Printing Office, 1976), p. 284.
45. Applying a machinery exchange rate of $1.6 = 1 ruble (see Hanson, "International Technology Transfer") to the total project cost of 722 million rubles (see G.T. Savel'ev, "Na stroitel'stve Cherepovetskogo zavoda," *Khimicheskaya promyshlennost'*, no. 8 [1975], p. 568-71).
46. Kostandov, *Khimicheskaya promyshlennost'*, p. 22.
47. BBC SWB SU/W764/A/14 (1974).
48. BBC SWB SU/W809/A/15 (1974).
49. K. Bush in *Radio Liberty Research Bulletin*, RL 119/76 (March 2, 1976), p. 2.
50. *Pravda*, December 4, 1968, p. 2. The plant's foreign origin is not mentioned, of course.
51. BBC SWB SU/W619/A/14 (1971).
52. A. Detyna, "Polish-Soviet Trade in Complete Sets of Industrial Equipment," *Foreign Trade*, no. 9 (1976), pp. 10-16.

53. Harold Lent, "East European Chemical Production and Trade" in US Congress, Joint Economic Committee, *Reorientation and Commercial Relations of the Economies of Eastern Europe* (Washington, D.C.: Government Printing Office, 1974), pp. 394-406, esp. pp. 400 and 404. See also *Chemical Industry Projects and Equipment: A Market Assessment for Poland* (Washington, D.C.: Bureau of East-West Trade, US Department of Commerce). In general, currency allocations for the import of machinery are supposed to be made only if the application from the would-be machinery-user is backed by statements from the relevant Soviet machine-building ministry that it cannot itself supply machinery of the requisite quantity in the time limits set by the investment program. *Metodicheskie ukazaniya k razrabotke planov razvitiya narodnogo khozyaistva SSSR* (Moscow: Gosplan, 1974), p. 595. How CMEA arrangements fit in with this rule is not revealed.

54. Kostandov, "Khimicheskaya promyshlennost," pp. 71-77.

55. *European Chemical News,* September 24, 1976, p. 45.

56. D.W. Green and H.S. Levine, "Soviet Machinery Imports" (Paper presented to the National Science Foundation Workshop on Soviet Science and Technology, Airlie House, November 1976).

57. R. Amann, J.M. Cooper, and R.W. Davies, ed., *The Technological Level of Soviet Industry* (New Haven: Yale University Press, 1977).

Ofer, "Growth Strategy, Specialization in Agriculture, and Trade"

1. Gur Ofer, "Industrial Structure, Urbanization and the Growth Strategy of Socialist Countries," *Quarterly Journal of Economics* 90 (May 1976): 219-44; idem, "Economizing on Urbanization in Socialist Countries: Historical Necessity of Socialist Strategy," in *Internal Migration: A Comparative Perspective,* ed. Alan A. Brown and Egon Neuberger (forthcoming).

2. Input substitution is clearly not the *only* reason for the observed low *relative* total productivity in SOC agricultural sectors. It is, however, an important one. Low relative productivity tends to further increase the share of labor (and other inputs) employed in this sector.

3. Ofer, "Industrial Structure," pp. 242-43.

4. See, for example, Michael Kaser, *Comecon: Integration Problems of the Planned Economies* (London: Oxford University Press, 1967), pp. 105-106.

5. Ideology is used here in its broader meaning to encompass all aspects of a socialist economic system.

6. On the conflict, see Alan A. Brown, "Towards a Theory of Centrally Planned Foreign Trade," in *International Trade and Central Planning,* ed. Alan A. Brown and Egon Neuberger (Berkeley: University of California Press, 1968), pp. 75-77. On A-exports financing imports of machinery, see especially John M. Montias, "Socialist Industrialization and Trade in Machinery Products: An Analysis Based on the Experience of Bulgaria, Poland, and Rumania," in *International Trade and Central Planning,* pp. 130-65; and John M. Montias, *Economic Development in Communist Rumania* (Cambridge, Mass.: The MIT Press, 1967), pp. 182-86, 234 ff.

7. See more on this below.

8. The ideological constraints to such specialization are suggested by statements that only after the elimination of differences (in levels of production but presumably also in structure) among SOC can the "socialist division of labor" flourish; it cannot easily be used to effect this equalization. See J. Novazamski, "The Development of the International Division of Labour between Countries at Different Economic Levels," in *Economic Development for Eastern Europe,* ed. Michael Kaser (London: Macmillan, 1968), pp. 148-49.

9. See Sandor Ausch, *Theory and Practice of CMEA Cooperation* (Budapest: Akadémiai Kiadó, 1972), pp. 44-45; John P. Hardt, "East European Economic Development: Two Decades of Interrelationships and Interactions With the Soviet Union," in US Congress, Joint Economic Committee, *Economic Development in Countries of Eastern Europe* (Washington, D.C.: Government Printing Office, 1970), p. 10 (hereafter referred to as JEC-1970); Paul Marer, "Soviet Economic Policy in Eastern Europe," in US Congress, Joint Economic Committee, *Reorientation and Commercial Relations in*

the Economies of Eastern Europe (Washington, D.C.: Government Printing Office, 1974), p. 154 (hereafter referred to as JEC-1974); and Nicolas Spulber, *The State and Economic Development in Eastern Europe* (New York: Random House, 1966), p. 45.

10. Marer, "Soviet Economic Policy," p. 154; Zbigniew M. Fallenbuchl, "Comecon Integration," *Problems of Communism* 22 (March/April 1973): 32; "East European Integration: Comecon," in JEC-1974, pp. 84-87. See also Ausch, *CMEA Cooperation*, pp. 41-45, and Spulber, *The State and Economic Development*, pp. 45-46.

11. From a net importer of raw materials from CMEA during 1949-51, by the late 1960s the Soviet Union became a very large net exporter of such materials. The trend in net exports of A-products is in the opposite direction, based on Paul Marer, *Soviet and East European Foreign Trade 1946-1969* (Bloomington: Indiana University Press, 1972), pp. 87, 111. For later years, see Soviet Union, Ministerstvo Vneshney Torgovli SSSR, *Vneshnyaya Torgovlya SSSR za 1974 god* [The foreign trade of the USSR for 1974] (Moscow, annual), p. 21.

12. Marer, "Soviet Economic Policy," pp. 138-41, 151-54; Peter J. Wiles, "Foreign Trade of Eastern Europe: A Summary Appraisal," in *International Trade and Central Planning*, p. 170; and Hardt, "East European Economic Development," pp. 9-10.

13. See, for example, Alan A. Brown and Paul Marer, "Foreign Trade in the East European Reforms," in *Plan and Market: Economic Reform in Eastern Europe*, ed. Morris Bornstein (New Haven, Conn.: Yale University Press, 1973), pp. 190-91. On other consequences of the technological failure, see below.

14. See Ausch, *CMEA Cooperation*, pp. 85 ff., 100-101; Marer, "Soviet Economic Policy," pp. 147-50; Edward A. Hewett, *Foreign Trade Prices in the Council for Mutual Economic Assistance* (London: Cambridge University Press, 1974), chapters 2 and 3, and pp. 160-62.

15. See, for example, Ausch, *CMEA Cooperation*, pp. 97, 111 ff.; and Montias, *Economic Development*, pp. 243-44.

16. Kaser, *Comecon*, pp. 94-96.

17. This failure, though partly unexpected by the designers of the socialist growth strategy, is a direct result of the extensive nature of the industrialization drive and the total neglect of light-consumer industries in which some of the developed SOC were already advanced before World War II.

18. See, for example, Montias, *Economic Development*, pp. 234-47; Wiles, "Foreign Trade of Eastern Europe," pp. 163-74; Fallenbuchl, "Comecon Integration," pp. 34-35.

19. And even rapidly becoming a net exporter of manufacturers and net importer of primary goods.

20. Montias, *Economic Development*, chapters 3, 4, and 5; see esp. pp. 243-44. Montias seems to imply (pp. 244-45) that Poland in the past (pre-1967) and Bulgaria and Romania in the future may exhaust their potential to export hard goods too early.

21. See Frederic L. Pryor, *The Communist Foreign Trade System* (London: Allen and Unwin, 1963), pp. 23-28, esp. tables 1-2; Ausch, *CMEA Cooperation*, p. 37, and notes to table 3; Maurice Ernst, "Post-War Economic Growth in Eastern Europe: A Comparison with Western Europe," in JEC-1966, table 18, p. 900.

22. It is indeed the product (multiplication) of the two that makes up the effects and differential effects of trade or the industrial structure; but problems in evaluating the first prevent us from incorporating the total effect in the analysis.

23. H. Chenery and M. Syrquin, *Patterns of Development, 1950-1970* (London: Oxford University Press, 1975), pp. 16-18.

24. Equations without $(\ln Y)^2$ were also estimated and are used whenever they give significantly better results.

25. Categories 0, 1, 2, 4 *less* 27 and 28 of Standard International Trade Classification, Revised (hereafter referred to as SITC).

26. Categories 7 and 95 of SITC.

27. See also general note to tables 1 and 4.

28. R is needed to adjust the figure of net exports in cases where exports don't equal imports and a higher (lower) proportion of E_i (as compared to I_i) may represent smaller (larger) value of exports as compared to imports.

29. If $\Delta EA = 20$ and $\Delta IA = 10$, then (with $R = 1$) $\Delta FA = 10$ as it is if $\Delta EA = -10$ and $\Delta IA = -20$.

30. For details and sources see notes to tables 1 and 4.

31. Other relevant points shall be made in the discussion on the trade structure of SOC.

32. The residuals are based on equations for individual years. The residuals estimated on the basis of equations that combine observations from all years and on equations of type [1a], that is, $(\ln Y)^2$, are usually larger than presented in the table.

33. On biases, see notes (*) and (†) to table 2.

34. Bulgaria's small size contributes to a lower normal or expected level of EM than those of other less-developed SOC. Compare, for example, EM and ΔEM for Bulgaria and Romania.

35. Underlying data on the breakdown of OM into its components are from Marer, *Soviet and East European Foreign Trade,* pp. 44-67.

36. Montias has shown similar results using a similar method of analysis. See John M. Montias, "The Structure of Comecon Trade and the Prospects for East-West Exchanges," in JEC-1974, pp. 679-80.

37. Deviations from this normal socialist deficit are shown in line 7 of table 5.

38. Observations based on trade structure data in Marer, *Soviet and East European Foreign Trade,* pp. 44-79, and CMEA-1975, *Statistical Yearbook,* pp. 327-33.

39. As can be seen from figures 1 and 2, when the coefficients of $S \ln Y$ are non-zero, the meaning of the S coefficients (the differences in the intercepts) change. They do not represent a uniform shift of the function at all income levels but only the unimportant ones of points of $Y=0$. This is the reason that the S coefficients estimated for equations [3] are so different in magnitude from those estimated in equations [2].

40. Soviet trade structure with European CMEA countries is as follows:

	EA	IA	FA	EM	IM	FM
1959-61	33.6	11.8	24.2	14.6	46.1	-30.5
1968	22.4	11.4	10.1	25.2	49.2	-25.0

Soviet net exports of raw materials to European CMEA are 30.3% and 35.0% for the two periods respectively. Based on Marer, *Soviet and East European Foreign Trade,* pp. 87, 111. See also Fallenbuchl, "Comecon Integration," pp. 33-34.

41. Thus, FA residuals for both 1960 and 1970 are computed from IA equations with $S \ln Y$ and EA equations without it. The opposite holds for the FM residuals.

42. With a net import of 22.4% (of total imports) in 1960 and 23.7% in 1970, Bulgaria has the highest such deficit among SOC. On the other hand, Bulgaria's net exports of light industrial goods of 8.7% in 1960 and 10.3% in 1970 are quite normal (by SOC standards). The underlying data are from Council for Mutual Economic Assistance, *Statistical Yearbook* (Moscow, 1975), pp. 327, 330.

43. Gur Ofer, *Industrial Structure, Urbanization and Socialist Growth Strategy: An Historical Analysis, 1940-1967* (Jerusalem: The Hebrew University, 1974), pp. 18-25; Spulber, *The State and Economic Development,* pp. 78-79; Alfred Zauberman, *Industrial Progress in Poland, Czechoslovakia, and East Germany 1937-1962* (London: Oxford University Press, 1964), pp. 294-96.

44. Most of the data presented here are from Gregor Lazarcik, "Agricultural Output and Productivity in Eastern Europe and Some Comparisons with the USSR and USA," in JEC-1974, pp. 328-93. Output growth data are on pp. 337, 339. Lazarcik's definition of agriculture excludes forestry and fishery, as does most of the evidence presented here. In forestry products, Bulgaria is a net importer, increasingly so over time.

45. These findings are also supported by a comparative study of Eastern Europe prepared for the United Nations. UN, Economic Commission for Europe, *Economic Survey of Europe, 1969* (Geneva, 1970), chapter 2, pp. 1-53 (hereafter cited as ECE-69). The data presented here are for 1950-67, pp. 12-13.

46. Lazarcik, "Agricultural Output," p. 353.

47. Ibid., pp. 358, 360.

48. Ibid., pp. 363, 365.

49. CMEA-1975, *Statistical Yearbook,* pp. 190-96.

50. Lazarcik, "Agricultural Output," pp. 362, 363.

51. Ibid., p. 367. See also ECE-69, p. 17, for 1950-67. The acceleration of the movement out of agriculture in the late 1960s may be one of the causes for the slowdown in growth. See Bogoslav Dobrin, *Bulgarian Economic Development Since World War II* (New York: Praeger, 1973), pp. 57-58.

52. See Lazarcik, "Agricultural Output," pp. 339, 360, 372, 378. See also Alton, *Economic Growth,* pp. 280, 281; and Ofer, "Industrial Structure," pp. 235-40.

53. Alton, *Economic Growth,* p. 267.

54. Lazarcik's use of 1953-57 as a base obscures the fact that by that time Bulgaria had advanced in these fields more than other SOC. See Lazarcik, "Agricultural Output," pp. 337, 339, 355.

55. Ibid., pp. 355, 371, 372.

56. ECE-69, p. 21. See similar results for 1960-72 in Alton, *Economic Growth,* p. 279.

57. Lazarcik, "Agricultural Output," p. 373.

58. See Alton, *Economic Growth,* pp. 256-57; ECE-69, pp. 11-12, 16; CMEA-1975, *Statistical Yearbook,* pp. 42-43.

59. Alton, *Economic Growth,* p. 263; ECE-69, p. 18; CMEA-1975, *Statistical Yearbook,* pp. 393-96. Since East European national accounts have a bias toward labor, I suspect that the Bulgarian A-share is relatively underestimated.

60. Based on Alton, *Economic Growth,* pp. 279, 281.

61. Bulgarian collective farms are the largest in Eastern Europe. See J. Wilczynski, *Technology in Comecon* (London: Macmillan, 1974), p. 211.

62. Lazarcik, "Agricultural Output," pp. 348, 349.

63. Ibid., p. 351.

64. Bulgaria's total exports grew at an annual rate of about 17% that of A-goods at about 13% over 1950-70. The corresponding figures for 1955-70 and 1960-70 are 17.5% and 15.5% for total exports and 15% and 12.5% for exports of A-goods. The growth of A-goods exports can only be explained by a simultaneous increase of its processed proportion: it grew from 76% to 84% in 1970. Presumably, the "depth" of processing grew even more. Based on Bulgaria, *Statisticheski Godishnik na Naroda Republika B'lgaria, 1971* [Statistical yearbook of the Bulgarian Republic] (Sofia, annual), pp. 312-14.

65. See, for example, Dobrin, *Bulgarian Economic Development,* pp. 43-65, 87.

66. There is conflicting evidence about whether or not the growth of agricultural output of Bulgaria actually slowed down during the late 1960s. While Lazarcik gives figures of 1% ("Agricultural Output," p. 337) per year for 1965-70, the official Bulgarian figure is 4.4% as compared with 4.1% during 1960-65 (*Bulgarian Statistical Yearbook,* 1971, p. 190). Lazarcik's 1960-65 figure is 5.2%. The differences may lie in different periodization and in different weights.

67. Edwin M. Snell, "Economic Efficiency in Eastern Europe," in JEC-1970, p. 243; Alton, *Economic Growth,* pp. 274, 275. Lately, Romania is clearly taking the lead.

68. ECE-69, p. 16.

69. Alton, *Economic Growth,* pp. 256-57.

70. Ibid., p. 263; ECE-69, p. 18.

71. CMEA-75, *Statistical Yearbook,* p. 66. Similar data are presented by Fallenbuchl, "Comecon Integration," p. 67. Distribution of employment is from Alton, *Economic Growth,* p. 265.

72. The level reached by most other SOC and the USSR. See CMEA-1975, *Statistical Yearbook,* p. 66.

73. Alton, *Economic Growth,* p. 265.

74. Ibid., p. 268.

75. Perkins states a similar argument, also in a counterfactual context, for China. A higher investment rate in and growth of agriculture in China could have raised exports and, hence, imports of equipment, thus allowing for a higher growth rate of the economy. See Dwight H. Perkins, "The International Impact on Chinese Central Planning," in *International Trade,* pp. 186-98, esp. pp. 193-94, 198.

Allen, "Discussion"

1. J. Michael Montias, "Socialist Industrialization and Trade in Machinery Products: An Analysis Based on the Experience of Bulgaria, Poland, and Rumania," in *International Trade and Central Planning*, ed. Alan A. Brown and Egon Neuberger (Berkeley: University of California Press, 1968), pp. 130-65.

2. *Statisticheski godishnik na N.R. Bulgariia* (Sofia: Central Statistical Office, 1975).

Montias, "Romania's Foreign Trade"

1. For example, see Michael C. Kaser, *Comecon: Integration Problems of the Planned Economies*, 2d ed. (London: Oxford University Press, 1967); Peter J. D. Wiles, *Communist International Economics* (New York: Praeger, 1969); and John Michael Montias, *Economic Development in Communist Rumania* (Cambridge, Mass.: The MIT Press, 1967). See also Jozef M. P. van Brabant, *Bilateralism and Structural Bilateralism in Intra-CMEA Trade* (Rotterdam: Rotterdam University Press, 1973) and the bibliography therein.

2. These initial results were published in Montias, *Economic Development in Communist Rumania*, chapters 3 and 5.

3. Directia Centrala de Statistica, *Anuarul Statistic al R.S.R. 1976* (Bucharest, 1976), p. 53. The official statistical yearbooks will hereafter be cited as *A.S.* and the date.

4. Thad P. Alton, "Economic Growth and Resource Allocation in Eastern Europe," in *Reorientation and Commercial Relations of the Economies of Eastern Europe*, A Compendium of papers presented to the Joint Economic Committee, 93rd Congress, 2d Session (Washington, D.C.: Government Printing Office, 1974), pp. 274-75. The Compendium will hereafter be cited as J.E.C. 1974.

5. Ibid., and *A.S. 1975*, p. 90.

6. *A.S. 1975*, pp. 57, 93; *Revista economica*, no. 5 (1976), p. 4; and Thad P. Alton, et al., *Economic Growth in Eastern Europe 1965-1975*, Occasional Papers of the Research Project on National Income in East Central Europe, no. OP-50 (New York: L.W. International Financial Research, 1976), p. 11.

7. Official Romanian statistics.

8. Since collectivization was completed in 1962, the farm sector remains backward. A comparison of the value of production per hectare in different CMEA countries shows that Romania lags appreciably behind Bulgaria and Hungary in this respect. The ratio of productivity per laborer in agriculture to productivity per laborer in industry turns out to be much lower in Romania than in any other East European country (22% in 1972 compared to 30% in Poland and 47% in Bulgaria). *Revista economica*, no. 16 (1974), p. 16.

9. *A.S. 1976*, p. 53.

10. Cf. the data in Montias, *Economic Development in Communist Rumania*, p. 56.

11. *A.S. 1976*, p. 76.

12. Unless otherwise indicated, reference is to the value of foreign-trade aggregates in current devisa prices.

13. Note that this rate of increase was slightly less than that of the Alton index of industrial output and roughly a third less than the official index of net output. An index of exogenous materials consumed in industry, in which imported materials were given a preponderant weight, lagged substantially behind our independently constructed index of industrial output for the benchmark years 1950, 1955, 1958, 1960, and 1963 (Montias, *Economic Development in Communist Rumania*, p. 56).

14. The petroleum industry, spearheaded by its oil-refining sector, expanded at approximately 4% per year from 1966 to 1972, but domestic requirements must have increased at an even faster rate.

15. The textile industry grew at approximately 11% per year during the period. This rate of expansion is meaningful on the reasonable assumption that prices of raw materials for light industry, expressed in foreign-exchange lei, were roughly on the same level at the beginning and end of the period.

16. The coefficient of variation of this estimate was equal to 40%, denoting a good deal of irregularity.

17. The coefficient of variation of this estimate was less than 5%.

18. Current values of imports and exports of foodstuffs (both raw and processed) were deflated by indexes of Hungarian foreign-trade prices (Központi Statisztikai Hivatal, *Külkereskedelmi statisztikai evkönyv* [Budapest, 1975], pp. 410-12; *Statisztikai havi közcemenyek*, no. 3/4 [1975], p. 92). These indexes distinguish, for both imports and exports, trade in rubles and trade in "dollars and other accounts." I assumed, for the purpose of these rough calculations, that the ruble area coincided with CMEA and the rest of the world with "dollars and other accounts." To the extent that Romania's trade with CMEA was actually carried on in dollar accounts (as in the case of certain transactions in foodstuffs), this assumption leads to an underestimation of price increases in trade with CMEA in the period 1973-75.

19. The widespread meat shortages the second half of 1975, which are said to have touched off popular disturbances in Romanian provincial centers, were probably caused at least in part by this export drive.

20. See table 3.

21. Machinery trade with the OSCs and LDCs combined was obtained as a residual from the data in table 1.

22. The data on Romanian trade by nine commodity groups divided according to trading area (CMEA, other socialist, MDCs, and LDCs) on which the following analysis is based are presented in an appendix to J. M. Montias, "Romania's Foreign Trade: An Overview," in *East European Economies Post Helsinki*, A Compendium of papers presented to the Joint Economic Committee, 95th Congress, 1st Session (Washington, D.C.: Government Printing Office, 1977), supplemented by Vanous, *Data Bank*.

23. For a more optimistic judgment on these possibilities, see Marvin R. Jackson's comment on this paper.

24. Computed from the country data in Ministerul Comerţului Exterior, *Comerţul exterior al R.S.R. 1973* (Bucharest, n.d.), pp. 76-77.

25. Ibid., pp. 102-103.

26. For estimates of trade in armaments, see sources and methods to table 2.

27. To calculate this surplus as a residual, an estimate was needed of the balance-in-trade in consumer goods with CMEA in 1972. From percentages in Chamber of Commerce of the Socialist Republic of Romania, Propaganda Department, *Economic and Commercial Guide to Romania 1974* (Bucharest, 1974), trade in this group with all socialist countries may be derived. To arrive at trade with CMEA alone it was assumed that the ratio of trade with CMEA to trade with socialist countries in group 9 was the same in 1972 and 1973. Only a small error can arise from this assumption.

28. J. M. Montias, "The Structure of Comecon Trade and the Prospects for East-West Exchange," in J.E.C. 1974, pp. 662-81; and idem, "Socialist Industrialization and Trade in Manufactures," in *Quantitative and Analytical Studies in East-West Economic Relations*, ed. Josef C. Brada, Studies in East European and Soviet Planning, Development, and Trade (Bloomington, Ind.: International Development Research Center, 1976), pp. 17-35.

29. Data on imports of consumer goods from the MDCs, which typically make up less than 10% of total imports of manufactures from these countries, are not available for 1968 and 1969. I could have filled this gap by making estimates for the missing years, but I could not do this without prejudicing in one way or another the results of the tests.

30. Data on CMEA and "world market" prices originated in Sandor Ausch, *A KGST együttmüködés helyzete, mechanizmusa, távlatai* (Budapest: Közgazdasági és Jogi Könyvkiadó, 1969), pp. 242-45, and were presented in Paul Marer, *Postwar Pricing and Price Patterns in Socialist Foreign Trade (1946-1971)*, IDRC Report 1 (Bloomington, Ind.: International Development Research Center, 1972), pp. 86-88.

31. On the dependence of imports on the supply of foreign exchange, see William H. Hemphill, "The Effect of Foreign Exchange Receipts on Imports of Less Developed Countries," *IMF Staff Papers*, no. 1 (1975), pp. 637-77.

426   Notes

32. $MACH^W = 1013 + 1.29D^W - 0.316S^W$ $R^2 = 0.543$
     (2.22)   (3.56)   (1.05)
The t-values are shown in parentheses.
33. The result of this regression is:
     $MACH^T = 607.8 + 0.11INV$ $R^2 = 0.94$,
                (2.5)   (14.8)
where INV stands for total investments in machinery at 1959 prices (computed from
A.S. 1966, pp. 374-75; *A.S. 1971*, pp. 482-83; *A.S. 1975*, pp. 292-93; and *Era socialistâ*,
no. 11 [1975], p. 9). For a more detailed econometric analysis of the dependence of
machinery imports on machinery investments in Eastern Europe, see Jozef M. P. van
Brabant, "Specialization and Import-dependence of Some East European Countries:
The Case of Investments in Machinery and Equipment," *Jahrbuch der Wirtschaft
Osteuropas*, vol. 5 (Munich: Günter Olzog Verlag, 1974), pp. 285-89.
34. Kindly made available by Lawrence Brainard.
35. Marvin R. Jackson, "Industrialization, Trade, and Mobilization in Romania," in
East European Economies Post Helsinki, p. 937.
36. Ibid., table 16.
37. Ibid., table 15.
38. In every five-year period from 1951 to 1970, the share of total investments going
to agriculture was higher in Bulgaria than in Romania. From 1971 to 1973, 18% of total
investments went to agriculture in Bulgaria and 14% in Romania (Gregor Lazarcik,
"Agricultural Output and Productivity in Eastern Europe and Some Comparisons with
the U.S.S.R. and U.S.A.," in J.E.C. 1974, p. 378).
39. *A.S. 1975*, pp. 254 and 257.
40. Iulian Dănescu, "Optimizarea exportului de mașini și utilajè al României in
perspectiva anilor 1975-1980" (Ph.D. diss., Bucharest, 1973), pp. 96-98.
41. Ibid., pp. 111-12.

Jackson, "Discussion"
1. For a survey of recent and planned agricultural development, see Marvin R.
Jackson, "Industrialization, Trade, and Mobilization in Romania's Drive For Economic Independence," in *East European Economies Post-Helsinki*, Joint Economic
Committee, 93d Congress, 2d Session, (Washington, D.C.: Government Printing Office,
1977), pp. 925-36.
2. Directia centrala de statistica, *Anuarul statistic al Republicii Socialiste România
1978* (Bucharest, 1979), pp. 86 and 454-55; and Radio Free Europe, "Romanian Situation Report 27," *Radio Free Europe Research* 3:45 (November 9-15, 1978): 6-8.
3. Jackson, "Industrialization, Trade, and Mobilization," pp. 900-901, 926.
4. *Scinteia*, February 15, 1975, p. 1. A means to achieve the increase, if not also a
possible change in Romanian statistical practice, was suggested by President Ceausescu
in 1974 when, noting that trade with LDCs was only about 9% of total trade, said, "It is
correct that, because of the methodology of calculation, these figures do not mirror all
of our economic relations with the [LDC] countries. Trade in convertible currencies is
included under the heading of exchanges with capitalist countries. Probably it will be
necessary to review this form of accounting in order not to deform reality. In reality
[trade with LDCs] has a weight much greater than is shown in the statistics." *Cuvintare
la consfatuirea cu activul de partid și de stat din domeniul comertului exterior și
cooperarii economice internationale, 16 mai 1976* (Bucharest, 1974), p. 8.
5. Details of foreign-trade organization may be found in Josef C. Brada and Marvin
R. Jackson, "Strategy and Structure in the Organization of Romanian Foreign Trade
Activities, 1967-75," in *East European Economies Post-Helsinki*, pp. 1264-75. The
suitability of its organizational system in Western markets is considered in Marvin R.
Jackson, "The CPE export System as a Marketing Organization," in *East-West Trade:
Theory and Evidence,* ed. Josef C. Brada and V.S. Somanath (Bloomington, Ind.: In-
ternational Development Institute, 1978), pp. 3-22.
6. These and subsequent trade data, unless otherwise noted, are from Jan Vanous,
*Project CMEA-FORTRAM Data Bank of Foreign Trade Flows and Balances of CMEA
Countries* (Vancouver: University of British Columbia, 1977), pp. 219-36.

7. Trade shares for country groups in 1976 and 1977 are from Radio Free Europe, "Romanian Situation Report No. 1," *Radio Free Europe Research* 4:4 (January 18-24, 1979): 7-8; and *Anuarul statistic 1978*, pp. 446-55.

8. Estimates of Romanian foreign prices are based on Jan Vanous, "An Econometric Model of World Trade of Member Countries of the Council of Mutual Economic Assistance" (Ph.D. diss., Yale University, May 1979), as privately communicated by the author.

9. See Jackson, "Industrialization, Trade, and Mobilization," pp. 906-11.

10. Joan Parpart Zoeter, "Eastern Europe: The Growing Hard Currency Debt," in *East European Economies Post-Helsinki*, pp. 1362-63. It should be pointed out that if Romania had earned CC balances with LDCs in these amounts, then her CC trade with CMEA would have been in deficit.

11. From 1965 through 1969, Romania, on balance, also exported hard goods to LDCs.

12. From 1970 through 1974, Romania experienced net imports of foodstuffs from LDCs and OSCs. Usually these net imports are offset by net exports of consumer manufactures, but in 1971, following the 1970 floods, net imports of foodstuffs from LDC/OSCs were possibly so large that industrial material imports were reduced.

13. In the case of petroleum there was never an actual shift, since Romania has not imported from the Soviet Union. As imports have been required, Romania turned to Iran and recently to Arab exporters. An actual shift from CMEA to LDC sources has taken place in the case of iron ore, and a shift may be in progress with coal imports. The shift from coke imports was actually a case of import substitution of domestic capacity.

14. The extent to which Romania might have been deprived of industrial raw material supplies from CMEA sources is not known.

15. Export-supply constraints are often mentioned by Romanian trade officials. For evidence of the possible importance of export-supply constraints on Romania's direction of exports, see Josef C. Brada and Larry J. Wipf, "Romanian Exports to Western Markets," in *Quantitative and Analytical Studies in East-West Economic Relations*, ed. Josef C. Brada (Bloomington, Ind.: International Development Institute, 1976), pp. 37-49.

Grossman, "Discussion"

1. For Romania's indebtedness to the industrial West to the end of 1976, see Joan P. Zoeter, "Eastern Europe: the Hard Currency Debt," US Congress, Joint Economic Committee, in *East European Economies Post-Helsinki*, 93rd Congress, 2d Session (Washington, D.C., Government Printing Office, 1974), pp. 1352, 1357. See also Richard Portes, "East Europe's Debt to the West," *Foreign Affairs* (July 1977), p. 757; and Kathryn Melson and Edwin M. Snell, "Estimating East European Indebtedness to the West," *East European Economies Post-Helsinki*, pp. 1369-95. Zoeter estimates Romania's net hard-currency debt as of the end of 1976 to have been about $3.3 billion; Portes's estimate is $2.8 billion. Romania's hard-currency exports in that year were approximately $2.3 billion.

2. The computations are in terms of SDRs according to a complicated procedure that I shall not take the space to reproduce here. The category "food" encompasses live animals, raw foodstuffs, and processed foodstuffs (CTN classes 6, 7, and 8). The underlying data are from the data bank of Project CMEA-FORTRAM (Foreign Trade Model), University of Pennsylvania. I take this opportunity to express my sincere gratitude to Professor Vanous, now at the University of British Columbia.

3. The data are from Gregor Lazarcik, "Comparative Growth and Levels of Agricultural Output and Productivity in Eastern Europe," *East European Economies Post-Helsinki*, p. 292. The GNP percentages are projections of estimates by Thad P. Alton in "Comparative Structure and Growth of Economic Activity in Eastern Europe," ibid., pp. 199-266; these percentages are in local 1968 or 1969 prices, and their mutual comparability may not be very good. For comparative data and analysis see also Karl-Eugen Wädekin, "The Place of Agriculture in the European Communist Economies," *Soviet Studies* 29 (April 1977): pp. 238-54. The appendix to this article

contains valuable cautionary observations on the sort of statistics used in this Comment.

4. Lazarcik, "Levels of Agricultural Output and Productivity," p. 303.

5. Sovet ekonomicheskoi vzaimopomoshchi, *Statisticheskii ezhegodnik stranchlenov S.E.V., 1976*. (Moscow, 1976), pp. 139, 141 (hereafter cited as *Ezhegodnik*).

6. Ibid., pp. 228, 231.

7. C. Sporea and K.-E. Wädekin, "Arbeitskräfte und Landwirtschaft Rumäniens," *Osteuropa* 27 (March 1977): 232ff. This is the second of a series of three articles by the same authors on Romanian agricultural and rural labor. See also Marvin R. Jackson, "Industrialization, Trade, and Mobilization in Romania's Drive for Economic Independence," *East European Economies Post-Helsinki*, pp. 934ff.

8. C. Sporea and K.-E. Wädekin, "Arbeitseinkommen und Lohnsystem in der rumänischen Landwirtschaft," *Osteuropa* 27 (April 1977): 331-39; Jackson, "Romania's Drive for Economic Independence." Earnings data are tabulated by Jackson on p. 935.

9. Cf. Sporea and Wädekin, "Arbeitskrafte," *passim*.

10. K.-E. Wädekin, "Agro-industrielle Integration in Bulgarien," *Agrarwirtschaft* 2 (1977): 51-56.

11. Jackson, "Romania's Drive for Economic Independence," chart on p. 927.

12. Ibid., p. 928.

13. Ibid.

14. *Ezhegodnik*, pp. 303, 307, 308. The Romanian data exclude private trade; those for the other East European countries generally include it.

15. A thorough study of four countries, though not Romania, is Bogdan Mieczkowski's *Personal and Social Consumption in Eastern Europe*. (New York: Praeger, 1975).

16. She has been rather successful in penetrating the US market as well. US imports of manufactures, mostly consumer goods, from Romania rose nearly fourfold between 1975 and 1977, to exceed (by very wide margins) those from any other East European country except Poland.

Errata
(Insert after page 428.)

Korbonski, "Poland and the CMEA"

1. The literature on CMEA is by now fairly extensive. Among the most interesting studies are: Michael Kaser, *Comecon,* 2d ed. (London: Oxford University Press, 1967); J. M. Montias, "Obstacles to the Economic Integration of Eastern Europe," *Studies in Comparative Communism* 2:3-4 (1969):38-60; Sandor Ausch, *Theory and Practice of CMEA Integration* (Budapest: Akademiai Kiado, 1972); Henry W. Schaefer, *Comecon and the Politics of Integration* (New York: Praeger, 1972); I. P. Olenyik and V. P. Sergeev, eds., *Problemy sotsialisticheskoi ekonomicheskoi integratsii* (Moscow: Mysl, 1974); Jozef M. P. van Brabant, *Essays on Planning, Trade and Integration in Eastern Europe* (Rotterdam: Rotterdam University Press, 1974); Zbigniew M. Fallenbuchl, "East European Integration: Comecon," in *Reorientation and Commercial Relations of the Economies of Eastern Europe* (Washington, D.C.: Government Printing Office, 1974), pp. 79-134; Paul Marer, "Has Eastern Europe Become a Liability to the Soviet Union? The Economic Aspects," in *The International Politics of Eastern Europe,* ed. Charles Gati (New York: Praeger, 1976), pp. 59-81; and idem, "Prospects for Integration in the Council for Mutual Economic Assistance," *International Organization* 30:4 (1976):631-48.

2. David Pfotenhauer and William A. Welsh, "The Economic Dimension of Integration in Eastern Europe" (Paper presented at a Conference on Trends in Integration of the East European Community, The University of South Carolina, Columbia, April, 1972), and David D. Finley, "Some International Pressures and Political Change in Eastern Europe" (Paper presented at the Western Slavic Conference, San Francisco, California, October, 1973). For a more recent statement, see idem, "Economic Linkage and Political Dependency in Eastern Europe" (Paper presented at the Annual Meeting of the American Association for the Advancement of Slavic Studies, St. Louis, Missouri, October, 1976).

3. Donna Bahry and Cal Clark, "A Dependence Theory of Soviet-East European Relations: Theory and Empirical Testing" (Paper presented at a Conference on Integration in Eastern Europe and East-West Trade, Indiana University, Bloomington, October, 1976).

4. For the most recent version, see J. S. Nye, *Peace in Parts* (Boston: Little, Brown, 1971), pp. 55-107.

5. Ernest B. Haas, "The Study of Regional Integration: Reflections on the Joy and Anguish of Pretheorizing," in *Regional Integration,* ed. Leon N. Lindberg and Stuart A. Scheingold (Cambridge, Mass.: Harvard University Press, 1971), p. 23.

6. Ibid., p. 23.

7. Roger E. Kanet, "Integration Theory and the Study of Eastern Europe," *International Studies Quarterly* 18:3 (1974): 388. For a somewhat different view, see Cal Clark, "The Study of East European Integration: A 'Political Perspective'," *East Central Europe* 2:2 (1975): 143ff.

8. Kanet, "Integration Theory," p. 373.

9. Nye, *Peace in Parts,* pp. 71-72.

10. Ibid., p. 99.

11. Ernest B. Haas, *The Obsolescence of Regional Integration Theory* (Berkeley: University of California, Institute of International Studies, 1975), p. 1.

12. For an interesting discussion of this question, see J. M. Montias, "The Industrialization of Eastern Europe and East-West Trade," in William E. Griffith, ed., *The Soviet Empire: Expansion and Detente* (Lexington, Mass.: D. C. Heath, 1976), pp. 384-396 and 396-97.

13. J. Wilczynski, *Technology in Comecon* (New York: Praeger, 1974), pp. 273-86.

14. John Michael Montias, *Economic Development in Communist Rumania* (Cambridge, Mass.: The MIT Press, 1967), chapters 4 and 5.

15. For an analysis of Gomulka's policies in 1956-57, see Zbigniew Brzezinski, *The Soviet Bloc,* rev. ed. (Cambridge, Mass.: Harvard University Press, 1967), pp. 263-65, 274-77, 289, 294-96, 303-305.

16. Andrzej Brzeski, "Poland as a Catalyst of Change in the Communist Economic System," *Polish Review* 16:2 (1971):3-24.

17. It is estimated that export price levels of CMEA countries in intrabloc trade have been significantly higher than in East-West trade during 1958-64 and 1966-70. For manufactured goods, CMEA countries tended to earn (and pay) between one-third to one and one-third more in intrabloc trade than the hypothetical price they would have received exporting the same good to the West. For primary products, the price differential was betwen 5 and 50%. Paul Marer, *Postwar Pricing and Price Patterns in Socialist Foreign Trade (1946-1970)* (Bloomington, Ind.: International Development Research Center 1972), pp. 52 and 55.

18. In fact, the planned Soviet oil deliveries to Eastern Europe (excluding Romania) in 1976-80 were estimated to be considerably above the actual deliveries in 1971-75. John Haberstroh, "Eastern Europe: Growing Energy Problems," in *East European Economies Post-Helsinki*, ed. John P. Hardt (Washington, D.C.: Government Printing Office, 1977), pp. 379-380.

19. For example, in 1960 EEC witnessed a "package deal" that combined a reduction in internal tariffs (to satisfy those interested in strengthening the Common Market) with a lowering of external duties (to satisfy those worried about possible decline in foreign trade). See Nye, *Peace in Parts*, p. 68.

20. After a rather lengthy hiatus, the literature on economic nationalism in Eastern Europe has increased in the last few years. Among the more interesting items, see J. M. Montias, "Economic Nationalism in Eastern Europe: Forty Years of Continuity and Change," in *Eastern Europe in Transition*, ed. Kurt London (Baltimore: Johns Hopkins Press, 1966), pp. 173-203; Jerzy F. Karcz, "Reflections on the Economics of Nationalism and Communism in Eastern Europe," *East European Quarterly* 5:2 (1971):232-59; and Vaclav Holesovsky, "The Conflict of Integration Concepts and National Self Assertion in Eastern Europe" (Paper presented at the National Convention of the American Association for the Advancement of Slavic Studies, Dallas, Texas, March, 1971). For a recent treatment, see Andrzej Korbonski, "Reconciling the Demands of National Identity and Economic Rationality in Eastern Europe" (Paper presented at a Conference on The Impact of Communist Modernization on National Identity and State Integration in Eastern Europe, The Pennsylvania State University, University Park, October, 1975).

21. This was a very frequent comment that I encountered in my interviews with Czechoslovak and Polish economists during my stay in Prague and Warsaw in 1966-67.

22. J. M. Montias, "Uniformity and Diversity in the East European Future" (Paper presented at the Annual Convention of the American Association for the Advancement of Slavic Studies, New York City, April, 1964), pp. 7-10.

23. Eugene Babitchev, "The International Bank for Economic Cooperation," in *Money and Plan*, ed. Gregory Grossman (Berkeley: University of California Press, 1968), pp. 147-51.

24. Andrzej Korbonski, "Theory and Practice of Regional Integration: The Case of Comecon," in *Regional Integration*, pp. 351-352.

25. Adam Zwass, "Costs and Benefits of CMEA Integration: Poland's Perspectives" (Paper presented at the Conference on Integration in Eastern Europe and East-West Trade," Indiana University, Bloomington, October, 1976), p. 11.

26. For a description of CMEA's institutional structure in the mid-1970s, see Harry Trend, "Comecon's Organizational Structure," Radio Free Europe Research *RAD Background Report/114*, July 3, 1975.

27. Nye, *Peace in Parts*, p. 70.

28. For a detailed account, see Schaefer, *Politics of Integration, passim.*

29. An interesting discussion of one of these conflicts can be found in Zygmunt Bauman, "Twenty Years After: The Crisis of Soviet-Type Societies," *Problems of Communism* 20:6 (1971):45-53.

30. Brzezinski, *The Soviet Bloc*, pp. 363-366.

31. Andrzej Korbonski, "External Influences on Eastern Europe," in *International Politics of Eastern Europe*, pp. 253-74.

32. Nye, *Peace in Parts*, p. 71.

33. It has been suggested that it was the failure of CMEA to achieve closer integration, especially at its "Summit Meeting" in Moscow in April 1969, that persuaded Gomulka to turn to the West and to seek accommodation with West Germany. Schaefer, *Politics of Integration*, p. 55.

34. *New York Times*, February 8, 1975.

35. *The Economist*, October 2, 1976.

36. *New York Times*, November 16, 1976.

37. Because of the newly imposed 200 miles EEC fishing zone, Poland and East Germany were forced to sign special fishery agreements with the European Community in February 1977 which represented a *de facto* recognition of the EEC.

38. Marer, "Prospects for Integration," pp. 642-47.

39. Interestingly enough, Poland appeared to be the only junior CMEA country that was fulfilling its obligations with regard to the construction of the Orenburg pipeline. Haberstroh, "Eastern Europe," p. 392.

40. One recent example of difficulties faced by CMEA countries was the embargo on the import of beef from Eastern Europe imposed by the EEC between July and October 1974. It was estimated to have cost Hungary alone the equivalent of $100 million. Radio Free Europe Research, *Situation Report Hungary/3*, January 21, 1975. Interestingly enough, the actual loss to Hungary was reduced due to the fact that the Soviet Union purchased some of the beef originally earmarked for EEC.

41. According to Polish data, the Soviet trade deficit in 1975 amounted to $3,536 million while the Polish deficit was $2,256 million. *Rocznik Statystyczny*, 1976, pp. 608-09.

42. In some cases, however, the Poles themselves have been reluctant to accept credits which the West was eager to grant. *New York Times*, April 4, 1977.

43. Nye, *Peace in Parts*, pp. 75-76.

44. Ibid., pp. 77-81. For a summary of the discussion of this issue as it related to CMEA, see Jozef M. P. van Brabant, "Communism, International Trade and the Level of Development," in *Planning, Trade, and Integration*, pp. 64-80.

45. There is by now a considerable body of literature dealing with economic reforms in Eastern Europe. Among the better known are: Gregory Grossman, "Econonic Reforms: A Balance Sheet," *Problems of Communism* 15:6 (1966):43-55; Morris Bornstein, "Introduction," in *Plan and Market*, ed. Morris Bornstein (New Haven, Conn.: Yale University Press, 1973), pp. 8-11; Radoslav Selucky, *Economic Reforms in Eastern Europe* (New York: Praeger, 1972), pp. 57-171; Karl C. Thalheim and Hans-Germann Hohmann, eds., *Wirtschaftsreformen in Osteuropa* (Cologne: Verlag Wissenschaft und Politik, 1968); Gregory Grossman, ed., *Money and Plan* (Berkeley: University of California Press, 1968); H. Flakierski, "The Polish Economic Reform of 1970," *The Canadian Journal of Economics* 6:1 (1973): 1-15; David Granick, "The Hungarian Economic Reform," *World Politics* 25:3 (1973):414-29; Michael Gamarnikow, "Balance Sheet on Economic Reforms," in *Reorientation and Commercial Relations of the Economies of Eastern Europe*, pp. 164-213; Oldrich Kyn, "The Rise and Fall of Economic Reform in Czechoslovakia," *The American Economic Review* 9:2 (1970):300-06; Richard D. Portes, "Economic Reforms in Hungary," ibid., pp. 307-13; Frederic L. Pryor, "Barriers to Market Socialism in Eastern Europe in the Mid 1960s," *Studies in Comparative Communism* 3:2 (1970):31-64; and Leon Smolinski, "Planning Reforms in Poland," *Kyklos* 21:3 (1968):498-511.

46. For a perceptive account of the Polish economic situation in the 1960s, see Jozef M. van Brabant, "Reflections on Poland's Economic Policies in the 1960s," *Berichte des Osteuropainstituts an der preien universitat Berlin*, no. 99 (1973).

47. Speeches by Jozef Cyrankiewicz and Mieczyslaw Moczar at the Polish Communist Party Central Committee plenum on February 6-7, 1971, as reported in a special undated issue of *Nowe Drogi*, and translated in Radio Free Europe, *Polish Press Survey*, no. 2314 and 2320, July 16 and August 19, 1971.

48. This was particularly true for the works of Brus and Kalecki, which were translated and made required reading for students at the High School of Economics in Prague where I attended seminars in 1966-67.

49. Personal interviews, Warsaw, Spring 1976.

50. Report of the Politburo to the Eighth Plenum of the Central Committee of the Polish Communist Party, February 6-7, 1971, Part 4, "The Economic Situation and the Most Pressing Economic Tasks," as reported in a special undated issue of *Nowe Drogi*, and translated in Radio Free Europe, *Polish Press Survey*, no. 2316, August 5, 1971.

51. An extensive discussion of this question can be found in Imre Vajda and Mihaly Simai, eds., *Foreign Trade in Planned Economy* (Cambridge, England: Cambridge University Press, 1971).

52. Nye, *Peace in Parts*, p. 81.

53. Andrew Janos, "Group Politics in Communist Society," in *Authoritarian Politics in Modern Society*, ed. Samuel P. Huntington and Clement H. Moore, (New York: Basic Books, 1970), pp. 437-50.

54. Andrzej Korbonski, "Bureaucracy and Interest Groups in Communist Societies: The Case of Czechoslovakia," *Studies in Comparative Communism* 4:1 (1971):57-79; and Andrzej Korbonski, "Political Aspects of Economic Reforms in Eastern Europe," in *Economic Development in the Soviet Union and Eastern Europe*, ed. Zbigniew M. Fallenbuchl, vol. 1 (New York: Praeger, 1975), pp. 8-41.

55. One of the more interesting aspects of the decentralization process was the granting of autonomy in foreign-trade transactions to a number of industrial enterprises which, as a result, were

able to negotiate their own contracts with Western firms.

56. This problem is discussed in Marer, "Has Eastern Europe Become a Liability to the Soviet Union?" pp. 65-69.

57. Marshall D. Shulman, "The Communist States and Western Integration," *Problems of Communism* 12:5 (1963):47-54.

58. Good examples of "political" credits were those provided by France and West Germany. A credit of 7 billion francs was announced by President Giscard d'Estaing on the occasion of his visit to Warsaw in May 1975, and a credit of 1 billion marks was approved in March 1976 following a meeting between Chancellor Helmut Schmidt and Gierek at Helsinki in August 1975. As a result of Gierek's visit to Bonn in June 1976, Poland received an additional investment credit of 3 billion marks. Moreover, in March 1976 Poland was granted a lump sum of 1.3 billion marks in settlement of Polish claims against German social security.

59. Edwin M. Snell, "Eastern Europe's Trade and Payments with the Industrial West," in *Reorientation*, p. 712; and Joan C. Zoeter, "Eastern Europe: The Growing Hard Currency Debt," in *East European Economies Post Helsinki*, pp. 1350-68.

60. Marer, "Prospects for Integration," pp. 643-47.

61. Paul Marer, "Soviet Economic Policy in Eastern Europe," in *Reorientation*, pp. 139-40.

Zwass, "Discussion"

1. See Brainard's contribution to this volume and my comments on his paper for a more detailed disucssion of the issues.

2. J. Soldaczuk: "Intergracja czynnikiem poglebienia wspolpracy" [Integration as a factor of enlarged cooperation], in *Integracja Ekonomiczna Krajow Socjalistycznych* [Economic integration of the socialist countries] (Warsaw, 1974), p. 37.

3. *Rocznik statystyczny*, 1976, p. 75.

4. Ibid., p. 340.

5. N. N. Inoziemcew, Vice President of the Planning Board of the USSR, "Strengthening of the Planning Aspects of Cooperation Among the CMEA-Member Countries," *Gospodarka planowa* (Warsaw, 1977), p. 236.

6. *Zycie gospodarcze*, April 20, 1976.

7. *Trybuna ludu*, July 9, 1976.

8. *Rocznik statystyczny*, 1976, pp. 494 and 496.

Bornstein, "Comparing Romania and Poland"

1. Soviet Ekonomicheskoi Vzaimopomoshchi, Sekretariat (Council for Mutual Economic Assistance, Secretariat), *Statisticheskii ezhegodnik stran-chlenov Soveta Ekonomicheskoi Vzaimopomoshchi 1976* [Statistical yearbook of the member-countries of the Council for Mutual Economic Assistance 1976] (Moscow: Statistika, 1976), pp. 339, 341. Figures for regional shares of total trade can be misleading when the same goods are traded with different areas at different prices as a result of trade agreements that cause prices to vary to different degrees from current world market prices. However, if adjustment for such price differences could be made in this case, it would not be large enough to alter significantly these basic conclusions about the relative importance of LDC trade for Romania versus Poland.

2. Kindly supplied by Lawrence J. Brainard.

3. "The New Sophistication in East-West Banking," *Business Week*, March 7, 1977, p. 40.

Index

absorption: domestic, 100, 102-103, 110, 220; model, 88, 90, 91, 97-98, 109, 403n
Afghanistan, 29, 35, 229
Aganbegyan, A. K., 250
agricultural-industrial units, 311
agricultural sector, 25, 104, 157, 220, 255, 262, 264, 266, 273-75, 277-78, 279, 283-320, 352-54, 391
Albania, 22, 33
Algeria, 17
Allen, Mark, 25, 129
Alton, Thad, 309, 322, 323
aluminum, 236-37
ammonia, 268-69, 272, 280; Black Sea-Tolyatti pipeline, 270
asbestos, 237-39
Ausch, Sandor, 122
Austria, 229, 230
autarky, 44, 45, 73, 152, 168, 218, 220, 259, 284, 285, 288, 289, 290, 297, 317, 359, 375

Balassa, Bela, 14
bilateralism, 48, 78, 111, 122, 123, 125, 126, 127, 128, 130, 134, 136, 137, 139, 140, 160, 173-74, 176, 177, 179, 181, 182, 184, 186, 189, 190, 191, 193, 194, 195, 209, 211, 213, 215, 278, 287, 316, 330, 348, 386, 391, 392, 395n; agreements on, 66, 70, 131; structural, 49, 122, 213
Birmingham University project, 280
Black Sea-Tolyatti pipeline, 270. See also Ammonia
Brainard, Lawrence, 17, 38, 139, 141, 142
Bretton Woods, 86, 145
Brezhnev, Leonid, 365
Brown, Alan, 44, 45, 63
Bulgaria, 9, 14, 20, 25, 26, 29, 33, 45, 48, 70, 71, 130, 162, 176, 189, 190, 191, 192, 193, 194, 226, 227, 229, 231, 232, 234, 241, 242, 244, 278, 342, 343, 350, 351, 352, 354, 363, 364, 371, 373, 381, 383, 386; Great Leap Forward, 319; growth strategy, 283-320

Cambodia, 29, 35
Canada, 238, 291
Caporaso, James A., 79
Ceausescu, 338, 360, 378, 391

Chase Manhattan Bank, 340, 392
chemicalization drive, 256, 258, 277
chemicals, 239-41, 243, 255, 256-61, 275, 278, 279; nitrogen fertilizers, 240; petrochemicals, 240-41, 244; phosphates, 239, 330, 358; potash, 239-40
Chemico, 268, 269
Chenery, H., 52, 290, 314
Chilas, John G., 14
China, Republic of, 35, 319, 330, 361, 423n
CMEA: Joint Commission on Cooperation, 34-35; membership of, 29, 366, 377; types of membership, 33-35; organization, 34, 35-38; sessions, 25, 157, 387, 388, 389
CMEA-Fortram, 188
coal: and coke, 231, 243, 363-64; in the Donets and Kuznetsk Basins, 231, 243; strikes, 345
Commission of European Communities, 153-54
commodity: convertibility, 140-41, 142-43, 176, 177, 181, 182, 189, 193, 290; groups, 49; structures of East-West trade, 54, 321, 342. See also Food sector
communications-transactions analysis, 76, 78, 79
Comprehensive Program (1971), 23, 156, 158, 387
concentration ratios, 63
consumer goods, 25, 49, 157, 178, 182-83; 187, 188, 193-94, 216, 299, 306, 312, 315, 325, 329, 331, 391, 394n
convertible currency (CC): attainment of, 16, 24, 28, 33, 38, 93, 121, 122, 125, 129-38, 139, 140, 142, 144, 158, 363, 386, 387, 391, 392; lack of, 17, 23, 32; trade, 126, 127, 128, 408n. See also Commodity, Financial convertibility
cooperation projects, 102, 103, 110, 216, 346, 348, 389; International Harvester-BUMAR, 27; National Steel and Earth Sciences, 271
Copenhagen Summit Meeting, 153, 154
credit settlement system, 386, 387
Creusot Loire, 268, 269
Cuba, 29, 33, 71, 195
currency convertibility. See Convertible currency
customs union, 5, 151, 153, 218, 219